Instructor's Resource
and
Solutions Manual

to accompany

Financial Statement
Analysis
Theory, Application,
and Interpretation

Sixth Edition

Leopold A. Bernstein
CUNY–Baruch College

John J. Wild
University of Wisconsin–Madison

D1368500

Prepared by
Mark P. Bauman
University of Illinois–Chicago

Boston   Burr Ridge, IL   Dubuque, IA   Madison, WI   New York   San Francisco   St. Louis
Bangkok   Bogotá   Caracas   Lisbon   London   Madrid
Mexico City   Milan   New Delhi   Seoul   Singapore   Sydney   Taipei   Toronto

Irwin/McGraw-Hill

A Division of The McGraw·Hill Companies

Instructor's Resource and Solutions Manual to accompany
FINANCIAL STATEMENT ANALYSIS: THEORY, APPLICATIONS, AND INTERPRETATION

3 4 5 6 7 8 9 0 BKM/BKM 9 0 9 8

ISBN 0-256-16705-2

http://www.mhhe.com

TABLE OF CONTENTS

Chapters

Case and Supplements

PREFACE

This *Instructor's Resource and Solutions Manual* is a teaching supplement to ***Financial Statement Analysis: Theory, Application, and Interpretation***, by Leopold A. Bernstein and John J. Wild. The purpose of this manual is to help instructors in teaching financial statement analysis. All thirteen chapters, the comprehensive case, and supplements B and C have corresponding chapters in this manual. Instructors should feel free to use material in this manual as transparency masters in the classroom.

Organization of the Book
An explanation of the organization of the book and its contents is provided to help the instructor in constructing course materials.

Explanation of Assignment Material
Assignment material is identified and described in several ways. First, we explain the organization of assignment material. Second, we note the inclusion in this new edition of a short description for all exercises, problems, cases and internet activities. Third, we discuss the importance of assignment material taken or drawn from actual practice in the field.

Financial Statement Analysis Project
The structure for a financial statement analysis project assignment is provided for the instructor. This reinforces the comprehensive case chapter in this edition.

Supplement Package
A description of the supplement package supporting this edition is provided for the instructor.

Suggested Course Outlines
Suggested course outlines are provided for the instructor's convenience in designing course syllabi. We present them for both accounting and accounting-related (e.g., finance, investment, lending, consulting, auditing) majors/fields. We also split these by undergraduate and graduate level backgrounds of the students.

Transition of Topics from 5th Edition to 6th Edition
A cross reference of the topics from the fifth edition to the sixth edition permits the instructor to easily identify your previously selected topics for assignment with the revised and new topic material in this edition. All topics from the fifth edition are updated to reflect new developments in practice.

Transition of Assignment Material from 5th to 6th Edition
A cross reference of the assignment materials from the fifth edition to the sixth edition enables the instructor to easily identify previously selected assignment material with the revised and new assignment material in this edition. Assignments from the fifth edition are revised to reflect any new developments in the field.

Learning Objectives

Learning objectives are set in large, bold-face print for transparencies.

Chapter Review

A condensed review provides a quick summary of the chapter material.

Acknowledgement

Mark P. Bauman of the University of Illinois at Chicago did an exceptional job in revising the material contained in this manual. We gratefully acknowledge his valuable contribution.

Organization and Content

Flexibility and innovation are increasingly important in financial statement analysis education. This book's design encourages unique teaching strategies in presenting material to students. While the book is comprehensive in covering all topics of relevance for financial statement analysis, its organization encourages instructors to choose topics and depth of coverage as desired.

Many books lack a tight, integrated flow of topics from chapter to chapter. In this book students are told in Chapter 1 how the book's topics are related to each other. One way integration is acheived is by organizing material into three parts: Overview; Accounting Analysis; and Financial Analysis.

■ **Overview.** *Part One* is an overview of financial statement analysis. It emphasizes understanding business activities--planning, financing, investing and operating. It describes strategies underlying business activities and their effects on financial statements, and it discusses the objectives of analysis. Important tools and techniques in analyzing and interpreting financial statements are illustrated. Attention is directed at users of financial statements whose well-being depends on reliable and relevant analysis. An important and unique feature is the book's use of Adaptec's annual report as a means to instill in students both the relevant and interesting nature of analysis. Two chapters comprise Part One.

◆ **Chapter 1**. This chapter begins the analysis of financial statements by considering their relevance in business decisions. This leads naturally to a focus on users, their needs, and how analysis addresses these needs. Business activities and how they are captured in financial statements is thoroughly explained.

◆ **Chapter 2**. This chapter describes the analysis objectives of users. It discusses both stock and debt valuation. The importance and limitations of accounting data for analysis are described and assessed.

■ **Accounting Analysis.** *Part Two* describes the accounting measurement and reporting practices underlying financial statements. Presentation is organized around financing (liabilities and equity), investing (assets), and operating (income and cash flow) activities. The book shows how operating activities are outcomes of changes in investing and financing activities. It provides insights into income determination, and asset and liability measurement. Procedures and clues for analysis are discussed. The book emphasizes that for students to effectively reap the benefits from financial statement analysis, they must understand accounting measurement and reporting practices. Five chapters comprise Part Two.

◆ **Chapter 3**. Chapter 3 begins the analysis of financial numbers reflecting business activities, and explains how these numbers are the *raw material* for all analyses. The focus is on explaining, analyzing and interpreting financing activities. The relevance of book values and the implications of off-balance-sheet financing are explored. Analyzing and adjusting accounting numbers for understanding financing activities are stressed.

◆ **Chapter 4**. Analysis of financial numbers is extended to investing activities. This chapter explores how to analyze assets like cash, marketable securities, receivables, derivatives, inventories, property, equipment, and intangibles. An understanding of what these numbers reveal about company performance and financing is provided.

- ◆ **Chapter 5**. Chapter 5 extends the analysis to special investing activities--*intercompany and international activities*. It analyzes both intercorporate investments and business combinations from the perspective of a "parent" company. It also examines international investments and their reporting in financial statements. This chapter shows how interpreting disclosures on intercompany and international activities is an important part of analysis.
- ◆ **Chapter 6**. Chapter 6 broadens the analysis to operating activities. It analyzes *accrual* measures of both revenues and expenses in yielding net income. Understanding recognition methods of both revenues and expenses is important and emphasized. The chapter interprets the income statement and its components for analysis purposes.
- ◆ **Chapter 7**. Chapter 7 expands analysis of business activities to cash flows. It analyzes cash flow measures for insights into *all* business activities, but with special emphasis on operations. Attention is directed at understanding company and business conditions when interpreting cash flows.

■ **Financial Analysis**. *Part Three* examines the processes and methods of financial statement analysis. The objectives of users and their analytical tools and techniques for meeting those objectives are emphasized. The means of analysis range from computation of ratio and cash flow measures to earnings prediction and valuation techniques. This section applies analysis tools showing students how to reconstruct the economic reality embedded in financial statements. It demonstrates how analysis tools and techniques enhance users' decisions--including company valuation and lending decisions. It also shows how financial statement analysis reduces uncertainty and strengthens confidence in making timely business decisions. Throughout the book it is stressed to students how an understanding of accounting along with knowledge of the analysis tools and techniques improves their decisions. This perspective reinforces the integrated presentation of financial statement analysis in this book. Six chapters and a comprehensive case comprise Part Three.

- ◆ **Chapter 8**. Chapter 8 begins the study of the application and interpretation of analysis tools. It presents analysis tools as means to reveal insights into company operations and future performance. Special emphasis is on assessing liquidity. Attention is directed at accounting-based ratios, turnover, and operating activity measures.
- ◆ **Chapter 9**. This chapter studies forecasting and pro forma analysis of financial statements. It explains the flow of cash through a company's business activities and its implications for liquidity. Both short and long-term forecasting of cash flows are described. Attention is directed at applying these analysis tools in practice.
- ◆ **Chapter 10**. This chapter focuses on capital structure and its implications for solvency. It explains the importance of financial leverage and its effects on risk and return. Analytical adjustments to accounting book values are evaluated for solvency assessments. It also describes earnings coverage measures and their interpretation.
- ◆ **Chapter 11**. Chapter 11 emphasizes return on invested capital and explains variations in its measurement. Special attention is directed at *return on assets* and *return on common equity*. It explores disaggregations of both these return measures and describes their relevance. Financial leverage is explained and analyzed.
- ◆ **Chapter 12**. This chapter expands returns analysis to emphasize profitability. It emphasizes the components of income and their evaluation. Special attention is directed at sales, cost of sales, taxes, selling and financing expenses. Break-even analysis and its relevance for assessing profitability are explained. Profitability analysis tools are demonstrated, including their interpretation and adjustment.
- ◆ **Chapter 13**. Chapter 13 concludes returns analysis with earnings-based analysis and valuation. Earnings-based analysis focuses on assessing earnings quality, earnings persistence and earning power. Attention is directed at techniques to aid users in measuring and applying analysis concepts. Discussion of earnings-based valuation focuses on issues in estimating company value and forecasting earnings.

◆ **Comprehensive Case**. This case is a comprehensive analysis of financial statements and related notes. It describe steps in analyzing statements and the essential attributes of an analysis report. Analysis is organized around the building blocks of financial statement analysis: liquidity, cash analysis, capital structure, solvency, return on invested capital, asset utilization, operating performance, and profitability.

Explanation of Assignment Material

The book contains a rich set of assignment materials. These assignments are sufficiently diverse, and are suited for basic courses as well as for more advanced undergraduate and graduate courses and professional programs. Following each chapter is a comprehensive list of questions and a wide selection of exercises, problems, cases and internet activities. Each exercise, problem, case and activity is prefaced with a brief caption describing its emphasis. The time required and difficulty of assignment material is generally less for exercises and greatest for cases, with problems somewhere in the middle. Internet activities are similar to exercises and problems.

Instructors at all levels should note the series of exercises, problems and cases based on the financial statements of Adaptec, Campbell Soup Company, and Quaker Oats Company. All these financial statements are reproduced in Supplement A to the text, and Adaptec's annual report is shrink-wrapped with all new books. While these assignments from practice are dispersed among the various chapters to which they relate, there is an integrating feature to them in that they focus on many aspects of the analysis of a single comprehensive financial report. These questions can also be used as a model for the creation of additional assignments or examination materials based on current financial reports selected by the instructor. Additional integrating problems, such as those based on the financial statements of ZETA Company in the Comprehensive Case chapter, are also provided.

Problems which draw on and are based on published financial statements have a number of advantages from an educational standpoint. Being based on facts and transactions that actually transpired imparts a sense of reality to the educational process which heightens student interest and motivation. Moreover, unlike "created" problems, these financial reports come complete with ambiguities, questionable accounting presentations, and similar features of the reality with which the student must ultimately deal with in practice. These problems build on the two major foundations of knowledge from where financial statement analysis rests: (1) understanding the complex financial communications embodied in published financial reports, and (2) mastering analytical tools and techniques to draw insights and conclusions.

The ability to understand fully the financial communications embodied in financial statements and to derive from it all important information are crucial analytical skills that can be perfected only through practice.

[Note on Examination Material: Assignment material at the end of each chapter is abundant and sufficiently varied to provide ample material for examinations. Assignment material can be used as is or can be adapted for examination purposes. It can also be effectively adapted for examinations using published financial statements. The end-of-chapter Questions often provide the basis for many essay-type and multiple choice questions.]

Financial Statement Analysis Project

The most interesting and challenging projects in financial statement analysis involve the analysis of published financial statements. A financial statement analysis project is also a superb means of synthesizing the material covered in the course. Students can be assigned either individual or groups projects, both requirements have merits. One example of a financial statement analysis project assignment is described below (the Comprehensive Case chapter illustrates a similar project using Campbell Soup Company):

Select a company from a non-regulated industry where you can obtain financial statements for at least five previous years.

A.   **Part I**. Using the financial statements, background information on both the company and its industry, as well as financial measures of other companies in the industry, prepare a comprehensive analysis report covering the following specific points:

1. General (brief) description of the company and its industry.
2. An evaluation of the following areas:
   a. Short-term liquidity
   b. Cash forecasting and pro forma analysis
   c. Capital structure and solvency
   d. Return on invested capital
   e. Asset utilization
   f. Profitability and earnings-based analysis

The evaluation should emphasize areas that are likely to expose a prospective investor or lender (or other user) to significant risk. Considerable analyses must be performed before one can identify areas of significant risk or opportunity, and not all investigations will yield important conclusions. The report is expected to include a clear description of the analyses that yield significant conclusions, as well as some limited discussion on analyses not yielding important conclusions. There should be clear identification and focus on those areas and inferences viewed as most significant.

3. Comment on the usefulness of the financial statement disclosures for the analysis.

4. Explain how the alternative accounting principles used in the financial statements affected the analytical measures used in the report.

The analysis project is expected to require a broad variety of financial analysis tools leading to a conclusion regarding the six areas detailed above. The book contains a thorough discussion of all major areas or building blocks of analysis with which this report is concerned. To complete work on the report by the end of the course, the student will likely have to read material in advance of the class schedule. The Comprehensive Case chapter contains an especially useful discussion about preparing a comprehensive financial analysis report.

B.   **Part II**. The second part of the financial statement analysis project requires an analysis and reconstruction of significant business transactions reflected in the financial statements. Nearly all chapters in the book provide examples of how such analysis and reconstruction can be applied to the financial statements of Campbell Soup, Quaker Oats and Adaptec. Examples include the reconstruction of transactions by use of statements of cash flows, reconstruction of income taxes, analysis of cash from operations and the analytical recasting and adjusting of income statements.

Supplement Package

This book is supported with a wide array of supplements aimed at the needs of both students and instructors of financial statement analysis. They include:

● **Financial Statement Analysis--_The Wall Street Journal Edition_**. This version of the book includes a 10-week subscription to *The Wall Street Journal*, the leading business daily newspaper. The *Journal's* coverage of financial statement analysis issues illustrates many of this book's topics.

● **Web Site**. The internet is increasingly important for financial statement analysis. This book is designed to take advantage of internet resources and to help students learn about this important medium. Chapter materials direct readers to World Wide Web sites relevant for financial analysis. This book has its own Web site:

http://www.mhhe.com/business/accounting/wild

It is an excellent starting point for financial analysis resources on the web. This site includes current links to a large number of relevant sites as well as additional information for both instructor and student, including: financial statement databases; up-to-date stock quote information; accepted accounting standards; regulatory agencies; and IEM assignment material.

● **Instructor's Solutions Manual**. A *Solutions Manual* contains complete solutions for assignment material. It is carefully prepared, reviewed and exhaustively checked for accuracy, and is available in both printed and electronic forms.

● **Instructor's Resource Manual**. An *Instructor's Resource Manual* contains chapter summaries, learning objectives, chapter outlines and other helpful teaching materials.

● **Instructor Resource File**. A *Resource File* is available comprising material contained in the *Instructor's Resource Manual*.

● **Case Support (ISBN: 0-256-12584-8)**. An accompanying casebook is available. It includes analyses from practice drawing on financial statements and related disclosures and includes a model case using Coca-Cola along with cases of other "high profile" companies like GE, Apple, Abbott, Whirlpool, Pfizer, and Waste Management.

● **Custom Cases by Darden and Insead**. The instructor has the opportunity to select from a large database of accounting cases developed and used at Darden and Insead.

- **IEM: Iowa Electronics Market**. *IEM* is a fully interactive, real money electronics futures market designed as a teaching supplement. Students use real money accounts to trade contracts with payoffs based on actual events like companies' earnings announcements. Students have incentives to learn about markets and follow company, industry and economic news. *IEM* is a user friendly, menu-driven technology and is easily accessed. Visit the *IEM* Web site at **http://www.biz.uiowa.edu/iem** or telnet directly to **iem.biz.uiowa.edu**, and log into a free practice session.

- *Financial Accounting Video Library*. The *Financial Accounting Video Library* includes short, action-oriented videos for lively classroom discussion of accounting topics including Ben & Jerry's disclosure practices, the purpose of the International Accounting Standards Committee, and the role of the Financial Accounting Standards Board.

- **Computerized Practice Sets**. Computerized Windows©-based practice sets, by L. Mansuetti and K. Weildkamp, help students understand basic accounting underlying financial statements. A corporate simulation practice set is provided with *Wild Goose Marina, Inc.*

- **Case Accompaniments**. Many instructors augment this book with additional case materials. While practical illustrations and case materials are abundant within the text, more are available:
  - **Financial Statement Analysis** by R.J. Ball and S.P. Kothari (ISBN: 0-070-04645-X). This supplement contains research for using financial statement information in financial markets. It focuses on investing and lending decisions, risk assessment, bankruptcy prediction, takeovers and management buyouts, and forecasting.
  - **International Accounting: A Case Approach** by J.A. Schweikart, S.J. Gray, and C.B. Roberts (ISBN: 0-070-55599-0). This case book consists of 40 class tested international cases divided into five sections: financial reporting, financial statement analysis, management and control, auditing, and taxation.
  - **Financial Accounting and Corporate Reporting: A Casebook** by K. Ferris (ISBN 0-256-11996-7). This case book contains over 70 cases on financial accounting and analysis topics-- most cases use actual company data and five are international.

- **Customer Service**. Irwin/McGraw-Hill provides complimentary services, supplements, and supplement packages to adopters. They can be reached at 1-800-634-3963 or at Irwin/McGraw-Hill, 1333 Burr Ridge Parkway, Burr Ridge, IL 60521-6489.

Suggested Course Outlines

Organization of courses using this book depends on the instructor's preferences and the students' background knowledge. Also, the time allocated to the study of financial statement analysis will, of necessity, determine the extent and selection of coverage. Nevertheless, certain commonalities in course content and coverage are normal. Accordingly, some guidance is offered for material coverage to meet certain conditions and objectives.

For the suggested course outlines, the following terms are used:

Intensive coverage–means full coverage of the subject matter in a chapter and includes the assignment of a number of representative end-of-chapter materials comprising varying degrees of difficulty.

Selective coverage--means coverage of a portion of the material in a chapter. Coverage can focus on elementary concepts or on more advanced topics. The assignment material is sufficiently varied to allow for a choice of various levels of difficulties to correspond to the desired level of coverage. Strategic use of appendixes allows added flexibility.

Background reading--means obtaining a general knowledge of the subject matter in a chapter. It does not normally entail extensive formal class coverage or require the assignment of end-of-chapter material.

Courses Emphasizing Analysis

Courses with students that have sufficient accounting knowledge (e.g., accounting majors or practicing accountants) can proceed directly to more advanced analysis topics. Guidance for both undergraduate and graduate courses is offered below:

Undergraduate (or less advanced) Level Courses or Programs:

Chapters intensively covered	Chapters selectively covered	Chapters as background reading
1-2, 7-8, 10-11	9, 12-13, Comp. Case	3-6, Supp. B & C

Graduate (or more advanced) Level Courses or Programs:

Chapters intensively covered	Chapters selectively covered	Chapters as background reading
1-2, 7-13, Comp. Case	3-6	Supp. B & C

Courses Emphasizing Analysis and Accounting

Courses with students that have little accounting knowledge (e.g., finance, investment, lending, and consulting majors or professionals) typically require additional study or review in accounting before moving to advanced analysis topics. Guidance for both undergraduate and graduate courses for these students is offered below:

Undergraduate (or less advanced) Level Courses or Programs:

Chapters intensively covered	Chapters selectively covered	Chapters as background reading
1-2, 7-8, 10-12	9, 13, Comp. Case	3-6, Supp. B & C

Graduate (or more advanced) Level Courses or Programs:

Chapters intensively covered	Chapters selectively covered	Chapters as background reading
1-2, 7-13, Comp. Case	3-6	Supp. B & C

Professional Development, Training and Review Courses

This book is widely used for professional development, training and review courses and programs. A brief listing of professionals educated using this book include: *accountants, actuaries, auditors, bank examiners, bank lenders, business appraisers, chief financial officers, economists, financial planners, planning analysts, management, investment bankers, consultants, investment managers, investment policy consultants, investment sales consultants, investment strategists, management consultants, marketers, options/futures analysts, commodity analysts, portfolio managers, portfolio performance evaluators, portfolio strategists, product/software developers, professors/instructors, quantitative investment analysts, real estate investment managers, securities analysts, securities regulators, securities traders, securities underwriters, stockbroker/registered representatives, valuators of closely held business, valuators of mergers/acquisitions, and venture capital investors.*

Depending on the areas emphasized (e.g., equity investment, credit analysis), the time available, and the training objectives, this book contains a wealth of material for professional programs. Experience shows this book is useful in strengthening and updating professionals' knowledge of financial statement analysis. It is also valuable in exposing professionals to the accounting communications and measurements on which financial statement analysis crucially depends.

Financial statement analysis is an interdisciplinary area. It is common to the fields of accounting, finance, economics and many other business and nonbusiness areas. Decisions requiring analysis of financial statements use data reported from the accounting system. Consequently, to most effectively analyze financial statements, an understanding of accounting measurements and disclosures is crucial. Similarly, to most effectively practice in accounting, a thorough and up-to-date understanding of the analysis needs of users is necessary. Accordingly, sound financial statement analysis involves important elements of both accounting and analysis.

Transition of Topics from 5th to 6th Edition

Chapter 1

Topic	5th edition	6th edition
Users' Objectives	Ch. 1, pp. 3-10; 23-25	Ch. 2, pp. 52-59
Investment theory	Ch. 1, 12-22	Ch. 1, 33-36; 39-42

Chapter 2

Topic	5th edition	6th edition
Accounting and data	Ch. 2, pp. 27-40	Ch. 2, pp. 59-66
Financial statements	Ch. 2, 40-42	Ch. 1, 6-17

Chapter 3

Topic	5th edition	6th edition
Conceptual framework	Ch. 3, pp. 43-55	Ch. 2, pp. 78-82
Accounting standards	Ch. 3, 55-66	Ch. 2, 75-77

Chapter 4

Topic	5th edition	6th edition
Transaction reconstruction	Ch. 4, pp. 71-74	Ch. 2, pp. 66-68
Sources of information	Ch. 4, 75-77	Ch. 1, 17-22
Principal analysis tools	Ch. 4, 77-85	Ch. 1, 22-33
Comparability of data	Ch. 4, 85-88	Ch. 2, 69-72
Computer-assisted analysis	Ch. 4, 94-97	Ch. 2, 83-84
Comparative data sources	Ch. 4, 101-104	Ch. 2, 84-87

Chapter 5

Topic	5th edition	6th edition
Current assets	Ch. 5	Ch. 4, pp. 154-182

Chapter 6

Topic	5th edition	6th edition
Noncurrent assets	Ch. 6	Ch. 4, pp. 182-197

Chapter 7

Topic	5th edition	6th edition
Liabilities	Ch. 7	Ch. 3, pp. 100-129

Chapter 8

Topic	5th edition	6th edition
Shareholders' Equity	Ch. 8	Ch. 3, pp. 129-140

Chapter 9

Topic	5th edition	6th edition
Intercorporate investments, business combinations & foreign operations	Ch. 9	Ch. 5

Chapter 10

Topic	5th edition	6th edition
Analysis of income	Ch. 10	Ch. 6, pp. 258-276

Chapter 11

Topic	5th edition	6th edition
Analysis of income	Ch. 11	Ch. 6, pp. 276-307

Chapter 12

Topic	5th edition	6th edition
Earnings per share	Ch. 12	Appendix 6A

Chapter 13

Topic	5th edition	6th edition
Statement of cash flows	Ch. 13	Ch. 7

Chapter 14

Topic	5th edition	6th edition
Effects of price changes	Ch. 14	Supplement C

Chapter 15

Topic	5th edition	6th edition
Auditor's opinion	Ch. 15	Supplement B

Chapter 16

Topic	5th edition	6th edition
Short-term liquidity	Ch. 16	Ch. 8

Chapter 17

Topic	5th edition	6th edition
Funds analysis & forecasts	Ch. 17	Ch. 9

Chapter 18

Topic	5th edition	6th edition
Capital structure & solvency	Ch. 18	Ch. 10

Chapter 19

Topic	5th edition	6th edition
Return on investment and asset utilization	Ch. 19	Ch. 11

Chapter 20

Topic	5th edition	6th edition
Results of operations I	Ch. 20	Ch. 12

Chapter 21

Topic	5th edition	6th edition
Results of operations II	Ch. 21	Ch. 12

Chapter 22

Topic	5th edition	6th edition
Evaluation and projection of earnings	Ch. 22	Ch. 13

Chapter 23

Topic	5th edition	6th edition
Comprehensive analysis	Ch. 23	Comprehensive Case

Transition of Assignment Material from 5th to 6th Edition

[Key: Q = Questions; E = Exercises; P = Problems; C = Cases]

Chapter 1

5th	6th		5th	6th
Q1	deleted		Q9	Q1-22,26
Q2	Q2-4		Q10	Q2-6
Q3	Q2-5		Q11	deleted
Q4	Q2-3		Q12	Q2-2
Q5	Q1-23		Q13	deleted
Q6	Q1-24		Q14	Q2-7
Q7	Q1-21		Q15	Q2-8
Q8	Q1-25			

Chapter 2

5th	6th		5th	6th
Q1	Q1-1		Q6	Q2-11
Q2	deleted		Q7	Q2-9
Q3	Q1-6		Q8	Q2-10
Q4	Q2-12		Q9	deleted
Q5	Q2-13			

Chapter 3

5th	6th		5th	6th
Q1	deleted		Q14	Q2-21
Q2	Q2-22		Q15	Q2-14
Q3	Q2-23		P1	P2-1
Q4	Q2-24		P2	P2-2
Q5	deleted		P3	P2-3
Q6	Q2-25		P4	E2-1,2
Q7	deleted		P5	P2-4
Q8	Q2-26		P6	P2-5
Q9	Q2-27		P7	P2-6
Q10	Q2-18		P8	E2-3
Q11	Q2-19		P9	P2-7
Q12	Q2-20		P10	C2-2
Q13	deleted			

Chapter 4

5th	6th		5th	6th
Q1	Q2-15		Q21	deleted
Q2	deleted		Q22	Q1-18
Q3	Q2-1		Q23	Q2-16
Q4	deleted		Q24	Q2-28
Q5-6	Q1-10		Q25	Q2-29
Q7	Q1-9		P1	C1-1 (Adaptec)
Q8	Q1-11		P2	C1-2
Q9	Q1-12		P3	E1-1
Q10	Q1-13		P4	E1-2
Q11	Q1-14		P5	P1-1
Q12	Q1-15		P6	P1-2
Q13-14	Q1-16		P7	P2-10
Q15	Q1-17		P8	P1-3
Q16	Q1-18		P9	P1-4
Q17-19	Q1-19		P10	P1-5
Q20	Q1-20		P11	E1-3

Chapter 5

5th	6th		5th	6th
Q1	Q4-1		Q13	Q4-13
Q2	Q4-3		Q14	deleted
Q3	Q4-4		P1	E4-6
Q4	Q4-2		P2	P4-1
Q5	Q4-5		P3	E4-1
Q6	Q4-6		P4	E4-2,3
Q7	Q4-7		P5	P4-2
Q8	Q4-8		P6	E4-4
Q9	Q4-9		P7	P4-3
Q10	Q4-10		P8	E4-5
Q11	Q4-11		P9	C4-2
Q12	Q4-12		P10	C4-3

Chapter 6

5th	6th		5th	6th
Q1	Q4-14		Q12	Q4-24
Q2	Q4-15		P1	P4-4
Q3	Q4-16		P2	P4-5
Q4	Q4-17		P3	E4-7
Q5	deleted		P4	E4-8, P4-6
Q6	Q4-18		P5	P4-7
Q7	Q4-19		P6	P4-8
Q8	Q4-20		P7	E4-9
Q9	Q4-21		P8	P4-9
Q10	Q4-22		P9	E4-10
Q11	Q4-23			

Chapter 7

5th	6th		5th	6th
Q1	Q3-2		Q19	Q3-20
Q2	Q3-3		Q20	Q3-23
Q3	Q3-4		Q21	Q3-24
Q4	Q3-5		Q22	Q3-21
Q5	Q3-6		Q23	Q3-22
Q6	deleted		Q24	Q3-25
Q7	Q3-7		Q25	Q3-19
Q8	Q3-8		P1	P3-1
Q9	Q3-9		P2	E3-1
Q10	Q3-10		P3	E3-2
Q11	Q3-11		P4	E3-3
Q12	Q3-12		P5	P5-2
Q13	Q3-13		P6	P3-3
Q14	Q3-14		P7	E3-4,5
Q15	Q3-15		P8	E3-6
Q16	Q3-16		P9	P3-4
Q17	Q3-17		P10	P3-5
Q18	Q3-18		P11	E3-7

Chapter 8

5th	6th		5th	6th
Q1	Q3-26		Q11	Q3-36
Q2	Q3-27		P1	E3-8
Q3	Q3-28		P2	E3-9
Q4	Q3-29		P3	P3-6
Q5	Q3-30		P4	E3-10
Q6	Q3-31		P5	E3-11
Q7	Q3-32		P6	E3-12
Q8	Q3-33		P7	P3-7,8
Q9	Q3-34		P8	P3-9
Q10	Q3-35			

Chapter 9

5th	6th		5th	6th
Q1	Q5-1		Q22	Q5-19
Q2	Q5-2		Q23	Q5-20
Q3	Q5-3		Q24	Q5-21
Q4	deleted		Q25	deleted
Q5	deleted		Q26	Q5-22
Q6	Q5-4		Q27	Q5-23
Q7	Q5-5		P1	P5-1
Q8	Q5-6		P2	P5-2
Q9	Q5-7		P3	E5-1
Q10	Q5-8		P4	P5-3
Q11	Q5-9		P5	E5-2
Q12	Q5-10		P6	P5-4
Q13	Q5-11		P7	P5-5
Q14	Q5-12		P8	E5-3
Q15	Q5-13		P9	C5-2
Q16	Q5-14		P10	E5-4
Q17	Q5-15		P11	E5-5
Q18	E5-5		P12	C5-3
Q19	Q5-16		P13	E5-6
Q20	Q5-17		P14	C5-4
Q21	Q5-18			

Chapter 10

5th	6th		5th	6th
Q1	Q6-1		Q14	deleted
Q2	Q6-2		Q15	deleted
Q3	Q6-3		P1	E6-1
Q4	Q6-4		P2	P6-1
Q5	Q6-5		P3	P6-1
Q6	Q6-6		P4	P6-2
Q7	deleted		P5	C6-3
Q8	deleted		P6	E6-3
Q9	Q6-7		P7	E6-4
Q10	deleted		P8	C6-4
Q11	Q6-8		P9	E6-5
Q12	Q6-9		P10	E6-6
Q13	Q6-10			

Chapter 11

5th	6th		5th	6th
Q1	deleted		Q22	deleted
Q2	Q3-16		Q23	deleted
Q3	deleted		Q24	Q6-32
Q4	deleted		Q25	Q6-33
Q5	Q6-15		Q26	Q6-34
Q6	Q6-16		Q27	Q6-35
Q7	Q6-17		P1	P6-3
Q8	Q6-18		P2	P6-4
Q9	Q6-19		P3	P6-5
Q10	Q6-20		P4	E6-7
Q11	Q6-21		P5	E6-8
Q12	Q6-22		P6	P6-6
Q13	Q6-23		P7	P6-7
Q14	Q6-24		P8	P6-8
Q15	Q6-25		P9	P6-9
Q16	Q6-26		P10	E6-9
Q17	Q6-27		P11	E6-10
Q18	Q6-28		P12	P6-10
Q19	Q6-29		P13	E6-11
Q20	Q6-30		P14	E6-12
Q21	Q6-31			

Chapter 12

5th	6th		5th	6th
Q1	Q6A-1		Q16	Q6A-11
Q2	deleted		Q17	deleted
Q3	Q6A-2		Q18	Q6A-12
Q4	Q6A-3		Q19	Q6A-13
Q5	Q6A-4		P1	E6A-1
Q6	deleted		P2	E6A-2
Q7	Q6A-5		P3	E6A-3
Q8	Q6A-6		P4	P6A-1
Q9	deleted		P5	P6A-2
Q10	Q6A-7		P6	P6A-3
Q11	deleted		P7	C6A-1
Q12	Q6A-8		P8	C6A-2
Q13	deleted		P9	P6A-4
Q14	Q6A-9		P10	P6A-5
Q15	Q6A-10			

Chapter 13

5th	6th		5th	6th
Q1	Q7-1		P10	P7-5
Q2	deleted		P11	P7-6
Q3	Q7-2		P12	E7-6
Q4	Q7-3		P13	P7-7
Q5	Q7-4		P14	P7-8
Q6	Q7-5		P15	E7-7
Q7	Q7-6		P16	C7-3
Q8	Q7-7		P17	C7-3
Q9	Q7-8		P18	P7-9
Q10	Q7-9		P19	P7-10
Q11	Q7-10		P20	E7-8
P1	E7-1		P21	P7-11
P2	E7-2		P22	P7-12
P3	E7-3		P23	P7-13
P4	P7-1		P24	E7-9
P5	P7-2		P25	E7-10
P6	P7-3		P26	P7-14
P7	E7-4		P27	E7-10
P8	E7-5		P28	P7-15
P9	P7-4			

Chapter 14

5th	6th		5th	6th
Q1	deleted		Q8	Q C-6
Q2	deleted		P1	E C-1
Q3	Q C-1		P2	E C-2
Q4	Q C-2		P3	P C-1
Q5	Q C-3		P4	P C-2
Q6	Q C-4		P5	E C-3
Q7	Q C-5		P6	E C-4

Chapter 15

5th	6th		5th	6th
Q1	Q B-1		Q9	Q B-9
Q2	Q B-2		Q10	deleted
Q3	Q B-3		Q11	Q B-10
Q4	Q B-4		Q12	Q B-11
Q5	Q B-5		Q13	Q B-12
Q6	Q B-6		Q14	Q B-13
Q7	Q B-7		Q15	Q B-14
Q8	Q B-8			

Chapter 16

5th	6th		5th	6th
Q1	Q8-1		Q25	Q8-25
Q2	Q8-2		Q26	Q8-26
Q3	Q8-3		Q27	Q8-27
Q4	Q8-4		Q28	Q8-28
Q5	Q8-5		Q29	Q8-29
Q6	Q8-6		Q30	Q8-30
Q7	Q8-7		Q31	Q8-17
Q8	Q8-8		Q32	Q8-31
Q9	Q8-9		Q33	Q8-32
Q10	Q8-10		P1	C8-2
Q11	Q8-11		P2	P8-1
Q12	Q8-12		P3	E8-1
Q13	Q8-13		P4	E8-2
Q14	Q8-14		P5	E8-3
Q15	Q8-15		P6	P8-2
Q16	Q8-16		P7	C8-3
Q17	Q8-17		P8	P8-3
Q18	Q8-18		P9	C8-4
Q19	Q8-19		P10	P8-4
Q20	Q8-20		P11	C8-5
Q21	Q8-21		P12	P8-5
Q22	Q8-22		P13	E8-4
Q23	Q8-23		P14	P8-6
Q24	Q8-24			

Chapter 17

5th	6th		5th	6th
Q1	Q9-1		Q14	Q9-14
Q2	Q9-2		Q15	Q9-15
Q3	Q9-3		Q16	Q9-16
Q4	Q9-4		P1	E9-1
Q5	Q9-5		P2	P9-1
Q6	Q9-6		P3	P9-2
Q7	Q9-7		P4	E9-2
Q8	Q9-8		P5	E9-3
Q9	Q9-9		P6	P9-3
Q10	Q9-10		P7	C9-2
Q11	Q9-11		P8	C9-3
Q12	Q9-12		P9	C9-4
Q13	Q9-13			

Chapter 18

5th	6th		5th	6th
Q1	Q10-1		Q24	deleted
Q2	Q10-5		Q25	Q10-4
Q3	Q10-6		Q26	Q10-24
Q4	Q10-7		Q27	Q10-25
Q5	Q10-8		Q28	Q10-26
Q6	Q10-9		Q29	Q10-27
Q7	Q10-10		P1	P10-1
Q8	Q10-11		P2	E10-1
Q9	Q10-2		P3	P10-2
Q10	Q10-3		P4	E10-2
Q11	Q10-12		P5	E10-3
Q12	Q10-13		P6	P10-3
Q13	Q10-14		P7	P10-4
Q14	deleted		P8	E10-4
Q15	Q10-15		P9	P10-5
Q16	Q10-16		P10	P10-6
Q17	Q10-17		P11	P10-7
Q18	Q10-18		P12	E10-5
Q19	Q10-19		P13	P10-8
Q20	Q10-20		P14	C10-2
Q21	Q10-21		P15	C10-3
Q22	Q10-22		P16	P10-9
Q23	Q10-23			

Chapter 19

5th	6th		5th	6th
Q1	Q11-1		P1	C11-2
Q2	Q11-2		P2	P11-3
Q3	Q11-3		P3	P11-1
Q4	Q11-4		P4	E11-1
Q5	Q11-5		P5	E11-2
Q6	Q11-6		P6	E11-3
Q7	Q11-7		P7	E11-4
Q8	Q11-8		P8	E11-5
Q9	Q11-9		P9	E11-6
Q10	Q11-10		P10	E11-7
Q11	Q11-11		P11	P11-2
Q12	Q11-12		P12	P11-5
Q13	Q11-13		P13	P11-6
Q14	Q11-14		P14	C11-3
Q15	Q11-15		P15	P11-4

Chapter 20

5th	6th		5th	6th
Q1	Q12-1		Q10	Q12-10
Q2	Q12-2		Q11	Q12-11
Q3	Q12-3		Q12	Q12-12
Q4	Q12-4		P1	P12-1
Q5	Q12-5		P2	P12-2
Q6	Q12-6		P3	E12-1
Q7	Q12-7		P4	E12-2
Q8	Q12-8		P5	C12-2
Q9	Q12-9			

Chapter 21

5th	6th		5th	6th
Q1	Q12-13		P5	E12-6
Q2	Q12-19		P6	E12-7
Q3	Q12-20		P7	P12-4
Q4	Q12-21		P8	E12-8
Q5	Q12-22		P9	E12-9
Q6	Q12-23		P10	E12-10
Q7	Q12-24		P11	P12-5
Q8	Q12-14		P12	P12-6
Q9	Q12-15		P13	E12-11
Q10	Q12-16		P14	C12-3
Q11	Q12-17		P15	C12-4
Q12	Q12-18		P16	P12-7
P1	E12-3		P17	C12-5
P2	P12-3		P18	P12-8
P3	E12-4		P19	P12-9
P4	E12-5			

Chapter 22

5th	6th		5th	6th
Q1	Q13-1		Q21	Q13-21
Q2	Q13-2		Q22	Q13-24
Q3	Q13-3		Q23	Q13-25
Q4	Q13-4		Q24	deleted
Q5	Q13-5		Q25	Q13-26
Q6	Q13-6		Q26	Q13-27
Q7	Q13-7		Q27	Q13-28
Q8	Q13-8		Q28	Q13-29
Q9	Q13-9		Q29	Q13-30
Q10	Q13-10		P1	P13-1
Q11	Q13-11		P2	E13-1
Q12	Q13-12		P3	P13-2
Q13	Q13-13		P4	C13-2
Q14	Q13-14		P5	P13-3
Q15	Q13-15		P6	P13-4
Q16	Q13-16		P7	C13-3
Q17	Q13-17		P8	E13-2
Q18	Q13-18		P9	E13-3
Q19	Q13-19		P10	E13-4
Q20	Q13-20		P11	E13-5

Chapter 23

5th	6th		5th	6th
Q1	Q CC-1		P3	C CC-1
Q2	Q CC-2		P4	P CC-1
Q3	Q CC-3		P5	C CC-2
Q4	Q CC-4		P6	C CC-3
Q5	Q CC-5		P7	P CC-2
P1	E CC-1		P8	P CC-3
P2	E CC-2			

◄ CHAPTER 1 ►

Overview of Financial Statement Analysis

◄ CHAPTER REVIEW ►

Financial statement analysis applies analytical tools and techniques to general-purpose financial statements and related data to derive estimates and inferences useful in business decisions. It transforms *raw data* into valuable information for decision making. The process of financial statement analysis depends on users' objectives. It is useful as a *screening* tool in selecting investment or merger candidates, as a *forecasting* tool of future financial conditions and consequences, as a *diagnostic* tool in assessing financing, investing, operating, or other business ventures, and as an *evaluation* tool of managerial and other business decisions. Financial statement analysis reduces our reliance on hunches, guesses, and intuition, and in turn diminishes our uncertainty in decision-making. It does not lessen the need for expert judgment, but rather establishes an effective and systematic basis for business decisions.

This chapter describes users of financial statements and the business activities underlying financial statements. We also introduce several fundamental tools and techniques of financial statement analysis. Special attention is devoted to a preliminary financial statement analysis of an actual company--Adaptec, Inc.

◄ CHAPTER OUTLINE ►

► **Users of Financial Statements**

► **Business Activities in a Market Economy**

    Planning Activities

    Financing Activities

    Investing Activities

    Operating Activities

► **Financial Statements Capture Business Activities**

    Balance Sheet

    Income Statement

    Statement of Shareholders' Equity

    Statement of Cash Flows

    Links between Financial Statements

► **Information Accompanying Financial Statements**

    Management's Discussion and Analysis (MD&A)

    Management Report

    Auditor Report

    Explanatory Notes

    Supplementary Information

    Social Responsibility Reports

    Proxy Statements

► **Preview of Financial Statement Analysis**

    Building Blocks of Analysis

    Comparative Financial Statement Analysis

    Common-Size Financial Statement Analysis

    Ratio Analysis of Financial Statements

    Specialized Analysis Tools

► **Financial Statement Analysis in an Efficient Capital Market**

    Capital Market Efficiency

    Market Efficiency Implications of Financial Statement Analysis

► **Preview of This Book's Organization**

► **Appendix 1A Investment Theory and Financial Statement Analysis**

◄ Learning Objectives ►

- **Explain why financial statement analysis is important.**

- **Identify financial statement users and information relevant for their decisions.**

- **Describe major types of business activities and their impact on financial statements.**

- **Explain the purpose of each financial statement and the linkages between them.**

- **Identify additional information in a financial reporting system and its relevance.**

- **Analyze and interpret the financial statements of an actual company as a preview to more fundamental analysis.**

- **Describe several financial statement analysis techniques and their relevance.**

◄ Learning Objectives ►

- **Explain the purpose of financial statement analysis in an efficient market.**

- **Describe important investment theories and their implications for financial analysis (Appendix 1A).**

◄ Answers to Questions ►

1. Financial statement analysis is the judgmental process which has as its aim the evaluation of the current and the past financial conditions and results of operations of an enterprise. One of its major objectives is to arrive at the best possible estimated predictions about future financial conditions and performance.

2. Financial statement users can be broadly classified into two groups. *Internal users*, primarily the managers of a company, are involved in making operating and strategic decisions regarding the business. *External users* are individuals not directly involved in the company's operations.

   Several primary external users of financial statements are introduced in the chapter. *Creditors* are bankers, bondholders, and other individuals who lend money to business enterprises. *Equity investors* include existing and potential shareholders of a company. Other external users include *merger and acquisition analysts*, *auditors*, a corporation's *board of directors*, *regulatory agencies*, *employees*, *intermediaries*, *suppliers*, and *customers*.

3. A business enterprise pursues four major activities in a desire to provide a saleable product and to yield a satisfactory return on investment:

   Planning activities. A company exists to implement specific goals and objectives. A company's goals and objectives are captured in a business plan or strategy, describing the company's purpose, its strategy, and its tactics for activities. A business plan assists managers in focusing their efforts and identifying expected opportunities and obstacles.

   Financing Activities. A company requires financing to carry out its business plan. Financing activities are the means companies use to pay for these ventures. Because of their magnitude, and their potential to determine success or failure of a venture, companies must take care in acquiring and managing their financial resources. There are two main sources of business financing: equity investors (sometimes referred to as owners or shareholders) and creditors.

   Investing Activities. Investing activities are the means a company uses to acquire and maintain investments for obtaining, developing, and selling products or services. Financing provides the funds necessary for acquisition of investments needed to carry out business plans. Investments include land, buildings, equipment, legal rights (patents, licenses, and copyrights), inventories, human capital (managers and employees), accounting systems, and all components necessary for the company to operate.

   Operating Activities. Operating activities represent the "carrying out" of the business plan, given necessary financing and investing. These activities involve at least five basic components--research, purchasing, production, marketing, and labor. Operating activities are a company's primary source of income. Income measures a company's success in buying from input markets and selling in output markets. How well a company does in devising business plans and strategies, and with decisions on materials comprising the mix of operating activities, determines business success or failure.

4. Business activities--planning, financing, investing, and operating--can be synthesized into a cohesive picture of how businesses function in a market economy. Step one is the company's formulation of plans and strategies. Next, a company obtains necessary financing from equity investors and creditors. Financing is used to acquire investments in resources to produce goods or services. The company uses these investments to undertake operating activities.

   At the end of a period of time--typically quarterly or annually--financial statements are released. These statements update listings of financing and investing activities, and summarize operating activities for the most recent period(s). This is the role of financial statements and our object of analysis. Financial statements report on business activities, and disclosure is at a point in time. Financial statements' listing of financing and investing activities are reported for a *point in time*, whereas operating activities are reported for a *period of time*.

5. The four primary financial statements published by companies are the balance sheet, the income statement, the statement of owners' equity, and the statement of cash flows.

Balance Sheet. The accounting equation is the basis for our system of financial accounting:

$$\text{Assets} = \text{Liabilities} + \text{Owners' Equity}.$$

The left-hand side of the equation relates to the economic resources controlled by the firm, or *assets*. These resources are valuable in the sense that they represent potential sources of future revenues for the firm. The firm uses these resources to carry out its operating activities. In order to engage in its operating activities, the firm must obtain funds to invest in the necessary asset base. The right-hand side of the fundamental accounting equation details the sources of these funds. *Liabilities* represent funds obtained from creditors. These amounts represent obligations of the firm or, alternatively, the claims of creditors on the assets of the firm. *Owners' equity*, also referred to as shareholders' equity, represents two amounts: (1) the funds invested or contributed by owners, or "contributed capital", and (2) those accumulated earnings since inception of the firm in excess of distributions to owners, or "retained earnings". From the owners' point of view, these amounts represent their claim on the firm's assets.

It is helpful to rewrite the accounting equation in terms of the underlying business activities ("economics"):

$$\text{Investing Activities} = \text{Financing Activities}.$$

Recognizing the two basic sources of financing for investments, this can be rewritten as:

$$\text{Investments} = \text{Creditor Financing} + \text{Owner Financing}.$$

Income Statement. The income statement is designed to measure a company's financial performance between balance sheet dates, hence, it references a period of time. An income statement lists revenues, expenses, gains, and losses of a company over this period. The "bottom line" of the income statement, net income, measures the increase (or decrease) in the net worth of the firm (i.e., assets minus liabilities), before consideration of any distributions to owners. Most contemporary accounting systems, the U.S. included, determine net income using the *accrual basis of accounting*. Under this method, revenues are recognized when the company sells goods and/or renders services, independent of the receipt of cash. Expenses, in turn, are recognized during the period in which any related revenue is recorded, independent of the payment of cash.

Statement of Owners' Equity. The statement of owners' equity discloses changes in the component accounts comprising owners' equity. The statement is useful in identifying the reasons for changes in owners' claims on the assets of the company. In addition, accepted practice excludes certain gains and losses from net income which, instead, are directly reported in the statement of owners' equity.

Statement of Cash Flows. Under the accrual basis of accounting, net income equals net cash flow only over the life of the firm. This creates a demand for periodic reporting on the amount of cash generated by a firm. The statement of cash flows details the cash inflows and outflows related to a company's operating, investing, and financing activities over a period of time.

6. Of the data which are available for meaningful analysis, financial statements are important because they are objective in that they portray actual events which already happened, they are concrete in that they can be quantified, and being quantifiable, they can be measured. This attribute of measurability endows financial statement data with another important characteristic: since they are expressed in the common denominator of money this enables us to add and combine the data, to relate them to other data, and to otherwise manipulate them arithmetically. The above attributes contribute to the great importance of financial accounting data, both historical or projected, to the decision-making process.

Financial accounting as a social science is subject to many shortcomings, imperfections and limitations. It is also an evolving discipline subject to continuous change and improvement, based mostly on experience.

Some users of accounting data, particularly those from other disciplines, became at times so impatient with these shortcomings, imperfections and limitations as to suggest that some substitute be used instead. There is no such substitute. Double entry bookkeeping, an ingenious recording and accounting system spawned in the middle ages and perfected ever since into the modern discipline of accounting is and remains the only viable system for the systematic recording classification and summarization of myriads of business activities. The only realistic hope for improvement lies in the improvement of this time-tested system rather than in its substitution by some other method which, while possessing theoretical elegance, cannot be implemented in practice.

It is thus incumbent on anyone who desires to analyze intelligently the financial position and the results of operations of an enterprise, to study the accounting framework its terminology, and its conventions, as well as the imperfections and limitations to which it is subject.

7. Formal financial statements are not the sole output of the financial reporting system. Additional information is communicated by firms through the following sources.

Management's Discussion and Analysis (MD&A). Companies with publicly-traded debt and equity securities are required by the SEC to provide a discussion of their financial condition and results of operations in the MD&A section of all quarterly and annual reports.

Management Report. The management report sets out the responsibilities of management in preparing the company's financial communications.

Auditor Report. The external auditor is an independent certified public accountant hired by management to assess whether the company's financial statements are prepared in conformity with generally accepted accounting principles. Auditors provide an important "check" on financial statements prior to their release to the public.

Explanatory Notes. Notes are a means of communicating additional information regarding items included in and excluded from the body of the statements.

Supplementary Information. Certain supplemental schedules are required by the accounting regulatory agencies. These schedules can appear in notes to financial statements or, in the case of companies with publicly-held securities, in exhibits to the Form 10-K filed with the Securities and Exchange Commission.

Social Responsibility Reports. Companies increasingly recognize their need for social responsibility. While reports of community-related activities are increasing, there is no standard format or accepted standard.

Proxy Statements. A proxy statement is the document containing the information necessary to assist shareholders in voting on the matters for which the proxy is solicited.

8. Whatever approach to financial statement analysis is taken and whatever methods are used, we always must examine one or more important aspects of an enterprise's financial condition and results of operations. Our financial analysis, motivated by any set of objectives, can be structured within any or all of six areas of inquiry. These six areas of inquiry and investigation are considered "building blocks" of financial statement analysis.

Short-term liquidity refers to a company's ability to meet short-term obligations at a particular point in time.

Funds flow relates to the forecasting of future availability and disposition of cash.

Capital structure and long-term solvency refer to a company's ability to meet long-term obligations and weather random shocks.

Return on investment measures the company's ability to provide financial rewards sufficient to attract and retain suppliers of funds.

Asset utilization relates to the intensity that assets are used to generate revenues needed to reach a sufficient level of profitability.

Operating performance pertains to the measurement and analysis of a company's periodic performance.

9. a. Comparative financial statements
        (1) Year-to-year changes
        (2) Trend analysis
    b. Common-size financial statements
    c. Ratio analysis
    d. Other specialized analyses such as cash forecasts, statements of variation in gross margin, etc.

10. a. In financial analysis, no number standing by itself can be meaningful and it gains meaning only when it is related to some other comparable quantity. Comparative analysis focuses on exceptions and variations and helps the analyst to make decisions for selecting among alternative choices.

    b. Comparison can be made against (1) past experience, (2) external data in the industry, and (3) some compiled yardsticks such as standards, budgets, and forecasts.

    c. A comparison, to be meaningful and fair, must be made between data which are prepared on a similar basis. If data are not directly comparable, the analyst should make appropriate adjustments before he attempts to make meaningful comparison. He must also keep in mind the fact that the past is seldom an unqualified guide to the future.

11. The trend of the past should be a fairly good predictor of the future if all the relevant variables remain constant or nearly constant. In practice, however, this is rarely the case. Therefore, the analyst should use the results of the trend analysis and adjust them in the light of other available information including the expected state of the general economy. Trend analysis will, in any case, reveal the direction of change in operating performance, and the velocity as well as the magnitude of change in various related variables.

12. One indicator in the absence of the other has only limited usefulness. An increase to $4.00 from a base year of $1.00 will indicate a 400 percent increase; however, the percentage in this case has hardly any meaning. Both have to be considered simultaneously. Reference to the absolute dollar amounts has to be made in order to retain the proper perspective when a significant change in percentage is revealed by analysis.

13. Since a division by zero is not mathematically defined, it is impossible to get changes in percentage when there is no figure for the base year. Also, if there is a negative figure in the base year and a positive figure in another year, or vice versa, a mere mathematical computation of percentage changes does not make much sense.

14. In index number analysis, all figures are expressed with reference to a base year figure. Since the base serves as a frame of reference, it is desirable to choose a year which is "typical" for the business. If the earliest year in the series analyzed cannot be regarded as typical, then another year should be chosen as a base year.

15. By utilizing index numbers, the analyst can measure change over time. Such analysis enables the financial analyst to assess management's policies and, when examined in the light of the economic environment of the periods studied. the ability of the enterprise to adapt to adversities and opportunities. Moreover, trend analysis enables the correlation of change among the various components of the financial statements and the evaluation of the relative change in them. For example, changes in sales and in accounts receivable are logically correlated and can be expected to display such correlation in an examination of relative trends.

16. a. While index number analysis compares changes between years in terr of base year, common-size financial statements enable comparisons of changes in the elements which make up the financial statements. The figures in each line item of the financial statements are divided by the total and are expressed in percentages. The total should add up to 100°6. Thus, internal structural changes which occur in the financial statements over the years can be assessed.

   b. The analysis of common-size financial statements focuses on major aspects of the internal structure of the financial statements such as:

   1. capital structure and sources of the capital,
   2. distribution of assets in which funds are invested,
   3. the composition of important segments of financial statements such as, for example, the current assets,
   4. the relative magnitude of various expenses in relation to sales.

   Very useful information can be obtained by a comparison of common-size statements of a single enterprise over the years. The advantage of this tool is even more evident in the case of comparisons between two enterprises of different sizes. Since analyses can be made on a uniform basis, it greatly facilitates the comparisons.

17. No. Some items in the financial statements have no a priori or logical relationship to other items. To be significant, the ratio must express a relationship that has significance.

18. Since not all relationships have meaning and not all ratios are useful for all analytical purposes, the financial analyst should be experienced in the selection of ratios which are useful for the particular problem at hand. Unfortunately, ratios are frequently misunderstood and their significance is often overrated. Ratios can provide the analyst with clues and symptoms of underlying conditions. Ratios can highlight the areas which require further investigating and inquiry. Ratios, like all other analytical tools, cannot predict the future. Moreover, the usefulness of the analytical information developed by means of ratios depends largely on the intelligent and skillful interpretation by the financial analyst.

   Of the several limitations on ratio analysis, two of the most significant are:

   a. Changing Price Levels. Different items on the balance sheet and income statement are valued as of different times, with the result that ratios can change over time even though underlying factors do not. For example, a plant constructed in 1950 and running at full capacity ever since might be compared to dollar sales , in 1972 dollars for a sales/gross plant ratio. Once we begin multiplying ratios together, it becomes difficult (if not impossible) to view everything in comparable real dollar terms.

   b. Diverse Underlying Businesses. In most cases for a multimarket company, even one reporting some breakdown of sales and earnings, ratios calculated from published statements represent averages or approximations and obscure what may be very significant differences by product line. For example, a utilization ratio may conceal the fact that there are different levels of facility utilization for different products. Yet, the overall utilization ratio would show a balanced picture with no great bottlenecks or problems.

   (CFA)

19. a. Current ratio, Acid-test ratio, Working capital to total liabilities, Net worth to total debt, Net worth to long-term debt, Net worth to fixed assets

   b. Times interest earned, Gross margin ratio, Operating profits to sales, Pretax income to sales, Net income to sales

   c. Inventory turnover, Days' sales in receivables, Return on total assets, Return on equity capital, Sales to cash, Sales to accounts receivable, Sales to inventory, Sales to working capital, Sales to fed assets, Sales to other assets, Sales to total assets

20. a. Cash forecasts
    b. Statement of changes in financial position (sources and uses of funds)
    c. Statements of variation in gross margin
    d. Break-even analysis

21. The efficient market hypothesis (EMH) deals with the reaction of market prices to financial and other data in various ways. First, it should be noted that the Efficient Market Hypothesis has its origins in the random walk hypothesis which states that at any given point in time the size and direction of the next price change is random relative to what is known about an investment at that given time. There are three derivatives of this hypothesis: The first is known as the *weak form* of the EMH and it states that current prices reflect fully the information implied by historical price time series. The second is the *semi strong form* which states that prices fully reflect all publicly available information. The third is the *strong form* and it asserts that prices reflect *all* information including that which is considered inside information.

The EMH, in all its forms, has undergone extensive empirical testing with much of the evidence seeming to be supportive of the theory.

22. The EMH is almost completely dependent on the assumption that competent and well- informed analysts, using certain tools of analysis, will constantly strive to evaluate and act upon the ever-changing stream of new information entering the marketplace. However, even the theory's proponents claim that since all that is known is already instantly reflected in market prices, there is no need for financial statement analysis.

This situation presents an unexplained and unresolved paradox. For when thousands of intelligent analysts are assumed to be capable enough to keep our security markets efficient through their efforts, they are not intelligent enough to realize that their efforts can yield no individual advantage. Moreover, should they suddenly realize that their efforts are unrewarded, the market would cease to be efficient.

There are a number of factors which may explain this paradox The fact is that the entire EMH is built on evidence based on an evaluation of aggregate rather than individual investor behavior. The focusing on macro or aggregate behavior results not only in highlighting of average performance and results but also ignores and masks the results achieved by individual ability, hard work, and ingenuity as well as by superior timing in acting on information as it becomes available.

Few would doubt that important information travels fast. After all, enough is at stake to make it travel fast. Nor is it surprising that the securities markets are rapid processors of information. In fact, using the same type of deductive reasoning as used by the efficient market proponents, we could conclude that the speed and the hard working efficiency of the market must be evidence that the market participants who make it happen are motivated by substantial rewards.

The reasoning behind the EMH's alleged implication for the usefulness of security analysis fails to recognize the essential difference between information and its proper interpretation. Even if all the information available on a security at a given point in time is impounded in its price, that price may not reflect value. It may be under- or overvalued depending on the degree to which an incorrect interpretation or evaluation of the available information has been made by those whose actions determine the market price at a given time.

The work of financial statement analysis is complex and demanding. The spectrum of users of financial statements varies all the way from the institutional analyst who concentrates on only a few companies in one industry to one who merely looks at the pictures of an annual report. All act on financial information but surely not with the same insights and competence.

The competent evaluation of "new information" entering the marketplace requires the possession of a prior fund of knowledge, of an information mosaic into which the new information can be fitted, as part of a link in a chain of

---

analytical information, before it can be evaluated and interpreted. Only few have the ability and are prepared to expend the efforts and resources needed to produce such information mosaics and it is only natural that they would reap the rewards by being able to act both competently and confidently on the new information received. This advantage in timing is all important in the marketplace.

The vast resources that must be brought to bear on the competent analysis of equity securities has caused some segments of the securities markets to be more efficient than others. Thus, the market for shares of the largest companies is more inefficient because many more analysts follow such securities in comparison to those who follow small and lesser known companies.

The function and purpose of the analysis of equity securities is construed much too narrowly by those who judge its usefulness in an efficient market. While the search for overvalued and undervalued securities is an important function of security analysis, the importance of risk assessment and loss avoidance, in the total framework of investment decision making, cannot be overemphasized. Security analysis can evaluate the justification of risk premium associated with a security. Thus, the prevention of serious investment errors is at least as important as the discovery of undervalued securities. Yet, a review of the CAPM and of beta theory tends to explain why this important function of analysis is neglected by adherents to these macro-oriented models of the security markets. For to some it is a basic premise of these theories that the analysis of unsystematic risk is not worthwhile because that kind of risk taking is not rewarded by the market. They maintain that such risks should be diversified away and that the portfolio manager should look only to systematic or market risk for his rewards.

Investment results are achieved through the careful study and analysis of individual enterprises rather than by an exclusive focus on market aggregates. Our approach in this area is to emphasize the value of fundamental investment analysis not only as a means of keeping our securities markets efficient and our capital markets rational and strong but also as the means by which those investors who, having obtained information. are willing and able to apply knowledge, effort, and ingenuity to its analysis. For those investors, the fruits of fundamental analysis and research, long before being converted to a "public good,. will provide adequate rewards. These rewards will not be discernable, however, in the performance of investors aggregated to comprise mayor market segments, such as mutual funds. Instead they will remain as individual as the efforts needed to bring them about.

23. Systematic risk is that portion of total risk which is attributable to the movement of the market as a whole. Unsystematic risk is the residual risk that is unique to a specific security. While the elements of unsystematic risk cannot be neatly separated from the systematic variety, the various components of the unsystematic risk, broadly speaking, are:

(1) *Economic Risk* which reflects risks of the overall economic environment in which the enterprise operates including general economic risk (fluctuations in business activity!, capital market risk (including changes in interest rates), and purchasing power risk (due to inflation and the consequent decrease in the purchasing power of the dollar).

(2) *Business Risk* which is concerned with the ever-present uncertainty regarding a business enterprise's ability to earn a satisfactory return on its investments as well as with the multitude of cost and revenue factors which enter into the determination of such a return. It includes the factors of competition, product mix, and management ability. Because of the effect of the market discount rate on systematic risk we cannot look at business risk as distinctive from investment risk

(3) *Financial Risk* is basically concerned with capital structure and with the ability of an enterprise to meet fixed and senior charges and claims.

(4) *Accounting Risk* which is inherent in the existence of alternative accounting principles, the loose criteria which define them, and the consequent loose standards Of practice. This lack of assurance about the principles used or the

method or rigor of their application may lead to a wide variety of results and hence to a great degree of uncertainty. The accounting risk may also include the degree of conservatism of accounting principles in use or the lack of it.

24. The capital asset pricing model (CAPM) is based on the assumption that investors desire to hold securities in portfolios which are efficient in the sense that they provide a maximum return for a given *level* of risk. The model was derived under the following simplifying assumptions:

    (1)   that there exists a riskless security.
    (2)   that investors are able to borrow or lend unlimited amounts at the riskless rate, and
    (3)   that all investors have identical investment horizons and act on the basis of identical expectations and predictions.

    Based on these assumptions, it can be shown that when capital markets are in a state of equilibrium, the expected return on an individual security $E(R_i)$, is related to its systematic risk β_i in the following linear form:

    $$E(R_i) = E(R_0) + [E(R_M) - E(R_0)]\, \beta_i$$

    The above formulation states, in essence, that under conditions of equilibrium, a security's expected return equals the expected return of a riskless security, $E(R_0)$, plus a premium for risk taking. This risk premium consists of a constant, $[E(R_M) - E(R_0)]$, which is the difference between the return expected by the market and the return on a riskless security (such as a short-term government bond) multiplied by the systematic risk of the security, which is known as beta. Thus under the CAPM, each security has an expected return which is related to its risk. This risk is measured by the security's systematic movements with the overall market and it cannot be eliminated by portfolio diversification.

25. The concept of trade-off between risk and return means that the higher the risk the higher the expected return and the lower the risk the lower the expected return. It is quite obvious that the greater the perceived degree of risk of an investment or of a loan, the greater the required rate of return to compensate for such greater risk. This concept is very significant to portfolio construction provided that there is a formal framework for quantifying both risk and return.

    This two-dimensional risk-return approach offers the investor an ability to choose in the trade-off between risk and return. It begins with the observation that the future return on a security can be estimated in the form of a probability distribution. Under certain assumptions this distribution could be summarized in terms of two variables risk and return. Using these variables a framework for deciding how much of each security to hold in constructing a portfolio could be devised.

26. The function and purpose of the analysis of equity securities is construed much too narrowly by those who judge its usefulness in an efficient market. While the search for overvalued and undervalued securities is an important function of security analysis, the importance of risk assessment and loss avoidance, in the total framework of investment decision making, cannot be overemphasized. Security analysis can evaluate the justification of risk premium associated with a security. Thus, the prevention of serious investment errors is at least as important as the discovery of undervalued securities. Yet, a review of the CAPM and of beta theory tends to explain why this important function of analysis is neglected by adherents to these macro-oriented models of the security markets. For to some it is a basic premise of these theories that the analysis of unsystematic risk is not worthwhile because that kind of risk taking is not rewarded by the market. They maintain that such risks should be diversified away and that the portfolio manager should look only to systematic or market risk for his rewards.

    Investment results are achieved through the careful study and analysis of individual enterprises rather than by an exclusive focus on market aggregates. Our approach in this area is to emphasize the value of fundamental investment analysis not only as a means of keeping our securities markets efficient and our capital markets rational and strong but also as the means by which those investors who, having obtained information. are willing and able to apply knowledge, effort, and ingenuity to its analysis. For those investors, the fruits of fundamental analysis and research, long before being converted to a "public good,. will provide adequate rewards. These rewards will not be discernable, however, in the performance of investors aggregated to comprise mayor market segments, such as mutual funds. Instead they will remain as individual as the efforts needed to bring them about.

28. The use of computers on investment analysis can be broken down into four major functions:

   I. Screening
      - performs numerous calculations
      - chooses only those issues meeting certain tests
      - or lists in order (rate of return, for instance) of performance

   II. Security Analysis
      - performs numerous calculations on past data
      - spot trends
      - simple calculations
      - regression analysis
      - predictive capabilities
      - projections based on regression data
      - simple models
      - sensitivity analysis
      - complex, probabilistic analysis

   III. Market timing
      - technical analysis
            - price changes
            - volume
            - momentum
      - economic analysis
            - past data
            - regression projections

   IV. Portfolio Management
      - computation of past performance
      - optimization objectives through linear programming
      - Markowitz's model which takes into account covariances of stocks.

   In sum, the computer's fabulous computational ability allows for (1) detailed analysis of past data, and (2) sophisticated, statistically sound, complex projections of future expectations.

   (CFA)

29. Limitations or disadvantages to the application of computers to security analysis revolve primarily around the data bank

   1. Lack of uniformity in accounting principles applied by different companies. The seeming comparability of corporate data is sometimes quite illusory.
   2. Lack of information in the data bank to tell the analyst how the accounting of the company was done. In this case the analyst has to rely on more traditional sources.
   3. It is frequently the case that there are "bugs" in the actual data bank. Examples are failure to change previous years' data for stock splits, outright absence of data, etc.
   4. Retroactive changes cannot be made accurately because companies only change final figures.

5. Some companies don't provide as full information as others for analytical purposes and therefore some comparisons cannot be done for all companies.
6. Absence of footnotes on data banks, and other written material which could at the analysis.

(CFA)

◄ Answers to Exercises ►

Exercise 1-1

	Yr. 6	Yr. 5	Yr. 4	Cumulative Amount	Annual Average Amount
Net Sales	6,880			13,230	4,410
Cost of Goods Sold		2,810	1,810	7,830	
Gross Profit				5,400	
Total Operating Expenses	930	465	945	2,340	780
Income Before Taxes				3,060	1.020
Net Income				1,688	563

Comments: Overall, the results are rather volatile. Net sales have steadily increased, almost doubling in Year 6. Gross profit dipped in Year 5, but increased considerably in Year 6. Total operating expenses were unusually low in Year 5, when the income tax rate was unusually high.

Exercise 1-2

a.

	Year 7		Year 6
	Index No.	Change in %	Change in %
Net Sales	129		11.1
Cost of Goods Sold		39	17.6
Gross Profit		26	25
Total Operating Expenses	120		53.8
Income Before Taxes	114		42.9
Net Income		29	33.3

b. The growth in cost of goods sold exceeded growth in net sales in Years 6 and 7. A continuation of this trend will limit future growth in net income. The growth in total operating expenses has been erratic -- 53.8% in Year 6 and 20% in Year 7.

Exercise 1-3

a. Single-year statements represent but a short segment of a firm's history. They are essentially interim reports on a going concern's continuing business activities. The allocation of costs and revenues to these short periods of time is, to a considerable extent, based upon convention, judgment, and estimates. The shorter the time period, the more difficult becomes the matching process and the more it is subject to error. Further, single-year statements may not be representative of a going concern's long-run progress because of the abnormally favorable or unfavorable economic or other conditions experienced in that year.

An analysis of single-year statements does not, therefore, provide information concerning trends and the changing relationships that occur over time. For this reason the information generated by the application of analytical procedures to a set of single-year statements is of limited interpretive value. Information concerning trends and relationships in the periodic changes in financial position and operating results can best be presented by the use of comparative statements.

Financial statements also have limitations for analytical and interpretive purposes by virtue of the inherent limitations of the accounting function. Many factors which significantly affect the progress and success of a firm are not of a financial character, and are not, therefore, capable of being expressed directly in financial statements. Included among these factors are general economic conditions, labor relations, customer attitudes, and the like. The preparation of comparative statements would not alleviate these limitations.

b. Changes or inconsistencies in accounting methods, policies, or classifications during the years covered by comparative statements may result in the misinterpretation of reported trends or changing relationships. For example, a change in a firm's depreciation or inventory valuation methods, even though the alternative procedures are acceptable, could easily destroy the comparability of corresponding items in two or more of the periods covered.

Material errors, and their correction in a subsequent period, material nonrecurring gains or losses, mergers or other acquisitions, and changes in corporate activities can also contribute to the misinterpretation of corresponding items on comparative statements.

To avoid the misinterpretations which may result from these factors, footnotes, explanations, and accountants' qualifications which appeared on the individual statements for the years covered should be repeated or referred to in the comparative statements to the extent that they continue to be required for full disclosures.

Changing price levels during the periods covered may also distort comparative statements. To begin with, even the items on a comparative balance sheet or income statement that pertain to a specific year are not all expressed in dollars having the same purchasing power. For example, in an era of rising prices a given year's depreciation charges will represent older dollars having greater purchasing power than other income statement items. Inventory methods other than LIFO also add to the inflationary distortion of the income statement. Similarly, balance sheet items for a given year are expressed in dollars of varying purchasing power.

Added to these vertical distortions which exist within the individual years covered by comparative statements are horizontal distortions in the trends

---

and relationships of corresponding items between years. An upward trend in sales, for example, may actually represent a constant level of or even decline in physical volume which is being sold at increasingly higher prices.

Because of the misunderstanding which is likely to result from conventionally prepared comparative statements during periods of fluctuating price levels, their usefulness as an analytical and interpretative tool can be severely restricted. Price level fluctuations can completely destroy the comparability of the data contained in the statements.

Supplementary comparative statements fully adjusted for the effects of fluctuations in the price level would restore the comparability of the financial position and operating data and thereby enhance their usefulness as tools of analysis and interpretation.

Exercise 1-4

Adaptec's MD&A includes disclosures under the following headings.

Fiscal 1996 Compared to Fiscal 1995.

a. Adaptec "began shipping products incorporating newer technologies such as RAID, ATM and CD-Recordable (CD-R) software." This has implications for future sales growth.

b. The increase in gross margin percent was due to "increased revenues from the Company's higher margin products" and "efficiencies in the manufacturing process." Adaptec has been able to earn increasing gross margin percentages over time. Its future success depends in part on it's ability to maintain these margins.

c. Adaptec "anticipates actual [research and development] spending in fiscal 1997 will increase." In addition, "sales and marketing expenditures will increase in fiscal 1997," while an increase in general and administrative expenditures is also planned. These disclosures indicate that the company is very aggressively pursuing future growth.

d. Adaptec "concluded negotiations with the Singapore government extending the tax holiday for the Company's manufacturing subsidiary." This is a very positive development as this tax benefit has been crucial to Adaptec's profitability.

e. Adaptec warns that "various factors could adversely effect its results of operations in the future including its reliance on the high-performance microcomputer and server markets, changes in product mix, competitive pricing pressures,..." This disclosure provides a 'laundry list' of key considerations for current and potential investors.

Liquidity and Capital Resources--Operating Activities.

a. "During fiscal 1996, the Company signed an agreement with Taiwan Semiconductor Manufacturing Co., Ltd. (TSMC) that will ensure availability of a portion of the Company's wafer capacity..." Such agreements will enable Adaptec to avoid raw material shortages.

Liquidity and Capital Resources--Investing Activities.

a. "The Company made payments of $31 million in connection with acquisitions...acquired Incat through the issuance of 385,000 shares of common stock..." The success of these acquisitions will impact future growth. The use of common shares to acquire other companies dilute the holdings of existing shareholders.

b. "During the 1997 fiscal year, the Company anticipates it will invest approximately $75 million in equipment..." This has implications for short-run cash flow.

c. During 1996, Adaptec "signed an agreement with AT&T Corporation...that will ensure availability of a portion of the Company's wafer capacity...in return for an investment in fabrication equipment of up to $25 million for AT&T's fabrication facility..."

d. "Subsequent to year end, the Company acquired certain assets and the ongoing business of Western Digital's Connectivity Solutions Group...paid $33 million cash...includes in-process technology that will be written off." Write offs of acquired technology may become more common in the future.

Liquidity and Capital Resources--Financing Activities.

a. "Subsequent to year end, the Company acquired all of the outstanding capital stock of Cogent Data Technologies, Inc. (Cogent) in a $68 million stock transaction." The use of common shares to acquire other companies dilute the holdings of existing shareholders.

b. "...the Company believes that existing working capital combined with expected cash generated from operations and available sources of bank and equipment financing will be sufficient to meet its cash requirements throughout fiscal 1997." Adaptec may resort to additional borrowings, thereby increasing its risk to creditors.

◄ Answers to Problems ►

Problem 1-1

Step 1: Compute net income for the year

Sales	920,000	
CGS	690,000	(75% of total sales)
Gross Profit	230,000	(25% of total sales)
Expenses	180,000	
Income before Tax	50,000	
Tax Expense	20,000	(tax at 40% rate)
Net Income	30,000	

Step 2: Compute Stockholders' Equity

Common Stock ($15 par × 10,000)		150,000
APIC ($21 - $15) × 10,000		60,000
		210,000
Retained earnings, 12/31/x4	98,000	
Net income for the year	30,000	
Retained earnings, 12/31/x5		128,000
Total		338,000

Step 3   Net worth   338,000
                       ÷ 4
          Total debt   84,500

Step 4
$$\frac{\text{CGS}}{\text{Inventory}} = \frac{690,000}{\text{Inventory}} = 8$$

Inventory = 86,250

$$\frac{\text{Receivables}}{\text{Credit Sales} \div 360} = 18 \ (\text{days}) = \frac{\text{Receivables}}{920,000/360}$$

∴Receivables = 46,000

Step 5   Total assets   = net worth + total liabilities
                          = 338,000 + 84,500
                          = 422,500

          Current assets = total assets - noncurrent assets
                          = 422,500 - 280,000
                          = 142,500

          Cash = 142,500 - 46,000 - 86,250
                = 10,250

Step 6   Acid test   = (Cash + Accounts Receivable) ÷ Current Liab = 2.5
                Current liab   = (10,250 + 46,000)/2.5 = <u>22,500</u>

                Noncurrent liab   = Total liab - current liab
                                  = 84,500 - 22,500 = <u>62,000</u>

THE MESCO COMPANY
Balance Sheet
As at Dec. 31, x5

Assets:

Current Assets		
Cash	10,250	
A/R	46,000	
Inventories	<u>86,250</u>	
Total Current Assets		142,500
Noncurrent Assets		<u>280,000</u>
Total Assets		<u>422,500</u>
Liabilities and Stockholders' Equity:		
Current Liabilities	22,500	
Noncurrent Liabilities	<u>62,000</u>	
Total Liabilities		84,500
Stockholders' Equity		
Common Stock	150,000	
APIC	60,000	
Retained Earnings	<u>128,000</u>	
Total Stockholders' Equity		<u>338,000</u>
Total Liabilities and Stockholders' Equity		<u>422,500</u>

Problem 1-2
Step 1: Compute net income for the year

Sales	1,000,000	
CGS	<u>500,000</u>	(50% of sales)
Gross Profit	500,000	(50% of sales)
Expenses	<u>450,000</u>	(given)
Net Income	50,000	

Step 2.   Return on equity = 20% = net income ÷ equity

$$50,000 ÷ equity = .2$$
$$∴ equity = \underline{250,000}$$

Step 3.   Debt to equity = 1:1

$$\frac{Debt}{Equity} = \frac{X}{250,000} = 1$$

∴Debt = 250,000

Step 4.   Accounts receivable turnover = Sales ÷ Average A/R

$$\frac{1,000,000}{\frac{(50,000+X)}{2}} = \frac{16}{1}$$

X = Ending accounts receivable = <u>75,000</u>

Step 5.   Inventory turnover   = CGS ÷ Ending inventory
           10   = 500,000 ÷ X
           ∴Ending inventory = <u>50,000</u>

Step 6.   Total assets = Debt + Equity = 250,000 + 250,000 = 500,000

           Current assets   = Total assets - noncurrent assets
                             = 500,000 - 300,000 = 200,000

           Current ratio   = Current assets ÷ Current liabilities
           2   = 200,000 ÷ X

           ∴Current liabilities = <u>100,000</u>

           Noncurrent liabilities   = Debt - Current liabilities
                                     = 250,000 - 100,000 = <u>150,000</u>

Step 7.   Cash = Current assets - Accounts receivable - Inventory
                 = 200,000 - 75,000 - 50,000
                 = <u>75,000</u>

THE FOX COMPANY
Balance Sheet
As of December 31, X2

Assets:		Liabilities and Equity:	
Current Assets		Current liabilities	100,000
Cash	75,000	Noncurrent liabilities	<u>150,000</u>
Accounts receivable	75,000	Total liabilities	250,000
Inventory	50,000	Equity	250,000
Noncurrent assets	<u>300,000</u>		
Total Assets	<u>500,000</u>	Total Liabilities and Equity	<u>500,000</u>

<u>Problem 1-3</u>

VAGUE COMPANY
Balance Sheet
December 31, x6

Assets:

    Current Assets:
        Cash $3,900
        Accounts receivable   2,600
        Inventory   1,820
        Prepaid expenses   <u>1,430</u>
             Total Current Assets $ 9,750
    Fixed Assets:
        Plant and Equipment, net   <u>6,000</u>
           Total Assets   <u>$15,750</u>

Liabilities and Equity:
    Current Liabilities $ 6,500
    Bonds Payable   6,500
    Stockholders' Equity   <u>2,750</u>
        Total Liabilities and Equity   <u>$15,750</u>

1.   Sales = Net Income ÷ Net Income to Sales
         = 1300 ÷ .10 = 13,000

2.   Gross Margin   = Sales × Gross margin ratio
                      = 13,000 × .30 = 3,900

    Cost of good sold = Sales - Gross margin
                      = 13,000 - 3,900 = 9,100

    Inventory   = COGS ÷ Inventory turnover
              = 9,100 ÷ 5 = <u>1,820</u>

3.   A/R   = Sales ÷ A/R turnover
         = 13,000 ÷ 5 = <u>2,600</u>

4.   Working capital   = Sales ÷ Sales to Working Capital
                   = 13,000 ÷ 4 = 3,250

    Current assets   = Current Liabilities + Working Capital
    Current assets   = Current Liabilities + 3,250
    Current liabilities   = Current Assets - 3,250

    Current ratio   = Current Assets ÷ Current Liabilities
                  = Current Assets ÷ Current Assets - 3,250 = 1.5
    Current assets   = (Current Assets - 3,250) 1.5
    Current assets   = 1.5 Current Assets - 4,875
    .5 Current assets   = 4,875
    Current assets   = <u>9,750</u>

Current liabilities = 9,750 - 3,250 = <u>6,500</u>

5.   Acid test ratio = 1.0

      Then: Cash + Accounts Receivable = Current Liabilities
            Cash = 6,500 - 2,600 = <u>3,900</u>

6.   Prepaid expenses   = Total Current Assets - Cash - Accounts Rec. - Inventory
                         = 9,750 - 3,900 - 2,600 - 1,820 = <u>1,430</u>

7.   Times interest earned   = (Income before Tax + Interest Exp.) ÷ Interest Exp.
      5   = (1,300 + Interest Expense) ÷ Interest Expense
      5 (Interest Expense)   = 1,300 + Interest Expense
      4 (Interest Expense)   = 1,300
      Interest Expense   = 325

      Par Value of Bonds Payable   = Interest Expense ÷ Interest Rate on Bonds
                                   = 325 ÷ .05 = <u>6,500</u>

8.   Shareholders' Equity   = Total Assets - Current Liabilities - Bonds Payable
                             = $15,750 - $6,500 - $6,500 = <u>2,750</u>

9.   Par Value of Preferred Stock   = Dividend on Preferred ÷ Dividend Rate
                                     = 40 ÷ .08   = 500

10.   EPS = (Net Income - Preferred Dividend) ÷ # Common Stock Shares Outstanding
      3.75 = (1,300 - 40) ÷ # Common Stock Shares Outstanding
      3.75 × # Common Shares Outstanding = 1,260
      # Common Shares Outstanding = 336
      Par Value of Common Stock = 336 × 5 = <u>1,680</u>

11.   Retained Earnings = Stockholders' Equity - Common Stock - Preferred Stock
                        = 2,750 - 1,680 - 500 = <u>570</u>

      <u>Dividends Paid on Common Stock:</u>

      Retained Earnings on 1/1/x6 $ 350
      + Net Income for 19x6   1,300
                                             1,650
      - Dividends Paid on Preferred   40
                                             1,610
      - Dividends Paid on Common - Plug   1,040
      = Retained Earnings at 12/31/x6 $ 570

      Dividends paid on common stock =   1,040

Problem 1-4

a.   (Cash + Accounts receivable) ÷ Total current liabilities
       (325 + 3,599) ÷ 3,945 = .99

b.   [Net income + Interest expense (1-tax rate)] ÷ Avg. total assets
       [1,265 + 78 (1 - .40)] ÷ [(4,792 + 8,058) ÷ 2] = 20.4%

c.   (Net income - Preferred dividends) ÷ Avg. Common equity
       [1,265 - 45] ÷ [(2,868 - 500 + 3,803 - 450) ÷ 2] = 42.7%

d.   (Net income - Preferred dividends) ÷ Avg. common shares o/s
       [1,265 - 45] ÷ [(550 + 829) ÷ 2] = 1.77

e.   (Net sales - Cost of goods sold) ÷ Net sales
       (12,065 - 8,048) ÷ 12,065 = 33.3%

f.   (Net income before tax + Interest expense) ÷ Interest expense
       (2,259 + 78) ÷ 78 = 30

g.   Avg. inventory ÷ (Cost of goods sold ÷ 360)
       [(2,423 + 1,415) ÷ 2] ÷ [8,048 ÷ 360] = 85.8 days

h.   (Long-term debt + Other liabilities) ÷ Shareholders' equity
       (179 + 81) ÷ 3,803 = 6.8%

i.   Total liabilities ÷ Total liabilities and shareholders' equity
       4,255 ÷ (3,803 + 4,255) = 0.53

j.   Net sales ÷ Working capital
       12,065 ÷ (6,360 - 3,945) = 5

Problem 1-5

	X5	X4
At December 31:		
Current ratio	2.3	1.95
Acid test ratio	1.05	.8
Book value per share	$12.50	$9.25
Year ended December 31:		
Gross profit ratio	35%	30%
Days to sell inventory	82	86
Times interest earned	18.0	12.5
Price-earnings ratio	17.5	15.4
Gross expenditures for P&E	$1,105,000	$975,000

Current ratio:

	Current assets	$13,570,000	$12,324,000
	÷ Current liabilities	5,900,000	6,320,000
a.	Current ratio	2.3	1.95

Acid test ratio:

	Cash, marketable securities, A/R (net)	$6,195,000	$5,056,000
	÷ Current liabilities	5,900,000	6,320,000
b.	Acid test ratio	1.05	.8

Book value per common share:

	Stockholders' equity	$11,875,000	$10,090,000
	- Preferred stock at liquidating value	5,000,000	5,000,000
	Common stockholders' equity	$ 6,875,000	$ 5,090,000
	÷ Equivalent shares o/s at year end	550,000	550,000
c.	Book value per common share	$12.50	$9.25

Gross margin rate:

	Gross margin (Sales - Cost of sales)	$16,940,000	$12,510,000
	÷ Net sales	48,400,000	41,700,000
d.	Gross profit ratio	35%	30%

Days to sell inventory:

	Inventories:		
	Beginning of year	$ 7,050,000	$ 6,850,000
	End of year	7,250,000	7,050,000
		14,300,000	13,900,000
	(A) Average inventories (÷ 2)	7,150,000	6,950,000
	(B) Cost of sales ÷ 360	87,389	81,083
e.	Days to sell inventory (A ÷ B)	82	86

Times interest earned:

	Income before taxes	$4,675,000	$3,450,000
	+ Interest expense	275,000	300,000
		4,950,000	3,750,000
	÷ Interest expense	275,000	300,000
f.	Times interest earned	18	12.5

Common stock, price-earnings ratio:

	Market value, at end of year	$73.50	$47.75
	÷ Earnings per share	4.20	3.10
g.	Common stock, price-earnings ratio	17.5	15.4

Gross expenditures for plant and equipment:

Plant and equipment at cost:			
End of year		$22,750,000	$22,020,000
Beginning of year		22,020,000	21,470,000
		730,000	550,000
Add sales and retirements at cost		375,000	425,000
h. Gross expenditures for P&E		$ 1,105,000	$ 975,000

Comparative Analysis:

   Lowland's financial statements reveal significant improvements across the board. In terms of liquidity, both the current and acid test ratios increased while the days to sell inventory dropped by 4 days. The nearly 50% increase in times interest earned further indicates a solid financial position. Profitability improved as evidenced by the 5% increase in gross profit margin. Lowland is poised for additional earnings growth based on its increasing capital expenditures. The improved performance has not gone unnoticed by the stock market as the price-earnings ratio increased from 15.4 to 17.5. Additional analysis is clearly needed before determining an appropriate price for the proposed acquistion.

◄ Answers to Cases ►

Case 1-1

	1996	1995
S/T Liquidity Ratios:		
Current Ratio	3.57	6.21
Acid Test Ratio	2.95	5.38
Collection Period	40	43
Days to Sell Inventory	57	62
Capital Structure & L-T Solvency Ratios:		
Total Debt to Total Capital	20.8%	14.7%
Long-Term Debt to Equity Capital	0.8%	2.1%
Times Interest Earned	165.3	106.6
Return on Investment Ratios:		
Return on Total Assets	19.2%	23.7%
Return on Common Equity Capital	23.4%	27.9%
Operating Performance Ratios:		
Gross Margin Ratio	58.2%	55.9%
Operating Profits to Sales	19.1%	25.3%
Pretax Income to Sales	20.9%	26.7%
Net Income to Sales	15.7%	20.0%

Asset-Utilization Ratios:

Sales to Cash	8.34	9.12
Sales to Accounts Receivable	9.03	8.34
Sales to Inventories	15.20	13.20
Sales to Working Capital	2.10	1.73
Sales to Fixed Assets	8.21	7.81
Sales to Total Assets	1.22	1.17

Market Measures:

Price-Earnings Ratio	25.53	18.86
Earnings Yield	3.9%	5.3%
Dividend Yield	0.0%	0.0%
Dividend Payout Ratio	0.0%	0.0%
Price-Book Ratio	5.00	4.59

Comments on changes in ratios from 1995 to 1996:

F = favorable . . . . A = adverse

Both the current and acid test ratios declined (A). However, this is not necessarily bad news, given the relatively large 1995 values (extremely high liquidity ratios may imply excessive working capital). Decreases in the collection period (F) and days to sell inventory (F) indicate improved working capital management.

Total debt to total capital increased (A) due to the note payable. On the other hand, long term debt to equity capital decreased (F) and times interest earned increased (F) from its high 1995 level.

Both return on total assets and return on equity capital decreased (A) by 4.5%. While some might argue that the decrease was due to the "write-off of acquired in-process technology," Adaptec's plans to continue acquiring companies with in-process technology indicate that the charge is of a recurring nature.

In terms of operating performance, the gross margin ratio increased (F). However, the remaining ratios decreased significantly (A).

The sales to total assets ratio increased slightly (F). The increases in sales to accounts receivable (F), inventories (F), working capital (F), and fixed assets (F) were offset by the increase in "Other assets." Only the sales to cash ratio decreased (A).

In terms of market measures, both the price-earnings and price-book ratios increased. These increases, coupled with the decrease in earnings yield reflect the stock market's favorable opinion of Adaptec.

COMPUTATIONS FOR 1995

Short-term liquidity ratios:

$$Current\ ratio = \frac{Current\ assets}{Current\ liabilities} = \frac{350,472}{56,414} = 6.21$$

$$\text{Acid test ratio} = \frac{\text{Cash} + \text{cash equivs.} + \text{Marketable sec.} + A/R}{\text{Current liabilities}} = \frac{66,835 + 179,911 + 56,495}{56,414} = 5.38$$

$$\text{Collection period} = \frac{\text{Average accounts receivable}}{\text{Credit sales} \div 360} = \frac{(55,334 + 56,495) \div 2}{466,194 \div 360} = 43 \text{ days}$$

$$\text{Days 2 sell inventory} = \frac{\text{Average inventory}}{\text{Cost of revenues} \div 360} = \frac{(38,940 + 31,712) \div 2}{205,596 \div 360} = 62 \text{ days}$$

Capital structure and long-term solvency ratios:

$$\text{Total debt / total capital} = \frac{\text{Current liabs.} + \text{Long-term liabs.}}{\text{Equity capital} + \text{Total liabs.}} = \frac{56,414 + 7,650}{371,644 + 56,414 + 7,650} = 14.70\%$$

$$\text{Long-term debt / equity capital} = \frac{\text{Long-term liabilities}}{\text{Equity capital}} = \frac{7,650}{371,644} = 2.06\%$$

$$\times \text{ interest earned} = \frac{\text{Income before income taxes} + \text{Interest expense}}{\text{Interest expense}} = \frac{124,537 + 1,179}{1,179} = 106.63$$

Return on investment ratios:

$$\text{Return on total assets} = \frac{\text{NI} + \text{Interest expense } (1 - \text{Tax rate})}{\text{Average total assets}} = \frac{93,402 + 1,179 \, (1 - 0.34)}{(358,475 + 435,708) \div 2} = 23.72\%$$

$$\text{Return on equity capital} = \frac{\text{Net income}}{\text{Average equity capital}} = \frac{93,402}{(297,616 + 371,644) \div 2} = 27.91\%$$

Operating performance ratios:

$$\text{Gross profit ratio} = \frac{\text{Gross profit}}{\text{Net revenues}} = \frac{260,598}{466,194} = 55.90\%$$

$$\text{Operating profit / Sales} = \frac{\text{Income operations}}{\text{Net revenues}} = \frac{117,784}{466,194} = 25.27\%$$

$$\text{Pretax income / Sales} = \frac{\text{Income before income taxes}}{\text{Net revenues}} = \frac{124,537}{466,194} = 26.71\%$$

$$\text{Net income / Sales} = \frac{\text{Net income}}{\text{Net revenues}} = \frac{93,402}{466,194} = 20.04\%$$

Asset utilization ratios:

$$\text{Sales / cash} = \frac{\text{Net revenues}}{\text{Average cash}} = \frac{466,194}{(35,387 + 66,835) \div 2} = 9.12$$

> **NOTE:** **Cash balance for beginning of 1995 appears on the statement of cash flows.**

$$\text{Sales / accounts receivable} = \frac{\text{Net revenues}}{\text{Average accounts receivable}} = \frac{466,194}{(55,334 + 56,495) \div 2} = 8.34$$

$$\text{Sales / inventories} = \frac{\text{Net revenues}}{\text{Average inventories}} = \frac{466,194}{(38,940 + 31,712) \div 2} = 13.20$$

$$\text{Sales / working capital} = \frac{\text{Net revenues}}{\text{Average working capital}} = \frac{466,194}{(243,451 + 294,058) \div 2} = 1.73$$

$$\text{Sales / fixed assets} = \frac{\text{Net revenues}}{\text{Average fixed assets}} = \frac{466,194}{(51,522 + 67,863) \div 2} = 7.81$$

$$\text{Sales / total assets} = \frac{\text{Net revenues}}{\text{Average assets}} = \frac{466,194}{(358,475 + 435,708) \div 2} = 1.17$$

Market measures:

$$\text{Price / earnings ratio} = \frac{\text{Market price}}{\text{Earnings per share}} = \frac{33}{1.75} = 18.86$$

$$\text{Earnings yield} = \frac{\text{Earnings per share}}{\text{Market price}} = \frac{1.75}{33} = 5.30\%$$

$$\text{Dividend yield} = \frac{\text{Dividends per share}}{\text{Market price}} = \frac{0}{33} = 0\%$$

$$\text{Dividend payout ratio} = \frac{\text{Dividends per share}}{\text{Earnings per share}} = \frac{0}{1.75} = 0\%$$

$$Price \ / \ book \ ratio = \frac{Market \ price}{Book \ value \ per \ share} = \frac{33}{371,644 \div 51,677} = 4.59$$

Case 1-2

a.

	11	10
S/T Liquidity Ratios:		
Current Ratio (A)	1.357	1.30
Acid Test Ratio (B)	0.778	0.569
Collection Period (C)	43	43
Days to Sell Inventory (D)	64	57
Capital Structure & L-T Solvency Ratios:		
Total Debt to Total Capital (E)	0.70	0.69
Long-Term Debt to Equity Capital (F)	1.31	1.15
Times Interest Earned (G)	4.95	4.09
Return on Investment Ratios:		
Return on Total Assets (H)	8.6%	7.7%
Return on Common Equity Capital (I)	21.0%	15.2%
Operating Performance Ratios:		
Gross Margin Ratio (J)	48.3%	46.6%
Operating Profits to Sales (K)	9.3%	10.0%
Pretax Income to Sales (L)	7.5%	7.6%
Net Income to Sales (M)	3.7%	3.4%
Asset-Utilization Ratios:		
Sales to Cash (N)	181.83	284.21
Sales to Accounts Receivable (O)	7.95	7.99
Sales to Inventories (P)	13.0	10.62
Sales to Working Capital (Q)	16.58	14.68
Sales to Fixed Assets (R)	4.45	4.36
Sales to Total Assets (S)	1.82	1.51
Market Measures:		
Price-Earnings Ratio (T)	19.8	26.3
Earnings Yield (U)	5.0%	3.8%
Dividend Yield (V)	3.0%	2.5%
Dividend Payout Ratio (W)	58.8%	65.1%
Price to Book Ratio (X)	4.449	4.198

b. *Comments:*

The current ratio and the acid test ratio both increased due to larger cash and receivables relative to current liabilities. Accounts payable and inventories both decreased while receivables increased. Days sales in receivables increased slightly but a complete analysis requires that we look at the terms of receivables and make industry comparisons. Inventory turnover showed an improvement, changing from 5.64 to 6.34.

Total debt to total capital changed very slightly but long-term debt to equity capital increased by almost 14%. In addition, the times interest earned ratio increased from 4.09 to 4.95.

Quaker Oats' return on investment ratios showed significant improvements over 1990 primarily due to the rise in net income to sales and reduced interest expense.

In the operating performance group, gross margin ratio increased due to larger sales relative to CGS. Because of the 15% increase in SGA expenses, both operating profits to sales and pretax income to sales fell slightly. In addition, net income to sales managed to increase from 3.4% to 3.7% due to a smaller loss from discontinued operations.

Price-earnings ratio dropped in 1991 due to higher earnings per share and a lower average stock price. With a higher dividends per share in 1991, dividend yield showed a slight increase. Finally, the dividend payout ratio decreased because of higher net income and a proportionally lower dividend increase.

Computations:

A. Current ratio

$$\frac{\text{Current Assets}}{\text{Current Liabilities}}$$

10

$$\frac{1481.3}{1138.5} = \underline{1.30}$$

11

$$\frac{1258.1 \ [62]}{926.9 \ [78]} = \qquad\qquad \underline{1.357}$$

B. Acid test ratio

$$\frac{\text{Cash + Cash Equiv + A/R}}{\text{Current Liabilities}}$$

10

$$\frac{17.7 + 629.9}{1138.5} = \underline{.569}$$

11

$$\frac{30.2 \ [53] + 691.1 \ [55]}{926.9 \ [78]} = \qquad\qquad \underline{.778}$$

C. Collection period

$$\frac{\text{Avg. Accounts Receivable}}{\text{Credit Sales} \div 360}$$

10

$$\frac{(594.4+629.9)/2}{5030.6/360} = \underline{43}$$

11

$$\frac{(629.9+691.1)/2 \ [55]}{5491.2 \ [1]/360} \qquad = \underline{43}$$

D.   Days to sell inventory

Avg. Inventory
Cost of Goods Sold ÷ 360

10

$$\frac{(479.1+473.9)/2}{2685.9/360} = \underline{64}$$

11

$$\frac{(473.9+422.3[59])/2}{2839.7[2]} = \underline{57}$$

E.   Total debt to total capital

Current Liab + L/T Liab
Total Liab and Equity

10

$$\frac{1138.5+1168.3}{3326.1} = \underline{.69}$$

11

$$\frac{926.9[78]+1183.4[79+80+81]}{3016.1[92]} = \underline{.699}$$

F.   Long-term debt to
     equity capital

Long-Term Debt
Equity Capital

10

$$\frac{740.3 + 100.3 + 327.7}{100 - 98.2 + 1017.5}$$

$$= \frac{1168.3}{1019.3} = \underline{1.146}$$

11

$$\frac{701.2[79]+115.5[80]+366.7[81]}{100[82]-94.5[83]-0.7[84]+901[91]}$$

$$= \frac{1183.4}{905.8} = \underline{1.306}$$

G.   Times interest earned[a]

Income before Interest & Taxes
Interest Expense

10

$$\frac{382.4 + 120.2}{120.2 + 2.8} = \underline{4.086}$$

11

$$\frac{411.5 [7] + 101.9 [156]}{101.9 [156] + 1.9 [156]} = \underline{4.946}$$

H.   Return on total assets

NI + Int Exp (1 - Tax Rate)[b]
Avg Total Assets

10

$$\frac{169 + 120.2 (1 - .34)}{(3125.9 + 3326.1)/2}$$

$$= \underline{.077}$$

11

$$\frac{205.8 [11] + 101.9 [156] (1 - .34)}{(3326.1 [69] + 3016.1 [69]/2}$$

$$= \underline{.086}$$

I. Return on common equity $\dfrac{\text{NI - Preferred Dividend}}{\text{Avg Common Capital}}$

10

$\dfrac{169 - 4.5}{(1137.1 + 1017.5)/2}$

$= \dfrac{163.5}{1077.3} = \underline{.152}$

11

$\dfrac{205.8\ [11] - 4.3\ [12]}{(1017.5\ [91] + 901\ [91])/2}$

$= \dfrac{201.5}{959.25} =$ .21

J. Gross margin ratio $\dfrac{\text{Gross Profit}}{\text{Sales}}$

10

$\dfrac{2344.7}{5030.6} = \underline{.466}$

11

$\dfrac{2651.5\ [1 - 2]}{5491.2\ [1]} =$ .483

K. Operating profit to sales $\dfrac{\text{Income before Interest \& Taxes}}{\text{Sales}}$

10

$\dfrac{382.4 + 120.2}{5030.6} = \underline{.0999}$

11

$\dfrac{411.5\ [7] + 101.9\ [156]}{5491.2\ [1]} =$ .0934

L. Pretax income to sales $\dfrac{\text{Pretax Income}}{\text{Sales}}$

10

$\dfrac{382.4}{5030.6} = \underline{.076}$

11

$\dfrac{411.5\ [7]}{5491.2\ [1]} =$ .0749

M. Net income to sales $\dfrac{\text{NI}}{\text{Sales}}$

10

$\dfrac{169}{5030.6} = \underline{.0336}$

11

$\dfrac{205.8\ [11]}{5491.2\ [1]} =$ .0374

N. Sales to cash $\dfrac{\text{Sales}}{\text{Cash}}$

10

$\dfrac{5030.6}{17.7} = \underline{284.21}$

11

$\dfrac{5491.2\ [1]}{30.2\ [53]} =$ 181.83

O.   Sales to A/R   Sales
                                     Accounts Receivable

     10   11

     5030.6   5491.2 [1]
     629.9 = 7.986   691.1 [55] =   7.945

P.   Sales to inventories   Sales
                                     Inventories

     10   11

     5030.6   5491.2 [1]
     473.9 = 10.62   422.3 [59] =   13.0

Q.   Sales to working capital   Sales
                                     Working Capital

     10   11

     5030.6   5491.2 [1]
     1481.3 - 1138.5 = 14.675   1258.1 [62] - 926.9 [78] =   16.579

R.   Sales to fixed assets   Sales
                                     Fixed Assets

     10   11

     5030.6   5491.2 [1]
     1154.1 = 4.358   1232.7 [66] =   4.454

S.   Sales to total assets   Sales
                                     Total Assets

     10   11

     5030.6   5491.2 [1]
     3326.1 = 1.512   3016.1 [69] =   1.82

T.   Price-earnings ratio   Market Price
                                     Earnings per Share

     10   11

     56.5   52.5 [137][c]
     2.15 = 26.3   2.65 [16] =   19.8

U.	Earnings yield	Earnings per Share	
		Market Price	
	10	11	
	$\dfrac{2.15}{56.5}$ = 3.8%	$\dfrac{2.65\ [16]}{52.5\ [137]^c}$ =	5.0%

V.	Dividend Yield	Dividends per Share	
		Market Price per Share	
	10	11	
	$\dfrac{1.40}{56.5}$ = 2.47%	$\dfrac{1.56\ [17]}{52.5\ [137]^c}$ =	2.97%

W.	Dividend payout ratio	Dividends per Share	
		Earnings per Share	
	10	11	
	$\dfrac{1.40}{2.15}$ = .651	$\dfrac{1.56\ [17]}{2.65\ [16]}$ =	.588

X.	Price to book ratio	Market Price	
		Book value per share	
	10	11	
	$\dfrac{56.5}{13.46}$ = 4.198	$\dfrac{52.5}{11.80\ [130]}$ =	4.449

[a]Simplified version
[b]Using Marginal Corporate Tax Rate [158]
[c]Average market price [137]

Case 1-3

A business enterprise pursues four major activities in a desire to provide a saleable product and to yield a satisfactory return on investment:

Planning activities. A company exists to implement specific goals and objectives. A company's goals and objectives are captured in a business plan or strategy, describing the company's purpose, its strategy, and its tactics for activities. A business plan assists managers in focusing their efforts and identifying expected opportunities and obstacles.

Financing Activities. A company requires financing to carry out its business plan. Financing activities are the means companies use to pay for these ventures. Because of their magnitude, and their potential to determine success or failure of a venture, companies must take care in acquiring and managing their financial resources. There are two main sources of business financing: equity investors (sometimes referred to as owners or shareholders) and creditors.

Investing Activities. Investing activities are the means a company uses to acquire and maintain investments for obtaining, developing, and selling products or services. Financing provides the funds necessary for acquisition of investments needed to carry out business plans. Investments include land, buildings, equipment, legal rights (patents, licenses, and copyrights), inventories, human capital (managers and employees), accounting systems, and all components necessary for the company to operate.

Operating Activities. Operating activities represent the "carrying out" of the business plan, given necessary financing and investing. These activities involve at least five basic components--research, purchasing, production, marketing, and labor. Operating activities are a company's primary source of income. Income measures a company's success in buying from input markets and selling in output markets. How well a company does in devising business plans and strategies, and with decisions on materials comprising the mix of operating activities, determines business success or failure.

◄ CHAPTER 2 ►

Analysis Objectives and Financial Reporting

◄ CHAPTER REVIEW ►

Financial statement analysis depends on the objectives of its users. While similarities exist, there are unique circumstances and objectives facing every user. To master financial statement analysis, we must understand users and their objectives. Financial statement analysis depends also on the accounting numbers comprising the statements. The recording function, the double-entry system, and classification are an integral part of accounting, a part we must understand to fully exploit our analysis. Accounting information is subject also to certain limitations impairing our analysis. We must recognize and adapt our analysis for these limitations.

This chapter describes the objectives and applications of primary users of financial statements. We also introduce several important accounting functions, and discuss their implications for analysis. Techniques of analysis that exploit our accounting knowledge are discussed.

◄ CHAPTER OUTLINE ►

▸ **Objectives of Financial Statement Analysis**

 Creditors

 Equity Investors

 Management

 Auditors

 Directors

 Mergers and Acquisition Analysts

 Regulators

 Other Important Users

▸ **Accounting Information: Basis of Analysis**

 Accounting Measurement and Reporting of Business Activity

 Relevance of Accounting Information

 Information Environment for Financial Statement Analysis

▸ **Accounting Principles and Limitations**

 Monetary Expression

 Simplification and Summarization

 Judgement and Incentives

 Interim Disclosures and Estimates

 Historical Cost Measurement

 Unstable Monetary Unit

 Need to Understand Accounting Measurements and Disclosures

 Implications of Accounting Risk

▸ **Additional Analysis Techniques**

 Reconstruction of Business Activities and Transactions

 Indirect Evidence and Evaluation

 Industry Comparability Analysis of Financial Statements

 Analytical Use of Accounting Standards and Assumptions

 Traditional Market Measures

▸ **Appendix 2A**

 Accounting Principles Underlying Financial Statements

 Additional Tools and Sources for Financial Statement Analysis

▸ **Appendix 2B**

 Describe the Role of Technology in Financial Statement Analysis

 Identify Sources of Information for Financial Statement Analysis

◄ Learning Objectives ►

- **Identify the primary users of financial statements and discuss their objectives and information needs.**

- **Describe common stock valuation and compare it with the valuation of debt.**

- **Explain double-entry accounting and how it aids in measuring business activities.**

- **Describe the relevance of accounting information in financial statement analysis.**

- **Identify limitations of accounting data and their consequences for financial statement analysis.**

- **Discuss specialized financial statement analysis techniques.**

◄ Learning Objectives ►

- **Explain how accounting rules are determined (Appendix 2A).**

- **Describe the role of technology in financial statement analysis (Appendix 2B).**

- **Identify sources of information for financial statement analysis (Appendix 2B).**

◄ Answers to Questions ►

1. Request the president to provide the audited financial statements of his company. In addition to any other available information about the company, analyze the statements, particularly with respect to:

    a. How has the company handled its borrowings in the past?
    b. Has the company's operating performance been stable enough as to assure scheduled payment of interest and repayment of principal?

    Also, analyze the company's plan to use loans and examine whether the underlying reasons are consistent with the findings of the financial statement analysis.

2. As we have seen in the answer to question 2, the equity investor bears the mayor risk of the enterprise and also is exposed to reaping all the rewards remaining after the claims of fixed interest securities are met. Consequently, he is interested in operating performance and in all other aspects of an enterprise's financial condition.

    One outstanding characteristic of all pure credit extension relationships is the fixed nature of the rewards accruing to the credit grantor. Thus, should the enterprise prosper, the credit grantor will still be limited to his contractually fixed rate of interest, or to the profit on the goods supplied. However, should the enterprise incur losses or meet other adversities, the credit grantor's principal may be placed in jeopardy. This uneven nature of the lender's risk-reward ratio has a major effect on his point of view and on the manner in which he analyzes the possibilities of credit extension.

    The difference in the point of view of the lenders as compared to that of the equity investor results in differences in the way they analyze future prospects and in the objectives they seek. The equity investor looks for his reward primarily in future prospects of earnings and to changes in those earnings. The credit grantor, on the other hand, is concerned primarily with specific security provisions of his loan, such as the fair market value of assets pledged. For repayment of principal and interest he/she looks to the existence of resources and to the projections of future flows of funds and the reliability and stability of such flows. The equity investor, as a result of the theoretically unlimited nature of his rewards, is receptive to highly abstract descriptions of "concepts," potentials, and future probabilities, while the lender, on the other hand, requires a more definite link between the projections of the future and the resources already at hand as well as the demonstrated ability to achieve results. Thus, credit grantors generally are more conservative in their outlook and approach and rely on financial statement analysis to an even greater extent than do investors, for it serves to reassure them regarding the borrower's demonstrated ability to control the flow of funds and to maintain a sound financial condition under a variety of economic and operating circumstances.

3. The essential difference is that whereas a bond coupon and the bond principal both are discounted to present value in the bond valuation model are known amounts and are subject only to financial ability to pay, both future earnings and future market prices, on which a similar stock valuation model is based are, in most cases, much more subject to conjecture and doubt.

4. As the ownership group exposed to the greatest risks and also to all the residual rewards of an enterprise, the equity owners are concerned with all aspects of its financial position and results of operations. To assess the risk inherent in that ownership they want to know all they can about the short-term liquidity as well as the long-term solvency of the enterprise. In order to determine whether the prospective rewards are worth the potential risks which they face, the equity holders are interested in operating performance, return on investment, and asset utilization. Thus, the informational needs of the equity holders are among the most demanding of all parties interested in a company's financial statements.

5. Most modern theories of stock valuation focus on the present value of a future stream of dividends and a residual value equal to the market value of the common stock. Regardless of what form these future returns take they

represent earnings and derivatives of earnings since both dividends and market values depend in large measure on earning power.

6.   Whatever method of stock valuation is used by the security analyst, be it a simple short-term projection of earn to be capitalized at a predetermined rate or be it a complex and sophisticated formula involving elegant mathematical techniques, the results can never reach a higher level of accuracy or be more reliable than the inputs used in such calculations. The reliability and the validity of these inputs. be they earnings projections, expected payout ratios or various risk factors such as those inherent in capital structure, depends on the quality of the financial statement analysis performed.

Financial statement analysis, while certainly not providing answers to all the problems of security analysis, at least keeps the decision maker in touch with the underlying realities of the enterprises which he investigates. It imposes the discipline of comparing the results already attained with the wide-ranging promises made for the future. As a very minimum it represents a safeguard against the repetition of the grievous mistakes of judgment recurringly made by analysts in time of speculative euphoria.

Not all needed information can be obtained by means of financial statement analysis nor is the information so obtainable always the most critical one in the determination of security values. However, it is clear that any rational and systematic approach to the valuation of common stocks must involve the use of quantified data which are the end product of financial statement analysis, evaluation, and interpretation.

7.   Management's interest in an enterprise's financial condition, profitability, and progress is pervasive and all-encompassing. Management has a number of methods, tools, and techniques available to it in monitoring and keeping up with the ever changing condition of the enterprise. Financial data analysis is one important category of such methods. Financial data analysis can be undertaken by management on a continuous basis because it has unlimited access to internal accounting and other records. Such analysis encompasses changes in ratios, trends, and other significant relationships. Ratio, change, and trend analysis is based on an intelligent, alert, and systematic surveillance of significant relationships in a business situation and the timely detection and interpretation of problem areas by an analysis of change. Management's primary objective in utilizing tools of analysis is to exercise control and to view the enterprise the way important outsiders. such as creditors and investors, view it. Ratio, change, and trend analysis makes use of the numerous and inevitable relationships and interrelationships among the variables occurring in any business situation. Constant surveillance over the size and amplitude of change in these interrelationships provides valuable clues to important changes in underlying financial and operating conditions. Recognition of such changes and timely action to check adverse trends is the essence of control. Management derives a number of important advantages from a systematic monitoring of financial data and the basic relationships which they display:

(1)   There is recognition that no event in a business situation is isolated and that it represents a cause or the effect of a chain of events of which it is but a link. This approach aims at discovering whether a given event or relationship is the cause or the effect of an underlying situation.

(2)   There is a recognition that one should not act on an isolated event, but rather by an examination of related changes, one should determine the basic courses of the event. Thus, an event cannot be judged as positive or negative until it has been properly related to other factors which have a bearing on it.

(3)   It prevents management from getting submerged in a maze of facts and figures which, in the typical business situation, consists of a great variety of factors of varying sizes, velocities of change, and degrees of impact. Instead, it organizes the data and relates them to a pattern of prior experience and external standards.

(4)   It calls for prompt and effective action as the situation unfolds rather than for "post mortem" analyses of causes and effects.

8. The end product of the financial audit is an expression of opinion on the fairness of presentation of financial statements setting forth the financial conditions and the results of operations of an enterprise. The basic objective of the audit process is to obtain the greatest possible degree of assurance about the absence of errors and irregularities, intentional or otherwise, which if undetected can materially affect the fairness of presentation of financial summarizations or their conformity with generally accepted accounting principles.

    Financial statement, as well as ratio change and trend analysis, represents an important group of audit tools which can significantly supplement other audit tools such as procedural and validation tests. This is so because errors and irregularities, whatever their source, can, if significant, affect the various financial operating and structural relationships and the detection and analysis of such changes can lead to the detection of errors and irregularities. Moreover, the process of financial analysis requires of the auditor, and imparts to him, the kind of understanding and grasp of the audited enterprise of which the soundest type of audit evidence is made.

    The application of financial statement analysis as part of the audit program is best undertaken at the very beginning of the audit because such analysis will often reveal the areas of greatest change and vulnerability, areas to which the auditor will want to direct most of his attention.

    In 1978 the accounting profession formally recognized the importance of analytical audit approaches through issuance of Statement of Auditing Standards No. 23 "Analytical Review Procedures."

9. Accounting is concerned with the quantitative measurement and expression of economic phenomena. One of its most important and vital functions is that of providing a system of measurement. As will be seen throughout this work, great controversy exists regarding some of the methods of measurement in accounting and regarding the very validity of others. The nature of these differences of opinion is such that thy will not be definitively settled in the foreseeable future. The analyst must understand the salient factors behind these differences in point of view and, above all, he must form his own opinion on the implications which they hold for the use of the results of these measurements in his own analyses and decisions. When we use accounting measurements we should never forget the reality behind these measurements and the compressed simplified and summarized picture which they represent.

10. One level is the recording function which is concerned with the mechanics of recording and summarizing the multitude of transactions which occur in an enterprise.

    The other level governs the methods, procedures, principles, and standards by which economic events are measured and the method of their presentation. It is this level which calls for most judgment and which is the subject of most of the controversy in this discipline.

11. The analysis of financial statements and data is an indispensable component of most lending, investing and other related decisions. It is, however, important to understand that its relative importance in the total decision context can vary significantly.

    In the lending decision the lender looks mainly to the enterprise for his rewards which come in the form of interest and principal repayment. We are not concerned here with interim changes in interest rates which depend on factors outside the scope of our discussion in this work. Since almost all the rewards (returns) which the lender expects come directly from the enterprise, financial statement analysis is a relatively large and important part of the total decision process. It is, in fact, the most important element in the entire decision set (*A decision set consists of the totality of all factors which enter into the making of a decision. The lending decision set includes many other important factors such as management ability and integrity, industry as well as broad economic conditions.) with which the lending officer or bond investor is concerned. mis is why most banks regard the ability to understand and analyze financial statements as one of the most critical skills to be possessed by the lending officer.

The role which financial statement analysis plays in the equity investing decision is quite different. One important reason for this is that the equity investor looks for his reward to two different sources: dividends and capital appreciation.

Dividends depend in the long run directly on profitability, growth and liquidity, elements which lend themselves to evaluation by means of an analysis of the financial statements of the paying enterprise. But dividends, which come from and are subject to enterprise discretion, are only one part, and often the smaller element, of the total sought for reward (return). In fact, many growing and successful enterprises pay minimal or no dividends.

The other, and often major portion, of the expected rewards comes not from the company directly but rather from other investors who it is expected will be willing, at some future time, to pay more for the equity investment than did our decision making investor. While the willingness of investors to pay higher prices for an equity security depends importantly on earnings power and earnings growth it often depends even more so on the state of the marketplace as well as on factors such as the rates of return available from other investments.

Thus, the investor's decision set must include considerations of market psychology and confidence which are factors of great importance not subject to analysis by use of the enterprise's financial statements. Consequently investors in many successful and growing companies often do not obtain the expected returns when the marketplace, in its collective wisdom, refuses to capitalize the earn they bought at prior or even higher multiples.

For these reasons, the relationship between the rates of return realized by the enterprise and those which the investor in it actually realizes in the marketplace is far from direct. This is often puzzling to those who do not fully appreciate the great importance of the marketplace as the final validator of value. Equity security markets are both logical and psychological and the relative importance of these two is ever changing. Since the analysis of financial statements relates to the logical processes, the relative importance of financial statement analysis in the equity investing decision set varies with circumstances and the time on the market clock. Its importance is relatively greater when market valuations are low than when these valuations are determined by general market euphoria. Its relative importance is always greater when it is directed to the assessment of risk and to the detection of areas of vulnerability or of potential problems. The value of financial statement analysis in defensive investing and in the avoidance of loss is far clearer and direct than is its value in the detection of investment opportunity.

12. The intelligent use of accounting data requires an understanding of the limitations to which they are subject. Some of the more important of these limitations are:

Monetary expression, i.e., that only those data which are subject to quantification are generally found in financial statements but that these can by no means include all the information necessary for most of the decisions made on the basis of accounting information.

Simplifications and rigidities inherent in the accounting framework. The classification and summarization of the great amounts of financial facts and details in the accounting system and, finally in the financial statements, require simplifications which tend to hide or obscure many important aspects of the reality which they are intended to portray. Furthermore, the large degree of estimation on which financial statements are inevitably based introduces into their determination judgments of various qualities and degrees of competence.

The generality of purpose for which financial statements are prepared precludes them from being necessarily responsive to the informational needs of users with specific purposes in mind.

Other limitations relate to the *interim nature* of most financial determinations, to the fact that the quest for objectivity of accounting has resulted in the use of *historical costs* rather than current fair market values, and to the lack of stability of most monetary units in terms of the purchasing power which they command.

13. Refer to the answer to the preceding question which covers also the answer to this question.

14. Accounting is a social science and consequently no assessment of the value or the reliability of accounting concepts or standards or of the financial statements that are based on them can be complete without a consideration of the pervasive influence of human nature on them.

While formally the objective of accounting is to supply information useful for making economic decisions, we must recognize that in fact many interested parties engaged in the accounting function have more specific (and more narrow or selfish) objectives in mind. For example:

(1)   Management or individual executives of an enterprise may want accounting presentations to help them with individual and specific objectives such as:

    (a)   Obtaining credit in order to insure the survival of an enterprise in financial difficulties.

    (b)   The ability to sell securities in the open market in order to insure survival, growth, the preservation of lobs or similar objectives.

    (c)   To enhance the compensation of executives or employees or to reflect favorably on their operating performance or their egos.

    (d)   To help management fend off hostile takeover attempts.

    (e)   To enhance the wealth of present owners of the enterprise.

(2)   Governments may want accounting to promote objectives such as helping to control inflation, enhance labor peace, foster economic growth, aid in antitrust enforcement, enlarge tax revenues, or help industries in distress.

(3)   Public Accountants may want accounting to increase the market for their services, help maintain positive relations with important clients as well as help those clients attain their own objectives.

Examples of the use of accounting for the attainment of such, often more narrow objectives abound in practice and are illustrated in this work. For example, Chapter 4 refers to Datapoint Corporation's reversal of questionable sales booked in an attempt to improve operating results. Chapter 13 discusses the H. J. Heinz case of income smoothing by "second tier" executives and the J.W.T. Group case in which fictitious assets and revenues were created by divisional executives who desired to look good by meeting increasing performance goals. Moreover, Chapter 6 refers to Itel Corporation's philosophy of "programmed" earnings as a means of promoting the corporate image of growth. Chapter 6 refers to the Yale Express case of substantial underaccruals of costs and of auditor carelessness in detecting them. Finally, Supplement B describes the huge and protracted Equity Funding fraud which involved management greed and deception and luckily, as a rare exception) auditor collusion in management's deception for purposes of achieving its own accounting "goals."

Now, as we all know, these narrow interests are not, nor should they be, the objectives of accounting. The FASB, now a body independent of all parties at interest, including the accounting profession, is in fact society's representative charged with the unwritten mission of insuring that, at least in theory, the objectives of accounting coincide with those of society at large.

Human nature being what it is, analysts must be ever aware that those with strong personal interests at stake will continue to try to bend the theory so that the practice favors their own more narrow interests. Society's most powerful countermeasures include institutions such as the SEC, the courts as well as the organized auditing profession. While significant progress has been made in improving e overall integrity and reliability of financial reporting in this country, the analyst must be aware that individual exceptions have occurred, are occurring and are likely to recur in the future.

15. The accountant's effort and skill is first directed to understanding the reality of the transactions or events to be recorded. Next there must be brought to bear the knowledge of the accounting framework, the generally accepted accounting standards which govern the recording of the transaction, its expression in the form of a journal entry and

its accumulation in accounts. No matter what form data recording and accumulation take in this electronic age, the basic concepts of the journal entry and the T account prevail. These, as we shall see, are particularly useful in analytical work. Finally, continuing to be guided by accepted standards of the accounting framework, the account summarizes all accounts of a period in the format of financial statements.

The flow of the analyst's work is basically in reverse order. He or she starts with the financial statements made available by the enterprise. The basic task is to recapture, as far as possible, the reality that is imbedded and summarized in these financial statements"the degree to which this is done being dependent on the particular analytical objectives at hand. This analytical process requires that the analyst visualize the journal entries made and that he or she reconstruct, in summary fashion, all or selected accounts in the financial statements. It also requires an understanding of the reality underlying such business transactions as well as knowledge of the accounting standards employed in recording it properly within the accounting framework.

By these means the analyst will be able to understand the changes in specific balance sheet items, trace the effect of a given transaction or specific accounts and answer questions such as the following:

• What was the reason for the increase or the decrease in the investment in X Company?

• What effect did the debt refunding have on working capital?

• How much long term debt was repaid this year?

• What was the effect of income taxes on the financial statements and how much tax was actually paid this year?

16. A number of circumstances require that financial statements be restated:

   1. The merger of entities under the pooling method of accounting requires that prior years be restated as if the entities had been merged from inception. As a practical matter only the financial statements presented at the time the merger is reported will be presented in restated form.
   2. Discontinuances or disposals of segment of a business require that revenues and expenses of the disposed units as well as losses expected on disposal be classified in the income statement under "discontinued operations." Similarly, the net assets of business expected to be discontinued are shown as a sine category on the balance sheet. Financial statements presented at the time the discontinuances are reported must be restated accordingly.
   3. Certain accounting principles changes (e.g. changes in inventory cost flow assumptions or changes in income recognition on long-term contracts) require that the prior years of financial statements presented at the time the change is reported be restated to reflect the newly adopted accounting method.

17. Traditional market measures include the price-earnings ratio, earnings yield, dividend yield, dividend payout ratio, and price-book ratio.

18. Accounting principles or standards are the rules and operative guides of accounting. These rules and guides are used in such determinations as the measurement of assets and liabilities, the recognition of revenue, and the measurement and accrual of costs, expenses, and losses.

19. The development of accounting standards is largely an evolutionary process. They have generally been established or promulgated, mostly by bodies of the AICPA, in response to perceived needs and developments. Thus they tend to lag after practice, rather than lead it. For example, in the 1920s there occurred a wave of abuses in the writing up of assets and so this practice was prohibited. Abuses in the field of lease accounting have in turn led to *APB Opinion No. 5* and consequently to issuance of *SFAS 13*. Again, improvements in accounting for business combinations, real estate sales, and income from franchises have generally followed abuses in practice. Thus, the analyst can expect that in the future, as in the past, accounting improvements are going to be undertaken in response to abuses which have already worked to the disadvantage of some investors or lenders.

20. The FASB does represent a very significant improvement over its predecessors for the following reasons:

(1) Before issuing a Financial Accounting Standard on a subject, the Board issues, in most cases, a Discussion Memorandum which is exposed for public comment. Written comments can be filed with the Board and oral comments can be voiced at public hearings which generally precede the issuance of an exposure draft of a *Statement of Financial Accounting Standards (SFAS)*. After further exposure and comment, a final *SFAS is* usually issued.

(2) Another significant improvement in procedure is the inclusion in SFAS of careful and elaborate explanations of the rationale of the Board for the Statements it issues, explanations of how comments to the Board were dealt with, as well as examples of actual applications.

21. Financial analysis bears on decisions of such importance and involves the commitment of such substantial resources that the analyst can never place complete reliance on the data with which he works without examining it carefully, understanding the bases on which it is prepared and adjusting it to conform to his own particular objectives. This is especially true for the following major reasons:

   a. There is a serious gulf between accounting theory and its implementation in practice. The attesting auditor is as yet unable and/or unwilling to resist the pressures of managements and other special interest factors.
   b. A number of important areas in accounting theory are as yet unsettled.
   c. Accounting theory formulation generally lags behind accounting practice. In general accounting theory is developed to cope with abuses after they happen rather than to anticipate them.

22. The purpose of the *FASB's* Conceptual Framework (CF) is the establishment of a coherent system of interrelated objectives and concepts that are expected to lead to consistent financial accounting and reporting. These concepts are expected to guide the selection of events to be accounted for, the measurement of those events as well as the means of their summarization and their communication to interested users.

The CF should enable investors, creditors and others to obtain increased understanding of and confidence in financial reporting. A CF centered on objectives can help narrow the range of acceptable accounting methods as well as promote increased comparability of financial information.

The *FASB* believes that without conceptual underpinnings, measures provided by accounting and financial reporting are essentially matters of judgment and personal opinion. Thus the more precise definitions provided by the CF are expected to narrow subjectivity, circumscribe the areas for applying judgments as well as provide a frame of reference for those judgments.

23. SFAC 1 establishes the objectives of general purpose external financial reporting by loudness enterprises. The Statement in essence states that financial reporting can best serve investors and creditors to predict the amount, timing and uncertainty of future cash flows to *them by* facilitating the prediction of the amount, timing and uncertainty of future cash flows to *the business entity.* Moreover, financial reporting should provide information about the economic resources of an enterprise, the claims to those resources and the effects of transactions, events and circumstances that change its resources and claims to those resources.

A primary focus of financial reporting is information about earnings and its components. Financial reporting is also expected to provide information about an enterprise's financial performance during a period and about how management has discharged its stewardship responsibility to owners.

24. SFAC 2 (1980) "Qualitative Characteristics of Accounting Information. is designed to examine the characteristics of accounting information that make it useful.

These characteristics are viewed as a hierarchy of qualities which separates user specific qualities (e.g., understandability) from qualities inherent in the information. Information cannot be useful to decision makers unless it is understood by them regardless of how relevant it may otherwise be.

Relevance and *reliability* are two primary qualities that make accounting information useful for decision making. Information is relevant if it has the capacity to confirm or change a decision maker's expectations.

If information is received by a user too late to have an effect on a decision it cannot have an impact on that decision. Hence, *timeliness* is an important aspect of relevance. So are *predictive value*, i.e., value as an input into a predictive process, as well *as feedback value* which is *a* characteristic of information that helps to confirm and to correct earlier predictions.

Information is *reliable* if it can be verified by agreement among a number of independent observers and if it represents what it purports to represent, I e., it has *representational faithfulness*. Reliability also implies completeness and neutrality of information.

Comparability, which includes consistency, interacts with relevance and reliability to contribute to the usefulness of information.

Comparison is one of the most basic tools of analysis for decision making. Almost all evaluations and alternative-choice judgments involve comparisons of one sort or another. Thus, the ability to compare sets of accounting data of the same enterprise over time, or those of one enterprise with that of another, is very important to the decision making process.

25. SFAC 3 (1980) "Elements of Financial Statements of Business Enterprises" defines the following 10 elements of financial statements of business enterprises:

(1) Assets are probable future economic benefits obtained or controlled by a particular entity as a result of past transactions or events.

• An asset has three essential characteristics:

   • It embodies a probable future benefit that involves a capacity, singly or in a combination with other assets, to contribute directly or indirectly to future net cash inflows.

   • The enterprise can obtain the benefit and control others' access to it. [Legal enforceability of a claim to the benefit is not a prerequisite for a benefit to qualify as an asset if its receipt by the enterprise is otherwise probable.]

   •The transactions or other events giving rise to the enterprise's-right to or control of the benefit has already occurred.

(2) Liabilities are probable future sacrifices of economic benefits arising from present obligations of a particular entity to transfer assets or provide services to other entitles in the future as a result of past transactions or events.

• A liability has three essential characteristics:

   •It embodies a present duty or responsibility to one or more other entities that entails settlement by probable future transfer or use of assets at a specified or determinable date on occurrence of a specified event, or on demand.

   • The duty or responsibility obligates a particular enterprise, leaving it little or no discretion to avoid the future sacrifice.

•The existence of a legally enforceable claim is not a prerequisite for an obligation to qualify as a liability if the future payment of cash or other transfer of assets to settle the obligation is otherwise probable.

•The transaction or other event obligating the enterprise has already happened.

• Once incurred, a liability continues as a liability of the enterprise until the enterprise settles it, or another event or circumstance discharges it or removes the enterprise's responsibility to settle it.

(3)　*Equity* is the residual interest in the assets of an entity that remains after deducting its liabilities.

• In a business enterprise, the equity is the ownership interest (owners' equity).

(4)　*Investment by owners* are increases in net assets of a particular enterprise resulting from transfers to it from other entities of something valuable to obtain or increase equity (ownership interests).

• That which is received includes most commonly assets. but may also include services or satisfaction or conversion of liabilities of the enterprise.

• Investments by owners increase equity (ownership interests).

(5)　*Distributions to owners* are decreases in net assets of a particular enterprise resulting from transferring assets, rendering services, or incurring liabilities by the enterprise to owners. Distributions to owners decrease equity (owners' interest).

• When dividends are declared, the enterprise incurs a liability to transfer assets to owners in the future, resulting in equity being reduced and liabilities increased.

Reacquisition by an entity of its own equity securities by transferring assets or incurring liabilities to owners is a distribution to owners.

(6)　*Comprehensive income is* the change in equity (net assets) of an enterprise during a period from transactions and other events and circumstances from nonowner sources. It includes all changes in equity during a period except those resulting from investment by owners and distributions to owners.

• Over the life of a business enterprise, its comprehensive income equals the net of its cash receipts and cash outlays (excluding cash investments by owners and cash distributions to owners).

• Comprehensive income results from:

- Exchange transactions and other transfers between the enterprise and other entities that are not its owners.

- The enterprise's productive efforts.

- Price changes, casualties, and other effects of interaction between the enterprise and its economic, legal, social, political and physical environment.

• Comprehensive income, as defined, is a return on financial-capital as distinguished from a return on physical capital.

• The major difference between the two capital maintenance concepts is that "holding gates and losses. are included in return on capital under the financial capital concept, but these are called "capital maintenance adjustments. under the physical capital concept and are included directly in equity and are not included in return on capital. (See also Supplement C.)

The term "earnings. has not been used because it may be used to designate a different concept that is a component part of (narrower or less than) comprehensive income, and earnings, when defined, may be a return on physical capital or may be a return on financial capital.

(7)   Revenues are inflows or other enhancements of assets of an entity or settlements of its liabilities (or a combination of both) during a period from delivering or producing goods, rendering services, or other activities that constitute the entity's ongoing mayor or central operations.

- Revenues represent actual or "expected cash inflows (or the equivalent) that have occurred or will eventuate as a result of the enterprise's ongoing major or central operations during the period.

(8)   Expenses are outflows or other using up of assets or incurrences of liabilities (or a combination of both) during a period from delivering or producing goods, rendering services, or carrying out other activities that constitute the enterprise's ongoing mayor or central operations.

- Expenses represent actual or expected cash outflows (or the equivalent) that have occurred or will eventuate as a result of the enterprise's ongoing mayor or central operations during the period.

(9)   Gains are increases in equity et assets) from peripheral or incidental transactions of an entity and from all other transactions and other events and circumstances affecting the entity during a period except those that result from revenues or investments by owners.

(10)   *Losses* are decreases in equity (net assets) from peripheral or incidental transactions of an entity and from all other actions and other events and circumstances affecting the entity during a period except those that result from expenses or distributions to owners.

26.   The basic approach to the recognition issue is the identification of the information that financial statements should show. According to the Board, the primary financial statements consist of elements--assets, liabilities, revenues, and expenses. To be included in the financial statements, the recognition of an item is required when all of the following four criteria are met:

1. The item must meet the definition of an element of financial statements as defined by SFAC 3.
2. The item is reliably measurable.
3. The item is relevant, i.e., the information about it is capable of making a difference in user decisions.
4. The information about the item is reliable, that is, it is representationally faithful, verifiable and neutral.

This Statement did not resolve the mayor measurement dilemma of current value versus historical cost. Several measurement attributes are used in present practice, and the Board expects the use of different attributes to continue. However, the Board gives itself an option to pursue more extensive use of current values, stating that: "Information based on current prices should be recognized if it is sufficiently relevant and reliable to justify the costs involved and more relevant than alternative information.

27.   The CF project represents an earnest attempt by the *FASB* to establish a logical and coherent framework of interrelated objectives and concepts that are intended to enhance the conceptual foundations of accounting standards and to promote confidence in and acceptance of these standards.

The analyst must understand that, contrary to what some would have us believe, accounting is *not* a science (concerned as science is with natural laws and predictions based on them) but rather a service activity which, in order to be useful to society, draws for its execution and improvement on related fields of science and particularly, social science.

Being rooted in the social system of which it is part accounting, whose issues affect different parties at interest in different ways, is always subject to political processes. Thus, the setting of accounting concepts and standards is in itself a political process.

Analysts should be understanding of the accounting profession's efforts in its attempts to establish a sound CF and should be supportive of its goals which are, ultimately, in the analyst's best interests. At the same time analysts must be aware of the fact that previous attempts at establishing conceptual frameworks have not yielded universally accepted concepts or "truths"—universal in the sense that men would settle differences of opinion by referring to them.

Analysts must also realize that agreements on accounting objectives or standards is often obtained by couching such statements in language that is vague enough so as to allow room for various interest groups to adopt their own interpretations of their operational meaning. It follows that in using the accountant's product, analysts must be alert to the fact that in practice considerations of self-interest can govern accounting presentations just as much as can logic and rational objectives.

According to FASB chairman Kirk SFAC 5 represents the "end of the trail. for the CF. The Board seems to have come to the conclusion that change in accounting will continue as an evolutionary process and will *not* come as the result of the CF. Since up to now accounting change has always come about as the result of an evolutionary process the question arises of whether this entire exercise of establishing a CF has been worthwhile. If SFAC 5, on which most hopes were pinned, merely describes and endorses present accounting practices what is its contribution? Substantial questions regarding the nature of earnings and of comprehensive income and the differences between them were left unanswered. Similarly the resolution of questions relating to accounting for changing prices (inflation), the recognition of executory contracts and a host of other problem areas were left on the knees of future evolving conditions.

The CF has had some positive results. It has contributed to a good debate on the objectives of accounting and identified the major users of financial statements. It also identified the qualitative characteristics of accounting information and the qualities which make it useful. Moreover, it defined elements of financial statements such as assets, liabilities, owners' equity, revenues, expenses, gains, losses and comprehensive income. It has resulted in some better and more thought-through terminology and superior definitions of accounting related concepts. It may even contribute to a higher degree of internal consistency in promulgated standards. But it has disappointed those who thought that the seven people in Stamford were going to come up with a solid framework for resolving today's as well as tomorrow's vexing problems of accounting. By stating its reliance on gradual change and evolution the Board has admitted that it cannot meet the great expectations many placed in it. From the point of view of users and analysts of financial statements this admission is a healthy development which will give them a more realistic view of what can and cannot be accomplished in financial reporting standard setting.

Change in accounting has come mostly as a process by which the standard set of the time addressed the problems which demanded prompt solutions. The motivations for diligent effort and for compromise were at hand and so solutions were found. And so it will probably continue in the future. The resolution of these problems will always be influenced by the cries and protestations of those most affected by them.

To many observers, including the author, this does not come as a surprise. For one, social sciences, such as accounting is, do not have codified conceptual frameworks. There are none for law, for economics or finance. Moreover, Board members who have experienced first hand how difficult it is to settle even more limited problems of practice, such as those of foreign operations, or pensions or taxes, realize that to settle great issues of accounting in advance is beyond them. The limited areas which have been addressed so far have required a great many compromises and adjustments to contemporary conditions and forces. The CF remains a shining theoretical ideal worthy of trial but, in large part, unattainable.

◀ Answers to Exercises ▶

Exercise 2-1
The most practical solution is the diligent and impartial application of the accrual method of accounting measurement. We need a method of profit determination on a periodic basis and we obviously cannot liquidate a business every time we need to measure its profitability.

Exercise 2-2
Apparently, the analyst is referring to a more reliable and valid earnings measure than that produced by the accounting process. It is, however, entirely unclear what source is to be used to produce such earnings figures.

Exercise 2-3
a. Perhaps the most important disadvantage of complete uniform accounting is that it would be inflexible and, if nationally or internationally adopted, it would be exceedingly difficult to change and to utilize new ideas. In short, total uniformity might freeze the state of accounting at its current level of development.

Second, complete standardization might stifle new approaches and ideas. This would be particularly true from the technical approach to accounting (as contrasted with the economic and business approaches).

Third, entirely uniform accounting might not be appropriate for all industries and all countries. Different countries have different economic objectives. For example, uniformity in accounting is more desirable in France where economic planning is important than in Germany, where the long-term trend in accounting has been toward less uniformity. Furthermore, the same accounting system may not be appropriate for the utility industry as opposed to railroads. Accounting must in some respects be tailored to the nature of the business.

An additional problem is that total uniformity in accounting would be difficult and expensive to implement. Accountants and regulatory authorities would disagree on the standardized form, and small firms would have difficulty shouldering the cost of adopting the full standardized form.

b. Uniform accounting does not necessarily mean comparability. Uniform accounting can mean: (a) uniform classification of accounts (a classification system), (b) a uniform plan (a system of procedures), or (c) total uniformity. The latter would not seem to be desirable in view of the different characteristics of different businesses.

For example, different pieces of equipment may have different lives and should be depreciated accordingly. Different mines have different expected reserves and should be depleted accordingly. Different lists of receivables have different quality, and bad debts reserves should accordingly vary. It would seem very unfair and inadvisable to apply the same depreciation rate, the same depletion rate, the same bad debts reserves for all companies regardless of the nature of their businesses. Thus, comparability might include uniform classification of accounts and a uniform plan but not total uniformity.

Exercise 2-4

a. Price = PV of principal + PV of interest   [5 periods, 11%]

= (1,000)(.59345) + (1,000)(.09)(3.6959)

= 593 + 333 = $\underline{\$~926}$

b. Price = PV of principal + PV of interest   [5 periods, 7%]

= (1,000)(.71299) + (1,000)(.09)(4.1002)

= 713 + 369 = $\underline{\$1,082}$

Exercise 2-5

Price = BV + PV of abnormal earnings

= 100 + 84.37 [see table] = $\underline{\$184.37}$

Year	NI	BV, beg[1]	abnormal NI[2]	PV factor	PV
1	30	100	15	.86957	13.04
2	35	130	15.5	.75614	11.72
3	40	165	15.25	.65752	10.03
4	45	205	14.25	.57175	8.15
5	50	250	12.5	3.31453[3]	41.43
				Total	$84.37

[1] BV, end = BV, beg + NI - dividends

[2] abnormal NI = NI - (.15)(BV, beg)

[3] (.49718)(1/.15)

◄ Answers to Problems ►

Problem 2-1

The standard setting process is of great relevance to the financial analyst because it provides insight into the final product of this process, i.e., accounting standards.

The financial analyst, in order to analyze financial statements intelligently, must have a sound understanding of the standards that underlie the preparation of these financial statements. Since financial accounting standards are the result of the standard setting process, the nature of this process affects the soundness and the lack of ambiguity of the standards. The standard-setting process is at risk to subversion by special interests and by standard setters trying to accommodate all. For example, if standards are written in such a way so as to satisfy different conflicting interests then they are likely to be "soft," i.e., subject to a wide variety of interpretations. That, in turn, can lead to practice which avoids the letter as well as the spirit of the standard.

Problem 2-2

a. Neutrality lies at the heart of reliability--it implies accounting devoid of ulterior motives and devoid of interests other than that of objective and fair presentation and reporting. It is even-handed with respect to the impact of the information on user's behavior.

b. Accounting which slants presentations so as to make financial statements present a financial position superior to that which in fact prevails or to present results of operations more favorable than were in fact achieved. The motives for such presentations which lack in neutrality between the parties at interest are as obvious as they are numerous.

Problem 2-3

a. Under present generally accepted accounting standards, measurement means determination of the cost or net realizable value of an asset or liability.

   Determining the original cost of an asset, say, in the purchase of bonds, involves nothing more than recording the purchase price. Measuring the fair value of accounts receivable involves estimating how much will ultimately be collected. Here we deal with probabilities based on experience, and this is a different level of precision in measurement.

b. Many analysts seem to be offended by the precision implied in the accountant's use of the word "measurement." Equity analysts want the measurement to have a link to or relevance to the ultimate valuation by the market place. This is, however, an altogether different level of measurement and estimation. Analysts may start with accounting measurements but they must build on these their assessment of how the market will (1) adjust these accounting measurements to its perception of relevant valuation factors and (2) value these, e.g., determine what price-earnings ratios it will accord the adjusted earnings.

c. The two measurement objectives are different. Accountants lay no claim to engaging in valuation. They merely provide the raw material for this process. Accounting measurements aim to estimate the most probable cash flows which will ultimately be realized from an asset or be devoted to the repayment of a liability. Measurement is only selectively concerned with the time value of money.

   Analysts seek measurements which are relevant to the valuation of the aggregate business enterprise in the context of the market place. Measurement is concerned with the timing of these cash flows and their valuation. In many cases, as a practical matter, it is concerned with the capitalization of the most relevant earnings number. The analyst's measurement *starts* with that of the accountant and builds on it.

Problem 2-4

Pure rules of measurement are possible only when the process of measuring is scientific, objective, and generally incontrovertible. In accounting, rules of measurement cannot be "sold" to those who have to live with them solely on that basis. These rules must be made acceptable to a majority of those who must abide by them. It is this requirement that gives them the character of rules of conduct to be abided by. To many, abiding by such rules may involve sacrifices. Hence, the need for acceptability as well as fairness.

The process by which acceptability is secured is basically a political process. It requires that those whose concurrence is sought be involved in the decision process, have a voice in the consideration of alternatives, be persuaded that compromises which have to be reached are fair, and recognize the theoretical soundness of the proposed solution.

Purists would argue that accounting is a science and that solutions to questions of accounting standards should be arrived at by the "scientific method" of observation, experimentation, and verification.

In the final analysis, accounting is more of a service activity than a service governed by natural law. To the extent that accounting is a science, it is a social science subject to the mores of the society of which it is part.

Problem 2-5

a. FASB's conceptual framework study should provide benefits to the accounting community such as

   •   guiding the FASB in establishing accounting standards on a consistent basis.

   •   determining bounds for judgment in preparing financial statements by prescribing the nature, functions, and limits of financial accounting and reporting.

   •   increasing users' understanding of and confidence in financial reporting.

b. *Statement of Financial Accounting Concepts No. 2* identifies the most important quality for accounting information as usefulness for decision-making. Relevance and reliability are the primary qualities leading to this decision usefulness. Usefulness is the most important quality because, without usefulness, there would be no benefits from information to set against its costs.

c. A number of key characteristics or qualities that make accounting information desirable are described in the *Statement of Financial Accounting Concepts No. 2*. The importance of three of these characteristics or qualities is discussed below.

- *Understandability*—information provided by financial reporting should be comprehensible to those who have a reasonable understanding of business and economic activities and are willing to study the information with reasonable diligence. Financial information is a tool and, like most tools, cannot be of much direct help to those who are unable or unwilling to use it or who misuse it.

- *Relevance*—the accounting information is capable of making a difference in a decision by helping users to form predictions about the outcomes of past, present, and future events or to confirm or correct expectations.

- *Reliability*—the reliability of a measure rests on the faithfulness with which it represents what it purports to represent, coupled with an assurance for the user, which comes through verification, that it has representational quality.

Problem 2-6

a. Society has brought increasing pressure to bear on accountants in its desire to improve the efficiency with which its assets are priced and its capital investment directed. It has also chosen to exploit the notion that corporations are an appropriate point at which to extract taxes from the economy and control economic activity.

Aspects of pressure on accountants include the increasing role of securities commissions requiring "full disclosure," the emergence of class action suits, the growing taxation bureaucracy, and the increasing literacy of the populace, including the press, corporate clients, and securities analysts. Indeed, society's developing objectives have made the practice of accounting and auditing increasingly demanding, if not hazardous.

Recent reports and hearings by Congressional committees are part of society's pressures on accountants so that it is better served.

b. Accountants' accommodation consists mainly of educating the profession and the public and enlarging the professional membership. Standards boards and research committees I view mainly and sympathetically as devices to protect accountants by providing them an authority with which to counter and modify the thrusts of society.

The accounting profession can enhance its position and at the same time improve its service to society by insisting that, while numbers are not possible without definitions, by recognizing the uniqueness of each enterprise, qualifications and descriptions enhance meaning and reduce possibilities for abuse of numbers and generally applied definitions.

The organized profession's response to Congressional action has been to organize politically as well as to promote and promise self-reform. Among these measures are the establishment of a Public Oversight Board by the AICPA, and the establishment of Peer Review as well as the institution of continuing Professional Education.

(CFA)

<u>Problem 2-7</u>

a. The professor's view is certainly skeptical, bordering on the cynical, and there is a good deal of misunderstanding regarding the function of general purpose financial reports in what he says.

It appears that the professor is confusing the function of the corporate controller (management accountant) with that of the independent public accountant whose function it is indeed to probe and to reveal.

While we have come a long way from the time when almost any financial disclosure was viewed as the giving away of competitive information, there remains a great deal that is not disclosed primarily for competitive reasons. Present-day financial disclosure requirements do not require details about the physical composition of inventories or the identification of specific slow-paying customers. Much additional information which analysts may view as essential need similarly not be disclosed. It is this lack of requirements rather than the accountant's subservience to management that represents the main reason why such information is rarely found in published financial reports. That independent public accountants, whose primary function it is to serve the public interest, are sometimes unduly influenced by management's desires is well known and a problem much in the forefront of public discussion today. (See examples in Supplement B and elsewhere in this book.) However, the degree of public disclosure necessary is a matter depending on public policy which is importantly influenced by the SEC. The day is long past when accountants were the sole setters of disclosure policy.

For reasons of competition, cost, and other considerations, it is unlikely that *all* information desired by financial analysts will ever be provided in general purpose public reports. Consequently, this will remain an area where analysts will have to exercise their information-gathering ingenuity to the fullest extent. Much additional information of a statistical nature is often available on request.

b. The omitted information which the writer is referring to is the type every serious financial analyst would like to get as much as possible of in order to assess the risks inherent in a business enterprise as well as the rewards which can be expected from it. Such quantified data as product sales breakdowns, inventory composition, and customer-paying records are indeed data needed by any good management in the conduct and planning of business operations. While analysts will not find these data in most financial statements, they attempt to obtain them, if they need them, from managements or from other sources.

In a report based on a survey of financial reports, the Financial Analysts Federation's corporate information committee listed the following most prevalent problem areas:

Lack of detail in production costs and marketing types of information.

Lack of nonstatement detail, such as labor costs or contracts, pension information, regulations, etc.

Limited discussion on economic and industry developments that represent current or recent problems, unusual developments or facts not generally available to average investors or shareholders.

A need for more disclosure of operating statistics already on file with regulatory agencies such as the ICC, FCC, CAB, etc.

A very important source of narrative as well as quantified information which is now available is "Management's Discussion and Analysis of Financial Condition and Results of Operations" which, because of specific SEC requirements, must now contain significant and meaningful information.

Problem 2-8

a. Price = PV of principal + PV of interest   [20 periods, 3%]
            = (10,000)(.55368) + (10,000)(.04)(14.87747)
            = 5,537 + 5,951 = $11,488

b. Price = PV of principal + PV of interest   [20 periods, 5%]
            = (10,000)(.37689) + (10,000)(.04)(12.46221)
            = 3,769 + 4,985 = $ 8,754

Problem 2-9

Price = BV + PV of abnormal earnings
     = 50 + 13.90 [see table] = $63.90

Year	NI	BV, beg[1]	abnormal NI[2]	PV factor	PV
1	8	50	-2.00	.83333	-1.67
2	11	58	-0.60	.69444	-0.42
3	20	69	6.20	.57870	3.59
4	40	89	22.20	.48225	10.71
5	30	129	4.20	.40188	1.69
6+			0		0
				Total	$13.90

[1] BV, end = BV, beg + NI - dividends
[2] abnormal NI = NI - (.2)(BV, beg)
[3] (.49718)(1/.15)

Problem 2-10

1. Debt to Equity = 1

$$\frac{Debt}{Equity} = 1 = \frac{300}{X} = 300$$

2. Return on Equity = 20% = $\dfrac{\text{Net Income}}{\text{Equity}}$ = $\dfrac{X}{300}$

   Net Income = 60

3. Net Income   60
   + Expenses   540
   Gross Profit   600

4. $\dfrac{\text{Gross Profit}}{\text{Sales}} = 0.5$ = $\dfrac{600}{0.5}$ = 1,200

   Cost of Goods Sold = Sales - Gross Profit = 1,200 - 600 = 600

5. Inventory Turnover = $\dfrac{\text{Cost of Goods Sold}}{\text{Ending Inventory}}$

   Ending Inventory = $\dfrac{\text{Cost of Goods Sold}}{\text{Inventory Turnover}}$ = $\dfrac{600}{10}$ = 60

6. Acid test = $\dfrac{\text{Cash + Accounts Receivable}}{\text{Current Liabilities}}$

   $0.6 = \dfrac{90 + X}{300}$

   Accounts Receivable = X = 90

7. Total Assets = Cash + Accounts Receivable + Inventory + Land + Building
   600 = 90 + 90 + 60 + Land + Building
   Land + Building = 360
   2/3x + x = 360
   x = 216 (Building)
   2/3x = 144 (Land)

8. Equity = Common Stock + Retained Earnings
   300 = Common Stock + 120
   Common Stock = 180

FLAM BAY INC.
Balance Sheet
As of December 31, X3

Assets:		Liabilities and Owner's Equity:	
Cash	$ 90	Total Liabilities	$300
Accounts Receivable	90	Common Stock	180
Inventory	60	Retained Earnings	120
Land	144	Total Liabilities and	
Building	216	Owners' Equity	$600
Total Assets	$600		

◀ Answers to Cases ▶

Case 2-1

a. Possible answers include: (1) detailed information regarding research and development projects, (2) market share data, (3) identification of major competitors, etc.

b. Adaptec has not paid dividends in the past and does not plan to pay dividends in the near future. The dividend discount formula is not helpful in valuing such a firm. [NOTE: According to its statement of shareholders' equity, Adaptec engaged in repurchases of common stock in fiscal 1995 and 1994. Under the clean surplus relation, share repurchases are considered dividends.]

c. abnormal NI = NI - (.15)(BV, beg)

1996: 103,375 - (.15)(371,644) = $47,628
1995: 93,402 - (.15)(297,616) = $48,760
1994: 58,950 - (.15)(225,155) = $25,177
1993: 49,390 - (.15)(117,742) = $31,729

d. Note one includes the following examples of managerial judgement: (1) disclosure of contingent assets and liabilities, (2) provisions for sales returns, (3) classification of marketable securities, (4) allowance for doubtful accounts, (5) useful lives of assets, (6) impairment of fixed assets, and (7) recording of deferred tax assets.

e.

	Marketable Securities		
beg	179,911		
SCF	24,372		
end	204,283		

	Accounts Receivable		
beg	56,495		
sales	659,347	626,355	collect.
end	89,487		

	Note Payable		
		0	beg
		46,200	loan
		46,200	end

	Long-term Debt		
		7,650	beg
SCF	3,400		
		4,250	end

f. 12/31/95: 30,587 + 557 + 31,163 + 29,949 = $92,256
9/30/95: 557 + 31,163 + 29,949 + 27,403 = $89,072
6/30/95: 31,163 + 29,949 + 27,403 + 18,458 = $106,973

Case 2-2

a. Political influences on accounting are and remain strong. The SEC's resistance to the adoption of the preferred successful accounting method was strongly influenced by pressure not only from affected oil companies but also by congressmen from oil-producing states.

The bending of rules was narrowly avoided when the commission stood up to the companies and to its staff. Had the SEC acquiesced to this bending of rules in time of stress, accounting integrity would have suffered another blow.

b. Tenneco's change in accounting method seems designed to avoid a writeoff to income of capitalized production costs that exceed the SEC-defined ceiling which are affected by dropping oil prices.

Tenneco had demonstrated how companies could use accounting rules to their advantage. Tenneco's past drilling expenses would be offset against past reported results and would never appear on a current income statement. Those costs will now be matched against revenues earned at a time when oil prices were much higher than at present.

While analysts may be able to adjust for the effects of Tenneco's accounting strategy their task in assessing the company's real earning power will be rendered more difficult.

◄ CHAPTER 3 ►

Analyzing Financing Activities

◄ CHAPTER REVIEW ►

Business activities are financed through either liabilities or equity. Liabilities are obligations requiring payment of money, rendering of future services, or dispensing of specific assets. They are claims against a company's present and future assets and resources. Such claims are usually senior to holders of equity securities. Liabilities include current obligations, long-term debt, capital leases, and deferred credits. This chapter also considers securities straddling the line separating liabilities from equity. Equity refers to claims of owners to the net assets of a company. While claims of owners are junior to creditors, they are residual claims to *all* assets once claims of creditors are satisfied. Equity investors are exposed to the maximum risk associated with a business, but are entitled to all residual rewards associated with it. Our analysis must recognize the claims of both creditors and equity investors, and their relationship, when analyzing financing activities.

This chapter describes business financing and how this is reported to external users. We describe two major sources of financing--credit and equity--and the accounting underlying reports of these activities. We also consider off-balance-sheet financing, the relevance of book values, and liabilities "at the edge" of equity. Techniques of analysis exploiting our accounting knowledge are described.

◄ CHAPTER OUTLINE ►

Section 1: Creditor Financing

► **Current and Noncurrent Liabilities**

    Current Liabilities

    Noncurrent Liabilities

    Analysis Implications of Liabilities

► **Lease Obligations**

    Lessee's Reporting

    Lessor's Reporting

    Special Leases

    Capital and Operating Lease Implications

    Analysis Implications of Lease Obligations

► **Pension Liabilities**

    Accounting and Reporting for Pensions

    Analysis Implications of Pension Liabilities

► **Postretirement Obligations Other than Pensions**

    Accounting and Reporting for Postretirement Obligations

    Analysis Implications of Postretirement Obligations

► **Contingent Liabilities**

    Accounting and Reporting for Contingencies

    Analysis Implications of Contingencies

► **Commitments**

► **Deferred Credits or Income**

    Nature of Deferred Credits

    Deferred Taxes

    Analysis Implications of Deferred Credits and Income

► **Off-Balance-Sheet Financing**

► **Liabilities at the "Edge" of Equity**

    Redeemable Preferred Stock

    Minority Interest

Section 2: Equity Financing

▸ **Reporting for Shareholders' Equity**

▸ **Classification of Common Stock**

  Preferred Stock

  Common Stock

  Reporting of Capital Stock

  Contributed Capital

  Treasury Stock

  Analysis Implications for Capital Stock

▸ **Retained Earnings**

  Cash and Stock Dividends

  Prior Period Adjustments

  Appropriations of Retained Earnings

  Restrictions on Retained Earnings

  Analysis Implications for Retained Earnings

▸ **Book Value per Share**

  Computation of Book Value per Share

  Relevance of Book Value per Share

◄ Learning Objectives ►

■ **Identify principal characteristics distinguishing liabilities and equity.**

■ **Interpret lease disclosures and their implications for future company performance.**

■ **Analyze pension disclosures and their consequences for company valuation.**

■ **Interpret postretirement obligations and funding implications for future performance.**

■ **Analyze contingent liability disclosures and risks.**

■ **Interpret deferred credits with reference to underlying transactions and events.**

■ **Identify off-balance-sheet financing and consequences to risk analysis.**

- **Analyze and interpret liabilities at the edge of equity.**

- **Interpret capital stocks and identify their distinguishing features.**

- **Describe retained earnings and their distribution through dividends.**

- **Explain and interpret book values and their relevance in business valuation.**

◄ Answers to Questions ►

1. Current liabilities may arise from operating or financial activities. Current liabilities of an operating nature--including accounts payable and operating expense accruals--represent spontaneous sources of funds. Current liabilities such as notes payable and current maturities of long-term debt arise from financing transactions.

2. The major disclosure requirements (in SEC FRR Section 203) regarding the terms of short-term debt are:

   a. Footnote disclosure of compensating balance arrangements including those not reduced to writing
   b. Balance sheet segregation of (1) legally restricted compensating balances and (2) unrestricted compensating balances relating to long-term borrowing arrangements if the compensating balance can be computed at a fixed amount at the balance sheet date.
   c. Disclosure of short-term bank and commercial paper borrowings:
       i.   Commercial paper borrowings separately stated in the balance sheet.
       ii. Average interest rate and terms separately stated for short-term bank and commercial paper borrowings at the balance sheet date.
       iii. Average interest rate, average outstanding borrowings, and maximum month-end outstanding borrowings for short-term bank debt and commercial paper combined for the period.
   d. Disclosure of amounts and terms of unused lines of credit for short-term borrowing arrangements (with amounts supporting commercial paper separately stated) and of unused commitments for long-term financing arrangements.

   It should be noted that the above disclosures are required for filing with the SEC but not necessarily in the published annual reports. It should also be noted that SFAS No. 6 stated that certain short-term obligations should not necessarily be classified as current liabilities if the company intends to refinance them on a long-term basis and can demonstrate its ability to do so.

3. The conditions required by SFAS No. 6 that will demonstrate the ability of the company to refinance it short-term debt on a long-term basis are:

   a. The company has actually issued a long-term obligation or equity securities to replace the short-term obligation after the date of the company's balance sheet but before it is released;
   b. The company has entered into an agreement with a bank or other source of capital that clearly permits the company to refinance the short-term obligation when it becomes due.

   It should be noted that financing agreements which are cancelable for violation of a provision that can be evaluated differently by the parties to the agreement (such as "a material adverse change" or "failure to maintain satisfactory operations") do not meet the second condition. Also, an operative violation of the agreement should not have occurred.

4. Since the exact interest rate which will prevail in the bond market at the time of issuance of bonds can never be predetermined, bonds are sold in excess of par, or at a premium, or below par, i.e., at a discount. The premium or discount represents, in effect, an adjustment of the effective interest rate. The premium received is amortized over the life of the issue, thus reducing the coupon rate of interest to the effective interest rate incurred. Conversely, the discount allowed is similarly amortized, thus increasing the effective interest rate paid by the borrower.

5. The following accounting is presently in use:

   a. In the case of convertible features, through their effect on the computation of diluted earnings per share and in no other way in the financial statements.
   b. In the case of warrants, by assigning a discount factor at the time of debt issuance which charge is amortized to income. In addition, the dilutive effects of warrants are given recognition in earnings per share computations.

6. SFAS 47 requires footnote disclosure of commitments under unconditional purchase obligations that provide financing to suppliers. It also requires disclosure of future payments on long-term borrowings and redeemable stock. Among required disclosures are:

For purchase obligations not recognized on purchaser's balance sheet:
1. Description and term of obligation.
2. Total fixed and determinable obligation. If determinable, also show these amounts for each of the next five years.
3. Description of any variable obligation.
4. Amounts purchased under obligation for each period covered by an income statement.

For purchase obligations recognized on purchaser's balance sheet, payments for each of the next five years.

For long-term borrowings and redeemable stock:
1. Maturities and sinking fund requirements for each of the next five years.
2. Redemption requirements for each of the next five years.

7. If short-term bank debt is included in the current liability section, it may mean that the company does not plan to refinance or the company cannot get a refinancing agreement with a lender that meets the requirements of SFAS No. 6. The analyst should attempt to determine the reason for the current liability classification of bank debt since an inability to secure a satisfactory refinancing agreement could indicate the company has problems beyond those revealed it its financial statements. The analyst must be aware of the possibility that understatement of liabilities can occur and, when it does, income will most likely be adversely affected.

8. The means by which auditors satisfy themselves that all liabilities have been properly recorded are such procedures as scrutiny of board of director meeting minutes, the reading of contracts and agreements, and inquiry of those who may have knowledge of company obligations and liabilities. Since the nature of double-entry bookkeeping requires that for every asset, resource, or cost, a counterbalancing obligation, or payment, or investment must be booked, the areas subject to considerable difficulty are those relating to commitments and contingent liabilities because they do not involve the commensurate recording of assets or costs. Here, the analyst must rely on the information which is provided in the notes to financial statements and in the general management commentary found in the text of the annual report and elsewhere.

Due to the uncertainties involved, the descriptions of commitments and especially of contingent liabilities in footnotes are often vague and indeterminate. In effect, this means that the burden of assessing the possible impact of the contingencies as well as the probabilities of their occurrence is passed on to the reader. The analyst should always determine whether the auditors feel that a contingency is serious enough and material enough to call for a qualification in their report.

The disclosure of the terms and conditions of regular recorded indebtedness and liabilities is another area deserving the analyst's careful attention. Here, the analyst must examine critically the description of debt, its terms, conditions, and encumbrances with a view to satisfy himself as to the term's feasibility and completeness. Important in the evaluation of a liability's total impact are such features as:

The terms of the debt,
Restrictions on deployment of resources and freedom of action,
Ability to engage in further financing,
Requirements relating to maintenance of working capital, debt to equity ratio, etc.
Dilutive conversion features to which the debt is subject.

The analyst, while utilizing all the information available must nevertheless bring his/her own critical evaluation to bear on the assessment of all the contingencies to which the company may be subject. This process must draw not only on available disclosures and information, but also on an understanding of industry conditions and practices.

9. a. SFAS No. 13 requires that a lease be classified and accounted for as a capital lease if at the inception of the lease it meets one of four criteria: (1) The lease transfers ownership of the property to the lessee by the end of the lease term; (2) the lease contains an option to purchase the property at a bargain price; (3) the lease term is equal to 75 percent or more of the estimated economic life of the property; or (4) the present value of the rentals and other minimum lease payments, at the beginning of the lease term, equals 90 percent of the fair value of the leased property less any related investment tax credit retained by the lessor. If the lease does not meet any of those criteria, it is to be classified and accounted for as an operating lease.

With regard to the last two of the above four criteria, if the beginning of the lease term falls within the last 25 percent of the total estimated economic life of the leased property, neither the 75 percent of economic life criterion nor the 90 percent recovery criterion is to be applied for purposes of classifying the lease and as a consequence, such leases will be classified as operating leases.

b. Summary of accounting for leases by lessees (SFAS No. 13):

1. The lessee shall record a capital lease as an asset and an obligation at an amount equal to the present value of minimum lease payments during the lease term, excluding executory costs (if determinable) such as insurance, maintenance, and taxes to be paid by the lessor together with any profit thereon. However, the amount so determined should not exceed the fair value of the leased property at the inception of the lease. If executory costs are not determinable from the provisions of the lease, an estimate of the amount shall be made.

2. Amortization, in a manner consistent with the lessee's normal depreciation policy, is called for over the term of the lease except where the lease transfers title or contains a bargain purchase option; in the latter cases amortization should follow the estimated economic life.

3. In accounting for an operating lease the lessee will charge rentals to expenses as they become payable, except when rentals do not become payable on a straight-line basis, in which case they should be expensed on such a basis or on any other systematic or rational basis which reflects the time pattern of benefits serviced from the leased property.

10. a. The different classifications of leases by lessors (according to SFAS No. 13) are:

1. Sales-type leases
2. Direct financing leases
3. Operating leases

The criteria for classifying each type are as follows: if a lease meets any one of the four criteria for capitalization (see question 9a above) plus two additional criteria, it is to be classified and accounted for as a sales-type lease (if manufacturer or dealer profit is involved), or as a direct financing lease. The additional criteria are: (1) collectibility of the minimum lease payments is reasonable predictable; and (2) no important uncertainties surround the amount of unreimbursable costs yet to be incurred by the lessor under the lease. A lease not meeting those tests is to be classified and accounted for as an operating lease.

b. The accounting procedures for leases by lessors according to SFAS No. 13 are as follows:

<u>Sales-type leases</u>

1. The minimum lease payments plus the unguaranteed residual value accruing to the benefit of the lessor shall be recorded as the gross investment in the lease.

2. The difference between gross investment and the sum of the present value of its two components shall be recorded as unearned income. The net investment equals gross investment less unearned income. Unearned income shall be amortized to income over the lease term so as to produce a constant periodic rate of return on the net investment in the lease. Contingent rentals shall be credited to income when they become receivable.

3. At the termination of the existing lease term of a lease being renewed, the net investment in the lease shall be adjusted to the fair value of the leased property to the lessor at that date, and the difference, if any, recognized as gain or loss. The same procedure applies to direct financing leases (see below.)

4. The present value of the minimum lease payments discounted at the interest rate implicit in the lease shall be recorded as the sales price. The cost, or carrying amount, if different, of the leased property, and any initial direct costs (of negotiating and consummating the lease), less the present value of the unguaranteed residual value shall he charged against income in the same period.

5. The estimated residual value shall be periodically reviewed. If it is determined to be excessive, the accounting for the transaction shall be revised using the changed estimate. The resulting reduction in net investment shall be recognized as a loss in the period in which the estimate is changed. No upward adjustment of the estimated residual value shall be made. (A similar provision applies to direct financing leases.)

Direct-financing leases

1. The minimum lease payments (net of executory costs) plus the unguaranteed residual value plus the initial direct costs shall be recorded as the gross investment.

2. The difference between the gross investment and the cost, or carrying amount, if different, of the leased property, shall be recorded as unearned income. Net investment equals gross investment less unearned income. The unearned income shall be amortized to income over the lease term. The initial direct costs shall be amortized in the same portion as the unearned income. Contingent rentals shall be credited to income when they become receivable.

Operating leases

The lessor will include property accounted for as an operating lease in the balance sheet and will depreciate it in accordance with his normal depreciation policy. Rent should be taken into income over the lease term as it becomes receivable except that if it departs from a straight-line basis income should be recognized on such basis or on some other systematic or rational basis. Initial costs should be deferred and allocated over the lease term.

11. Where land only is involved the lessee should account for it as a capital lease if either of the enumerated criteria (1) or (2) is met. Land is not usually amortized.

In a case involving both land and building(s), if the capitalization criteria applicable to land (see above) are met, the lease will retain the capital lease classification and the lessor u ill account for it as a single unit. The lessee will have to capitalize the land and buildings separately, the allocation between the two being in proportion to their respective fair values at the inception of the lease.

If the capitalization criteria applicable to land are not met, and at the inception of the lease the fair value of the land is less than 25 percent of total fair value of the leased property both lessor and lessee shall consider the property as a single unit. The estimated economic life of the building is to be attributed to the whole unit. In this case if either of the enumerated criteria (3) or (4) is met the lessee should capitalize the land and building as a single unit and amortize it.

If the conditions in (c) above prevail but the fair value of land is 25 percent or more of the total fair value of the leased property, both the lessee and the lessor should consider the land and the building separately for purposes of applying capitalization criteria (3) and (4). If either of the criteria is met by the building element of the lease it should be accounted for as a capital lease by the lessee and amortized. The land element of the lease is to be accounted for as an operating lease. If the building element meets neither capitalization criteria, both land and buildings should be accounted for as a single operating lease.

Equipment which is part of a real estate lease should be considered separately and the minimum lease payments applicable to it should be estimated by whatever means are appropriate in the circumstances.

Leases of certain facilities such as airport, bus terminal, or port facilities from governmental units or authorities are to be classified as operating leases.

12. The principal items of information required to be described by <u>lessees</u> are: (1) future minimum lease payments, separately for capital leases and operating leases, in total and for each of the five succeeding years and (2) rental expense for each period for which an income statement is presented.

Information required to be disclosed by <u>lessors</u> includes: (1) future minimum lease payments to be received, separately for sales-type and direct financing leases and for operating leases, and (2) the other components of the investment in sales-type and direct financing leases: estimated residual values, and unearned income.

13. SFAS No. 13 represents a major step in the direction of providing the analyst with the information required for the proper reflection of leases in the financial statements and the evaluation of their impact on the financial position and results of operations of an enterprise. The criteria as well as the disclosure requirements embodied in this Statement are much more comprehensive and explicit than those contained in any former pronouncements and this should assure that the abuses and distortions of the past will not inhibit the process of analysis. Nevertheless, the analyst, mindful of the historical tendencies and developments in this area of accounting which is affected by strong special interests, should be ever alert to the possibility that management, aided by the seemingly inexhaustible ingenuity of their accountants, lawyers, and other financial advisers will often attempt to devise ways to circumvent this statement.

While, under the standards which preceded SFAS No. 13, only relatively few leases were capitalized, the new rules will require the capitalization of most leases where there is an effective transfer of substantially all of the benefits and risks of ownership from lessor to lessee.

The effect of these changes will result in the increase of debt and of fixed assets, the impairment in debt/equity ratios, the reduction in current and acid-test ratios (the current portion of long-term lease obligations will increase current liabilities) and in the increase of expenses in the early stages of a lease. Because of the requirement that enterprises use their "normal. depreciation policies in accounting for the depreciation of leased property the income of entities using accelerated depreciation methods for book purposes will be more substantially affected.

The provisions of SFAS No. 13 which entail assumptions of fair values, selling prices, salvage or residual values, implicit rates of interest and incremental borrowing rates are not so tight as to preclude substantial changes in accounting through a manipulation of these relatively "soft" factors. Thus, as in the past, the analyst will also in the future have to be alert and vigilant when analyzing the impact of leases on financial statements.

14. Property, plant, and equipment can be financed by having an outside party acquire the facilities while the company agrees to do enough business with the facility to provide funds sufficient to service the debt. Examples of these kinds

of arrangements are through-put agreements, in which the company agrees to run a specified amount of goods through a processing facility or "take or pay" arrangements in which the company guarantees to pay for a specified quantity of goods whether needed or not.

A variation of the above arrangements involves the creation of separate entities for ownership and the financing of the facilities (such as joint ventures or limited partnerships) which are not consolidated with the company's financial statements and are, thus, excluded from its liabilities.

Companies have attempted to finance inventory without reporting on their balance sheets the inventory or the related liability. These are generally product financing arrangements in which an enterprise sells and agrees to repurchase inventory with the repurchase price equal to the original sales price plus carrying and financing costs or other similar transactions such as a guarantee of resale prices to third parties.

15. SFAS 125, "Accounting for Transfers and Servicing of Financial Assets and Extinguishment of Liabilities," allows companies which sell their receivables with recourse (i.e., retaining some risk of loss) to book them as a sale rather than as a loan if they meet three criteria regarding surrender of control:

    1. the receivables are isolated from the seller
    2. the purchaser obtains the right to pledge or exchange the receivables
    3. the seller does not maintain effective control through an agreement entitling or obligating the seller to repurchase the receivables

    If any one of the above three conditions is not met, the transfer of the receivable is considered as a loan with the receivables pledged as security for such loan.

16. a. The *accumulated benefit obligation* is an estimate of the employer's obligation for pensions based on current and past compensation levels. No assumption regarding future compensation levels is included and for pension plans, such as flat benefit plans or those with non-pay related formulas the accumulated benefit obligation accurately measures the entire or final obligation.

    b. The *projected benefit obligation* takes into consideration the effect of future salary increases as is necessary in order to determine the full obligations in pension plans such as those based on career-average pay or final pay.

    Contrary to the position taken by APB Opinion 8, which recognized essentially no obligation in excess of amounts accrued as the pension expense, SFAS 87 recognizes an additional minimum liability. Since this additional liability is based on the accumulated rather than on the projected benefit obligation, it represents a compromise position between the full fledged recognition of pension liabilities and their much less adequate recognition before SFAS 87.

17. One such difference relates to the accounting for the unfunded OPEB obligation. When a company adopts SFAS 106, the unfunded OPEB obligation at the date of adoption, also referred to as the "transition obligation" can be recognized as either (1) a cumulative effect of an accounting change (included as a charge to income) or (2) over future periods as a component of the annual OPEB expense (see Chapter 6) over a period not to exceed 20 years. Thus, if a company elects to amortize its transition obligation over future years, then, unlike under pension accounting, it will not be required to recognize immediately a minimum liability on the balance sheet for the unfunded OPEB obligation attributable to present retired and active employees that are eligible to receive benefits.

    The other major difference from pension accounting relates to funding. Because there are no legal requirements for OPEB benefits ,similar to ERISA requirements for pensions, and also because funding OPEB benefits does not enjoy the favorable tax treatment accorded to the funding of pension plans, few companies have funded their OPEB liabilities or are likely to do so in the near future. Thus, we have sizable unrecorded as well as increasing amounts of recorded OPEB liabilities which are unfunded and are consequently backed by assets on the companies balance sheets rather than assets in the hands of independent trustees.

18. Under SFAS 106, the required disclosures include:
    1. Description of the plan
    2. Net periodic postretirement benefit cost and its components.
    3. Reconciliation of funded status of the plan with amounts reported in balance sheet.
    4. Assumed health-care cost trend rate used to measure covered benefit costs for the next year. Also, a description of the direction and pattern of change in the assumed trend rates thereafter.
    5. Weighted average discount rate, rate of compensation, and expected long-term rate of return used to measure the APBO.
    6. The effect on various amounts reported of a 1% increase in the health-care cost trend rate.
    7. Amounts and types of employer securities held.

19. a. A loss contingency is any existing condition, situation, or set of circumstances involving uncertainty as to possible loss that will be resolved when one or more future events occur or fail to occur. Examples of loss contingencies are: litigation, threat of expropriation, uncollectibility of receivables, claims arising from product warranties or product defects, self-insured risks, and possible catastrophe losses of property and casualty insurance companies.

    b. The two conditions specified by SFAS No. 5 that must be met before a provision for a loss contingency should be charged to income are: First, it must be probable that an asset had been impaired or a liability incurred at a date of a company's financial statements. Implicit in that condition is that it must be probable that a future event or events will occur confirming the fact of the loss. Second, the amount of loss can be reasonably estimated. The effect of applying these criteria is that a loss will be accrued only when it is reasonably estimable and relates to the current or a prior period.

20. Some equity securities (typically preferred stock) have mandatory redemption provisions which make them more akin to debt than they are to equity. Whatever their name, these securities impose upon the issuing companies obligations to lay out funds at specified dates which is precisely a burden which a true equity security is not supposed to impose. The analyst must be alert to the existence of such equities and look to substance over form when analyzing them.

21. In order to facilitate their understanding and analysis, reserves and provisions can be redivided into a number of major categories.

    The first category is most correctly described as comprising provisions for liabilities and obligations which have a high probability of occurrence, but which are in dispute or are uncertain in amount. As is the case with many financial statement descriptions, neither the title nor the location in the financial statement can be relied upon as a rule-of-thumb guide to the nature of an account. Thus, the best key to analysis is a thorough understanding of the business and financial transactions which give rise to the account. The following are representative items in this group: provisions for product guarantees, service guarantees and warranties which are established in recognition of the fact that these undertakings involve future costs which are certain to arise though presently impossible to measure exactly. Consequently, the provision is established by a charge to income at the time products covered by guarantees are sold, in an amount estimated on the basis of experience or on the basis of any other reliable factor.

    Another type of obligation which must be provided for on the best basis available is the liability for unredeemed trading stamps issued. To the company issuing the trading stamps, there is no doubt about the liability to redeem the stamps for merchandise. The only uncertainty concerns the number of stamps which will be presented for redemption.

    The second category comprises reserves for expenses and losses, which by experience or estimate are very likely to occur in the future and which should properly be provided for by current charges to operations.

    One group within this category comprises reserves for operating costs such as maintenance, repairs, painting, or furnace relining. Thus, for example, since furnace relining jobs may be expected to be required at regularly recurring intervals, they are provided for ratably by charges to operations in order to avoid charging the entire cost to the year in which the actual relining takes place.

Another category comprises provisions for future losses stemming from decisions or actions already taken. Included in this group are reserves for relocations, replacement, modernization, and discontinued operations.

Reserves for contingencies comprise the third group in the reserves category. Reserves for self-insurance are designed to provide the accumulation against which specific types of losses, not covered by insurance, may be charged. Although the term self-insurance contradicts the very concept of insurance, which is based on the spreading of risks among many business units, it nevertheless is a practice which has a good number of adherents.

Other contingencies provided against by means of reserves are those arising from foreign operations and exchange losses due to official or de facto devaluations.

Provisions, such as for service guarantees and warranties. represent, in effect, revenue received for services yet to be performed. Of importance to the analyst ifs the adequacy of the provision which is often established on the basis of prior experience or, that, absent on the basis of other estimates. Concern with adequacy of amount is a prime factor in the analysis of all other reserves, whatever their purpose. Reserves and provisions appearing above the equity section should almost invariably be created by means of charges to income. They are designed to assign charges to the income statement based on when they are incurred rather than when they are paid.

Another important group of future costs which must be provided for is that of employee compensation. These, in turn, give rise to provisions for vacation pay, deferred compensation, incentive compensation, supplemental unemployment benefits, bonus plans, welfare plans, and severance pay.

Finally the category of estimated liabilities includes provisions for claims arising out of pending or existing litigation.

22. Reserves for future losses represent a category of accounts which require particular scrutiny. While conservatism in accounting calls for recognition of losses as they can be determined or clearly foreseen, companies tend, particularly in loss years, to over-provide for losses yet to be incurred such as disposal of assets, relocation, or plant closings. Overprovision does, of course, shift expected future losses to a present period which already shows adverse results.

The problem with such reserves is that once established there is no further accounting for the expenses) and losses which are charged against them. Only in certain financial statements required to be filed with the SEC (such as Form 10K) are details of changes in reserves required. Recent requirements have tightened the disclosure rules (EITF 94-3 and EITF 95-3).

A basic reason why we have overprovisions of reserves is that the income statement effects are accorded much more importance than the residual balance sheet effects. While a provision for future expenses and losses establishes a reserve account which is analytically in the "never-never land" between liabilities and the ownership (equity) accounts, it serves the important purpose of creating a cushion which can absorb future expenses and losses, thus shielding the all-important income statement from them. The analyst should endeavor to ascertain that provisions for future losses reflect losses which can reasonably be expected to have already occurred rather than be used as a means of artificially benefiting future income by adding excessive provisions to present adverse results.

23. An ever-increasing variety of items and descriptions is included in the "deferred credits" group of accounts. In many cases these items are akin to liabilities; in others, they represent deferred income yet to be earned, while in a number of cases, they serve as income-smoothing devices. The confusion confronting the analyst is compounded by a lack of agreement among accountants as to the exact nature of these items or the proper manner of their presentation. Thus, regardless of category or presentation, the key to their analysis lies in an understanding of the circumstances and the financial transactions which brought them about.

At one end of this group's spectrum we find those items which have the characteristics of liabilities. Here we may find included such items as advances or billing on uncompleted contracts, unearned royalties and deposits, and customer service prepayments. guise clearly, the outstanding characteristics of these items is their liability aspects even though, as in the case of advances of royalties, they may, after certain conditions are fulfilled, find their way into the company's income stream. Advances on uncompleted contracts represent primarily methods of financing the work in progress while deposits of rent received represent, as do customer service prepayments, security for performance of an agreement. Even though found sometimes among "deferred credits" such items are more properly classified as liabilities, or current liabilities if due within the company's operating cycle.

24. One of the most complicated and controversial, as well as the most substantial, of deferred credits is deferred income taxes.

Tax allocation, which is the accounting process giving rise to deferred tax credits (or debits in reverse circumstances), is primarily a device for matching the applicable tax expense with corresponding pretax income.

The accounting profession, which in SFAS 109 retained the concept of comprehensive tax allocation, states that it does regard deferred taxes as a liability. The analyst must understand what this account represents when he finds it included within the deferred tax liabilities.

The location of the deferred tax credit in the "twilight zone" between liabilities and equity indicates that it is neither, but that in itself does not shed light on its true nature.

The reason that the deferred tax credit is not a liability is that it has some of the more important characteristics of debt. The government has no present claim for taxes nor is there a timetable for payment. While the deferred tax account represents the loss of future deductibility of assets for tax purposes, the drawing down of this account to reduce tax expenses depends on future developments, such as asset acquisition and depreciation policies which are not predictable with certainty.

This kind of uncertainty attests to the fact that the deferred tax credit is also not in the nature of equity capital because it represents a tax benefit in the nature of a postponement of taxes rather than a savings of taxes.

The most meaningful thing that can be said about this account from the point of view of financial analysis is that it represents a temporary source of funds derived from the postponement of taxes and that the duration of the overall postponement depends on factors such as the future growth or stability of the company's depreciable assets pool. It is the assessment of such factors and their future likelihood that will be helpful to the analysis of the deferred tax account.

25. Under SFAS 105 entities will be required to discloses the following information about financial instruments with off-balance-sheet risk of accounting loss:

1. The face, contract, or notional principal amount.
2. The nature and terms of the instruments and a discussion of their credit and market risk, cash requirements, and related accounting policies.
3. The accounting loss the entity would incur if any party to the financial instruments failed completely to perform according to the terms of the contract, and the collateral or other security, if any, for the amount due proved to be of no value to the entity.
4. The entity's policy for requiring collateral or other security on financial instruments it accepts, and a description of collateral on instruments presently held.

Information about significant concentrations of credit risk from an individual counter-party or groups of counterparties for all financial instruments is also required.

26. The accounting for the equity section as well as the presentation, classification, and footnote disclosure have certain basic objectives, the most important among which are:

1. To classify and distinguish among the major sources of capital contributed to the entity.
2. To set forth the priorities of the various classes of stockholders and the manner in which they rank in partial or final liquidation.
3. To set forth the legal restrictions to which the distribution of capital funds may be subject for whatever reason.
4. To disclose the contractual, legal, managerial, or financial restrictions to which the distribution of current or retained earnings may be subject.

The accounting principles which apply to the equity section do not have a marked effect on income determination and, as a consequence, do not hold many pitfalls for the analyst. From the analyst's point of view, the most significant information here relates to the composition of the capital accounts and to the restrictions to which they may be subject.

The composition of the equity capital is important because of provisions affecting the residual rights of the common equity. Such provisions include dividend participation rights, and the great variety of options and conditions which are characteristic of the complex securities frequently issued under merger agreements, most of which tend to dilute the common equity.

Any analysis of restrictions imposed on the distribution of retained earnings by loan or other agreements will usually shed light on a company's freedom of action in such areas as dividend distributions and required levels of working capital. Such restrictions also shed light on the company's bargaining strength and standing in credit markets. Moreover, a careful reading of restrictive covenants will also enable the analyst to assess how far a company is from being in default of these provisions.

27. The preferred stock is usually preferred in liquidation and preferred as to dividends. It may be entitled to par value in liquidation or it may be entitled to a premium. On the other hand, its rights to dividends are generally fixed although they may be cumulative, which means that preferred shareholders are entitled to arrearages of dividends before the common stockholders get any dividends. The preferred features as well as the fixed nature of the dividend give the preferred stock some of the earmarks of debt with the important difference that preferred stockholders are not generally entitled to demand redemption of their shares. Nevertheless, there are preferred stock issues which have set redemption dates and which may require sinking funds to be established for that purpose.

Characteristics of preferred stock which may make them more akin to common stock are dividend participation rights, voting rights, and rights of conversion into common stock.

28. In APB Opinion No. 10, the Board stated:

"Companies at times issue preferred (or other senior) stock which has a preference in involuntary liquidation considerably in excess of the par or stated value of the shares. The relationship between this preference in liquidation and the par or stated value of the shares may be of major significance to the users of the financial statements of those companies and the Board believes it highly desirable that it be prominently disclosed. Accordingly, the Board recommends that, in these cases, the liquidation preference of the stock be disclosed in the equity section of the balance sheet in the aggregate, either parenthetically or in short rather than on a per share basis or by disclosure in notes."

Such disclosure is particularly important since the discrepancy between the par and liquidation value of preferred stock can be very significant.

29. a. Such distributions are dividends in name only. In substance they represent a return *of* capital, not a return *on* capital.

b. Presidential Realty, like many other companies in the real estate field, makes distributions because the large amounts of depreciation which they charge to revenue result in sources of funds from operations even though the operations result in losses. Unless the depreciation expense is, as some of these companies claim, overstated the depreciation recovery from operations represents funds of a capital, not income, nature.

30. This question is answered in a SEC release (dated June 1, 1972), entitled "Pro Rata Distribution to Shareholders":

Several instances have come to the attention of the Commission in which registrants have made pro rata stock distributions which were misleading. These situations arise particularly when a registrant makes distributions at a time when its retained earnings or its current earnings are substantially less than the fair value of the shares distributed. Under present generally accepted accounting rules, if the ratio of distribution is less than 25 percent of shares of the same class outstanding, the fair value of the shares issued must be transferred from retained earnings to other capital accounts. Failure to make this transfer in connection with a distribution or making a distribution in the absence of retained or current earnings is evidence of a misleading practice. Distributions of over 25 percent (which do not normally call for transfers of fair value) may also lend themselves to such an interpretation if they appear to be part of a program of recurring distribution designed to mislead shareholders.

It has long been recognized that no income accrues to the shareholder as a result of such stock distributions or dividends, nor is there any change in either the corporate assets or the shareholders' interest therein. However, it is also recognized that *many recipients of such stock distributions, which are called or otherwise characterized as dividends, consider them to be distributions of corporate earnings equivalent to the fair value of the additional shares received.* In recognition of these circumstances, the American Institute of Certified Public Accountants has specified in Accounting Research Bulletin No. 43, Chapter 7, paragraph 10, that "... the corporation should in the public interest account for the transaction by transferring from earned surplus to the category of permanent capitalization (represented by the capital stock and capital surplus accounts) an amount equal to the fair value of the additional shares issued. Unless this is done, the amount of earnings which the shareholder may believe to have been distributed will be left, except to the extent otherwise dictated by legal requirements, in earned surplus subject to possible further similar stock issuances or cash distributions. Both the New York and American Stock Exchanges require adherence to this policy by their listed companies.

31. SFAS 16 requires that, except for corrections of errors in the financial statements of a prior period and adjustments that result from realization of income tax benefits of preacquisition operating loss carry forwards of purchased subsidiaries all items of profit and loss recognized during a period, including accruals of estimated losses from loss contingencies be included in the determination of net income for that period. The statement permits limited restatements in interim periods of an enterprise's current fiscal year.

32. a. Minority interests are the claims of shareholders of a majority owned subsidiary whose total net assets are included in a consolidated balance sheet.

b. Consolidated financial statements show minority interests as liabilities: however, they are fundamentally different in nature from legally enforceable obligations. Minority shareholders do not have any legally enforceable rights for payments of any kind from the parent company. Therefore, the financial analyst may justifiably classify minority interest as equity funds in most cases.

33. Book value per share is the stockholders' equity divided by the number of common shares outstanding. If preferred stock is outstanding, an amount allocable to that should be taken out of stockholders' equity before the computation is made. It has little significance in terms of the market value per share or the liquidation value per share for several reasons. First, intangible assets may be included which would overstate the book value per share if it were being used as a measure of the company's liquidation value. Assets such as investment, land, building, and equipment are all at cost less accumulated depreciation and thus do not necessarily bear any resemblance to market value or replacement value. Inventory can be valued in a number of ways and is again valued at cost, not worth, in current terms.

Lastly, there are credits that perhaps should be included in stockholders' equity which are not. Such items might be deferred tax liabilities if they represent a permanent tax savings, and certain "reserve" accounts which may not represent real liabilities.

34. According to the accounting-based equity valuation formula, book value is the starting point in valuing a company's stock. Estimates of future profitability are based directly on the earnings capacity of the asset base.

   Other reasons for the continued use of book value per share include:

   1. Book value, properly adjusted, is often used in an assessment of merger terms.

   2. Due to the fact that the rate base of public utilities often approximates its book value, this measure is important in this industry.

   3. The analysis of companies which have mostly liquid assets such as those in the finance, investment, insurance, and banking fields, rightfully affords greater than usual importance to book values.

   4. The analyst of high-grade bonds and preferred stock usually attaches considerable importance to asset coverage in addition to earning capacity.

   There are other factors which make net assets a measure of some importance in financial analysis. A company's earnings growth is sooner or later dependent on growth in assets and consequently, on a choice of how to finance them. A large asset base has, depending on its compensation, a certain potential of profitable utilization.

35. The accounting considerations that enter into computation of book value should be thoroughly understood by any user of this statistic:

   1. The carrying values of assets, particularly long-lived assets such as plant and equipment, long-term investments and some inventories, is usually at cost and may differ significantly from current market values. Moreover, such carrying values will, as was seen in the preceding chapters, vary according to the accounting principles selected. Thus, for instance, in times of rising prices the carrying value of inventories under the LIFO method of inventory accounting will be lower than under the FIFO method.

   2. Intangible assets of great value may not be reflected in book value nor are contingent liabilities, which may have a high probability of occurrence, usually BO reflected.

36. The blanket exclusion from book value of goodwill, patents, franchises, and other intangibles cannot make up for the lack of the analysis required to adopt this measure to the particular objective it is designed to meet. Either book value is computed on a "current value" basis or on a cost basis. In the latter case, the arbitrary exclusion of intangible assets makes no sense. If, for example, book value is to be used in comparing the relative value of two companies engaged in merger negotiations, adjustments such as the following may be required so that an intelligent comparison can be made:

   1. The carrying value of assets should be adjusted to current market values.
   2. Differences in the application of accounting principles should be adjusted for.
   3. Unrecorded intangibles should be given recognition to.
   4. Contingent liabilities should be assessed and given appropriate recognition.
   5. Accounting and other errors should be adjusted on the books of both companies.

   Other adjustments may also be called for. For example, if the preferred stock has the characteristics of debt. it may be appropriate to capitalize it at the prevailing interest rate, thus reflecting the benefit or disadvantage of it to the company.

The emphasis of earning power has resulted in a de-emphasis of asset size. Sterile or unproductive assets are worse than worthless. They are often a drag on earnings because they require a minimum of upkeep and management expenses. Like any other analytical tools, book value is a measure which can be useful for certain purposes provided it is used with discrimination and understanding.

◄ Answers to Exercises ►

Exercise 3-1
a.

Long-term debt [79]

		740.3	beg
C	39.7	141.1	A
D	142.3	1.8	B
		701.2	end

Current portion of long-term debt [71]

		32.3	beg
E	39.1	39.7	C
		32.9	end

A.   Proceeds from issuance of debt for spin-off [39].
B.   Proceeds from long-term debt [42].
C.   Reduction of long-term debt to current portion [43].
D.   This is a plug number to show the unexplained decrease in long-term debt. Item 142 describes long-term decrease due primarily to debt spun off with the Fisher Price business. Therefore, the unexplained reduction is probably related to the reduction of assets of discontinued operations.
E.   This is a plug number representing amount of long-term debt paid in 1991.

b.   According to disclosure in the "Liquidity and Capital Resources" section [142] of the MD&A the issuance of this debt was primarily driven by the company's common share repurchase program (see also Note 7).

Exercise 3-2
a.   The economic effects of a long-term capital lease on the lessee are similar to that of an equipment purchase using installment debt. Such a lease transfers substantially all of the benefits and risks incident to the ownership of property to the lessee, and obligates the lessee in a manner similar to that created when funds are borrowed. To enhance comparability between a firm that purchases an asset on a long-term basis and a firm that leases an asset under substantially equivalent terms, the lease should be capitalized.

b.   A lessee should account for a capital lease at its inception as an asset and an obligation at an amount equal to the present value at the beginning of the lease term of minimum lease payments during the lease term, excluding any portion of the payments representing executory costs, together with any profit thereon. However, if the present value exceeds the fair value of the leased property at the inception of the lease, the amount recorded for the asset and obligation should be the fair value.

c. A lessee should allocate each minimum lease payment between a reduction of the obligation and interest expense so as to produce a constant periodic rate of interest on the remaining balance of the obligation.

d. Von should classify the first lease as a capital lease because the lease term is more than 75 percent of the estimated economic life of the machine. Von should classify the second lease as a capital lease because the lease contains a bargain purchase option.

Exercise 3-3

The economic nature of the timing difference and, therefore, the nature of the item for accounting purposes depends on whether the timing difference impacts taxable income currently or whether the impact on taxable income will occur in a future period. In the case of the chocolate chip miller, the economic effect is an immediate cash saving of $60,000 in taxes due to depreciation, and this effect precedes recognition (of the depreciation and tax effect) in the accounting statements. Since the effect is immediate the deferred tax account should not be interpreted as a liability but rather as a valuation account, in this case a reduction in the value of the chocolate chip miller. For the installment sales the economic effect is a $32,000 cash payment of taxes in the next year, and the economic effect (actual payment of taxes) will follow the recognition in the accounting statements. In this case the deferred tax is in the nature of a liability.

Exercise 3-4

a. A lessee would account for a capital lease as an asset and an obligation at the inception of the lease. Rental payments during the year would be allocated between a reduction in the obligation and interest expense. The asset would be amortized in a manner consistent with the lessee's normal depreciation policy for owned assets, except that in some circumstances the period of amortization would be the lease term.

b. No asset or obligation would be recorded at the inception of the lease. Normally, rental on an operating lease would be charged to expense over the lease term as it becomes payable. If rental payments are not made on a straight-line basis, rental expense nevertheless would be recognized on a straight-line basis unless another systematic or rational basis is more representative of the time pattern in which use benefit is derived from the leased property, in which case that basis would be used.

Exercise 3-5

a. The gross investment in the lease is the same for both a sales-type lease and a direct-financing lease. The gross investment in the lease is the minimum lease payments (net of amounts, if any, included therein for executory costs such as maintenance, taxes, and insurance to be paid by the lessor, together with any profit thereon) plus the unguaranteed residual value accruing to the benefit of the lessor.

b. For both a sales-type lease and a direct-financing lease, the unearned interest income would be amortized to income over the lease term by use of the interest method to produce a constant periodic rate of return on the net investment in the lease. However, other methods of income recognition may be used if the results obtained are not materially different from the interest method.

c. In a sales-type lease, the excess of the sales price over the carrying amount of the leased equipment is considered manufacturer's or dealer's profit and would be included in income in the period when the lease transaction is recorded.

In a direct-financing lease, there is no manufacturer's or dealer's profit. The income on the lease transaction is composed solely of interest.

Exercise 3-6
A number of major companies have a small debt ratio. However, where a company shows little, if any debt on its balance sheet, it may have considerable long-term liabilities. This can reflect one or more of several factors.

Lease commitments, while detailed in footnotes, are not in the balance sheet for most companies. This could be a critical problem for companies that have expanded by leasing rather than buying property. These lease commitments, while carrying different covenants from debt, are just as surely long-term obligations.

Many companies have very large unfunded pension liabilities. These are not carried on the balance sheet, but are noted (though in a manner very often hard to determine the long-term liability) in the footnotes. At one time, a case could have been made that such obligations were not a problem, for as long as the business operated, payments would be made, and if it went bankrupt, the liability would end. Now, under ERISA, the company has a real long-term obligation to employees.

Another problem is when a company may have guaranteed the debt of another company. The most typical is a nonconsolidated lease subsidiary. Although noted in the footnotes, this debt, which is real and can be large, is not shown on the parent's balance sheet.

Off-balance-sheet debt--such as industrial revenue bonds or pollution control financing where a municipality sells tax-free bonds guaranteed for payment--are clearly cases where a supposedly debt-free balance sheet could look much worse if these obligations had been included.

Finally, the practice of deferred taxes--reflecting taking some expenses for tax, but not book purposes, or through the difference in timing to recognize sales--is one which, while on the balance sheet, is normally not recognized as a long-term obligation. However, if the rate of investment slows dramatically for some reason or the sales trend is reversed, the sudden coming due of the tax liabilities could be a major problem.

(CFA)

Exercise 3-7

a. An estimated loss from a loss contingency shall be accrued by a charge to income if both of the following conditions are met:

    •   Information available prior to issuance of the financial statements indicates that it is probable that an asset had been impaired or a liability had been incurred at the date of the financial statements. It is implicit in this condition that it must be probable that one or more future events will occur confirming the fact of the loss.

    •   The amount of loss can be reasonably estimated.

b. Disclosure should be made for an estimated loss from a loss contingency that need not be accrued by a charge to income when there is at least a reasonable possibility that a loss may have been incurred. The disclosure should indicate the nature of the contingency and should estimate the possible loss or range of loss or state that such an estimate cannot be made.

    Disclosure of a loss contingency involving an unasserted claim is required when it is probable that the claim will be asserted and there is a reasonable possibility that the outcome will be unfavorable.

Exercise 3-8

a. Note: Unless otherwise indicated, the information below can be found in item (68) of the financial statements.

Millions		11		10	
Net Income		$401.5		$ 4.4	(28)
Cash Dividends		(142.2)	(89)	(126.9)	(87)
Treasury Stock Purchase		(175.6)		(41.1)	(78)
Treasury Stock Issued—Capital Surplus		. 45.4	(91)	11.1	(87)
—Treas. Stock		12.4	(91)	4.6	(87)
Translation Adjustment		(29.9)	(92)	61.4	(87)
Sale of foreign operations		(10.0)	(93)		
Increase in Stockholders' Equity . . .		101.6[a]		(86.5)[b]	

    [a]1,793.4   [54]   [b]1,691.8 [54]
    -1,691.8   1,778.3 [87]
       101.6   (86.5)

b. *Book Value per share of Common Stock:*

        1,793.4 [54]
        ─────────── = 14.12   which is equal to the company's computed
          127.0*   amount (185) of 14.12.

    *135.6 [49] - 8.6 [52]

    Note: There is no preferred stock outstanding.

c. According to note 24 to the financial statements, Campbell's stock traded between $72.38 and $84.88 during the last quarter of Year 11. Investors apparently have high expectations regarding future profitability.

Exercise 3-9
a.

	11	10
Stockholders' Equity (6/30) [91]	901.0	1017.5
Stockholders' Equity (7/1) [91]	1017.5	1137.1
Decrease in Shareholders' Equity	(116.5)	(119.6)
Net Income [11]	205.8	169.0
Cash Dividend paid [38]	(123.0)	(110.5)
Common stock issued for Stock Purchase and		
Incentive Plan [113] [104]	28.2	16.1
Repurchases of Common Stock [105]	–	(223.2)
Translation Adjustments [114] [106] . . .	(23.6)	27.3
Distribution of Equity to Shareholders from spin-off		
o f Fisher-Price [112]	(200.0)	–
Deferred Compensation [115] [107]	(3.9)	1.7
Change Account for	(116.5)	(119.6)

b. 1. Book value of common stock

$$\frac{901,000,000^a}{76,328,721^b} = \underline{\$11.80} \ [130]$$

2. Book value of preferred stock

$$\frac{4,800,000^c}{1,271,962^d} = \underline{\$3.77}$$

[a]Total common stockholders' equity [91]
[b]Common shares outstanding (issued [85] - treasury [90])
[c]Preferred stock (net of deferred compensation) [82-83-84]
[d]Shares outstanding (issued [82] - treasury [84])

c. Details regarding the preferred stock are included in note 8 to Quaker's financial statements. The Deferred Compensation account relates to an employee stock ownership plan.

According to note 20 to the financial statements, Quaker's stock traded between $55.13 and $64.88 during the last quarter of Year 11. Investors apparently have high expectations regarding future profitability.

Exercise 3-10
a. A "secret reserve" is created when stockholders' equity is understated. Generally, such reserves, often called hidden assets, are created or enlarged by practices which understate assets and/or overstate liabilities. Such practices often result from the application of the accounting convention or principle of conservatism.

b. Both of the practices cited tend to cause assets to be stated at lower amounts than would be the case with other acceptable alternatives. The use of LIFO during a period of steadily rising prices tends to cause the inventory cost to be stated in terms of prices that prevailed when the method was adopted. When such prices are compared to current prices they are low; hence income and stockholders' equity are correspondingly low. The expensing of all human resource costs as they are incurred, in effect, denies that such costs have produced any future benefits. To the extent that such expenditures produce future benefits, a portion of the costs should be capitalized as intangible assets. "Secret reserves" exist to the extent that assets have been understated by the expensing of all human resource costs immediately.

c. It is not impossible to create a "secret reserve" by overstating liabilities. This could most readily occur in recording estimated liabilities such as for product warranties or pensions at amounts in excess of actuarially determined amounts or for the restoration of property at the termination of a lease. Any such overstatement of the ultimate liability overstates current expenses and thereby understates stockholders' equity. A "secret reserve" also would exist when a firm has long-term, fixed interest debt outstanding during periods when interest rates are increasing and much higher than on the debt.

In a sense the concept of "secret reserves" also can be extended to include the effects of holding an excess of monetary liabilities over monetary assets. During a period of inflation the "reserve" is in terms of general purchasing power whereas the previously discussed "reserves" have been due to differences in money amounts.

d. There are several objections to the creation of "secret reserves." Only insiders are likely to know of their existence and value. Statement readers who are unaware of the existence of "secret reserves" may regard a company's securities as overvalued when, in fact, they may be undervalued or valued correctly. As a result, stockholders may be willing to part with their shares for too little consideration.

The creation of "secret reserves" also tends to shift income between periods and usually to have a smoothing effect on reported income. If an asset is understated or a liability is overstated in the current period, it usually means that some expense is going to be correspondingly overstated with the result that current income is understated. In some subsequent period the service potential of the unrecognized or undervalued asset will be consumed. If its cost were understated or not recognized, expenses of the later period also will be understated and income of the later period will be overstated. Somewhat the same effect can be achieved through overaccrual of estimated expenses. There are practical limits as to how large an estimated liability for estimated expenses can become before it will be discovered and investigated. In the period when the carrying value of the estimated liability reaches its upper limit, usually no accrual or an inadequate accrual is recognized.

Involved also is an application of the concept of organization slack. During expansionary periods a cushion is accumulated by overstating expenses or understating revenues. This cushion can be utilized when the environment becomes unfavorable such as during a period of depressed income caused by either external or internal factors. Thus "secret reserves" are a form of organization slack that gives management "squirming room" and helps it to smooth unfavorable reports under the assumption that bad news should be softened to prevent expectations (aspirations) from fluctuating widely.

The purpose of financial statements is to inform, not to mislead. The existence of "secret reserves" makes the statement misleading to the extent that assets are understated or liabilities are overstated because the extent of the under- or overstatement is not reported.

e. 1. A corporation's stock can be said to be "watered" if the stockholders' equity is overstated because assets are correspondingly overstated or because liabilities are understated.

2. "Watered stock" most commonly arises because assets for which the stock is issued are overvalued. One common motivation for such an issuance is to avoid showing a discount on capital stock when stock has been recorded as issued at par for assets having a fair market value equal to or greater than par when the value of the assets received was much less. Somewhat less likely is the understatement of liabilities in connection with the issuance of stock. If stock is issued for property subject to a mortgage, understating or ignoring the actual liability could result in an overvaluation of the stock.

3. The writing down of overstated assets or the writing up of understated liabilities would eliminate "water" from the stock. The offsetting charge to such credits might be made to retained earnings or preferably to another capital account. If some of the excess shares are recaptured, the appropriate charge would be to a capital stock account.

(AICPA)

Exercise 3-11

a. The principal transactions or items that reduce the amount of retained earnings include the following:

1. Operating losses (including extraordinary losses and other debit adjustments).
2. Stock dividends.
3. Dividends distributing corporate assets.
4. Recapitalizations such as quasi-reorganizations.

b. The principal reason for making the distinction between contributed capital and earned capital in the stockholders' equity sections is to enable stockholders and creditors to identify dividend distributions as actual distributions of earnings or as returns of capital. This identification is necessary to comply with the various state statutes which provide that there should be no impairment of the corporation's legal or stated capital by the return of such capital to owners in the form of dividends. This concept of legal capital generally provides a measure of protection to creditors and imposes a liability upon the stockholders in the event of such impairment.

A knowledge of the distinction between contributed capital and earned capital provides a guide to the amount of dividends that may be distributed by the corporation . Assets represented by the earned capital, if in liquid form, may properly be distributed as dividends; but invested assets represented by contributed capital should ordinarily remain for continued operation of the corporation. If assets represented by contributed capital are distributed to shareholders, the distribution should be identified as a return of capital and hence in the nature of a liquidating dividend.

A knowledge of the amount of capital that has been earned over a period of years after adjustment for dividends is also of value to the stockholders in judging dividend policy and obtaining an indication of past profits to the extent not distributed as dividends.

c. The acquisition and reissuance of its own stock by a corporation results only in the contraction or expansion of the amount of capital invested in it by stockholders. In other words, an acquisition of treasury shares by a corporation is viewed as a partial liquidation and their subsequent reissuance is viewed as an unrelated capital-raising activity.

To characterize as gain or loss the changes in owners' equity resulting from a corporation's acquisition and subsequent reissuance of its own shares at different prices is a misuse of accounting terminology. When a corporation acquires its own shares, it is not "buying" anything nor has it incurred a "cost." The price paid merely represents the amount by which the corporation has reduced its net assets or "partially liquidated." Similarly, when the corporation reissues these shares it has not "sold" anything. It has merely increased its total capitalization by the amount received.

Thus it is the practice of referring to the acquisition and reissuance of treasury shares as a buying and selling activity that gives the superficial impression that, in this process, the corporation is acquiring and disposing of assets and that, if different amounts per share are involved, a gain or loss results. It is obvious, however, that when a corporation "buys" treasury shares it is not acquiring assets; nor is it disposing of any assets when these shares are subsequently "sold."

Exercise 3-12
a. There are four basic rights inherent in ownership of common stock. The first right is that common shareholders may participate in the actual management of the corporation through participation and voting at the corporate stockholders meeting. Second, a common shareholder has the right to share in the profits of the corporation through dividends declared by the board of directors (elected by the common shareholders) of the corporation. Third, a common shareholder has a pro rata right to the residual assets of the corporation if it liquidates. Finally, common shareholders have the right to maintain their interest (percent of ownership) in the corporation if additional common shares are issued by the corporation, by being given the opportunity to purchase a proportionate number of shares of the new offering. This last is most commonly referred to as a "preemptive right."

b. Preferred stock is form of capital stock that is afforded special privileges not normally afforded common shareholders in return for giving up one or more rights normally conveyed to common shareholders. The most common right given up by preferred shareholders is the right to participate in management (voting rights), and, in return, the corporation grants one or more preferences to the preferred shareholder. The most common preferences granted to preferred shareholders are these:

1. Dividends may be paid to common shareholders only after dividends have been paid to preferred shareholders.

2. Claim ahead of common shareholders to residual assets (after creditors have been paid) in the case of corporation liquidation.

3. Although the board of directors is under no obligation to declare dividends in any particular year, preferred shareholders may be granted a cumulative provision stating that any dividends not paid in a particular year must be paid in subsequent years before common shareholders may be paid any dividend.

4. Preferred shareholders may be granted a participation clause that allows them to receive additional dividends beyond their normal dividend if common shareholders receive dividends of greater percentage than preferred shareholders. This participation may be on a one-to-one basis (fully participating); common shareholders may be allowed to exceed the rate paid to preferred shareholders by a defined amount before preferred shareholders begin to participate: or, the participation clause may have a maximum rate of participation to which preferred shareholders are entitled.

5. Preferred shareholders may have the right to convert their preferred shares to common shares at a set future price no matter what the current market price of the common stock is.

6. Preferred shareholders may also agree to have their stock callable by the corporation at a higher price than when the stock was originally issued. This item is generally coupled with another preference item to make the issue appear attractive to the market.

c. 1. *Treasury stock* is stock previously issued by the corporations but subsequently repurchased by the corporation and not retired but available for use at a subsequent date by the corporation.

2. *Legal capital* is that portion of corporate capital required by statute to be retained in the business to afford creditors a minimum degree of protection.

3. A *stock right* represents a privilege extended by the corporation to acquire additional shares (or fractional shares) of its capital stock.

4. A *stock warrant* is physical evidence of stock rights. The warrant specifies the number of rights conveyed, the number of shares to which

the rightholder is entitled, the price at which the rightholder may purchase the additional shares, and the life of the rights (time period over which the rights may be exercised).

Exercise 3-13
Amount required on retirement = (20,000)(8.559480) = $171,189.60

Yearly payments = 171,190 ÷ 40.99549 = $4,175.83

◄ Answers to Problems ►

Problem 3-1

a. 1. $200 million

2. As the maturity date approaches the liability will be shown at increasingly larger amounts to reflect the accrual of interest that will be due at maturity.

3. The journal entry will be:

Interest expense
            Unamortized discount

b. The $28 million will be paid out and this figure will include $6.5 million of interest implicit in the leases.

c. Only in the footnote. These lease payments will be expensed as they occur over the years.

Problem 3-2

a. 1/1/x1 Leased Property under Capital Leases   39,390
                    Obligation under Capital Leases   39,930

12/31/x1   Payment of Rental:
            Interest on Leases   3,194.40 (1)
            Obligations under Capital Leases   6,805.60
                    Cash   10,000

            Amortization of Property Rights:
            Amortization of Leased Property under
               Capital Leases   7,986 (2)
                    Leased Property under Capital Leases   7,986

b.   Balance Sheet
                              12/31/x1

            Assets   Liabilities

Leased property under   Obligations under
capital leases $31,944   capital leases $33,124.40 (4)

Income Statement
For Year Ended 12/31/x1

Amortization of leased property	$ 7,986.00
Interest on eases	3,194.40
Total lease-related cost for 19x1	$11,180.40 (5)

(1) $39,930 × .08 = $3,194.40
(2) $39,930 ÷ 5 = $7,986
(3) $39,930 - $7,986 = $31,944
(4) $39,930 - $6,805.60 = $33,124.40
(5) To be contrasted to rental costs of $10,000 when no capitalization takes place.

c.

TABLE I
Payments of Interest and Principal

Year	Total Payment	Interest @ 8%	Payment of Principal	Mortgage Balance
				$39,930.00
1	$10,000	$ 3,194.40	$ 6,805.60	33,124.40
2	10,000	2,649.95	7,350.05	25,774.35
3	10,000	2,061.95	7,938.05	17,836.30
4	10,000	1,426.90	8,573.10	9,263.20
5	10,000	736.80	9,263.20	___
	$50,000	$10,070.00	$39,930.00	–

TABLE II
Expenses to Be Charged to Income Statement

Expenses if equipment was purchased

Year	Lease Expense	Amortization	Interest	Total
1	$10,000	$ 7,986.00	$ 3,194.40	$11,180.40
2	10,000	7,986.00	2,649.95	10,635.95
3	10,000	7,986.00	2,061.95	10,047.95
4	10,000	7,986.00	1,426.90	9,412.90
5	10,000	7,986.00	736.80	8,722.80
	$50,000	$39,930.00	$10,070.00	$50,000.00

TABLE III

Expenses to Be Charged to Income Statement

Expenses if equipment was purchased

Year	Lease Expense	Amortization	Interest	Total
1	$10,000	$ 7,986.00	$ 3,194.40	$11,180.40
2	10,000	7,986.00	2,649.95	10,635.95
3	10,000	7,986.00	2,061.95	10,047.95
4	10,000	7,986.00	1,426.90	9,412.90
5	10,000	7,986.00	736.80	8,722.80
	$50,000	$39,930.00	$10,070.00	$50,000.00

Problem 3-3

a. A lease should be classified as a capital lease when it transfers substantially all of the benefits and risks inherent to the ownership of property by meeting any one of the four criteria established by FAS 13 for classifying a lease as a capital lease.

Lease J should be classified as a capital lease because the lease term is equal to 80 percent of the estimated economic life of the equipment, which exceeds the 75 percent or more criterion.

Lease K should be classified as a capital lease because the lease contains a bargain purchase option.

Lease L should be classified as an operating lease because it does not meet any of the four criteria for classifying a lease as a capital lease.

b. For Lease J, Borman Company should record as a liability at the inception of the lease an amount equal to the present value at the beginning of the lease term of minimum lease payments during the lease term, excluding that portion of the payments representing executory costs such as insurance, maintenance, and taxes to be paid by the lessor, including any profit thereon. However, if the amount so determined exceeds the fair value of the equipment at the inception of the lease, the amount recorded as a liability should be the fair value.

For Lease K, Borman Company should record as a liability at the inception of the lease an amount determined in the same manner as for Lease J, and the payment called for in the bargain purchase option should be included in the minimum lease payments.

For Lease L, Borman Company should not record a liability at the inception of the lease.

c. For Lease J, Borman Company should allocate each minimum lease payment between a reduction of the liability and interest expense so as to produce a constant periodic rate of interest on the remaining balance of the liability.

For Lease K, Borman Company should allocate each minimum lease payment in the same manner as for Lease J.

For Lease L, Borman Company should charge minimum lease (rental) payments to rental expense as they become payable.

d. From an analytical viewpoint, both capital and operating leases represent economic liabilities as they involve commitments to make fixed payments. The fact that companies can structure leases as "operating leases" to avoid balance sheet recognition is also problematic from the asset side. If the leased assets are used to generate revenues, they should be considered in ratios such as return on assets.

Problem 3-4

a. Because detachable stock purchase warrants are equity instruments that have a separate fair value at the issue date, the portion of the proceeds from bonds issued with detachable stock purchase warrants allocable to the warrants should be accounted for as paid-in capital. The remainder of the proceeds should be allocated to the debt security portion of the transaction. This usually results in issuing the debt security at a discount (or, occasionally, a reduced premium).

b. A serial bond progressively matures at a series of stated installment dates, for example, one-fifth each year. A term (straight) bond completely matures on a single date.

c. The amortization in the first year of the life of a five-year term bond issued at a premium would differ using the interest method instead of the straight-line method because the interest method employs a uniform interest rate based upon a changing balance, whereas the straight-line method provides for the recognition of an equal amount of premium amortization each period. Because the interest method provides for an increasing premium amortization each period, the amount of amortization in the first year of the life of the bond would be lower.

d. The journal entry to record a bond issue sold between interest dates is as follows:

- Debit cash for the price of the bond plus the accrued interest from the last interest date.
- Debit discount on bonds payable for the amount of discount to be amortized over the remaining life of the issue.
- Credit bonds payable for the par value of the bonds.
- Credit accrued interest payable (or interest expense) for the accrued interest from the last interest date.

The subsequent amortization of bond discount is affected when a bond issue is sold between interest dates because the discount should be amortized over the period from the date of sale (not the date of the bond) to the maturity date.

e. The gain or loss from the reacquisition of a long-term bond prior to its maturity should be included in the determination of net income for the period reacquired and, if material, classified as an extraordinary item, net of related income taxes.

f.   Current accounting standards require many useful bond-related disclosures, including: amounts borrowed, interest rates, due dates, encumbrances, restrictive covenants, events of default, etc. While bonds are reported at their fair value at the date of issuance, subsequent changes in fair value are not recognized on the balance sheet. If the analyst is interested in the fair value of a firm's bonds, he/she must examine the footnote disclosures mandated by SFAS 107.

(AICPA)

Problem 3-5

a.   The 11% term bonds were sold at a discount (less than face value) because the effective annual interest rate (yield) of 12% was higher than the stated interest rate of 11%. The bonds provide for the payment of interest of 11%; however, this rate was less than the prevailing or market rate for bonds of similar quality at the time the issue was sold. Therefore, the market value of the bonds at the date of sale must be less than face value so that investors may receive the effective annual interest rate (yield) on their investments.

b.   In a balance sheet prepared immediately after the term bond issue was sold, a noncurrent liability, term bonds payable, would be presented at an amount equal to the face value of the bonds less the discount. At December 31, x5, a noncurrent liability, term bonds payable, would be presented in the balance sheet at the face value of the bonds, less the unamortized discount. Therefore, the amortization of bond discount for November and December x5 would increase the amount of term bonds payable, net of discount.

The bond issue costs incurred in preparing and selling the bond issue could be presented in one of three ways in a balance sheet prepared immediately after the term bond issue was sold:

• Noncurrent asset, deferred charge
• Reduction of the noncurrent liability, term bonds payable
• Not presented in balance sheet (expensed as incurred in x5)

At December 31, x5, the bond issue costs could be presented in one of three ways:

• If the bond issue costs were presented in the balance sheet of a noncurrent asset, deferred charge, the amortization of bond issue costs for November and December x5 would decrease the amount of the deferred charge.
• If the bond issue costs were presented in the balance sheet as a reduction of the noncurrent liability, term bonds payable, the amortization of bond issue costs for November and December x5 would increase the amount of the term bonds payable, net of discount.
• If the bond issue costs were expensed as incurred in x5, there would be no effect from the date the term bond issue was sold to December 31, x5.

A current liability, accrued interest payable, would be presented in a balance sheet prepared immediately after the term bond issue was sold for accrued interest received for October x5. At December 31, x5, the accrued interest payable would include accrued interest received for October x5 and accrued interest for November and December x5.

c. Bond discount for bonds sold between interest dates should be amortized over the period the bonds will be outstanding, that is, the period from the date of sale (November 1, x5) to the maturity date (October 1, x10).

d. The straight-line method of amortization provides an even dollar amount of amortization each year allocated over the period the bonds are outstanding. The interest method of amortization provides for an increasing dollar amount of amortization each year.

The interest method of amortization is preferable to the straight-line method because it provides a constant interest rate when applied to the increasing carrying value.

e. The proceeds from the sale of the 9% nonconvertible bonds with detachable stock purchase warrants should be accounted for as paid-in capital and long-term debt. Because the detachable stock purchase warrants are equity instruments which have a separate fair value at the issue date, the portion of the proceeds allocable to the warrants should be accounted for as paid-in capital. Because the bonds are debt instruments, the remainder of the proceeds, including the premium, should be accounted for as long-term debt.

(AICPA)

Problem 3-6

a.
Par (liquidation) Value . . .	$15,000,000
Net Deficit[1]	(4,500,000)
Total	$10,500,000

Number of Shares	200,000
Book Value Per Share	$52.50

1) Net deficit:
R. E. Deficit	(2,100,000)
Paid-in Excess	100,000
Dividends in arrears* .	(1,500,000)
Liquidation premium** .	(1,000,000)

*   Dividend in arrears = 100,000 (Shares) * $150 (Par) * 0.05 (Annual Dividend) * 2 years

**   100,000 x (160 - 150)

b. The carrying value of assets, particularly of long-lived assets such as plant and equipment, long-term investments and some inventories, is usually at cost and may differ significantly from current market values. Moreover, such values will sometimes vary according to the accounting principles selected. These values must be adjusted to reflect the current market values. Part of this adjustment is the recognition that some assets may be impaired or actually obsolete. Additionally, intangible assets of great value may not be reflected in book values. These intangibles must be identified and their value estimated. Contingent liabilities, sometimes of high probability, may also not have been disclosed and must be identified and valued. The preferred stock including dividends in arrears should be reclassified as debt in the capital structure to recognize its negative impact on the value of the common stock. Finally, it is clear that the value may be situation specific, and that the market value of groups of assets sold as productive entities may differ from assets sold quickly and singly.

Problem 3-7

10% cumulative preferred stock	$100,000
Common stock	50,000
Net income for 1981 (retained earnings)	450,000
Stockholders' equity 12/31/81	$600,000
Less: Preferred stock liquidation value	
(1,000 × $100)	$100,000
Less: Dividends in arrears on preferred stock	
($100,000 × 10%)	10,000
Total deduction for preferred	(110,000)
Net amount applicable to common stockholders . .	$490,000
Common stock outstanding	$ 10,000
Book value per share ($490,000/10,000)	$49

Problem 3-8

a. Cumulative dividend to preferred stock = $100 × 1,000 × 10% = $10,000

$$BV \text{ of } P/S = \frac{105,000 + 10,000}{1,000} = 115$$

b. BV of common stock

$$\frac{OE - \text{liquidation value of } P/S - \text{cumulative div. to } P/S}{\# \text{ of shares of } C/S}$$

$$\frac{\$800,000 - 105,000 - 10,000}{10,000}$$

= $68.50

Problem 3-9

a. Superior Oil sells possibly for more because for a given amount of shareholders' equity, there are fewer shares issued and outstanding.

b. It is not possible to reach any conclusions about relative profitability simply by looking at the stock selling prices. In order to determine profitability, information about earnings and dividends per share would have to be known.

c. In terms of absolute amounts, Superior Oil had the greatest price rise, $21 to Getty's $2 increase. However, Getty Oil had the greater relative increase, 3.1 percent to 1.4 percent for Superior Oil. For shareholders, the relative increase is more important than the absolute increase, so the Getty Oil shareholders benefited more than those of Superior Oil.

d.   There would be no effect upon the equity of stockholders shown on the Getty Oil Company's books. The only change would be the change of the shareholders' names in the corporate records maintained to keep track of share ownership.

◄ Answers to Cases ►

Case 3-1

a.   At 3/31/96, Adaptec's three largest liabilities were accrued liabilities ($56,717), note payable ($46,200), and accounts payable ($23,974). Of these three categories, only the note payable requires recognition of interest expense.

b.

	Long-term debt		
		7,650	beg
payment (SCF)	3,400		
		4,250	end

c.   Under the subheading *Fair Value of Financial Instruments*, Adaptec reports that "amounts shown for long-term debt...approximate fair value because current interest rates offered to the Company for debt of similar maturities are substantially the same." In addition to changes in interest rates, the value of debt is affected by the creditworthiness of the issuer.

d.   At 3/31/96, Adaptec's accrued liabilities consisted of accrued compensation and related taxes ($22,440), sales and marketing related items ($7,443), tax related items ($16,218), and other ($10,616).

e.   Note three to the financial statements indicates that Adaptec has available a $17 million line of credit.

f.   According to note four, the long-term debt bears interest at 7.65%. Principal and interest are payable in quarterly installments of $850 thousand. The loan matures in June 1998.

g.   1.   No, Adaptec does not disclose the future minimum lease payments for each of the next five years.
       2.   Future cash outflows not reflected on the balance sheet include (i) $7,290,000 under operating leases, (ii) purchase commitments of $19,800,000 in 1997 and $4,950,000 in 1998, and (iii) investment in fabrication equipment of up to $25 million.

Case 3-2

a.   1993: $225,155 ÷ 50,714 = $4.44
       1994: $297,616 ÷ 52,291 = $5.69
       1995: $371,644 ÷ 51,677 = $7.19
       1996: $511,945 ÷ 53,020 = $9.66

b. 1. 1993: 12.75 ÷ 4.44 = 2.87
1994: 18.125 ÷ 5.69 = 3.19
1995: 33 ÷ 7.19 = 4.59
1996: 48.25 ÷ 9.66 = 4.99

2. The price-to-book value (P/B) ratio will exceed 1 whenever the present value of future abnormal earnings is greater than zero. Since Adaptec's P/B ratio has increased steadily from 1993 through 1996, investors are apparently quite positive regarding Adaptec's future profitability.

c. 1994: common stock sold under employee purchase and option plans (per share amount = 13,511 ÷ 1,577 = $8.57)

1995: common stock sold under employee purchase and option plans (17,174 ÷ 1,426 = $12.04)

1996: common stock sold under employee purchase and option plans (27,459 ÷ 1,218 = $22.54)

Common shares issued in connection with acquisition (17,232 ÷ 385 = $44.76)

d. 1994: no shares repurchased

1995: 2.04 million shares repurchased @ $17.92 (36,548 ÷ 2,040). Debit to retained earnings of $10.42 per share (21,248 ÷ 2,040) implies that shares were initially sold for $7.50 (17.92 - 10.42).

1996: 260 thousand shares repurchased @ $29.87 (7,765 ÷ 260). Debit to retained earnings of $22.37 per share (5,815 ÷ 260) implies that shares were initially sold for $7.50 (29.87 - 22.37).

Under GAAP, Adaptec did not report a loss on these treasury stock transactions. Notice, however, that the excess of repurchase price over issue price is eventually debited to retained earnings.

e. Adaptec's common shares do not have a par value. Normally, par value is disclosed on the face of the balance sheet.

f. 1995: 200,000,000 authorized; 51,677,000 issued and outstanding
1996: 200,000,000 authorized; 53,020,000 issued and outstanding

◄ CHAPTER 4 ►

Analyzing Investing Activities

◄ CHAPTER REVIEW ►

Assets are the driving force of profitability for a company. Assets produce revenues that compensate workers, repay lenders, reward owners, and fund growth. Current assets are resources or claims to resources readily convertible to cash. Major current assets include cash and cash equivalents, marketable securities, receivables, derivative financial instruments, inventories, and prepaid expenses. Our analysis of current assets provides us insights into a company's liquidity. Liquidity is the length of time until assets are converted to cash. It is an indicator of a company's ability to meet financial obligations. The less liquid a company, the lower its financial flexibility to pursue promising investment opportunities, and the greater its risk of failure. Noncurrent assets are resources or claims to resources expected to benefit more than the current period. Major noncurrent assets include property, plant, equipment, intangibles, investments, and deferred charges. Our analysis of noncurrent assets provides us insights into a company's solvency and operational capacity. Solvency refers to the ability of a company to meets its long-term (and current) obligations. Operational capacity is the ability of a company to generate future profits.

This chapter shows how we use financial statements to better assess liquidity, solvency, and operational capacity using asset values, and to critically evaluate a company's financial performance and prospects. The accounting practices underlying the measurement and reporting of current and noncurrent assets are described. We discuss the accounting for these assets and its implications for analysis of financial statements. Special attention is given to various analytical adjustments helping us better understand current and future prospects.

◄ CHAPTER OUTLINE ►

Section 1: Current Assets

▸ **Cash and Cash Equivalents**

    Analysis Implications of Cash and Cash Equivalents

▸ **Marketable Securities**

    Classification of Marketable Securities

    Financial Statement Consequences

    Analysis Implications of Marketable Securities

▸ **Receivables**

    Valuation of Receivables

    Analysis Implications of Receivables

▸ **Financial Instruments**

    Disclosure and Analysis of Financial Instruments

▸ **Inventories**

    Inventory Costs

    Inventory Cost Flows

    Inventory Valued at Lower of Cost or Market

    Purchase Commitments for Inventory

    Inventory Disclosures under Long-Term Contracts

    LIFO and Changing Inventory Prices

    Analysis Implications of Inventory When Prices are Changing

    Analysis Implications of Inventory

Section 2: Noncurrent Assets

▸ **Noncurrent Investments**

      Noncurrent Investments in Equity Securities

      Noncurrent Investments in Debt Securities

      Analysis Implications of Noncurrent Investments

▸ **Plant Assets and Natural Resources**

      Valuing Property, Plant, and Equipment

      Valuing Natural Resources

      Analysis Implications of Plant Assets and Natural Resources

▸ **Intangible Assets**

      Identifiable Intangibles

      Unidentifiable Intangibles

      Amortizing Costs of Intangibles

      Analysis Implications of Intangibles

▸ **Deferred Charges**

      Rationale for Cost Deferral

      Research and Development Costs

      Computer Software Costs

      Additional Deferred Charges

      Analysis Implications of Deferred Charges

▸ **Unrecorded Intangibles and Contingent Assets**

◄ Learning Objectives ►

- **Explain cash management and its interpretation for financial statement analysis.**

- **Analyze financial statement disclosures for marketable securities.**

- **Analyze receivables and provisions for uncollectible accounts.**

- **Describe analytical adjustments to receivables to reflect risk of ownership.**

- **Analyze disclosures for financial instruments.**

- **Interpret effects of inventory methods for analysis under varying business conditions.**

◄ Learning Objectives ►

- **Analyze financial statement disclosure for noncurrent investments.**

- **Interpret valuations and disclosures for plant assets and natural resources.**

- **Describe and analyze intangible assets and their disclosures.**

- **Explain and interpret deferred charges for financial statement analysis.**

- **Analyze statements for unrecorded and contingent assets.**

◂ Answers to Questions ▸

1. a. No. When considering this most liquid of current assets the analyst is interested in the availability of cash in meeting the enterprise's needs for current means of payments. A restriction under compensating balances arrangements does, at worst, remove these cash balances from immediate availability as means of payment and at least can set off through their use repercussions which can affect the enterprise's future access to bank credit.

    b. The analyst should exclude cash restricted under compensating balance agreements from current assets. Securities and Exchange Commission Accounting Series Release 148 requires that a company which has borrowed money from a bank segregate on its balance sheet any cash subject to withdrawal or usage restrictions under compensating balance agreements with the lending bank. These requirements may, as is often the case in such situations, move companies and their banker to alter the form of their contractual agreements while retaining their substance. The analyst must be ever alert to such attempts to distort his measurements by presentations whose form is not a true reflection of their substance. Vulnerability in this area can be measured by computing the ratio of restricted cash to total cash.

2. a. The normal operating cycle is a concept which is important in the classification of items as current or noncurrent. The operating cycle generally encompasses the full period of time from the commitment of cash for purchases until the collection of receivables resulting from the sale of goods or services. The diagram on page 155 of the text illustrates the concept.

    b. If the normal collection interval of a receivables is longer than a year (e.g., longer term installment receivables), then their inclusion as current assets is proper provided the collection interval is normal and expected for the type of business the enterprise is engaged in. Similarly, if inventories, by business need or custom, have to be kept on average for more than 12 months, then this normal inventory holding period becomes part of the operating cycle and such inventories are included among current assets.

    c. The limitations of the current ratio (which is computed by use of items defined as "working capital") as a measure of short-term liquidity are discussed in Chapter 8. If we accept the proposition that it is useful to measure the current resources which are available to pay current obligations, then it is hard to see how the extension of the definition of "current" from the customary 12 months to periods of 36 months and longer can serve such a useful purpose. The "operating cycle" concept may help businessmen show the kind of positive current position which they otherwise may not be able to show, but this concept is of doubtful value or validity from the point of view of the financial analyst charged with analyzing an enterprise's short-term liquidity.

    d. (1) Tobacco Industry. The tobacco leaf must go through an aging, curing, and drying process extending over a number of years. Nevertheless, such tobacco inventory (green leaf) which may not be used in the production of a salable product for many years is classified as current under the "operating cycle" theory. This is so even if the long-term loans taken out to finance the carrying of such inventory are classified among noncurrent liabilities.

    (2) Liquor Industry. Like the tobacco industry, the liquor industry prolongs the "operating cycle" far beyond the customary 12 months. Here the keeping of inventory of liquor for aging over many years provides justification for inclusion of such inventories among current assets.

    (3) In retailing, the sale of "large ticket" items on the installment plan can extend the operating cycle to 36 months or even longer. Such installment receivables are, consequently, shown among current assets.

3.   a. Following are some of the salient provisions of SFAS 115:

A debt security represents a creditor relationship with another entity. An equity security encompasses any instrument representing ownership shares or the right to acquire or dispose of ownership shares in an enterprise (this definition specifically excludes convertible bonds,treasury stock, and redeemable preferred stock).

Debt securities are classified as trading, held-to-maturity, or available-for-sale. Equity securities are classified as trading, held-to-maturity, available-for-sale, influential, or controlling. These classifications are largely determined by management intent.

Trading, and available-for-sale securities are reported at fair value at each balance sheet date. Changes in fair value of trading securities are reported as part of net income, while changes in fair value of available-for-sale securities are reported as a separate component of shareholders' equity. Held-to-maturity securities are reorted at amortized cost. Influential securities are accounted for under the equity method. Controlling securities are not reported in consolidated financial statements (see Chapter 5). Transfers between categories are accounted for at fair value.

The fair value approach is based on the aggregate value of the portfolio of marketable equity securities rather than on the values of individual securities. A parent must group its securities with those of its consolidated subsidiaries for the current and noncurrent classification.

   b. The following disclosures are required by SFAS 115:

Individual amounts for the investment categories.

For securities classified as available-for-sale and separately for securities classified as held to maturity: (1) aggregate fair value, gross unrealized holding gains/losses, amortized cost basis, and (2) information regarding contractual maturities of debt securities.

For each period for which an income statement is presented: (1) proceeds from sales of available-for-sale securities and gross gains/losses on sales, (2) basis for determining cost in computing gains/losses, (3) gross gains/losses from transfers of available-for-sale securities to trading securities, and (4) change in net unrealized holding gain/loss on available-for-sale securities.

4.   Following are some of the gaps and inconsistencies in SFAS 115 of which the analyst must be aware:

The definition of equity securities in the statement is somewhat arbitrary and inconsistent. Often convertible bonds derive all or most of their value from their conversion feature and are much more akin to equity securities than to debt instruments. The exclusion of these securities from the equity classification is not logical. Nor, for that matter, is there a sound reason for excluding from the valuation process debt securities and marketable mortgages which can fluctuate in value significantly either due to interest rate changes or to changes in credit standing. The continued carrying at cost and above market of debt obligations of issuers in default is particularly unwarranted.

SFAS 115 does not clearly define when marketable securities should be carried as trading and when as available-for-sale, thus introducing a degree of arbitrariness in the decisions of how change in the market value of such securities should be accounted for. It is by no means self-evident that the manner of classifying securities in the balance sheet should determine whether changes in their value are reflected in income or not. While the statement requires the transfer of a marketable security from one category to the next at fair value, category switching could still allow a company some leeway in the determination of future results.

The accounting is one-sided in that changes in the fair value of liabilities are not acoounted for.

Companies may engage in "gains trading" by selling available-for-sale and held-to-maturity with unrealized gains while holding those with unrealized losses.

While the statement does not address the question of how "cost" is determined, the analyst must be aware that a number of methods of determining the cost of marketable securities exist (e.g., specific identification, average, first-in first-out) and that they can affect reported results.

As illustrated, the aggregation of unrealized gains and losses can have an inconsistent effect on income recognition.

5. a. The two most important questions facing the financial analyst with respect to receivables are: (1) Is the receivable genuine, due, and enforceable?, and (2) Has the probability of collection been properly assessed? While the unqualified opinion of an independent auditor should lend assurance with regard to these questions, the financial analyst must recognize the possibility of an error of judgment as well as the lack of it.

    b. The description of the receivables or the notes to the financial statement will usually not contain sufficient clues which would allow a judgment to be made as to whether a receivable is genuine, due, and enforceable. Consequently, a knowledge of industry practices and supplementary sources of information must be used for additional assurance. For example, in some industries, such as compact discs, toys, or bakery, a substantial right of merchandise return exists and allowance must be made for this.

    Most provisions for uncollectible accounts are based on past experience although they should also make allowance for current and emerging industry conditions. In actual practice the accountant is likely to attach more importance to the former than to the latter. The analyst must, in such cases, use his own judgment and knowledge of industry conditions to assess the adequacy of the provision for uncollectible accounts.

    Unfortunately, information that would be helpful in assessing the general level of collection risks in the receivables is not usually found in published financial statements. Such information can, of course, be sought from the company directly. Examples of such information are:

    (1)   What is the customer concentration? What percentage of total receivables is due from one or a few mayor customers? Would failure of any one customer have a material impact on the company's financial condition?
    (2)   What is the age pattern of the receivables?
    (3)   What proportion of notes receivable represent renewals of old notes?
    (4)   Have allowances been made for trade discounts, returns, or other credits to which customers are entitled?

    The financial analyst, in assessing the current financial position and a company's ability to meet its obligations currently, as expressed by such measures as the current ratio, must recognize the full impact of accounting conventions which relate to the classification of receivables as "current." Thus, the operating cycle theory allows the inclusion of installment receivables which may not be fully collectible for years. In balancing these against current obligations, allowance for these differences in timing should be made.

6. With the possible exception of some service organizations, in most businesses inventories represent assets of great importance. From the point of view of the analyst of financial statements inventories are significant for two main reasons:

    (1)   They are a significant component of the assets devoted to the conduct of the business.
    (2)   They enter importantly in the determination of net income.

7. a. Very few useful generalizations about the effect of differing methods of inventory valuation on financial analysis can be made. We know, for instance, that under conditions of fluctuating price levels, the LIFO inventory method will have a smoothing effect on income. Moreover, this method results, in times of price inflation, in an unrealistically low book inventory figure. This in turn will lower the current ratio of a company and at the same time tend to increase its inventory turnover ratio. We also know that the LIFO method affords management an opportunity to manipulate profits by allowing inventory to be depleted in poor years, thus drawing on the low cost base pool. A judgment on all these effects can only be made on the basis of an assessment of all surrounding circumstances. Thus, for example, a slight change in a current ratio of 4:1 may be of no significance, whereas the same change in a ratio of 1.5:1 may be of far greater importance.

   The use of FIFO in the valuation of inventories will generally result in a higher inventory on the balance sheet and a lower cost of goods sold than under LIFO resulting in a higher net income.

   The average cost method smoothes out cost fluctuations by using a weighted average cost in value of inventories and in pricing and cost of goods sold. The resulting net income will be close to an average of the net income under LIFO and FIFO.

   The "lower-of-cost-or-market" principle of inventory accounting has additional implications for the analyst. In times of rising prices it tends to undervalue inventories regardless of the cost method used. This in turn will depress the current ratio below its real level since the other current assets (as well as the current liabilities) are not valued on a consistent basis with the methods used in valuing inventories.

   b. In practice we can find wide variations in the kinds of costs which are included in inventory. Practice varies particularly with respect to the inclusion or exclusion of various classes of overhead costs, freight-in, as well as general and administrative costs. This variety of practices can have a significant effect on comparability among enterprises.

8. The allocation of overhead costs to all units of production must be done on a rational basis designed to get the best approximation of actual cost. However, this is far from an easy matter. The greatest difficulty stems from the fact that a good part of overheads are "fixed" costs, i.e., costs which do not vary with production but vary mostly with the lapse of time. Examples are rent payments and the factory manager's salary. Thus, assuming for a moment that only a single product is produced, if the fixed costs are $100,000 and 10,000 units are produced, each unit will absorb $10 of fixed costs. However, if only 5,000 units are produced, each unit will have to absorb $20 of fixed costs. Clearly, then, the level of activity itself is an important determinant of unit cost. In other words, wide fluctuations in output can result in wide fluctuations in unit cost.

   In order to allocate fixed costs over output, an assumption must be made at the outset of the fiscal period as to how many units the company expects to produce and that in turn will determine over how many units the overhead costs will be allocated. That entails estimates of sales and related production. To the extent that the actual production differs from estimated production, the overhead will be either overabsorbed or underabsorbed. That means that production and inventory are charged with more than total overhead costs or with an insufficient amount of overhead costs.

9. The mayor objective of the LIFO method of inventory accounting is to charge cost of goods sold with the most recent costs incurred. Where the price level remains stable the results under either the FIFO or the LIFO method will be the same, but under changing price levels the results in the use of these methods can differ significantly. The use of the LIFO method has increased greatly due to its acceptance for tax purposes. The tax law stipulates that its use for tax purposes makes mandatory its adoption for financial reporting. The aim is to obtain a better matching of costs and revenues in times of inflation. However, this objective is not always achieved.

Under the LIFO method the income statement is given priority over the balance sheet. Thus, while a matching of more current costs with revenues occurs in times of price inflation, the inventory carrying amounts in the balance sheet will be unrealistically low.

10. It is a fact that in most published reports insufficient information is given to allow the analyst to convert inventories accounted for under one method to a figure reflecting a different method of inventory accounting. Most analysts would want such information in order to be able to better compare the financial statements of companies which use different inventory accounting principles. Converting an inventory figure from one method to another is made even more difficult by the use of different methods for various components of inventory.

Financial analysts will, in most cases, have to make an overall assessment of the impact of differing inventory methods on the comparability of inventory figures. Such an assessment should be based on a thorough understanding of the inventory methods in use and the effect they are likely to have on inventory values. The differences between such informed approximations and the exact figures that can be arrived at only with use of additional data will, in most cases, not be material from the analyst's point of view.

To be useful, disclosure of inventory methods would have to give, in addition to methods used, an identification of the segments (in amounts) in which such methods are used and, if possible, the dollar difference that the method used makes compared to the method most prevalent in the industry.

11. a. Cost, which has been defined generally as the price paid or consideration given to acquire an asset, is the primary basis for accounting for inventories. As applied to inventories, cost means, in principle, the sum of the applicable expenditures and charges directly or indirectly incurred in bringing an article to its existing condition and location. These applicable expenditures and charges include all acquisition and production costs but exclude all selling expenses and that portion of general and administrative expenses not clearly related to production.

   b. Market, as applied to the valuations of inventories, means the current bid price prevailing at the date of the inventory for the particular merchandise in the volume in which is usually purchased by the company. The term is applicable to inventories of purchased goods and to the basic elements of cost (materials, labor, and overhead) of goods that have been manufactured. Therefore, market means current replacement cost except that it should not exceed the net realizable value (estimated selling price less predicted cost of completion and disposal) and should not be less than net realizable value reduced by an allowance for a normal profit margin.

   c. The usual basis for carrying forward the inventory to the next period is cost. Departure from cost is required, however, when the utility of the goods included in the inventory is less than their cost. This loss in utility should be recognized as a loss of the current period, the period in which it occurred. Furthermore, the subsequent period should be charged for goods at an amount that measures their expected contribution to that period. In other words, the subsequent period should be charged for inventory at prices no higher than those which would have been paid if the inventory had been obtained at the beginning of that period. (Historically, the lower-of-cost-or-market rule arose from the accounting convention of providing for all losses and anticipating no profits.) In accordance with the foregoing reasoning the rule of "cost or market, whichever is lower" may be applied to each item in the inventory, to the total of the components of each major category, or to the total of the inventory, whichever most clearly interprets operations. The rule is usually applied to each item, but if individual inventory items enter into the same category or categories of finished product, alternative procedures are suitable.

   d. The arguments against the use of the lower-of-cost-or-market method of valuing inventories include the following:

      (1) The method requires the reporting of estimated losses (all or a portion of the excess of actual cost over replacement cost) as definite income charges even though the losses have not been sustained to date and may never be sustained. Under a consistent criterion of realization a drop in selling price below cost is no more a sustained loss than a rise above cost is a realized gain.

(2) A price shrinkage is brought into the income statement before the loss has been sustained through sale. Furthermore, if the charge for the inventory write-down is not made to a special loss account, the cost figure for goods actually sold is inflated by the amount of the estimated shrinkage in price of the unsold goods. The title "Cost of Goods Sold" therefore becomes a misnomer.

(3) The method is inconsistent in application in a given year because it recognizes the propriety of implied price reductions but gives no recognition in the accounts or financial statements to the effect of price advances.

(4) The method is also inconsistent in application in one year as opposed to another because the inventory of a company may be valued at cost at one year-end and at market at the next year-end.

(5) The lower-of-cost-or-market method values the inventory in the balance sheet conservatively. Its effect on the income statement, however, may be the opposite. Although the income statement for the year in which the unsustained loss is taken is stated conservatively, the net income on the income statement of the subsequent period may be distorted if the expected reductions in sales prices do not materialize.

(6) In the application of the lower of cost or market rule a prospective "normal profit" is used in determining inventory values in certain cases. Since "normal profit" is an estimated figure based upon past experiences (and might not be attained in the future), it is not objective in nature and presents an opportunity for manipulation of the results of operations.

12.   LIFO tends to lead to lower reported earnings during rising price periods than FIFO.

Period	Units in Inventory	Cost per Unit	Total Cost
Period 1	5	5	25
Period 2	5	10	50
Period 3	5	15	75

If 10 items are sold, using LIFO, the cost of goods sold would be $(5 \times 15) + (5 \times 10) = 125$ and the inventory value would be $5 \times 5 = 25$. If each is sold for 20, the gross profit would be $10 \times 20 - 125 = 75$. If FIFO were used, the cost would be $(5 \times 5) + (5 \times 10) = 75$ and gross profit would be $200 - 75 = 125$. Inventory would be valued at $5 \times 15 = 75$, thus inflating the balance sheet. FIFO, therefore tends to increase reported earnings and taxes during inflationary periods.

13.   FIFO and LIFO are inventory costing methods employed to measure the flow of cost. FIFO matches the first cost incurred with the first revenue produced while LIFO matches the last cost incurred with the first revenue produced after the cost is incurred. (This, of course, assumes a perpetual inventory system is in use and may not be precisely true if a periodic inventory system is employed.) If prices are changing, different costs would be matched with revenue for the same quantity sold depending upon whether the LIFO or FIFO system is in use. In a period of rising prices FIFO tends to value inventories at approximate market value in the balance sheet and LIFO tends to match approximately the current replacement cost of an item with the revenue produced.

14.   Marketable securities that are temporary investments of cash specifically designated for special purposes such as plant expansion or sinking fund requirements are classified as noncurrent.

Trading securities are never classified as noncurrent. Held-to-maturity securities are classified as noncurrent except for the reporting period immediately prior to maturity. Available-for-sale securities are classified as current or noncurrent based on management's intent regarding sale. Influential securities are noncurrent unless their sale is imminent.

15. Long-term investments are usually investments in assets such as debt instruments, equity securities, real estate, mineral deposits, or joint ventures acquired with longer-term objectives in mind. Such objectives may include the ultimate acquisition of control or affiliation with other companies, investment in suppliers, securing of assured sources of supply, etc.

Held-to-maturity securities are reported at amortized cost. Available-for-sale securities classified as noncurrent are reported at fair value. Influential securities are accounted for under the equity method.

APB Opinion No. 18 concluded that even a position of less than 20% of the voting stock may give the investor the ability to exercise significant influence over the operating and financial policies of the investee. When such an ability to exercise influence is evident the investment should be accounted for under the equity method. Basically this means at cost plus the equity in the earnings or losses of the investee since acquisition, with the addition of certain other adjustments.

Evidence of the investor's ability to exercise significant influence over operating and financial policies of the investee may be indicated in several ways, such as management representation and participation, but in the interest of uniformity of application the APB concluded that, in the absence of evidence to the contrary, an investment (direct or indirect) in 20% or more of the voting stock of an investee should lead to the presumption of an ability to exercise significant influence over the investee. Conversely, an investment of less than 20% in the voting stock of the investee leads to the presumption of a lack of such influence unless the ability to influence can be demonstrated.

While the eligibility to use the equity method is based on the percentage of voting stock outstanding, which may include, for example, convertible preferred stock, the percentage of earnings which may be picked up under the equity method depends on ownership of common stock only.

Joint ventures should be accounted for under the equity method. Subsidiaries (i.e., companies over 50% owned), should be consolidated. In certain cases, use of the "equity method" may be appropriate.

16. a. The accounting for investments in common stock has undergone significant improvement. The carrying of investments representing over 20% control at equity is an improvement over the practice, which prevailed prior to the issuance of APB Opinion No. 18, of carrying such investments at cost. While the equity method is more realistic than cost it must be borne in mind that it is not the equivalent of fair market value which, depending on circumstances, may be significantly larger or lower than the carrying amount at equity.

   The analyst must remember that the assumption that an investment in 20% or more of the voting securities of an investee results in significant influence over that investee is an arbitrary one which had to be made in the interest of accounting uniformity. If such influence is indeed absent then there may be some question regarding the investor's ability to realize the amount stated at equity. The marketplace does not necessarily pay close attention to book values. An improvement brought about by APB Opinion No. 18 is the requirement that, where available, the market value of investments in common stock (other than in subsidiaries) be disclosed.

   b. APB Opinion No. 18 states that "a loss in value of an investment which is other than a temporary decline should be recognized the same as a loss in value of other long-term assets." This leaves a great deal to judgment and interpretation and in the past this approach has resulted in companies being very slow to recognize losses in their investments. Since the Opinion does not consider a decline in market value to be conclusive evidence of such a loss the analyst must be alert to detect situations where hope rather than reason supports the carrying amount of an investment. It must be recognized that the equity method reflects only current operating losses rather than the capital losses which occur when the earning power of an investment deteriorates or disappears.

17. Following are some flaws and inconsistencies pertaining to the accounting for marketable securities carried as noncurrent assets:

The classification of securities as noncurrent investments is based on management intent, a subjective notion.

Under Statement 115, changes in the fair value of noncurrent available-for-sale securities bypass the income statement.

Equity securities of companies in which the enterprise has a 20 percent or larger interest, and in some instances an even smaller interest than 20 percent, need not be adjusted to market but must instead be carried at equity which may at times be significantly below and at other times above, market. Thus, with regard to such relatively substantial blocks of securities, the values at which they are carried on the balance sheet may be substantially in excess of their realizable values.

18. The Property, Plant and Equipment account is assumed to include assets in active or productive use. If such assets are temporarily idle, disclosure of this fact will usually be made in notes or comments in order to explain the resulting excess costs and lower profit margins.

Should a substantial segment of assets be idle for a longer period of time and without definite prospects of use, they should no longer be included in the property, plant and equipment designation where their inclusion would distort such relationships as sales to plant or return on fixed assets. Instead, they should be segregated away from other assets pending their reactivation, sale, or other disposition. Such idle assets represent not only an investment on which no return is earned, but they often involve expenses of upkeep and maintenance.

19. a. Generally accepted accounting principles require that wasting assets be stated at original cost plus costs of discovery, exploration, and development. This means that the very significant value increment which occurs following the discovery of natural resources is not given immediate accounting recognition, but shows up only through the income stream when and as the resource is exploited.

    b. When an enterprise acquires natural resources from another entity then the cost is more likely to reflect the values of such resources. In such a situation the relationship between the cost of the assets and the revenues they generate is likely to be more logical and reasonable.

20. In valuing property, plant and equipment and in presenting it in conventional financial statements accountants are concerned with the objectivity of original cost, and the conservatism implicit therein, and with an accounting for the number of dollars originally invested in such assets. Judging from the resulting figures they are quite clearly not overly concerned with the objectives of those who analyze financial statements. They are content to proclaim that "a balance sheet does not purport to reflect and could not usefully reflect the value of the enterprise." Not that the accountant is necessarily unmindful of the interests of those who use his statements, it is rather that his/her overwhelming concern lies in the real or imagined problems of his own art.

Only by sheer coincidence can historical costs be useful to analysts. They are not relevant to questions of current replacement or of future needs. They are not directly comparable to similar data in other companies' reports. They do not enable us to measure the opportunity cost of disposal and alternative use of funds nor do they provide a valid yardstick against which to measure return. Moreover, in times of changing price levels they represent an odd conglomeration of a variety of purchasing power disbursements.

21. a. The basic rule in accounting for intangibles is that they be carried at cost. If property other than cash is given in exchange for the intangible it must be recorded at the fair market value of the consideration given.

    If a company spends material and labor in the construction of a "tangible" asset, such as a machine, these costs are capitalized and recorded as an asset which is depreciated over its estimated useful life. On the other hand, if a company spends a great amount of resources advertising a product or training a sales force to sell and service it, which is a process of creating "goodwill," it cannot usually capitalize such costs even though they may be as, or more, beneficial to the company's future operations than is the "tangible" machine. The reason for this inconsistency in accounting for the two assets is steeped in such basic accounting conventions as conservatism which casts greater doubt on the future realization of intangible costs (such as advertising or training) than costs sunk into tangible "hard" and visible goods.

b. Goodwill is an important asset in the intangible category, but it represents the only case where the valuation of the asset is restricted to its cost of acquisition from a third party. Thus the costs of developing and defending a patent, or copyright, or a trademark are properly included as part of the cost of these intangible assets. The same holds generally for other categories such as the cost of leases or leasehold improvements, or processes, licenses, and franchises. Internally developed goodwill, on the other hand, cannot be capitalized and carried as an asset.

c. APB Opinion No. 17 distinguishes between identifiable and unidentifiable intangible assets.

Identifiable intangibles can be separately identified and given reasonably descriptive names such as patents, trademarks, franchises, and the like. Identifiable intangibles can be developed internally, acquired singly or as part of a group of assets. In either case, they should be recorded at cost and amortized over their useful lives. Write-down or complete write-off at date of acquisition is not permitted.

Unidentifiable intangibles can be developed internally or purchased from others. They cannot, however, be acquired singly but from part of a group of assets or part of an entire enterprise. The excess of cost of an acquired company over the sum total of identifiable net assets is the most common unidentifiable intangible asset. APB Opinion No. 17 refers to this unidentifiable mass of assets as "goodwill. and this is actually a residual amount in an acquisition after the amount of tangible and identifiable intangibles have been determined. It represents an expansion of the goodwill concept from what has been obtained before this Opinion was issued.

The costs of developing, maintaining or restoring intangibles which are unidentifiable, have indeterminate lives, or are inherent in a continuing enterprise should be expensed as incurred. By contrast, such intangible assets which are purchased must be carried at cost and amortized over their useful lives and cannot be written down or written off at date of acquisition.

d. Both types of intangibles, those identifiable as well as those unidentifiable are believed to have limited useful lives and must be amortized accordingly. Depending on the type of intangible asset, its useful life may be limited by such factors as legal, contractual, or regulatory provisions; demand and competition; life expectancies of employees; and economic factors. The cost of each intangible should be amortized over its individual useful life taking into account all factors which determine its length. The period of amortization may not, however, exceed 40 years.

22. Goodwill is often a sizable asset. Since it can only be recorded on acquisition from a third party, it can be recorded only upon the purchase of an ongoing business enterprise. The description of what is being paid for varies greatly and the variety of views add to the confusion surrounding this subject. Some refer to the ability to attract and keep satisfied customers, while others point to qualities, inherent in an enterprise that is well organized and is efficient in production, service, and sales.

Having understood the accounting conventions governing the recording of goodwill, the analyst realizes that only purchased goodwill will be found among the recorded assets and that more "goodwill" may exist off the balance sheet than on it.

Another key point here is that if there is value in goodwill it must be reflected in earnings. True, if a mismanaged situation with great potential was purchased, the profits may not become visible immediately, but if there is value to goodwill then such an asset should give rise to superior earnings within a reasonably short time after acquisition.

If those earnings are not in evidence, it is a fair assumption that the investment in goodwill is of no value regardless of whether it is found on the balance sheet.

Another important factor of which the analyst must be aware is that, in practice, the accounting for goodwill is far from faithful to the theory. Due to the beneficial effect that an absence of write-off of assets has on the results of operations, goodwill and other intangibles may not be written off as speedily as a realistic assessment of their useful life may require. While the overall limitation of 40 years on the assumed useful life of intangibles is arbitrary and may, in some instances, result in excessive amortization it is safe to assume that in most cases the bias will be in the direction of too slow a rate of amortization. The analyst must be alert to this possibility.

Regardless of the amount of outlays incurred in the acquisition or in the internal development of an intangible, the rule applicable to the carrying amount of any asset is that it be carried at an amount not in excess of realizable value in terms of sales price or future utility. That, at least, is the intention and the theory. But, as in most other categories of accounting theory, actual implementation in practice is another matter, and the analyst must be prepared to form his/her own judgment on the amounts at which intangible assets are carried. The analyst must also bear in mind that goodwill recorded as a result of business combinations initiated before November 1, 1970 does not have to be amortized at all and that at the cutoff date there were billions of dollars of unamortized goodwill on corporate balance sheets in this country.

The analyst must also be alert to the consideration with which the enterprise has parted in the acquisition of goodwill, for this may affect the amount of the intangible recorded. Payments in promoter stock should be thoroughly scrutinized. Also of concern to the analyst is the rate at which goodwill is amortized. The 40-year maximum, after all, is a long period exceeding a generation. The assumption of useful life should be realistic and should reflect the proper allocation of costs to revenues. A lump-sum write-off of an intangible may bring the asset down to its proper realizable value but by no means does it make up for the implicit overstatement of earnings of prior years and should be segregated and allocated to the years to which it pertains in a restatement of income for purposes of comparability.

23. The following are a number of categories of deferred charges. In each of the above cases, the rationale for deferral is that these outlays hold future utility (benefits) for the enterprise.

(1) Business development, expansion, merger, and relocation costs.
   a. Preoperating expenses, initial start-up costs, and tooling costs.
   b. Initial operating losses or preoperating expenses of subsidiaries.
   c. Moving, plant rearrangement, and reinstallation costs.
   d. Merger or acquisition expenses.
   e. Purchased customer accounts.
   f. Noncompete agreements.

(2) Deferred expenses.
   a. Advertising and promotional expenses.
   b. Imputed interest.
   c. Selling, general and administrative expenses.
   d. Pension plan costs.
   e. Property and other taxes.
   f. Rental and leasing costs.
   g. Vacation pay.
   h. Seasonal growing and packing expenses.

(3) Intangible costs.
   a. Intangible drilling and development costs.
   b. Contracts, films, copyright materials, art rights
   c. Costs of computer software

(4) Debt discount and expenses.

(5) Future income tax benefits.

(6) Organization costs.

(7) Advance royalties.

24. a. One category of assets which is not recorded on the balance sheet is internally created goodwill. In this case if the intangible is internally developed, rather than purchased from an outside party, it cannot normally be capitalized and results instead in a charge to current operations. Thus, to the extent that a valuable asset has been created, one that can be either sold or which possesses earning power, the income charged with the expense of its development has been understated.

Contingent assets are another category of unrecorded assets. Under the principle of conservatism, these rights/claims to resources are not recognized due to their uncertainty.

   b. The analyst must realize that reported book values are not a substitute for market values. As illustrated by the accounting-based equity valuation model, unrecorded assets must eventually be realized in the form of abnormal earnings.

◄ Answers to Exercises ►

Exercise 4-1

a. Cash normally consists of coins and currency on hand, bank deposits, and various kinds of orders for cash such as bank checks, money orders, traveler's checks, demand bills of exchange, bank drafts, cashier's checks, and letters of credit. Balances on deposit in banks which are subject to immediate withdrawal are properly included in cash. There is some question as to whether deposits not subject to immediate withdrawal are properly included in cash or whether they should be set out separately. Savings accounts, time certificates of deposit, and time deposits fall in this latter category. Unless restrictions on these kinds of deposits are such that they cannot be converted (withdrawn) within one year or the operating cycle of the entity, whichever is longer, there can be little question but that they are properly classed as current assets. At the same time, they may well be presented separately from other cash and their restrictions as to convertibility reported.

b. Valuation problems can arise where cash balances are in foreign countries or where a domestic entity holds a bill of exchange payable in foreign money. All balances expressed in foreign money must be converted into domestic dollar equivalents. While the conversion of cash items is fairly simple and is ordinarily done in terms of the exchange rate prevailing at the close of a fiscal period, a problem can arise as to a choice of rates where there are both official and free market rates which do not coincide. The latter has generally been interpreted to be the most clearly realistic and appropriate.

Valuation problems can also arise where there is cash in a domestic bank which has closed or is in receivership. In such cases, an estimate must be made or obtained from the receiver which reflects the probable amount to be realized in excess of balances covered fully by deposit insurance.

There is some potential of loss any time an entity accepts checks. However, only those entities which handle a substantial volume of checks giving rise to losses from insufficient funds or forgeries would ordinarily reflect a valuation allowance in respect to bank checks which have not yet cleared payor banks.

Exercise 4-2

a. The allowance method based on credit sales attempts to match bad debts with the revenues generated by the sales in the same period. Thus, it focuses on the income statement rather than the balance sheet.

On the other hand, the allowance method based on the balance in the trade receivables accounts attempts to value the accounts receivable at the end of a period at their future collectible amounts. Thus, it focuses on the balance sheet rather than the income statement.

It should be noted, however, that both the allowance method based on credit sales and the allowance method based on the balance in the trade receivables accounts are acceptable under generally accepted accounting principles.

b. Carme Company should report on its balance sheet at December 31, Year 1, the balance in the allowance for bad debts account as a valuation or contra asset account; that is, a subtraction from the asset accounts receivable.

Bad debt expense may be presented in the income statement as a selling expense, general and administrative expense, or as a subtraction to arrive at net sales.

c. When examining the reasonableness of the allowance for bad debts, the analyst is interested in assessing the collectibility of accounts receivable. The analyst is especially interested in changing or emerging business/economic conditions and their impact on the allowance. In addition, the analyst must assess any changes in collectibility assumptions as they have a direct impact on net income through the determination of bad debt expense.

Exercise 4-3

a. Carmen Company should report a portion of the interest income from the note receivable in Year 1 (interest earned for the six-month period from July 1, Year 1, to December 31, Year 1) and a portion in Year 2 (interest earned for the six-month period from January 1, Year 2, to June 30, Year 2). Interest accrues with the passage of time, and should be accounted for as an element of income over the life of the note receivable.

b. First, determine the maturity value of the note receivable (the face value of the note receivable plus the interest income to be earned over the life of the note receivable [twelve-month period from July 1, Year 1 to June 30, Year 2]). Then, multiply the maturity value of the note receivable by one half of the discount rate (six-month period from December 31, Year 1, to June 30, Year 2) to arrive at the amount of the discount.

To account for the discounting transaction, cash would be debited for the amount received from the bank. Notes receivable would be credited for the face value of the note receivable. Interest expense for the amount of the discount would be debited and interest revenue for the interest income to be earned over the life of the note receivable would be credited. These latter two entries, however, are usually netted against each other instead of being recognized separately.

c. The primary concern is collectibility of interest and principal. Thus, the liquidity position of the customer is a concern. The analyst should be aware that many firms accept notes receivable from customers who are unable to pay accounts receivable on a timely basis.

Exercise 4-4

a. Inventory cost should include all reasonable and necessary costs of preparing inventory for sale. These costs include not only the purchase price of the inventories, but also other costs associated with readying inventories for sale.

b. The lower of cost or market rule produces a realistic estimate of future cash flows to be realized from the sale of inventories. This is consistent with the principle of conservatism, and recognizes (matches) the anticipated loss in the income statement in the period in which the price decline occurs.

c. Steel's inventories should be reported on the balance sheet at market. According to the lower of cost or market rule, market is defined as replacement cost. Market cannot exceed net realizable value and cannot be less than net realizable value less the normal profit margin. In this instance, replacement cost is between net realizable value and net realizable value less the normal profit margin. Therefore, market is established as replacement cost. Since market is less than original cost, inventory should be reported at market.

d. Ending inventories and net income would have been the same under either lower of average cost or market or lower of FIFO cost or market. In periods of declining prices, the lower of cost or market rule results in a write-down of inventory cost to market under both methods, resulting in the same inventory cost. Therefore, net income using either inventory method is the same.

Exercise 4-5

a. The average cost method is based on the assumption that the average costs of the goods in the beginning inventory and the goods purchased during the period should be used for both the inventory and the cost of goods sold.

The FIFO (first-in, first-out) method is based on the assumption that the first goods purchased are the first sold. As a result, the inventory is at the most recent purchase prices, while cost of goods sold is at older purchase prices.

The LIFO (last-in, first-out) method is based on the assumption that the latest goods purchased are the first sold. As a result, the inventory is at the oldest purchase prices, while cost of goods sold is at more recent purchase prices.

b. In an inflationary economy, LIFO provides a better matching of current costs with current revenue because cost of goods sold is at more recent purchase prices. Net cash inflow is generally increased because taxable income is generally decreased, resulting in payment of lower income taxes.

c. Where there is evidence that the utility of goods to be disposed of in the ordinary course of business will be less than cost, the difference should be recognized as a loss in the current period, and the inventory should be stated at market value in the financial statements. In accordance with the concept of conservatism, inventory should be valued at the lower of cost or market.

(AICPA)

Exercise 4-6

a.

	LIFO		FIFO	
Beginning Inventory	816.0	(a)	904.0	(b)
Cost of Goods Purchased	4,262.0	(c)	4,262.0	(c)
Goods Available for Sale	5,078.0		5,166.0	
Less Ending Inventory	819.8	(34)	904.4	(152A)
Cost of Goods Sold	4,258.2	(14)	4,261.6	
Revenues	6,205.8	(13)	6,205.8	(13)
CGS—as above	4,258.2		4,261.6	
Gross Profit—				
As reported	1,947.6			
Under FIFO			1,944.2	

(a) From Comprehensive Case.
(b) 816.0 + 88.0 (given)
(c) CGP same under either method—derived.

b. The major purpose for making the LIFO-to-FIFO restatement is to achieve comparability between firms using different inventory methods.

Exercise 4-7
In addition to excess replacement value of plant over cost and LIFO inventory reserve, assets not presently included on corporate balance sheets include:

1. Excess of market value over adjusted cost of equity in nonconsolidated subsidiaries and in affiliates.

2. Intangibles—widely recognized corporate name or product name not now capitalized.

3. "Successful" R&D, such as a new drug that has passed all but the final clearance of the Food & Drug Administration.

4. Proved reserves of extractive-type companies carried at substantially less than market value of product less extraction costs.

5. Human capital.

6. Value of savings on short-term credit lines where maximum interest payable is currently below bank prime rate.

The analyst must remember that book value is only the starting point for accounting-based stock valuation. If unrecorded assets have economic value, they will eventually be recognized through higher future abnormal earnings. Thus, the analyst must consider the impact of unrecorded assets when projecting future profitability for valuation purposes.

(CFA)

Exercise 4-8

a. Current: for temporary investment of excess cash in highly liquid investments. Noncurrent: for investment income, appreciation, control, or to secure sources of supply.

b. Trading securities are always classified as current. Held-to-maturity securities are classified as noncurrent, except for the reporting period immediately prior to maturity. Available-for-sale securities are classified as current or noncurrent based on management's intent regarding sale. Influential securities are noncurrent unless their sale is imminent. Marketable securities that are temporary investments of cash specifically designated for special purposes such as plant expansion or sinking fund requirements are classified as noncurrent.

Unrealized losses on trading securities (which are classified as current assets) are the only unrealized losses to flow through the income statement. Unrealized losses on noncurrent investments as included as a separate component of shareholders' equity.

Exercise 4-9

a. The value of assets which are generally acquired for purposes of economic performance (as opposed to, say, esthetic pleasure) is determined by their expected future utility, i.e., the future net cash inflows or cost savings which they can be expected to bring.

b. Accounting principles for fixed assets focus on recording them at original cost reduced by accumulated depreciation, as applicable. Under SFAS 121, declines in economic value should be recognized when the assets are impaired. However, the determination of whether an asset has been impaired and the amount of any impairment are driven by management estimates of future cash flows. This permits much leeway in the recording of asset write-downs.

Regardless of what the tanker is booked at by its owners, real support for its economic value can come only through the income statement, i.e., through the excess of revenues over operating costs (including recovery of the investment in the ship).

c.   Asset valuation rules under GAAP are heavily influenced by the principle of conservatism. Thus, market values of firms often exceed their book values. The analyst must remember that conservatively-stated asset values must eventually result in abnormal earnings.

Exercise 4-10
c, e, g, h, i, j, m, p, q

◄ Answers to Problems ►

Problem 4-1

a.

	11 Mostly LIFO	11 Average Cost			10 Mostly LIFO	10 Average Cost	
Revenues [1]	5491.2	5491.2			5030.6	5030.6	
Cost of sales:							
Beg. Inv. [59]	473.9	501.8	(B)	[59]	479.1	510.1	(C)
+ Purchases (A) . .	2788.1	2788.1		(A)	2680.7	2680.7	
Cost of Goods Avail	3262.0	3289.9			3159.8	3190.8	
- Ending Inv. [59] . .	422.3	441.2	(B)	[59]	473.9	501.8	(B)
Cost of Sales [2] .	2839.7	2848.7			2685.9	2689.0	
Gross Profit	2651.5	2642.5			2344.7	2341.6	

(A)   Purchases = CGS [2] + End Inv [59] - Beg Inv [59]
      Purchases (11) =   2839.7 + 422.3 - 473.9 = 2788.1
      Purchases (10) =   2685.9 + 473.9 - 479.1 = 2680.7

(B)   Avg Cost Beg Inv (11) = 473.9 [59] + 27.9 [143] = 501.8
      Avg Cost End Inv (11) = 422.3 [59] + 18.9 [143] = 441.2

(C)   Avg Cost Beg Inv (10) = 479.1 [59] + 31.0 [143] = 510.1

b.   *Effect on net income of using LIFO instead of valuing the entire inventory under average cost methods for the year ended June 30.*

	11	10
Gross Profit (LIFO) . .	2651.5	2344.7
Gross Profit (Avg Cost)	2642.5	2341.6
LIFO is higher	9.0	3.1
Taxes at 34% . . .	3.1	1.1
Effect on Net Income . .	5.9	2.0

In 10 amd 11, the net income is larger under LIFO because inventory reductions occurred in both years possibly causing LIFO liquidations to occur. In other words, LIFO layers that were recorded at lower prices were used resulting in higher net income.

c.   *Restatement of Financial Statements from a LIFO to an Average Cost Basis:*

	11	10
Excess of Average Cost over LIFO [143]	18.9	27.9

Therefore, if Average Costs were used for all inventory, the ending inventory would be higher than it is under LIFO by the above amounts.

Restatement of 11 balance sheet to the Avg Cost Basis:

Inventories (A)	18.9	
Deferred Taxes Payable (B)		6.43
Retained Earnings (C) . .		12.47

(A)   Inventories increased to a closer estimate of current replacement costs. However, not as close as they would be if stated under FIFO.

(B)   Using Average Costs increases Inventories and therefore a provision for taxes payable in the future on this increase must be made (tax rate = .34).

(C)   If inventories are higher then CGS is lower and Income is higher and therefore, cumulative Net Income must be increased and this is done by a credit to retained earnings.

<u>Problem 4-2</u>

a.   Under the FIFO method of accounting for inventories, cost-of-goods-sold reflects the cost of inventories purchased earlier. During periods of rising costs, operating margins are higher under FIFO because sales at current prices are matched with older, lower cost inventory. During periods of declining costs, operating margins are compressed because older, higher cost inventories are matched with current, lower cost sales.

1.   During the period 1985-1987, according to Table 4, cost per pound produced declined from 34 cents to 31 cents to 29 cents. The use of FIFO compressed Avon's margins because higher cost, older inventory was being expensed.

2.   During the period 1987-1989, unit costs were rising. Unit costs rose from 29 cents in 1987 to 35 cents and 39 cents in 1988 and 1989 respectively. The use of FIFO increased Avon's operating margins during this period as older, lower cost inventory was being expensed first.

b.   According to Table 4, prices and costs are expected to decline in 1990. Prices (and presumably costs) are expected to increase. Adopting LIFO at 1/1/91, prior to expected rise in prices will produce tax savings, better cash flow, and a better matching of costs and revenues.

Problem 4-3

a. $(50,000)(1 - .35) = \underline{\$32,500}$

b. $(4,000)(1 - .35) = \underline{\$2,600}$

c. The major purpose for making the LIFO-to-FIFO restatement is to achieve comparability between firms using different inventory methods.

Problem 4-4

Property, Plant & Equipment (gross)

[161A] beg	2,734.9		
[186] additions	371.1	156.7	retirements/sales [186]
[186] acqd. assets	4.7	32.1	rate variance [186]
[161A] end	2.921.9		

Accumulated Depreciation

		1,117.2	beg [162]
[187] retire./sales	69.5	194.5	ordinary deprec. [162A]
[187] translation adj.	10.7		
		1,131.5	end [162]

The reconstruction of transactions through T-account analysis enables the financial statement reader to examine the economic substance behind the accounting entries.

Problem 4-5

Year 11:

Property, Plant & Equipment (gross)

[64] beg	1,745.6		
[32] additions	240.6	42.7	retirements/sales [146]
		18.1	translation adj. [146]
		10.8	other [146]
[64] end	1,914.6		

Accumulated Depreciation

		591.5	beg [65]
[146] retire./sales	24.8	128.6	additions to A/D [146]
[146] other	13.4		
		681.9	end [65]

Year 10:

Property, Plant & Equipment (gross)

[64] beg	1,456.9			
[32] additions	275.6	38.7	retirements/sales	[146]
[146] translation adj.	22.7			
[146] other	29.1	_____		
[64] end	1,745.6			

Accumulated Depreciation

		497.3	beg	[65]
[146] retire./sales	24.8	106.5	additions to A/D	[146]
[146] other	13.4	14.6	other	[146]
		591.5	end	[65]

The reconstruction of transactions through T-account analysis enables the financial statement reader to examine the economic substance behind the accounting entries.

Problem 4-6

I.   Since the *aggregate* market value of the *portfolio* exceeds cost, there is no writedown of the individual security whose market value declined to less than one-half of cost. Stockholders' equity will be increased (decreased) to the extent that the excess of market over cost has increased (decreased) over the period. There is no effect on the income statement.

II.   This situation is similar to I above. The only difference is that the firm in question does not use the classified balance sheet format. In this case, the analyst must be sure to examine footnote disclosure regarding the classification of investments (if not provided on the face of the balance sheet).

III. This is not a reclassification between categories as the securities remain in the available-for-sale category. However, the analyst should note that management is contemplating a sale in the near future.

IV.   The increase in fair value of the security should be credited to shareholders' equity. (Since the security is classified as noncurrent, it cannot be a trading security).

Problem 4-7

a.   The expenditures that should be capitalized when equipment is acquired for cash should include the invoice price of the equipment (net of discounts) plus all incidental outlays relating to its purchase or preparation for use, such as insurance during transit, freight, duties, ownership search, ownership registration, installation, and breaking-in costs. Any available discounts, whether taken or not, should be deducted from the capitalizable cost of the equipment.

b. 1. When the market value of the equipment is not determinable by reference to a similar cash purchase, the capitalizable cost of equipment purchased with bonds having an established market price should be the market value of the bonds.

2. When the market value of the equipment is not determinable by reference to a similar cash purchase, and the common stock used in the exchange does not have an established market price, the capitalizable cost of equipment should be the equipment's estimated fair value if that is more clearly evident than the fair value of the common stock. Independent appraisals may be used to determine the fair values of the assets involved.

3. When the market value of equipment acquired is not determinable by reference to a similar cash purchase, the capitalizable cost of equipment purchased by exchanging similar equipment having a determinable market value should be the lower of the recorded amount of the equipment relinquished or the market value of the equipment exchanged.

c. The factors that determine whether expenditures relating to property, plant, and equipment already in use should be capitalized are as follows:

- Expenditures are relatively large in amount.
- They are nonrecurring in nature.
- They extend the useful life of the property, plant, and equipment.
- They increase the usefulness (e.g., quantity or quality of goods produced) of the property, plant, and equipment.

d. The net book value at the date of the sale (cost of the property, plant, and equipment less the accumulated depreciation) should be removed from the accounts. The excess of cash from the sale over the net book value removed is accounted for as a gain on the sale, while the excess of net book value removed over cash from the sale is accounted for as a loss on the sale.

e. Considerations in analyzing property, plant, and equipment include: (1) reporting at historical cost, (2) need for sufficient capacity to meet anticipated demand, (3) need for writedowns of impaired assets, (4) effect of changes in price level, (5) use of assets under operating lease arrangments, and (6) existence of idle facilities.

Problem 4-8

a. A firm may wish to construct its own fixed assets rather than acquire them from outsiders to utilize idle facilities and/or personnel. In some cases fixed assets may be self-constructed to effect an expected cost saving. In other cases the requirements for the asset demand special knowledge, skills, and talents not readily available outside the firm. Also, the firm may want to keep the manufacturing process for a particular product as a trade secret.

b. Costs which should be capitalized for a self-constructed fixed asset include all direct and indirect material and labor costs identifiable with the construction. All direct overhead costs identifiable with the asset being constructed should also be capitalized. Examples of costs elements which should be capitalized during the construction period include charges for licenses, permits, and fees, depreciation of equipment used in the construction, taxes, insurance, interest on borrowings, and similar charges related to the assets being constructed.

c. 1. The increase in overhead caused by the self-construction of fixed assets should be capitalized. These costs would not have been incurred if the assets had not been constructed. This proposition holds regardless of whether or not the plant is operating at full capacity. It is improper to increase the cost of finished goods with costs which were not incurred in their manufacture and which would not have been incurred if fixed assets had not been produced. However, if the total construction costs on self-constructed fixed assets were substantially in excess of their business and economic usefulness, the excess cost should not be capitalized but should instead be recorded as a loss.

    2. It is clear that the capitalized costs of self-constructed assets should include a proportionate share of overhead on the same basis as that applied to goods manufactured for sale when the plant is operating at full capacity at the time the fixed asset is constructed. Under these circumstances costs of finished goods produced should not be increased for overhead for goods for which production was foregone. The activity replacing the production of goods for sale should be charged with the related overhead.

        When idle plant capacity is used for the construction of a fixed asset, opinion varies as to the propriety of capitalizing a share of general factory overhead allocated on the same basis as that applied to goods manufactured for sale. The arguments to allocate overhead maintain that constructed fixed assets should be accorded the same treatment as inventory, new products, or joint products. It is maintained that this procedure is necessary, or special favors or exemptions from undercosting of fixed assets will cause a consequent overcosting of inventory assets.

        Those arguing against allocating overhead to fixed assets where the assets are constructed when ideal capacity exists maintain that, since normal production will not be affected or overhead increased, capitalization will result in increased reported income for the period resulting from construction rather than production of goods for sale. It is also sometimes maintained that the full cost of the constructed asset should not include overhead that would be incurred in the absence of such construction.

d. The $90,000 cost by which the initial machine exceeded the cost of the subsequent machines should be capitalized. Without question there are substantial future benefits expected from the use of this machine. Because future periods will benefit from the extra outlays required to develop the initial machine, all development costs should be capitalized and subsequently associated with the related revenue produced by the sale of products manufactured. If, however, it can be determined that the excess cost of producing the first machine was the result of inefficiencies or failure which did not contribute to the machine's successful development, these costs should be recognized as an extraordinary loss. Subsequent periods should not be burdened with charges arising from costs which are not expected to yield future benefits.

Capitalizing the excess costs as a cost of the initial machine can be justified under the general rules of asset valuation. That is, an asset acquired should be charged with all costs incurred in obtaining the asset and placing it in service.

(AICPA)

Problem 4-9

a. *Intangible assets*, like other monetary assets, represent rights to future benefits. An intangible asset is usually defined as a capital asset having no physical existence, its value being dependent upon the rights that possession confers upon the owner. The term "capital" implies they are non-current.

A few assets which fit the definition are not classified as intangible assets. For example, long-term receivables and long-term investments ordinarily are classified elsewhere in the balance sheet.

b. 1. A dollar to be received in the future is worth less than a dollar received today because of an interest or discount factor—often referred to as the time value of money. The discounted value of the expected royalty receipts can be thought of either in terms of the present value of an annuity of 1 or in terms of the sum of several present values of 1.

2. If the royalty receipts are expected to occur at regular intervals and the amounts are to be fairly constant, their discounted value can be calculated by multiplying the value of one such receipt by the present value of an annuity of 1 for the number of periods the receipts are expected. On the other hand, if receipts are expected to be irregular in amount, or if they are to occur at irregular intervals, each expected future receipt would have to be multiplied by the present value of 1 for the number of periods of delay expected.

In each case some interest rate (discount factor) per period must be assumed and used. As an example, if receipts of $10,000 are expected each six months over the next 10 years and an 8 percent annual interest rate is selected, the present value of the 20 $10,000 payments is equal to $10,000 times the present value of an annuity of 1 for 20 periods at 4 percent. Twice as many periods as years and half the annual interest rate of 8 percent are used because the payments are expected at semiannual intervals. Thus the discounted (present) value of these receipts is $135,903 ($10,000 x 13.5903). Because of the interest rate, this discounted value is considerably less than the total expected collections of $200,000. Continuing the example, if instead it is expected that $10,000 will be received six months hence, $20,000 one year from now, and a terminal payment of $15,000 is expected 18 months hence, the calculation is as below:

$10,000 \times$ present value of 1 at 4% for 1 period = $10,000 \times .96154$
$20,000 \times$ present value of 1 at 4% for 2 periods = $20,000 \times .92456$
$15,000 \times$ present value of 1 at 4% for 3 periods = $15,000 \times .88900$

Adding the results of these three calculations yields a total of $41,441 (rounded), considerably less than the $45,000 total collections, again due to the discount factor.

c. The basis of valuation for the patents that is generally accepted in accounting is cost. Evidently the cartons were developed and the patents obtained directly by the client corporation. Therefore, their cost would include applicable experimental and developmental costs, government and legal fees, and the costs of any models and drawings. The proper initial valuation would be the sum of these costs plus any other costs incident to obtaining the two patents. This is in accord with the accounting principle that the initial valuation of any asset generally includes virtually all costs necessary to acquire and make it ready for normal use. Such values are objectively determined and rest upon actual completed transactions rather than upon estimates and future expectations.

d. 1. Intangible assets represent rights to future benefits. The ideal measure of the value of intangible assets is the discounted present value of their future benefits. For the Vandiver Corporation, this would include the discounted value of expected net receipts from royalties as suggested by the financial vice-president as well as the discounted value of the expected net receipts to be derived from the Vandiver Corporation's production. Other valuation bases that have been suggested are current cash equivalent or fair market value.

    2. The amortization policy is implied in the definition of intangible assets as rights to future benefits. As the benefits are received by the firm, the cost or other value should be charged to expense or to inventory to provide a proper matching of revenues and expenses. Under the discounted value approach the periodic amortization would be the decline during the year in the present value of expected net receipts.

e. The litigation can and probably should be mentioned in notes to the financial statements. Some indication of the expectations of legal counsel in respect to the outcome can properly accompany the statements. It would be inappropriate to record a contingent asset reflecting the expected damages to be recovered. Costs incurred to September 30, 1970 in connection with the litigation should be carried forward and charged to expense (or to loss if the cases are lost) as royalties (or damages) are collected from the parties against whom the litigation has been instituted; however, the conventional treatment would be to charge these costs as ordinary legal expenses. If the final outcome of the litigation is successful, the costs of prosecuting it should be capitalized. Similarly, if the client were the successful defendant in an infringement suit on these patents, the generally accepted accounting practice would be to add the costs of the legal defense to the Patents account.

Developments to the time that the statements are prepared and released can be reflected in notes to the statements as a post-balance sheet (or subsequent event) disclosure.

(AICPA)

◄ Answers to Cases ►

Case 4-1

a. At 3/31/96, Adaptec reported the following current assets: cash and cash equivalents, marketable securities, accounts receivable, inventories, and prepaid expenses/other.

b. Marketable securities

c. $4,220 of $93,707 (89,487 + 4,220), or 4.5%

d. "Cash and cash equivalents consist of funds in checking accounts, money market funds and marketable securities with original maturities of three months or less."

Case 4-2

a. The main determinants of the valuation of feature films, television programs, and general release feature productions by Columbia are: (1) the cost of productions, and (2) estimates on how to allocate those costs over the earnings-generating capacity of the films.

b. The reasonableness of the bases of valuation depends almost entirely on the reasonableness of the estimates of the expiration of value of the inventory costs. Judging from the third paragraph of the quoted footnote it appears that some of the company's estimates of the value of films were overoptimistic and that this required subsequent substantial writedowns. If this is an indication of management's ability to estimate the potentials of its film releases, then the analyst should treat the inventory values with suspicion and caution.

c. An unsecured lender would want to carefully evaluate the valuation of film inventories in the light of past experience and of future prospects in the industry, particularly because inventories form such an important part of total assets in this industry. He/she would want to know what the experience of valuation has been in the past (from available evidence in Columbia's footnote—not too reassuring). He/she would compare the estimation process with that followed by other companies in the industry and would also compare the estimates with conditions and trends in the industry which are expected to prevail in the future.

<u>Case 4-3</u>

a. 1. FIFO (first-in, first-out) allocates cost of goods sold to sales in the order goods were purchased:

Sales, 1,000 units at $1.70	$ 1,700
Cost of goods sold (1,000 units at $1.00 which is inventory at the beginning of the year)	<u>1,000</u>
Net income before taxes	$ 700
Provision for federal income taxes (50%)	<u>350</u>
Net Income Transferred to Retained Earnings	$ 350

2. LIFO (last-in, first-out) allocates recent cost to sales:

Sales, 1,000 units at $1.70	$ 1,700
Cost of goods sold (the last 1,000 units acquired—1,000 at $1.50)	<u>1,500</u>
Net income before taxes	$ 200
Provision for federal income taxes (50%)	<u>100</u>
Net Income Transferred to Retained Earnings	$ 100

b. FIFO: Current Assets:

Cash	$ 200
Inventory (FIFO method)	<u>1,500</u>
Total Assets	$ <u>1,700</u>

Current Liabilities:

Federal income taxes payable	$ 350
Net worth	<u>1,350</u>
Total Liabilities and Stockholders' Equity . . .	$ <u>1,700</u>

LIFO: Current Assets:

Cash	$ 200
Inventory (LIFO method)	<u>1,000</u>
Total Assets	$ <u>1,200</u>

Current Liabilities:

Federal income taxes payable	$ 100
Net worth	<u>1,100</u>
Total Liabilities and Stockholders' Equity . . .	$ <u>1,200</u>

c. During a period of rising prices, the LIFO method is more conservative in profit determination and the evaluation of the financial position of a company than the FIFO method. LIFO allocates recent costs of inventory to sales, the result being that these costs are higher in the light of price increases. Accordingly, inventory is valued more and more conservatively, and profits reported are lower than those under the FIFO method. Parts (a) and (b) clearly reveal this: Under LIFO, profit reported is $100 after taxes as compared to $350 under FIFO. Likewise, inventory is reported at $1,000 under LIFO as opposed to $1,500 under FIFO. Evidence of rising prices is the fact that existing inventory was valued at $1.00 per unit while goods purchased during the year ran at $1.50 per unit. Tax considerations are important. As we can see from (a) and (b) the LIFO method produced a tax liability of only

$100.00 whereas taxes under the FIFO method amounted to $350.00. As long as inventory is maintained at a given level or increased, LIFO produces an interest-free perpetual loan from the government. Of course, should inventory be liquidated, cost of goods sold will be very low compared to sales, with a resulting higher income tax liability.

d.   Companies use a dollar pool LIFO method in order to prevent liquidation of low-cost LIFO inventory units. Under this method, groups of items are viewed as a dollar pool, and if one item is sold, it may be replaced by new items of the same or greater dollar value, and there is no liquidation of the pool. The problem for a company which prepares interim statements is to decide whether liquidated items in one quarter will be replaced before the end of the fiscal year. If the items are replaced, income taxes allocated to profits of the current quarter will be lower than if the items are not replaced.

(CFA)

Case 4-4

a.

	FIFO	LIFO	Average cost
Sales:			
1,000 @ $25	$25,000	$25,000	$25,000
Cost of sales:			
Beginning inventory	0	0	0
Purchases	23,200	23,200	23,200
Less: Ending inventory	11,700	9,100	10,312
Cost of sales	11,500	14,100	12,888
Gross profit	13,500	10,900	12,112
Operating expenses	5,000	5,000	5,000
Net income	$8,500	$5,900	$7,112
Net income per share	$4.25	$5.90	$3.56

NOTES: (1)   The FIFO inventory computation is based on 500 units at $15 and 300 at $14.

            (2)   The LIFO inventory computation is based on 100 units at $10, 300 units at $11, and 400 units at $12.

            (3)   The average cost is obtained by dividing $23,200 by 1,800 units purchased, yielding an average unit price of $12.89.

b.

	FIFO	LIFO	Avg. Cost
Current ratio (1)	2.47	2.36	2.41
Debt-to-equity ratio (2)	19.0%	20.4%	19.9%
Inventory turnover (3)	2.00	3.10	2.50
Return on total assets (4)	9.8%	7.0%	8.3%
Gross margin ratio	54.0%	43.6%	48.5%
Net profit as percent of sales	34.0%	23.6%	28.5%

(1) (ending inventory + 50,000) ÷ 25,000
(2) 10,000 ÷ (ending inventory + 40,000)
(3) cost of sales ÷ (ending inventory ÷ 2)
(4) net income ÷ (ending inventory + 75,000)

c.   Under conditions of fluctuating price levels, the LIFO inventory method will have a smoothing effect on income. Moreover, this method results, in times of price inflation, in an unrealistically low book inventory figure. This in turn will lower the current ratio of a company and at the same time tend to increase its inventory turnover ratio. We also know that the LIFO method affords management an opportunity to manipulate profits by allowing inventory to be depleted in poor years, thus drawing on the low cost base pool.

The use of FIFO in the valuation of inventories will generally result in a higher inventory on the balance sheet and a lower cost of goods sold than under LIFO resulting in a higher net income.

The average cost method smoothes out cost fluctuations by using a weighted average cost in value of inventories and in pricing and cost of goods sold. The resulting net income will be close to an average of the net income under LIFO and FIFO.

Case 4-5

a.   At 3/31/96, Adaptec reported the following noncurrent assets: property and equipment and other (noncurrent) assets.

b.   At 3/31/96, Adaptec's property and equipment account included the following:

Land	$25,154
Buildings and improvements	20,328
Machinery and equipment	59,290
Furniture and fixtures	22,944
Leasehold improvements	5,245

These dollar amounts represent the original cost of the assets.

c.   In terms of dollars, machinery and equipment experienced the largest increase ($16,480). In percentage terms, land increased by 90%. Increases in productive capacity should lead to increased sales revenues.

d.   Adaptec does not expect that adoption of SFAS 121 will have a material impact on its financial condition and results of operations. This fact increases our confidence in the stated balance sheet amounts.

e.   Adaptec acquired $68,621 thousand of assets as the result of several
     acquisitions: tangible assets ($8,108), in-process technology ($52,313), and
     goodwill ($8,200). The in-process technology was written off in 1996.

f.   Adaptec's manufacturing facility is located in Singapore. The location
     decision was surely influenced by the tax holiday offered by the Singapore
     government. Labor costs were probably another motivation.

g.

                        Other assets ($millions)

     ───
                    A   66,000
                    B   14,650 │ 422   D
                    C   8,200 │ ─────
                   end   88,428 │

     A   advance payments to TSMC (20,000 + 46,000)
     B   deposit paid to TSMC
     C   goodwill from acquisitions
     D   unexplained difference (probably due to goodwill amortization)

◄ CHAPTER 5 ►

Analyzing Investing Activities: Special Topics

◄ CHAPTER REVIEW ►

Intercompany and international activities play an increasingly larger role in business activities. Companies pursue intercompany activities for several reasons including diversification, expansion, and competitive opportunities and returns. International activities provide similar opportunities but offer unique and often riskier challenges. This chapter considers our analysis and interpretation of these company activities as reflected in financial statements.

We consider current reporting requirements from our analysis perspective--both for what they do *and* do not tell us. We describe how current disclosures are relevant for our analysis, and how we might usefully apply analytical adjustments to these disclosures to improve our analysis. We direct special attention to the unrecorded assets and liabilities in intercompany investments, the interpretation of international operations in financial statements, and the risks assumed in intercompany and international activities.

◄ CHAPTER OUTLINE ►

Section 1: Intercompany Activities

▸ **Intercorporate Investments**

    Consolidated Financial Statements

    Equity Method Accounting

    Analysis Implications of Intercorporate Investments

▸ **Business Combinations**

    Pooling versus Purchase Accounting for Business Combinations

    Accounting Mechanics of Business Combinations

    Analysis Implications of Business Combinations

Section 2: International Activities

▸ **Reporting of International Activities**

    International Accounting and Auditing Practices

    Translation of Foreign Currencies

    Analysis Implications of Foreign Currency Translation

◄ Learning Objectives ►

- **Analyze financial reporting for intercorporate investments.**

- **Interpret consolidated financial statements.**

- **Analyze implications of purchase and pooling accounting for business combinations.**

- **Interpret goodwill arising from business combinations.**

- **Describe international accounting and auditing practices.**

- **Analyze foreign currency translation disclosures.**

- **Distinguish between foreign currency translation and transaction gains and losses.**

◄ Answers to Questions ►

1. Liabilities shown in the consolidated financial statements do not operate as a lien upon a common pool of assets. The creditors, secured and unsecured, have recourse in the event of default only to assets owned by the individual corporation which incurred the liability. If, on the other hand, a parent company guarantees a specific liability of a subsidiary then the creditor would, of course, have the guarantee as additional security.

   The consolidated balance sheet obscures rather than clarifies the margin of safety enjoyed by specific creditors. To gain full comprehension of the financial position of each part of the consolidated group, the analyst needs to examine the individual financial statements of each subsidiary.

2. From the legal standpoint, the statement is basically correct. However, consolidated financial statements are not prepared as a legal document. Consolidated financial statements disregard the legal technicalities in favor of business substance and reflect the economic reality of a business entity under centralized control. From the financial analysts' viewpoint, consolidated statements are often more meaningful than separate financial statements for a fair presentation of financial condition and results of operation.

3. a.   NC (no consolidation)
   b.   NC
   c.   NC
   d.   NC
   e.   C   (consolidation)
   f.   NC
   g.   C

4. Consolidated financial statements generally represent the most meaningful presentation of the financial condition and the results of operations of a group. However, they do have limitations:

   (1)   The financial statements of the individual companies in the group may not be prepared on a comparable basis. Accounting principles applied and valuation bases/amortization rates used may differ thereby destroying homogeneity and the validity of ratios, trends, and relationships.

   (2)   Companies in relatively poor financial condition may be combined with sound companies, obscuring information necessary for analysis.

   (3)   The extent of intercompany transactions is unknown unless *consolidating* financial statements are presented. The latter reveal the adjustments involved in the consolidation process.

   (4)   Unless specifically disclosed, it may be difficult to establish how much of consolidated retained earnings is actually available for payment of dividends.

(5)   The composition of the minority interest (e.g., as between common and preferred) cannot be determined because the minority interest is generally shown as a combined amount in the consolidated balance sheet.

(6)   Consolidated financial statements do not reveal restrictions on use of cash for individual companies or intercompany cash flows.

(7)   Consolidation of nonhomogeneous subsidiaries (e.g., finance or insurance subsidiaries) can distort ratios and other relations.

5. a. Yes. It is a subsequent event required to be disclosed. Conditions of contingent additional consideration are adequately disclosed; however, it would have been more informative had the note disclosed the market value of net assets or stocks issued.

    b. The acquisition does not qualify as a pooling of interests because there is contingent additional consideration involved. It has to be accounted for by the purchase method. Since the more readily determinable value in this case is the consideration given in the form of the Best Company's stock, the investment should be recorded at $1,057,386 (48,063 shares x $22.00). In a consolidated statement there may or may not be goodwill to be recognized because net book value of $1,016,198 may not reflect market value of the net assets.

    c. In this case, the contingency is based on the performance of the acquired companies over the next five years but the total amount payable in stock is limited to $2 million.

    d. During the course of the next five years, if the acquired companies earn cumulatively over $1 million, then the Best Company will record the additional payment when the outcome of the contingency is determined beyond a reasonable doubt. The payments are considered additional consideration in the purchase and will either increase the carrying values of tangible assets or the "excess of cost over net tangible assets" (i.e., goodwill) account.

6. a. The total cost of the assets is the present value of the amounts to be paid in the future. If the debt security has been issued at an interest rate which is substantially above or below the current effective rate for a similar security, the appropriate amount of premium or discount should be recorded.

    b. The general rule for determining the total cost of the assets acquired is to value the assets acquired at the fair value of the stock given (as traded in the market) or fair value of assets received, whichever is more clearly evident. If there is no ready market for either the securities or the assets acquired, the valuation has to be based on the best means of estimation, including a detailed review of the negotiations leading up to the purchase and the use of independent appraisals.

7. a. Goodwill represents the excess of the total cost over the fair value assigned to identifiable assets acquired less liabilities assumed.

    b. It is possible that market values of identifiable assets acquired less liabilities assumed exceed the cost of the acquired company. In this case, the values otherwise assignable to noncurrent assets acquired should be reduced by a proportionate part of the excess (except for marketable securities). Negative goodwill should not be recorded unless the value assigned to such long-term assets is first reduced to zero. If negative goodwill is justifiably recorded, it should be amortized to income over the period estimated to be benefited (but not in excess of 40 years).

    c. Marketable Securities: Recorded at current net realizable values.

    d. Receivables: Recorded at the present value of amounts to be received, determined at appropriate current interest rates, less allowances for uncollectibility and collection costs.

    e. Finished Goods: Recorded at selling prices less cost of disposal and reasonable profit allowance.

    f. Work-in-Process: Recorded at estimated selling price of finished goods less the sum of the costs to complete, costs of disposal, and a reasonable profit allowance.

    g. Raw Materials: Recorded at current replacement costs.

    h. Plant and Equipment: Recorded at current replacement costs unless the expected future use of the assets indicates a lower value to the acquirer.

    i. Land and Mineral Reserves: Recorded at appraised values.

    j. Payables: Recorded at present values of amounts to be paid, determined at appropriate current interest rates.

    k. The goodwill of the acquired company cannot be carried forward to the acquiring company's books.

8. No. If the acquiring company's stock is an acceptable consideration to seller, it is proof that the stock has a value equivalent to the assets given up by the seller. Stock which represents a claim to a share of a company is as valid a resource as is cash. The mere fact that stock is given in the exchange is not a sufficient reason for accounting under the pooling-of-interests method.

9. Since Company A will record assets acquired at the book values carried on Company B's books, such nonrecording of asset values for which Company A actually paid generally results in an overstatement of income and an understatement of assets. This is the primary reason why earnings which are the result of pooling combinations are viewed as being of lower quality than similar earnings resulting from purchase accounting.

10. Goodwill is simply ignored under the pooling-of-interests method even though consideration may have in fact been given for it. Assets acquired are carried at book value rather than the fair (market) value and the goodwill is omitted from the acquiring company's balance sheet.

11. a. Since assets are understated, the fundamental equation of a double-entry bookkeeping system results in an understatement of the capital account. This, in turn, will result in the overstatement of the return on investment.

    b. The understatement of assets such as inventory, property, plant and equipment, as well as goodwill and other intangibles will lead to an understatement of expenses such as cost of goods sold, depreciation, and amortization. The result is an overstatement of income.

    c. Since assets were originally recorded at an unrealistically low amount, disposition of such assets invariably will result in a gain on sale which is not truly attributable to the acquiring entity. When this gain is included in the results of operations, the reported income is overstated. Note, however, that sales of significant assets are generally prohibited within the first two years after the combination.

12. A crude way of adjusting for omitted values in a pooling is to determine the difference between the market value and the recorded value of net assets acquired and to amortize the difference on some reasonable basis. The result would be approximately comparable to the income achieved under purchase method. However, the information usually available for such adjustments is limited.

13. Generally, the purchase method is preferable from the analyst's viewpoint. Since purchase accounting recognizes the acquisition values on which the buyer and seller actually bargained, the balance sheet reflects more realistically the valuation of assets and the income statement better reflects the actual results of operations.

14. The analyst should be alerted to the propriety of the valuation of the net assets acquired in the combination. In periods of high market price levels, purchase accounting may introduce inflated values when net assets, and particularly the intangibles, of acquired companies are valued on the basis of the market price of the stock issued. Such values, while determined on the basis of temporarily inflated stock prices, remain on a company's balance sheet and affect its operating results on a long-term basis.

15. Although APB Opinion No. 17 allows that a payment made in anticipation of future earnings (goodwill) should be recovered from those earnings over a period which cannot exceed 40 years, the analyst must be alert to the possibility that many companies will use the maximum period of amortization rather than the reasonable estimate of useful life which is also called for by APB Opinion No. 17. Moreover, the amount at which goodwill is often carried on the acquirer's books bears little relationship to its real value which must be based on the demonstrated superior earning power of the acquired enterprise.

16. a.   By purchasing companies with lower P/E ratios, Company X can, in effect, "buy" earnings. For example, let us say that Company X earns $1,000,000 or $1.00/share on 1,000,000 shares, and that its P/E = 50x. Let us say that it purchases Company Y for 10x earnings of $5,000,000, or 1,000,000 shares.

The new earnings: X $5,000,000
                Y   +1,000,000
                    $6,000,000

The new number of shares outstanding is 2,000,000, providing an EPS of $3.00. Therefore, the earnings per share has increased from $1.00 to $3.00 by means of this acquisition.

Synergistic effect (1+1=3): Sometimes two companies combined can do better than the total effect of each separately, through combination of producing and selling companies, or combining sales and accounting for better distribution, or saving freight by better geographical spread of plants.

Company S: P/E = 10x
                     EPS = $1.00
                     Earnings= $1,000,000
                     Number of shares= 1,000,000

Company Y: P/E = 10x
                     Earnings= $1,000,000

X buys Y for a steal at 10x earnings and assumes $1,000,000 after-tax savings from efficiencies.

New earnings:

X earnings	$1,000,000
Y earnings	1,000,000
Savings resulting from merger	1,000,000
New earnings	$3,000,000
New number of shares	2,000,000
New EPS	$1.50

Therefore, the EPS increased 50 percent as a result of the merger.

b.   Statements should be pooled as if X and Y had been merged prior to the years under consideration with intercompany sales, if any, eliminated. This would give the best indication of the earnings potential. Adjusting backwards to reflect merger savings subsequently realized is considered a bit tenuous. It is recommended to use the actual combined figures, with mental adjustments by the analyst. Too many of these "adjusted for merger savings" statements bear little relation to the historical record. Also, the analyst may want to compare Company X's actual results with the new merged company's record to get an idea of the success of the program.

One trick is to look for companies with a fair Year 1 and Year 2 and a good Year 3 as acquisition candidates, since the Year 3 pooled statements then look good in comparison with pooled years 1 and 2. "Company X only" figures would show if this device is being used.

17. All factors supporting the original estimates should be reexamined in the light of current conditions. Some examples of circumstances which could affect these factors are:

- A new invention which renders a patented device obsolete.
- Significant shifts in customer preferences for styling.
- Regulatory sanctions against a segment of the business.
- Reduced market potential because of increase in number of competitors.

18. Problems in accounting for foreign operations can be grouped into two broad classifications:

   (1)   Those problems related to differences in accounting principles, auditing standards, and practices which are peculiar to the foreign country in which the operations are conducted.

   (2)   Those problems which arise from the translation of foreign assets, liabilities, equities, and results of operations into the U.S. dollars.

19. The analyst should realize that there are differences in accounting principles among countries and should become familiar with the foreign accounting practices. The analyst should also verify the reputation of foreign independent auditors before relying on them. The analyst should also be familiar with the provisions of SFAS 52 governing the translation of foreign financial statements into dollars.

20. SFAS 52 has as its major objectives: (1) to provide information that is generally compatible with the expected economic effects of a change in exchange rate on an enterprise's cash flows and equity, and (2) to reflect in consolidated statements the financial results and relationships as measured in the primary currency of the economic environment in which the entity operates which is referred to as its functional currency.

In adopting the functional currency approach, the Board had the following objectives of foreign currency translation in mind:

   (1)   To present the consolidated financial statements of an enterprise in conformity with U.S. generally accepted accounting principles.

   (2)   To reflect in consolidated financial statements the financial results and relationships of the individual consolidated entities as measured in their functional currencies.

The Board's approach is to report the adjustment resulting from translation of foreign financial statements not as a gain or loss in the income of the period but as a separate accumulation as part of equity.

21. The major provisions of SFAS 52 are:

The translation process requires that the functional currency of the entity be identified first. Ordinarily it will be the currency of the country in which the entity is located or the U.S. dollar. All financial statement elements of the foreign entity must then be measured in terms of the functional currency in conformity with U.S. generally accepted accounting principles.

Translation from the functional currency into the reporting currency, if they are different, is to be at the current exchange rate except that revenues and expenses are to be translated at the average exchange rates prevailing during the period. The functional currency translation approach generally considers the effect of exchange rate changes to be on the net investment in a foreign entity rather than on its individual assets and liabilities (which was the focus of SFAS 8).

Translation adjustments are not included in net income but are disclosed and accumulated as a separate component of stockholders' equity until such time that the net investment in the foreign entity is sold or liquidated. To the extent that the sale or liquidation represents realization, the relevant amounts should be removed from the separate equity component and included as a gain or loss in the determination of the net income of the period during which the sale or liquidation occurs.

Exchange gains and losses attributable to intercompany foreign currency transactions and balances that are of a trading nature, are to be included in income, while those that are of a long-term financing or capital nature for which settlement is not contemplated in the foreseeable future are to be reported in the separate component of shareholders' equity.

22. The following two circumstances require use of the temporal method of translation.

(1) When by its nature, the foreign operation is merely an extension of the parent and consequently the dollar is its functional currency.

(2) When hyperinflation (as defined) causes the translation of nonmonetary assets at the current rate to result in unrealistically low carrying values. In such cases, in effect, the foreign currency has lost its usefulness as a measure of performance and a more stable unit (i.e., the dollar) is used.

23. The following are some implications for analysis:

(1) While unquestionably insulating income from balance sheet translation gains and losses, as opposed to transaction gains and losses and income statement translation effects, SFAS 52 introduced a translation exposure which differs from that of SFAS 8.

(2) Under SFAS 8, the translation exposure was measured by the excess of monetary assets over monetary liabilities (or vice versa). Under SFAS 52 all balance sheet items, except the net equity, are translated at the current rate; thus, the exposure is measured by the size of the net equity or net investment.

(3) While under SFAS 52 net income is not affected by balance sheet translation, the equity capital is. This affects the debt-equity ratio (the level of which may be specified by certain debt covenants) and book value per share of the translated balance sheet, but not of the foreign currency balance sheet. Since the entire equity capital is the measure of exposure to balance sheet translation gain or loss, that exposure may be even more substantial than that under SFAS 8 particularly with regard to a subsidiary financed with low debt and high equity. The analyst can estimate the translation adjustment impact by multiplying year-end equity by the estimated change in the period to period rate of exchange.

(4) The effect of a change in exchange rates on the translation of the income statement is another matter. Under SFAS 52 translated reported earnings will vary directly with changes in exchange rates, and this makes estimation by the analyst of the "income statement translation effect" easier. Estimation of earnings under SFAS 8 was more difficult.

The analyst must also be aware that in addition to the above, income will also include the results of completed foreign exchange transactions. Also, any gain or loss on the translation of a current payable by the subsidiary to parent (which is not of a long-term capital nature) will pass through consolidated net income.

◄ Answers to Exercises ►

Exercise 5-1

a. Each of the four corporations will maintain separate accounting records based on its own operations (e.g., C1's accounting records are not affected by the fact that it has only one stockholder).

b. For public reporting, consolidated statements would be presented for Co. X + C1 + C2 as if the three separate legal entities were *one* entity. C1 or C2 would probably not be consolidated if controlled only temporarily. C3 would be shown as a *one-line consolidation* (both balance sheet and income statement) under the equity method.

c. The financial analyst could request as much of the following as needed for the analysis assuming that he/she is able to convince the company of these needs (since only the consolidated statements would normally be available publicly).

    1. Consolidated Co. X plus subsidiaries C1 and C2 (C3 would be a one-line consolidation).

    2. Co. X statements only (all three investee companies, C1, C2, and C3 would be one-line consolidations).

3.   Separate statements for one or more of the investee companies (C1, C2, and C3).

4.   Consolidating statements (which would provide everything in 1-3 above except separate statements for C3, and would also show the elimination entries).

5.   Sometimes partial consolidations (e.g., Co. X plus C2) or combining statements (e.g., only C1 and C2) may be useful. For example, if C1 is a foreign subsidiary, the analyst may ask for a partial consolidation excluding C1, with separate statements for C1. Also, loan covenants (or loan collateral) frequently cover only selected companies, and a partial consolidation or combined statements are necessary.

d.   Co. X will show an asset "investment in common stock of subsidiary" valued at either cost or equity. (The equity method would be required only if no consolidated statements were presented.) Note: Co. X owns shares of common stock of C1--Co. X does not own any of C1's assets or liabilities.

e.   Instead of an "investment in subsidiary," Co. X's balance sheet would now include all of the assets and liabilities of C1.

f.   No change. Consolidated financial statements present two or more legal entities as if they are one.

g.   100 percent of C2's assets and liabilities are included in the consolidated balance sheet. The stockholders' equity of C2 is split into two parts: 80 percent is added to the stockholders' equity of Co. X and 20 percent is shown on a separate line (above Co. X's stockholders' equity) as "minority ownership of C2" (frequently just "minority interest"). The portion of the 80 percent representing the past purchase by Co. X would be eliminated (in consolidation) against the "investment in subsidiary."

h.   Co. X must purchase enough additional common stock from other stockholders in C3 or new shares issued by C3 to increase its ownership to more than 50 percent of C3's common stock. (Or C1 or C2 could purchase the additional shares.)

i.   Probably. There would be no intercompany investment or intercompany dividends. But any other intercompany transactions must be eliminated (e.g., intercompany sales, intercompany receivables and payables).

j.   No change. There would be a two-step consolidation (first C1 plus C2, then Co. X plus C1 consolidated). Any gain or loss on the transaction would be eliminated in consolidation.

k.   No change. The additional investment for Co. X would be eliminated against the additional invested capital for C1 in the consolidation.

<u>Exercise 5-2</u>

a. Goodwill does not arise and, therefore, should not be reported if the business combination is accounted for as a pooling of interests. The recorded assets and liabilities of the separate companies generally become the recorded assets and liabilities of the combined corporation. However, goodwill should be reported if the business combination is accounted for as a purchase.

b. All identifiable assets acquired, either individually or by type, and liabilities assumed in a business combination, whether or not shown in the financial statements of Moore, should be assigned a portion of the cost of Moore, normally equal to their fair values at date of acquisition. Then, the excess of the cost of Moore over the sum of the amounts assigned to identifiable assets acquired less liabilities assumed should be recorded as goodwill.

c. Minority interest should be reported whether the business combination is accounted for as a purchase or a pooling of interests. The amount of minority interest reported would be the same whether the business combination is accounted for as a purchase or a pooling of interests.

d. Consolidated financial statements should be prepared in order to present financial position and operating results in a manner more meaningful than in separate statements.

e. The usual first necessary condition for consolidation is control, as evidenced by ownership of a majority voting interest. As a general rule, ownership by one company, directly or indirectly, of over fifty percent of the outstanding voting shares of another company is a condition necessary for consolidation.

f. Consolidated financial statements should be prepared whether a business combination is accounted for as a purchase or a pooling of interests. Control exists and is independent of the method of accounting used.

<u>Exercise 5-3</u>

a. *Comparable Approach*: This approach attempts to restate the earnings figures on a comparable basis using US GAAP, International Accounting Standards Committee standards, or another enterprise's accounting practices in an appropriate model developed by the investor.

   Assessment of the Quality of Earnings: In assessing the quality of earnings, a scale or standard is developed by the investor. This scale or standard may incorporate considerations for such accounting choices as inventory valuation, depreciation methods, accounting for pensions as well as the treatment of accounting for research and development.

   Cash Flow Basis: Applied on a world-wide basis, an attempt is made to analyze the cash flows of the investment. Consideration of cash flow definitions may include cash from operations, earnings before interest and taxes (EBIT), or changes in the financial position. The overriding rule is analyze the investment from a cash flow perspective.

Adopt the Foreign Corporation's Financial Statements: Here an attempt is made to analyze the foreign corporation's financial statements from the perspective of a local investor and apply local valuation methods. This may include a comparison with local enterprises since their financial statements are assumed to be prepared on a similar and comparable basis.

Asset Valuation Model: A financial analyst may attempt to mark the assets to market values and then subtract the indebtedness to arrive at a value for the enterprise.

Dividend Valuation Model: Using a dividend valuation approach, the investor may focus on dividends (and not earnings) to arrive at an estimated value of the investment.

b. 1. An upward revaluation of fixed assets would increase depreciation expense on the income statement and reduce net income. A downward revaluation of fixed assets would reduce depreciation expense on the income statement and increase net income. Under US GAAP, except in rare cases, only the downward revaluation of fixed assets is permitted. In some foreign countries, upward revaluation is also permitted as well as current expensing of a fixed asset which can greatly distort net income for an accounting period.

2. The amortization of goodwill reduces net income. Under US GAAP, goodwill can only be amortized if purchased and is carried on the balance sheet. The amortization is for forty years or the useful life of the goodwill, whichever is less.

In some foreign countries, purchased goodwill can be written off against shareholders' equity immediately. Immediate write off of goodwill against shareholders' equity results in higher future earnings due to the absence of amortization charges. In countries where goodwill is recorded and amortized, the longer (shorter) the amortization period, the higher (lower) reported earnings will be. The International Accounting Standards Committee has a proposal that provides for five years amortization unless a longer period can be justified.

3. As the name implies, discretionary reserves are up to the discretion of management. The primary impact of discretionary reserves on net income is to smooth the net income, allowing management to "look better" in bad years.

The creation of a discretionary reserve, when charged to income, lowers net income in that year. Absence of the charge in a later year, or use of the reserve to cover expenses of that year, increases net income in the later year.

Discretionary reserves against fixed assets (revaluation or impairment) will affect future depreciation charges and therefore net income. "Excess" depreciation charges can also be used to lower net income in a good year.

<u>Exercise 5-4</u>

a. 1. *Functional currency*: The functional currency approach presumes an enterprise may operate and generate cash flows in a number of separate economic environments. The currency in that primary economic environment is the functional currency for those operations. It is also presumed that the company may commit to a long-term position in a specific economic environment and does not currently intend to liquidate that position.

Most companies will probably consider each foreign country in which they do business as a primary economic environment for operations in that country and, therefore, the functional currency for the company's operation will probably be the local currency.

2. *Translation*: This is where a company converts a financial statement in foreign currency to dollar financial statements. As exchange rates move, translation adjustments are produced during this process because assets and liabilities are translated in current exchange rates while equity accounts are translated in historical rates. Because the translation process is performed only for the purpose of preparing financial statements and it does not anticipate that the foreign currency accounts will be liquidated and exchanged into dollars, translation adjustments are not included in income but are deferred as adjustments to the equity (net worth) section in the balance sheet.

Essentially, the translation process expresses the functional currency net assets, at their dollar equivalent--using the current rate--and creates an adjusting entry to balance the dollar net worth. The translation adjustment does not affect net income until a specific investment is wholly or substantially liquidated. At that time, the component of the translation adjustment account related to that specific investment is removed from the translation adjustment account and included in the determination of gain or loss on sale of the investment.

3. *Remeasurement*: Transactions may be denominated in a foreign currency (e.g. purchases payable in French francs), but these transactions may be measured also in another currency different from where they are denominated. This process is called *remeasurement*. It is accomplished by assuming that an exchange of currencies will occur at the exchange rate prevailing on the date of the remeasurement. This may produce a foreign exchange gain or loss if the exchange fluctuates between the date of the original transaction and the date of the assumed exchange. Foreign exchange gains or losses are similar to other trading activities that are included in income.

Remeasurement under FASB 52 is very similar to translation under FASB No. 8. Under the functional currency approach, which does accept multiple units of measure, remeasurement is required only when:

  ■   the accounts of an entity are maintained in a currency other than its functional currency is, or

- an entity is a party to a transaction which produces a monetary asset or liability denominated in a currency other than its functional currency.

b. A fundamental problem arises in the translation of foreign currency financial statements when non-monetary assets are translated in current exchange rates and the functional currency is highly inflationary. This situation is referred to as "disappearing plant." FASB 52 has tried to address itself to this problem. The special provision of FASB 52 requires that the dollar be the presumptive functional currency when the economic environment is highly inflationary. The prescribed test for a highly inflationary economy is the accumulative inflation of approximately 100% over a three-year period. Therefore, by requiring companies in highly inflationary economies to be remeasured to a dollar basis, FASB 52 avoids the erosion of non-monetary accounts (e.g., property and plant) that otherwise would arise from translation and current exchange rates.

Exercise 5-5

a. In pooling, acquisition is made by payment in stock rather than in cash and/or debt as in the purchase method of acquisition. Where consolidation is on a pooling basis:

- Assets of the acquired firm are carried at book value (with a purchase they are restated to fair value plus perhaps a "goodwill" item).
- The total retained earnings of the acquired firm are carried on the consolidated statement (with a purchase only the retained earnings from the date of acquisition).

The "hidden" items are best viewed in terms of what is *not* shown in pooling that is shown in purchasing.

- The payment for a pooling is by stock. Because the assets of the acquired are at book value, the offsetting entry for the issuance of the stock is at that same value. For instance, there may have been one million shares given (market value $100 million) but they may only show up at $10 million on the consolidated statement—if the net book value acquired is only $10 million. Therefore, the total capital invested is greatly understated and the rate of return is automatically higher.

- In a purchase, goodwill will be amortized and will reduce the profits after the merger. As no goodwill is recorded in pooling, reported profits are higher.

- In a purchase, the depreciation charges may be higher because fixed assets are stated at fair value (assumed greater than book). Because of this, the profits will be less. There is no restatement in pooling so higher profit is reported.

- In a purchase, the inventory may be revalued (fair value) which would probably increase the Cost of Goods Sold, thus decreasing profits. This does not occur in pooling (assets at book value); therefore, profits are reported higher.

b. All in all, the pooling "hides" the cost of the acquired firm, and overstates resulting profits and return on investment—compared to the purchase method. Analysis is obviously affected in all the above ways. One *crude* way to at least partially adjust for this is to value the stock given at market and put in some part of the excess as goodwill, which you would then amortize in an attempt to get at more realistic profits and rate of returns.

Exercise 5-6

a. The choice of the functional currency would make no difference on reported sales because sales are translated at rates on the transaction date or average rates regardless of the choice of the functional currency.

b. When the functional currency is the local currency (Star Company), all assets and liabilities are translated at current exchange rates, and common and preferred stock are translated at historic rates. The translation gain or loss is based on the net investment in each local currency.

When the U.S. dollar is the functional currency (Bethel), then some assets and liabilities (mainly inventory and fixed assets) are translated at historic rates. Monetary assets and liabilities are translated at current exchange rates. Therefore, the translation gain or loss is based only on those assets and liabilities which are translated at current rates.

c. When the functional currency is the local currency, the translation gain or loss appears on the balance sheet as a separate component of shareholders' equity, thus bypassing the income statement. However, remeasurement gains or losses are included in net income.

When the U.S. dollar is the functional currency, all translation gains or losses are included in reported net income.

(CFA)

◄ Answers to Problems ►

Problem 5-1

a. They are shown in "other assets" [166] at $155.8 million under investments in affiliates, which includes $28.3 million as goodwill.

b. No

c. It indicates that of $180.1 million paid, $132.3 million was for intangibles, principally goodwill [107]. This means that most of the purchase price was in effect for some form of superior earning power assumed to be enjoyed by the acquired companies.

d.

Working capital items	5.1
Fixed assets—net	4.7
Intangibles, principally goodwill	132.3
Other assets	1.5
Minority interest	36.5
Cash (or other consideration)	180.1

e. The change in the cumulative translation adjustment accounts [101] for Europe is most likely due to significant translation losses in Year 11. In Australia the decrease in the credit balance of the account may be due to sales of businesses by Armotts Ltd. [169A] which may have involved the removal of a proportionate part of the account as well as gains or losses on translation in Year 11. This is corroborated by item [93] showing a reduction in the cumulative translation account due to sales of foreign operations.

Problem 5-2

a. The assets of and liabilities to Fisher Price have been aggregated and segregated in the following accounts:
- [61] Net current assets of discontinued operations
- [68] Net non-current assets of discontinued operations
- [76] Payable to Fisher-Price

b. The intangible account [67] which is primarily goodwill has been level, with only small declines, being less than amortization reported [143]. There seems to be no disclosure which would explain the increasing level of goodwill amortization (Year 9=$55.6, Year 10=$71.2, and Year 11=$86.5 million.)

c. Gains and losses on these foreign currency forward contracts [160] would be reflected in the cumulative exchange adjustment account [88].

d. Because of the hyper-infationary conditions the functional currency of these subsidiaries will be deemed to be the U.S. dollar. Consequently, the temporal method of translation will apply and translation gains and losses will be reflected in income.

Problem 5-3

a. For Year 6:
- No effect on sales.
- Net income equals dividend income of $10 (1% of $1,000, or $1 per share). Assuming the shares are classified as available-for-sale (a reasonable assumption given the subsequent purchases), the price appreciation of $1 per share will bypass the imcome statement.
- Cash flow equals dividend income of $10. (If the outflow due to the stock purchase is included: Net cash flow = dividend income less purchase price = $10 - $100 = -$90).

For Year 7, the equity method applies:
- No effect on sales.
- Net income equals percentage share of Francisco earnings for Year 7, or 30% of $2,200 = $660.

- Cash flow equals dividend income or 30% of $1,200 = $360. (If the outflow due to the stock purchase is included: Net cash flow = dividend income less purchase price = $360 - 3,190 = -$2,830).

b. At December 31, Year 6, the carrying value of the investment in Francisco is $110 (10 shares @ $11 per share). The $11 per share figure is the fair value at 1/1/Year 7.

For Year 7, the equity method applies:

First, the equity method should be applied retroactively to the prior years of ownership (i.e., Year 6):

Original cost (10 shares @ $10)	$100
Add: Percentage share of Year 6 earnings (1% of $2,000)	20
Less: Dividends received in Year 6	(10)
Net carrying value—January 1, Year 7	$110

Second, the equity method should be carried through the end of Year 7.

Net carrying value—January 1, Year 7	$ 110
Add: Original cost of additional shares (290 shares @ $11)	3,190
Add: Percentage share of Year 7 earnings (30% of $2,200)	660
Less: Dividends received in Year 7	(360)
Net carrying value—December 31, Year 7	$3,600

c. For Year 8, with ownership in excess of 50% (i.e., 100%), the financial statements of Francisco would be consolidated with those of Potter. Two basic methods of consolidation are available in accounting for the investment: pooling of interests and purchase. This situation does not meet several of the mandatory requirements to allow a pooling of interests:

- Potter is not allowed to hold more than 10% of the outstanding common stock of Francisco prior to the combination. (It held 30% in Year 7.)
- The combination should be effected in a single transaction (not 3 as in this case), or within one year (not 2+ as in this case).
- The combination should involve the issuance of voting common stock for voting common stock for at least 90% of the purchase price (not sold for cash as in this case).

Therefore, the purchase method is the only available choice. Under this method, all assets and liabilities for Francisco are restated to fair market value. In order to do this, one needs to know fair market values. Also, information about off-balance sheet items (e.g., contingencies, pensions) which may need to be recognized would need to be known. Due to these changes in asset and liability values, an initial purchase price in excess of the book value does not necessarily indicate that goodwill exists.

Problem 5-4

a.

Current Assets	$135
Land	70
Building	130
Equipment	130
Goodwill	35 *
Total Assets	500
Current Liabilities	$140
Long-term Liabilities	180
Shareholders' Equity	180
Total Liab/Equity	$500

*Goodwill:

Payment	$180
Fair value of net assets (165 - 20)	145
	35

b.   The basic difference between pooling and purchase is that in the pooling case the unrecording or suppression of assets values for which the acquiring company paid generally results in an understatement of assets and an overstatement of income. Pooling only uses current book values, which do not necessarily reflect current fair market values; thus it tends to understate assets. The understatement of assets under the pooling method leads to not only an understatement of expenses but to an overstatement of gains realized on their disposition.

Problem 5-5

a.

	Investment	Income
Cost of Acquisition	40,000	
Earnings for Year 6	1,600 (1)	
Amortization of goodwill	(500) (2)	
Dividends for Year 6	(800) (3)	
Earnings pickup, Year 6		1,100 (4)
Loss for Year 7	(480) (5)	(480) (5)
Amortization of goodwill	(500) (2)	(500) (2)
Dividends for Year 7	(640) (6)	
Earnings pickup, Year 7		(980) (4)
Investment @ 12/31/Year 7	38,680	

(1)	80% of 2,000		
(2)	Cost of 80% interest in Bowman	=	40,000
	Less 80% of net assets of 25,000	=	20,000
	Excess of cost over net assets	=	20,000
	Amortization over 40 years	=	20,000 + 40 = 500
(3)	80% of 1,000		
(4)	earnings - amortization		
(5)	80% of (600)		
(6)	80% of 800		

b.   Strengths associated with use of the equity method include:
•   Reduction in balance of investment account in Year 7 due to net loss. Just recording dividend income would obscure the loss.
•   Recognition of goodwill on balance sheet reflects full cost of investment.

Possible weaknesses include:
•   Lack of detailed information (one-line consolidation).
•   Unrealistic amortization of goodwill.
•   Dollar earned by Bowman may not be equivalent to dollar earned by Burry.

◄ Answers to Cases ►

Case 5-1
a.   Future Domain: $25 million cash purchase

Power I/O: $7 million cash purchase

Trillium: $3 million cash purchase

Incat: $17 million purchase via issuance of 385,000 common shares plus contingent consideration

b.   Connectivity Solutions Group (CSG) of Western Digital: $33 million cash purchase plus contingent consideration

Cogent Data Technologies, Inc.: $68 million pooling via issuance of $68 million in common stock

c.   The companies listed in part a "design and develop high performance I/O products, networking technologies and software for recordable CD peripherals for both consumer and enterprise computing markets." The CSG "designs, manufactures and markets controller Ics for high-capacity disk drives." Cogent "provides high performance Fast Ethernet products for the networking market."

All of the acquisitions are related to Adaptec's core business. Given that the operating results of the acquired companies are immaterial relative to Adaptec's reported results, there is no track record to examine. Thus, to assess the business potential of the acquired entities, the analyst must seek information outside of Adaptec's financial statements (e.g, trade publications, management, etc.).

d.   1. $52 million
       2.   If Adaptec was not permitted to write off in-process technology, this amount would probably be treated as goodwill. Thus, the accounting permits Adaptec to "front load" the expense and avoid annual amortization.
       3.   The write off reduces current assets, book value, and earnings. Future earnings will appear larger.

e. According to note five, $8,200 thousand of goodwill was recorded in fiscal 1996. The amount amortized in 1996 is not stated, nor is the amount (if any) existing at the beginning of 1996. It appears that Adaptec reports goodwill under "Other assets."

f. According to note one, Adaptec minimizes its exposure to foreign currency exchange risk by selling primarily in U.S. dollars.

Case 5-2

a. 1.
Investment in Wheal	110,000	
Capital Stock		110,000

2.
Investment in Wheal	350,000	
Capital Stock		110,000
Other Contributed Capital		240,000

b. 1.
Capital Stock S	100,000	
Other Contributed Capital S	10,000	
Investment in Wheal		110,000

2.
Inventory	25,000	
Property, Plant, and Equipment	100,000	
Secret Formula	30,000	
Goodwill	40,000	
Long-Term Debt	2,000	
Accounts Receivable		5,000
Accrued Employee Pensions		2,000
Investment in Wheal		190,000

Capital Stock S	100,000	
Other Contributed Capital S	35,000	
Retained Earnings S	35,000	
Investment in Wheal		160,000

c. Consolidated Retained Earnings, 12/31/x4

	Pooling	Purchase
Retained Earnings, Axel	$150,000	$150,000
Retained Earnings, Wheal	35,000	--
Consolidated Retained Earnings . . .	$185,000	$150,000

Case 5-3

a.   With the dollar as the functional currency, FI originally translated using
      the "temporal method" per FASB 52. Now that the pont is the functional
      currency, FI must use the "all-current method" as follows:

	Ponts (Millions)	Exchange Rate Ponts/$	Dollars (Millions)
Balance Sheet			
Cash	82	4.0	20.50
Accounts receivable	700	4.0	175.00
Inventory	455	4.0	113.75
Fixed assets (net)	360	4.0	90.00
	1,597		399.25
Accounts payable .	532	4.0	133.00
Capital stock . . .	600	3.0	200.00
Retained earnings .	465		132.86
Translation adjustment =			(66.61)*
	1,597		399.25
Income Statement			
Sales	3,500	3.5	1,000.00
Cost of sales .	(2,345)	3.5	(670.00)
Depreciation Expense	(60)	3.5	(17.14)
Selling expense .	(630)	3.5	(180.00)
	465		132.86

*Translation Adjustment = 600 (1/3 - 1/4)   = 600 (1/12) =   (50)
                        + 465 (1/3.5 - 1/4) = 465 (1/28) =   (16.61)
                                                              (66.61)

b.   1.   Dollar: Inventory and fixed assets translated at historical rates.
                       Translation gain (loss) computed based on net monetary
                       assets.

            Pont: All assets and liabilities translated at current exchange
                       rates. Translation gain (loss) computed based on net
                       investment (all assets and liabilities).

      2.   Dollar: Cost of sales and depreciation expenses translated at
                       historical rates. Dollar: Translation gain (loss) included
                       in net income (volatility increased).

            Pont: All revenues and expenses translated at average rates for
                       period. Translation gain (loss) in separate component of
                       stockholder equity. Net income less volatile.

      3.   Dollar: Financial statement ratios skewed.
            Pont: Ratios in dollars same as ratios in ponts.

a.

SWISCO
12/31/19x8

	Trial Balance (in SFR)	Translation Rate $/SFR		Trial Balance (in Dollars)
Cash	50,000	C	.38	19,000
Accounts Receivable	100,000	C	.38	38,000
Property, Plant, and Equipment, net	800,000	C	.38	304,000
Depreciation Expense	100,000	A	.37	37,000
Other Expenses (including taxes) .	200,000	A	.37	74,000
Inventory 1/1/19x8	150,000	A	(1)	56,700
Purchases	1,000,000	A	.37	370,000
	2,400,000			898,700
Sales	2,000,000	A	.37	740,000
Allowance for Doubtful Accounts . .	10,000	C	.38	3,800
Accounts Payable	80,000	C.	.38	30,400
Note Payable	20,000	C	.38	7,600
Capital Stock	100,000	H	.30	30,000
Retained Earnings 1/1/19x8	190,000		(2)	61,000
Translation Adjustment			(3)	25,900
	2,400,000			898,700

   (1) = Forced dollar amount needed to state cost of goods sold at average rate as follows:

	SFR		Rate	$	
Inventory 1/1/19x8	150,000			56,700	Plug
Purchases	1,000,000	A	.37	370,000	
	1,150,000			426,700	
Inventory 12/31/x8	120,000	C	.38	45,600	
Cost of Goods sold	1,030,000	A	.37	381,100	

(2)   Dollar balance at 12/31/x7
(3)   Forced Amount

C = Current rate; A = Average rate; H = Historical rate

b.

SWISCO
Income Statement (In Dollars)
For the Year ending 12/31/19x8

Sales		$740,000	
Beginning Inventory	$56,700		(1)
Purchases	$ 370,000		
	426,700		
Ending Inventory (SFR 120,000 = $.36)	45,600		(1)
Cost of Goods Sold		381,100	
Gross Profit		358,900	
Depreciation Expense	37,000		
Other Expenses (including taxes) .	74,000	111,000	
Net Income		$247,900	

(1) See Note 1 to translated trial balance.

SWISCO CORP.
Balance Sheet (In Dollars)
At 12/31/19x8

Assets

Cash		$19,000	
Accounts Receivable	$38,000		
Less: Allowances for Doubtful Accounts . . .	3,800	34,200	
Inventory		45,600	A
Total Current Assets		98,800	
Property, Plant, and Equipment, net		304,000	
Total Assets		$402,800	

Liabilities and Equity

Accounts Payable		$30,400	
Note Payable		7,600	
Total Liabilities		38,000	
Capital Stock		30,000	
Retained Earnings: 1/1/19x8	$61,000		
Add: Income for 19x8	247,900	308,900	
Equity Adjustment from Translation of Foreign Currency			
Statements		25,900	B
Stockholders' Equity		364,800	
Total Liabilities and Equity		$402,800	

A.   Ending Inventory SFR 120,000 × .38
B.   First time this account appears in financial statements.

c.   Investment in Swisco Corporation   185,925
         Equity in Subsidiary's Income   185,925

To record 75% equity in Swisco Subsidiary's reported
earnings (in dollars) of $247,900.

Note: While not specifically required by the problem, it should be noted that the parent will also pick up the translation adjustment as follows:

Investment in Swisco Corporation   19,425
      Equity adjustment from translation of
        foreign currency statements (75% × $25,900)   19,425

◄ CHAPTER 6 ►

Analyzing Operating Activities: Income

◄ CHAPTER REVIEW ►

Income is the residual of revenues and gains *less* expenses and losses. Net income is measured using the accrual basis of accounting. Accrual accounting recognizes revenues and gains when earned, and recognizes expenses and losses when incurred. The income statement (also referred to as statement of operations or earnings) reports net income during a period of time. This statement also reports income components--revenues, expenses, gains, and losses. We analyze income and its components to *evaluate company performance, assess risk exposures, and predict amounts, timing, and uncertainty of future cash flows*. While "bottom line" net income frames our analysis, income components provide pieces of a mosaic revealing the economic portrait of a company.

This chapter examines the analysis and interpretation of income components. We consider current reporting requirements and their implications for our analysis of income components. We describe how we might usefully apply analytical adjustments to income components and related disclosures to better our analysis. We direct special attention to revenue recognition and the recording of major expenses and costs. Further use and analysis is made of income components in Part Three of the book.

◄ CHAPTER OUTLINE ►

▸ **Income Measurement**

▸ **Revenue and Gain Recognition**

       Guidelines for Revenue Recognition

       Uncertainty in Revenue Collection

       Revenue When Right of Return Exists

       Franchise Revenues

       Products Financing Arrangements

       Transfers of Receivables with Recourse

       Recognition at Completion of Production

       Revenue under Contracts

       Unearned Finance Charges

       Recognizing "Sales" to Leasing Subsidiaries

       Analysis Implications of Revenue Recognition

▸ **Expense and Loss Accruals**

       Depreciation and Depletion

       Pensions

       Other Postretirement Employee Benefits

       Supplementary Employee Benefits

       Research, Exploration, and Development

       Goodwill Amortization

       Interest on Liabilities

       Income Taxes

       Extraordinary Items and Discontinued Operations

▸ **Accounting Changes**

       Change in Accounting Principle

       Change in Accounting Estimate

       Change in Reporting Entity

       Correction of an Error

       Analysis Implications of Accounting Changes

▸ **Comments on Income Analysis**

▸ **Appendix 6A Earnings per Share: Computation and Analysis**

◄ Learning Objectives ►

- **Analyze revenue recognition and its risks for financial analysis.**

- **Describe depreciation and depletion of assets.**

- **Evaluate pension and other postretirement costs.**

- **Analyze expenditures for research, development, and exploration.**

- **Interpret goodwill and its implications for financial analysis.**

- **Describe interest expense and accounting for income taxes.**

- **Analyze extraordinary items and discontinued operations.**

- **Interpret accounting changes and error corrections.**

- **Analyze and interpret earnings per share data (Appendix 6A).**

◄ Answers to Questions ►

1. The income statement portrays the net results of operations of an enterprise. Since results are what enterprises are supposed to achieve and since their value is, in large measure, determined by the size and quality of these results, it follows that the analyst attaches great importance to the income statement.

2. The following criteria exemplify the rules which have been established to prevent the premature anticipation of revenue. Realization is deemed to take place only after the following conditions have been met:

   (1) The earning activities undertaken to create revenue have been substantially completed, e.g., no significant effort is necessary to complete the transaction.

   (2) In the case of a sale, the risk of ownership has been effectively passed on to the buyer.

   (3) The revenue, as well as the associated expenses, can be measured or estimated with substantial accuracy.

   (4) The revenue recognized should normally result in an increase in cash, receivables, or marketable securities and, under certain conditions, in an increase in inventories or other assets, or a decrease in a liability.

   (5) The business transactions giving rise to the income should be at arm's-length with independent parties (i.e., not with controlled parties).

   (6) The transactions should not be subject to revocation, e.g., carrying the right of return of merchandise sold.

3. SFAS 48, "Revenue Recognition When Right of Return Exists," specifies that revenue from sales transactions in which the buyer has a right to return the product should be recognized at the time of sale only if all of the following conditions are met:

   ■ At the date of sale, the price is substantially fixed or determinable.
   ■ The buyer has paid the seller, or is obligated to pay the seller (not contingent on resale of the product).
   ■ In the event of theft or physical damage to the product, the buyer's obligation to the seller would not be changed.
   ■ The buyer acquiring the product for resale has economic substance apart from that provided by the seller.
   ■ The seller does not have significant obligations for future performance to directly bring about resale of the product.
   ■ Product returns can be reasonably estimated.

If these conditions are not met, revenue recognition is postponed; if they are met, sales revenue and cost of sales should be reduced to reflect estimated returns and expected costs or losses should be accrued. Note: The Statement does not apply to accounting for revenue in service industries if part or all of the service revenue may be returned under cancellation privileges granted to the buyer, transactions involving real estate or leases, or sales transactions in which a customer may return defective goods, such as under warranty provisions.

4. Some of the factors that might impair the ability to predict returns (when right of return exists in the transaction) are: (1) susceptibility to significant external factors, such as technological obsolescence or swings in market demand, (2) long return privilege periods, and (3) absence of appropriate historical return experience.

5. Unlike SFAS 45 and 48, which deal with the timing of revenue recognition, SFAS 49, "Accounting for Product Financing Arrangements," is concerned with the issue of whether revenue has been earned.

A product financing arrangement is an agreement involving the transfer or sponsored acquisition of inventory which, although it resembles a sale, is in substance a means of financing inventory through a second party. For example, if a company transfers inventory to another company in an apparent sale, and in a related transaction agrees to repurchase the inventory at a later date, the arrangement may be a product financing arrangement rather than a sale and subsequent purchase of inventory.

If the party bearing the risks and rewards of ownership transfers inventory to a purchaser, and in a related transaction agrees to repurchase the product at a specified price, or guarantees some specified resale price for sales of the product to outside parties, the arrangement is a product financing arrangement and should be accounted for as such.

6. The *percentage-of-completion method* is preferred when estimates of costs to complete and estimates of progress toward completion of the contract can be made with reasonable dependability. A common basis of profit estimation is to record that part of the estimated total profit which corresponds to the ratio that costs incurred to date bear to expected total costs. Other methods of estimation of completion can be based on units completed or on qualified engineering estimates or on units delivered.

The *completed-contract method* of accounting is preferable where the conditions inherent in the contract present risks and uncertainties which result in an inability to make reasonable estimates of costs and completion time. Problems under this method concern the point at which completion of the contract is deemed to have occurred as well as the kind of expenses to be deferred. For example, some companies defer all costs to the completion date, including general and administrative overhead while others consider such costs as period costs to be expensed as they are incurred.

Under either of the two contract accounting methods, losses, present or anticipated, must be fully provided for in the period in which the loss first becomes apparent.

7. The recording of revenue is the first step in the process of income determination and one on which the recognition of any and all profit depends. The analyst should be particularly inquisitive about the accounting methods chosen.

One element which casts doubt on the recording of revenue is uncertainty about the collectibility of the resulting receivable. Special problems of collectibility exist with respect to installment sales, real estate sales, and franchise sales. Problems of collection exist, however, in the case of all sales and the analyst must be alert to them.

The analyst must also be alert to the problems related to the timing of revenue recognition. The present rules generally do not allow for recognition of profit in advance of sale--increases in market value of property such as land or equipment, the accretion of values in growing timber, or the increase in the value of inventories are not recognized in the accounts. As a consequence, income will not be recorded before sale and the timing of sales is a matter which lies within the discretion of management. That, in turn, gives management a certain degree of discretion in the timing of profit recognition.

In the area of contract accounting, the analyst should recognize that the use of the completed contract method is justified only in cases where reasonable estimates of costs and the degree of completion are not possible. Yet, some companies consider the choice of method a matter of discretion.

Other alternative methods of taking up revenue, as in the case of lessors or finance companies, must be fully understood by the analyst before he/she attempts an evaluation of a company's earnings or a comparison among companies in the same industry.

8. *Variable costs* are those which vary in direct proportion to activity, whether the latter is measured by means of sales, production, or other gauges. For example, in the manufacture of electric cable, the consumption of copper wire may be said to vary in direct proportion to a given unit of wire length. The higher the cable sales figure the higher the copper wire cost. In practice many costs, while varying somewhat in proportion to activity, do not vary in exact proportion to it and are usually referred to as *semivariable costs*.

   Fixed costs are those which remain relatively constant over a considerable range of activity. Rent, property taxes, and insurance are examples of fixed costs. No category of cost can remain fixed indefinitely. For example, after reaching a certain level of activity an enterprise will have to rent additional space, thus bringing the rent expense to a higher level.

9. The quoted observation is correct in pointing out that the analyst must subject the data available on an entity's depreciation policies to critical analysis and scrutiny. On the basis of such analysis, in the absence of more precise data, the analyst is still better off in adjusting the depreciation charges on the basis of his/her estimates and assumptions than not adjusting them at all.

10. There are a number of measures relating to plant assets which are useful in comparing depreciation policies over time as well as for intercompany comparisons.

The *average total life span* of plant and equipment can be approximated as follows:

Gross Plant and Equipment ÷ Current Year Depreciation Expense.

The *average age* of plant and equipment can be computed as follows:

Accumulated Depreciation ÷ Current Year Depreciation Expense.

The *average remaining life* of plant and equipment is computed as follows:

Net Depreciated Plant and Equipment ÷ Current Year Depreciation Expense.

As can be seen from the computations above, and as is logical:

Average Total Life Span = Average Age + Average Remaining Life.

The above ratios are helpful in assessing an enterprise's depreciation policies and assumptions over time. The ratios can be computed on a historical cost basis as well as on a current cost basis.

11. The reason pension costs are reduced by the expected (rather than actual) return on plan assets is that use of the actual return would subject pension costs to the fluctuations of the financial markets, creating volatility in annual costs.

12. Periodic pension costs are smoothed by several aspects of pension accounting including: (1) use of expected versus actual return on plan assets, (2) valuing pension assets on a market-related versus a market basis (3) amortization of deferred cost elements such as prior service cost, net gains/losses, and unrecognized transition costs.

13. Management can exercise latitude over the amount of pension expense recorded through its selection of expected return on plan assets and choice of assumptions regarding future levels of inflation.

14. Pension costs may appear as part of a company's operating expenses (e.g., cost of goods sold or compensation expense) or capitalized into assets such as inventory.

15. The following three fundamental aspects of pension accounting are retained by the accounting firm OPEB:

Net cost reporting. The consequences of events and transactions affecting the OPEB plans are reported as a single amount. That amount includes at least three components: (1) the present value of the accrued cost of the promise of deferred compensation in the form of OPEB in exchange for employee service, (2) the interest cost accruing from the passage of time until these benefits are paid and (3) the returns from the investment in plan assets.

Delayed Recognition. Certain changes in OPEB obligations, including those arising as a result of a plan initiation or amendment, and certain changes in the value of plan assets set aside to meet that obligation are recognized systematically over future periods rather than as they occur. These measures are designed to insulate current costs from fluctuations in values and other factors.

Offsetting. Plan assets restricted for the payment of OPEB benefits offset the Accumulated Postretirement Benefit Obligation {APBO) in determining amounts recognized in the employer's statement of financial position.

16. While the estimation process for OPEB costs is similar to that of estimating pension costs it is more difficult and more subjective. First, data about current costs are harder to obtain. Pension benefits involve either fixed dollar amounts or a defined dollar amount, based on pay levels. Health benefits, by contrast, are estimates not easily computed by actuarial formula. Many factors enter in to such estimates, including deductibles, ages, marital status, number of dependents, etc. Second, more assumptions than those governing pension calculations are needed. In addition to retirement dates, life expectancy, turnover, and discount rates there is a need for estimates of the medical costs trend rate, Medicare reimbursements, etc.

17. Accounting for stock options has improved with the introduction of SFAS 123, "Accounting for Stock-Based Compensation." Until this pronouncement, the accounting was based on the notion that an option to buy stock at a price as of the date of grant for a number of years was not a measurable value. Thus, there was a failure to reflect in operating expenses the compensation granted to employees.

Under SFAS 123 companies may continue to avoid expense recognition of the cost of options granted, but must provide disclosure of pro forma net income and earnings per share numbers using an estimate of the fair value of the options granted.

18. SFAS 2, "Accounting for Research and Development Costs," offers a simple solution to the complex problem of accounting for research and development costs--they should be charged to expense when incurred.

The Board defines research and development activities as follows:

(1)   *Research activities* are aimed at discovery of new knowledge for the development of a new product or process or in bringing about a significant improvement to an existing product or process.

(2)   *Development activities* translate the research findings into a plan or design for a new product or process or a significant improvement to an existing product or process.

(3)   R&D specifically excludes routine or periodic alterations to ongoing operations and market research and testing activities. The Board recommended the following accounting treatment for R&D costs:

  (a)   The majority of expenditures incurred in research and development activities as defined above constitutes the costs of that activity and should be charged to expense when incurred.

(b)   Costs of materials, equipment, and facilities that have alternative future uses (in research and development projects or otherwise) should be capitalized as tangible assets.

(c)   Intangibles purchased from others for R&D use that have alternative future uses should also be capitalized.

(d)   Indirect costs involved in acquiring patents should be capitalized as well.

(4)   Elements of costs that should be identified with R&D activities are:

    (a)   Costs of materials, equipment, and facilities that are acquired or constructed for a particular research and development project and purchased intangibles, that have no alternative future uses (in research and development projects or otherwise).

    (b)   Costs of materials consumed in research and development activities, the depreciation of equipment or facilities, and the amortization of intangible assets used in research and development activities that have alternative future uses.

    (c)   Salaries and other related costs of personnel engaged in R&D activities.

    (d)   Costs of services performed by others.

    (e)   A reasonable allocation of indirect costs. General and administrative costs that are not clearly related to R&D activities should be excluded.

The disclosure requirements as stipulated by SFAS 2 are as follows: (1) for each income statement presented, the total R&D costs charged to expense shall be disclosed, and (2) government-regulated companies that defer R&D costs in accordance with the addendum to SFAS 2 must make certain additional disclosures to that effect.

19.   In order to form an opinion on the quality and the future potential value of research outlays, the analyst needs to know a great deal more than the totals of periodic research and development outlays. The analyst needs information on (1) the types of research performed, (2) the outlays by category, (3) the technical feasibility, commercial viability, and future potential of each project assessed and reevaluated at the time of each periodic report, and (4) information on a company's success-failure experience in its several areas of research activity to date. Of course, present disclosure requirements will not give the analyst such information and it appears that, except in cases of voluntary disclosure, only the investor or the lender with the necessary clout will be able to obtain such information.

In general, one can assume that the outright expensing of all research and development outlays will result in more conservative balance sheets and fewer painful surprises stemming from the wholesale write-offs of previously capitalized research and development outlays. However, the analyst must realize that along with a lack of knowledge about future potential he/she may also be unaware of the potential disasters which can befall an enterprise tempted or forced to sink ever greater amounts of funds into research and development projects whose promise was great but whose failure is nevertheless inevitable.

20.   One of the most common solutions applied by analysts to the complex problem of the analysis of goodwill is to simply ignore it. That is, they ignore the asset

shown on the balance sheet. As for the income statement they have the assistance of accountants in trying to ignore its effect, i.e., the amortization of goodwill has in the past been the exception rather than the rule. Moreover, even in those cases where amortization occurred, the expense is treated with a skepticism which implies a questioning of its real nature. In fact, by ignoring goodwill, analysts ignore investments of very substantial resources in what may often be a company's most important asset.

Ignoring the impact of goodwill on reported periodic income is no solution to the analysis of this complex cost. Even considering the limited amount of information available to the analyst, it is far better that he/she understand the effects of accounting practices in this area on reported income rather than dismiss them altogether.

Goodwill is measured by the excess of cost over the fair market value of tangible net assets acquired in a transaction accounted for as a purchase. It is the excess of the purchase price over the fair value of all the tangible assets acquired, arrived at by carefully ascertaining the value of such assets. That is the theory of it.

The financial analyst must be alert to the makeup and the method of valuation of the Goodwill account as well as to the method of its ultimate disposition. One way of disposing of the Goodwill account, frequently chosen by management, is to write it off at a time when it would have the least serious impact on the market's judgment of the company's earnings, e.g., a time of loss or reduced earnings.

Under normal circumstances goodwill is not indestructible but is rather an asset with a limited useful life. Whatever the advantages of location, market dominance and competitive stance, sales skill, product acceptance, or other benefits are, they cannot be unaffected by the passing of time and by changes in the business environment. Thus, the amortization of goodwill gives recognition to the expiration of a resource in which capital has been invested, a process which is similar to the depreciation of fixed assets. The analyst must recognize that a forty-year amortization period, while adhering to minimum accounting requirement of APB Opinion No. 17, which represents a compromise position, may not be realistic in terms of the time expiration of economic values. Thus, he/she must assess the propriety of the amortization period by reference to such evidence of continuing value as the profitability of units for which the goodwill consideration was originally paid.

21. The interest cost to an entity is the nominal rate paid including, in the case of bonds, the amortization of bond discount or premium. A complication arises when companies issue convertible debt or debt with warrants, thus achieving a nominal debt coupon cost which is below the cost of similar debt not enjoying these added features.

   After trial pronouncements on the subject and much controversy, APB Opinion No. 14 concluded that in the case of convertible debt the inseparability of the debt and equity features is such that no portion of the proceeds from the issuance should be accounted for as attributable to the conversion feature.

In the case of debt issued with stock warrants attached, the proceeds of the debt attributable to the warrants should be accounted for as paid-in capital. The corresponding charge is to a debt discount account which must be amortized over the life of the debt issue thus increasing the effective interest cost.

22. a.   SFAS 34, "Capitalization of Interest Cost," requires capitalization of interest cost as part of the historical cost of "assets that are constructed or otherwise produced for an enterprise's own use (including assets constructed or produced for the enterprise by others for which deposits or progress payments have been made)." Inventory items that are routinely manufactured or produced in large quantities on a repetitive basis do not qualify for interest capitalization. The objectives of interest capitalization according to the FASB are (1) to measure more accurately the acquisition cost of an asset, and (2) to amortize that acquisition cost against revenues generated by the asset.

      b.   The amount of interest to be capitalized is based on the entity's actual borrowings and interest payments. The rate to be used for capitalization may be ascertained in this order: (1) the rate of specific borrowings associated with the assets and (2) if borrowings are not specific for the asset, or the asset exceeds specific borrowings therefore, a weighted average of rates applicable to other appropriate borrowings may be used. Alternatively, a company may use a weighted average of rates of all appropriate borrowings regardless of specific borrowings incurred to finance the asset.

      c.   Interest capitalization may not exceed total interest costs for any period, nor is imputing interest cost to equity funds permitted. A company without debt will have no interest to capitalize. The capitalization period begins when three conditions are present: (1) expenditures for the asset have been made by the entity, (2) work on the asset is in progress, and (3) interest cost is being incurred. Interest capitalization ceases when the asset is ready for its intended use.

23. The net income computed on the basis of generally accepted accounting principles (also known as "book income") is often not identical to the "taxable income" computed on the entity's tax return. This is due to two types of difference. Permanent differences (discussed here) and temporary, or timing, differences (see question 26).

Permanent differences result from provisions of the tax law under which:

      a.   Certain items may be nontaxable--e.g., income on tax exempt obligations and proceeds of life insurance on an officer

      b.   Certain deductions are not allowed--e.g., penalties for filing certain returns; fines, officer life insurance premiums.

      c.   Special deductions granted by law--e.g., dividend exclusion on dividends from unconsolidated subsidiaries and from dividends reserved from other domestic corporations.

24. The effective tax rate paid by a corporation on its income will vary from the statutory rate (e.g., 34 percent) because:

   a.   The basis of carrying property for accounting purposes may differ from that for tax purposes as a result of reorganizations, business combinations, etc.

   b.   Nonqualified as well as qualified stock-option plans may result in book-tax differences.

   c.   Certain industries, such as savings and loan associations, shipping lines, and insurance companies enjoy special tax privileges.

   d.   Up to $100,000 of corporate income is taxed at lower tax rates.

   e.   Certain credits may apply, e.g., R&D credits, foreign tax credits.

   f.   State and local income taxes, net of federal tax benefit, is included in total tax expense.

   What makes these differences and factors permanent is the fact that they do not have any future repercussions on a company's taxable income. Thus, they must be taken into account when reconciling a company's actual (effective) tax rate to the statutory rate.

25. SFAS 109, "Accounting for Income Taxes," establishes financial accounting and reporting standards for the effects of income taxes that result from an enterprise's activities during the current and preceding years, and requires an asset and liability approach. SFAS 109 requires that deferred taxes should be determined separately for each tax paying component (an individual entity or group of entities that is consolidated for tax purposes) in each tax jurisdiction. The determination includes the following procedures:

   - Identify the types and amounts of existing temporary differences and the nature and amount of each type of operating loss and tax credit carry forward, plus the remaining length of the carry forward period.
   - Measure the total deferred tax liability for taxable temporary differences, using the applicable tax rate.
   - Measure the total deferred tax asset for deductible temporary differences and operating loss carry forwards, using the applicable tax rate.
   - Measure deferred tax assets for each type of tax credit carry forward.
   - Reduce deferred tax assets by a valuation allowance if based on the weight of available evidence. it is more likely than not (a likelihood of more than 50 percent) that some portion or all of the deferred tax assets will not be realized. The valuation allowance should be sufficient to reduce the deferred tax asset to the amount that is more likely than not to be realized.

   Deferred tax assets and liabilities should be adjusted for the effect of a change in tax laws or rates. The effect should be included in income from continuing operations for the period that includes the enactment date.

26. 1.   Revenues or gains are included in taxable income later than they are included in pretax accounting income.

    2.   Expenses or losses are deducted in determining taxable income later than they are deducted in determining pretax accounting income.

    3.   Revenues or gains are included in taxable income earlier than they are included in pretax accounting income.

    4.   Expenses or losses are deducted in determining taxable income earlier than they are deducted in determining pretax accounting income.

27. The components of the net deferred tax liability or asset recognized in an enterprise's balance sheet should be disclosed as follows:

    ■   The total of all deferred tax liabilities.
    ■   The total of all deferred tax assets.
    ■   The total valuation allowance recognized for deferred tax assets.

    Additional disclosures include the significant components of income tax expense attributable to continuing operations for each year presented which include, for example:

    a.   Current tax expense or benefit.
    b.   Deferred tax expense of benefit (exclusive of the effects of other components listed below).
    c.   Investment tax credits.
    d.   Government grants (to the extent recognized as a reduction of income tax expense).
    e.   The benefits of operating loss carry forwards.
    f.   Tax expense that results from allocating certain tax benefits either directly to contributed capital or to reduce goodwill or other noncurrent intangible assets of an acquired entity.
    g.   Adjustments of a deferred tax liability or asset for enacted changes in tax laws or rates or a change in the tax status of the enterprise.
    h.   Adjustments of the beginning-of-year balance of a valuation allowance because of a change in circumstances that causes a change in judgment about the realizability of the related deferred tax asset in future years.

    Also to be disclosed is a reconciliation between the effective income tax rate and the statutory federal income tax rate. In addition, the amounts and expiration dates of operating loss and tax credit carry forwards for tax purposes shall be disclosed.

28. One of the flaws remaining in tax allocation procedures is that no recognition is given to the fact that a future obligation, or loss of benefits, should be discounted rather than shown at par as today's tax deferred accounts actually are. The FASB has reviewed the issue and decided not to address it because of the conceptual and implementation issues involved.

    Another flaw is that the Board allowed parent companies to avoid providing taxes on unremitted earnings of subsidiaries and other specialized exceptions to the requirements of deferred tax accounting.

29. APB Opinion No. 30 restricted the use of the "extraordinary" category by requiring that in order to qualify for this designation an item be both unusual in nature and infrequent of occurrence. It defined these terms as follows:

a. *Unusual nature* of the underlying event or transaction should possess a high degree of abnormality and be of a type clearly unrelated to, or only incidentally related to, the ordinary and typical activities of the entity, taking into account the environment in which the entity operates.

b. *Infrequency of occurrence* of the underlying event or transaction should be of a type that would not reasonably be expected to recur in the foreseeable future, taking into account the environment in which the entity operates.

Three examples of extraordinary items are:

- A major casualty loss, such as an earthquake.
- An expropriation of property.
- A gain or loss from a condemnation of land by eminent domain.

30. To qualify as a prior period adjustment, an item must meet all of the following requirements:

- Material
- Specifically identifiable with the business activities of particular prior periods
- Not attributable to economic events occurring subsequent to the prior period
- Dependent primarily on determinations by persons other than management
- Not susceptible of reasonable estimation prior to such determination

31. While there is need for full details of all normal operating elements of revenue and expense, the need for information regarding the nature of extraordinary gains and losses is even more essential. This is true because of the material nature of such items as well as the need to form judgments and conclusions regarding how they should be treated in an assessment of the overall results of operations and what probability of recurrence should be assigned to them. To the analyst who most carefully analyzes all elements of the income statement the exact positioning of the extraordinary item within the income statement is not of great import. He/she is much more concerned with the adequate description of the extraordinary item as well as the circumstances which gave rise to it.

32. If we accept the proposition that there is such a thing as "true" or "real" income, i.e., income that could be determined when all the facts are known and all the uncertainties are resolved, then it is obvious that most reported income must deviate somewhat from this ideal figure. We can never be sure about the useful life of an asset until it has actually come to an end; we cannot be certain about the value of a research project until it has seen its fruition, nor can we be certain about the revenue received from a transaction until the sales price is actually collected. There is nothing one can do about these

uncertainties except to estimate their ultimate disposition on the basis of the best information and judgment available. Periodic income reporting requires that we do not wait for final disposition of uncertainties but that we estimate them as best as we can. Such a system is subject to many errors: errors of estimation, errors of omission, and errors of commission. The better and the more conscientious a company's management and the better its internal controls the less likely it is that such errors will substantially distort reported results.

33. Income and expense distortions can be accomplished by means of the timing of transactions, the choice from a variety of generally accepted principles, the introduction of conservative or alternatively, very optimistic estimates, and the arbitrary choice of methods by which elements of income and expenses are presented or their nature is disclosed.

Generally, an enterprise wishing to benefit current income at the expense of the future will engage in one or a number of practices such as the following:

(1)   It will choose inventory methods which allow for maximum inventory carrying values and minimum current charges to cost of goods or services sold.

(2)   It will choose depreciation methods and useful lives of property which will result in minimum current charges as depreciation expense.

(3)   It will defer all managed costs to the future such as, for example: preoperating, moving, rearrangement and start-up costs, marketing costs. Such costs would be carried as deferred charges or included with the costs of other assets such as property, plant, and equipment.

(4)   It will amortize assets and defer costs over the largest possible period. Such assets include: goodwill, leasehold improvements, patents, and copyrights.

(5)   It will elect the method requiring the lowest possible pension and other employment compensation cost accruals.

(6)   It will inventory rather than expense administrative costs, taxes, etc.

(7)   It will choose the most accelerated methods of income recognition such as in the areas of leasing, franchising, real estate sales, and contracting.

(8)   It will take into income right away rather than defer the taking up of benefits such as investment tax credits.

Enterprises which wish to "manage" the size of reported income can regulate the flow of income and expense by means of reserves for future costs and losses.

26. (1) Depreciation

Straight Line: This is calculated by taking the salvage value (S) from the original cost (C) and dividing by the useful life of the asset in question; i.e., [C-S] / [Number of years].

Sum-of-Years'-Digits: This depreciation formula is: X/Y (C - S), where C and S are the same as above, X is the remaining years (i.e., if object is being depreciated over 5 years and this was the first year, then X=5), and Y equals the "sum-of-years'-digits" (i.e., for a 5 year asset, Y=5+4+3+2+1=15).

Straight line is easily understood and provides level taxes, depreciation and earnings whereas the sum-of-the-years'-digits gives heavier weight to earlier years and causes lower taxes and earnings in the early years and higher earnings toward the end of the asset's life.

(2) Inventory--can be valued on the LIFO (last-in, first-out) method or FIFO (first-in, first-out) method. The LIFO method assumes the assets employed were those most recently acquired in the inventory whereas FIFO assumes the first assets acquired were used. The effect on earnings depends on whether the economy is in an inflationary or deflationary period. In times of inflation, the usual case, LIFO inventory accounting would result in lower earnings being reported than would be the case had FIFO been employed.

(3) Installment sales--can assume all income is realized when the sale is made (accrual method) or that income is only received as the various installments come due (installment method). The installment method is almost always used for tax purposes while the accrual method is employed in shareholder reporting. The accrual method would result in a higher earnings figure being reported than the installment method. The combination of accrual method for sales and installment for tax calculation also produces a misleadingly high earnings figure.

35.   1. Changes in accounting principle
      2. Changes in accounting estimate
      3. Changes in reporting entity

A1.   The determination of the earnings level of an enterprise which is relevant to the purpose of the analyst is a complex analytical process. This earnings figure can be converted into a per-share amount which is useful in evaluating the price of the common stock, its dividend coverage, and the potential effects of dilution. As with any measure, there are strengths and weaknesses associated with its computation. Thus, the analyst must have a thorough understanding of the principles which govern the computation of earnings per share.

A2.   Earnings per share are used in making investment decisions. They are used in evaluating the past operating performance of a business and in forming an opinion as to its potential. They are commonly presented in prospectuses, proxy material, and reports to stockholders. They are used in the compilation of business earnings data for the press, statistical services, and other publications. When presented with formal financial statements, they assist the investor in weighing the significance of a corporation's current net income and of changes in its net income from period to period in relation to the shares he/she holds or may acquire.

Current GAAP regarding EPS has been revised in order to conform with international standards. While a degree of uniformity will be achieved, the analyst must be aware that basic EPS does not take into account securities which, although not common stock, are in substance equivalent to common stock. The analyst must take care to focus on diluted EPS, which intends to show the maximum extent of potential dilution of current earnings which conversions of securities could create.

A3. Diluted earnings per share is the amount of current earnings per share reflecting the maximum dilution that would have resulted from conversions, exercises, and other contingent issuances that individually would have decreased earnings per share and in the aggregate would have had a dilutive effect. All such issuances are assumed to have taken place at the beginning of the period (or at the time the contingency arose, if later).

A4. The amount of the loss should be increased by any cumulative dividends.

A5. Yes, the computation would assume that all the conversions took place at the beginning of the year.

A6. No, it is included in diluted earnings per share.

A7. The amount of any dividends on preferred stock which have been paid (declared) for the year should be deducted from net income before computing earnings per share.

A8. Yes, if warrants or options are present, an increase in the market price of the common stock can increase the number of common equivalent shares by decreasing the number of shares repurchasable under the treasury stock method.

A9. Antidilution is an *increase* in earnings per share resulting from the assumption that convertible securities have been converted, options and warrants have been exercised, or other shares have been issued upon the fulfillment of certain conditions.

For example. antidilutive conditions would exist when the dividend or interest requirement of a convertible security exceeds the current EPS multiplied by the number of common shares issuable upon conversion of that security. This may be illustrated as follows. Assume that current EPS is $0.97, preferred stock has a dividend requirement of $5.00 per share, and each share is convertible into two shares of common stock.

	Actual	Assumed Conversion
Net income for the year	$10,200	$10,200
Dividends on 100 shares of preferred stock	500	
Income applicable to common stock	$ 9,700	$10,200
Common shares outstanding	10,000	10,000
Assume conversion of 100 shares of preferred at 2 to 1		200
Adjusted shares outstanding	10,000	10,200
Earnings per share	$ 0.97	$ 1.00

The assumed conversion would result in an increase in EPS and consequently would be antidilutive.

A10. For options and warrants the treasury stock method of computing the dilution to be reflected in EPS should be used. Under the treasury stock method:

■ EPS is computed as if the options and warrants were exercised at the beginning of the period (or at time of issuance, if later) and as if the funds obtained thereby were used to purchase common stock at the average market price during the period, but

■ The assumption of exercise is not reflected in EPS until the market price of the common stock obtainable has been in excess of the exercise price for substantially all of three consecutive months ending with the last month of the period to which earnings per share relate.

■ The proceeds that would be obtained upon exercise of options and warrants are assumed to be used to purchase common stock at the average market price during the period.

A11. There is one exception to the use of the treasury stock method. Warrants or debt indentures may permit or require certain uses of funds in connection with exercise of warrants. Examples include:

■ Debt is permitted or required to be tendered toward exercise price.
■ Proceeds of exercise are required to retire debt.
■ Convertible securities require cash payments upon conversion.

In these cases, an "if converted" method which assumes conversion or exercise at the beginning of the period should be applied as if retirement or conversion of the securities had occurred and as if the excess proceeds, if any, had been applied to the purchase of common stock under the "treasury stock" method.

A12. SFAS 128 has a number of flaws and inconsistencies which the analyst must consider in interpreting EPS data:

(1) The computation of basic EPS completely ignores the potentially dilutive effects of options and warrants.

(2) There is a basic inconsistency in treating certain securities as the equivalent of common stock for purposes of computing EPS while not considering them as part of the stockholders' equity in the balance sheet. Consequently, the analyst will have difficulty in interrelating reported EPS with the debt-leverage position pertaining to the same earnings.

(3) Generally, EPS are considered to be a factor influencing stock prices. Whether options and warrants are dilutive or not depends on the price of the common stock. Thus we can get a circular effect in that the reporting of EPS may influence the market price which, in turn, influences EPS. Under these rules earnings may depend on market prices of the stock rather than only on economic factors within the enterprise. In the extreme, this suggests that the projection of future EPS requires not only the projection of earnings levels but also the projection of future market prices.

A13. a. See answer to question 6A-1.

b. Earnings per common share are not fully relevant to the valuation of preferred stock. For purposes of preferred stock evaluation, the earnings coverage ratio of preferred stock is among the most relevant. It measures the number of times preferred dividends have been earned and thus is a measure of the safety of the dividend as well as the safety of the preferred issue.

◄ Answers to Exercises ►

<u>Exercise 6-1</u>

a. 1.   Average total life span of plant and equipment:

<u>Gross plant and equipment</u>
Current year depreciation expense

        11   *10*

$$\frac{1883.6^a}{125.2^b} = \underline{15.04} \text{ years} \qquad \frac{1714.6^a}{103.5^b} = \underline{16.56} \text{ years}$$

[a]Total plant equipment ($1914.6 in Year 11, $1745.6 in Year 10) less land ($31.0 in both years) [146].

[b]Depreciation expense [125].

2.   Average age of plant and equipment:

<u>Accumulated depreciation</u>
Current year depreciation expense

        11   *10*

$$\frac{681.9^c}{125.2} = \underline{5.45} \text{ years} \qquad \frac{591.5^e}{103.5} = \underline{5.71} \text{ years}$$

[c]From balance sheet [65].

3.   Average remaining life of plant equipment:

<u>Net plant and equipment</u>
Current year depreciation expense

        11   *10*

$$\frac{1883.6 - 681.9^d}{125.2} = \underline{9.59} \text{ yrs} \qquad \frac{1714.6 - 591.5^d}{103.5} = \underline{10.85} \text{ yrs}$$

[d]Gross plant and equipment minus accumuated depreciation

b.   These ratios can be used to assess a company's depreciation policies within the company over time and for comparison purposes with other companies in the same industry. Care must be taken whenever comparisons are made between companies, for the reason that different depreciation methods and assumptions are used, creating results that can be substantially different. For example, Quaker Oats uses straight line depreciation for plant and equipment; another company may use an accelerated method such as double-declining-balance. For capital intensive companies, profit margins may not reflect the higher costs that may be expended to replace an older plant.

All three measures for Quaker decreased measurably from Year 10 to Year 11. This is most likely the result of Quaker's disposition of assets with relatively long useful lives (see [138]). Comparisons with similar companies should be made.

Exercise 6-2

a.   1.   Average total life span of plant and equipment:

$$\frac{\text{Gross plant and equipment}}{\text{Current year depreciation expense}}$$

$$11 \qquad\qquad\qquad\qquad 10$$

$$\frac{2538.0^a}{194.5^b} = \underline{13.05} \text{ years} \qquad \frac{2404.1^a}{184.1^b} = \underline{13.06} \text{ years}$$

[a]Buildings [159] ($758.7 in Year 11, $746.5 in Year 10) plus machinery and equipment [160] ($1779.3 in Year 11 and $1657.6 in Year 10).

[b]From Form 10-K, item [187].

2.   Average age of plant and equipment:

$$\frac{\text{Accumulated depreciation}}{\text{Current year depreciation expense}}$$

$$11 \qquad\qquad\qquad\qquad 10$$

$$\frac{1131.5^c}{194.5} = \underline{5.82} \text{ years} \qquad \frac{1017.2^c}{184.1} = \underline{5.53} \text{ years}$$

[c]From note 16 [162].

3.   Average remaining life of plant equipment:

Net plant and equipment
Current year depreciation expense

          11   10

$$\frac{2538.0 - 1131.5^d}{194.5} = \underline{7.23} \text{ yrs} \qquad \frac{2404.1 - 1017.2^d}{184.1} = \underline{7.53} \text{ yrs}$$

^{d}Gross plant and equipment minus accumuated depreciation

b.   These ratios can be used to assess a company's depreciation policies within the company over time and for comparison purposes with other companies in the same industry. Care must be taken whenever comparisons are made between companies, for the reason that different depreciation methods and assumptions are used, creating results that can be substantially different. For example, Quaker Oats uses straight line depreciation for plant and equipment; another company may use an accelerated method such as double-declining-balance. For capital intensive companies, profit margins may not reflect the higher costs that may be expended to replace an older plant.

The measures reveal no unusual changes. Comparisons with similar companies should be made.

Exercise 6-3

a.   The point of sale is the most widely used basis for the timing of revenue recognition because in most cases it provides the degree of objective evidence accountants consider necessary to measure reliably periodic business income. In other words, sales transactions with outsiders represent the point in the revenue generating process when most of the uncertainty about the final outcome of business activity has been alleviated. It is also at the point of sale in most cases that substantially all of the costs of generating revenues are known, and they can at this point be matched with the revenues generated to produce a reliable statement of a firm's effort and accomplishment for the period. Any attempt to measure business income prior to the point of sale would, in the vast majority of cases, introduce considerably more subjectivity into financial reporting than most accountants are willing to accept.

b.   1.   Though it is recognized that revenue is earned throughout the entire production process, generally it is not feasible to measure revenue on the basis of operating activity. It is not feasible because of the absence of suitable criteria for consistently and objectively arriving at a periodic determination of the amount of revenue to take up.

Also, in most situations the sale represents the most important single step in the earning process. Prior to the sale the amount of revenue anticipated from the processes of production is merely prospective revenue; its realization remains to be validated by actual sales. The accumulation of costs during production does not alone generate revenue; rather, revenues are earned by the entire process including making sales.

Thus, as a general rule the sale cannot be regarded as being an unduly conservative basis for the timing of revenue recognition. Except in unusual circumstances, revenue recognition prior to sale would be anticipatory in nature and unverifiable in amount.

2.   To criticize the sales basis as not being sufficiently conservative because accounts receivable do not represent disposable funds, it is necessary to assume that the collection of receivables is the decisive step in the earning process and that periodic revenue measurement, and therefore net income, should depend on the amount of cash generated during the period. This assumption disregards the fact that the sale usually represents the decisive factor in the earning process and substitutes for it the administrative function of managing and collecting receivables. In other words, the investment of funds in receivables should be regarded as a policy designed to increase total revenues, properly recognized at the point of sale; and the cost of managing receivables (e.g., bad debts and collection costs) should be matched with the sales in the proper period.

The fact that some revenue adjustments (e.g., sales returns) and some expenses (e.g., bad debts and collection costs) may occur in a period subsequent to the sale does not detract from the overall usefulness of the sales basis for the timing of revenue recognition. Both can be estimated with sufficient accuracy so as not to detract from the reliability of reported net income.

Thus, in the vast majority of cases for which the sales basis is used, estimating errors, though unavoidable, will be too immaterial in amount to warrant deferring revenue recognition to a later point in time.

c.   1.   *During production.* This basis of recognizing revenue is frequently used by firms whose major source of revenue is long-term construction projects. For these firms the point of sale is far less significant to the earning process than is production activity because the sale is assured under the contract, except of course where performance is not substantially in accordance with the contract terms.

To defer revenue recognition until the completion of long-term construction projects could impair significantly the usefulness of the intervening annual financial statements because the volume of completed contracts during a period is likely to bear no relationship to production volume. During each year that a project is in process a portion of the contract price is therefore appropriately recognized as that year's revenue. The amount of the contract price to be recognized should be proportionate to the year's production progress on the project.

It should be noted that the use of the production basis in lieu of the sales basis for the timing of revenue recognition is justifiable only when total profit or loss on the contracts can be estimated with reasonable accuracy and its ultimate realization is reasonably assured.

2. *When cash is received.* The most common application of this basis for the timing of revenue recognition is in connection with installment sales contracts. Its use is justified on the grounds that, due to the length of the collection period, increased risks of default, and higher collection costs, there is too much uncertainty to warrant revenue recognition until cash is received.

   The mere fact that sales are made on an installment contract basis does not justify using the cash receipts basis of revenue recognition. The justification for this departure from the sales depends essentially upon an absence of a reasonably objective basis for estimating the amount of collection costs and bad debts that will be incurred in later periods. If these expenses can be estimated with reasonable accuracy, the sales basis should be used.

   (AICPA)

Exercise 6-4

a. Michael Company should earn revenue as it performs the work on the contract (the percentage-of-completion method) because the right to revenue is established and collectibility is reasonably assured. Furthermore, the use of the percentage-of-completion method avoids distortion of income from period to period and provides for better matching of revenues with the related expenses.

b. Progress billings would be accounted for by increasing Accounts Receivable and increasing Progress Billings on Contract, a contra asset account that is offset against the Construction Costs in Progress account. If the Construction Costs in Progress account exceeds the Progress Billings on Contract account, the two accounts would be shown in the current assets section of the balance sheet. If the Progress Billings on Contract account exceeds the Construction Costs in Progress account, the two accounts would be shown, in most cases, in the current liabilities section of the balance sheet.

c. The income recognized in the second year of the four-year contract would be determined as follows:

   • First, the estimated total income from the contract would be determined by deducting the estimated total costs of the contract (the actual costs to date plus the estimated cost to complete) from the contract price.

   • Second, the actual costs to date would be divided by the estimated total costs of the contract to arrive at a percentage completed, which would be multiplied by the estimated total income from the contract to arrive at the total income recognized to date.

• Third, the total income recognized in the second year of the contract would be determined by deducting the income recognized in the first year of the contract from the total income recognized to date.

d. Earnings in the second year of the four-year contract would be higher using the percentage-of-completion method instead of the completed-contract method because income would be recognized in the second year of the contract using the percentage-of-completion method, whereas no income would be recognized in the second year of the contract using the completed-contract method.

Exercise 6-5

a. Crime Control's revenue recognition practices, while not the most conservative, conform to present GAAP. The important issue is whether lessees will, in fact, continue for their eight-year terms. Should large cancellations occur, substantial portions of the revenue recognized in earlier years may have to be reversed in subsequent years. This would result in distortions of earning power and earning trends. Thus, a critical issue of this accounting is whether the company provides adequately for contingencies such as cancellations. Should the pace of newly written sales-type leases shrink, the company's earnings growth may stop or earnings may even decline.

b. While the tax return accounting does provide the company with significant funds from tax postponement, it does not affect reported results because under present GAAP the company is required to provide for deferred taxes which it is assumed will be payable in the future.

c. While it is true that the sale of the receivables without recourse would enable the company to book profits in the year the lease is originated, this practice would at the same time substantially increase the company's tax bill.

Exercise 6-6

a. Some costs are recognized as expenses on the basis of a presumed direct association with specific revenue. This has been identified both as "associating cause and effect" and as the "matching concept."

    Direct cause-and-effect relationships can seldom be conclusively demonstrated, but many costs appear to be related to particular revenue, and recognizing them as expenses accompanies recognition of the revenue. Generally, the matching concept requires that the revenue recognized and the expenses incurred to produce the revenue be given concurrent periodic recognition in the accounting records. Only if effort is properly related to accomplishment will the results, called earnings, have useful significance concerning the efficient utilization of business resources. Thus, applying the matching principle is a recognition of the cause-and-effect relationship that exists between expense and revenue.

    Examples of expenses that are usually recognized by associating cause and effect are sales commissions, freight-out on merchandise sold, and cost of goods sold or services provided.

b.   Some costs are assigned as expenses to the current accounting period because (1) their incurrence during the period provides no discernible future benefits; (2) they are measures of assets recorded in previous periods from which no future benefits are expected or can be discerned; (3) they must be incurred each accounting year, and no buildup of expected future benefits occurs; (4) by their nature they relate to current revenues even though they cannot be directly associated with any specific revenues; (5) the amount of cost to be deferred can be measured only in an arbitrary manner or great uncertainty exists regarding the realization of future benefits, or both; and (6) uncertainty exists regarding whether allocating them to current and future periods will serve any useful purpose. Thus, many costs are called "period costs" and are treated as expenses in the period incurred because neither do they have a direct relationship with revenue earned nor can their occurrence be directly shown to give rise to an asset. The application of this principle of expense recognition results in charging many costs to expense in the period in which they are paid or accrued for payment.

Examples of costs treated as period expenses would include officers' salaries, advertising, research and development, and auditors' fees.

c.   A cost should be capitalized, that is, treated as an asset, when it is expected that the asset will produce benefits in future periods. The important concept here is that the incurrence of the cost has resulted in the acquisition of an asset, a future service potential. If a cost is incurred that resulted in the acquisition of an asset from which benefits are not expected beyond the current period, the cost may be expensed as a measure of the service potential that expired in producing the current period's revenues. Not only should the incurrence of the cost result in the acquisition of an asset from which future benefits are expected, but also the cost should be measurable with a reasonable degree of objectivity, and there should be reasonable grounds for associating it with the asset acquired.

Examples of costs that should be treated as measures of assets are the costs of merchandise on hand at the end of an accounting period, the costs of insurance coverage relating to future periods, and the costs of self-constructed plant or equipment.

d.   In the absence of a direct basis for associating asset cost with revenue, and if the asset provides benefits for two or more accounting periods, its cost should be allocated to these periods (as an expense) in a systematic and rational manner. When it is impractical, or impossible, to find a close cause-and-effect relationship between revenue and cost, this relationship is often assumed to exist. Therefore, the asset cost is allocated to the accounting periods by some method. The allocation method used should appear reasonable to an unbiased observer and should be followed consistently from period to period.

Examples of systematic and rational allocation of asset cost would include depreciation of fixed assets, amortization of intangibles, and allocation of rent and insurance.

e. A cost should be treated as a loss when an unfavorable event results from an activity other than a normal business activity. The matching of losses to specific revenue should not be attempted because, by definition, they are expired service potentials not related to revenue produced. That is, losses resulting from extraneous and exogenous events that are not recurring or anticipated as necessary in the process of producing revenue.

There is no simple way of identifying a loss, because ascertaining whether a cost should be a loss is often a matter of judgment. The accounting distinction between an asset, expense, loss, and prior-period adjustment is not clear cut. For example, an expense is usually voluntary, planned, and expected as necessary in the generation of revenue. But a loss is a measure of the service potential expired that is considered abnormal, unnecessary, unanticipated, and possibly nonrecurring and is usually not taken into direct consideration in planning the size of the revenue stream.

(AICPA)

Exercise 6-7

a. Reinvested earnings [112]   200.0
    Unexplained debit*   212.7
        Change in net assets of discontinued
            operations [61 + 68]   412.7

    *   Based on the information given in the financial statements and footnotes, we can assume that part of the unexplained debit is related to the reduction of long-term debt. Also included is a $30 million after tax loss from discontinued operations.

b. Revenues [144]   702.6
    Operating loss-net of tax [144]   (59.9)
    Expenses—net of tax
        benefit of 36.3 [144]   762.5

c. When estimating future earning power, the results from discontinued operations should not be treated as recurring.

Exercise 6-8

a. Some transactions affect the determination of net income for accounting purposes in one reporting period and the computation of taxable income and income taxes payable in a different reporting period. In accordance with the matching principle, the appropriate income tax expense represents the income tax consequences of revenues and expenses recognized for accounting purposes in the current period, whether those income taxes are paid or payable in current, future, or past periods.

b. When depreciation expense for certain machinery purchased this year is reported using the MACRS for income tax purposes and the straight-line basis for accounting purposes, a timing difference arises. Because more depreciation expense is reported for income tax purposes than for accounting purposes this year, pretax accounting income would be more than taxable income. The difference would create a credit to deferred income taxes equal to the difference in depreciation multiplied by the appropriate income tax rate.

When rent revenues received in advance this year are included in this year's taxable income and as unearned revenues, i.e., a current liability, for accounting purposes, a timing difference arises. Because rent revenues are reported this year for income tax purposes but not for accounting purposes, pretax accounting income would be less than taxable income. The difference would create a debit to deferred income taxes equal to the difference in rent revenues multiplied by the appropriate income tax rate.

c.   The income tax effect of the depreciation timing difference should be classified on the balance sheet as a noncurrent liability because the asset to which it is related is noncurrent. The income tax effect of the rent revenues received in advance timing difference should be classified on the balance sheet as a current asset because the liability to which it is related is current. The noncurrent liability and the current asset should not be netted on the balance sheet because one is current and one is noncurrent.

On the income statement, the income tax effect of the depreciation timing difference and the rent revenues received in advance timing difference should be netted. The amount should be classified as a deferred component of income tax expense.

Exercise 6-9
a.   The two accounting problems resulting from the nature of the defined benefit pension plan are as follows:

•   Estimates or assumptions must be made concerning the future events that will determine the amount and timing of the benefit payments.

•   Some approach to attributing the cost of pension benefits to individuals years of service must be selected.

The two problems arise because a company must recognize pension costs before it pays pension benefits.

b.   Carson should determine the service cost component of the net pension cost as the actuarial present value of pension benefits attributable to employee services during a particular period based on the application of the pension benefit formula.

c.   Carson should determine the interest cost component of the net pension cost as the increase in the projected benefit obligation due to the passage of time. Measuring the projected benefit obligation requires accrual of an interest cost at an assumed discount rate.

d.   Carson should determine the actual return on plan assets component of the net pension cost as the change in the fair value of plan assets during the period, adjusted for (1) contribution and (2) benefit payments.

<u>Exercise 6-10</u>

a. 1. The overall size of the post-retirement benefit obligation to be recognized by the more labor-intensive firm (Firm L) will be larger than for the other firm (Firm O) because it has a higher ratio of retirees to active employees, possesses an older work force, and has a strong union.

The more labor intensive nature of Firm L indicates a larger number of future retirees to provide for and thus a larger obligation. The higher ratio of retirees to active employees would imply that Firm L, as the current older work force retires, a greater obligation will be incurred. Firm L has a stronger union than Firm O, which does not have a direct effect on the size of an obligation under the present plan, but it may make it more difficult to undertake "containment measures" such as a reduction in benefits which would affect the size of any future obligation.

2. Again, the overall size of the post-retirement benefit cost reported by Firm L will be greater. Since Firm L is more labor intensive, this indicates a larger number of future retirees and thus a greater annual cost. However, although the absolute size of the cost under the new standard will be higher for Firm L, the percentage increase in cost will probably be lower than for Firm O. This is because Firm L has a relatively high ratio of retirees so that its pay-as-you-go current plan is already very high. Also, the effect of the new standard on Firm O is relatively greater because its current plan cost is relatively low.

The older work force of Firm L suggests that more of its employees are nearing retirement and eligibility for benefits. Thus, the present value of benefits earned in the current year (service cost) is likely to be higher for Firm L under the new standard.

Although the stronger unionization of Firm L does not have a direct bearing on current costs, it will be more difficult for Firm L to undertake "containment measures" such as reduction in benefits which would affect the costs at some later date.

In summary, although Firm L has a greater exposure to the cost of post-retirement benefits, its high pay-as-you-go current plan will increase by a lower percentage rate than firms with lower pay-as-you-go current plans.

b. The efficient market hypothesis has three forms, the weak, semi-strong, and strong form.

The weak form refers only to historical trading data. As accounting changes do not change such data but will change reported net income, the new standard may have an impact on stock prices probably causing them to decline.

The semi-strong form applies to publicly available data. The new standard is public knowledge, but the exact impact on the financial statements can only be estimated. To the extent that these estimates are accurate, adoption of the new standard will not affect stock prices since it is already fully reflected in the stock prices. Adoption would affect stock prices to the extent that the estimates fail to reflect non-public information. Only the "surprise" part of the accounting impact will affect stock prices.

Under the strong form, all information is fully reflected in stock prices, and adoption of the new standard will not have an effect on stock prices.

Under the circumstances, the semi-strong form appears to be most applicable to the adoption of the new standard. The new standard has been widely discussed, and estimates for major firms are readily available. If the estimates are accurate, then adoption of the new standard should have no effect on stock prices. Inaccurate estimates would have an effect on stock prices as the new information becomes available.

Exercise 6-11

a. By the use of reserves, a company can allocate costs in excess of actual experience in the current period, based on estimates of additional costs in the future, or even based on the simple possibility of further costs in the future. Then, in later periods, actual costs can be written off against the reserve rather than reported in the company's income statement for those periods. The advantage to the company is that earnings trends can be "smoothed" to a degree, and a cushion of future earnings can be built up during good economic years for use during weaker periods. To the extent that stability and predictability of earnings are market virtues, the company's common might be accorded a higher multiple for these efforts, in effect lowering the cost of capital to the company.

The use of reserves also poses problems for the analyst as well as conflicting with some basic trends of accounting.

(1) Use of reserves contradicts the matching principle, by which revenues and related costs should be recognized in the same period.

(2) Reserving for future events (especially contingencies) is obviously subject to estimate, and accounting should attempt to record quantifiable value as much as possible.

(3) The reserving technique makes reported earnings less indicative of fundamental trends in the company. The effects of the economic cycle are reduced, making correlation techniques (e.g., GNP growth vs. EPS growth) invalid. The "uninformed" investor may be misled by these reported numbers. In contrast to the artificial smoothing referred to earlier, the company's growth rate may be exaggerated, by overreserving for losses in a bad year, and subsequent writing off of the reserve.

It should be mentioned that a reserve may be properly taken, however, when it recognizes a liability which may (1) exist in the relatively near future-- such as costs of winding up a plant shutdown with the next year or (2) which is subject to quantification--such as the outright expropriation of net assets in a foreign country.

b.   If the analyst is able to discern the impact of reserves, he/she should exclude the reserves' impact from reported earnings when assessing past trends. Only operating or normal earnings should be compared over the short-term trends. However, over a longer period of time the losses against which reserves have been taken should be included.

In estimating future earnings, the analyst must carefully consider the impact of reserves and exclude the impact when forecasting normal earnings. By doing this, the analyst will have a better understanding of the true operations of the company.

In valuation of the common stock, again the analyst must focus on the "normal" earning power of the company. Thus, earnings may have to be adjusted upward or downward depending on the degree of abuse of reserves.

(CFA)

Exercise 6-12

a.   A change from the sum-of-the-years'-digits method of depreciation to the straight-line method for previously recorded assets is a change in accounting principle. Both the sum-of-the-years'-digits method and the straight-line method are generally accepted. A change in accounting principle results from adoption of a generally accepted accounting principle different from the generally accepted accounting principle used previously for reporting purposes.

b.   A change in the expected service life of an asset arising because of more experience with the asset is a change in accounting estimate. A change in accounting estimate occurs because future events and their effects cannot be perceived with certainty. Estimates are an inherent part of the accounting process. Therefore, accounting and reporting for certain financial statement elements requires the exercise of judgment, subject to revision based on experience.

c.   1.   The cumulative effect of a change in accounting principle is the difference between: (1) the amount of retained earnings at the beginning of the period of change and (2) the amount of retained earnings that would have been reported at that date if the new accounting principle had been used in prior periods.

     2.   The cumulative effect, net of income taxes, should be shown as a separate item in the income statement for the period of change between the captions "extraordinary items" and "net income." Pro-forma disclosure of the effects of retroactive restatement should be shown on the face of the income statement.

d.   Consistent use of accounting principles from one accounting period to another enhances the usefulness of financial statements to users of comparative accounting data.

e. If a change in accounting principle occurs, the nature and effect of a change in accounting principle should be disclosed to avoid misleading financial statement users. There is a presumption that an accounting principle, once adopted, should not be changed in accounting for events and transactions of a similar type.

◄ Answers to Problems ►

Problem 6-1

I.	a
II.	b (40% of revenue and cost recognized)
III.	a
IV.	d
V.	a
VI.	c
VII.	d (120,000/.3 + 440,000/.4)

a. Straight line: Depreciation = $200,000/yr.

	X1	X2	X3	X4	X5
Earnings before taxes and depreciation:	$1,500,000	$2,000,000	$2,500,000	$3,000,000	$3,500,000
(a) Depreciation	200,000	200,000	200,000	200,000	200,000
Net Before Taxes	$1,300,000	$1,800,000	$2,300,000	$2,800,000	$3,000,000
(b) Income Taxes	650,000	900,000	1,150,000	1,400,000	1,650,000
(c) Net Income	$ 650,000	$ 900,000	$1,150,000	$1,400,000	$1,650,000
+ Depreciation	200,000	200,000	200,000	200,000	200,000
(d) Cash Flow	$ 850,000	$1,100,000	$1,350,000	$1,600,000	$1,850,000

b. Sum of the years' digits:

Depreciation   Year 1 = 364.6 (Thousand)   Year 3 = 290.9   Year 5 = 218.2
                Year 2 = 327.3   Year 4 = 254.5

In Thousands

	X1	X2	X3	X4	X5
Earnings before taxes and depreciation:	$1,500.0	$2,000.0	$2,500.0	$3,000.0	$3,500.0
(a) Depreciation	364.6	327.3	290.9	254.5	218.2
Net Before Taxes	$1,135.4	$1,672.7	$2,290.1	$2,745.5	$3,281.8
(b) Income Taxes	567.7	836.4	1,104.6	1,372.8	1,640.9
(c) Net Income	$ 567.7	$ 836.3	$1,104.5	$1,372.7	$1,640.9
+ Depreciation	364.4	327.3	290.9	254.5	218.2
(d) Cash Flow	$ 932.3	$1,163.6	$1,395.4	$1,627.2	$1,859.1

Cash flow larger; Net Income smaller; Depreciation larger

c. Double-Declining Balance:

X1 Depreciation = 400.00
X2 Depreciation = 320.0
X3 = 256.0
X4 = 204.8
X5 = 163.5 (In Thousands)

In Thousands

	X1	X2	X3	X4	X5
Earnings before taxes and depreciation:	$1,500.0	$2,000.0	$2,500.0	$3,000.0	$3,500.0
(a) Depreciation	400.0	320.0	256.0	204.8	163.8
Net Before Taxes	$1,100.0	$1,680.0	$2,244.0	$2,795.2	$3,336.2
(b) Income Taxes	550.0	840.0	1,122.0	1,397.6	1,668.1
(c) Net Income	$ 550.0	$ 840.0	$1,122.0	$1,397.6	$1,668.1
+ Depreciation	400.0	320.0	256.0	204.8	163.8
(d) Cash Flow	$ 950.0	$1,160.0	$1,378.0	$1,602.4	$1,831.9

Cash Flow higher than straight line, lower than S.O.Y.D. (except year X5).
Net income lower than straight line, higher than S.O.Y.D. (except year X5).
Depreciation higher than straight line, lower than S.O.Y.D. (except year X5).

(CFA adapted)

Problem 6-3

a. The service cost of $22.1 million for Year 11 is the present value of actuarial benefits earned by employees in Year 11.

b. Year 11: Discount rate = 8.75%
    Year 10: Discount rate = 9.00%

A higher discount rate will lead to a lower present value of service cost. With the reduction of discount rate from 9% to 8.75%, the service cost is increased.

c. The interest cost is computed by multiplying the projected benefit obligation (PBO) as of the end of the prior year by the discount rate of 8.75%.

d. The actual return on assets in Year 11 is $73.4 million [113]. It consists of investment income plus the realized or unrealized appreciation or depreciation of plan assets during the year. The expected return on plan assets is computed by multiplying the expected long-term rate of return (9%) on plan assets by the market value of plan assets at the beginning of the period, i.e., $773.9 million [120].

Therefore, expected return = 773.9 * 9% = $69.65 million

The actual return would subject pension cost too much to the fluctuation of the financial market and therefore, the annual pension cost would be too volatile. As a result, expected return is used in determining pension expense. The difference between actual and expected return will be amortized over an appropriate period.

e. Accumulated benefit obligation (ABO) is employer's obligation to employees' pension based on current and past compensation levels rather than future levels. Therefore, it could amount to the employer's current obligation if the plan were discontinued presently.

f. Projected benefit obligation (PBO) is employer's obligation to employees' pension based on future compensation level. The difference between PBO and ABO is due to the inclusion of a provision of 5.75% increase in future compensation level by PBO. In Year 11, the difference between PBO and ABO is $113.3 million [120].

g. Yes, there is a prepaid pension expense of $172.5 million in Year 11 [120].

Problem 6-4

a.

	11	10	9
(1) Depreciation expense per item [162A]	194.5	184.1	175.9
(2) Depreciation timing difference [128]	5.9	18.6	11.9
(3) (2)/.34 = "excess" depreciation	17.4	54.7	35.0
(1) + (3) = depreciation on tax return . . .	211.9	238.8	210.9

b. Identification of the following amounts (combining federal, state and foreign taxes):

		11	10	9
1.	Earnings before Income Tax [26]	667	179	107
2.	Expected income tax @ 34% (confirmed by Item [134])	226.9	61.0	36.2
3.	Total income tax expense [27]	265.9	175.0	93.4
4.	Total income tax due to governments*	230.4	171.1	161.2
5.	Total income tax due and not paid [44] . . .	67.7	46.4	30.1

*Items [122], [123], and [124]

c. The effective tax rate differs from the statutory rate (34%) due to the following (numbers are from item [76]):*

	11	%	10	%	9	%
[134] Tax at statutory rate	226.9	34.0	61.0	34.0	36.2	34.0
[135] State tax (net of fed benefit) . . .	20.0	3.0	6.6	3.7	3.8	3.6
[136] Nondeductible divestitures, re-structuring and unusual charges . .			101.4	56.5	51.9	48.7
[137] Nondeductible amortization of intangibles	4.0	0.6	1.6	0.9	1.2	1.1
[138] Foreign earnings not taxed or taxed at other than statutory rate . . .	(2.0)	(0.3)	2.2	1.2	0.2	0.2
[140] Tax at effective rate (includes deferred tax)	16.7	2.5	2.2	1.2	0.1	0.1
Totals	269.6	39.8	175.0	97.5	93.4	87.7

*By multiplying EBIT [26] by applicable percentage as given.

d. Campbell can probably deduct for tax purposes only cash actually spent in Year 10 for these charges. If this is so, a good estimate of cash spent is (item [105])

$$\$339.1 - \$301.6 = 37.5; \quad \frac{37.5}{.34} = \underline{\$110} \text{ million}$$

Problem 6-5

a.

		11	10	9
Depreciation ([125]	(A)	125.2	103.5	94.2
Excess tax depreciation [158A]	(B)	8.4	14.5	15.0
Gross amount of excess depreciation (divide excess tax by 34%) B ÷ .34	(C)	24.7	42.6	44.1
Depreciation shown on tax return . (A) + (C)		149.9	146.1	138.3

			11	10	9

b. 1. Earnings before Taxes [7] 411.5 382.4 239.1
      times statutory tax rate 34%

   2. Expected income tax [158C] 139.9 130.0 81.3
      . . . .
      Income tax at effective rate 175.7 153.5 90.2
      Difference to be reconciled 35.8   23.5   8.9

   3. Total income tax expense (actual tax provision)
      [158] 175.7 153.5 90.2

   4. Total income tax due to govts (total currently
      payable) [158] 161.4 134.9 49.6

      Total income tax due & not yet paid (taxes payable)
      [75] 45.1   36.3   8.0

c.

	11	%	10	%	9	%
Income tax at 34%	139.9	34.0	130.0	34.0	81.3	34.0
ANC benefit					(1.7)	(.7)
Repatriation of foreign earnings	4.3	1.0	4.8	1.3	(2.1)	(.9)
State and local taxes	16.7	4.1	11.9	3.1	7.7	3.2
Non-U.S. tax rate	8.2	2.0	9.8	2.5	8.8	3.7
U.S. tax credits	(.2)	—	(.1)	—	(.7)	(.3)
Miscellaneous items	6.8	1.6	(2.9)	(.8)	(3.1)	(1.3)
Tax at effective rate . . .	175.9	42.7	153.5	40.1	90.2	37.7

The largest percent increase due to state and local taxes and non-U.S.
tax rate are likely to continue if the earnings in the future continue
to increase.

d. The difference in Quaker Oats' effective tax rate for Years 10 and 11 was
    2.6%. This resulted primarily because in Year 10 there was a smaller amount
    at state and local tax rate.

e. Change in current portion of deferred tax cannot be determined because we
    have no balance sheet listing or other disclosure related to a
    deferred-current account.

f. Increase in deferred-noncurrent*   11   10   9
        (def income tax provision) [158]   14.3 18.6 40.6
    Change in deferred income taxes account in
    balance sheet [81]** . . . . 39.0 19.3   ?

    *   Change in statement of cash flows [21] is shown along with other
        changes.
    ** This change differs from that disclosed in [158] for undisclosed
        reasons.

BIG-DEAL CONSTRUCTION CO.

	Dam	X1	X2	X3	X4	X5	Total
1 Book income	1	$24,000	$ 72,000	$ 24,000	–	–	$120,000
2	2	–	37,800	75,600	$ 12,600	–	126,000
3	3	–	15,000	45,000	75,000	$ 15,000	150,000
4 Total		$24,000	$124,800	$144,600	$ 87,600	$ 15,000	$396,000
5							
6 Taxable income	1	–	–	$120,000	–	–	$120,000
7	2	–	–	–	$126,000	–	126,000
8	3	–	–	–	–	$150,000	150,000
9 Total		$24,000	$124,800	$120,000	$126,000	$150,000	$396,000
10							
11 Line 4—line 9		$24,000	$124,800	$ 24,600	$(38,400)	($135,000)	=

		X1	X2	X3	X4	X5
Added to def. tax (cr.)		$12,000	$ 64,200	$ 12,300		
Reduction in deferred taxes (dr.)					$ 19,200	$ 67,500

Problem 6-7

STEAD CORP.

		(000 omitted)	
	x4	x5	x6
a. TAX RETURN			
Taxable income (loss):			
Before loss carryforward	$ (400)	$ 1,000	$ 1,000
After deducting loss carryforward		$ 600	
Tax due (at 50%)	$ —	$ 300	$ 500
INCOME STATEMENT			
Sales $10,000	$10,000	$10,000	
Expenses*	9,000	9,000	10,400
Income before tax	$ 1,000	$ 1,000	$ (400)
Tax expense:			
Current	--	300	500
Deferred	500	200	(700)
Total	$ 500	$ 500	$(200)
Net Income (Loss)	$ 500	$ 500	$ (200

*Includes unusual expense of $1,400 in Year x6.

b. BALANCE SHEET			
Current tax payable	$—	$300	$500
Deferred tax payable	$500	$700	$—

Note: The timing difference regarding deferred preoperating costs is $1,400 in x4. However, only $1,000 of this amount results in a reduction of x4 taxable income (the remaining $400 becomes a loss carryforward and reduces taxable income in x5). The tax effect (at 50 percent) of these differences is $500 in x4 and $200 in x5. The entire timing difference reverses in x6.

Problem 6-8

	x1	x2	x3	x4	x5	x6	x7	x8
Tax Return:								
Taxable income	20	35	50	(300)	(65)[b]	185[c]	260	300
Tax due @ 50%	10	17.5	25	(52.5)[a]	0	92.5	130	150
Income Statement:								
Sales	50	80	120	100	200	400	500	600
Cost of sales	20	30	50	300	50	120	200	250
G&A	10	15	20	100	20	30	40	50
Net income before tax	20	35	50	(300)	130	250	260	300
Tax expense (refund):								
Current provision	10	17.5	25	—	—	92.5	130	150
Refund from carryback	—	—	—	(52.5)	—	—	—	—
Tax effect of loss carryforward	—	—	—	—	65	32.5	—	—
Total Tax	10	17.5	25	(52.5)	65	125	130	150
Income before extraordinary items	10	17.5	25	(247.5)	65	125	130	150
Extraordinary gain—reduction of taxes due to carryforward	—	—	—	—	65	32.5	—	—
Net Income (*)	10	17.5	25	(247.5)	130	157.5	130	150

(*) Footnote disclosure: Tax loss carryforwards are $195 at end of x4 and $65 at end of x5.

Journal Entries—Dr. (Cr.):								
Tax expense	10	17.5	25	52.5	65	125	130	150
FIT Receivable	—	—	—	52.5	—	—	—	—
FIT Payable	10	17.5	25	—	—	92.5	130	150
Extraordinary gains	—	—	—	—	65	32.5	—	—

Notes:

[a]Operating loss of $300 carried back to eliminate all taxable income for x1, x2 and x3 and secure refund of $52.5 for total taxes paid during those years.

[b]Income for x5 of $130 less loss carryforward of $195.

[c]Income for x6 of $250 less loss carryforward of $65.

Problem 6-9

Service Cost (586 × 1.1)	$645
Interest Cost (PBO × Discount Rate (2,212 × 0.085) . .	188
Return on plan assets (0.115 × 3,238)	(372)
Amortization of deferred loss (48/30)	2
Amortization of transition asset	(19)
Periodic pension cost	$444

Problem 6-10

a. The income statements of Disposo Corp. should be shown as follows:

	x8	x7
Continuing operations:		
Sales	775	600
Costs and expenses	657	576
Pretax income	118	24
Tax expense	59	12
Income from continuing operations . .	59	12
Discontinued operations:		
Operations (net of tax) (a)	(3)	8
Disposal (net of $6 tax) (b)	(6)	—
	(9)	8
Net Income	50	20

(a) Represents net income (loss) from operations for year x7 and for x8 until August 15.

(b) Represents:

Loss from operations August 15 to December 31	(1)
Loss on sale of assets (after $5 tax) .	(5)
Total	(6)

The $10 loss and related tax benefit of $5 would still be recorded (anticipated) at December 31, x8 (the asset would be reduced by $10 to market value).

◄ Answers to Cases ►

Case 6-1

a. Adaptec recognizes revenue "at the time of shipment or upon satisfaction of contractual obligations."

b. Yes, Adaptec may choose to accelerate shipments at the end of the year in order to increase revenues.

c. Probably not. Sales "borrowed" from the next year (as in part b) can only be recorded once. Adaptec would have to accelerate shipments year after year without detection by auditors or investors in order to exercise long-run discretion over revenue.

d. According to note one, Adaptec uses straight-line depreciation for property and equipment.

Note two discloses estimated useful lives for buildings and improvements (5-40 years), machinery and equipment (3-5 years), furniture and fixtures (3-8 years), and leasehold improvements (life of lease).

e. Life span (1996): (132,961-25,154) ÷ 17,593   = 7.56 years
    Life span (1995): (95,111-13,240) ÷ 15,662   = 5.23 years

    Age (1996): 40,183 ÷ 17,593   = 2.28 years
    Age (1995): 27,248 ÷ 15,662   = 1.74 years

    Remaining life (1996): 7.56 - 2.28   = 3.84 years
    Remaining life (1995): 5.23 - 1.74   = 3.49 years

Case 6-2

a. <u>1986 Employee Stock Purchase Plan</u>
    shares authorized: 2.8 million
    eligibility: "qualified" employees
    purchase price: 85% of market value

    <u>1990 Stock Plan</u>
    shares authorized: total not disclosed (4,098,315 available, 5,819,831 outstanding)
    eligibility: employees, officers, consultants
    purchase price: not less than 50% of market value

    <u>1990 Directors' Option Plan</u>
    shares authorized: total not disclosed (290,000 available, 326,250 outstanding)
    eligibility: directors
    purchase price: market value

    <u>Rights Plan</u>
    shares authorized: 120 million
    eligibility: shareholders
    purchase price: $50.00

b. 1. 1994: 1.577 million
        1995: 1.426 million
        1996: 1.218 million

    2. 1986 Employee Stock Purchase Plan   139,275
        1990 Stock Plan   1,017,131
        1990 Directors' Option Plan   55,000
        unexplained   6,594
                Total   1,218,000

c. 1990 Stock Plan   1,956,767
    1990 Directors' Option Plan   93,750
        Total   2,050,517

As discussed in the appendix, the dilutive effects of stock options are incorporated in the earnings per share computations. Note that Adaptec will be required to comply with SFAS 123 in fiscal 1997.

d. 1. 1994: $39.993 million
        1995: $60,848 million
        1996: $87,628 million

    2. In the short-run, a reduction in R&D expenditures would boost earnings.

    3. In the long-run, a reduction of R&D activities would hurt Adaptec's profitability as the company's financial health is predicated on developing new products.

e. The amortization period for goodwill is not disclosed.

f. 1. 1994: 70% domestic (54,972/78,603); 30% foreign
        1995: 60% domestic (74,397/124,537); 40% foreign
        1996: 42% domestic (57,882/137,989); 58% foreign

        Ignoring the write-off of in-process technology, the split in 1996 is 58% domestic [(57,882+52,313)/(137,989+52,313)]; 42% foreign

        The trend is toward more foreign pretax income, although the trend slowed in 1996 (after considering the write-off). As discussed in the note, foreign subsidiary income is taxed at a favorable rate.

    2. The effective tax rate paid on foreign income increased from 2.2% (1,106/50,140) in 1995 to 17.0% (13,583/80,107) in 1996. Possible causes include: (1) less favorable terms under the new tax holiday agreement with the Singapore government, (2) increased dividend payments to the parent in 1996, and (3) tax accruals due to other causes such as penalties. The tax footnote is not clear on the underlying cause(s). This is a case where the analyst must seek information from the company as changes in future effective tax rates directly impact Adaptec's profitability.

    3. Note eight indicates that deferred tax assets are included in prepaid expenses. As there is no indication of a valuation allowance, one can assume that Adaptec does not anticipate incurring losses in the future.

    4. Adaptec's effective tax rate was 25.1% in 1996 and 25.0% in 1995 and 1994. The effective rate is lower than the statutory rate due primarily to the tax holiday offered by the Singapore government. Adaptec's tax-exempt investments also lower the effective rate. As seen in part 2, additional information is needed to determine whether future effective rates will remain at a comparable level.

    5. Adaptec has not accrued income taxes on the undistributed earnings of its Singapore subsidiary because it expects these earnings to be reinvested indefinitely.

g. The analyst might be tempted to ignore this amount and consider it a one-time item. However, as disclosed in note six, Adaptec continues to make acquisitions which will require similar write-offs. Thus, the analyst must be alert to future write-offs and their effect on profitability.

Case 6-3

a. Accounting for depreciation is a system of accounting to distribute the cost (or other book value) of tangible capital assets, less salvage, over their useful lives in a systematic and rational manner. Under generally accepted accounting principles as presently understood, depreciation accounting is a process of cost allocation, not of valuation, through which the productive effort (cost) to be matched with productive accomplishment (revenue) for the period is measured. Depreciation accounting, therefore, is concerned with the timing of the expiration of the cost of tangible fixed assets.

b. The proposed depreciation method is, of course, systematic. Whether it is rational in terms of cost allocation depends on the facts of the case. It produces an increasing depreciation charge, which is usually not justifiable in terms of the benefit from the use of the asset because manufacturers typically prefer to use their new equipment as much as possible and their old equipment only as needed to meet production quotas during periods of peak demand. As a general rule, then, the benefit declines with age. Assuming that the actual operations (including equipment usage) of each year are identical, maintenance and repair costs are likely to be higher in the later years of usage than in the earlier years. Hence the proposed method would couple light depreciation and repair charges in the early years, while it would couple heavy depreciation and repair charges in the later years. Reported net income in the early years would be much higher than reported net income in the later years of asset life, an unreasonable and undesirable variation during periods of identical operation.

On the other hand, if the expected level of operations (including equipment usage) in early years of asset life is expected to be low as compared to that of later years because of slack demand or production policies, the pattern of the depreciation charges of the proposed method approximately parallels expected benefits (and revenues) and hence is reasonable. Although the units-of-production depreciation method is the useful selection to fit this case, the proposed method also conforms to generally accepted accounting principles in this case.

c. 1. Depreciation charges neither recover nor create cash. Revenue-producing activities are the sources of cash from operations: if revenues exceed out-of-pocket costs during a fiscal period, cash is available to cover other than out-of-pocket costs; if revenues do not exceed out-of-pocket costs, no cash is made available no matter how much, or little, depreciation is charged.

2. Depreciation may affect cash in two ways. First, depreciation charges affect reported income and hence may affect managerial decisions such as those regarding pricing, product selection, and

dividends. For example, the proposed method would result initially in higher reported income than would the straight-line method; consequently, shareholders might demand higher dividends in the earlier years than they would otherwise expect. The straight-line method, by causing a lower reported income during the early years of asset life and thereby reducing the amount of possible dividends in early years as compared with the proposed method, could encourage earlier reinvestment in other profit-earning assets in order to meet increasing demand.

Second, depreciation charges affect reported taxable income and hence affect directly the amount of income taxes payable in the year of deduction. Using the proposed method for tax purposes would reduce the total tax bill over the life of the assets (1) if the tax rates were increased in future years or (2) if the business were doing poorly now but were to do significantly better in the future. The first condition is political and speculative, but the second condition may be applicable to Toro in view of its recent origin and its rapid expansion program. Consequently, more funds might be available for reinvestment in fixed assets in years of larger deductions if the business is always profitable. If Toro is not profitable now, it would not benefit from higher deductions now and should consider an increasing charge method for tax purposes, such as the one proposed. If Toro is quite profitable now, the president should reconsider his proposal because it will delay the availability of tax-paid dollars. This decision should not affect the decision to use a depreciation method for stockholder reporting that is systematic and rational in terms of cost allocation under GAAP.

(AICPA)

Case 6-4

a.

Balance Sheet:

	Shipment	Coll.	Prod. (b)	Prod. (b)
Cash	1,670	1,670	1,670	1,670
Receivables	1,800	1,800	1,800	1,800
Inventory, at cost	700	700	--	--
Inventory, at market	--	--	900	790
Total Assets	4,170	4,170	4,370	4,260
Accrued shipping cost	--	--	20	--
Accrued sales commission	180	180	270	180
Deferred income	--	180a	--	--
Invested capital	3,000	3,000	3,000	3,000
Retained earnings	990	810	1,080	1,080
Total Liabilities and Equity	4,170	4,170	4,370	4,260

Income Statement:

	Shipment	Coll.	Prod. (b)	Prod. (b)
Sales	9,900	8,100	10,800	9,900
Costs and expenses:				
Cost of goods sold	7,700	6,300	8,400	7,610
Selling expense	990	810	1,080	990
Shipping expense	220	180	0240	220
Total	8,910	7,290	9,720	8,820
Net Income	990	810	1,080	1,080

Notes:

a. Deferred income: Sales—$1,800 less Costs ($1,400 + $180 + $40) = $180

b. Time of production—Figures may be reflected *gross* as in left column or *net* as in right column. Inventory, at net realizable value ($790) = $900 less $20 less $90.

Cost of goods sold is a "plug" figure based on inventory account (e.g., Beg. $-0- plus purchases $8,400 less End $790 = C/G/S $7,610). (Both presentations are used in practice.)

Note: There is only one legal reality. Notice that cash and accounts receivable are identical for all four presentations. Inventories are real, but the accounting valuation is not governed by law.

b. The installment method delays the reporting of profits and thereby delays the time of payment of taxes. The time value of money is a major motivation for delaying cash payments.

c. *Balance Sheet*: Some analysts prefer the installment method because it is more "conservative." However, the installment method attempts to value receivables (less deferred income) at the historical cost of the inventory. It would appear that the credit analyst should be future-oriented and view receivables at the expected future cash inflow.

Income Statement: some analysts prefer the installment method because it is more "conservative."

The installment method has two critical weaknesses:

(i) revenues and profits are not recognized when performance (earning) occurs but the recognition is delayed until cash is collected.

(ii) selling costs are mismatched (this is most dramatic in a period of rapid growth or decline in sales).

By definition, the installment method does not show economic reality.

◀ Appendix 6A ▶

Exercise 6A-1

a. The effects of dilutive stock options and warrants are *not* included in the computation of the number of shares for basic earnings per share. They are, however, included in diluted earnings per share.

b. The effects of dilutive convertible securities are *not* included in the computation of the number of shares for basic earnings per share. They are, however, included in diluted earnings per share.

c. Antidilutive securities are excluded from both basic and diluted earnings per share.

Exercise 6A-2

a. Basic earnings per share is the amount of earnings attributable to common shareholders (i.e., net income less preferred dividends) divided by the weighted average number of common shares outstanding during the period.

b. Diluted earnings per share is the amount of current earnings per share to reflect the maximum dilution that would result from the conversion of all convertible securities and the exercise of all warrants and options. The conversion of these securities individually would decrease earnings per share and in the aggregate would have a dilutive effect. The computation of diluted earnings per share should be based upon the assumption that all such issued and issuable shares were outstanding from the beginning of the period, or from their inception if after the beginning of the period.

Whereas basic earnings per share does not reflect any securities convertible or exercisable into common shares, diluted earnings per share includes all all such securities and considers their dilutive effect upon earnings per share, taking into account necessary adjustments to income resulting from the conversion process.

c. Basic earnings per share does not consider the dilutive effects of securities such as options, warrants, and convertibles. Primary earnings per share is the amount of earnings attributable to each share of issued common stock *and* *common stock equivalents*. A "common stock equivalent" represents any security which, because of its terms or the circumstances under which it was issued, is in substance equivalent to a common stock.

d. Diluted and fully diluted earnings per share are virtually identical, with two technical differences. First, the treasury stock method is modified for fully diluted EPS (as described on page 328) if the number of shares obtainable upon exercise of outstanding options and warrants in the aggregate exceeds 20% of the number of common shares outstanding at the end of the period. Second, for fully diluted EPS the market price at the end of the period should be used to determine the number of shares assumed to be repurchased under the treasury stock method if such price is greater than the average price during the period.

(CFA Adapted)

Exercise 6A-3
I.   b (110% of 2 million)
II.   a
III. a

Problem 6A-1
I.   c ($6,500,000/2,500,000 = $2.60)
II.   b

Diluted EPS = $$\frac{\text{Adjusted net income}}{\begin{array}{l}\text{wtd. avg. of } + \text{ wtd. avg. number} \\ \text{common stock} \quad \text{of common shares} \\ \text{outstanding} \qquad \text{issuable from options} \\ \qquad\qquad\qquad \text{and convertibles}\end{array}}$$

Since average market price of stock exceeds exercise price of options, the options are dilutive. Using treasury stock method for options:

200,000 shs. × $15 = $3,000,000 proceeds
$3,000,000/20 = 150,000 shs. purchased in open market
Thus, 50,000 additional shares would be issued.

Are the convertible debentures dilutive? No. Assuming conversion of debentures, 100,000 additional shares would be issued. The net income adjustment would be:

Interest expense for debentures	$500,000
Less taxes	
	(200,000)
Increase in net income	$300,000

EPS = (6,500,000+300,000)/(2,500,000+100,000) = $2.62

Diluted EPS = 6,500,000/(2,500,000+50,000) = $2.55

Problem 6A-2

a.   Weighted average shares outstanding during Year 6:

Jan. 1	200,000 sh.	1 yr.	200,000 sh.
Oct. 1	60,000 sh.	1/4 yr.	15,000 sh.
			215,000 sh.

Basic EPS:

Income before extraordinary item $\dfrac{\$800,000}{215,000 \text{ sh.}}$ = $3.72

Extraordinary item $\dfrac{\$(200,000)}{215,000 \text{ sh.}}$ = (0.93)

Basic EPS $2.22

b.   *Diluted EPS*:

Weighted average (from part a)	215,000 sh.
Convertible bonds	20,000 sh.
Convertible preferred stock	50,000 sh.
Options:	
Potential issuable . . . . 50,000 sh.	
Potential proceeds $2,250,000 ÷ $50 45,000 sh.	5,000 sh.
	290,000 sh.

Income before ext. item $\dfrac{\$800,000 + \$36,000*}{290,000 \text{ sh.}}$ = $2.88

*(1,000,000 × .6).6

Extraordinary item $\dfrac{(\$200,000)}{290,000 \text{ sh.}}$ = (0.69)

DEPS $2.19

c.   *Primary EPS:*
      Weighted average (from part a) . . . .   215,000 sh.
      Common stock equivalents:
          Convertible pfd. stock . . . .   50,000 sh.
          Options:
          Potential issuable . . . .   50,000 sh.
          Potential proceeds $2,250,000 ÷ $50 45,000 sh. 5,000 sh.
                                                          270,000 sh.

          Income before extraordinary item $800,000
                                              ─────────── = $2.96
                                               270,000 sh.

          Extraordinary item $(200,000)
                                              ─────────── = (0.74)
                                               270,000 sh.

          Primary EPS $2.22

d.   *Fully diluted EPS:*
      Weighted average (from part a) . . . .   215,000 sh.
      Convertible bonds . . . .   20,000 sh.
      Convertible preferred stock . . . .   50,000 sh.
      Options:
          Potential issuable . . . .   50,000 sh.
          Potential proceeds $2,250,000 ÷ $60 37,500 sh. 12,500 sh.
                                                          297,500 sh.

      Income before ext. item $800,000 + $36,000*
                                      ─────────────────── = $2.81
                                          297,500 sh.

          *(1,000,000 × .6).6

      Extraordinary item   ($200,000)
                                          ─────────── = (.67)
                                           297,500 sh.

      FDEPS $2.14

Problem 6A-3
a.   *Basic EPS* = $4,000,000 ÷ 3,000,000 = $1.33

      Diluted EPS:
      Since average market price of stock exceeds exercise price of options and
      warrants, the options and warrants are dilutive. Using treasury stock
      method:

          1,000,000 shs. × $15 = $15,000,000 proceeds
          $15,000,000/20 = 750,000 shs. purchased in open market
          Thus, 250,000 additional shares would be issued.

          DEPS = $4,000,000 ÷ 3,250,000 = $1.23

b.   *Basic EPS* = $4,000,000 ÷ 3,000,000 = $1.33

Diluted EPS:
Since average market price of stock exceeds exercise price of options and warrants, the options and warrants are dilutive. Using treasury stock method:

   1,000,000 shs. × $15 = $15,000,000 proceeds
   $15,000,000/18 = 833,333 shs. purchased in open market
   Thus, 166,667 additional shares would be issued.

   EPS = $4,000,000 ÷ 3,166,667 = $1.26

c and d.

Primary EPS:

	(a)	(b)
Reduction of Debt:		
Assumed proceeds = 1,000,000 × $15	$15,000,000	$15,000,000
Repurchase of 20% of outstanding common shares at applicable average market value:		
(a) 3,000,000 shares outstanding × 20% × $20	12,000,000	
(b) 3,000,000 shares outstanding × 20% × $18		$10,800,000
Reduction of debt	$3,000,000	$4,200,000

Adjusted Net Income:

	(a)	(b)
Net income before adjustments	$4,000,000	$3,000,000
Add back: Reduction in interest (at 6%) less 50% tax effect:		
(a) $3,000,000 × 6% × 50%	90,000	
(b) $4,200,000 × 6% × 50%		126,000
Adjusted net income (A)	$4,090,000	$3,126,000

Adjusted Number of Shares Outstanding

	(a)	(b)
No. of shares o/s before adjustment	3,000,000	3,000,000
Add: Incremental shares (1,000,000 - 600,000)	400,000	400,000
Adjusted number of shares o/s (B)	3,400,000	3,400,000
Primary EPS = (A) ÷ (B)	$1.20	$.92

Fully Diluted EPS:

Reduction of Debt:

	(a)	(b)
Assumed proceeds (as above)	$15,000,000	$15,000,000
Repurchase of 20% of outstanding common shares at applicable year-end market price:		
(a) 3,000,000 shares × 20% × $25	15,000,000	
(b) 3,000,000 shares × 20% × $20		12,000,000
Reduction of debt	---	$3,000,000

Adjusted Net Income:

```
Net income before adjustments . . . .   $4,000,000  $3,000,000
Add back: Reduction in interest (at 6%) less
      50% tax effect:
      (a) Zero . . . . . . . . . . . . . .  ---
      (b) $3,000,000 x 6% x 50%  . . . . . .              90,000
Adjusted net income (A) . . . . . . .   $4,000,000  $3,090,000

Adjusted Number of Shares Outstanding:
No. of shares o/s before adjustments  .  3,000,000   3,000,000
Add: Incremental shares (1,000,000
      - 600,000) . . . . . . . . . . .     400,000    $400,000
Adjusted number of shares o/s (B) . . .  3,400,000   3,400,000

Fully Diluted EPS = (A) ÷ (B) . . . . . .   $1.20*       $.91**
```

*No dilution, need not be reported.
**Dilution is less than 3 percent, need not be reported.

Problem 6A-4

Net income (consolidated) = $100,000 + $150,000 + $500,000 = $750,000

Average number of shares for Year 5:

```
Simon:    (25,000)(2) x 6 months    =      300,000
          (50,000)(2) x 3 months    =      300,000
Duke:     (30,000)(5) x 8 months    =    1,200,000
          (40,000)(5) x 1 month     =      200,000
Allen:    150,000 x 9 months        =    1,350,000
          450,000 x 3 months        =    1,350,000
                                         4,700,000
                                             ÷ 12
                                           391,667
```

EPS = $750,000 ÷ 391,667 = $1.91

Problem 6A-5

Net income (consolidated) = $200,000 + $300,000 + $500,000 = $1,000,000

Average number of shares for Year 5:

```
Afternoon:  (50,000)(2) x 6 months    =      600,000
            (100,000)(2) x 3 months   =      600,000
Evening:    (60,000)(5) x 8 months    =    2,400,000
            (80,000)(5) x 1 month     =      400,000
Morning:    300,000 x 9 months        =    2,700,000
            900,000 x 3 months        =    2,700,000
                                           9,400,000
                                               ÷ 12
                                             783,333
```

EPS = $1,000,000 ÷ 783,333 = $1.28

Case 6A-1

a.   *Basic EPS* = $1,500,000 ÷ 900,000 = <u>$1.67</u>

Diluted EPS:
The warrants are dilutive since the average market price of common stock ($13) exceeded the exercise price of the warrants ($10).

        900,000 shs. × $10 = $9,000,000 proceeds
        $9,000,000/13 = 692,307 shs. purchased in open market
        Thus, 207,693 additional shares would be issued.

        EPS = 1,500,000/(900,000+207,693) = $1.35

Are the subordinated convertible debentures dilutive? Yes. Assuming conversion, a total of 500,000 ($9,000,000/$18) additional common shares would be issued at June 30, Year 1. The net income adjustment would be:

        Interest expense for debentures $270,000
        Less taxes   <u>(135,000)</u>
        Increase in net income $135,000

        EPS = (1,500,000+135,000)/(900,000+250,000) = $1.42

DEPS = (1,500,000+135,000)/(900,000+207,693+250,000) = <u>$1.20</u>

b.   Interest expense (Year 2):
            Debentures (9,000,000)(.06) . . . $540,000
            Term loan: (3,000,000)(.07)/2 . .   105,000
                       (2,500,000)(.07)/2 . . .   <u>87,500</u>
            Total $732,500

      EBIT (Year 2):
            Net income $1,500,000
            Taxes (50%) 1,500,000
            Interest expense . . . . . <u>732,500</u>
                                      $3,732,500

      Times interest earned = 3,732,500/732,500 = <u>5.10</u>

Case 6A-2

I.   a. *Basic EPS* = [285,000-(2.4)(10,000)]/90,000 = <u>$2.90</u>

      b. *Diluted EPS:*

      Are the convertible bonds dilutive? Yes. Assuming conversion, the net income adjustment would be:

            Interest expense for debentures $80,000
            Less taxes   <u>(40,000)</u>
            Increase in net income $40,000

            EPS = (285,000+40,000)/(90,000+30,000) = $2.71

Is the convertible preferred dilutive? Yes. Assuming conversion:

$$EPS = 285,000/(90,000+20,000) = \$2.71$$

$$DEPS = (285,000+40,000)/(90,000+30,000+20,000) = \underline{\$2.32}$$

II.   Weighted average shares outstanding during Year 6:

Jan. 1	10,000 sh.	1 yr.	10,000 sh.
July 1	2,000 sh.	1/2 yr.	<u>1,000 sh.</u>
			11,000 sh.

Basic EPS = (10,000-1,000)/11,000 = $\underline{\$0.82}$

◄ CHAPTER 7 ►

Analyzing Business Activities: Cash Flows

◄ CHAPTER REVIEW ►

Cash is the residual of cash inflows *less* cash outflows for all prior periods of a company. Net cash flows, or simply cash flows, refers to the current period's cash inflows less cash outflows. Cash flows are different from accrual measures of performance. Cash flow measures recognize inflows when cash is received not necessarily earned, and outflows when cash is paid not necessarily incurred. The statement of cash flows reports cash flow measures for three primary business activities: operating, investing, and financing. Operating cash flows, or cash flows from operations, is the cash basis counterpart to accrual net income. Information on cash flows helps us assess a company's ability to meet obligations, pay dividends, increase capacity, and raise financing. It also helps us assess the quality of earnings and the dependence of income on estimates and assumptions regarding future cash flows.

This chapter describes cash flows and their relevance to our analysis of financial statements. We describe current reporting requirements and their implications for our analysis of cash flows. We explain useful analytical adjustments to cash flows using financial data to improve our analysis. We direct special attention to transaction reconstruction, T-account, and conversion analyses.

◄ CHAPTER OUTLINE ►

▸ **Relevance of Cash Flows**

▸ **Statement of Cash Flows**

　　　Cash Flow Relations

　　　Reporting by Activities

　　　Constructing the Cash Flow Statement

▸ **Reconstruction Analysis of Cash Flows**

　　　Determining Cash Flows by Activities

　　　Reconstruction of Transactions

　　　Derivation of the Statement of Cash Flows

▸ **Reporting Cash Flows from Operations**

　　　Indirect Method

　　　Direct Method

　　　Converting from Indirect to Direct Method

　　　Adjustments to Cash Flow Components

　　　Additional Disclosures and Adjustments

▸ **Analysis Implications of Cash Flows**

　　　Limitations in Cash Flow Reporting

　　　Interpreting Cash Flows and Net Income

　　　Alternative Cash Flow Measures

　　　Company and Economic Conditions

　　　Free Cash Flows

　　　Cash Flows as Validators

▸ **Appendix 7A Analytical Cash Flow Worksheets**

▸ **Appendix 7B Analytical Reconstruction of Transactions**

◄ Learning Objectives ►

- **Explain the relevance of cash flows in analyzing business activities.**

- **Describe reporting of cash flows by business activity.**

- **Analyze cash flows through T-accounts and transaction reconstruction.**

- **Interpret cash flows from operating activities.**

- **Analyze cash flows under alternative company and business conditions.**

- **Describe alternative measures of cash flows and their usefulness.**

- **Illustrate analytical tools in evaluating cash flows (Appendices 7A and 7B).**

◀ Answers to Questions ▶

1. While fragmentary information on sources and uses of funds can be obtained from comparative balance sheets and from income statements, a comprehensive picture of this important area of activity can be gained only from a statement of cash flows (SCF). The SCF provides information on questions such as:

    *   What was the cash generated by operations?
    *   What utilization was made of cash provided by operations?
    *   What was the source of cash invested in new plant and equipment?
    *   What use was made of cash derived from a new bond issue or the sale of common stock?
    *   How was it possible to continue the regular dividend in the face of an operating loss?
    *   How was the debt repayment achieved, or what was the source of cash used to redeem the preferred stock?
    *   How was the increase in investments financed?
    *   Why, despite record profits, is the cash position lower than last year?

2. SFAS 95 requires that the SCF classify cash receipts and payments by operating, financing and investing activities.

    Operating activities encompass all the earning-related activities of the enterprise. They encompass, in addition to all the income and expense items found in the income statement, all the net inflows and outflows of cash that operations impose on the enterprise as a result of activities such as the extension of credit to customers, investment in inventories and obtaining credit from suppliers. Thus, operating activities relate to all items in the statement of income (with minor exceptions) as well as to balance sheet items that relate to operations--mostly working capital accounts such as accounts receivable, inventories, prepayments, accounts payable and accruals. SFAS 95 also specifies that operating activities include all transactions and events that are not of an investing or financing nature.

    Financing activities include obtaining resources from owners and providing them with a return *of* or a return *on* (i.e., dividends) their investment. They also include obtaining resources from creditors and repaying the amounts borrowed or otherwise settling the obligations.

    Investing activities include acquiring and selling or otherwise disposing of securities which are not cash equivalents and productive assets that are expected to generate revenues over the long-term. They also include lending money and collecting on those loans.

3. We can distinguish among three categories of adjustments which convert accrual basis net income to CFO:

    I.   Expenses, losses, revenues and gains which do not use or generate cash, i.e. those involving non-cash accounts (except those in II, below).

    II.   Net changes in non-cash accounts (mostly in the operating working capital group) which relate to operations. These modify the accrual-based revenue and expense items included in income.

    III.   Gains or losses (such as on sales of assets) which are transferred to other sections of the SCF so as to show there the entire cash proceeds of the sale.

4. The following are the two methods of determining CFO:

Indirect Method: Under this method net income is adjusted for non-cash items required to convert it to CFO. The advantage of this method is that it is a reconciliation which discloses the differences between net income and CFO. Some analysts estimate future cash flows by first estimating future income levels and then adjusting these for leads and lags between income and CFO (i.e., non-cash adjustments).

Direct (or Inflow-Outflow) Method: This method lists the gross cash receipts and disbursements related to operations. Most respondents to the Exposure Draft which preceded SFAS 95 preferred this method because this presentation discloses the total amounts of cash which flowed into the enterprise and out of the enterprise due to operations. This gives analysts a better measure of the size of cash inflows and outflows over which management had some degree of discretion. As the risks to which lenders are exposed relate more to fluctuations in CFO than to fluctuations in net income, information on the amounts of operating cash receipts and payments is important in assessing the nature of those fluctuations.

5. The function of the income statement is to measure the profitability of the enterprise for a given period. This is done by relating, as well as is possible, expenses and revenues. While no other statement measures profitability as well as the income statement, it does not show the timing of cash flows and the effect of operations on liquidity and solvency. This is done by the SCF which represents a different aspect of the same reality.

Cash from operations (CFO) encompasses the broader concept of operations of the two measures. It encompasses all earning-related activities of the enterprise. CFO is concerned not only with costs and revenues but also with the cash demands of these activities, such as investments in customer receivables and in inventories as well as the financing provided by suppliers of goods and services. CFO focuses on the liquidity aspect of operations and is not a measure of profitability because it does not include important items of cost such as the use of long-lived assets in operations or revenue items such as the equity in the earnings of nonconsolidated subsidiaries or affiliates.

6. The term "cash flow" was probably first coined by financial analysts. They recognized, long before accountants were ready to admit it, that the accrual system of income measurement permits the introduction of a variety of alternative accounting treatments and consequent distortions. The crude concept of cash flow--net income plus the best known non-cash expense (depreciation)--was invented in order to bypass such distortions and to bring income measurement closer to the discipline of actual cash flows. This cash flow measure, a popular surrogate for cash from operations (CFO), is crude because it falls far short of even approximating in most cases the correct measure of CFO. It stayed crude because the people who developed and used it lacked the will or the accounting sophistications to improve it.

One source of confusion stems from the incorrect computation of the crude measure of cash flow as noted above. The figure is simply represented to be what it is not.

Another and even more serious confusion arises from the assertion of some, and particularly those managements that are dissatisfied by the level of their reported net income, that cash flow is a measure of performance superior to or more valid than net income. This is like saying that depreciation, or other costs not involving the use of cash, are not genuine expenses. Only net income can be properly regarded as a measure of performance and can be validly related to the equity investment as an indicator of operating performance. If we add back depreciation to net income and compute the resulting return on investment, we are, in effect, confusing the return on investment with an element of return of investment in fixed assets.

7. The SCF sheds light on the effects of earning activities on cash resources, and on what assets were acquired and how they were financed. It can highlight more clearly the distinction between net income and cash provided by operations.

The ability of an enterprise to generate cash from operations on a consistent basis is an important indicator of financial health. No business can survive over the long-term without generating cash from its operations. However, the interpretation of CFO figures and trends must be made with care and with a full understanding of all surrounding circumstances.

Prosperous as well as failing entities may find themselves unable to generate cash from operations at any given time, but for different reasons. The entity caught in the "prosperity squeeze" of having to invest its cash in receivables and inventories in order to meet ever-increasing customer demand will often find that its profitability will facilitate financing by equity as well as by debt. That same profitability should ultimately turn CFO into a positive figure. The unsuccessful firm, on the other hand, will find its cash drained by slowdowns in receivable and inventory turnovers, by operating losses, or by a combination of these factors. These conditions usually contain the seeds of further losses and cash drains and may also lead to the drying up of trade credit. In such cases, a lack of CFO has different implications. Even if the unsuccessful firm manages to borrow, the costs of borrowing will only magnify the ultimate drains of its cash. Thus, profitability is a key consideration, and while it does not insure CFO in the short run, it is essential to a healthy financial condition in the long run.

The unsuccessful or financially pressed firm can increase its CFO by reducing accounts receivable and inventories, but usually this is done at the expense of services to customers which may lower future profitability.

Changes in operating working capital items must be interpreted in the light of attending circumstances. An increase in receivables may mean expanding consumer demand for enterprise products or it may mean an inability to collect amounts due in a timely fashion. Similarly, an increase in inventories (and particularly of the raw material component) may mean preparations for an increase in production in response to consumer demand. It may also mean (particularly if the finished goods component of inventories is increasing) an inability to sell, i.e., that anticipated demand has not materialized.

As the above discussion suggests, the evaluation and the interpretation of CFO must be done with great care and with a consideration of all surrounding circumstances.

8. A valuable analytical derivative of the SCF is "free cash flow." As with any other analytical measure, analysts must pay careful attention to components of the computation. Here, as in the case of cash flow measures, ulterior motives may sometimes affect the validity of the computation.

One of the analytically most useful computations of free cash flow is as follows:

Cash from Operations (CFO)
Less: Capital expenditures required to maintain productive capacity used up in the production of income
Less: Dividends (on preferred stock and maintenance of desired payout on common stock)
Equals Free Cash Flow (FCF)

Positive FCF implies that this is the amount available for corporate purposes after provisions for financing outlays and expenditures to maintain productive capacity at current levels. Internal growth and financial flexibility depend on an adequate amount of FCF.

It should be noted that the amount of capital expenditures needed to maintain productive capacity at current levels is generally not disclosed by companies. It is included in total capital expenditures which may also include outlays for expansion of productive capacity. Breaking down capital expenditures between these two components is difficult. The repeal of mandatory inflation disclosures (SFAS 89) made this task even more difficult. The FASB considered this issue and in SFAS 95 decided not to require classification of investment expenditures into maintenance and expansion categories.

9. To the financial analyst, the SCF provides clues to important matters such as:

    *   Feasibility of financing capital expenditures and possible sources of such financing.
    *   Sources of cash to finance an expansion in the volume of business.
    *   Dependence of the enterprise on external sources of financing (e.g., borrowing or new equity).
    *   Future dividend policies.
    *   Ability to meet future debt service requirements.
    *   Financial flexibility, i.e., the firm's ability to generate sufficient cash so as to respond to unanticipated needs and opportunities.
    *   An insight into the financial habits of management and resulting indications of future policies.
    *   Indications regarding the quality of earnings.

10. The reconstruction, in the aggregate, of all transactions for a period can determine whether the SCF satisfactorily explains all the changes in the balance sheet accounts, can provide additional information that is helpful in understanding the SCF and generally can provide analytically useful insights into the aggregate transactions of a period and the relationships among them.

    In the process of reconstruction light is shed on those summary transactions which management, for whatever reason, has chosen not to disclose and to combine in categories usually designated as "other, net." While this category can relieve the SCF of unimportant detail (such as stock dividends or the write-off of fully depreciated assets) it can also hide significant transactions (such as new investments) about which the analyst needs to know. This process also provides a check on management's classification and descriptions of items in the SCF.

◄ Answers to Exercises ►

Exercise 7-1

a. SFAS 95 requires that the SCF classify cash receipts and payments by operating, financing, and investing activities.

Operating activities encompass all the earning related activities of the enterprise. They encompass, in addition to all the income and expense items found in the income statement, all the net inflows and outflows of cash that operations impose on the enterprise as a result of activities such as the extension of credit to customers, investment in inventories, and obtaining credit from suppliers. Operating activities relate to all items in the statement of income (with minor exceptions) as well as to balance sheet items that relate to operations--mostly working capital accounts such as accounts receivable, inventories, prepayments, accounts payable, and accruals. SFAS 95 also specifies that operating activities include all transactions and events that are not of an investing or financing nature.

Financing activities include obtaining resources from owners and providing them with a return of or a return on (i.e. dividends) their investment. They also include obtaining resources from creditors and repaying the amounts borrowed or otherwise settling the obligations.

Investing activities include acquiring and selling or otherwise disposing of securities which are not cash equivalents and productive assets that are expected to generate revenues over the long term. They also include lending money and collecting on those loans.

b. SFAS 95 requires that all significant financing and investing activities be disclosed. For example, noncash transactions which include the conversion of debt to equity, the acquisition of assets through the issuance of debt, and exchanges of assets or liabilities, should be disclosed in a separate schedule of noncash investing and financing activities.

c. 1. The amount net income is the starting point of the computation of CFO. SFAS 95 does not require the separate disclosure of extraordinary items in the SCF.

2. Depreciation is added back as an expense not requiring cash.

3. The write-off of uncollectible receivables does not affect cash. The bad debt expense does not require an outlay of cash. Because we use the indirect method of presentation of CFO no additional adjustment is needed beyond the adjustment for the change in the net receivable, which includes the credit to the allowance for doubtful accounts.

4. The increase in accounts receivable means that some sales have not been collected in cash, and net income is reduced by $140,000 in arriving at CFO.

The decline in inventories means that cost of goods sold includes inventories paid for in prior years, and did not require cash this year. Net income is increased by $60,000 in arriving at CFO.

5. This is an expense requiring cash--no adjustment is called for. This amount must be disclosed as part of supplemental disclosure.

6.
Cash	30,000	
Accumulated Depreciation	50,000	
PPE		75,000
Gain on sale of machine		5,000

$30,000 will be shown as a source from investing activities. The $5,000 will be deducted from (i.e. removed from) net income so entire proceeds of sale are shown as part of investment activities.

7. Only the cash payment of $100,000 will be shown in the SCF as an investing activity outflow. In a separate schedule, the purchase of building and land for noncash considerations will be detailed.

8. This is a noncash transaction which will be disclosed in a separate schedule of noncash investing and financing activities.

9. The declaration of a cash dividend creates a current liability. During Year 8 no cash outflow occurred and there is nothing to report on the SCF.

10. This event has no effect on cash nor need it be reported in conjunction with the SCF.

Exercise 7-2

a.
Net income		$10,000
Add (deduct) items to convert to cash basis:		
Depreciation, depletion, and amortization	$8,000	
Deferred income taxes	400	
Amortization of bond discount	50	
Increase in accounts payable	1,200	
Decrease in inventories	850	10,500
		$20,500
Undistributed earnings of unconsolidated subsidiaries and affiliates	$(200)	
Amortization of premium on bonds payable	(60)	
Increase in accounts receivable	(900)	(1,160)
Cash provided by operations		$19,340

b. 1. The issuance of treasury stock for employee stock plans (as compensation) requires an addback to net income because it is an expense not using cash.

2. The cash outflow for interest is not included in expense and must be included as cash outflow in investing activities (as part of outlays for property.)

3.   If the difference between pension expense and actual funding is an accrued liability the unpaid portion must be added back to income as an expense not requiring cash. If the amount funded exceeds pension expense net income must be reduced by that excess amount.

Exercise 7-3

a.

Opening balance of accounts receivable	$ 305,000
Net sales	1,937,000
Total	$2,242,000
Ending balance of accounts receivable	- 295,000
Cash collected for sales	$1,947,000

b.

Ending balance of inventory	$ 549,000
Cost of sales	+1,150,000
Total	$1,699,000
Beginning balance of inventory	- 431,000
Purchases	$1,268,000
Beginning balance of A/P	$ 563,000
+ Purchases	1,268,000
Total	$1,831,000
Ending balance of A/P	- 604,000
Cash payments for A/P	$1,227,000

c.

Increase in common stock	$81,000
Sales of treasury stock	17,000
Total	$98,000

d.

Increase in land	$150,000
Increase in plant and equipment	18,000
Total	$168,000

Exercise 7-4

	Source	Use	Adjustment	Category
a.		X	X	O
b.		X		F
c.	X			F
d.	X			I
e.		X		F
f.				NCN
g.		X		I
h.				NCS
i.		X		F
j.	X		X	O

Exercise 7-5

	Source	Use	Adjustment	Category
a.	X		X	O
b.		X		F
c.				NCN
d.		X		I
e.				NCS
f.				NCN
g.	X			I
h.				NCS
i.				NE
j.				NE

Exercise 7-6

	Net income	Cash from operations	Cash position
1.	NE	NE	+
2.	NE	NE	+
3.	+	+	+
4a.	-	NE	NE
4b.	NE[1]	+[2]	+[2]
4c.	-	+[2]	+[2]
5.	NE	+	+
6.	-	+	+
7.	-	-[5]	+
8.	+	NE	NE
9.	+[3]	+[4]	+[4]

[1]   Deferred tax accounting
[2]   Depends on whether tax savings are realized in cash
[3]   If profitable
[4]   If A/R collected
[5]   Depends on whether interest is paid or accrued

Other effects:

1.   Substituting payment in stock for payment in cash for dividends will not affect income or CFO but will increase cash position by cash savings.

2.   In the short run, postponement of capital expenditures will save cash but have no effect on income or CFO. In the longer term both income and CFO may suffer due to lower operating efficiency.

3.   Cash not spent on repair and maintenance will increase all three measures. However, the skimping on necessary discretionary costs will affect adversely future operating efficiency, and hence, profitability.

4.   Those advocating an increase in depreciation may have spoken in the mistaken belief that depreciation is a source of cash and that consequently increasing it would result in a higher cash inflow. In fact, the level of depreciation expense has no effect on cash flow--the

same amount of depreciation deducted in arriving at net income is added back in arriving at CFO.

Increasing depreciation for tax purposes will in all cases result in at least a short-term savings.

5. Quicker collections will not affect income but will increase CFO because of lower accounts receivable. Cash will also increase by the speedier conversion of receivables into cash. In the longer run this stiffening in the terms of sale to customers may result in sales lost to competition.

6. Payment stretch-out will lower income because of lost discounts but does affect CFO positively by increasing the level of accounts payable. Cash conservation will result in a higher cash position. Relations with suppliers may be affected adversely.

7. Borrowing will result in interest costs which will decrease income and CFO. Cash position will increase.

8. This change in depreciation method will increase income in the early stages of an asset's life. The opposite may hold true in the later stages of the asset's life.

9. In the short term, higher sales to dealers will result in higher profits (assuming we sell above all costs) and if they pay promptly CFO and cash will increase. However, unless the dealers are able to sell to the ultimate consumer such sales will be made at the expense of future sales.

Exercise 7-7

a. Depreciation is neither a source nor a use of cash but rather a bookkeeping allocation of the cost of an asset over its useful life.

b. A major cause of the belief that depreciation is a source of cash is the "add back" presentation in most SCF. This presentation adds depreciation to net income and gives the impression that it increases cash from operations.

c. There is one sense in which depreciation is a source of cash, and for this reason we must not overemphasize the idea that depreciation is not a source of cash. When selling prices are sufficient to recover the depreciation expense allocated to products sold, revenues do provide management with a discretionary, even if temporary, inflow of cash (assuming no significant change in operating working capital). Normally, management will have to invest this cash in fixed assets replacements in order to continue in business on a long-term basis. However, in the event of an emergency or a financial stringency, management has the option of diverting such cash to uses which will avert a liquidity crisis. This is the one exception which may let us regard depreciation as a temporary "source" of cash.

Exercise 7-8

The CFO of Campbell is higher (by $403.7 million) than its Year 11 net income for two major reasons:

1. Some items decreased net income but did not use cash:

    a. Depreciation and amortization are expenses not requiring a cash outlay ($208.6)

    b. Deferred income taxes similarly are an expense which involves no present cash payment ($35.5)

    c. Several charges and expenses did not require outlays of cash ($63.2)

    d. A decrease in inventory means that cost of sales were charged by reducing inventory levels rather than by making cash payments of $48.7

2. Some items generated operating cash inflow but did not enter the determination of net income (adding to the effect of the above):

    a. The decrease in accounts receivable means that cash was collected beyond the amounts booked as sales revenue in the income statement ($17.1)

    b. There were a number of other items which had a similar effect for $30.6.

Exercise 7-9

a.

Accounts Receivable (Net)			
Beg (a)	564.1		
3ales [13]	6205.8	6145.4	Plug = collections (b)
End [33]	624.5		

    (a)   Balance at 7/29/Year 10 $624.5 [33]
                Less: increase in Year 10   (60.4) [61]
                                        $564.1

    (b)   This amount is overstated by the provision for doubtful accounts expense which is included in some expense category.

b.

Dividends Payable			
Dividend paid [77]	137.5	32.3	Beg [43]
		142.2	dividend declared (a) [89]
		37.0	End [43]

    (a)   Item [89] represents dividends declared, not dividends paid (see also Item [77]).

c.

Inventories			
Beg [34]	819.8	4095.5	Cost of products sold [14]
- plug -	3982.4		
End [34]	706.7		

d.   Entry for income tax provision for Year 11:

```
Income tax expense [27]                    265.9
   Deferred income tax (current)--plug        12.1
   Income tax payable                         230.4
   Deferred income tax (noncurrent) (1)        23.4
```

    (1)   Difference in balance of noncurrent deferred income tax item [176] = \$258.5 - \$235.1 = \$23.4

Note: \$23.4 + \$12.1 = \$35.5 total deferred tax [59] or [127A]

This entry increases current liabilities by \$12.1 since deferred income tax (current) is credited by this amount. It also increases current liabilities by \$230.4, the amount of income taxes payable.

e.   Depreciation expense had no effect on cash from operations. The credit, when booking the depreciation expense, goes to accumulated depreciation, a noncash account.

f.   Because the provision affected only noncash accounts, the charge to earnings had to be removed in converting these to the cash basis.

g.   It represents translation adjustments (differences) arising from the translation of cash from foreign currencies to the U.S. dollar.

h.   Under "other net" item [60].

Exercise 7-10

a.

Receivables [55]			
Beginning balance	594.4		
Revenue [1]	5,030.6	4,995.1	Collections (a)
Ending balance	629.9		

   (a)   This plug figure is overstated by the provision for doubtful accounts. This account is part of Quaker Oats' expense categories.

b.

	(in millions)
Total cash dividends paid in Year 11 [38]	123.0
Less: Dividends on preferred stock [111]	4.3
Dividends paid on common stock *	118.7

   * Item [110] indicates $118.7 million as common dividends.

c.

Inventories [59]			
Beginning balance	473.9		
(a)	2,788.1	2,839.7	COGS [2]
Ending balance	422.3		

   (a) Cost of goods and services produced and otherwise generated (plug)

d.   Quaker Oats did not acquire any property through the issuance of common stock. If they had, this would appear in a noncash transaction schedule which is disclosed with the statement of cash flows.

e.   The entry establishing the income tax provision for Year 11 follows:

Provision for income taxes [8]	175.7	
Deferred income tax--noncurrent [158]		14.3
Tax currently payable [158]		161.4

The company does not appear to have a current deferred tax account. The deferred tax provision was noncurrent, having no effect on current liabilities.

f.   Depreciation is an expense that is credited to accumulated depreciation which is, in turn, netted against gross fixed assets. It is an expense that does not require the use of cash. For that reason, it is added back to net income to arrive at cash provided by operations.

g.   The year-to-year increase of $97.8 million in receivables means that sales exceeded collections (on a net basis) by this amount.

h.   Yes. See items [29] and [30] which relate to discontinued operations.

i. The difference of $326.6 ($532.4 - 205.8) is explained as follows:

Items Decreasing Cash

[25] Asset prepaid for which will be recognized as an expense in the future (i.e., increase in other current assets)

                                                                                    (13.7)

[23] Cash collected this year is less than sales (increase in receivables)

                                                                                    (97.8)
                                                                                   (111.5)

Items Increasing Cash

[24+30] Assets that were purchased in past periods and expensed in the current period (i.e., reduction in inventory and current assets, that are expenses not using cash in this period)

                                                                                     96.7

[26+27+ Expenses recognized in the current period, that will be paid for in
+28+29] future periods (i.e., an increase in accounts payable, accrued liabilities and others)

                                                                                    108.4

[20] Expenses recognized this period but paid for in prior periods (i.e., depreciation and amortization)

                                                                                    177.7

[21+22] Expenses recognized this period that will not be paid until future periods (i.e., noncurrent deferred taxes and provision for restructuring charges)

                                                                                     55.3
                                                                                    438.1
       Difference between net income and cash from operations   326.6

j. The provision for uncollectible accounts is probably buried in Selling, General and Administrative Expenses. The entry to record this provision is:

    Provision for Doubtful Accounts (SGA)
        Allowance for Doubtful Accounts

The provision for doubtful accounts is assumed to be using cash, the allowance for doubtful accounts (credit) results in a decrease in accounts receivable showing an increase in cash. Therefore, cash receipts and cash disbursements are overstated. However, the net effect on cash is zero.

k. Cash provided by operations $ 532.4
    Less: Change in payables to Fisher Price $ 29.6
        Change in net current assets of discontinued operations   66.0   95.6
    Cash provided by continuing operations $ 436.8

◄ Answers to Problems ►

Problem 7-1
a. T-accounts required to prepare statement of cash flows:

Cash		
Beg	34,000	

Operations			
Net income (a)	7,000	3,000	Gain on sale of invest. (i)
Depreciation (c)	5,000	5,000	Increase in receivables (x)
Loss on fixed assets (f)	1,000	7,000	Decrease in A/P (z)
Decrease in inventory (y)	2,000		

Investing Activities			
Sale of fixed assets (f)	6,000	4,000	Purchase of fixed assets (g)
Sale of investments (i)	9,000		

Financing Activities			
Sale of common stock (n)	1,000	11,500	Purch. of treasury stock (j)

Noncash Transactions			
Bonds issued to acquire fixed assets (h)	30,000	30,000	Fixed assets purchase by issuance of bonds (h)
Issuance of common stock in exchange of bonds (k)	10,000	10,000	Conversion of bonds (k)
End	34,500		

Investments			
Beg	6,000		
		6,000	(i)
End	- 0 -		

Treasury Stock			
Beg	- 0 -		
(j)	11,500		
End	11,500		

Bonds Payable			
		10,000	Beg
(k)	10,000	30,000	(h)
		30,000	End

Inventory			
Beg	16,000		
		2,000	(y)
End	14,000		

Accounts Receivable		
Beg	12,000	
(x)	5,000	
End	17,000	

Fixed Assets			
Beg	80,000	21,000	(f)
(g)	4,000		
(h)	30,000		
End	93,000		

Accumulated Depreciation			
(g)	14,000	48,000	Beg
		5,000	(c)
		39,000	End

Common Stock			
		50,000	Beg
		10,000	(k)
		1,000	(n)
		61,000	End

Retained Earnings			
		21,000	Beg
		7,000	(a)
		28,000	End

Accounts Payable			
		19,000	Beg
(z)	7,000		
		12,000	End

Zett Company
Statement of Cash Flows
For the Year Ended 12/31/Year 2

Cash flows from operating activities:		
Net Income	7,000	
Add (deduct) items to convert to cash basis		
Depreciation	5,000	
Loss on sale of fixed assets	1,000	
Gain on sale of investment	(3,000)	
Decrease in inventory	2,000	
Increase in receivables	(5,000)	
Decrease in accounts payables	(7,000)	
Net cash provided from operating activities		- 0 -
Cash flows from investing activities:		
Sale of fixed assets	6,000	
Sale of investments	9,000	
Purchase of fixed assets	(4,000)	
Net cash provided from investing activities		11,000
Cash flows from financing activities:		
Sale of unissued common stock	1,000	
Purchase of treasury stock	(11,500)	
Net cash used by financing activities	(10,500)	
Net Increase in cash		500

Supplemental disclosure of Cash Flow information:
Cash paid during the year for
  Interest   4,000
  Income taxes   6,000

Schedule of noncash investing and financing activities:
Acquisition of fixed assets by issue of bonds   30,000
Conversion of bonds into common stock   10,000

b.

Zett Company
Comparison of two bases of reporting

	Income Statement	Cash from operations	
Sales	70,000	65,000	Collection from customers
Gain on sale of investments	3,000	- (a)	
	73,000	65,000	
Purchases	(40,000)	(47,000)	Payments to suppliers (b)
Decrease in inventory	(2,000)	--	
Depreciation	(5,000)	(c)	
Expenses paid	(18,000)	(18,000)	
Loss on sale of fixed assets	(1,000)	(d)	
Net income	7,000		
Cash from operations		- 0 -	

(a)   Omitted because it is linked up with proceeds from sale of investment (investing activities).

(b)   Purchase of $40,000 + decrease in accounts payable of $7,000.

(c)   No cash required.

(d)   Linked up with sale of fixed assets (investing activities).

c.   The income statement prepared on the accrual basis is designed to reflect profitability. Cash from operations measures the effects on cash of operating activities.

Problem 7-2

a.

Cash	
Beg	640

Operations			
Net income (1)	160	310*	(4) Inc. in A/R
Amortization (2)	10	145	(5) Inc. in inventories
Depreciation (3)	95	25	(6) Inc. in prepaid expenses
Inc. in accounts payable (7)	30		
Inc. in deferred income tax (8)	12		
Inc. in other C. Liabs (9)	7		

Investing			
		140	(10) purchase of patents
		700	(1) Addition to plant and equipment
		25	(12) Addition to other assets

Financing			
Addition to L.T. debt (13)	800	109	(15) Cash dividends
Issuance of common stock (14)	200		
End	500		

* Because we are preparing the CFO segment under the indirect method, the noncash charge for bad debt expense has no effect on the presentation. Under the direct presentation, cash inflows would be decreased by $40,000 and so would cash outflows for expenses.

Patents			
Beg	0	10	(2)
(10)	140		
End	130		

Other Assets		
Beg	175	
(12)	25	
End 200		

Prepaid Expenses		
Beg	0	
(6)	25	
End	25	

Plant and Equipment		
Beg	1,950	
(11)	700	
End	2,650	

Accumulated Depreciation		
	535	Beg
	95	(3)
	630	End

Accounts Receivable		
Beg	550	
(4)	310	
End	860	

Inventories		
Beg	790	
(5)	145	
End	935	

Retained Earnings		
(15)	109	197	Beg
		160	(1)
		248	End

Long-term Debt		
	850	Beg
	800	(13)
	1,650	End

Other Current Liabilities		
	78	Beg
	7	(9)
	85	End

Common Stock		
	1,800	Beg
	200	(14)
	2,000	End

Accounts Payable		
	600	Beg
	30	(7)
	630	End

Deferred Income Tax		
	45	Beg
	12	(8)
	57	End

Dax Corporation
Statement of Cash Flows
For the Year Ended Dec. 31, Year 2
(In thousands of dollars)

Cash provided from (used for) operations:		
Net Income	160	
Add (deduct) items to convert to cash basis:		
Amortization	10	
Depreciation	95	
Inc. in accounts payable	30	
Inc. in deferred income tax	12	
Inc. in other current liabilities	7	
Inc. in accounts receivable	(310)	
Inc. in inventories	(145)	
Inc. in prepaid expenses	(25)	
Net cash used for operations		(166)
Cash provided from (used for) investing activities:		
Purchase of patents	(140)	
Addition to plant and equipment	(700)	
Addition to other assets	(25)	
Net cash used for investing activities		(865)
Cash provided from (used for) financing activities:		
Addition to long-term debt	800	
Issuance of common stock	200	
Dividends paid	(109)	
Net cash provided from financing activities		891
Net Decrease in Cash		140

Supplemental disclosure of cash flow information:
Cash paid during year for
Interest	$28,000
Income taxes	$70,000

b. The major reasons for the difference between net income of $160 and cash outflow for operations of $166 are the heavy investments in inventories of $145 and the financing of customers through higher receivables by $310. Compared to these heavy investments in operating assets, accounts payable have increased very modestly. With rising sales and profits the company is experiencing a prosperity squeeze.

c. This situation must be addressed before the liquidity problems become more serious. The following actions could be taken:

1.   The larger volume of purchases justifies more trade credit and an expansion of accounts payable will increase cash from operations.

2.   The company needs a larger equity capital base. With increasing profits
        and with the company being in a growth industry this may be a good time
        to sell stock without diluting earnings per share.

3.   Sale of equity will form a good base for further borrowing should
        business continue to expand rapidly.

4.   After additional equity capital has been obtained the company should
        consider lowering the dividend payout. For a fast growing and
        profitable company like Dax a dividend payout ratio of 68% (109/160)
        is quite high. Given present profit opportunities more earnings should
        be retained in the business.

Problem 7-3

Sales	$1,000	
Less increase in receivables	(20)	
Cash collections		$980
Cost of goods sold	$(650)	
Add increase in inventories	(20)	
		(670)
Sales and general expense	$(100)	
Less increase in payables	25	
		(75)
Interest expense	$(50)	
Less increase in interest payable	10	
		(40)
Income tax expense	$(40)	
Less increase in deferred income tax	10	
		(30)
CASH FROM OPERATIONS		$165
Purchase of fixed assets	$(150)	
CASH USED IN INVESTING ACTIVITIES		(150)
Decrease in notes payable	$(25)	
Increase in long term debt	50	
Dividends paid	(30)	
CASH USED IN FINANCING ACTIVITIES		(5)
NET INCREASE IN CASH		$10
BEGINNING CASH		50
ENDING CASH		$60

Note: Purchase of fixed assets is computed from depreciation expense plus change in fixed assets (100 + 50). Dividends paid is computed from net income and change in retained earnings (60 - 30).

Supporting schedule for CFO:

Net income	$60
Depreciation	100
Increase in deferred tax	10
Increase in receivables	(20)
Increase in inventory	(20)
Increase in accounts payable	25
Increase in interest payable	<u>10</u>
CFO	$165

Problem 7-4

	EFFECTS	ENTRIES		
a.	[-Y, 11,000]	Bad debt expense	11,000	
	[CC, 11,000]	Allowance for bad debt		11,000
b.	[-Y, 16,000]	Depreciation	16,000	
	[YA, 16,000]	Accum. depreciation		16,000
c.	[NAA, 100,000]	Building	100,000	
	[NDE, 90,000]	LT note payable		100,000
d.	none			
e.	none			
f.	[+C, 10,000]	Cash	10,000	
	[-Y, 2,000]	Loss	2,000	
	[CC, 12,000]	Inventory		12,000
g.	[+C, 35,000]	Cash	35,000	
	[DC, 5,000]	A/R	5,000	
	[CC, 25,000]	Inventory		25,000
	[+Y, 15,000]	Gain		15,000
h.	[CC, 3,000]	Allowance	5,000	
	[-Y, 3,000]	Bad debt expense	3,000	
		A/R		8,000
i.	[AA, 100,000]	Assets	100,000	
	[-C, 100,000]	Cash		100,000
	[-Y, 20,000]	Depreciation expense	20,000	
	[YA, 20,000]	Accum. depreciation		20,000
j.	[+C, 8,000]	Cash	8,000	
	[AD, 8,000]	Loss on sale	1,000	
	[YA, 1,000]	Machinery (net)		9,000
	[-Y, 1,000]			

Problem 7-5

I.

	EFFECTS	ENTRIES		
a.	[DL, 100,000]	Curr. Portion LTD	100,000	
	[-C, 100,000]	Cash		100,000
b.	[+C, 4,000]	Cash	4,000	
	[AD, 4,000]	Loss	1,000	
	[YA, 1,000]	Equipment		5,000
	[-Y, 1,000]			
c.	[-Y, 75,000]	Loss	75,000	
	[CC, 75,000]	Inventory		75,000
d.	[+C, 28,000]	Cash	28,000	
	[DE, 28,000]	P.I.C.	2,000	
		Treasury stock		30,000
e.	[NAA, 300,000]	Plant	300,000	
	[NDE, 300,000]	Mortgage Payable		250,000
		Mortgage Payable—Current		50,000
f.	[+C, 6,000]	Investment	30,000	
	[+Y, 30,000]	Equity in NI of sub		30,000
	[YS, 24,000]	Cash	6,000	
		Investment		6,000
g.	[+C, 10,000]	Cash	10,000	
	[+Y, 40,000]	A/R, current	10,000	
	[DC, 10,000]	A/R, noncurrent	20,000	
	[NC, 20,000]	Sales		40,000
h.	[DC, 9,000]	Inventory	9,000	
	[+Y, 9,000]	Cost of Goods Sold		9,000
i.	[DC, 260,000]	Current Assets	260,000	
	[CC, 160,000]	PPE	600,000	
	[AA, 670,000]	Goodwill	70,000	
	[DE, 410,000]	Curr. Liabs.		160,000
	[-C, 360,000]	LTD		410,000
		Cash (400-40)		360,000
j.	[-Y, 60,000]	Expense	60,000	
	[CC, 60,000]	Allowance for doubtful accounts		60,000

II.

	EFFECTS	ENTRIES		
a.	[AA, 120,000]	Investment	120,000	
	[-C, 120,000]	Cash		120,000
b.	[YS, 7,500]	Investment	7,500	
	[+Y, 7,500]	Equity in earnings		7,500
c.	[+C, 3,000]	Investment	9,000	
	[+Y, 9,000]	Equity in earnings		9,000
	[YS, 6,000]	Cash	3,000	
		Investment		3,000
d.	[+C, 4,000]	Cash	4,000	
	[AD, 4,000]	Equipment (net)		3,000
	[YS, 1,000]	Gain on Sale		1,000
	[+Y, 1,000]			
e.	[+C, 60,000]	Cash	60,000	
	[IL, 60,000]	Note Pay. (current)		60,000
f.	[NDR, 9,000]	Bonds Payable	9,000	
	[NDE, 9,000]	Common stock		2,000
		PIC		7,000
g.	[+C, 6,000]	Cash	6,000	
	[DE, 6,000]	Treasury stock		4,000
		PIC		2,000
h1.	[AA, 200,000]	Investment	200,000	
	[DE, 100,000]	Common stock		100,000
	[-C, 100,000]	Cash		100,000
h2.	[DC, 80,000]	Current Assets (120-40)	80,000	
	[AA, 180,000]	PPE	150,000	
	[CC, 60,000]	Goodwill	30,000	
	[DE, 140,000]	Current Liabilities		60,000
	[-C, 60,000]	LTD		40,000
		Common stock		100,000
		Cash (100-40)		60,000
i.	[-Y, 4,000]	Minority Int. Exp.	4,000	
	[YA, 4,000]	Minority Interest		4,000
j.	[-Y, 50,000]	Inventory Loss	50,000	
	[CC, 50,000]	Inventory		50,000
k.	none	Allow for doubtful accounts	1,200	
		Accounts receivable		1,200

```
l.   [NAA, 120,000]    Leased Equipment          120,000
     [NDE, 120,000]        Long-term debt                  120,000

m.   none              Retained earnings         180,000
                           Common stock                   120,000
                           Paid in Capital                 60,000

n.   [-Y, 27,000]      Bad debts expense          27,000
     [CC, 27,000]          Allow for doubtful accts        27,000

o.   none

     or

     [ID, 40,000]      Retained earnings          40,000
     [IL, 40,000]          Dividends payable               40,000
     (should be eliminated)
```

Problem 7-6

Cash		
Beg — plug —	50,000	

Operations			
Net income (1)	150,000	50,000	(5) Gain on sale of inventory
Depreciation expense (2)	85,000	30,000	(6) Increase in A/R
Loss on sale of equip (3)	5,000	20,000	(7) Increase in inventory
Increase in A/P (4)	40,000		

Investing			
Sale of equipment (8)	10,000	150,000	(10) Add. to POL Equip.
Sale of investments (9)	95,000		

Financing			
Issuance of common stock (11)	10,000	80,000	(13) Cash dividends
Additions to LTD (12)	15,000	30,000	(14) Decrease in current portion of LTD
End	100,000		

Retained Earnings			
(13)	80,000	80,000	Beg
		150,000	(1)
		150,000	End

Property, Plant, and Equipment			
Beg	465,000		
(10)	150,000	65,000	(3), (8) & (a)
End	550,000		

Other Noncurrent Investments		
Beg	245,000	45,000 (5),(9)
End	200,000	

Accumulated Depreciation		
(a)	50,000	235,000 Beg
		85,000 (2)
		270,000 End

Long-term Debt		
	185,000	Beg
	15,000	(12)
	200,000	End

Common Stock		
	290,000	Beg
	10,000	(11)
	300,000	End

Accounts Receivable		
Beg	90,000	
(6)	30,000	
End	120,000	

Inventory		
Beg	110,000	
(7)	20,000	
End	130,000	

Accounts Payable		
	60,000	Beg
	40,000	(4)
	100,000	End

Current Portion of LTD		
(14)	30,000	110,000 Beg
		80,000 End

BIRD CORPORATION
Balance Sheet
January 1, Year 1

Assets:
Cash		$ 50,000
Accounts receivable		90,000
Inventory		110,000
Current assets		$250,000
Property, plant, and equipment	$465,000	
Less—Accumulated depreciation	235,000	230,000
Other noncurrent investments		245,000
Total assets		$725,000

Liabilities and Equity:
Accounts payable	$ 60,000
Current portion of long-term debt	110,000
Current liabilities	$170,000
Long-term debt	185,000
Common stock	290,000
Retained earnings	80,000
Total liabs. and equity	$725,000

	Current Ratio	Working Capital Effect	Cash From Operations Amount	Cash From Operations Effect	Amount	Journal Entries DR	Journal Entries CR
a.	+	0	0	-	$1,000	Accrued wages	Cash
b.	-	0	0	0	0	Purchases	A/P
c.	-	-	70,000	-	0	Loss	A/P
d.	0	0	0	+	8,000	Cash	A/R
e.	-	-	100,000	0	0	PPE	Cash
f.	+	0	15,000	0	0	Note Payable	Cash
g.	+	+	15,000	0	0	Note Rec	Land
h.	+	+	90,000	0	0	Cash	APIC
i.	-	-	20,000	0	0	PPE	Cash / Current Liabs / LT Liabs
j.	-	-	50,000	0	Premium	Bond Payable	Cash / Gain
k.	-	-	10,000	0	0	RE	Div Payable
l.	+	0	0	0	0	Div Payable	Cash
m.	0	0	0	0	0	RE	Stock Div Payable
n.	0	0	0	0	0	Stock Div Payable	APIC / Capital Stock
o.	0	0	0	0	0	No entry	
p.	-	0	0	0	0	Cash	Notes Payable
q.	+	0	20,000	-	20,000	A/P	Cash
r.	-	-	20,000	0	0	Patent	Cash
s.	-	-	15,000	-	15,000	Loss	Marketable Sec
t.	0	0	0	0	0	Loss	Organization Exp
u.	0	0	0	0	0	Depr Exp	Accum Depr
v.	+	+	28,000	0	0	A/R	Sales
w.	+	+	90,000	0	0	Cash	Building / Gain
x.	+	+	5,000	0	0	Cash / Notes Rec	PPE
y.	-	-	40,000	0	0	Inc Tax Exp	Inc Tax Payable / Def Inc Tax (NC)

<u>Problem 7-8</u>

a.   We are considering here two statements (or portions of statements) which
         deal with operations--the income statement and cash from operations (CFO).
         There seems to be an endless confusion, particularly among users of
         financial statements, about the concept of "operations" and about the
         different aspects of operations which these two statements are designed
         to portray.

The function of the *income statement* is to measure the *profitability* of the
enterprise for a given period. This is presently done by matching, as well as is
possible, costs and revenues. However, costs incurred during the period which do
not create future utility must be charged to income regardless of the availability
of related revenues against which they can be matched. While no other statement
measures profitability as well as does the income statement, it does not show the
timing of cash flows and the effect of operations on liquidity and solvency.
Consequently, other specialized statements are needed to focus on the latter
which are different dimensions of earnings related activities.

Cash from operations (CFO) encompasses the broader concept of operations of these
two measures. Here we encompass all earning related activities of the enterprise
and are not concerned only with costs and revenues but also with the cash demands
of these activities such as investments in customer receivables and in inventories
as well as the financing provided by suppliers of goods and services. We arrive
at operating cash receipts and disbursements by adjusting net income for items
needed to convert it to the cash basis.

CFO focuses on the liquidity aspect of operations and is not a measure of
profitability because it does not include important items of cost such as the use
of long-lived assets in operations, or income items such as the equity in the
earnings of nonconsolidated subsidiaries or affiliates.

b.

	Income	CFO
1.	+	NE
2.	+	NE
3.	NE	NE
4.	NE	NE
5.	NE	+
6.	-	NE
7.	NE	NE
8.	-	NE
9.	NE	-
10.	-	NE
11.	NE	NE
12.	-	NE
13.	-	NE
14.	-	NE
15.	NE	NE
16.	+	NE
17.	-	NE
18.	NE	NE
19.	-	NE
20.	-	NE
21.	NE	NE
22.	NE	-

Problem 7-9

a.   As an initial step, the effect of the Kraft acquisition must first be removed. Balance sheet changes:

	Year 7	Year 8	Change	Kraft	Change
A/R	$2,065	$2,222	$157	$758	$(601)
Inv.	4,154	5,384	1,230	1,232	(2)
PP&E	6,582	8,648	2,066	1,740	326
Goodwill	4,052	15,071	11,019	10,361	658
S-T Debt	1,440	1,259	(181)	1,700	(881)
A/P	4,791	1,777	1,986	1,578	408
Accr. liab.	2,277	3,848	1,571	1,530	1,041
L-T Debt	6,293	17,122	10,829	1,900	9,929

Under the indirect method, the following presentation is appropriate:

PHILIP MORRIS COMPANIES, INC.
Statement of Cash Flows
For the Year Ended December 31, Year 8   ($ millions)

Cash flows from operating activities:
Net income $2,337
Add (deduct) adjustments to cash basis:
   Depreciation expense   654
   Amortization of goodwill   125
   Decrease in accounts receivable   601
   Decrease in inventories   2
   Decrease in deferred taxes   (325)
   Increase in accounts payable   408
   Increase in accrued liabilities   1,041
   Increase in income taxes payable   362
Net cash flow operating activities $ 5,205

Cash flows from investing activities:
Increase in property, plant & equipment
   (before depreciation) $ (980)
Increase in goodwill (before amortization)   (783)
Decrease in investments   405
Acquisition of subsidiary—Kraft*   (11,383)
Net cash used by investing activities   (12,741)

Cash flows from financing activities:
Decrease in short-term debt $ (881)
Increase in long-term debt   9,929
Decrease in stockholders' equity (repurchase)**   (540)
Dividends declared   (941)
Increase in dividends payable   47
Net cash provided by financing activities   7,614
Net increase in cash $ 78

Supplemental disclosure of cash flow information:
   Interest paid during year $ 670
   Income taxes paid during the year $1,353

*   Total of Kraft assets and liabilities removed from year to year changes
    and shown as cash outlay for investing activity.

** The net issuance or repurchase of equity is computed by reconciling the stockholders' equity account:

12/31/Year 7 balance	$6,823
Year 8 net income	2,337
Dividend declared	(941)
Total	$8,219
12/31/Year 8 balance	(7,679)
Decrease in equity (repurchase)	$ 540

b. If the direct method is utilized, the following presentation of CFO would be added to the Statement of Cash Flows previously shown under the indirect method or used to replace the "cash flows from operating activities" section of the Statement of Cash Flows:

PHILIP MORRIS COMPANIES, INC.
Cash Flow From Operations
For Year Ended December 31, Year 8 ($ Millions)

Operating cash receipts and disbursements:
Cash receipts from operations:

Sales	$31,742		
Decrease in accounts receivable	601		
Cash collections			$32,343
Cash disbursements for operations:			
Cost of goods sold	$(12,156)		
Decrease in inventories	2		
Increase in accounts payable	408		
		(11,746)	
Selling and administrative expense	$(14,410)		
Increase in accrued liabilities	1,041		
		(13,369)	
Interest expense		(670)	
Income tax expense	$(1,390)		
Increase in income taxes payable	362		
Decrease in deferred income taxes	(325)		
		(1,353)	
Total cash outflows			$(27,138)
Cash from operations			$ 5,205

c. Free cash flow can be defined in various ways. The starting point is cash flow from operating activities of $5,205 million. Students may want to remove interest expense from operating cash flow; if they do so, it should be on an after tax basis.

From operating cash flow, capital expenditures should be deducted. It would be proper to differentiate capital expenditures required to maintain existing business from those which generate growth. The simplest calculation would be operating cash flow less capital expenditures: $5,205 - 980 = $4,225 million. But many variations are possible. Students should also subtract dividends paid of $894 leaving free cash flow of $3,331.

Possible uses of free cash flow include:

1. Repayment of debt resulting in lower interest cost and higher earnings. This also reduces debt ratios and improves interest coverage, possibly leading to higher debt ratings.

2. Repurchase of equity may be able to raise earnings per share and (if repurchased below stated book value or real value per share) increase these.

3. Used to make acquisitions (such as Kraft) which may provide future growth, better diversification, lower risk, etc.

4. Used to fund internal growth through capital spending, research and development, new product introduction costs, etc.

5. Increase dividends, providing larger payout of earnings to equity investors.

6. Held to increase liquidity (financial flexibility) allowing the firm to respond to unexpected needs and opportunities.

Problem 7-10

a.
　　　　　WORKSHEET TO COMPUTE CASH FLOW FROM OPERATIONS
　　　　　　　　　　　DIRECT PRESENTATION
　　　　　　　　ZETA CORPORATION (000s omitted)

		Year 6	Year 5
OPERATING CASH RECEIPTS & DISBURSEMENTS			
Cash Receipts from Operations:			
Net sales (a) (186,000 + 18,000)			
(155,000 + 23,000) (A)	1*	$204,000	$178,000
Other revenue and income	2*		
(I) D in current receivables	3	(3,000)	(2,400)
(I) D in non-current receivables (b)	4		
Other adjustments (c)	5		
= CASH COLLECTIONS	6	201,000	175,600
Cash Disbursements for Operations:			
Total expenses (a) (B)	7*	196,000	170,000
Less—Expenses & Losses not using cash			
- Depreciation & amortization	8	(6,000)	(4,000)
- Noncurrent deferred income taxes	9	(1,600)	(1,000)
- Other minority interest	10	(200)	
- Other loss on discontinued operations	11	(700)	
- Other	12		
Changes in Current Assets and Liabilities			
related to Operations			
I (D) in inventories	13	15,900	6,000
I (D) in prepaid expense	14	—	200
(I) D in accounts payable and accruals	15	(2,500)	(2,000)
(I) D in taxes payable	16	(5,700)	(1,000)
(I) D in accruals	17		
I or D other	18		
I or D other	19		
I or D in noncurrent accounts (b)	20		
= CASH DISBURSEMENTS FOR OPERATIONS	21	195,200	168,200
Dividends Received:			
Equity in income of unconsolidated affiliates	22*	2,000	(1,000)
- Undistributed equity in income of affiliate	23	(1,400)	1,300
= DIVIDENDS FROM UNCONSOL AFFILIATES	24	600	300
Other Cash Receipts (Disbursements)	25*		
CASH FLOW FROM OPERATIONS (d)	26	6,400	7,700

(*)　These five lines must equal reported net income per income statement [Year 6:
　　　204,000 -196,000 + 2,000 = 10,000].
(a)　Including adjustments (grossing-up) of revenue and expense of discontinued
　　　operations disclosed in footnote.
(b)　Which have been determined to relate to operations (describe in footnotes).
(c)　Such as removal of gains included above (describe in footnotes).

(d)   Reconcile to amount reported by company. If not reported, reconcile to change
      in cash for period.

(A)   Sales from discontinued operations (Note 4)

	Year 6	Year 5
(B) Expenses per income statement	167,000	138,000
Income taxes	10,000	7,800
Minority interest	200	—
Discontinued operations	1,100	1,200
Loss on disposal	700	—
Cum. effect of accounting change	(1,000)	-
	178,000	147,000
Expenses of discont. ops	19,100	24,200
Loss on discontinued operations	(1,100)*	(1,200)**
	196,000	170,000

*   Replaced by sales 18,000 (Note 4) - expenses $19,100
** Replaced by sales 23,000 (Note 4) - expenses $24,200

Note: Due to the acquisition of TRO Company in Year 6, the operating working
capital accounts include amounts so acquired and may distort cash inflows and
outflows from operations.

b.

	Year 6	Year 5*
Income tax expense	10,000	7,800
Taxes in below line items:		
+ Tax on cum. effect	1,000	---
- Tax on disc. operations	(1,100)	(1,200)
- Tax on loss on disp.	(700)	
	9,200	6,600
Incr. in def. income tax	1,600	800
Incr. in taxes payable	5,000	1,000
Income taxes paid	2,600	4,800

*   Data for Year 5 not given in financial statements.

c.   Note 4 describes the loss on disposal which can be summarized as follows:

Loss on disposal	1,400	
Property, plant & equipment		1,000
Inventories*		100
Accounts payable & accruals*		300

Tax payable*	700	
Loss on disposal		700

Clearly no cash was involved in this loss. However, if the operating working
capital items (marked *) involved in this entry are not adjusted, the
operating cash flows will be distorted. Thus, the effect of this entry on
these accounts must be eliminated.

The balance sheet year to year change in the "Accounts payable and accruals" account is an increase of $6,000. However, the change related to cash effects of operations is $300 less because the $300 credit to the account represents a noncash entry. Thus, the adjustment in SCF is $5,700.

The total adjustment due on loss on disposal in the SCF can be summarized as follows:

Inventories (increase)	100	
Accounts payable and accruals (decrease)	300	
Property, plant and equipment (increase)	1,000*	
Loss on discontinued operations (addback to income)		700
Taxes payable (increase)		700

* The amount of $6,500 for additions to PPE reflects this adjustment.

Note 3 describes the acquisition of TRO Company. Zeta assumed accounts payables and accruals of $3,200. These must be removed from the determination of CFO in order not to distort this figure. The 3,200 is shown as part of the amount determining the acquisition price of TRO.

In summary:

Change in balances of A/P and Accruals per balance sheet		$6,000
Less—Adjustment due to disposal	$ 300	
Less—Adjustment due to TRO acquisition	3,200	3,500
Adjustment to Net Income to arrive at CFO		$2,500

Problem 7-11

FORM A
WORKSHEET TO COMPUTE CASH FLOW FROM OPERATIONS (in millions)
DIRECT (INFLOW-OUTFLOW) PRESENTATION
CAMPBELL SOUP YEAR ENDED JULY 28, YEAR 11

OPERATING CASH & DISBURSEMENTS	Ref.	Reported	Adj.	Revised
Cash Receipts from Operations:				
Net Sales	13	$6,204.1	$7.5	$6,211.6
Other revenue and income	19	26.0	—	26.0
(I) D in current receivables	61	17.1	—	17.1
(I) D in non-current receivables				
= CASH COLLECTIONS		$6,247.2	$7.5	$6,254.7
Cash Disbursements for Operations:				
Total expenses (include min int & taxes)[a]		5,831.0	7.5	5,838.5
Less—Expenses & losses not using cash:				
- Depreciation & amortization	57	(208.6)		(208.6)
- Non-current def. income taxes	59	(35.5)		(35.5)
- Other, net	60	(63.2)		(63.2)
Change in Current Assets and Liabilities related to Operations:				
I (D) in inventories	62	(48.7)		(48.7)
I (D) in prepaid expenses	35	(25.3)		(25.3)
(I) D in accounts payable	41	42.8		42.8
(I) D in taxes payable	44	(21.3)		(21.3)
(I) D in accruals, payrolls, etc.[b]	175	(26.8)		(26.8)
I or D in noncurrent accounts[c]		5.8	0.0	5.8
= CASH DISBURSEMENTS FOR OPERATION		$5,450.2	$7.5	$5,457.7
Dividends Received:				
Equity in income of unconsolidated affiliates	24	2.4		2.4
Distributions beyond equity in income of affiliates[c]		5.8	0.0	5.8
= Divs from unconsol affiliates	169A	$8.2	$0.0	$8.2
CASH FLOW FROM OPERATIONS		$805.2	$0.0	$805.2

[a] Total costs and expenses [22A] + Taxes on earnings [27] + Minority interests [25] + Interest income [19] = $5,531.9 + $265.9 + $7.2 + $26.0 = $5,831

[b] It is assumed that accruals, payrolls, etc. are part of item [175].

[c] A reconciling amount to tie in with the $8.2 dividends from affiliates (item 169A) vs. equity in earnings of affiliates (item 24).

Problem 7-12

a.

FORM A

WORKSHEET TO COMPUTE CASH FLOW FROM OPERATIONS (in millions)
DIRECT (INFLOW—OUTFLOW) PRESENTATION
CAMPBELL SOUP YEAR ENDED JULY 29, YEAR 10

OPERATING CASH & DISBURSEMENTS	Ref.	Reported	Adj.	Revised
Cash Receipts from Operations:				
Net Sales	13	$6,205.8	$7.5	$6,213.3
Other revenue and income				
(I) D in current receivables	61	(60.4)		(60.4)
(I) D in non-current receivables				
Effect of translation adjustments		0.0	0.0	0.0
= CASH COLLECTIONS		6,145.4	7.5	6,152.9
Cash Disbursements for Operations:				
Total expenses (include interest & taxes) [22A] + [27] + [25]		6,214.9	7.5	6,222.4
Less—Expenses & Losses not using cash				
- Depreciation & amortization	57	(200.9)		(200.9)
- Non-current deferred income taxes	59	(3.9)		(3.9)
- Other—Provision for restructuring and writedowns	58	(339.1)		(339.1)
- Other*	60	(24.7)		(24.7)
- Other				
Changes in Current Assets and Liabilities related to operations				
I (D) in inventories	62	(10.7)		(10.7)
I (D) in prepaid expense				
(I) D in accounts payable				
(I) D in taxes payable				
(I) D in accruals, payrolls, etc.				
(I) D in dividends payable				
I or D other **	63	68.8		68.8
I or D in noncurrent amounts		0.0	0.0	0.0
= CASH DISBURSEMENTS FOR OPERATIONS		5,704.4	7.5	5,711.9
Dividends Received:				
Equity in income of unconsolidated affiliates	24	13.5		13.5
- Undistributed equity in income of affiliates	169A	6.1	0.0	6.1
= Divs from unconsol affils		7.4		7.4
Other Cash Receipts (Disbursements)				
CASH FLOW FROM OPERATIONS		448.4		448.4

* Other, net [60] $18.6 + [169A] $6.1 = $24.7

** Campbell presents a combined figure instead of details of operating assets and liabilities.

b.

ANALYTICAL STATEMENT OF CASH FLOWS

Campbell Soup Co.--Year Ended July 28, Year 10 (in thousands)

			Year 10
CASH FLOW FROM OPERATIONS:			
[28]	Income before extraordinary items	1	$ 4.4
Add (deduct) adjustments to cash basis:			
[57]	Depreciation & Amortization	2	200.9
[59]	Deferred income taxes	3	3.9
Equity in income of investees		4	
[58]	Divestitures and restructuring provisions	5	339.1
[60]	Other—Net	6	18.6
[61]	(I) D in receivables	7	(60.4)
[62]	(I) D in inventories	8	10.7
(I) D in prepaid expenses		9	
I (D) in accounts payable		10	
I (D) in accruals		11	
I (D) in taxes payable		12	
[63]	I or D in other current operating accts	13	(68.8)
I in dividends payable		14	
Extraordinary items net of noncash items		15	
Discount. ops--net on noncash items		16	0.0
CASH FROM OPERATIONS		17	$448.4
CASH FLOWS FROM INVESTING ACTIVITIES:			
[65]	Additions to properties	18	(387.6)
[70]	Additions to investments (advances)	19	3.7
Additions to other assets		20	
[67]	Cost of acquisition—net of cash	21	(41.6)
Disposals of properties [66]+[68]		22	56.6
[69]	Decreases in other assets	23	(18.6)
Other		24	0.0
CASH FROM INVESTING		25	$(387.5)
CASH FLOWS FROM FINANCING ACTIVITIES:			
Net I (D) in short-term debt [74]+[75]+[76]		26	61.2
I (D) in long-term debt [72]+[73]		27	(9.9)
I (D) of common & preferred stock			
Treasury stock—net [78]+[79]		28	(28.7)
[77]	Dividends paid	29	(124.3)
[80]	Other—net	30	(0.1)
CASH FROM FINANCING		31	(101.8)
[82]	Effect of exchange rate changes on cash	32	0.7
[83]	NET INCREASE IN CASH & EQUIV.	33	$(40.2)
NON CASH ACTIVITIES			
[183]	Capital lease obligations incurred	34	$10.0
ADDITIONAL DATA			
[180]	Interest paid—net of amounts capitalized		$116.3
[182]	Income taxes paid		$152.8

CAMPBELL SOUP COMPANY
Reconstruction of T-Accounts
For the Year Ended July 28, Year 10

Cash and Equivalents		
Beg	120.9	

Operations			
[56] Net income	4.4	60.4	[61] Increase in A/R
[57] Depr & amort	200.9	68.8	[63] Net change in other
[58] Divestiture &	339.1		current assets and liabs
restructuring provision			
[59] Deferred taxes	3.9		
[60] Other, net	18.6		
[62] Decr in inventories	10.7		

Investing, Financing, and Other			
[66] Sales of plant assets	34.9	387.6	[65] Purch of plant assets
[68] Sales of business	21.7	41.6	[67] Business acquired
[70] Net change in other	3.7	18.6	[69] Incr in other assets
temporary investments		22.5	[73] Repayment of
[72] Long-term borrowings	12.6		LT borrowings
[75] Other short-term borrowings	153.7	2.7	[74] Decr in borrowings with
[79] Treasury stock issued	12.4		less than 3 mos maturities
[82] Exchange rate effect	0.7	89.8	[76] Repayments of other
			ST borrowings
		124.3	[77] Dividends paid
		41.1	[78] Treasury stock purch
		0.1	[80] Other, net
End	80.7		

Temporary Investments			
Beg	26.2	3.7	[70]
End	22.5		

Accounts Receivable		
Beg	538.0	
[61]	60.4	
[A]	26.1	
End	624.5	

Inventories			
Beg	816.0	10.7	[62]
[B]	14.5		
End	819.8		

Prepaid Expenses		
Beg	100.4	
[C]	17.6	
End	118.0	

Plant Assets			
Beg	2,543.0	195.7	[D]
[65]	387.6		
End	2,734.9		

Accumulated Depreciation			
[E]	169.3	1,002.4	Beg
		184.1	[57]
		1,017.2	End

Intangible Asset—Net			
Beg	466.9	16.8	[57]
		66.7	[F]
End	383.4		

Other Assets		
Beg	323.1	
[69]	18.6	
[G]	7.3	
End	349.0	

Notes Payable			
[74]	2.7	271.5	Beg
[76]	89.8	153.7	[75]
[H]	130.4		
		202.3	End

Payable to Suppliers & Others			
		508.2	Beg
		17.0	[I]
		525.2	End

Accrued Liabilities			
		392.6	Beg
		99.3	[J]
		491.9	End

Dividend Payable			
		29.7	Beg
		2.6	[K]
		32.3	End

Accrued Income Taxes			
		30.1	Beg
		16.3	[L]
		46.4	End

Long-term Debt			
[73]	22.5	629.2	Beg
		12.6	[72]
		186.5	[M]
		805.8	End

Deferred Income Taxes		
	218.0	Beg
	3.9	[59]
	13.2	[N]
	235.1	End

Other Liabilities		
	19.6	Beg
	8.9	[O]
	28.5	End

Minority Interest		
	54.9	Beg
	1.4	[P]
	56.3	End

Common Stock		
	20.3	Beg
	20.3	End

Capital Surplus		
	50.8	Beg
	11.1	[Q]
	61.9	End

Retained Earnings			
[77]	124.3	1,775.8	Beg
[R]	2.6	4.4	[56]
		1,653.3	End

Treasury Stock			
Beg	70.7	12.4	[79]
[78]	41.1		
[S]	7.8		
End	107.2		

Cum. Translation Adj.		
	2.1	Beg
	61.4	[T]
	63.5	End

Unexplained Differences			
[63] Net change in other current assets and liabs	68.8	339.1	[58] Divestiture & restructuring provision
[67] Business acquired	41.6	18.6	[60] Other, net
[80] Other, net	0.1	34.9	[66] Sales of plant assets
[D] Plant assets—net	195.7	21.7	[68] Sales of business
[F] Intangible assets	66.7	0.7	[82] Exchange rate effect
[I] Payable to suppliers and others	17.0	26.1	[A] Account receivable
		14.5	[B] Inventories
[J] Accrued liabilities	99.3	17.6	[C] Prepaid expenses
[K] Dividend payable	2.6	169.3	[E] Accumulated depr
[L] Accrued income taxes	16.3	7.3	[G] Other assets
[M] Long-term debt	186.5	130.4	[H] Notes payable
[N] Deferred income taxes	13.2	2.6	[R] Retained earnings
[O] Other liabilities	8.9	7.8	[S] Treasury stock
[P] Minority interest	1.4		
[Q] Capital surplus	11.1		
[T] Cum. transl. adj.	61.4		
	790.6	790.6	

CAMPBELL SOUP COMPANY
Summary of Various Account Balances and Sources
For Years 10 and 9 (in millions)

Accounts	Year 10	Year 9	
Cash and cash equivalents	$80.7	$120.9	[84]
Other temporary investments [32]+[70]	22.5	26.2	
Accounts receivable	624.5	538.0*	
Inventories	819.8	816.0*	
Prepaid expenses	118.0	100.4*	
Plant assets	2,734.9	2,543.0	[186]
Accumulated depreciation	(1,017.2)	(1,002.4)	[187]
Intangible assets, net of amortization	383.4	466.9*	
Other assets	349.0	323.1	plug #1
Total assets	$4,115.6	$3,932.1	
Notes payable	$202.3	$271.5*	
Payable to suppliers and others	525.2	508.2*	
Accrued liabilities	491.9	392.6*	
Dividend payable	32.3	29.7 *	
Accrued income taxes	46.4	30.1	plug #2
Long-term debt	805.8	629.2	[185]
Deferred income taxes	235.1	218.0*	
Other liabilities	28.5	19.6 *	
Minority interest	56.3	54.9	plug #3
Common stock	20.3	20.3	[87]
Capital surplus	61.9	50.8	[87]
Retained earnings	1,653.3	1,775.8	[87]
Treasury stock	(107.2)	(70.7)	[87]
Cumulative translation adjustments	63.5	2.1	[87]
Total liabs and shareowners' equity	$4,115.6	$3,932.1	

Plug #1:   Calculated using the data on total assets [185]
Plug #2:   Calculated using the data on working capital [185]
Plug #3:   Force the balance sheet to balance
*   Data extracted from financial statements for Year 9

The following journal entries are used here to explain in detail the posting of each item in Campbell's SCF to the related T-accounts.

[56]	Cash—Operations	4.4	
	Retained Earnings		4.4

[57]	Cash—Operations	200.9	
	Accumulated Depreciation		184.1
	Intangible Assets—Net		16.8

[58]	Cash—Operations	339.1	
	Unexplained Differences		339.1

We don't know enough about this so we post this amount to unexplained differences.

| [59] | Cash—Operations | 3.9 | |
| | Deferred income taxes | | 3.9 |

| [60] | Cash—Operations | 18.6 | |
| | Unexplained Differences | | 18.6 |

We know this amount to be composed of a number of items. We transfer it to the unexplained T-account. After all items are posted we will be in a better position to assign its amount to the proper accounts.

| [61] | Accounts receivable | 60.4 | |
| | Cash—Operations | | 60.4 |

| [62] | Cash—Operations | 10.7 | |
| | Inventories | | 10.7 |

| [63] | Unexplained Differences | 68.8 | |
| | Cash—Operations | | 68.8 |

This amount is also composed of a number of items related to current assets and liabilities. Therefore, we post it to the unexplained T-account.

| [65] | Plant Assets—Net | 387.6 | |
| | Cash—Investing | | 387.6 |

| [66] | Cash—Investing | 34.9 | |
| | Unexplained Differences | | 34.9 |

Since we do not know the book value of assets sold, we transfer this amount to unexplained T-account.

| [67] | Unexplained Differences | 41.6 | |
| | Cash—Investing | | 41.6 |

This amount represents business acquired which relates to a number of different accounts. So, the best way is to post it to the unexplained T-account.

| [68] | Cash—Investing | 21.7 | |
| | Unexplained Differences | | 21.7 |

We do not have enough information on the sales of business. Hence, we transfer this amount to the unexplained T-account.

| [69] | Other Assets | 18.6 | |
| | Cash—Investing | | 18.6 |

| [70] | Cash—Investing | 3.7 | |
| | Temporary Investments | | 3.7 |

| [72] | Cash—Financing | 12.6 | |
| | Long-term Debt | | 12.6 |

| [73] | Long-term Debt | 22.5 | |
| | Cash—Financing | | 22.5 |

| [74] | Notes Payable | 2.7 | |
| | Cash—Financing | | 2.7 |

| [75] | Cash—Financing | 153.7 | |
| | Notes Payable | | 153.7 |

| [76] | Notes Payable | 89.8 | |
| | Cash—Financing | | 89.8 |

| [77] | Retained Earnings | 124.3 | |
| | Cash—Financing | | 124.3 |

| [78] | Treasury Stock | 41.1 | |
| | Cash—Financing | | 41.1 |

| [79] | Cash—Financing | 12.4 | |
| | Treasury Stock | | 12.4 |

| [80] | Unexplained Differences | 0.1 | |
| | Cash—Financing | | 0.1 |

We post it to unexplained T-account because we do not know which accounts this amount is related to.

| [82] | Cash—Financing | 0.7 | |
| | Unexplained Differences | | 0.7 |

We do not know to what specific accounts these translation adjustments relate, so they are posted to unexplained T-account.

CAMPBELL SOUP COMPANY
Analysis of Unexplained Differences
For Year Ended July 29, Year 10

Ref.
Items

	<1>		
R	Retained Earnings	2.6	
K	Dividend Payable		2.6

Non-cash entry

	<2>		
H	Notes Payable	130.4	
M	Long-term Debt		130.4

Transfer from current to long-term debt, unexplained = 186.5 - 130.4 = 56.1

```
             <3>
    Cash and/or Mgt. Compensation              15.7
S           Treasury Stock                                      4.6
Q           Capital Surplus                                    11.1
```

Treasury stock issued—Management Incentive and Stock Option Plan—see data in [87]—Partial explanation.

```
             <4>
             Unexplained*                     143.1
A            Accounts Receivable               26.1
B            Inventories                       14.5
C            Prepaid Expenses                  17.6
63              Net change in other current assets
                     and liabilities (related to operations)   68.8
I            Payable to suppliers and others          17.0
J            Accrued Liabilities                      99.3
L            Accrued Income Taxes                     16.3
```

* Must represent changes in current assets and liabilities related to others thru operations, such as acquisitions, divestitures, etc.

```
             <5>
66           Cash—Sales of Plant Assets        34.9
68           Cash—Sales of Businesses          21.7
E            Accumulated Depreciation         169.3*
T            Translation Adjustments             ?
N               Deferred Income Taxes                     13.2
P               Minority Interest                          1.4
D               Plant Assets                             195.7
F               Intangible assets                          ?
```

Incomplete entry relating to asset and business disposition—some added detail available from items [186] and [187].

```
    *    Per item [187]:
         Retirements & sales              $187.2
         - Translation Adjustments          17.9
                                          $169.3
```

```
             <6>
G&O          Other Assets & Liabilities        7.3        8.9
F            Intangible Assets                  ?
T            Translation Adjustments            ?
67              Cash—Business Acquired                     41.6
```

Assets and Liabilities Acquired (part of unexplained entry <4>. Incomplete entry relating to business and assets acquired.

```
        <7>
58        Divestiture & restructuring provision    339.1
          Assets and Liabilities affected
          by this provision                             ?              ?
```

Changes in these assets and liabilities are part of unresolved differences above.

Problem 7-14

WORKSHEET TO COMPUTE CASH FLOW FROM OPERATIONS
INFLOW-OUTFLOW PRESENTATION
QUAKER OATS

		Year 11	Year 10	Year 9
OPERATING CASH RECEIPTS & DISBURSEMENTS				
Cash Receipts from Operations:				
[1] Net sales (a)	*1	6,092.2	5,733.2	5,724.2
Other revenue and income	*2			
[23] (I) D in current receivables	3	(97.8)	(55.9)	(77.1)
(I) D in noncurrent receivables	4			
Other adjustments	5			
CASH COLLECTIONS FROM OPERATIONS	6	5,994.4	5,677.3	5,647.1
Cash Disbursements for Operations:				
Total expenses				
(incl. int. & tax)(b)	*7	5,886.4	5,564.2	5,421.2
Less Expenses & Losses not using cash:				
[20] -Depreciation & amortization	8	(177.7)	(162.5)	(135.5)
[21] -Noncurrent deferred income taxes				
and other items	9	(45.3)	(15.2)	(79.9)
[22] -Restructuring charges	10	(10.0)	17.5	(124.3)
[28] -Other (net)	11	(9.5)	(0.4)	8.4
Changes in current operating assets and liabilities:				
[24] I (D) in inventories	13	(30.7)	2.2	90.3
I (D) in prepaid expense	14			
[26] (I) D in accounts payable	15	(26.1)	(31.4)	(102.2)
[29] (I) D payable to Fisher Price	16	(29.6)		
(I) D in accruals	17			
[25+30] I or D other current assets	18	(52.3)	(60.8)	34.4
[27] I or D other current liabs.	19	(43.2)	(83.4)	53.1
I or D in noncurrent accounts	20			
CASH DISBURSEMENTS FROM OPS.	21	5,462.0	5,230.2	5,265.5
Dividends Received:				
Equity in NI of unconsol. affiliates	*22			
-Undistr. equity in NI of affils.	23			
=Dividends from unconsol. affiliates	24			
Other cash receipts (disbursements)	*25			
NET CASH FLOW FROM OPERATIONS	26	532.4	447.1	381.6

* These five lines must equal reported net income per income statement.

(a)		Year 11	Year 10	Year 9
	Net Sales [1]	5,491.2	5,030.6	4,879.4
	plus Net Sales of disc. Ops. [144]	601.0	702.6	844.8
	Total	6,092.2	5,733.2	5,724.2

(b)	Costs and Expenses	Year 11	Year 10	Year 9
	Cost of Sales [2]	2,839.7	2,685.9	2,655.3
	Selling, General and Admin. Exp. [4]	2,121.2	1,844.1	1,779.0
	Interest Expense [5]	86.2	101.8	56.4
	Other [6]	32.6	16.4	149.6
	Tax Expense [8]	175.7	153.5	90.2
	Expenses from Discontinued Operations*	631.0	762.5	790.7
	Total Costs and Expenses	5,886.4	5,564.2	5,521.2
	* Net sales of disc. ops. [144]	601.0	702.6	844.8
	Less op. income (loss) net of tax [10]	(30.0)	(59.9)	54.1
	Total expenses of discont. ops.	631.0	762.5	790.7

RECONCILIATION:

	Year 11	Year 10	Year 9
From the inflow-outflow statement:			
Net sales	6,092.2	5,733.2	5,724.2
Less: Total expenses	5,886.4	5,564.2	5,521.2
Reconciliation number (see below)	205.8	169.0	203.0
From the income statement:			
Income from continuing ops. [9]	235.8	228.9	148.9
Add op. income or less (loss) from			
discontinued operations [10]	(30.0)	(59.9)	54.1
Reconciliation (see above)	205.8	169.0	203.0

Problem 7-15

Quaker Oats Company
Reconstruction of T-Accounts
For the Year Ended June 30, Year 11

Cash and Cash Equivalents		
Beginning balance	17.7	

Operations			
[19] Net income	205.8	97.8	[23] Increase in receivables
[20] Depreciation & amortization	177.7	13.7	[25] Incr. in other current assets
[21] Deferred income taxes and other items	45.3		
[22] Provision for restructuring	10.0		
[24] Decrease in inventories	30.7		
[26] Increase in accounts payable	26.1		
[27] Increase in other curr. liab.	43.2		
[28] Other-net	9.5		
[29] Incr. in payable to Fisher-Price	29.6		
[30] Decrease in net current assets of discontinued operations	66.0		

Investing			
[35] Disposals of PP&E	17.9	240.6	[32] Additions to PP&E
		10.7	[34] Incr. in other receivables and investments
		19.8	[36] Other-discontinued ops.

Financing			
[39] Proceeds from issuance of debt for spin-off	141.1	123.0	[38] Cash dividends
		0.2	[40] Change in deferred comp.
[42] Proceeds from long-term debt	1.8	265.6	[41] Change in short-term debt
[44] Issuance of common treas. stock	25.6	39.7	[43] Reduction of long-term debt
		0.7	[47] Purchase of preferred stock

Other			
		6.0	[49] Effect of exchange rate changes on cash & cash equivalents
Ending balance	30.2		

Short-Term Investments [54]		
Beg	0.6	
		0.6 [a]
End	0.0	

Accounts Receivable, net [55]		
Beg	629.9	
[23]	97.8	36.6 [b]
End	691.1	

Inventories [59]		
Beg	473.9	
		30.7 [24]
		20.9 [c]
End	422.3	

Other Current Assets [60]		
Beg	107.0	
[25]	13.7	6.2 [d]
End	114.5	

Net Current Assets of Discontinued Operations [61]		
Beg	252.2	
		66.0 [30]
		186.2 [e]
End	0.0	

Other Receivables and Investments [63]		
Beg	63.5	
[34]	10.7	
[f]	4.9	
End	79.1	

PP&E [64]		
Beg	1,745.6	
[32]	240.6	42.7 [35]
		28.9 [g]
End	1,914.6	

Accumulated Depreciation [65]		
		591.5 Beg
[35]	24.8	125.2 [20] & [125]
[h]	13.4	3.4 [i]
		681.9 End

Intangible Assets—Net [67]		
Beg	466.7	
[j]	1.9	22.4 [20] & [157]
End	446.2	

Net Noncurrent Assets of Disc. Ops. [68]		
Beg	160.5	
[36]	19.8	180.3 [k]
End	0.0	

Short-Term Debt [70]		
		343.2 Beg
[41]	265.6	3.0 [l]
		80.6 End

Current Portion of LT Debt [71]		
		32.3 Beg
		0.6 [m]
		32.9 End

Trade Accounts Payable [72]		
	354.0	Beg
[n] 29.2	26.1	[26]
	350.9	End

Accrued Payrolls, Pensions and Bonuses [73]		
	106.3	Beg
	10.0	[o]
	116.3	End

Accrued Advertising & Merch. [74]		
	92.6	Beg
	13.1	[p]
	105.7	End

Income Taxes Payable [75]		
	36.3	Beg
	8.8	[q]
	45.1	End

Payables to Fisher-Price [76]		
	0.0	Beg
	29.6	[29]
	29.6	End

Other Accrued Liabilities [77]		
	173.8	Beg
[r] 8.0		
	165.8	End

Long-Term Debt [79]		
	740.3	Beg
[43] 39.7	141.1	[39]
[s] 142.3	1.8	[42]
	701.2	End

Other Liabilities [80]		
	100.3	Beg
	15.2	[t]
	115.5	End

Deferred Income Taxes [81]		
	327.7	Beg
	39.0	[u]
	366.7	End

Deferred Compensation [83]+[89]		
Beg	262.3	
[40]	0.2	
End	262.5	

Preferred Stock [82]		
100.0		Beg
	100.0	End

Treasury Preferred Stock [84]		
Beg	0.0	
[47]	0.7	
End	0.7	

Common Stock [85]		
	420.0	Beg
	420.0	End

APIC [86]		
	12.9	Beg
[v] 5.7		
	7.2	End

Reinvested Earnings [87]			
		1,164.7	Beg
[38]	123.0	205.8	[19]
[w]	200.0		
		1,047.5	End

Cumulative Exchange Adjustment [88]		
Beg	29.3	
[49]	6.0	
[x]	17.6	
End	52.9	

Treasury Common Stock [90]			
Beg	386.7		
		25.6	[44]
		8.3	[y]
End	352.8		

Unexplained Differences				
[a]	Short-term investment	0.6	30.1	[20] Depreciation & amortization
[b]	Receivables	36.6	45.3	[21] Deferred income taxes
[c]	Inventories	20.9		and other items
[d]	Other current assets	6.2	10.0	[22] Provision for restructuring
[e]	Net current assets of		43.2	[27] Incr. in other current liabs.
	discontinued operations	186.2	9.5	[28] Other-net
[g]	Property, plant & equipment	28.9	4.9	[f] Other receivables and invest.
[i]	Accumulated depreciation	3.4	13.4	[h] Accumulated depreciation
[k]	Net noncurrent assets of		1.9	[j] Intangible assets
	discontinued operations	180.3	29.2	[n] Trade accounts payable
[l]	Short-term debt	3.0	8.0	[r] Other accrued liabilities
[m]	Current portion of LT debt	0.6	142.3	[s] Long-term debt
[o]	Accrued payrolls, pensions		5.7	[v] APIC
	and bonuses	10.0	200.0	[w] Reinvested earnings
[p]	Accrued advertising and		17.6	[x] Cumulative exchange adjustment
	merchandising	13.1		
[q]	Income taxes payable	8.8		
[t]	Other liabilities (8.9+6.3)	15.2		
[u]	Deferred income taxes	39.0		
[y]	Treasury common stock	8.3		
		561.1	561.1	

Journal entries based on SCF:

[19]	Cash—operations	205.8	
	Reinvested earnings		205.8

[20]	Cash—operations	177.7	
	Accumulated depreciation [125]		125.2
	Intangible assets [157]		22.4
	Unexplained		30.1

| [21] | Cash—operations | 45.3 | |
| | Unexplained | | 45.3 |

| [22] | Cash—operations | 10.0 | |
| | Unexplained | | 10.0 |

| [23] | Receivables | 97.8 | |
| | Cash—operations | | 97.8 |

| [24] | Cash—operations | 30.7 | |
| | Inventories | | 30.7 |

| [25] | Other current assets | 13.7 | |
| | Cash—operations | | 13.7 |

| [26] | Cash—operations | 26.1 | |
| | Trade accounts payable | | 26.1 |

| [27] | Cash—operations | 43.2 | |
| | Unexplained | | 43.2 |

| [28] | Cash—operations | 9.5 | |
| | Unexplained | | 9.5 |

| [29] | Cash—operations | 29.6 | |
| | Payable to Fisher-Price | | 29.6 |

| [30] | Cash—operations | 66.0 | |
| | Net current assets of disc. ops. | | 66.0 |

| [32] | PPE—purchased | 240.6 | |
| | Cash—investing | | 240.6 |

| [34] | Other receivables and investments | 10.7 | |
| | Cash—investing | | 10.7 |

[35]	Cash—investing	17.9	
	Accumulated depreciation [146]	24.8	
	PPE—disposals [146]		42.7

| [36] | Net non-current assets of disc. ops. | 19.8 | |
| | Cash—investing | | 19.8 |

| [38] | Reinvested earnings—dividends | 123.0 | |
| | Cash—financing | | 123.0 |

| [39] | Cash—financing | 141.1 | |
| | Long-term debt | | 141.1 |

| [40] | Deferred compensation | 0.2 | |
| | Cash—financing | | 0.2 |

[41]	Short-term debt	265.6	
	Cash—financing		265.6
[42]	Cash—financing	1.8	
	Long-term debt		1.8
[43]	Long-term debt	39.7	
	Cash—financing		39.7
[44]	Cash—financing	25.6	
	Treasury common stock		25.6
[47]	Treasury preferred stock	0.7	
	Cash—financing		0.7
[49]	Cumulative exchange adjustment	6.0	
	Cash—other		6.0

(I) Analysis of differences--[20], [22], (g), (h), (i), (j), and part of (x).

The provision for restructuring charges is added back to income because it does not use cash. Although explanation is not provided, it probably relates to writedowns of PP&E and the related accumulated depreciation account. In addition, a portion of the depreciation and amortization is unexplained, the related accounts are accumulated depreciation, PP&E and intangible assets. Another possible explanation for the sum of these unexplained differences is the exchange adjustment. Therefore, a credit of $23.1 resulted as a plug and the cumulative exchange adjustment account remains a debit of $40.7 ($17.6 + $23.1) unexplained.

Depreciation and amortization [20]	30.1	
Provision for restructuring [22]	10.0	
Accumulated depreciation (h)	13.4	
Intangible assets (j)	1.9	
Accumulated depreciation (i)		3.4
PP&E (g)		28.9
Exchange adjustment--plug (x)		23.1

(II) Analysis of differences--[21], (u) and part of (t).

The statement of cash flows reports a debit of $45.3 related to deferred income taxes and other items. Assuming the other items are related to the other liabilities accounts, $6.3 of the unexplained liabilities is explained, a credit of $8.9 remains to be explained (15.2-6.3).

Deferred income taxes & other items [21]	45.3	
Deferred income taxes (u)		39.0
Other liabilities (t)		6.3

(III) Analysis of differences--part of [27], (r), (1), (o), (p), (q) & rest of (t).

The statement of cash flows reports an aggregated amount for the changes in
other current liabilities. While most of it is explained by the unexplained
balances in the liabilities account and a plug of $35.8, there remains $7.4
unexplained. (43.2-35.8 =7.4).

Other current liabilities-plug [27]	35.8	
Other accrued liabilities (r)	8.0	
Short-term debt (1)		3.0
Accrued payrolls, pensions (o)		10.0
Accrued advertising (p)		13.1
Income taxes payable (q)		8.8
Other liabilities (t)		8.9

(IV) Analysis of differences--(w), (s), (e) and (k).

Item [112] shows a $200 charge to retained earnings as distribution in
spin-off of Fisher-Price. Also, item [142] reveals that long-term debt
decreased in Year 11 due primarily to proceeds from debt spun off with the
Fisher-Price business. Therefore, the unexplained reduction of long-term debt
and reinvested earnings can now be explained by the decrease of assets of
discontinued operations. Putting all these related unexplained differences
together, a debit of $24.2 remains unexplained.

Reinvested earnings (w)	200.0	
Long-term debt (s)	142.3	
Unresolved debit	24.2	
Net current assets of discontinued operations		186.2
Net non-current assets of discontinued operations		180.3

(V) Analysis of differences--(v) and (y).

Item [113] describes common stock issued for stock purchase and incentive
plans, the only related unexplained entry is the reduction of APIC. As a
result, a debit of $2.6 remains unexplained.

APIC (v)	5.7	
Unresolved debit	2.6	
Treasury common stock (y)		8.3

(VI) Analysis of differences--(a), (b), (c), (d), (n) and (f).

Spin-off of discontinued operations (and possibly acquisitions) require adjustments of operating accounts so as to distinguish operating and investing cash flows. The following items may represent such adjustments:

Other receivables and investments (f)	4.9	
Trade accounts payable (n)	29.2	
Short-term investments (a)		0.6
Receivables (b)		36.6
Inventories ©		20.9
Other current assets (d)		6.2
(partial entry)		

◄ Answers to Cases ►

Case 7-1

a.   **1994 (NI=$58,950, CFO=$43,063):**
   Largest additions to NI were depreciation/amortization and increase in accrued liabilities. Largest deductions were increases in A/R and other assets.

   1995 (NI=$93,402, CFO=$118,089):
   Largest additions to NI were depreciation/amortization and decrease in inventories. Largest deductions was increase in other assets.

   1996 (NI=$103,375, CFO=$103,379):
   Largest additions to NI were write-off of in-process technology, increase in accrued liabilities, and depreciation/amortization. Largest deductions were increases in A/R, inventories, and other assets.

b.   DIRECT PRESENTATION -- ADAPTEC, INC. (in $ thousands)

		1996	1995
OPERATING CASH RECEIPTS & DISBURSEMENTS			
Cash Receipts from Operations:			
Net sales	1*	$659,347	$466,194
Other income (interest)	2*	12,694	7,932
(I) D in current receivables	3	(30,727)	(1,311)
= CASH COLLECTIONS	6	641,314	472,815
Cash Disbursements for Operations:			
Total expenses	7*	568,666	380,724
Less—Expenses & Losses not using cash			
- Depreciation & amortization	8	(17,593)	(15,662)
- Noncurrent deferred income taxes	9		
- Other--write-off, net of tax	10	(39,686)	
- Other--doubtful accts (a)	11	(250)	(150)
Changes in Current Assets and Liabilities related to Operations			
I (D) in inventories	13	20,516	(7,228)
I (D) in prepaid expenses	14	8,973	(460)
I (D) in other assets	15	19,111	4,107
(I) D in accounts payable	16	167	(2,354)
(I) D in accrued liabilities	17	(21,969)	(4,251)
I or D in noncurrent accounts	20	0	0
= CASH DISBURSEMENTS FOR OPERATIONS	21	537,935	354,726
Dividends Received:			
Equity in NI of unconsol. affils.	22*		
- Undistributed equity in NI	23		
= DIVIDENDS FROM UNCONSOL AFFILS	24		
CASH FLOW FROM OPERATIONS	26	$103,379	$118,089

   (*)   These lines must equal reported net income per income statement.
   (a)   Disclosed in SCF.

---

c.   Per note seven, advance payments to suppliers of wafer capacity are debited to Other Assets. As discussed in Appendix 7A, practice requires management to use their informed judgment when classifying items in the SCF. Given that silicon wafers are raw materials for Adaptec's products, management believes they are of an operating nature.

Case 7-2

a.

WYATT CORPORATION
STATEMENT OF CASH FLOWS
For the Year ended December 31, Year 10

Net Income *	$186,000	
Depreciation	246,000	
Gain on sale of equipment **	(4,000)	
		$428,000
Change in:		
Accounts receivable	$(111,000)	
Inventory	(218,000)	
Accounts payable	103,000	
Taxes payable	(25,000)	
Other payables	92,000	
		(159,000)
Cash from operations		269,000
Other sources of cash:		
Proceeds from sale of equipment	$34,000	
Issuance of stock	17,000	
		51,000
Uses of cash:		
Additions to plant and equipment	$(212,000)	
Dividends	(74,000)	
Reduction of debt	(17,000)	
		(303,000)
CHANGE IN CASH		$17,000
CASH, 12/31/Year 9		175,000
CASH, 12/31/Year 10		$192,000

* Determination of Year 10 NI:

Retained earnings, 12/31/Year 10	$1,638,000
Retained earnings, 12/31/Year 9	$1,526,000
	112,000
Plus: Dividends Paid	74,000
Year 10 Net Income	$186,000

** Derivation of gain on sale of equipment:

Accum. deprec., 12/31/Year 9	$916,000
Depreciation expense	246,000
Subtotal	$1,162,000
Accum. deprec. 12/31/Year 10	1,131,000
Accum. deprec. on equip. sold	$31,000
Original Cost	$61,000
Accum. deprec. on equip. sold	31,000
Basis of equipment	$30,000
Proceeds from sale	34,000
Gain on sale	$4,000

b.   In Year 10, Wyatt Corp. generated cash from operations of $269,000 after considering operating working capital needs. Subtracting projected debt service of $300,000 per year and estimated capital spending of $325,000 per year from that figure leaves a decidedly negative number--i.e., there isn't enough cash to fund both for any extended period of years. Therefore, the leveraged buyout and the capital spending plan are mutually incompatible goals; Wyatt cannot do both. In fact, it probably cannot do either one with any margin of safety.

Case 7-3
NOTE: T-accounts include amounts in $ thousands.

Cash		
Beg	307	

Operating				
(1) Loss on sale of equip	10	(2) Gain on sale of sec		34
(4) NI	305	(c) Equity in Top Corp.		30
(b) Decrease in Inventory	80	(a) Increase in A/R		35
(e) Amortization of patent	9	(g) Decrease in A/P		115
(f) Depreciation	82			

Investing			
(1) Proceeds from sale of equipment	18	(d) Additions to PPE	120
(2) Proceeds from sale of securities	119		

Financing			
(3) Issue of common stock	260	(h) Increase in note payable	300
		(5) Dividends	85
End	471		

MES, at cost			
Beg	250	(2)	100
End	150		

Allow. to Reduce MES to Market			
(2)	15	25	Beg
		10	End

Accounts Receivable			
Beg	515		
(a)	35		
End	550		

Inventories			
Beg	890	80	(b)
End	810		

Investment in Top Corp. (at equity)			
Beg	390		
(c)	30		
End	420		

PP&E			
Beg	1,070	45	(1)
(d)	120		
End	1,145		

Patent			
Beg	118	9	(e)
End	109		

Accum. Depreciation			
(1)	17	280	Beg
		82	(f)
		345	End

LT Note Payable			
(h)	300	900	Beg
		600	End

A/P and Accrued Liabs.			
(g)	115	960	Beg
		845	End

Common Stock			
		650	Beg
		200	(3)
		850	End

Deferred Inc. Taxes			
		190	Beg
		190	End

Retained Earnings			
(5)	85	365	Beg
		305	(4)
		585	End

APIC			
		170	Beg
		60	(3)
		230	End

DOVER CORP.
STATEMENT OF CASH FLOWS
For the Year Ended December 31, Year 8

Cash flows from operating activities:

Net income	$305,000
Adjustments to reconcile net income to net cash provided by operating activities:	
Depreciation	82,000
Amortization of patent	9,000
Loss on sale of equipment	10,000
Equity in income of Word Corp.	(30,000)
Gain on sale of marketable equity securities	(19,000)
Decrease in allowance to reduce marketable equity securities to market	(15,000)
Increase in accounts receivable	(35,000)
Decrease in inventories	80,000
Decrease in A/P and accrued liabilities	(115,000)
Net cash provided by operating activities	$272,000

Cash flows from investing activities:

Sale of marketable equity securities	$119,000
Sale of equipment	18,000
Purchase of equipment	(120,000)
Net cash provided by investing activities	17,000

Cash flows from financing activities:

Issuance of common stock	$260,000
Cash dividend paid	(85,000)
Payment on note payable	(300,000)
Net cash used in financing activities	(125,000)

Net increase in cash	164,000
Cash at beginning of year	307,000
Cash at end of year	$471,000

Cash from operations, Year 8	272
Additional interest cost	(200)
Annual equipment investments	(180)
Less: Year 8 outlay	120
Annual inventory buildup	(60)
Projected cash shortfall	48

Other considerations:
Cash balance cannot be considered a recurring source to finance new structure. On balance, non-CFO cash flows in Year 8 were negative by $108,000. However, dividend payments may be reduced. A big question is whether the investment in equipment add to CFO.

◄ CHAPTER 8 ►

Short-Term Liquidity

◄ CHAPTER REVIEW ►

Liquidity refers to the availability of resources to meet short-term cash requirements. A company's short-term liquidity risk is affected by the timing of cash inflows and outflows along with its prospects for future performance. Our analysis of short-term liquidity is aimed at companies' operating activities, their ability to generate profits from the sale of goods and services, and working capital requirements and measures.

This chapter describes several financial statement analysis tools to assess short-term liquidity risk for a company. We begin with a discussion of the importance of liquidity and its link to working capital. We explain and interpret useful ratios of both working capital and a company's operating cycle for assessing liquidity. We also discuss potential adjustments to these analysis tools and the underlying financial statement numbers. What-if analysis of changes in a company's conditions or strategies concludes our discussion.

◄ CHAPTER OUTLINE ►

► **Importance of Short-Term Liquidity**

► **Analyzing Working Capital**

    Current Assets

    Current Liabilities

    Working Capital Measure of Liquidity

    Current Ratio Measure of Liquidity

    Using the Current Ratio for Analysis

    Cash-Based Ratio Measures of Liquidity

► **Operating Activity Analysis of Liquidity**

    Accounts Receivable Liquidity Measures

    Inventory Turnover Measures

    Liquidity of Current Liabilities

► **Additional Short-Term Liquidity Measures**

    Current Assets Composition

    Liquidity Index

    Acid-Test (Quick) Ratio

    Cash Flow Measures

    Financial Flexibility

    Management's Discussion and Analysis

► **What-If Analysis**

◄ Learning Objectives ►

■ **Explain the importance of liquidity in analyzing business activities.**

■ **Describe working capital measures of liquidity and their components.**

■ **Interpret the current ratio and cash-based measures of liquidity.**

■ **Analyze operating cycle or turnover measures of liquidity and their interpretation.**

■ **Describe other short-term liquidity measures and their usefulness for analysis.**

■ **Illustrate what-if analysis for evaluating changes in company conditions and policies.**

◄ Answers to Questions ►

1. Short-term liquidity is an indicator of an entity's ability to meet its current obligations. An entity in a weak short-term liquidity position will have difficulty in meeting short-term obligations. Lack of liquidity would affect major parties in some of the following ways:

   Ownership: The enterprise is unable to avail itself of favorable discounts and to take advantage of profitable business opportunities as they arise. It could even mean loss of control and partial or total loss of the capital investment eventually.

   Creditors: Delay in collection of interest and principal due can be expected and there is a possibility of the partial or total loss of the amounts due.

2. A major limitation is that working capital (in dollars) is more meaningful when related to other amounts, such as current liabilities or total assets.

   In addition, the importance attached to working capital by various parties provides a strong incentive for an entity (especially the ones in a weak financial position) to stretch to the limit the definition of what constitutes a current asset and a current liability in order to present their current position in the most favorable light. There are many possibilities of stretching the definitions of current items. For this reason the analyst must use his own judgment in evaluating the proper classification of items included in working capital.

3. Cash equivalents are temporary investments of cash in excess of current requirements made for the purpose of earning a return on these funds. The analyst must be alert to the fact that such investments yield relatively low returns and should be minimized.

4. In classification of accounts as to current and noncurrent, the intention of the management and normal practice in the industry serve as a guide. However, mere intention is not a controlling factor in classification. The cost of fixed assets which are intended to be sold should be included in current assets only if the enterprise has a definite contractual commitment from a buyer to purchase the assets at a given price within the following year (or operating cycle).

5. Installment receivables derived from sales in the regular course of business are deemed to be collectible within the operating cycle of an enterprise. Therefore, such installment receivables may be included in current assets.

6. No. The amounts in excess of current requirements should be excluded from current assets. Current requirements include quantities to be used within the following year or within the normal operating cycle. Business at times builds up its inventory in excess of current requirement in order to hedge against an increase in price or in anticipation of a strike. Such excess inventories beyond the requirements of one year should be classified as noncurrent.

7. Prepaid expenses represent advance payments for services and supplies which would otherwise require the current outlay of funds during the succeeding 12 months.

8. Banks usually reserve the right not to renew the whole or part of a loan at their option when they sign a revolving loan agreement. The fact that a bank agrees informally to renew short-term notes does not make them noncurrent. The possibility that the company under analysis included such notes under long-term liabilities should be carefully evaluated.

9. Some of these special characteristics, such as the absence of any distinction between current and noncurrent on the balance sheet in the real estate industry, may indeed require special treatment. However, even in such cases, analysts should be careful to consider whether the "special" circumstances in fact change the relationship existing between current obligations and the liquid funds available, or reasonably expected to become available, to meet them.

10. No. The absolute amount of working capital has significance only when related to other variables such as sales, total assets, etc. The absolute amount only has at best a limited value for intercompany comparison purposes. A better gauge of liquidity when focusing on working capital is to relate the size of current assets to that of current liabilities.

11. The current ratio is the ratio of current assets to current liabilities. It is a static measure of resources available at a given point in time to meet current obligation. The reasons for its widespread use include:

    * It measures the degree to which current assets cover current liabilities.
    * It measures the margin of safety available to allow for possible shrinkage in the value of current assets.
    * It measures the margin of safety available to meet the uncertainties and the random shocks to which the flows of funds in an enterprise are subject.

12. Cash inflows and outflows are rarely balanced in the short run. In the case of a business downturn, sales may fall more rapidly than do outlays for purchases and expenses. The amount of cash held at a safe minimum is in the nature of a precautionary reserve intended to take care of short-term imbalances in cash flows.

13. Yes, as sales increase the inventory level generally increases also. However, inventories are a direct function of sales only in rare cases. Scientific methods of inventory management generally establish that inventory increments vary not in proportion to demand (sales) but rather with the square root of demand.

14. The major objectives in the determination of receivable and inventory size are the promotion of sales, profitability, and the efficient utilization of assets.

15. The current ratio is a static measure. The value of the current ratio as a measure of liquidity is limited for the following reasons:

    * Future liquidity depends on prospective cash flows and the current ratio alone does not indicate what these future cash flows will be.
    * There is no direct or established relationship between balances of working capital items and the pattern which future cash flows are likely to assume.
    * Managerial policies directed at optimizing the levels of receivables and inventories are oriented primarily toward the efficient and profitable utilization of assets and only secondarily at liquidity considerations.

16. The limitations to which the current ratio is subject should be recognized and its use should be restricted to the type of analytical job it is capable of serving--that is, measuring the adequacy of present current assets to discharge existing current liabilities and considering the excess, if any, as a liquid surplus available to meet imbalances in the flow of funds, shrinkages in value, and other contingencies.

17. Cash ratios are ratio of cash and cash equivalents to total current assets or total current liabilities, depending on the purpose of analysis. The higher the ratio to total current assets the more liquid the current asset group is. This means that this portion of the total current assets is subject only to a minimal danger of loss in value in case of liquidation and that there is practically no waiting period for conversion of these assets into usable cash.

    The ratio of cash to total current liabilities measures how much cash and cash equivalents are available to pay current obligations immediately. This is a severe test which ignores the revolving nature of current liabilities. It supplements the cash ratio to total current assets in that it measures cash availability from a somewhat different point of view.

18. An important measure of the quality of current assets such as receivables and inventories is their turnover. The faster the turnover--collections in case of receivables and sale in case of inventories--the smaller the likelihood of loss on ultimate realization.

19. The average accounts receivable turnover measures in effect the speed of their collection during the period. The higher the turnover figure the faster the collection must have been on average.

20. The collection period (or days' sales in accounts receivable) measures the number of days' sales uncollected. It can be compared to an enterprise's credit terms in order to evaluate the quality of its collection activities.

21. Either one or all of the following can be possible reasons for this increase in the collection period:

    * A relatively poorer collection job.
    * Difficulty in obtaining prompt payment for various reasons from customers in spite of diligent collection efforts.
    * Customers in financial difficulty, which in turn may imply a poor job by the credit department.
    * Change of credit policy or of sales terms to increase sales.
    * Excessive delinquency of one or a few substantial customers.

22. An accounts receivable aging schedule is simply a listing of accounts receivable classified according to the length of time they have been outstanding. By revealing the age distribution of the receivables, the aging schedule will lead to better informed conclusions regarding the quality and the liquidity of the receivables as well as the kind of action which is necessary to remedy an unfavorable situation.

23. If the inventory level is inadequate the sales volume may decline to below the level of sales otherwise attainable. A loss of customers in the future may also be the result.

    On the other hand, excessive inventories expose the enterprise to expenses such as storage costs, insurance, and taxes as well as to risks of loss of value through obsolescence and physical deterioration. Excessive inventories also tie up funds which can be used more profitably elsewhere.

24. The LIFO method of inventory valuation in time of inflation may render both the inventory turnover ratio as well as the current ratio practically meaningless. Information regarding the LIFO reserve is available in published financial statements to enable the analyst to adjust the unrealistically low LIFO inventory valuations to more meaningful inventory figures. In intercompany comparative analysis, even if two companies use LIFO cost methods for their inventory valuation, the ratios based on such inventory figures may not be comparable because their respective LIFO inventory pools (bases) may have been acquired in years of significantly different price levels.

25. Not all current liabilities represent equally urgent and forceful calls for payment. Some claims, such as for taxes and wages, must be paid promptly regardless of current financial difficulties. Trade bills and other debts may not represent equally urgent calls for payment.

26. Changes in the current ratio over time do not automatically imply changes in liquidity or operating results. In a prosperous year, growing liabilities for taxes may result in a lowering of the current ratio. In times of business expansion working capital requirements increase with a resulting contraction of the current ratio, i.e., "prosperity squeeze." Conversely, during a business contraction current liabilities may be paid off while there may be a concurrent involuntary accumulation of inventories and uncollected receivables causing the ratio to rise.

27. "Window dressing" is manipulation of year-end balances of current items in order to show a more favorable current ratio than is otherwise warranted. This can be accomplished, for example, by temporarily stepping up the efforts for collection, by temporarily recalling advances and loans to officers, and by reducing inventory to below the normal level and use the proceeds from these steps to pay off current liabilities. The analyst should go beyond year-end measures and try to obtain as many interim readings of the current ratio as possible. Even if the year-end current ratio is very strong, interim ratios may reveal that the enterprise is dangerously close to insolvency. The analyst must always be aware of the possibility of manipulation.

28. The rule of thumb regarding the size of the current ratio is a popular belief that if the current ratio is 2 to 1, it is sound and anything below that norm is bad. The rule of thumb may go even further in believing that the higher the current ratio above the norm the better. The following, however, should be noted:

   * A current ratio much higher than 2 to 1, while implying a superior coverage of current liabilities, may also mean a wasteful accumulation of liquid resources.
   * It is the quality of the current assets and the nature of the current liabilities that are most significant in evaluating the meanings of the current ratio rather than a mere mechanical relationship.
   * The need of an enterprise for working capital varies with industry conditions as well as with the length of its own particular net trade cycle.

29. In an assessment of the overall liquidity of current assets, the trend of sales is an important factor. Since it takes sales to convert inventory into receivables and/or cash, an uptrend in sales indicates that the conversion of inventories into more liquid assets will be easier to achieve than when sales remain constant. Declining sales, on the other hand, will retard the conversion of inventories into cash.

30. The liquidity index is a measure of short-term liquidity, computed by according different weights (according to their convertibility into cash) to items among the current assets. The index as a number has no significance in itself. It has meaning only when it is compared with the index number for other periods or for other companies. Its reliability depends on the validity of the assumptions implicit in the weighting process.

31. In addition to the tools of analysis of short-term liquidity which lend themselves to quantification there are important qualitative considerations which also have an important bearing on the short-term liquidity of an enterprise. These can be usefully characterized as depending on the financial flexibility of an enterprise.

   Financial flexibility is the ability of an enterprise to take steps to counter unexpected interruptions in the flow of funds for. It means the ability to borrow from a variety of sources, to raise equity capital, to sell and redeploy assets and to adjust the level and the direction of operations in order to meet changing circumstances.

   The capacity to borrow depends on numerous factors and is subject to rapid change. It depends on profitability, stability, relative size, industry position, asset composition and capital structure. It will depend, moreover, on such external factors as credit market conditions and trends.

   The capacity to borrow is important as a source of funds in time of need for funds and is also important when an enterprise must roll over its short-term debt. Prearranged financing or open lines of credit are more reliable sources of funds in time of need than is potential financing.

   Other factors which bear on the assessment of the financial flexibility of an enterprise are the ratings of its commercial paper, bonds and preferred stock, restrictions on the sale of its assets, the degree to which expenses are of a discretionary nature as well as the ability to respond quickly to changing conditions such as strikes, shrinking demand or the cessation of sources of supply.

   The SEC requires an expanded "Management's Discussion and Analysis of Financial Condition and Results of Operations" (MD&A). The financial condition portion requires a discussion of liquidity factors--including known trends, demands, commitments or uncertainties likely to have a material impact on the enterprise's ability to generate adequate amounts of cash. If a material deficiency in liquidity is identified management must discuss the course of action it has taken or proposes to take in order to remedy the deficiency. In addition, internal and external sources of liquidity as well as any material unused sources of liquid assets must be identified and described.

32. The importance of projecting the effects of changes in conditions and policies on the cash resources of an enterprise is to allow for proper planning. For example, if management decides to ease the credit terms to its customers,

knowing the impact of the new policy on cash resources will help it make a more informed decision. It may seek easier terms from suppliers or make arrangements to get a loan.

◄ Answers to Exercises ►

Exercise 8-1

	Current Ratio	Quick Ratio	Working Capital
1.*	No change	No change	No change
2.	No change	No change	No change
3.	Increase	Increase	Increase
4.	Decrease	No change	Decrease
5.	Decrease	Decrease	Decrease
6.	Decrease	Decrease	Decrease
7.	Increase	Increase	No change
8.	Decrease	Decrease	No change
9.	Increase	Increase	Increase
10.	No change	No change	No change

*   Assuming that a sufficient amount had been provided for Allowance for Bad Debts.

Exercise 8-2

	A	B	C	Journal Entry	Explanation
1.	NE	NE	D	CGS 500 R.E. 500	Cost of goods sold increases by 500; average inventory increases by 250; ratio C decreases.
2.	I	D	NE	A/R Sales	Denominator will increase by half the amount of the numerator causing the A ratio to increase. Denominator of ratio B will increase causing the ratio to decrease. There is no effect on the components of ratio C.
3.	I	D	NE	Allow for Bad Debts A/R	The numerator in ratio A won't change and the denominator will decrease thus increasing the ratio. Because ratio A will increase, ratio B will decrease as the average accounts receivable turnover increases. Ratio C is not affected.
4.	I	D	NE	Bad Debt Expense A/R	Ratio A will increase due to the decrease in the denominator. Ratio B will decrease due to the increase in the denominator which is due to the increase in ratio A. Ratio C is unaffected.
5.	NE	NE	I	CGS Inventory	Only ratio C is affected. The numerator increases while the denominator decreases.

6. NE NE I R.E. 500 Neither ratio A nor B are affected. The
                 CGS 500 average inventory will decrease by 50%
                          of the decrease in the numerator in
                          ratio C due to the averaging effect,
                          thus increasing the ratio.

Exercise 8-3

	A	B	C	Journal Entry	Explanation

1. NE NE NE Allow for Bad Debts Since we use A/R in
                    A/R   net in computation of ratio—no effect.

2. NE NE D CGS Neither ratio A nor B is affected. The
                 RE cost of goods sold increases by $1,000,
                     and average inventory will increase by
                     $500 (due to the averaging effect), thus
                     decreasing ratio C.

3. NE NE I CGS Only ratio C is affected. The
                 Inventory numerator increases while the
                            denominator decreases.

4. N N I Loss Neither ratio A nor B is affected.
                 Inventory Average inventory will decrease by
                            $1,500 (half of $3,000), increasing
                            ratio C.

5. N N I RE Neither ratio A nor B is affected. The
                 CGS average inventory will decrease by half
                      of the decrease in the numerator.

6. I D N Sales Denominator of ratio A decreases by
                 A/R half the amount the numerator decreases,
                      causing ratio A to increase. Denominator
                      of ratio B will increase, causing it to
                      decrease. There is no effect on ratio C.

Exercise 8-4

a. 1. They could pay off accounts payable with cash. This would have the effect
        of reducing both current assets and current liabilities by the same amount,
        thus increasing the current ratio and quick ratio.

    2.* They could inject additional capital funds at year-end. This would increase
        cash without affecting current liabilities so the effect would be even more
        pronounced.

    3.* They could sell fixed assets for cash or short-term notes. This would
        increase current assets, but decrease only fixed assets. Thus, the current
        and quick ratios would improve.

4.* They could borrow cash by incurring long-term liabilities (notes or bonds). This would increase cash, but would not affect current liabilities, since the purpose is to make them long-term liabilities.

5.* They could defer incurring various expenses, such as advertising, research and development, and capital expenditures.

6. They could keep the cash receipts books open longer, in an effort to show higher receivables or collections. This method is a highly irregular and manipulative device.

* These procedures are normal business transactions which cannot usually be considered manipulative in character. They may become manipulative when they have no sound business justification and are undertaken solely to influence the measures used by outside analysts.

b. The analyst could, if all underlying evidence and documents were available, detect any of these devices. However, such evidence, such as invoices and the books of original entry, will most likely not be available for inspection. These devices may not be recognizable by inspection solely of the financial statements and 10-Ks of the company, even if they are compared with those of prior years or statements of other companies in the industry. If all evidence were available, the following are the techniques which may be used to detect the devices illustrated.

1. The analyst could determine the company's usual payment policies, and compare them with those employed at year-end. He/she could look at the terms of the liabilities, to see if they were paid at the most beneficial time--in other words, if any economic benefit was derived by paying them earlier than due or when normally paid. He/she could inspect also the payments in the first month of the following year, to see if liabilities were paid disproportionately to year-end, taking into account due dates and normal requirements. An unusually low inventory at year-end might also indicate failure to purchase merchandise at year-end in an effort to improve the quick ratio.

2. The analyst could analyze the timing of investments and the use to which they were put. If he/she sees large capital infusions at year-end, and that these investments were represented by idle cash, or by marketable securities which are not related to operations, and where there is little probability of such funds being required for operations in the near future, the reason might be window dressing.

3. Contracts and invoices might be examined to see when they were entered into and when they were recorded.

4. The procedures for investigation of excessive borrowing at year-end are the same as those for excessive investments of equity funds (2. above). Also, the contracts should be studied to determine if they are bona fide loans.

5. The purchase journal and cash disbursements journal should be examined, to compare expenses incurred towards the end of the year with expenses at the beginning of the following year, and the reasons for large differences.

6. To determine if the books are being kept open too long, the analyst would study such documents as the underlying invoices and canceled checks to determine their actual dates, and to compare this with the dates recorded. He/she might also confirm material accounts with customers as of the year-end.

◀ Answers to Problems ▶

Problem 8-1
a. Short-term liquidity ratios for Campbell Soup:

1. [36] ÷ [45] = 1665.5 ÷ 1298.1 = <u>1.28</u>

2. (80.7 [31] + 22.5 [32] + 624.5 [33]) ÷ 1298.1 [45] = <u>0.56</u>

3. Year 9 A/R = 624.5 [33] - 60.4 [61] = 564.1
   6205.8 [13] ÷ [(624.5 + 564.1)/2] = <u>10.44</u>

4. 4258.2 [14] ÷ [(819.8 [34] + 816)/2] = <u>5.21</u>

5. 624.5 [33] ÷ (6205.8 ÷ 360) = <u>36.23</u>

6. 819.8 ÷ (4258.2 ÷ 360) = <u>69.31</u>

7. 36.23 + 69.31 = <u>105.54</u>

8. (80.7 + 22.5) ÷ 1665.5 = <u>0.062</u>

9. (80.7 + 22.5) ÷ 1298.1 = <u>0.0795</u>

10.	Amount	Days from cash	Product $ x days
Cash & equivalents	103.20	—	—
Account receivables	624.50	36.23	22,625.64
Inventories	819.80	105.54	86,521.69
Prepaid expenses	<u>118.00</u>	100	<u>11,800.00</u>
	1,665.5		120,947.33

   Liquidity index = 120,947.33 ÷ 1,665.5 = <u>72.62</u>

11. EI	819.8	[34]
+ CGS	4,258.2	[14]
- BI	816.0	(given)
- Depreciation	<u>184.1</u>	[187]
= Purchases	4,077.9	

   525.2 [41] ÷ (4077.9 ÷ 360) = <u>46.36</u>

12. 105.54 - 46.36 = <u>59.18</u>

13. 448.4 [64] ÷ 1298.1 [45] = <u>34.54%</u>

b. Current assets using FIFO = 1665.5 [36] + 84.6 [153] = 1750.1

COGS (FIFO) = COGS (LIFO) + ΔLIFO reserve
             = 4258.2 + [84.6 - (904 - 816)] = 4254.8

1. 1,750.1 ÷ 1,298.1 = <u>1.35</u>

4. 4254.8 ÷ [(904.4 + 904)/2] = <u>4.71</u>

5. 624.5 [33] ÷ (6205.8 [13] ÷ 360) = <u>36.23</u>

6. 904.4 ÷ (4258.2 ÷ 360) = <u>76.46</u>

7. 36.23 + 76.46 = <u>112.69</u>

c. Disregarding, for purposes of this analysis, prepaid expenses and similar unsubstantial items entering the computation of the current ratio, we are left with the four major elements that comprise this ratio: i.e., cash, accounts receivable, inventories, and current liabilities. If we define liquidity as the ability to balance required cash outflows with adequate inflows, including an allowance for unexpected interruptions of inflows or increases in outflows, we must ask-- Does the relationship of these four elements at a given point in time:

1. Measure and predict the pattern of future fund flows?

2. Measure the adequacy of future fund inflows in relation to outflows?

Unfortunately, the answer to these questions is mostly negative. The current ratio is a static concept of what resources are available at a given moment in time to meet the obligations at that moment. The existing reservoir of net funds does not have a logical or causative relationship to the future funds that will flow through it. And yet it is the future flows that are the subject of our greatest interest in the assessment of liquidity. These flows depend importantly on elements *not* included in the ratio itself, such as sales, profits, and changes in business conditions.

There are a number of conclusions that can be reached:

1. Liquidity depends to some extent on cash or cash equivalents balances and to a much more significant extent on prospective cash flows.

2. There is no direct or established relationship between balances of working capital items and the pattern that future cash flows are likely to assume.

3. Managerial policies directed at optimizing the levels of receivables and inventories are oriented primarily towards efficient and profitable assets utilization and only secondarily towards liquidity.

Given these conclusions, which obviously limit the value of the current ratio as an index of liquidity, and given the static nature of this ratio and the fact that it is composed of items that affect liquidity in different ways, we may ask why this ratio enjoys such widespread use and in what way, if any, it can be used intelligently by the analyst.

d. Accounts receivable turnover rates or collection periods can be compared to industry averages or to the credit terms granted by the enterprise.

When the collection period is compared with the terms of sale allowed by the enterprise, the degree to which customers are paying on time can be assessed. In assessing the quality of receivables, the analyst should remember that a significant conversion of receivables into cash, except for their use as collateral for borrowing, cannot be achieved without a cutback in sales volume. The sales policy aspect of the collection period evaluation must also be kept in mind. An enterprise may be willing to accept slow-paying customers who provide business that is, on an overall basis, profitable; that is, the profit on sale compensates for the extra use by the customer of the enterprise funds. This circumstance may modify the analyst's conclusions regarding the *quality* of the receivables but not those regarding their *liquidity*.

The current ratio computation views its current asset components as sources of funds that can, as a means of last resort, be used to pay off the current liabilities. Viewed this way, the inventory turnover ratios give us a measure of the quality as well as of the liquidity the inventory component of the current assets.

The quality of inventory is a measure of the enterprise's ability to use it and dispose of it without loss. When this is envisaged under conditions of forced liquidation, then recovery of cost is the objective. In the normal course of business, the inventory should, of course, be sold at a profit. Viewed from this point of view, the normal profit margin realized by the enterprise assumes importance because the funds that will be obtained, and that would theoretically be available for payment of current liabilities, will include the profit in addition to the recovery of cost. In both cases, costs of sale will reduce net proceeds.

In practice, a going concern cannot use its investment in inventory for the payment of current liabilities because any drastic reduction in normal inventory levels will surely cut into the sales volume.

The turnover ratio is a gauge of liquidity in that it conveys a measure of the speed with which inventory can be converted into cash. In this connection, a useful additional measure is the conversion period of inventories.

Problem 8-2

Sales: 450,000 × 1.05 = 472,500

Cost of goods sold 312,000 × .98 = 305,760

Cash Forecast for Year 2:

Cash 1/1/Year 2			42,000
Cash Collections:			
Accounts Receivable, 1/1/Year 2	90,000		
Sales	472,500		
	562,500		
(a) Less Discount on Sales	(4,630)		
(b) Less A/R, 12/31/Year 2	(70,875)	486,995	
Total Cash Available			528,995
Cash Disbursements:			
Accounts Payable, 1/1/Year 2	78,000		
(c) Purchases	356,760		
(d) Less: A/P, 12/31/Year2	(132,510)	302,250	
Accrued Taxes paid		10,800	
(e) Other expenses—Cash		97,650	410,700
Cash Available 12/31/Year 2			118,295
Cash needed for machinery			(175,000)
Cash balance desired			(30,000)
Deficiency in Cash (need to borrow)			(86,705)

(a) 472,500 × .1 × .98 = 4,630 (Discount on Sales)

(b) 472,500 × .9 × (60/360) = 70,875 (A/R, 12/31/Year 2)

(c)

Year 2 Cost of Goods Sold	305,760
Ending Inventory	90,000 (given)
Goods Available for Sale	395,760
Beginning Inventory	39,000
Purchases	356,760

(d) A/P, 12/31/Year 2 = Yr 2 Purchases × (A/P, 12/31/Year 1 ÷ Yr 1 Purchases)

    A/P, 12/31/Year 2 = 356,760 × (78,000 ÷ 210,000) = 132,510

(e) Year 1:

Sales	450
Cost of Goods Sold	(312)
Depreciation	(25)
Net Income	(20)
Other Expenses	93

Other expenses (Year 2) = 93 x 1.05 = 97,650

Problem 8-3

Exhibit I -- Cash Forecast before Contemplated Changes:

Cash, January 1, Year 2			80,000
Cash Collections:			
Accounts receivable, beg.		150,000	
Sales (800,000 x 1.1)		880,000	
Less: Accounts receivable, end (a)		(165,000)	865,000
Total Cash Available			945,000
Cash Disbursements:			
Accounts payable, beg.	130,000		
Purchases (b)	657,000		
Less: Accounts payable, end (c)	(244,000)	543,000	
Increase in Notes payable		(15,000)	
Accrued taxes		20,000	
Cash expenses (d)		258,500	
			806,500
Net cash flow			138,500
Cash balance desired			50,000
Cash excess			88,500

(a)   360 days ÷ (800/150) = 67.5 days
     Applied to Year 2 sales: 880,000 x (67.5/360) = 165,000

(b)	Year 2 Cost of Sales (520,000 x 1.1)	572,000
	Ending Inventory (given)	150,000
	Goods available for sale	722,000
	Beginning Inventory	65,000
	Purchases	657,000

(c)   Purchases x (Year 1 A/P ÷ Year 1 Purchases)
     = 657,000 x (130,000/350,000) = 244,000

(d)	Gross profit (880,000 - 572,000)		308,000
	Less: NI (110% of 20,000 Year 1 NI) +		
	(10% of Year 1 depr.*) (22,000 + 2,500)	24,500	
	Depreciation—noncash	25,000	49,500
	Other cash expenses		258,500

    *   Because depreciation expense did not increase by 10%.

a.	A/R, end [880,000 (sales) x (90/360)]	220,000
	Less A/R from Exhibit I	165,000
	Additional cash needed	55,000
	Cash excess per Exhibit I	88,500
	Cash excess for this alternative	33,500

b.	A/R, end [880,000 (sales) x (120/360)]	293,000
	Less A/R from Exhibit I	165,000
	Additional cash needed	128,000
	Cash excess per Exhibit I	88,500
	Cash to be borrowed	39,500

```
c.   A/P, end [657,000 (purch) × (60/360)]        109,500
     A/Pper Exhibit I                             244,000

     Additional cash needed                       134,500
     Cash excess per Exhibit I                     88,500
     Cash to be borrowed                           46,000
```

Problem 8-4

```
Cash balance (1/1/Year 6)                                         35,000
Cash receipts:
    Accounts receivable, beg.                    75,000
    Sales                                       412,500
    Accounts receivable, end
        (Sales 412,500 × 90/360)                103,125
    Cash collections                                            384,375
Total cash inflows                                              419,375
Cash disbursements:
    Accounts payable, beg.          65,000
    Purchases (1)                  331,750
    Accounts payable, end          122,000
                                                274,750
    Payment of Notes payable                      2,500
    Accrued taxes                                 9,000
    Cash expenses (2)                           110,250         396,500
Estimated cash balance                                           22,875
Minimum cash required                                            50,000
Required to borrow                                               27,125
```

```
(1)  Beginning inventory                         32,000
     + Purchases (plug)                         331,750
     Goods available                            363,750
     - Ending inventory                          75,000
     COGS (412,500 × .70)                       288,750

(2)  Gross profit (30% of sales)                123,750
     Depr. expense (25,000 - 21,500)              3,500
     NI (excl. other exp.)                      120,250
     Other expenses (plug)                      110,250
     Net Income (given)                          10,000
```

Problem 8-5

a.   Information which could probably be derived from the notes to the financial statements:

   1.   Details of Gant's bank credit facility (e.g., total line of credit, portion currently unused, rates, term of credit facility).

   2.   Assess the impact consolidated subsidiaries have on liquidity constraints of the consolidated balance sheet of Gant. Very often, subsidiaries maintain separate credit facilities; therefore, solvency of a subsidiary may not necessarily be accessible to the parent company's creditors.

3. Gant's pension funding obligations. Is there an unfunded liability? If so, what are the future financial obligations?

Information which you should attempt to get from Gant's management:

1. A past series (e.g., several years) of statements of cash receipts and payments.

2. A prospective statement (one year) of the due dates and amounts of receivables and payables.

3. A budget of planned capital expenditures.

4. A budget of planned long-term financings.

b. General assessments which you should make regarding Gant Corporation and its industry:

1. The financial flexibility of Gant in terms of its ability to actually liquidate assets without affecting profitability.

2. The apparent level of inflation applicable to Gant and its industry (i.e., raw materials, unionized labor, product price flexibility).

3. Gant's competitiveness in the domestic industry (i.e., how up-to-date is its plant and equipment?). Will a major capital expenditure program be required in the near term?

4. How does the industry compete internationally? Are there adverse international industry developments beyond the control of Gant?

Specifically, with respect to the background details provided on Gant, you should consider the following points:

Cost Control Program:

-   How has the cost cutting program impacted the company's financial flexibility?
-   How lean is the operation?
-   Are there still assets which could be disposed of without impacting productivity or profitability negatively?

-   Has the program been too intense, such that long-term opportunities will be lost?

"Commodity" Orientation of Product Line:

-   What has happened with commodity prices over the past several years? Are the markets for Gant's various product lines soft?

U.S. Plant Facilities:

- How has the strength/weakness in the U.S. dollar affected the company's competitive position over the past years?

- How competitive is Gant internationally?

- Will it be forced to diversify its operations internationally and/or upgrade plant productivity?

- How would a major sustained capital expenditure program affect solvency?

Problem 8-6

a. *Ratio:*

Year 5 Year 6

1. Current ratio

Year 5: 61,000/40,000	1.5	
Year 6: 84,000/54,000		1.6

2. Days' sales in receivables

5: 20,000 ÷ (155,000/360)	46	
6: 25,000 ÷ (186,000/360)		48

3. Inventory turnover

5: 99,000/[(32,000+38,000)÷2]	2.83	
6: 120,000/[(38,000+56,000)÷2]		2.55

4. Days' sales in inventory

5: 38,000/(99,000 ÷ 360)	138	
6: 56,000/(120,000 ÷ 360)		168

5. Days' purchases in accounts payable

5: 20,000/(105,000* ÷ 360)	69	
6: 25,000/(138,000* ÷ 360)		65

* Purchases	Year 5	Year 6
Cost of sales	99,000	120,000
+ Ending inventory	38,000	56,000
Goods available for sale	137,000	176,000
- Beginning inventory	32,000	38,000
Purchases	105,000	138,000

6. Cash flow ratio

5: 7,700 ÷ 40,000	0.19	
6: 5,400 ÷ 54,000		0.10

7. Liquidity index:
   5: 8,002,000/61,000   131
   6: 13,386,000/84,000   159

Year 5	Amount	x	Days Removed from Cash	=	Product
Cash	2,000		—		—
Accounts receivable	20,000		46		920,000
Inventories	38,000		184*		6,992,000
Prepaid expenses	1,000		90		90,000
	61,000				8,002,000

* 138 + 46 = 184 days

Year 6	Amount	x	Days Removed from Cash	=	Product
Cash	2,000		0		—
Accounts receivable	25,000		48		1,200,000
Inventories	56,000		216**		12,096,000
Prepaid expenses	1,000		90		90,000
	84,000				13,386,000

** 168 + 48 = 216 days

Summary	Year 6	Year 5
Current ratio	1.6	1.5
Days' sales in receivables	48	46
Inventory turnover	2.55	2.83
Days' sales in inventory	168	138
Days' purchases in A/P	65	69
Cash flow ratio	.1	.19
Liquidity index	159	131

b. Most liquidity measures of ZETA have not shown marked year-to-year changes. However, there is a deterioration in the inventory turnover and that is even more evident in the days' sales in inventory measures. The liquidity index indicates that, overall, the liquidity of ZETA has deteriorated somewhat year-to-year. However, due to the short time span involved in this analysis it will be necessary to evaluate the longer term trend. Because of a lower level of CFO, the cash flow ratio has dropped significantly.

◄ Answers to Cases ►

Case 8-1

a. 1.

Account	1996	1995
Cash & equivalents	20%	19%
Marketable securities	44	51
Accounts rec.	19	16
Inventories	12	9
Prepaid expenses	5	4

2.
Component	1996	1995
Raw materials	43%	39%
Work in process	23	18
Finished goods	34	43

		1996	1995
3.	96: 4220/(89,487+4220)	4.5%	
	95: 4431/(56,495+4431)		7.3%
4.	96: 465,280 - 130,291	334,989	
	95: 350,472 - 56,414		294,058
5.	96: 465,280/130,291	3.57	
	95: 350,472/56,414		6.21
6.	96: (91,211+204,283+89,487)/130,291	2.95	
	95: (66,835+179,911+56,495)/56,414		5.38
7.	96: (91,211+204,283)/465,280	0.64	
	95: (66,835+179,911)/350,472		0.70
8.	96: (91,211+204,283)/130,291	2.27	
	95: (66,835+179,911)/56,414		4.37
9.	96: 360/[659,347÷(89,487+56,495)/2]	39.85	
	95: 360/[466,194÷(56,495+55,334)/2]		43.18
10.	96: 360/[275,939÷(55,028+31,712)/2]	56.58	
	95: 360/[205,596÷(31,712+38,940)/2]		61.86
11.	96: 39.85 + 56.58	96.43	
	95: 43.18 + 61.86		105.03
12.	96: 103,379/130,291	0.79	
	95: 118,089/56,414		2.09

b. Review of note seven and the MD&A reveal the following concerning Adaptec's financial flexibility:

*   Adaptec has a $17 million unsecured revolving line of credit under which no borrowings were outstanding at 3/31/96. Given Adaptec's strong financial position, other sources of borrowings should be readily available.

*   Due to the strong performance of Adaptec's common stock, sales of shares under various stock plans has provided a continuing source of additional equity capital.

*   Despite the numerous commitments identified in note seven, Adaptec's management asserts (in the MD&A) that "existing working capital combined with expected cash generated from operations and available sources of

bank and equipment financing will be sufficient to meet its cash requirements throughout fiscal 1997."

c. Adaptec's liquidity position is extremely strong. While the values of certain liquidity measures (e.g., current ratio and cash flow ratio) have decreased from 1995 to 1996, they still remain quite high. These declines may be viewed as favorable since current assets are not income-producing. In addition, notable improvements in the company's operating cycle were made in 1996.

Case 8-2

I. a.   Short-term liquidity ratios for the three year period:

		11	10	9
Current ratio (A)	(times)	1.36	1.30	1.84
Acid-test ratio (B)	(times)	.78	.57	.75
Cash & cash equiv to current assets (C)	(%)	2.4	1.19	1.38
Avg accts receivable turnover (D)	(times)	8.31	8.22	8.21
Avg collection period (E)	(days)	43	44	44
Avg inventory turnover (F) . . .	(times)	6.34	5.64	5.54
Avg. # of days to sell inv (G) .	(days)	57	64	65
Avg. # of days to pay A/P (H) . .	(days)	45	48	—
Operating cycle (I) (E + G) . . .	(days)	100	108	109
Net trade cycle (E + G - H) . . .	(days)	55	60	—
Liquidity index (J)	(#)	62.9	70.3	71.4
Cash from operations to current liabilities (K)	(%)	57	39	46

For Year 11:

(A)   [62] ÷ [78] = 1258.1 ÷ 926.9 = 1.36

(B)   [53 + 55] ÷ [78] = (30.2 + 691.1) ÷ 926.9 = .78

(C)   [53] ÷ [62] = 30.2 ÷ 1258.1 = 2.4%

(D)   [1] ÷ [55, avg] = 5491.2 ÷ [(691.1 + 629.9)/2] = 8.31

(E)   360 ÷ (D) = 360 ÷ 8.31 = 43.3

(F)   [2] ÷ [59, avg] = 2839.7 ÷ [(422.3 + 473.9)/2] = 6.34

(G)   360 ÷ (F) = 360 ÷ 6.34 = 57

(H)   [72, avg] ÷ (Purchases*/360) = 350.9 ÷ (2788.1/360) = 45

        *Purchases = CGS + End Inv - Beg Inv (not avail in Year 9)
                    = 2839.7 + 422.3 - 473.9 = 2788.1

(I)   This computation adds the collection period of receivables to the days needed to sell inventories.

(J)   *Liquidity Index* $ ×   *days*   =   #
       Cash   30.2   ×   0   =   0
       A/R   691.1 ×   43   =   29,717
       Inventories   422.3 ×   100   =   42,230
                                   1143.6   71,947

       Liquidity Index = 71,947 ÷ 1143.6 = 62.9

(K)   [31] ÷ [78] = 532.4 ÷ 926.9 = 57%

b.   Both the current ratio and acid test ratio increased slightly in Year 11 after the significant decrease in Year 10. Both inventory and accounts receivable turnovers have been stable over these years. So has the conversion period which has declined slightly. Cash from operations to current liabilities has improved measurably while the liquidity index improved somewhat from Year 9 to Year 10 and significantly from Year 10 to Year 11.

II.   *Projected Income Statement for Year 12:*

Sales (5491.2 × 1.15) [1]   6314.9
Cost & Expenses:
       Cost of Sales (2839.7 × 1.15) [2]   3265.7
       SGA (2121.2 × 1.15) [4]   2439.4
       Interest Expense (103.8 × 1.15) [156]   119.4
       Interest Capitalized (1.9 × 1.15) [156]   (2.2)
       Other Expense (32.6 × 1.15) [6]   37.5
              Total Costs & Expenses   5859.8
Income before Income Tax   455.1
Income Taxes at 45%[E]
       Current (90%)   184.3
       Deferred (10%)   20.5   204.8
Net Income   250.3
Dividends[E] Preferred (110)   4.3
Dividends[E] Common (118.7 × 1.08)   128.2   132.5
Increase to Retained Earnings   117.8

Projected Statement of Cash Flows for Year 12:

Beginning Cash Balance [53]		30.2
Cash Receipts		
Beg. A/R [55]	691.1	
Sales[A]	6314.9	
Less Ending A/R[B]	(743.0)	
Collections from Customers		6263.0
Total Cash Receipts		6293.2
Cash Disbursements		
Beg. A/P [72]	350.9	
Purchases[C]	3040.0	
Less Ending A/P[D]	(380.0)	
Payments to Creditors	3010.9	
S-T Notes[E]	40.0	
SGA[A]	2439.4	
Interest Expense[A]	119.4	
Taxes—Current[A]	184.3	
Dividends[A]	132.5	
Total Cash Disbursements		5926.5
Net Cash Inflow (Outflow)		366.7
Less: Minimum Cash Balance[E]		(70.0)
Cash Available*		296.7

*The Company will not have to borrow in Year 12

[A]As per projected Income Statement for Year 12

[B]Ending A/R = Sales/(A/R Turnover[E]) = 6314.9/8.5 = 743

[C]Purchases = A/P x A/P turnover = 380 x 8 = 3,040

[D]Ending A/P (given)

[E]Other Assumptions:

Tax Rate = 45%. Common stock dividends increased 8%. Preferred as per Item [110]. $40 million in notes are paid off. Management desires to maintain a minimum cash balance of $70 million. A/R turnover will be 8.5.

Case 8-3

a. Statement of expected cash flow:

Beginning cash balance		30,000
Add: Cash Receipts:		
Beginning accounts receivable	52,000	
+ Sales for Year 2 (1)	1,104,000	
- Ending accounts receivable (2)	276,000	
Cash collections		880,000
Total cash inflows		910,000
Deduct: Cash disbursements:		
Beginning accounts payable	60,000	
+ Purchases for Year 2 (3)	600,000	
-Ending accounts payable (4)	75,000	
Payments to creditors	585,000	
Payments of cash expenses (5)	315,920	
Payment of notes payable	20,000	
Payment of long-term debt	25,000	
Total cash disbursements		945,920
Net cash flow		(35,920)
Less minimum cash balance		(20,000)
b. Cash borrowings—expected		(55,920)

(1)   Sales for Year 2 = Sales for Year 1 × 115% = 960,000 × 1.15 = 1,104,000

(2)   Ending A/R = Average daily sales × Collection period
                 = 1,104,000 × 90 = $276,000

(3)   Purchases (Year 2) = COGS + Ending inventory - Beginning inventory
        COGS (Year 2) = COGS (Year 1) × 110% = 550,000 × 1.1 = 605,000
        Avg Inventory   = COGS ÷ Average inventory turnover
                      = 605,000 ÷ 5.5 = 110,000
        Ending inventory = (Average inventory × 2) - (Beginning Inventory)
                      = 110,000 × 2 - 112,500 = 107,500
        Purchases (Year 2) = 605,000 + 107,500 - 112,500 = 600,000

(4)   Ending A/P = Purchases (Year 2) × (Beg. A/P ÷ Year 1 Purchases)
                 = 600,000 × (60,000 ÷ 480,000) = 75,000

(5)   Cash expenses (Year 2) = S&A exp. + taxes paid

        S&A (Year 2) = S&A (Year 1) × 110% = 160,000 × 1.1 = 176,000

        Income tax expense for Year 2
        = [Sales - (COGS + Depreciation + S&A)] .48
        = [1,104,000 - (605,000 + (30,000 × 1.05) + 176,000] × .48
        = 139,920

        cash expenses (Year 2) = 176,000 + 139,920 = 315,920

b.   It is expected that FAX will need to borrow $55,920 in Year 2.

<u>Case 8-4</u>

a. *Statement of expected cash flow:*

Beginning cash balance		30,000
Add: Cash receipts:		
Beg. accounts receivable	52,000	
+ Sales for Year 2 (1)	1,104,000	
- Ending accounts receivable (2)	276,000	
Cash collections		880,000
Total cash inflows		910,000
Deduct: Cash disbursements:		
Beg. accounts payable	60,000	
+ Purchases for Year 2 (3)	582,667	
- Ending accounts payable (4)	77,689	
Payments to creditors	564,978	
Payments for cash expenses (5)	315,920	
Payment of notes payable	20,000	
Payment of long-term debt	25,000	
Total cash disbursements		925,898
Net cash flow		(15,898)
Less: Minimum cash balance		(20,000)
b. *Cash borrowings—expected*		(35,898)

(1)   Year 2 Sales = Year 1 Sales × 115% = 960,000 × 1.15 = 1,104,000

(2)   Ending A/R = Average daily sales × Collection Period
                  = (1,104,000/360) × 90 = 276,000

(3)   Year 2 Purchases = COGS + Ending inventory - Beginning inventory
        Year 2 COGS = Year 1 COGS × 110% = 550,000 × 1.1 = 605,000
        Avg inventory   = COGS ÷ Average inventory turnover
                      = 605,000 ÷ 6 = 100,833.33
        Ending inventory = (Average inventory × 2) - (Beginning Inventory)
                      = (100,833.33 × 2) - 112,000 = 89,667

        Year 2 Purchases = 605,000 + 89,667 - 112,000 = 582,667

(4)   Ending A/P = Year 2 Purchases × (Beg. A/P ÷ Year 1 Purchases)
                  = 52,667 × (60,000/450,000) = 77,689

(5)   Year 2 cash expenses:

    a.   Year 1 S&A exp. × 110% = 160,000 × 1.10 = 176,000
    b.   Year 2 income tax expense = [Sales - (COGS + Depr. + S&A exp.)] .48
           = [1,104,000 - (605,000 + (30,000 × 105%) + 176,000)] × .48 = 139,920

    Cash expenses = 176,000 + 139,920 = 315,920

Case 8-5

a.
			Year 5	Year 4
1.	Working capital:			
		Current assets	342,000	198,000
		Current liabilities	177,800	64,800
		Working capital	164,200	133,200

2.   Current ratio   1.92   3.06

3.   Acid-test ratio:
      [($12,000 + $183,000) ÷ $177,800]   1.10
      [($15,000 + $80,000) ÷ $64,800]   1.46

4.   Accounts receivable turnover:
      $1,684,000 ÷ [($183,000 + $80,000) ÷ 2]   12.81
      $1,250,000 ÷ [($80,000 + $60,000) ÷ 2]   17.86

5.   Collection period of receivables:
            360 ÷ 12.81   28.10
            360 ÷ 17.86   20.16

6.   Inventory-turnover ratio:
      $927,000 ÷ [($142,000 + $97,000) ÷ 2]   7.76
      $810,000 ÷ [($97,000 + $52,000) ÷ 2]   10.88

7.   Days to sell inventory:
            360 ÷ 7.76   46.39
            360 ÷ 10.88   33.09

8.   Debt-to-equity ratio:
      (120 + 30 + 147.8) ÷ (110 + 94.2)   1.46
      (73 + 14.4 + 50.4) ÷ (110 + 60.2)   0.81

9.   Times interest earned:
            $87,000 ÷ $12,000   7.25
            $43,300 ÷ $7,300   5.93

b.   *Index-number trend series*

	5	4	3
Sales	160.4	119.0	100.0
Cost of goods sold	181.1	158.2	100.0
Gross margin	140.7	81.8	100.0
Marketing and admin.	143.2	84.8	100.0
Net income	112.5	54.0	100.0

c.   A loan should not be granted as it appears that the overall financial position
     of the company is deteriorating. The following points should be noted:

     1.   The current ratio went down from 3.06 to 1.92.

     2.   A similar reduction occurred in the acid-test ratio, indicating the
           company is in a weaker position.

3. The accounts receivable turnover decreased while the collection period increased. This indicates a greater investment in receivables although the collection period of 28 days is still within the firm's terms of net 30 days.

4. The inventory turnover deteriorated from 10.88 to 7.76 and the days to sell inventory increased to 46 days from 33 days. This means that the firm is carrying a larger investment in inventories which ties up its badly needed quick assets. In addition, the risk of obsolete inventory is increased.

5. The debt-to-equity ratio increased drastically. Both the short-term and long-term debt were affected. The firm will probably experience difficulty in meeting its current maturities (see current and acid-test ratio declines) because the firm is financing its increased working capital needs with debt instead of with equity.

6. Although sales increased dramatically, the firm incurred a greater proportional increase in its costs. In Year 4, the firm actually had a lower gross margin and a lower net income despite the increase in sales. In Year 5, gross margin increased, but at a slower rate than the increase in sales. This indicates that the firm is experiencing a cost/profit squeeze.

Before any loans are made to the company, the firm must address the issues noted above and an improved financial condition must be demonstrated.

◄ CHAPTER 9 ►

Forecasting and Pro Forma Analysis

◄ CHAPTER REVIEW ►

Future liquidity is as important to our analysis of financial statements as our assessment of past and current liquidity. This chapter shows how our analysis of future liquidity benefits from forecasts of cash inflows and outflows. For long-term cash forecasting horizons, we show the usefulness of forecasts framed by the statement of cash flows. These forecast tools and others described in this chapter are extremely useful in analyzing a company's future liquidity, solvency, and financial flexibility. We demonstrate these tools with financial statements taken from practice.

The analysis in this chapter relies on a more *dynamic* representation of liquidity than traditional static ratio analysis based on past financial statement data. The static nature of traditional analysis, relying on financial reports listing claims against an enterprise and the resources available to meet these claims, fails to capture the dynamic nature of liquidity. We show how the analysis techniques in this chapter build on reliable patterns of past performance, incorporate estimates of future plans and conditions, and forecast the future availability and disposition of cash. These techniques are subject to feasibility tests using pro forma analysis and the discipline inherent in the accounting system.

◄ CHAPTER OUTLINE ►

▸ **Cash Flow Patterns**

▸ **Short-Term Cash Forecasting**

      Importance of Forecasting Sales

      Cash Flow Forecasting with Pro Forma Analysis

▸ **Long-Term Cash Forecasting**

      Analysis of Prior Cash Flows for Forecasting

      Forecasting Sources and Uses of Cash Flows

▸ **Specialized Cash Flow Ratios**

      Cash Flow Adequacy Ratio

      Cash Reinvestment Ratio

◄ Learning Objectives ►

- **Describe cash flow patterns in a company's business activities.**

- **Explain short-term forecasting and pro forma analysis of financial statements.**

- **Analyze cash flow patterns for long-term forecasting.**

- **Describe forecasting of operating, investing and financing cash flows.**

- **Explain what-if forecasting scenarios and their relevance.**

- **Interpret special cash flow adequacy and reinvestment ratios.**

◄ Answers to Questions ►

1. Ratio analysis is a static measurement--it establishes various relationships among financial statement items as of a given moment. Funds flow analysis is a dynamic measure covering a period of time. Such a dynamic model of funds flow analysis uses the present only as a starting point and utilizes the best available estimates of future plans and conditions in order to forecast the future availability and disposition of cash or working capital. Analyzing funds flow also encompasses projected operations of an entity. Since one of the fundamental assumptions of accounting is the going-concern concept, it can be said that the dynamic model is more realistic and is superior to the static models. However, extreme care should be taken in building up such a dynamic model as it is primarily based on estimates rather than on fact.

2. Yes. Cash is the most liquid asset and when management needs urgently to purchase assets or incur expenses, cash is the only asset it can utilize without costly delay. Unless management has a credit line established with a reliable outsider (such as a revolving account at a bank), lack of cash may mean permanent loss of a profitable opportunity.

3. The two are highly interrelated. The two are parts of the whole circulation system of "business blood." A failure of any part of the system can affect the entire system. For example, a reduction or cessation of sales affects the vital conversion of finished goods into receivables or cash which in turn leads to a drop in the cash reservoir. If the system is not strengthened by "blood transfusion" (e.g., additional investment by owner, or incurring debt, or accounts payable), production cannot be continued. Lack of cash will cut down other expenses, such as advertising and marketing, which will further adversely affect sales.

4. The short-term cash forecast is the key to the measurement of short-term liquidity. An asset is called "liquid" because it will or can be converted into cash within the current period. The analysis of a short-term cash forecast will reveal whether an entity will be able to repay short-term loans as planned; therefore, the analysis is extremely important for the potential short-term credit grantor. Also, a short-term cash forecast can be relatively realistic and accurate because of the nearness of the time span covered.

5. Except for transactions involving raising money from external sources (such as loan or additional investment) and investment of money in long-term assets, almost all internally generated cash flows relate to and depend on sales. Therefore, the first step in preparing a cash forecast is to estimate sales for the period under consideration. The reliability of any cash forecast depends on the forecast of sales. In estimating the sales forecast, the analyst should consider: (1) past trends of sales volume, (2) share of the market, (3) industry and general economic conditions, (4) productive and financial capacity, and (5) competitive factors as well as other pertinent variables.

6. Pro forma financial statements are estimated financial statements prepared on the assumption that the future trends will reflect past patterns adjusted for known and expected changes.

    The reliability of the pro forma financial statements depends, of course, on how realistic the underlying assumptions used in their preparation have been. Once prepared, ratios and other relationships derived from the pro forma financial statements should be compared against their historical counterparts for feasibility. After proper adjustments, the information can be used as a basis for future decisions.

7. A cash forecast, to be meaningful, must be for a relatively short-term period of time. There are many unpredictable variables involved in the preparation of a reliable forecast for a highly liquid asset such as cash. Over a longer period of time (i.e., beyond the time span of one year), the difference in the degree of liquidity among the items in the current assets group is not significant. What is more important for such a longer time span are the projections of net income and other sources and uses of funds. The focus should be shifted to working capital from cash because over a period of, say, thirty months, the time required to convert current assets into cash is relatively insignificant.

8. The financial analyst who wants to estimate what future cash flows will be can get the most relevant information by analyzing the sources and uses of cash patterns of the recent past. If there is no drastic change in the management or in the nature of the enterprise, it is possible to assume that certain cash flow patterns will persist and that with proper adjustments a protection of cash flows by broad categories can be undertaken.

9. In evaluating sources and uses of cash, the analyst will focus on questions such as these:

   ■ Has the enterprise been able to finance fixed asset replacement from internally generated funds? Historical as well as current cost depreciation may be useful in this assessment. Many companies do not provide adequate information to enable the analyst to distinguish between replacement and capacity expansion.

   ■ How have expansion and business acquisitions been financed?

   ■ To what extent is the enterprise dependent on outside financing? How frequently is it required and what form does it take?

   ■ What does the company's need for and access to cash suggest as implications for its debt service ability and dividend policy?

10. The analysis of the SCF enables the analyst to appraise the quality of management's financing and investing decisions over time as well as their impact on the results of operations and financial condition of the enterprise. The analysis will reveal also what has been done with retained earnings over the years as well as how management has reinvested the internal cash inflow over which it had discretion. Moreover, in the process of such an evaluation, the financial analyst can also judge an entity's quality of earnings by the impact which changes in economic and industry conditions have on its cash flow.

11. A forecast of future statements of cash flow would have to take into consideration all trends which the enterprise has exhibited, such as those relating to income, the elements that convert it to sources of cash from operations, fixed assets additions, the relationship of sales to growth in working capital, and possibly to sources of cash provided by operations as well. The size of noncash adjustments, such as depreciation, depends on future depreciation policies and equipment acquisitions. The latter, as well as write-off methods to be used for tax purposes, will, in turn, determine the size of the deferred tax adjustments. The more we know about factors such as these the more reliable the forecast will be.

12. The short-term cash forecast is, as we have seen, a very useful and reliable aid in projecting the state of short-term liquidity. Such a detailed approach is, however, only feasible for the short term, that is, up to about 12 months. Beyond this time horizon the uncertainties become so great as to preclude detailed and accurate cash forecasts. Instead of focusing on collections of receivables and on payments for labor and materials the longer-term estimates focus on projections of net income and the resulting cash flows from operations as well as on other sources and uses of cash.

13. The common-size statement of cash flows facilitates the comparison and the analysis of the mayor components of sources and uses of cash over the years or of one enterprise as compared to another.

14. Past data are useful in evaluating past performance of an entity and in understanding managerial quality and habits. However, past data are historical in nature--the financial analyst is interested in the future. Unless there is a sound understanding about the size and the source of cash needed for future operations the analyst cannot assess the likelihood of their realization. For example, if a future expansion of sales and profits is forecast, the financial analyst must know whether the enterprise has the "financial horsepower" to generate internally the required cash and, if not, where the required future cash is going to come from.

15. The projected SCF provides a very useful frame of reference against which the impact on the enterprise of sudden adversity can be assessed. The projected statement will be a starting point in building up the defensive posture of an enterprise. The analysis is directed to a basic question: "What can the enterprise do and what resources, both internal and external, can it marshal to cope with a sudden and serious reduction in the inflows of cash?" The analysis of the statement represents an excellent tool in the assessment of risk for a prospective credit grantor.

16. Cash flow per share (often measured as net income plus depreciation) should not necessarily be used more in financial analysis largely because of the misconceptions which have arisen in connection with its use--namely, that cash flow represents profitability (which it does not) and that cash flow represents actual cash available (also which it does not due to the keeping of most accounting statements on an accrual basis). However, for certain types of analysis, for example to eliminate the effects of different depreciation policies of two companies being compared, cash flow analysis can be used effectively.

◄ Answers to Exercises ►

Exercise 9-1
Projected Income Statement for Year 12:

Revenues (given)		6000.0
Costs & Expenses:		
COGS (a)	3186.0	
SGA (b)	2439.4	
Other expenses (c)	35.2	
Interest (d)—net	91.4	
Total Expenses		5752.0
Income from continuing operations		248.0
Income taxes (e)		105.9
Income before discontinued operations . .		142.1
(Loss) on disposal of disc ops (given) . .		(2.0)
Net Income		140.1

a. Cost of sales is estimated to be at a level representing the average percentage of cost of sales to sales as prevailed in the four-year period ending June 30, Year 11, which is 53.1% (19909.2 - 9331.3)/19909.2. Therefore, 6,000 × .531 = $3,186.

b. Selling, general & administrative expenses in Year 12 are expected to increase by the same percentage as these expenses increased from Year 10 to Year 11, which is 15%. Therefore, $2121.2 × 1.15 = $2,439.4.

c. Other expenses are expected to be 8% higher in Year 12. Therefore, 32.6 × 1.08 = $35.2.

d. Interest expense (net of interest capitalized) and interest income will increase by 6% due to increased financial needs. Therefore, 86.2 × 1.06 = $91.4

e. The effective tax rate in Year 12 will equal that of Year 11, which is 42.7% (175.7/411.5). Therefore, tax expense = 248 × .427 = 105.9.

Exercise 9-2

a. *Cash flow adequacy ratio:*

3-year sum of cash from operations
3-year sum of capital expenditures,
inventory additions, and cash dividends

= 1361.1 (a) ÷ [852.3 (b) + 92.5 (c) + 328.7 (d)]
= 1361.1 ÷ 1273.5 = 1.069

(a) Cash from operations [31] = 532.4 + 447.1 + 381.6
(b) Capital expenditures [32+33] = 240.6 + 275.6 + 223.2 + 112.9
(c) Inventories additions [24] = 2.2 + 90.3
(d) Cash dividends [38] = 123.0 + 110.5 + 95.2

b. This ratio is a measure of the extent to which the company was able to cover their capital expenditures, inventory additions and cash dividends by cash generated from operations. If a ratio of 1 is reached, a company has covered itself at a particular growth level without outside financing. If the ratio falls below 1, the company has not been able to maintain current operating growth levels and dividends solely from internally generated funds.

The computation above indicates that Quaker Oats' cash from operations provided enough cash to cover their needs. Although the surplus is small, the company should be able to reduce their debt by the excess amount of cash available.

c. *Cash reinvestment ratio:*

Cash provided by operations - dividends
Gross plant + Other receivable & investment +
Other intangible assets + working capital

Year 11:   532.4 [31] - 123.0 [38]
            1914.6 [64] + 79.1 [63] + 446.2 [67] + 331.2 62-78]

            = 409.4/2771.1 = 14.77%

Year 10:   447.1 - 110.5
            1745.6 + 63.5 + 466.7 + 342.8

            = 336.6/2618.6 = 12.85%

d. Quaker Oats has a fairly good reinvestment ratio of greater than 12% in both years. This shows the potential for future strength by planning for the replacement of assets and operations growth. For 1991 the level of this ratio is higher.

Exercise 9-3

```
Beginning cash balance . . . . . . . . . . . .              20
Cash collections:
      Beginning accounts receivable  . . . .    20
      Sales for month  . . . . . . . . . . .   150
                                               170

      Less: Ending accounts receivable . . .    21         149
Cash available . . . . . . . . . . . . . . .               169
Cash disbursements:
      Beginning accounts payable . . . . . .    18
      Purchases (1)  . . . . . . . . . . . .   115
             . . . . . . . . . . . . . . . .   133
      Ending A/P (25% of purchases)  . . . .    29    104
      Miscellaneous outlays . . . . . . . . .          11   115

Cash balance . . . . . . . . . . . . . . . .                54
Minimum cash balance desired . . . . . . . . .             30
Excess cash  . . . . . . . . . . . . . . . .                24

(1)   Ending inventory  . . . . . . . . . . .        15
      Cost of goods sold (5/6 of sales)  . . .      125
                                                    140
      Less beginning inventory          . . .       25
      Purchases                         . . .      115
```

◄ Answers to Problems ►

Problem 9-1

Quaker Oats
Projected Statement of Cash Flows -- Year 12

Cash provided by (used for) continuing operations

Net income (a)	$ 225.0

Items in income not affecting cash

Depreciation & amortization (b)	185.2
Deferred income taxes (c)	54.7
Provision for restructuring charges (given)	0.0
	$ 464.9

Cash provided by (used for) operating working capital

Receivables (d)	(8.9)
Inventories (e)	(45.2)
Other current assets (f)	(25.6)
Accounts payable (g)	42.1
Other current liabilities (h)	24.5
Cash provided by operating activities	$ 451.8

Cash provided by (used for) investment activities

Capital expenditures—PP&E (given)	$ (300.0)
Asset retirements (given)	20.0
Other changes (given)	(30.0)
Cash used for investing activities	$ (310.0)

Cash provided by (used for) financing activities

Repayments of L-T debt (given)	$ (45.0)
Net decrease in S-T debt (given)	(40.0)
Cash dividend paid (given)	(135.0)
Additions to L-T debt—plug (i)	*81.0*
Cash provided by financing activities	$ (139.0)

Increase in cash (j)	2.8
Beginning balance	30.2
Balance at end of the year	33.0

Notes:

(a) Avg % of Net Income to sales, Years 9-11: [118]

Total Net Income	=	577.8	
Total Revenues		15401.2	= 3.75%

Net Income in 12 = $6,000 × .0375 = $225

(b) Depreciation & Amortization in 12 = 225 × .8233 = $185.2

(c) Avg % of deferred income taxes (noncurrent) and other items to net income, Years 9-11 [21]/[19] = 140.4/577.8 = 24.3%

Noncurrent deferred income tax in 12 = 225 × .243 = 54.7

(d)   Ending A/R = 6,000 x (42/360) = 700.0

For Year 12:   A/R, beg   691.1
                      A/R, end   700.0
                      Increase   8.9

(e)   Year 12 Cost of Sales = 6000 x .51 = 3060

Ending Inventory = 3060 x (55/360) = 467.5

For Year 12:   Inv, beg   422.3
                      Inv, end   467.5
                      Increase   45.2

(f)   Using item [25], (13.7 + 14.1 + 48.9)/3 = 25.6

(g)   Year 12 Purchases = 2807.2 x 1.12 = 3144.1

A/P, end = 3144.1 x (45/360) = 393.0

For Year 12:   A/P, beg   350.9
                      A/P, end   393.0
                      Increase   42.1

(h)   Using item [27], (43.2 + 83.4 - 53.1)/3 = 24.5

(i)   Amount required to balance statement

(j)   Percent of cash to revenues in Year 11 = 30.2/5491.2 = .55%
        Year-end cash in 12 = $6,000 x .55% = 33
        Increase in cash for Year 12 = 33-30.2 = 2.8

Problem 9-2

Quaker Oats
Common-Size Statement of Cash Flows
For the Three Years Ended June 30, Year 11

	11	10	9
	%	%	%
Sources (applications):			
Internally generated funds:			
Net income [19]	28.63	23.34	26.38
Depreciation & amortization [20]	24.72	22.44	17.60
Deferred income taxes and other items [21]	6.30	2.10	10.38
Provision for restructuring charges [22]	1.39	(2.42)	16.15
Cash provided by (used for) operating working capital:			
Receivables [23]	(13.60)	(7.72)	(10.02)
Inventories [24]	4.27	(0.30)	(11.73)
Other current assets [25]	(1.90)	(1.95)	(6.35)
Trade accounts payable [26]	3.63	4.34	13.28
Other current liabilities [27]	6.01	11.52	(6.90)
Other—net [28]	1.32	0.06	(1.09)
Payable to Fisher-Price [29]	4.12	0.00	0.00
Net current assets of discontinued ops [30]	9.18	10.35	1.88
Total from operations [31]	74.07	61.76	49.58
Disposals of PPE [35]	2.49	1.64	3.47
Proceeds from issue of debt for spin-off [39]	19.63	0.00	0.00
Proceeds from long-term debt [42]	0.25	34.83	32.64
Issuance of common treasury stock [44]	3.56	1.77	1.32
Issuance of preferred stock [46]	0.00	0.00	12.99
Total sources	100.00	100.00	100.00
Applications (sources):			
Additions to PPE [32]	33.47	38.07	29.00
Cost of acquisitions [33]	0.00	0.00	14.67
Other receivables and investments [34]	1.49	3.12	0.74
Other—discontinued operations [36]	2.75	8.07	6.07
Cash dividend [38]	17.11	15.26	12.37
Deferred compensation [40]	0.03	(0.48)	32.28
Short-term debt [41]	36.95	0.99	(5.47)
Reduction of long-term debt [43]	5.52	4.81	3.91
Purchase of common stock [45]	0.00	30.83	8.90
Purchase of preferred stock [47]	0.10	0.00	0.00
Total uses of cash	97.42	100.67	102.47
Effect of exchange rate [49]	0.84	(0.22)	0.96
Increase (decrease) in cash	1.74	(0.45)	(3.43)

In summary, during the three-year period the major sources of cash for Quaker Oats were operations, disposals of PPE, and proceeds from long-term debt. In addition, a small amount of cash was generated by the issuance of common and preferred stocks.

The major uses during this period were additions to PPE, reduction of debt, payment of dividends, and purchase of common and preferred stocks.

During this period, operations as a percentage of total sources fluctuated from a low of 49.58% in Year 9 to a high of 74.07% in Year 11. Proceeds from long-term debt as a percentage of total sources declined from a high of 34.83% in Year 10 to a low of 0.25% in Year 11. Cash provided by operating activities was strong for all years and in Year 11 showed a 19% growth over Year 10 cash flow from operations.

Problem 9-3
Use T-accounts to determine cost of goods sold:

Raw Material Inventory (in $ thousands)			
Beg	0		
Purchases (125 x 6 mos.)	750	715	To WIP inventory (plug)
End (given)	35		

Work in Process Inventory			
Beg	0		
From RM inventory	715	7	Prepaid product exp.
Labor (30.5 x 6)	183	1,299	To FG inventory (plug)
Variable overhead (22.5 x 6)	135		
Rent (10 x 6)	60		
Depreciation (35 x 6)	210		
Patent amort. (.5 x 6)	3		
End (given)	0		

Finished Goods Inventory			
Beg	0		
From WIP inventory	1,299	1,199	COGS (plug)
End (given)	100		

Telnet Corporation
Pro Forma Income Statement
Six Months Ended June 30, Year 2
(in $ thousands)

Sales revenue (250,000 x 6)	$1,500
Cost of goods sold (from above)	1,199
Gross margin	301
Selling and administrative expenses (47,500 x 6)	285
Expected pretax income	16
Estimated income taxes (at 50%)	8
Expected net income	$ 8

Pro forma Balance Sheet
June 30, Year 2

Cash 40		(minimum cash)
Accounts receivable 375		(45 days' sales)*
Inventories (35 + 100) 135		(given)
Prepaid expenses 7		(given)
Current assets	557	
Equipment 1,200		
Less accumulated depreciation 210		
. . . .	990	
Patents 40		(given)
Less—amortization 3		(500 × 6 months)
	37	
Total Assets	1,584	
Accounts payable	125	(30 days' purch)**
Accrued taxes	8	(from I/S)
Stockholders' equity	1,300	(given)
Retained earnings	8	(from I/S)
Additional funds needed	143	"plug"
Total Liabilities and Equity	1,584	

$$* \quad \frac{6 \times \$250,000}{180 \text{ days}} = \$8,333 \text{ per day} \times 45 \text{ days} = 375,000$$

$$** \quad \frac{\$125,000 \times 6}{180 \text{ days}} = \$4,166 \text{ per day} \times 30 \text{ days} = 125,000$$

Statement of Cash Flows
For Six Months Ended June 30, Year 2

Cash balance—beginning	60,000	
Add: Cash receipts		
Collection of accounts receivable* .	1,125,000	1,185,000
Less: Disbursements		
Material purchases**	625,000	
Labor	183,000	
Rent	60,000	
Overhead	135,000	
Selling expense	285,000	(1,288,000)
Tentative cash balance		(103,000)
Minimum cash balance required		40,000
Additional borrowing required		143,000
Ending cash balance		40,000
Loan balance		143,000

```
* Collection of A/R              Jan.  Feb.  Mar.  Apr.  May  June
Sales . . . . . . . . . . . . . . . . .  250   250   250   250   250   250
Collections . . . . . . . . . . . . . .    0   125   250   250   250   250
Accumulated Collections . . . . . . . .    0   125   375   625   875 1,125

** Payment of A/P                Jan.  Feb.  Mar.  Apr.  May  June

Purchases . . . . . . . . . . . . . . .  125   125   125   125   125   125
Payments . . . . . . . . . . . . . . .     0   125   125   125   125   125
    Accumulated Payments . . . . . . . .   0   125   250   375   500   625
```

◄ Answers to Cases ►

Case 9-1

a. 1.

Adaptec, Inc.
Common-Size Statements of Cash Flows
For the Years Ended March 31, 1996, 1995, and 1994

	1996	1995	1994
	%	%	%
Sources (applications):			
Internally generated funds:			
Net income	79.0	69.1	104.2
Write-off of in-process tech.	30.3	0.0	0.0
Depreciation & amortization	13.4	11.6	20.3
Provision for doubtful accounts	0.2	0.1	3.7
Cash provided by (used for) operating working capital:			
Receivables	(23.5)	(1.0)	(23.0)
Inventories	(15.7)	5.3	(9.8)
Prepaid expenses	(6.9)	0.3	(9.7)
Other assets	(14.6)	(3.0)	(20.3)
Accounts payable	(0.1)	1.7	(4.9)
Accrued liabilities	16.8	3.1	15.7
Total from operations	79.0	87.3	76.1
Issuance of common stock	21.0	12.7	23.9
Total sources	100.0	100.0	100.0
Applications (sources):			
Additions to PP&E	30.4	23.3	30.6
Cost of acquisitions	23.8	0.0	0.0
Repayment of debt	2.6	2.5	5.2
Purchase of treasury stock	5.9	27.0	0.0
Purchase of marketable securities	18.6	23.9	35.8
Total uses of cash	81.4	76.8	71.6
Increase (decrease) in cash	18.6	23.2	28.4

2.   Common-Size Statement of Cash Flows
               For the Three-Year Period Ended March 31, 1996

Sources (applications):
Internally generated funds:
    Net income 79.3
    Write-off of in-process tech. 12.3
    Depreciation & amortization 13.9
    Provision for doubtful accounts 0.8
Cash provided by (used for) operating working
    capital:
    Receivables . . . . (14.0)
    Inventories . . . . (5.8)
    Prepaid expenses . . . . (4.3)
    Other assets . . . . (10.8)
    Accounts payable . . . . (0.2)
    Accrued liabilities 10.9
Total from operations 82.0
Issuance of common stock 18.0
    Total sources 100.0

Applications (sources):
Additions to PP&E 9.7
Cost of acquisitions 27.5
Repayment of debt 23.8
Purchase of treasury stock 13.7
Purchase of marketable securities 3.0
    Total uses of cash 77.7
Increase (decrease) in cash 22.3

Discussion:
Over the period 1994-1996, cash from operations comprised 80% of sources of
cash. The only other source of cash Adaptec has relied on is issuance of
common stock under various stock purchase plans. Adaptec's stock price has
risen steadily over time. A decrease in stock price may reduce this source of
financing. However, the strong operating performance and low level of current
borrowings, Adaptec should have no problem borrowing on favorable terms, if
needed.

Adaptec's cash flow has been more than enough to finance its operations. Over
the period, 37.5% of cash sources have been directed to nonoperating uses--
purchases of marketable securities (23.8%) and purchases of treasury shares
(13.7%).

b. 1. *Cash flow adequacy ratio:*

<u>cash from operations</u>
sum of capital expenditures, inventory
additions, and cash dividends

1996: 103,379/(31,177 + 39,748 + 20,516) = <u>1.13</u>
1995: 118,089/31,576 = <u>3.74</u>
1994: 43,063/(17,314 + 5,563) = <u>1.88</u>

1994-96: 264,531/145,894 = <u>1.81</u>

The ratios indicate that Adaptec has had no problem financing operations from internally-generated cash.

2. *Cash reinvestment ratio:*

<u>Cash provided by operations - dividends*</u>
Gross plant + Other receivable & investment +
Other intangible assets + working capital

1996: 103,379/(132,961 + 88,428 + 465,280 - 130,291) = <u>18.6%</u>
1995: 118,089/(95,111 + 17,373 + 350,472 - 56,414) = <u>29.1%</u>
1994: balance sheet info n/a

1995-96: 264,531/962,920 = <u>27.5%</u>

*   Purchases of treasury shares may be considered as equivalent to cash dividends.

Relative to the rule-of-thumb range of 7% to 11%, Adaptec's ratio is quite high.

c. This problem has deliberately been left open-ended to force students to develop their own assumptions. A sample projected income statement is provided as a starting point. The common-size income statements on page 30 of the 1996 Adaptec annual report are a useful source of information.

Sales (given)	934,000
Cost of revenues	<u>392,280</u>
Gross margin (58% of sales) (a)	541,720
R&D (13%)	121,420
Sales and marketing (13%)	121,420
General and administrative (5%)	46,700
Write-off of in-process tech. (b)	<u>33,000</u>
Income from operations	219,180
Interest income, net (2%)	<u>18,680</u>
Income before income taxes	237,860
Provision for I/T (25% effective rate)	<u>59,465</u>
Net income	178,395

(a)   Based on gross margin in 1996. Other expenses comprise a fairly stable percentage of sales over the 1994-96 period.

(b)   Per note five, the 1996 write-off of $52.313 million was approximately equal to the purchase price of the companies acquired. Absent any additional information, the 1997 write-off (also mentioned in note five) is assumed to be equal to the purchase price of CSG.

Case 9-2
Schedule of interest and Commitment Fees:

	Amount of Loan	Interest or Fee
Year 2:		
To be borrowed 1/1	$ 800,000	
To be borrowed 4/1	500,000	
Commitment fee due 4/1 ($1,000,000 × 1% × 1/4)		$ 2,500
To be borrowed 7/1	300,000	
Commitment fee due 7/1 ($500,000 × 1% × 1/4)		1,250
To be borrowed 12/31	100,000	
Commitment fee due 12/31 ($200,000 × 1% × 1/2)		1,000
Interest due on loan:		
On $800,000 @ 5%		40,000
On $500,000 @ 5% × 3/4		18,750
On $300,000 @ 5% × 1/2		7,500
Total at 12/31/Year 2	$1,700,000	$71,000
Year 3:		
To be borrowed 4/1	100,000	
Commitment fee due 4/1 ($100,000 × 1% × 1/4)		$ 250
Repayment of loan:		
Due 6/30	(100,000)	
Due 12/31	(100,000)	
Interest due on loan:		
On $1,700,000 @ 5% × 1/4		21,250
On $1,800,000 @ 5% × 1/4		22,500
On $1,700,000 @ 5% × 1/2		42,500
Total at 12/31/Year 3	$1,600,000	$86,500
Year 4:		
Repayment of loan:		
Due 6/30	(100,000)	
Due 12/31	(100,000)	
Interest due on loan:		
On $1,600,000 @ 5% × 1/2		$40,000
On $1,500,000 @ 5% × 1/2		37,500
Total at 12/31/Year 4	$1,400,000	$77,500

	Year 2	Year 3	Year 4
Results of operations:			
Operating profit (at $.04 per ton handled)	$200,000	$212,000	$224,000
Interest and commitment fees (above)	71,000	86,500	77,500
Cash derived from operations	$129,000	$125,500	$146,500
Depreciation (at $.03 per ton handled) . .	$150,000	159,000	168,000
Operating loss	$21,000	$ 33,500	$ 21,500
Operating loss from prior year(s)		21,000	54,500
Accumulated operating loss		$ 54,500	$ 76,000

Miller Company
Cash Forecast
For Years Ended December 31, Years 2, 3, and 4

	Year 2	Year 3	Year 4
Cash forecast summary:			
Cash balance at beginning of period		$229,000	$154,500
Cash received from stockholders	$ 100,000		
Proceeds of loan	1,700,000	100,000	
Excess of cash income over cash expenses . .	129,000	125,500	146,500
Payments for construction	(1,700,000)	(100,000)	
Payments on loan		(200,000)	(200,000)
Cash balance at end of period	$ 229,000	$154,500	$101,000

Evaluation:

As noted in the "Results of operations" section, Miller will be booking
operating losses in each of the three years examined. However, Miller is
expected to generate sufficient cash flow to cover the debt service.

Case 9-3

Royal Co.
Cash Budget
For Years Ending March 31, Years 6 and 7

	Year 6	Year 7
Beginning balance of cash	$ 0	$ 75,000
Cash collections from customers (see Schedule A)	$825,000	$1,065,000
Disbursements:		
Direct materials—Schedule B	220,000	245,000
Direct labor	300,000	360,000
Variable overhead	100,000	120,000
Fixed costs	130,000	130,000
Total disbursements	$750,000	$ 855,000
Excess of collections over disbursements	$75,000	$210,000
Cash available from operations	75,000	285,000
Cash received from liquidation of existing A/R and inventories	90,000	0
Total cash available	$165,000	$285,000
Payments to general creditors	90,000	270,000[2]
Balance of cash at end	$ 75,000[1]	$ 15,000

[1]   This amount could have been used to pay general creditors or carried forward to the beginning of the next year.

[2]   ($600,000 × 60%) - ($50,000 + $40,000)

Schedule A   COLLECTIONS FROM CUSTOMERS

	Year 6	Year 7
Sales	$900,000	$1,080,000
Beginning accounts receivable	0	75,000
Total	$900,000	$1,155,000
Less: ending accounts receivable	75,000	90,000
Collections from customers	$825,000	$1,065,000

Schedule B   DISBURSEMENTS FOR DIRECT MATERIALS

	Year 6	Year 7
Direct materials required for production	$200,000	$240,000
Required ending inventory	40,000[3]	$50,000[4]
Total	$240,000	$290,000
Less: beginning inventory	0	$40,000
Purchases	$240,000	$250,000
Beginning accounts payable	0	$20,000
Total	$240,000	$270,000
Less: ending accounts payable	20,000	25,000
Disbursements for direct materials	$220,000	$245,000

[3]   12,000 units × 2/12 = 2,000; 2,000 × $20 per unit = $40,000
[4]   15,000 units × 2/12 = 2,500; 2,500 × $20 per unit = $50,000

Case 9-4

a.   1.   SCHEDULE A
                        ESTIMATED CASH RECEIPTS

	SEP	OCT	NOV	DEC
Total Sales	$40,000	$48,000	$60,000	$80,000
Credit Sales (25%)	10,000	12,000	15,000	$20,000
Cash Sales	$30,000	36,000	$45,000	$60,000
Collections—Prior Month's Credit Sales .		10,000	12,000	$15,000
Total Collections		$46,000	$57,000	$75,000

        2.   SCHEDULE B
                ESTIMATED CASH DISBURSEMENTS FOR PURCHASES

	OCT	NOV	DEC	TOTAL
Total Sales	$48,000	$60,000	$80,000	
Purchases	$42,000	$56,000	$25,200	$123,200
Less: 2% Purchase Discount	840	1,120	504	2,464
Disbursements	$41,160	$54,880	$24,696	$120,736

        3.   SCHEDULE C
        ESTIMATED CASH DISBURSEMENTS FOR OPERATING EXPENSES

	OCT	NOV	DEC	TOTAL
Sales	$48,000	$60,000	$80,000	
Salaries and Wages (15%)	$ 7,200	$ 9,000	$12,000	$28,200
Rent (5%)	2,400	3,000	4,000	9,400
Other Expenses (4%)	1,920	2,400	3,200	7,520
Total	$11,520	$14,400	$19,200	$45,120

3.

SCHEDULE D
ESTIMATED TOTAL CASH DISBURSEMENTS

	OCT	NOV	DEC	TOTAL
Purchases (Sch. B)	$41,160	$54,880	$24,696	$120,736
Operating Expenses (Sch. C)	11,520	14,400	19,200	45,120
Furniture and Fixtures (given) . . .	600	400		1,000
Total	$53,280	$69,680	$43,896	$166,856

4.

SCHEDULE E
ESTIMATED CASH RECEIPTS AND DISBURSEMENTS

	OCT	NOV	DEC	TOTAL
Receipts	$46,000	$57,000	$75,000	$178,000
Disbursements	53,280	69,680	43,896	166,856
Net Cash Increase			$31,104	$ 11,144
Net Cash Decrease	$ 7,280	$12,680		

5.

SCHEDULE F
FINANCING REQUIRED

	OCT	NOV	DEC	TOTAL
Opening Cash Balance	$12,000	$ 8,720	$ 8,040	$12,000
Net Cash Increase			31,104	11,144
Net Cash Decrease	7,280	12,680		
Cash Position before Financing . .	$ 4,720	$(3,960)	$39,144	$23,144
Financing Required	4,000	12,000		16,000
Interest Expense (1)			(180)	(180)
Financing Retired			(16,000)	(16,000)
Closing Cash Balance	$ 8,720	$ 8,040	$22,964	$22,964

(1)   (4,000)(.06)(3/12) + (12,000)(.06)(2/12)

b.   1.

FORECASTED INCOME STATEMENT
FOR THE QUARTER ENDING DECEMBER 31, YEAR 6

Sales (Schedule A)		$188,000
Deduct:		
Cost of Goods Sold (70% of sales)	$131,600	
Less: Purchase Discounts Taken (Schedule B) . . .	2,464	129,136
Gross Margin	$ 58,864	
Selling and Administrative Expenses:		
Salaries and Wages (Schedule C)	$ 28,200	
Rent (Schedule C)	9,400	
Other Expenses (Schedule C)	7,520	
Depreciation ($750 x 3 months)	2,250	
Total Selling and Administrative Expenses		47,370
Net Operating Income		$ 11,494
Interest Expense		180
Net Income		$ 11,314

2.

FORECASTED BALANCE SHEET
DECEMBER 31, YEAR 6

```
Current Assets:
     Cash (Schedule F)  . . . . . . . . . . . . . . .   $ 22,964
     Accounts Receivable (25% of December sales)   . . .   20,000
     Inventory ($30,000 + 70% of $36,000) (.98)  . . . .   54,696
          Total Current Assets  . . . . . . . . . . . . .            $ 97,660
Property, Plant, and Equipment:
     Furniture and Fixtures  . . . . . . . . . . . .   $101,000
          Less: Accumulated Depreciation  . . . . . . . .    2,250    98,750
               Total Assets . . . . . . . . . . . . . . . . . .      $196,410

Liabilities   . . . . . . . . . . . . . . . . . . . . . .          $  -0-
Stockholders' Equity . . . . . . . . . . . . . . . . . .            196,410
          Total Equities . . . . . . . . . . . . . . . . .          $196,410
```

◄ CHAPTER 10 ►

Capital Structure and Solvency

◄ CHAPTER REVIEW ►

Solvency is an important factor in our analysis of a company's financial statements. Solvency refers to a company's long-run financial viability and its ability to cover long-term obligations. All business activities of a company--financing, investing, and operating--affect a company's solvency. One of the most important components of solvency analysis is the composition of a company's capital structure. Capital structure refers to a company's sources of financing and its economic attributes.

This chapter describes capital structure and explains its importance to solvency analysis. Since solvency depends on success in operating activities, the chapter examines earnings and its ability to *cover* important and necessary company expenditures. Specifically, this chapter describes various tools of solvency analysis, including leverage measures, analytical accounting adjustments, capital structure analysis, and earnings-coverage measures. We demonstrate these analysis tools with data from financial statements. We also discuss the relation between risk and return inherent in a company's capital structure, and its implications for financial statement analysis.

◄ CHAPTER OUTLINE ►

▸ **Keys to Solvency Analysis**

▸ **Importance of Capital Structure**

      Characteristics of Debt and Equity

      Motivation for Debt Capital

      Measuring Effects of Financial Leverage

▸ **Accounting Implications for Capital Structure Analysis**

      Adjustments to Book Values of Liabilities

      Adjustments to Book Values of Assets

▸ **Capital Structure Composition and Solvency**

      Long-Term Projections in Analyzing Solvency

      Common-Size Statements in Solvency Analysis

      Capital Structure Measures for Solvency Analysis

      Interpretation of Capital Structure Measures

▸ **Asset-Based Measures of Solvency**

      Asset Composition in Solvency Analysis

      Asset Coverage in Solvency Analysis

▸ **Importance of Earnings Coverage**

      Relation of Earnings to Fixed Charges

      Times Interest Earned Analysis

      Relation of Cash Flow to Fixed Charges

      Earnings Coverage of Preferred Dividends

      Interpreting Earnings Coverage Measures

▸ **Capital Structure Risk and Return**

▸ **Appendix 10A Rating Debt Obligations**

▸ **Appendix 10B Predicting Financial Distress**

▸ **Appendix 10C Analytical Adjustments to the Long-Term Debt to Equity Ratio**

◄ Learning Objectives ►

- **Describe capital structure and its relation to solvency.**

- **Explain financial leverage and its implications for company performance and analysis.**

- **Analyze adjustments to accounting book values to assess capital structure.**

- **Describe analysis tools for evaluating and interpreting capital structure composition and assessing solvency.**

- **Analyze asset composition and coverage for solvency analysis.**

- **Explain earnings-coverage analysis and its relevance in evaluating solvency.**

◄ Learning Objectives ►

- **Describe capital structure risk and return and its relevance to financial statement analysis.**

- **Interpret ratings of organizations' debt obligations (Appendix 10A).**

- **Describe prediction models of financial distress (Appendix 10B).**

◄ Answers to Questions ►

1. The key elements in evaluating long-term solvency are:

   a. the analysis of the capital structure of the firm.
   b. the different degrees of risk associated with the holding of different types of assets.
   c. earnings, earning power, and earnings trend of the firm.
   d. earnings coverage of fixed charges.
   e. assets coverage of loans.
   f. the protection afforded by loan covenants and/or the pledges of specific assets as security.

2. The financial stability of an enterprise and the risk of insolvency to which it is exposed are dependent on the sources of its funds as well as on the type of assets it holds and the relative magnitude of such asset categories.

   There are essential differences between debt and equity, which are the two major sources of funds. Equity capital has no guaranteed return which must be paid out and there is no time-table for repayment of the capital investment. From the viewpoint of an enterprise, equity capital is permanent and can be counted on to remain invested even in times of adversity. Therefore, the enterprise can confidently invest such funds in long-term assets and expose them to the greatest risks. On the other hand, debts are expected to be paid at certain specified times regardless of an enterprise's financial condition.

   To the investor in common stock, the existence of debt contains an element of risk of loss of his/her investment. The creditors would want as large a capital base as is possible as a cushion which will shield them against losses which can result from adversity. Therefore, it is important for the financial analyst to review carefully all the elements of the capital structure.

3. Financial leverage is the result of borrowing and incurring fixed obligations for interest payments. The owners of a successful business that requires funds may not want to dilute their ownership of the business by issuing additional common stock. They can "trade on the equity" by borrowing the funds required on the strength of their equity capital as a borrowing base. Generally, they may rather borrow than share the ownership with new shareowners. Financial leverage will be most advantageous when the rate of return on total assets exceeds the net interest cost paid on debt. An additional advantage provided by financial leverage is that interest expense is tax deductible while dividend payments are not.

4. Leverage is a two-edged sword. In good times earnings benefit, and perhaps decisively so, from leverage. In a severe recession or when unexpected events occur, net income could turn out to be far less than total interest payments. Therefore, the use of leverage is acceptable to the financial markets only up to some undefined level. Ninety percent is higher than whatever that level is.

   At 90 percent debt to total capital, future financing flexibility would be extremely limited. Lenders would not loan money, and equity financing may cost more than the potential returns on incremental investments. A 90 percent debt level would make net earnings extremely volatile, with a sizable increase in fixed charges. The incremental cost of borrowing, including refunding of maturing issues, increases with the levels of borrowing done. A 90 percent debt level could pose the probability of default and receivership in the event that something goes wrong. The financial risk of Dynamic would be much too high for either stockholders or bondholders.

5. In making his/her judgment the analyst must recognize that under normal circumstances, deferred tax liabilities will reverse (i.e., become payable) only when a firm shrinks in size. Generally, a shrinkage in size is attended by losses rather than by taxable income. In such circumstances, the drawing down of the deferred tax account is more likely to involve credits to tax loss carryforwards or carrybacks, rather than to the cash account.

To the extent that such future "reversal" is only a remote possibility, the deferred credit should be viewed as a source of funds of such long-term nature as to be classifiable as equity. On the other hand, if the possibility of a "drawing down" of the deferred tax account in the foreseeable future is quite strong, then the account, or a part of it, is more in the nature of a long-term liability. In classifying the deferred tax account as between debt and equity, the analyst must be guided by considerations such as the ones discussed above.

6.   Present accounting requirements for the capitalization of leases are not rigorous and definite enough to insure that all leases which represent, in effect, installment purchases of assets are capitalized. Consequently, the analyst must evaluate leases which have not been capitalized with a view to including them among debt obligations.

      Leases which cover most (say 75-80 percent) of the useful life of an asset can generally be considered the equivalent of debt financing.

7.   Off-balance-sheet financing are attempts by management to structure transactions in such a way as to seemingly justify excluding debt (and related assets) from the balance sheet. This is usually done by emphasizing legal form over substance. Examples of such transactions are take or pay contracts, "sales" of receivables, and inventory repurchase agreements.

8.   SFAS 87 recognizes that if the fair value of pension assets falls short of the accumulated pension benefit obligation, a liability for pensions exists. However, this liability does not take into consideration the projected benefit obligation which recognizes an estimate for future pay increases. When pension plans base their benefits on future pay formulas, analysts, who judge such understatement as serious and who can estimate it, may want to adjust the pension liability for analytical purposes.

9.   The preferred method of presenting the financial statements of a parent and its subsidiary is in consolidated format. This is also the preferred method from the analyst's point of view for most analytical purposes although separate financial statements of the consolidated entitles are necessary in some cases, such as when the utilization of assets of a subsidiary (e.g., an insurance company or a bank) is not subject to the full discretion of the parent.

      Information on unconsolidated subsidiaries may also be important because bondholders of such subsidiaries can look only to the latter's assets as security for their bonds. Moreover, bondholders of the parent company (particularly holding companies) may derive a significant portion of their fixed charge coverage from the dividends of the unconsolidated subsidiaries. Yet, in the event of the subsidiary's bankruptcy the parent bondholders may be in a junior position to the bondholders of the subsidiary.

10.   a. Generally, the minority interest is shown among liabilities in consolidated financial statements. However, the minority interest differs from debt in that it has neither mandatory dividends payment requirements nor principal repayment requirements. Therefore, for the purpose of capital structure analysis, it may be classified as equity rather than as a liability.

      b. The purpose of appropriating retained earnings is to "set aside" a certain portion of retained earnings in order to prevent them from serving as a basis for the declaration of dividends. There exists no claim by an outsider to such an appropriation until the contingency materializes. Therefore, unless the loss reserved against is considered certain to occur, such appropriations should be considered as part of equity capital.

      c. A guarantee for product performance is the result of a definite contract with the buyer that commits the entity to correct product defects. Therefore, it is a potential liability and should be classified as such.

      d. Convertible debt is generally classified among liabilities. However, if the terms of conversion and the market price of the common stock are such that it is most likely to be converted into common stock, it should be considered as equity for the purpose of capital structure analysis.

e. Most preferred stock entails no absolute obligation for payment of dividends or repayment of principal, possessing thus the characteristics of true equity. However, preferred stock with a fixed maturity or subject to sinking fund requirements should, from an analytical point of view, be considered as debt.

11. a. Because the owner's equity of an enterprise is measured by the excess of total assets over total liabilities, any analytical revision of asset book values (i.e., amounts at which assets are shown in the financial statements) will also result in a change in the amount of owner's equity. For this reason, in assessing capital structure, the analyst must decide whether or not the book value amounts of assets are realistically stated.

b. The following are examples of the need for possible adjustments. Different or additional adjustments may be needed depending on circumstances:

Inventories carried at LIFO are generally understated in times of rising prices. The amount by which inventories computed under FIFO (which are closer to replacement cost) exceed inventories computed under LIFO is disclosed as the LIFO reserve. These disclosures should enable the analyst to adjust inventory amounts and the corresponding owner's equity amounts to more realistic current costs or values.

For fiscal years beginning before 12/16/93, marketable securities were generally stated at cost which may be below market value. Using parenthetical or footnote information, the analyst can make an analytical adjustment increasing this asset to market value and increasing owner's equity by an equal amount.

Intangible assets and deferred items of dubious value which are included on the asset side of the balance sheet have an effect on the computation of the total equity of an enterprise. To the extent that the analyst cannot evaluate or form an opinion on the present value or future utility of such assets, they may be excluded from consideration thereby reducing the amount of equity capital by the amounts at which such assets are carried. However, the arbitrary exclusion of all intangible assets from the capital base is an unjustified exercise in overconservatism.

12. Long-term creditors are interested in the future operations and cash flows in addition to the short-term financial condition of the debtor. For example, a creditor of a three-year loan would want to make an analysis of solvency assuming the worst set of economic and operating conditions. For such purposes, an analysis of short-term liquidity is usually not adequate. However, such a dynamic analysis for the long term is subject to substantial uncertainties and requires the making of assumptions over a much longer time horizon. The inevitable lack of detail and the uncertainties inherent in long-term projections do severely limit their reliability. However, this does not mean that long-term projections are not useful. It does mean that the analyst must be aware of the serious limitations to which they are subject.

13. Common-size analysis focuses on the composition of the funds which finance an enterprise and it thus measures the financial risk inherent in it. It shows clearly the relative magnitude of the sources of funds of the enterprise and allows the analyst to compare them with similar data of other enterprises.

The various capital structure ratios measure the financial risk in an enterprise by relating various components of the capital structure to each other or to their totals. One advantage of ratio analysis is that it can be used as a screening device and that it can go beyond relationships present in a single financial statement (e.g., the balance sheet).

14. The difference between the book value of the equity capital and its market value is usually caused by a number of factors. One of these is the effects price-level changes. These in turn are caused by two factors: change in the purchasing power of money and change in price due to economic factors such as the law of supply and demand. Therefore, with fluctuating prices it is unlikely that the historical cost will correspond to current market value. Accounting methods in use can also affect the book value of an asset significantly. For example, often a particular

depreciation method is adopted for tax reasons rather than in order to measure the loss of value of an asset due to wear and tear and obsolescence.

The financial analyst could possibly correct this distortion of current value by valuing the equity at market value. For actively traded securities this would not be too difficult; however, the stock market is often subject to substantial overvaluation and undervaluation depending on the degree of speculative sentiment.

15. Since the liability/equity side of the balance sheet shows the sources of funds of an entity and the asset side the investment of these funds, we can generally establish direct relationships between asset groups and selected items of capital structure. This does not, of course, imply that resources provided by certain liabilities or capital should be directly associated with the acquisition of certain assets. However, it is valid to assume that the type of assets an enterprise employs should determine to some extent sources of resources used to finance them. Therefore, in order to judge the risk exposure of a given capital structure, the analysis of asset distribution is one additional important dimension to consider. For example, if an entity acquired long-term assets by means of short-term borrowings, the analyst would conclude that this particular method of financing involves a considerable degree of risk.

16. The earnings to fixed charges ratio measures directly the relationship between debt-related and other fixed charges and the earnings available to meet these charges. It is a test of the ability of an enterprise to meet its fixed charges out of current earnings. Earnings coverage ratios are superior to other tools, such as debt-equity ratios which do not focus on the availability of funds. in that they measure directly the availability of funds for payment of fixed charges. Fixed charges are mostly a direct result of the incurrence of debt and an inability to pay them, with attendant repercussions, represents one of the most serious elements of risk stemming from debt.

17. What items to include in "fixed charges" depends on the purpose of analysis. Fixed charges can be defined narrowly to include only interest and interest equivalents or broadly to include all other outlay requirements under contractual obligations.

    (1)   Interest and interest equivalents:
      a.   Interest on long-term debt, including amortization of bond discounts and premiums.
      b.   The interest element included in long-term lease rentals.
      c.   Capitalized interest.

(2)   Other outlays under contractual obligations:

a.   Interest on income bonds (assuming profitable operations which are implicit assumptions in such borrowings).

b.   Required deposits to sinking funds and principal payments under serial bond obligations.

c.   Principal repayment included in lease obligations.

d.   Purchase commitments under noncancelable contracts to the extent that requirements exceed normal usage.

e.   Preferred stock dividend requirements of majority-owned subsidiaries.

f.   Interest on recorded pension liabilities.

g.   Guarantees to pay fixed charges of unconsolidated subsidiaries if the requirement to honor the guarantee appears imminent.

(3)   Other fixed charges, such as imputed interest in the case on non-interest or low interest-bearing obligations. These do not, however, represent genuine periodical fund drains.

For each of the above categories, the corresponding income to be included in the ratio computation should be adjusted accordingly.

Fixed charges which are not tax deductible must be tax adjusted. This is done by increasing them by an amount equivalent to the income tax that would be required to obtain an after-tax income sufficient to cover such fixed charges. The tax rate to be used should be based on the relationship of the provision for income tax expense applicable to income from continuing operations to the amount of pretax income from continuing operations, i.e., the company's normal effective tax rate.

18.   Normally an entity would sign a long-term purchase contract to insure that the required supply of essential raw material is not interrupted, to get a favorable purchase discount, or both. In times of favorable economic conditions, the analyst does not have to worry about such commitment (in fact, it is a positive factor) unless the committed amount is in excess of requirements for expected sales in the future. Therefore, if his or her analysis leads to the conclusion that the purchase commitment represents the minimum requirements of supplies for the entity which will be needed even in case of slack business conditions, he or she may be justified in excluding the commitment from fixed charges. If he or she decides to include it in fixed charges, income should be adjusted to reflect the tax deductible nature of the purchase which will eventually become the cost of goods sold. Proceeds from the forced sale of excess supplies may also be deducted on an estimated basis.

19.   Net income includes items of revenue which do not generate cash currently as well as expenses which do not require the current use of cash. For the measure of fixed charges coverage, the more relevant figure is "cash provided by operations" shown in the statement of cash flows. Net income, in most fixed charge coverage computations, is used as a surrogate of this more valid measure of cash availability.

20.   Since Company B is under the control of Company A, the latter can siphon off funds from it to the detriment of B's creditors. Moreover, the customer-supplier relationship with Company A means that Company A has considerable discretion in the allocation of revenues, costs, and expenses among the two entities in such a way as to determine which will show what portion of the total available profit. This can again work to the detriment of Company B's creditors.

A lender to Company B should write into the lending agreement conditions that would prevent parent Company A from exercising its controlling powers to the detriment of the lender.

21.   Because of the fixed nature of its rewards, debt can never be expected to carry the risks of ownership and, because it is repayable it cannot serve as the permanent risk capital of an enterprise. In fact, debt is incurred on the foundation of an equity base. The latter is the fund which shields the debt from risk and absorbs the losses to which an enterprise may be exposed.

22. The advantages of such a course of action are that the enterprise is able to potentially enlarge its equity base if it otherwise could not sell equity, to sell equity shares at prices in excess of current market and to obtain, in the interim, a lower interest cost on funds because of the conversion feature of the debt.

The disadvantage is that a decline in the market price of the stock may postpone conversion substantially and indefinitely, thus leaving the enterprise with a debt burden which it was not prepared to shoulder over the longer term. What may be conceived of as temporary financing may, in fact, become long-term debt.

23. a. Because it is at risk over such an extended period of time, the long term is subject to many uncertainties and imponderables of the future. In order to prevent, as much as is possible, deterioration in some key ratios and safe guards which exist at the time the loan is made, long-term creditors often insist on the maintenance of certain ratios at specified levels and/or other managerial actions and policies. Of course, no contractual arrangement can prevent operating losses which are the number one cause of failure of most enterprises.

    b. 1. The maintenance of a minimum degree of short-term liquidity.
       2. Provisions aimed at preventing the dissipation of equity capital by retirement, refunding, or the payment of excessive dividends.
       3. Preservation of equity capital for the safety of creditors.
       4. To insure the ability of creditors to protect their interests in a deteriorating situation.

24. The mayor reason why debt securities are widely rated while equity securities are not lies in the fact that there is a far greater uniformity of approach and homogeneity of analytical measures used in the evaluation of credit worthiness than there can be in the evaluation of the future market performance of equity securities. This wide agreement on what is being measured in credit risk analysis has resulted in a widespread acceptance of and reliance on published credit ratings.

25. In rating an industrial bond issue, rating agencies focus on the issuing company's asset protection, financial resources, earning power, management, and the specific provisions of the debt security.

Asset protection is concerned with measuring the degree to which a company's asset protection, financial resources, earning power, management, and the specific provisions of the debt security.

Financial resources encompass, in particular, such liquid resources as cash and other working capital items.

Future earning Power is a factor of great importance in the rating of debt securities because the level and the quality of future earnings determine importantly an enterprise's ability to meet its obligations. Earnings power is generally a more reliable source of security than is asset protection.

Management abilities, philosophy, depth, and experience always loom importantly in any final rating judgment. Through interviews, field trips and other analyses the raters probe into management's goals, the planning process as well as strategies in such areas as research and development, promotion, new product planning and acquisitions.

The specific provisions of the debt security are usually spelled out in the bond indenture. What is analyzed here are the specific provisions in the indenture which are designed to protect the interest of bondholders under a variety of future conditions.

26. a. Municipal securities, those issued by state and local authorities, comprise a number of varieties. Most are general obligation bonds backed by the full faith and credit of the governmental unit which issues them. Others are special tax bonds that are limited in security to a particular tax that will be used to service and retire them. Then there are revenue bonds secured only by revenues which are derived from the investment of the proceeds of the bond issue. Other categories comprise housing authority bonds, tax anticipation notes, etc.

b. Raters require a great variety of information from issuers of municipal debt. In case of general obligation bonds, the basic security rests on the issuer's ability and willingness to repay the debt from general revenues under a variety of economic conditions. The fundamental revenue source is the taxing power of the local authority. Thus, the information they require includes: current population and the trend and composition of population, the largest taxpayers, the current market value of taxable properties, the gross indebtedness and the net indebtedness (i.e., after deducting self-sustaining obligations, sinking fund, etc.), recent annual reports, budgets and estimates of capital improvement and future borrowing programs, as well as an overall description of the area's economy.

Other factors of interest include unfunded pension liabilities as well as the trend of indebtedness. A steady increase in indebtedness is usually a danger sign. As in all cases of debt rating, the factor of management, though largely intangible and subject to measurement only through ultimate results, is of critical importance.

27. As is true in any phase of security analysis the analyst who can, through superior analysis, improve on what is conventionally accepted stands to benefit accordingly and this is more true in the case of debt securities than in the case of equity securities. Bond ratings cover a wide range of characteristics and they consequently present opportunities for those who can identify these differences within a rating classification. Moreover, rating changes generally lag the market, and this presents additional opportunities to the analyst who with superior skill and alertness can identify important changes before they become generally recognized.

◄ Answers to Exercises ►

Exercise 10-1

a. $2,110,300,000^a/(76,328,721^b \times 53.3125^c) = \underline{0.52}$

^{a}Total Liabilities [78+79+80+81] = 926.9 + 701.2 + 115.5 + 366.7 = 2110.3
^{b}# of Common Shares Issued [85-90] = 83,989,396 - 7,660,675 = 76,328,721
^{c}Avg. stock price for 1991 [137] = (64.875 + 41.75)/2 = 53.3125

b.   Item [130] tells us that Quaker Oats' Year 11 book value for common stock is $11.80 which is much lower than the average market value. Market values are important in a company like Quaker Oats, because they take into consideration the fair values of the company intangible assets and earning power. If we compare the 0.52 ratio that we get when using the market value of the equity to the 2.33 ratio reached when using the book values we can see that the market value ratio is superior. This indicates that the market accords Quaker Oats' assets a value higher than book value and thus a better coverage for liabilities.

a.

	Alpha	Beta	Gamma
Operating income	80,000	210,000	300,000
Interest expense	30,000	0	60,000
Income before taxes	50,000	210,000	240,000
Taxes (40%)	20,000	84,000	96,000
Net income	30,000	126,000	144,000
Total assets	1,000,000	2,000,000	3,000,000
Stockholders' equity	700,000	2,000,000	1,800,000
Net income plus			
interest (1-tax rate)	48,000	126,000	180,000
Return on:			
Total assets	4.8%	6.3%	6%
Stockholders' equity	4.29%	6.3%	8%
Financial Leverage Index	0.89	1.00	1.33

b. For Alpha the index (0.89) indicates a negative effect of financial leverage--the company does not earn enough to justify the cost of borrowing. For Gamma the index (1.33) indicates a positive effect of financial leverage, which is due to a higher return on the company's assets compared to the cost of obtaining the debt capital. Beta has an index of 1, which is the neutral level, that is, the company neither gains nor loses from borrowing because, in this case, the company has no debt.

Exercise 10-3

A.	TOTAL DEBT/TOTAL EQUITY	
B.	LONG-TERM DEBT/TOTAL EQUITY	
C.	{PRETAX EARNINGS + FIXED CHARGES (FC)}/FC	
D.	{PRETAX CFO + FC}/FC	

	A	B	C	D
a.	NE	NE	I/I=D*	I/I=D*
b.	D/NE=D	D/NE=D	D/D=I	D/D=I
c.	I/NE=I	I/NE=I	I/I=D	I/I=D
d.	NE/I=D	NE/I=D	I/I=D	I/I=D
e.	NE	NE	D/NE=D	NE
f.	NE	NE	NE	I/NE=I
g.	NE	NE	I/I=D	I/I=D
h.	NE	NE	D/D=I	D/D=I
i.	D/I=D	D/I=D	NE	NE
j.	I/NE=I	NE	NE	NE

* If preferred stock outstanding

Exercise 10-4

I.   b

II. a

III. b

IV. b

V.   d

Exercise 10-5

a.   *Calculation of interest incurred (on outstanding debt):*

6,000,000 at 11% =	660,000
10,000,000 at 9% =	900,000
40,000,000 at 10% =	4,000,000
	5,560,000

Calculation of capitalized interest:

I.   specific borrowing:
     6,000,000 x 11% = 660,000

II. non-specific borrowing:
     (900,000 + 4,000,000)/(10,000,000 + 40,000,000) = 9.8%
     4,000,000 x 9.8% = 392,000

I + II = 660,000 + 392,000 = 1,052,000

Calculation of interest expense:

interest incurred - capitalized interest
5,560,000 - 1,052,000 = 4,508,000

b.   In order to evaluate the ability of a company such as Rogan to actually service its debt and to compare it to other companies within its industry, a bond analyst would supplement the times interest earned ratio by using cash flow from operations in the numerator instead of income and in the denominator interest incurred instead of interest expense.

◄ Answers to Problems ►

<u>Problem 10-1</u>

a.   *11*   *10*   *9*

1.	Financial leverage index	2.44	2.00	2.02
2.	Long-term debt to equity capital	1.31	1.15	1.02
3.	Total liabilities to total liabilities and equity capital	.70	.69	.64
4.	Total liabilities to total owners' equity	2.33	2.26	1.75
5.	Preferred stock to total owners' equity	.53%	.18%	—
6.	Analytically adjusted ratio of LT debt to equity	—	.77	—
7.	Earnings coverage of fixed charges	4.45	3.75	3.57
8.	Cash flow coverage of fixed charges	6.83	5.20	5.65
9.	Cash from operations to long-term debt	.45	.38	.33
10.	Earnings coverage of preferred dividends	4.22	3.58	3.57
11.	Equity capital to net fixed assets	.73	.88	1.19

Calculations:

1. $\underline{\text{(NI [11] - Pfd Div [111])/Avg. Owners' Equity [91]}}$
   (NI [11] + Net Int Exp [156] (1 - TR))/Avg Assets [69]

   11: $\underline{\text{(205.8 - 4.3)/((901 + 1017.5)/2)}}$
   (205.8 + 101.9 (1 - .34))/((3016.1 + 3326.1)/2)

   10: $\underline{\text{(169 - 3.6)/((1017.5 + 1137.1)/2)}}$
   (169 + 120.2 (1 - .34))/((3326.1 + 3125.9)/2)

   9: $\underline{\text{(203 - 0)/((1137.1 + 1251.1)/2)}}$
   (203 + 75.9 (1 - .34))/((3125.9 + 2886.1)/2)

2. Total Debt & Owners' Equity [92]
   $\underline{\text{- S/T Debt [78] - Owners' Equity**}}$
   Owners' Equity**

   11: $\underline{\text{3016.1 - 926.9 - 905.8}}$
   905.8

   10: $\underline{\text{3326.1 - 1138.5 - 1019.3}}$
   1019.3

   9: $\underline{\text{3125.9 - 824.1 - 1137.1}}$
   1137.1

   **Owners' Equity = [91 + 82 + 83 + 84]

3. $\underline{\text{Current Liab [78] + L/T Debt (2 above)}}$
   Total Liabilities and Equity [92]

   11: $\underline{\text{926.9 + 1183.4}}$
   3016.1

10: $\dfrac{1138.5 + 1168.3}{3326.1}$

9: $\dfrac{824.1 + 1164.7}{3125.9}$

4. Total Liabilities (3 above)
    Total Equity Capital (2 above)

11:	10:	9:
2110.3	2306.8	1988.8
905.8	1019.3	1137.1

5. Preferred stock at stated value [82-83-84]
    Total Owners' Equity (2 above)

11: $\dfrac{100 - 94.5 - .7}{905.8}$

10: $\dfrac{100 - 98.2 - 0}{1019.3}$

9: $\dfrac{100 - 100 - 0}{1137.1}$

Pfd Stock at stated value (or liquidating value if higher)
Total Stockholders' Equity

11: $\dfrac{99,213,036^a}{905,800,000}$ = 10.95%

[a] # of shares issued and outstanding [82, 84]
    (1,282,051 - 10,089) × $78 liquidating value

6. 10: $\dfrac{740.3^a + 32.3^b + 163.9^c}{1019.3^d + 163.8^e + 27.9^f}$

    [a] Long-term debt [79]
    [b] Current portion of long-term debt [71]
    [c] Deferred income taxes—50% considered a liability [81]
    [d] Total stockholders' equity (2 above)
    [e] Deferred income taxes—balance of 50% considered equity
    [f] Excess of cost method in use over LIFO [143]

7. Pretax inc. from cont operations [7] +
    Int exp [156] + Int portion of operating rentals [154]
    Int incurred [156] + Int portion of operating rentals [154]

    11: $\dfrac{411.5 + 101.9 + 44.5/3}{103.8 + 44.5/3}$

$10:$ $\dfrac{382.4 + 120.2 + 44.3/3}{123 + 44.3/3}$

$9:$ $\dfrac{239.1 + 75.9 + 42.4/3}{78.1 + 42.4/3}$

8. $\dfrac{\text{Cash provided by operating activities [31]} + \text{ Inc tax exp* [158]} + \text{Fixed charges (7 above)}}{\text{Fixed charges (7 above)}}$

*Except deferred—already added back in computing CFO.

$11:$ $\dfrac{532.4 + 161.4 + 116.7}{118.6}$

$10:$ $\dfrac{447.1 + 134.9 + 135}{137.8}$

$9:$ $\dfrac{381.6 + 49.6 + 90}{92.2}$

9. $\dfrac{\text{Cash from operations [31]}}{\text{Long-term debt (2 above)}}$

$11:$	$10:$	$9:$
$\dfrac{532.4}{1183.4}$	$\dfrac{447.1}{1168.3}$	$\dfrac{381.6}{1164.7}$

10. $\dfrac{\text{Income before tax [7]} + \text{Fixed charges (7 above)}}{\text{Fixed charges (7 above)} + \text{Preferred Dividend}/(1 - \text{TR})}$

$11:$ $\dfrac{411.5 + 116.7}{118.6 + 4.3/(1 - .34)}$

$10:$ $\dfrac{382.4 + 135}{137.8 + 4.5/(1 - .34)}$

$9:$ $\dfrac{239.1 + 90}{92.2 + 0/(1 - .34)}$

11.   Equity Capital (2 above)/PP&E—net [66]

$11:$	$10:$	$9:$
$\dfrac{905.8}{1232.7}$	$\dfrac{1019.3}{1154.1}$	$\dfrac{1137.1}{959.6}$

b.   The financial leverage index in Year 11 indicates that the use of leverage has been increasingly more advantageous for the common stockholder. The liability to equity ratios indicate an unfavorable increase of more than 12% in Years 11 and 10. The cash flow coverage ratio of fixed charges has improved from the low level in Year 10. The earnings coverage of fixed charges has exhibited more steady improvement. So has the ratio of cash from operations to long-term debt.

Problem 10-2

a. The computation of the capital structure and solvency ratios of Campbell requires that we determine the relevant capital structure for Year 10:

Long-term debt:

	Notes payable	792.9
	Capital lease obligations	12.9
[172]	Long-term debt	805.8
[176]	Deferred income taxes (50%)	117.6
[177]	Other Liabilities	28.5
[45]	Current Liabilities	1298.1
	Total debt	2250.0

Equity Capital:

[54]	Owners' equity	1691.8
[176]	Deferred income taxes (50%)	117.6
[178]	Minority interests	56.3
	Total equity	1865.7

1. 2250.0/1865.7 = 1.21

2. 2250.0/4115.7 = 0.55

3. (805.8 + 117.6 + 28.5)/1865.7 = 0.51

4.

	Numerator	*Denominator*
Long-term debt	805.8	—
Other LT Liabilities	28.5	—
Deferred taxes (50%)	117.6	—
Owners' equity	—	1865.7
LIFO reserve (904.4-819.8) [153]	=	84.6
	951.9	1950.3

Ratio = 951.9/1950.3 = 0.49

5. 1865.7/2250.0 = 0.83

6. 1717.7 [37]/1865.7 = 0.92

7. 1298.1/2250.0 = 0.58

8.

	Numerator	Denominator
Pretax income [26]	179.4	
Interest expense [100]	111.6	
Interest portion of op leases (1/3 of $62.4 [143])	20.8	20.8
Interest incurred [98]		121.9
Undistributed equity in earnings in non-consolidated subsidiaries [169A] (13.5 - 7.4)	(6.1)	0.0
	305.7	142.7

Ratio = 305.7/142.7 = 2.14

9.

	Numerator	Denominator
Cash from ops before tax*	619.5	
Interest expense	111.6	
Interest incurred		121.9
Interest portion of op leases	20.8	20.8
	751.9	142.7

*   Cash from ops [64] $448.4 + current tax expense $171.1 [124A] = 619.5

Ratio = 751.9/142.7 = 5.27

10. 367.4/2250.0 = 0.16

b.   We would compute the total debt to total capitalization as follows:

$$\frac{805.8(a)\ [46] + 28.5(b)\ [177] + 235.1(c)\ [176]}{1069.4(d) + 1691.8(e)\ [54] + 56.3(f)\ [178]}\ =\ 38.0\%$$

(a) Long term debt
(b) Other liabilities
(c) Deferred income taxes (assuming 100% considered as liabilities)
(d) a + b + c
(e) Total equity
(f) Minority interests

The closest we come to Campbell's computation of 33.7%, item [12], is:

(805.8 + 28.5)/(834.3 + 1691.8) = 33%,

omitting deferred taxes and minority interests from the computation.

<u>Problem 10-3</u>

a.   1.   *Ratio of Earnings to Fixed Charges:*

Reference to Text		Numerator	Denominator
a	Pretax income	4,600	
b	Interest expensed	400	
h	Interest incurred		440
d	Interest portion of operating rental expense	120	120
f	Amortization of previously capitalized interest	60	
g	Undistributed income of less than 50% owned affiliates	(300)	
		4,880	560

Ratio = 4,880/560 = <u>8.71</u>

2.   *Cash from operations coverage of fixed charges:*

	Numerator	Denominator
Pretax Income	4,600	
Add (Deduct) Adjustments:		
Depreciation	600	
Amort of bond premium	(300)	
Share of minority int in income	200	
Undistributed income of affils	(300)	
Increase in accounts receivable	(900)	
Decrease in inventory	800	
Increase in accounts payable	700	
Pretax cash provided by operations	5,400	
Interest expensed (400) + Bond premium amortization (300)	700	
Interest incurred		440
Interest portion of cap leases	120	120
	6,220	560

Ratio = 6,220/560 = <u>11.11</u>

3.   *Earnings Coverage of Preferred Dividends:*

$4,880/[560 + 400(1 - .40)] = $ <u>3.98</u>

b.   Considered alone, the company's coverage ratios seem fairly high. Values for other firms and additional years are needed for comparative analyses.

<u>Problem 10-4</u>
a.   1.   *Ratio of Earnings to Fixed Charges:*

	Numerator	Denominator
Pretax income	5,800	
Interest incurred — interest capitalized		
(880 + 340 - 120)	1,100	1,220
Amortization of bond discount 100	100	
Interest portion of rental expense	400	400
Amort of previously capitalized int	100	
Undistributed income of less than 50%		
owned affiliates	(400)	
Share of minority interest	<u>600</u>	<u> </u>
	7,700	1,720

Ratio = 7,700/1,720 = <u>4.48</u>

2.   *Cash from operations coverage of fixed charges:*

	Numerator	Denominator
Pretax income	5,800	
Add back expenses not requiring cash		
Depreciation (includes amortization of		
previously capitalized int)	1,200	
Amortization of bond discount	100	
Share of minority int in income	600	
Deferred taxes—already added back	—	
Increase in inventories	(2,000)	
Decrease in accounts receivable	1,600	
Increase in accounts payable	2,000	
Less—Undistributed income of affils	<u>(400)</u>	
Pretax cash provided by operations	8,900	
Interest expensed--bond discount		
added back	1,100	
Interest portion of rental expense	400	400
Interest incurred (1,220 + 100)	<u> </u>	<u>1,320</u>
	10,400	1,720

Ratio = 10,400/1,720 = <u>6.04</u>

3.   *Earnings Coverage of Preferred Dividends:*

Ratio = 7,700/[1,720 + 400(1 - .40)] = <u>3.22</u>

b.   Considered alone, the company's coverage ratios seem fairly high. Values for other firms and additional years are needed for comparative analyses.

Problem 10-5

a.   1.   *Ratio of Earnings to Fixed Charges:*

	Numerator	Denominator
Pretax income	6,200	
Interest expense (880 + 340 - 120)	1,100	
Interest incurred (880 + 340)		1,220
Amortization of bond discount	100	100
Interest portion of rental payments	400	400
Amort of capitalized interest	80	
Less undistributed income of less than 50% owned affiliates	(600)	___
	7,280	1,720

Ratio = 7,280/1,720 = <u>4.23</u>

2.   *Cash from operations coverage of fixed charges:*

	Numerator	Denominator
Pretax income	6,200	
Add (deduct) items to convert to cash basis		
Depreciation	1,200	
Amortization of bond discount	100	
Minority interest in income	600	
Undistributed income of affiliates	(600)	
Changes in:		
Accounts receivable	600	
Inventories	(160)	
Payable and accruals	<u>120</u>	
Pretax cash from operations	8,060	
Interest incurred (880 + 340)		1,220
Amortization of bond discount		100
Interest expense (880 + 340 - 120)	1,100	
Interest portion of rental expense	<u>400</u>	<u>400</u>
	9,560	1,720

Ratio = 9,560/1,720 = <u>5.56</u>

3.   *Earnings coverage of preferred dividends:*

Ratio = 7,280/[1,720 + 400(1 - .4) = <u>3.05</u>

b.   Based on the above calculations, the supervisor's concerns about the coverage ratios are misplaced. Considered alone, the company's coverage ratios seem fairly high. Values for other firms and additional years are needed for comparative analyses.

Problem 10-6
Interest incurred:

First Mortgage Bonds:	5% of 7,500	=	375
	6% of 17,500	=	1,050
			1,425
Sinking Fund Debentures	6.5% of 10,000	=	650
TOTAL			2,075

a. Earnings coverage for first mortgage bonds (calculated on a cumulative pretax basis) is:

   3.3 based on Year 7 earnings (4,750 ÷ 1,425)
   3.1 based on 5-year average [(4750+4500+4500+4250+4000)/5]/1425

   and for the sinking fund debentures (same method of calculation):

   2.3 based on Year 7 earnings (4,750 ÷ 2,075)
   2.1 based on 5-year average

b. Debt = 35/82 = .43, i.e., 43% of capital is debt

   Of the equity capital, 39% (20*/51.5) is senior to common stock

	*	$1.10 preferred (300,000 x 20) =	6
		Class A shares	14
			20

c. | Interest requirements for LT debt | 2,075 |
$1.10 preferred dividend--tax adjusted	
[(300,000)(1.1)]/[1-.5]	660
Required pre-tax	2,735

   Average 5-year coverage = 4400/2735 = **1.6**
   Year 7 coverage = 4750/2735 = **1.7**

d. Earnings per share assuming conversion:

4,750	Year 7 earnings before interest and taxes
(2,075)	interest
2,675	pre-tax income
1,337	taxes (50%)
1,338	after tax income
(330)	$1.10 preferred dividends (300,000 SH x $1.10)
1,008	available for common
÷1.8M	Common Shares 1 M + .8 M (Class A Conversion)
$0.56	per share

Problem 10-7

a.

	Debt	Equity
Earnings before interest and taxes—present	20,000,000	20,000,000
Added earnings—expansion	4,000,000	4,000,000
	24,000,000	24,000,000
Interest (.06)(20,000,000)+1,000,000	(2,200,000)	(1,000,000)
	21,800,000	23,000,000
Taxes (40%)	8,720,000	9,200,000
Net Income	13,080,000	13,800,000
Common shares outstanding	2,000,000	2,400,000
Earnings per share	$6.54	$5.75

b. $$\frac{(EBIT - 2,200,000)(1 - .4)}{2,000,000} = \frac{(EBIT - 1,000,000)(1 - .4)}{2,400,000}$$

EBIT = 8,200,000 (level where EPS under either alternative are equal)

Problem 10-8

a. 1. Add $250,000,000 to both long term debt and to fixed assets. Rationale: Under the equity method of accounting for joint ventures, the debt incurred is not reported on the balance sheet of the partners and therefore, this debt should be reflected in the adjusted debt ratio since Lubbock has guaranteed the total indebtedness of the joint venture.

   2. Add $200,000,000 to both inventories and to retained earnings (ignoring potential tax effects). Rationale: Under LIFO accounting Lubbock will report current prices for inventory transactions in its income statement but its balance sheet amount for ending inventory will reflect first-in, still-here, or FISH. Accordingly, the SEC requires companies using LIFO to disclose in notes to the financial statements the amounts by which LIFO inventories would have to be increased to reflect current cost. Lubbock has reported that using FIFO, its inventories would have exceeded reported amounts by $200,000,000. Accordingly, to hypothetically reflect current value, inventories should be stated on the basis of FIFO and retained earnings (excluding tax effects) credited by the same amount that inventories are debited by. An alternative approach is to recognize a deferred tax liability of $200,000 × current marginal tax rate.

   3. These long term operating leases could be capitalized. The present value of these long term leases must be calculated using a discount rate. Assuming 10% is the interest rate implicit in the lease, the present value is approximately $750,000,000. The present value amount should be added to long term debt and to fixed assets.

Long Term Debt Ratio Before Adjustments ($ millions):

Long Term Debt

Long Term Debt + Minority Interest + Shareholders' Equity

675/(675 + 100 + 400 + 1,650) = 23.9%

Adjusted Long Term Debt Ratio Formula ($ millions):

Long Term Debt + Guaranteed Debt + Leases
Long Term Debt + Minority Interest + Shareholders' Equity +
Guaranteed Debt + Inventory Adj. + Leases

$$(675+250+750)/(675+100+400+1650+250+200+750) = \underline{41.6\%}$$

b.   1.   For fiscal years beginning before 12/16/93, marketable securities were valued at the lower of cost or market under SFAS 12 (for marketable equity securities) and ARB No. 43 (for marketable debt securities). During this period the market value of securities were sometimes substantially higher than shown on the balance sheet, requiring analytical adjustment. Under current practice all marketable securities (except held-to-maturity debt securities) are valued at market. The analyst must realize, however, that the longer the time since the balance sheet date the greater the chance that market values have changed.

     2.   Deferred income taxes result when a company uses different accounting methods for income tax and financial reporting such that so called timing differences in income occur. One school of thought argues that deferred taxes should be recognized as a liability since the timing differences will reverse in the future and the taxes will become payable or that changes in tax law could accelerate payment of such taxes. However, opponents argue that deferred taxes should be included in shareholders' equity since if all timing differences of a company reconsidered in total, timing differences are unlikely to reverse and therefore the balance in deferred taxes will continue to grow and not become payable. Accordingly, the long term debt ratio of a company would be adversely affected if deferred taxes are considered long term debt and on the other hand, favorably impacted if such taxes are considered shareholders' equity.

Problem 10-9

a.   *Ratio Computations:*

     1.   Year 5 ROCE = 7,000/[(42,000+47,000)÷2] = 15.73%
          Year 6 ROCE = 10,000/[(47,000+54,000)÷2] = 19.80%

          Year 5 ROA = [7,000+6,000(1-.50)]/[(94,500+105,000)÷2] = 10.03%
          Year 6 ROA* = [10,000+10,000(1-.50)]/[(105,000+138,000)÷2] = 12.35%

              *Ignores minority interest in earnings.

          Year 5 Financial leverage index = 15.73/10.03 = <u>1.57</u>
          Year 6 Financial leverage index = 19.80/12.35 = <u>1.60</u>

2. Year 5: $57,200^a/105,000^b = \underline{.55}$
   Year 6: $82,600^a/138,000^b = \underline{.60}$

   ^{a}Includes (1) Total current liabilities,
              (2) Long-term debt due after one year, and
              (3) Deferred income taxes

   ^{b}Includes (1) All items in (a) above
              (2) Minority interest, and
              (3) Stockholders' equity

3. Year 5: $57,200/(57,200+800+40,000)^a = \underline{.58}$
   Year 6: $82,600/(82,600+1,400+49,500)^a = \underline{.62}$

   ^{a} This figure consists of total liabilities, minority interest and
        market value of common equity computed as: market value of common
        equity = number of shares x market price.

        Year 5: 1,000,000 shares (note 7) x $40 = 40,000,000
        Year 6: 1,100,000 shares (note 7) x $45 = 49,500,000

4. Year 5: $57,200/47,000 = \underline{1.22}$
   Year 6: $82,600/54,000 = \underline{1.53}$

5. Year 5: $17,200^a/47,800^b = \underline{.36}$
   Year 6: $28,600^a/55,400^b = \underline{.52}$

   ^{a}including deferred taxes.
   ^{b}stockholders' equity + minority interest.

6. Year 5:

   $$\frac{16,000^a + 4,000^b + 2,000^c + 16^d + 1,000^e + 1,000^{f*}}{5,000^g + 2,000^c + 16^d} = \underline{3.42}$$

   * Loss per income statement (additional 300 added back in funds
      statement represents dividends received).

   Year 6:

   $$\frac{21,000^a + 7,420^b + 2,500^c + 20^d + 1,200^e - 1,400^{f**}}{9,280^g + 2,500^c + 20^d} = \underline{2.61}$$

   ** From cash statement (income minus dividends received).

   ^{a}Pretax income
   ^{b}Interest incurred-interest capitalized
   ^{c}Amortization of bond discount
   ^{d}Interest portion of operating rental expense
   ^{e}Amount of previously capitalized interest amortized in this period
   ^{f}Reversal of undistributed income (loss) of associated companies
   ^{g}Interest incurred

7. Cash from operations* + income tax expense (except deferred taxes)
   <u>+ fixed charges**</u>
   Fixed charges**

   * depreciation added back here already includes amortization of interest previously capitalized
   ** as computed in 6 above

   Year 5 = [7,700+(7,800-1,000)+7,016]/7,016 = <u>3.07</u>

   Year 6 = [5,400+(10,000-1,600)+11,800]/11,800 = <u>2.17</u>

b.

Summary:	Yr. 6	Yr. 5
1. Financial leverage index	1.60	1.57
2. Total debt ratio	.60	.55
3. Total debt ratio (mkt value)	.62	.58
4. Total debt to equity	1.53	1.22
5. Long-term debt to equity	.52	.36
6. Earnings to fixed charges	2.61	3.42
7. CF to fixed charges	3.07	2.17

Comments:

The financial leverage index, which underwent only minimal change, is at a level which indicates that leverage benefits ZETA's stockholders. There has been a significant increase in leverage as is particularly indicated by the total debt to equity and the long-term debt to equity measures. With total liabilities exceeding equity by over 50 percent, the level of liabilities is significant. The relationship of long-term debt to equity is at a somewhat lower level.

The earnings and cash flow coverage of fixed charges are low on an absolute basis and have declined year-to-year primarily because fixed charges increased faster than net income. CFO actually declined in Year 6 compared to Year 5.

c. The analytically adjusted long-term debt to equity ratio is:

Year 5:

$$\frac{15,200^a + 1,200^b + 200^c + 2,800^d\ (1-.50)}{47,000^e + 800^f + 800^g + 4,500^h - 2,800^d\ (1-.50)} = \underline{.26}$$

Year 6:

$$\frac{25,000^a + 2,160^b + 200^c + 2,800^d\ (1-.50)}{54,000^e + 1,400^f + 1,440^g + 6,000^h - 2,800^d\ (1 - .50)} = \underline{.32}$$

[a]   Long-term debt
[b]   60% of deferred taxes
[c]   Present value of noncapitalized financing leases
[d]   Excess of projected pension benefit obligation over the accumulated pension
      benefit obligation
[e]   Stockholders' equity
[f]   Minority interest
[g]   40% of deferred taxes
[h]   Excess of disclosed FIFO value of ending inventory over LIFO amount (Note 2)

Comments:

ZETA's conventional long-term debt to equity ratio is:

Year 5: 17,200/(17,200+47,800) = .26

Year 6: 28,600/(28,600+55,400) = .34

Thus, in this case the analytically adjusted ratio is not significantly different from the conventionally computed ratio.

◄ Answers to Cases ►

Case 10-1

a.   1.   1995 ROCE = 93,402/[(297,616+371,644)÷2] = 27.91%
          1996 ROCE = 103,375/[(371,644+511,945)÷2] = 23.40%

          1995 ROA = [93,402+1,179(1-.35)]/[(358,475+435,708)÷2] = 23.71%
          1996 ROA = [103,375+840(1-.35)]/[(435,708+646,486)÷2] = 19.21%

          1995 Financial leverage index = 27.91/23.71 = $\underline{1.18}$
          1996 Financial leverage index = 23.40/19.21 = $\underline{1.22}$

     2.   1995: 435,708/371,644 = $\underline{1.17}$
          1996: 646,486/511,945 = $\underline{1.26}$

     3.   *1995*   *1996*
          Current liabilities   12.9%   20.2%
          LT debt   1.8%   0.7%
          Common stock   32.2%   28.3%
          Retained earnings   53.1%   50.9%

4. As many of the capital structure ratios are redundant, only the following
    two measures are computed:

    1995 debt-to-equity: (56,414+7,650)/371,644 = <u>17.24%</u>
    1996 debt-to-equity: (130,291+4,250)/511,945 = <u>26.28%</u>

    1995 debt-to-equity (@ market): 64,064/[(25.5*)(51,677)] = <u>4.86%</u>
    1996 debt-to-equity (@ market): 134,541/[(42.81**)(53,020)] = <u>5.93%</u>

    $\qquad$ * (14+37)/2
    $\qquad$ ** (29.25+56.375)/2

5.

	1995	1996
Cash	15.3%	14.1%
ST investments	41.3%	31.6%
Accounts receivable	13.0%	13.8%
Inventories	7.3%	8.5%
Prepaid expenses	3.6%	3.9%
Property & equipment	15.5%	14.4%
Other assets	4.0%	13.7%

6. 1995 tangible assets to LT debt: 435,708/7,650 = <u>56.96</u>
    1996 tangible assets to LT debt: (646,486-8,200*)/4,250 = <u>150.18</u>

    * goodwill per note five

7. 1995 earnings to fixed charges:
    [124,537+1,179+(2,377*/3)]/[1,179+(2,377/3)] = <u>64.17</u>

    1996 earnings to fixed charges:
    [137,989+840+(3,715*/3)]/[840+(3,715/3)] = <u>67.39</u>

    * rental expense per note seven

    1995 cash flow to fixed charges:
    $$\frac{(118,089-93,402+124,537)** + 1,179 + (2,377/3)}{1,179 + 2,377/3} = \underline{76.70}$$

    1996 cash flow to fixed charges:
    $$\frac{(103,379-103,375+137,989)** + 840 + (3,715/3)}{840 + 3,715/3} = \underline{67.40}$$

    ** CFO - NI + Pretax income

8. Possible answers include:

    Quality of management (as reflected in financial performance)
    Continued commitment to R&D program
    Financial flexibility (due to low degree of leverage)
    Lack of regulation
    Competition
    Sources of supply

Conclusion:

> Adaptec clearly possesses a strong capital structure which allows a great degree of financial flexibility. Some may argue that Adaptec could borrow more in an effort to increase ROCE.

b. Possible adjustments include: (1) deferred income taxes (notes two and eight), (2) operating leases and other commitments (note seven), and (3) recognition of market value of equity vs. book value. Note that Adaptec uses FIFO inventory method and reports marketable securities at fair value.

c. Companies rarely disclose the present value of minimum lease payments under noncancelable operating leases. However, footnote disclosures are provided to help analysts make reasonable estimates. Note seven indicates that Adaptec has entered into operating lease agreements through fiscal 2001, and that the minimum future rental payments total $7,290,000.

One way to estimate the present value is to divide the total payments by the number of remaining years. This results in an estimated annual payment of $1,458,00 ($7,290,000 ÷ 5 years). The present value of this annuity is $5,526,967, assuming a discount rate of 10%. Other methods are certainly possible.

Case 10-2

a. The following eight variables are relevant for beginning the task of analyzing credit:

1. *Economic cyclicality.* How closely do the tobacco, food, and beverage industries track GNP? Is tobacco consumption more tied to sociopolitical and regulatory factors more than to economic ones? Cyclicality of an industry is the starting point an analyst should consider in reviewing an industry. A company's earnings growth should be compared against the growth trend of its industry, with significant deviations carefully analyzed. Industries may be somewhat dependent on general economic growth, demographic changes, interest rates, etc. In general, however, industry earnings are not perfectly correlated with any one economic statistic. Not only are industries sensitive to many economic variables, but often segments within a company or industry move with different lags in relation to the overall economy.

2. *Growth prospects.* Are the businesses Philip Morris is in growing at a steady pace, or is growth slipping? Will European consumption of cigarettes begin to slow as they have in the U.S. due to more no smoking regulations? Related to the issue of growth, is there consolidation going on in tobacco, food or beverages? Alternate growth scenarios have different implications for a company. With high-growth industries, the need for additional capacity and related financing is an issue. With low-growth industries, movement toward diversification and/or consolidation strategies are a possibility. As a general proposition, companies in high-growth industries have greater potential for credit improvement than companies operating in lower-growth industries.

3. *Research & development.* R&D is not a big item in the tobacco, food or beverage industries, although some dollars are clearly spent on new product development. In general, it is safe to characterize these businesses as having a stable product line that will not vary much over time. For firms relying on such expenditures to maintain or improve market position, it is important to assess whether the compant in question has the financial resources to maintain a leadership position or at least expend a sufficient amount of money to keep technologically current.

4. *Competition.* How competitive are these industries? Are there players who are out to gain market share at the expense of profits? Is the industry trending toward oligopoly, which would make small companies in the industry vulnerable to the economies of scale the larger companies bring to bear? Economic theory shows us how competition within an industry relates to market structure and has implications for pricing flexibility. An unregulated monopoly is clearly in the position to price its goods at a level that will maximize profits. Most industries, however, encounter free market forces and cannot price their goods/services without consideration of supply and demand as well as the price charged for substitute goods/services. Oligopolies often have a pricing leader. Analysts must be concerned about small companies in an industry that is trending toward oligopoly. In such an environment, the small company's production costs may exceed those of the industry leaders. If a small firm is forced to follow the pricing of the industry leaders, the firm may be driven out of business.

5. *Sources of supply.* Are these businesses vulnerable to the cost of production inputs? Or is the market position of Philip Morris such that it can easily pass on higher raw material costs? Industry market structure often has a direct impact on sources of supply. From a competitive standpoint, the company which controls its factors of production is in a superior position.

6. *Degree of regulation.* Tobacco has faced some regulatory hurdles in the past (especially the recent past), as has food and beverage to a lesser degree. What does the future hold in this area? The analyst should be concerned with the direction of regulation and its effect on future profitability.

7. *Labor.* Are these businesses heavily unionized? What is the status of labor-management relations? When the labor market is "tight," this is an important consideration in nonunionized companies.

8. *Accounting.* Do these businesses have any unique accounting practices that warrant special attention? As stressed throughout the text, an analyst must become familiar with industry accounting practices before proceeding with a company analysis. To assess whether a company is liberal or conservative in applying GAAP industry practices should be examined.

b. 1. The ratios for Philip Morris for Year 9 *before* the acquisition of Kraft are:

Pretax interest coverage = (4,820+500)/500 = <u>10.64</u>

LT debt as % of capitalization = 3,883/(3,883+9,931) = <u>28.11%</u>

CF as % of total debt = (2,820+750+100-125)/(3,883+1,100) = <u>71.14%</u>

The ratios for Philip Morris for Year 9 *pro forma* for the acquisition of Kraft are:

Pretax interest coverage = (4,420+1,600)/1,600 = <u>3.76</u>

LT debt as % of capitalization = 15,778/(15,778+9,675) = <u>61.99%</u>

CF as % of total debt = (2,564+1,235+390-125)/(15,778+1,783) = <u>23.14%</u>

2. Relating these ratios to the median ratios for the various bond rating categories places Philip Morris in the position shown below:

Before Kraft	Ratio	*Implied Rating*
Pretax interest coverage	10.64	AA
LT debt as % of cap.	28.11%	A
CF as % of total debt	71.14%	A+/AA-

After Kraft	Ratio	*Implied Rating*
Pretax interest coverage	3.76	BBB
LT debt as % of cap.	61.99%	B
CF as % of total debt	23.14%	BB

The ratios suggest that Philip Morris bonds have deteriorated from a strong A rating to a BB rating, based on the median ratios for the various bond categories. Given that Philip Morris is in relatively stable businesses that tend to be much less cyclical than the economy overall (food and tobacco), an argument could be made that the bonds should be rated as a strong BB or even a BBB.

<u>Case 10-3</u>

a.   *Asset Protection*   *Year 7*   *Year 9*

	Year 7	Year 9
Net tangible assets to LT debt	52.0%	46.2%

> Moderate deterioration, but nothing serious. Large increase in goodwill account evidently a factor.

LT debt to total capitalization	64.0%	62.6%

> Modest improvement.

Debt to common equity	2.31	1.83

> Good improvement due to more rapid growth in retained earnings.

Total assets to total shareholders' equity	3.33	3.40

> Slight improvement.

Short-Term Liquidity	Year 7	Year 9
Collection period	68	90
Inventory turnover	12.0	4.7

> Petrochemicals acquisition has increased ABEX's working capital requirements, particularly accounts receivable and inventories.

% ST Debt to LT Debt	5.8%	9.3%

> The greater working capital requirements have evidently forced ABEX to rely more heavily on short-term debt.

Earning Power	Year 7	Year 9
Pretax interest coverage	1.80	1.84
Operating CF to LT Debt	20.9%	22.1%

> Pretax interest coverage was little different in Year 7 vs. Year 9, although it was significantly higher in Year 8 (2.54). Higher operating margins and improved cash flow helped in supporting the higher debt burden. This is particularly evident in the operating cash flow to LT debt ratio.

b.   Among the more qualitative considerations that should be reviewed in assessing the risk of downgrade are:

   (1) Economic cyclicality: The petrochemical business is likely to be more cyclical than the pipeline business, which is regulated and generally more of a cost pass-through operation.

(2) Growth prospects: Petrochemicals may have greater growth prospects than the pipeline business, but that growth is likely to be more erratic, due to economic cyclicality.

(3) Competition: The lack of regulation and the commodity nature of most of its products makes the petrochemical business generally more competitive than the pipeline business.

(4) Sources of supply: Both the petrochemical and the pipeline businesses have to deal with the problem of securing sufficient supplies of raw material. Again, the petrochemical business is probably more prone to disruption than the pipeline business.

Other possible considerations include: (5) management expertise, (6) environmental concerns, (7) debtor problems, (8) quality of earnings, (9) barriers to entry, and (10) the benefits of diversification.

c. One might conclude from the qualitative considerations in part b that the shift toward petrochemicals makes ABEX more vulnerable to the vagaries of the economic cycle, which will lead to a more volatile earnings stream going forward. To this extent, the risk of a rating downgrade is likely to increase.

Looking at the ratio analysis in part a, one might conclude that there is relatively little deterioration in credit quality. The modest deterioration in asset protection seems to be offset by higher cash flow margins, which allow the company to support the higher debt burden. The greater reliance on short-term debt to finance the increased working capital requirements is somewhat troublesome, however.

◄ CHAPTER 11 ►

Return on Invested Capital

◄ CHAPTER REVIEW ►

Return on invested capital is important in our analysis of financial statements. Financial statement analysis involves our assessing both risk and return. The prior three chapters focused primarily on risk, whereas this chapter extends our analysis to return. Return on invested capital refers to a company's earnings relative to both the level and source of financing. It is a measure of a company's success in using financing to generate profits, and is an excellent measure of a company's solvency risk.

This chapter describes return on invested capital and its relevance to financial statement analysis. We also explain variations in measurement of return on invested capital and their interpretation. We also disaggregate return on invested capital into important components for additional insights into company performance and future operations. The role of financial leverage and its importance for returns analysis is examined. This chapter demonstrates each of these analysis techniques using financial statement data.

◄ CHAPTER OUTLINE ►

▸ **Importance of Return on Invested Capital**

    Measuring Managerial Effectiveness

    Measuring Profitability

    Measure of Forecasted Earnings

    Measuring for Planning and Control

▸ **Components of Return on Invested Capital**

    Defining Invested Capital

    Defining Income

    Adjustments of Invested Capital and Income

    Computing Return on Invested Capital

▸ **Analyzing Return on Assets**

    Disaggregating Return on Assets

    Relation between Profit Margin and Asset Turnover

    Asset Turnover Analysis

▸ **Analyzing Return on Common Equity**

    Disaggregating Return on Common Equity

    Computing Return on Invested Capital

    Assessing Growth in Common Equity

    Financial Leverage and Return on Common Equity

    Return on Common Shareholders' Equity versus Investment

◄ Learning Objectives ►

- **Describe the usefulness of return measures in financial statement analysis.**

- **Explain return on invested capital and variations in its computation.**

- **Analyze return on total assets and its relevance in our analysis.**

- **Describe disaggregation of return on assets and the importance of its components.**

- **Analyze return on common shareholders' equity and its role in our analysis.**

◄ Learning Objectives ►

■ **Describe disaggregation of return on common shareholders' equity and the relevance of its components.**

■ **Explain financial leverage and how to assess a company's success in trading on the equity by individual financing sources.**

◄ Answers to Questions ►

1. Economic performance is the first and foremost purpose of a business enterprise. The effectiveness of operating performance determines the ability of the enterprise to survive financially, to attract suppliers of funds, and to reward them adequately. Return on invested capital is the prime measure of economic performance. The analyst uses it as: (1) an indicator of managerial effectiveness, (2) a method of projecting earnings, and/or (3) a measure of the enterprise's ability to earn a satisfactory return on investment.

2. The return achieved in any one period on the total investment of an enterprise is composed of the returns (and losses) realized by the various segments and divisions of which it is composed. In turn, these returns are made up of the results achieved by individual product lines, protects, etc. The well-managed enterprise exercises rigorous control over the returns achieved by each of its profit centers and rewards its managers on the basis of such results. Moreover, in evaluating the advisability of new investments of funds in assets or projects, management will compute the estimated returns it expects to achieve from them and use these estimates as a basis for its decision.

3. The motivation for excluding nonproductive assets from invested capital is based on the idea that management is not responsible for earning a return on non-operating invested capital. While this may be valid for internal analysis, external analysts must include these amounts as they are part of assessing overall management effectiveness.

    The exclusion of intangible assets from the investment base is often due to skepticism regarding their value or their contribution to the earning power of the enterprise. Under GAAP intangibles are carried at cost. However, if the cost exceeds their future utility they must be written down or else the analyst will at least find an uncertainty exception regarding their carrying value included in the auditor's opinion. The exclusion of intangible assets from the asset base must be based on more substantial evidence than a mere lack of understanding of what these assets represent or an unsupported suspicion regarding their value.

4. If the investment base is defined as comprising total assets, then income before interest cost is used. The exclusion of interest from income deductions is due to its being regarded as a payment for the use of money to the suppliers of debt capital in the same way that dividends are regarded as a reward to suppliers of equity capital. Income before deductions for interest or dividends is used when it is related to total assets or to long-term debt plus equity capital (assuming most of the interest expense is on long-term obligations).

5. Where convertible debt sells at a substantial premium above par and is clearly held by investors for its conversion feature, there is justification for treating it as the equivalent of equity capital. This is particularly true when the company can choose at any time to force conversion of the debt by calling it.

6. The income of a consolidated entity which includes a subsidiary which is partially owned by a minority interest usually reflects a deduction for the minority's share in that income. The consolidated balance sheet, however, includes all the assets of such a subsidiary, i.e., those belonging to the parent as well as those belonging to the minority (see also Chapter 5). Because the investment in the denominator includes all the assets of the consolidated entity, the income (in the numerator) should include all the income (or loss), not just the parent's share. For this reason the minority's share of earnings (or loss) must be added back to income in computing return on total assets. When the denominator is the equity capital only, the minority share in income (or loss) need not be added back, if the equity capital excludes minority interest.

7. The basic formula for computing the return on investment is net income divided by total assets. Whenever we modify the definition of the investment base by, say, omitting certain items (liabilities, idle assets, etc.) we must also adjust the corresponding income figure in order to make it consistent with the modified asset base.

8. The relationship of net income to sales measures operating performance and profitability. The relationship of sales to total assets is a measure of asset utilization or turnover, a means of determining how effectively (in terms of sales generation) the assets are utilized. It can be readily seen that both factors, profitability as well as asset utilization, determine the return realized on a given investment in assets. In the measurement of both of these elements sales is a factor.

9. Profitability, although important, is only one aspect of the return on investment formula. The other is asset turnover. Thus, while Company B's profitability may have been high, its asset turnover may have been such as to drag down the return on invested capital, leading to the shareholder's complaint.

10. The asset turnover of Company X is 3. The profitability percentage of Company Y is 0.5%. Since both companies are in the same industry, it is obvious to advise Company X to concentrate on improving its asset turnover and Company Y should concentrate on improving its profitability ratio.

11. The Sales/Total Assets element of the return on investment formula, while measuring the overall rate of asset utilization, does not measure the rate of utilization of the individual asset categories which enter into the overall asset turnover. In order to analyze the reasons for the level of asset turnover or the reasons for changes in that level, it is necessary to compute the rate of individual asset turnovers which make up the overall turnover figure.

12. The evaluation of return on invested capital involves many factors of great complexity. The inclusion of extraordinary gains and losses in a single period and average net income must be evaluated. Moreover, the effects of price-level changes on return calculations must be taken into account by the analyst.

   The analyst must bear in mind that return on invested capital calculations are most commonly based on book values appearing in the financial statements rather than on market values which, in most cases, may be more relevant and economically more significant. Also, quite often, a return is earned on assets which either do not appear in the financial statements or are significantly understated therein. Examples of such assets are intangibles such as patents, trademarks, expensed research and development costs, advertising and training costs, etc.

   In analyzing the trend of returns over the years, the effect of acquisitions accounted for as poolings-of-interest must be isolated and their chance of recurrence evaluated. The effect of discontinued operations must be similarly evaluated.

13. The equity growth rate by means of earnings retention can be calculated as follows:

   [Net Income - Payout] ÷ Common Shareholders' Equity

   This is the growth rate due to the retention of earnings and assures a constant divided payout over time. It indicates the possibilities of earnings growth without resort to external financing. These increased funds, in turn, can be expected to earn the rate of return which the enterprise can obtain on its assets and thus contribute to growth in earnings.

14. a. The rate of return on total assets and that on the stockholders' equity differ because a portion of the capital with which assets are financed is usually supplied by creditors who receive a fixed return or, in some cases, no return at all. Similarly, preferred stock usually receives a fixed dividend. These fixed returns differ from the rate earned on the assets (funds) which they provide, and this accounts for the difference in returns on assets and those on stockholders' equity. This is the concept of financial leverage.

b. ROCE can be disaggregated into the following elements which facilitate its analysis:

$$\frac{\text{Net Income - Preferred Dividends}}{\text{Sales}} \times \frac{\text{Sales}}{\text{Average Total Assets}} \times \frac{\text{Average Total Assets}}{\text{Average Common Stockholders' Equity}}$$

Descriptively we can express this formula as follows:

$$\text{Adjusted Profit Margin} \quad \times \quad \text{Asset Turnover} \quad \times \quad \text{Leverage}$$

The Adjusted Profit Margin represents the portion of the sales dollar which is left for common shareholders after providing for all costs and claims (e.g., those of the preferred shareholders). The Asset Turnover measures the relationship between sales and assets required to generate them. Leverage measures the extent to which total assets are financed by common stockholders. The larger this ratio is, the smaller the proportion of assets financed by common stockholders and the greater the extent of leverage.

15. a. ROCE is computed as:

$$\frac{\text{Net Income}}{\text{Sales}} \quad \times \quad \frac{\text{Sales}}{\text{Average Stockholder's Equity}}$$

So, it can be seen that equity turnover (sales/average stockholders' equity) is one of the two determinants of the rate of return on common shareholders' equity. Assuming a stable profit margin, the equity turnover can be used to determine the level and trend of ROCE. An increase in equity turnover will produce an increase in ROCE if the profit margin is stable or declines less than the equity turnover increases. For example, the objective of discount stores has been to lower prices by lowering profit margins, but to offset this by increasing equity turnover by more than the decrease in profit margin.

b. Equity turnover is a function of:

$$\frac{\text{Sales}}{\text{Net Operating Assets}} \quad \times \quad \frac{\text{Net Operating Assets}}{\text{Average Stockholder's Equity}}$$

The first factor shows how well assets are being utilized. If the ratio is rising, this may show either a technological advantage or undercapacity and the need for more capital for expansion. The second factor shows the use of leverage in the business. This ratio will be higher for those firms that have financed some of their assets by borrowing money.

By considering the factors which compose equity turnover, it is apparent that EPS cannot grow indefinitely from an increase in these factors since the factors themselves cannot grow indefinitely. Even if there is a technological advantage in production, the sales/operating assets ratio cannot increase indefinitely. This is because sooner or later they will have to expand its net operating asset base to meet the rising sales or else be unable to meet its sales and lose a share of the market.

Also, the net operating assets/equity ratio can be increased by financing new assets by debt. However, this can only be done safely up to a reasonable point and must then stop until the equity base is expanded again (which makes the ratio fall).

◄ Answers to Exercises ►

Exercise 11-1

a. Net income = 10,000,000 × .10 = 1,000,000
    Operating income = [1,000,000 ÷ (1-.4)] + 0 = <u>1,666,667</u>

b. After expansion, total assets = 10 + 6 = 16 million

    First alternative:
    Interest = 2,000,000 × .05 = 100,000

    $$\frac{NI + 100,000\ (1-.40)}{16,000,000} = .1 \qquad NI = 1,540,000$$

    Operating income = [1,540,000 ÷ (1-.4)] + 100,000 = <u>2,666,667</u>

    Second alternative:
    Interest = 6,000,000 × .06 = 360,000

    $$\frac{NI + 360,000\ (1-.40)}{16,000,000} = .1 \qquad NI = 1,384,000$$

    Operating income = [1,384,000 ÷ (1-.4)] + 360,000 = <u>2,666,667</u>

c. Under first alternative, ROCE = 1,540,000/(10,000,000 + 4,000,000) = <u>11%</u>

    Under second alternative, ROCE = 1,384,000/(10,000,000 + 0) = <u>13.84%</u>

d. ROCE is higher under the second alternative due to successful use of financial leverage.

Exercise 11-2

a. *First alternative:*

    $$\frac{NI + (1,000)(0.12)(1-0.4)}{4,000 + 2,000} = 0.1 \qquad NI = 528$$

    Operating income = 528 ÷ (1-.4) + (1,000 × 0.12) = <u>1,000</u>

    Second alternative:

    $$\frac{NI + (2,000)(0.12)(1-0.4)}{6,000} = 0.1 \qquad NI = 456$$

    Operating income = 456 ÷ (1-.4) + (2,000 × 0.12) = <u>1,000</u>

b. First alternative: ROCE = 528 ÷ 5,000 = <u>10.56%</u>

    Second alternative: ROCE = 456 ÷ 4,000 = <u>11.4%</u>

c. First alternative: 10.56% ÷ 10% = <u>1.056</u>

Second alternative: 11.4% ÷ 10% = <u>1.14</u>

d. Return on assets (ROA):

First alternative: 1,000 ÷ 6,000 = 16.67%
Second alternative: 1,000 ÷ 6,000 = 16.67%

Interest rate of 12% is less than ROA. Thus, company earns more on total assets than it pays on debt on after tax basis--(.12)(1 - .40) = .072. As the second alternative uses more debt, the financial leverage index of second alternative is higher.

Exercise 11-3

a.

	Year 5	Year 9
Pretax Profit Margin	0.112	0.109
Asset Turnover	0.46	0.44
Financial Leverage	3.25	3.40
After-Tax Income Retention *	0.570	0.556
ROCE (product of above)	9.54%	9.07%

* 1 - tax rate

ROCE declined because: (1) pretax margin declined by approx. 3%, (2) asset turnover declined by 2.25% approx., and (3) tax rate increased 2.5% approx. The combination of these factors was more than the slight improvements in financial leverage.

b. The primary reason EPS increased was that shareholders had a large amount of assets and equity working for them. The company got bigger while return on assets and return on equity remained fairly stable. In addition, the amount of preferred stock declined as did the amount of preferred dividends. With this net decline in the cost of carrying the preferred stock, earnings available to common stock increased.

(CFA Adapted)

Exercise 11-4

a. ROCE = Adjusted Profit Margin x Asset turnover x Leverage
        = 0.05 x 2 x 1.786 = <u>17.86%</u>

b. Total assets = Sales/Asset turnover = 5,000,000/2 = 2,500,000

Capital Structure:
Current Liabilities (2,500,000)(0.1)   250,000
Long-term debt (2,500,000)(.03)   750,000
Minority interests   100,000
                                        1,100,000

Common equity = 2,500,000 - 1,100,000 = 1,400,000

Net income = 5,000,000 × 0.05 = 250,000

Interest:
  Current Liabilities (250,000)(1/2)(0.05)   6,250
  Long-term debt (750,000)(0.06)   45,000
                                              51,250

ROA   =   NI + Interest(1-tax rate) + Minority interest in earnings
            Total assets

       =   250,000 + 51,250 (1 - 0.4) + 1,000
            2,500,000   = 11.27%

c.

Source of funds	Funds Supplied	Return @ 11.27%	Payment or Credit to Funds' Suppliers	Accruing to Common
Current liabilities (1/2)	125,000	14,087.5	—	14,087.5
Current liabilities (1/2)	125,000	14,087.5	3,750 [a]	10,337.5
Long-Term debt	750,000	84,525.0	27,000 [b]	57,525.0
Minority interests	100,000	11,270.0	1,000	10,270.0
				92,220.0

Net leverage advantage to common equity = 92,220/1,400,000 = 6.59%

Return on total assets   11.27%
+ Leverage advantage   6.59%
Return on equity   17.86%

  [a] (125,000)(.05)(1 - .4) = 3,750

  [b] (750,000)(.06)(1 - .4) = 27,000

Exercise 11-5
a. At the present level of debt, ROCE = 157,500 ÷ 1,125,000 = 14%

In the absence of leverage, the noncurrent liabilities would be substituted by equity, and consequently, there would be no interest expense. In this case, net income would be as follows:

Net income (before adjustment)   157,500
+ interest saved (675,000 × 8%)   54,000
- tax effect of interest expense   27,000   27,000
Net income in the absence of leverage   184,500

ROCE in absence of leverage = 184,500 ÷ 1,800,000 = 10.25%

Thus, existing leverage is beneficial to Rose's shareholders.

b. ROA = $\dfrac{\text{Net income + Interest (1 - tax rate)}}{\text{Total assets}}$

.20 = [NI + (675,000)(.08)(1-.50)] ÷ 2,000,000
NI   = 373,000

To achieve a 20% ROA, net income of 373,000 will have to be earned.

ROCE = 373,000/1,125,000 = <u>33.16%</u>

Financial leverage index = 33.16% ÷ 20% = <u>1.66</u>

c. Since the financial leverage index is substantially greater than 1, financial leverage is beneficial to shareholders.

<u>Exercise 11-6</u>
a. ROCE   = Adjusted Profit Margin x Asset turnover x Leverage
        = 0.07 x 3 x 1.667 = <u>35.01%</u>

b. Total assets = Sales/Asset Turnover = 12,000,000/3 = 4,000,000

Net income = 12,000,000 x 0.07 = 840,000

Capital Structure:
Current liabilities (4,000,000 x .15)   600,000
Long-term debt (4,000,000 x .20)   800,000
Common equity (4,000,000 x .60)   2,400,000
Minority interests   200,000
Total Assets   4,000,000

Interest:
On current liabilities (600,000)(1/3)(.04)   8,000
On LT debt (800,000)(.05)   40,000
                                              48,000

ROA   = $\dfrac{\text{NI + interest (1 - tax rate) + minority interest in earnings}}{\text{total assets}}$

       = $\dfrac{840{,}000 + 48{,}000\ (1 - .50) + 2{,}000}{4{,}000{,}000}$ = <u>21.65%</u>

c.

Source of Funds	Funds Supplied	Return at 21.65%	Payment or Credit to Funds' Suppliers	Accruing to Common Equity
Current liabilities	400,000	86,600	--	86,600
Current liabilities	200,000	43,300	4,000	39,300
Long-Term debt	800,000	173,200	20,000	153,200
Minority interests	200,000	43,300	2,000	41,300
				320,400

Net leverage advantage to common equity = 320,400/2,400,000 = 13.35%

ROA	21.65%
+ leverage advantage	13.35%
ROCE (diff due to rounding)	35.00%

Exercise 11-7

I.   c
II. b
III. a
IV. c

◄ Answers to Problems ►

Problem 11-1

a. 1. $\dfrac{\text{NI [28] + Interest Exp. [18]} \times \text{(1 - TR) + Minority Int. in Income [25]}}{\text{Average Total Assets} \{[39A] + [185A]\} \div 2}$

[4.4 + 111.6 (1-.34) + 5.7] ÷ [(4,115.6 + 3,932.1)/2] = 2.08%

2. $\dfrac{\text{Net Income - Preferred Stock Dividends}}{\text{Average Common Equity*}}$

$\dfrac{4.4 - 0}{(1691.8 \ [185] + .5 \times 235.1 \ [176] + 1778.3 \ [185] + .5 \times 218) \div 2}$

= 0.24%

* Excluding minority interest and including 50% of deferred taxes

3.   NI + Interest exp. x (1 - TR) + Minority Interest in Earnings
      Average of Long-term Liabilities and Equity

      4.4 + 111.6 (1 - .34) + 5.7
      (2817.5** + 2,700**) ÷ 2 = 3.04%

	Year 10	Year 9
L-T debt [185]	805.80	629.20
Other Liability [177]	28.50	19.60
50% deferred income taxes [176]	117.55	109.00
Total L-T debt	951.85	757.80
Shareholders' equity [185]	1691.80	1778.30
50% deferred income taxes [176]	117.55	109.00
Minority interest [178]	56.30	54.90
Total equity	1865.65	1942.20
** Total L-T debt & equity	2817.50	2700.00

4.   0.24% ÷ 2.08% = 0.12

5.   Net Income [28] - Dividends [87A]
      Average Common Equity

      (4.4 - 126.9) ÷ 1848.3 = - 6.63%

b. ROCE = Adjusted Profit Margin x Asset turnover x Leverage
           = (4.4/6,205.8) x (6,205.8/4,023.9) x (4,023.9/1,848.3)
           = 0.07 x 1.54 x 2.18 = 0.24%

Components of ROCE indicate that profit margin is the lowest component of the three, as is generally expected. Since both asset turnover and leverage are more than one, they contribute to enhancing ROCE. Fully evaluating the return requires comparison with prior year returns as well as industry returns over a number of years.

c.

Ratio	Numerator	Denominator	
Sales to cash equiv.	6,205.8 [13]	103.2 [31]+[32]	60.1
Sales to receivables	6,205.8	624.5 [33]	9.9
Sales to inventories	6,205.8	819.8 [34]	7.6
Sales to working capital	6,205.8	367.4 [36]-[45]	16.9
Sales to fixed assets	6,205.8	1,717.7 [37]	3.6
Sales to other assets	6,205.8	349.0 [39]	17.8
Sales to total assets	6,205.8	4,115.6 [39A]	1.5

d. Campbell's return on equity of 0.24% is clearly lower than the comparable company's 12.7% return. However, these are returns earned by the respective companies based on their book values. The return earned by the company for the individual stockholder is based on the cost of his or her shares. Thus, the market price per share is relevant to this decision as may be other factors such as yield, price-earnings ratios, etc.

<u>Problem 11-2</u>

a.
Sales (500,000 @ $10)	$5,000,000
Fixed Cost	1,500,000
Variable Costs (500,000 @ $4)	2,000,000
Labor Cost (20 x $35,000)	700,000
Total Costs	$4,200,000
Net profit before taxes	800,000
Taxes (@ 50%)	400,000
Net Income	$ 400,000

1. $[400,000+(2,000,000)(.075)(1-.5)] \div 8,000,000 = \underline{5.94\%}$

2. $[400,000+(2,000,000)(.075)(1-.5)] \div 6,000,000 = \underline{7.92\%}$

3. $[400,000-(1,000,000)(.06)] \div 3,000,000 = \underline{11.33\%}$

b. *Estimated Fiscal Year 9 Operations:*

Sales (550,000 units @ $10) . . .	$5,500,000
Fixed costs (1,500,000)(1.06) . .	1,590,000
Variable costs (550,000 @ $4) . .	2,200,000
Income before labor & taxes	$1,710,000

To obtain 10% return on long-term debt and equity capital, Zear will need a numerator of $600,000. The required net income is computed as:

NI + Interest exp. x (1 - .5) = 600,000
NI + (2,000,000)(.075)(1-.5) = 600,000
NI = 525,000

Assuming taxes of 50%, Zear needs pretax income of $1,050,000.

Income b4 labor & taxes	$1,710,000
Labor	?
Pretax Profit	$1,050,000

Labor = 660,000
Average wage/worker = 660,000/22 = 30,000

Current salary level is $35,000. Thus, Zear cannot acheive its target return level *and* give a raise.

(CFA Adapted)

<u>Problem 11-3</u>

a.   1.   Quaker does not specify its computation. Focusing on *one share* the dividend is $1.56 [121] for Year 11. The average between the beginning price of 48 and the ending price of $62 is $55. The price increase in Year 11 is $14:

<u>Dividend + Price increase</u>
Average Price   = 28%

Using the beginning price of 48 as a base we get closer to the company's 34% return:

(1.56 + 14) ÷ 48 = 32%

     2.   The return on equity is based on the relationship between net income and the *book value* of the equity capital. The return to shareholders uses dividends plus market value change in relation to the market price per share (i.e., cost of investment *to shareholders*.)

     3.   The concepts are similar but not identical in computation. The return on shareholder's investment focuses on the dividend plus the market's valuation on earnings retained. The return to shareholders focuses on dividends plus change in the market value of the stock. Both relate to shareholder's cost of investment rather than to book value.

     4.   As shown in part a.4. of Case 11-2, Quaker's Year 11 ROCE is computed as 21.01%. As the ROCE disclosed in the annual report (24.1%) is higher, it is possible that Quaker's figure ignores the effect of discontinued operations. ROCE ignoring the effect of discontinued operations is:

235.8/[(1,017.5 + 901 + 30)/2] = 24.2%

b.   The company must have derived the 3.6% from price, market, and other relationships which are not disclosed.

c.   The company does not reveal its computations. It discloses a variety of long term debt rates [148] to which it is subject. Based on data available to it, but not to the reader, it probably computed a weighted average interest rate from which it deducted the tax benefit in arriving at the 6.4% cost of debt.

<u>Problem 11-4</u>

a.   1.   <u>NI + Interest Exp. (1 - Tax Rate) + Minority Interest in Earnings</u>
          (Beginning Total Assets + Ending Total Assets) ÷ 2

Year 5:   <u>7,000 + 6,000 (1 - .5) + 0</u>
          (94,500 + 105,000) ÷ 2   = <u>10.03%</u>

Year 6:   <u>10,000 + 10,000 (1 - .5) + 200</u>
          (105,000 + 138,000) ÷ 2   = <u>12.51%</u>

2. $\dfrac{\text{NI + Interest exp.* (1 - Tax Rate) + Minority interest in earnings}}{\text{Average long-term liabilities** + equity capital***}}$

     *   On long-term debt
     **   Include deferred taxes
     ***   Include minority interest

Year 5: $\dfrac{7,000 + 3,000\ (1 - .5) + 0}{(12,200 + 17,200 + 42,800 + 47,800) \div 2} = \underline{14.17\%}$

Year 6: $\dfrac{10,000 + 4,000\ (1 - .5) + 200}{(17,200 + 28,600 + 47,800 + 55,400) \div 2} = \underline{16.38\%}$

3. $\dfrac{\text{Net income - preferred dividends}}{\text{Average common stockholders' equity}}$

Year 5: $\dfrac{7,000 - 0}{(42,000 + 47,000) \div 2} = \underline{15.73\%}$

Year 6: $\dfrac{10,000 - 0}{(47,000 + 54,000) \div 2} = \underline{19.80\%}$

4. $\dfrac{\text{Net income - Preferred dividends - Common dividends}}{\text{Average common shareholders' equity}}$

Year 5: $\dfrac{7,000 - 2,000}{(42,000 + 47,000) \div 2} = \underline{11.24\%}$

Year 6: $\dfrac{10,000 - 3,000}{(47,000 + 54,000) \div 2} = \underline{13.86\%}$

b.   All the return on investment measures for ZETA improved from Year 5 to Year 6. The return on shareholders' equity increased 25% and the increases in the other return measures are equally impressive.

The increase in the equity growth rate, a measure of the company's ability to finance further expansion through internally generated funds, seems to be due mainly to the increase in profit margin, a healthy sign.

c.   ROCE = Adjusted Profit Margin x Asset turnover x Leverage

Year 5:   (7,000/155,000) x (155,000/99,750) x (99,750/44,500)
         = 0.0452 x 1.554 x 2.241 = <u>15.73%</u>

Year 6:   (10,000/186,000) x (186,000/121,500) x (121,500/50,500)
         = 0.0538 x 1.531 x 2.406 = <u>19.80%</u>

Comments on the disaggregated ROCE:

By disaggregating ROCE, the analyst can evaluate the factors that affect that ratio. The adjusted profit margin represents the portion of each sales dollar which is left for the common shareholder after providing for all costs. The asset turnover measures the utilization of assets, i.e., how many dollars of sales are generated by each dollar of assets. The leverage ratio measures how many dollars of assets are financed by each dollar of equity invested.

ZETA's ROCE increased significantly in Year 6 due to an increase in profitability (net income to sales) as well as an increase in leverage.

d. From part a, ROA = 10.03%

Category of Fund Supplier	Avg. Funds Supplied	Earnings on funds supplied at rate of 12.5%	Payment to supplier of funds	Accruing to (detracting from) return on common stock
Current liabilities	45,500	5,688	3,000[a]	2,688
Long-term debt	21,600	2,700	2,000[b]	700
Deferred taxes	2,800	350	0	350
Minority interest	1,100	138	200	(62)
Earnings in excess of compensation of suppliers of funds . . .				3,676
Add common stock, equity . .	50,500	6,313		6,313
Total income to stockholders' equity				9,989[c]

[a]Interest cost of $6,000 less 50% tax.
[b]Interest cost of $4,000 less 50% tax.
[c]The slight difference of $11 between the statement figure and $10,000 is due to rounding.

e. The analysis of the composition of return on shareholders' equity focuses on the contribution of each fund category to the return realized by the common equity. Current liabilities, because they are largely interest cost free, are the largest contributors. So are deferred taxes but they are much smaller in size. While the computation considers the minority interest, their share in profits does not truly represent a "payment" to suppliers of funds.

Problem 11-5
a.

	Year 5	Year 9
Profit margin	(38-3)/542 = 6.46%	(76-9)/979 = 6.84%
Asset turnover	542/245 = 2.21	979/291 = 3.36
Interest burden	3/245 = 1.22%	0/291 = 0
Leverage	245/159 = 1.54	291/220 = 1.32
Effective tax rate	13/32 = 40.36%	37/67 = 55.22%

b.   ROCE = [(Profit Margin x Asset Turnover) - Interest Burden]
         x Leverage x (100% - Income Tax Rate)

       Year 5: [(6.46% x 2.21) - 1.22%] x 1.54 x .5937 = <u>11.94%</u>

       Year 9: [(6.48% x 3.36) - 0] x 1.32 x .4478 = <u>13.58%</u>

c.   Asset turnover measures the ability of a company to minimize the level of
       assets (current and fixed) to support its level of sales. The asset turnover
       increased substantially over the period, contributing to an increase in the
       ROE. Financial leverage measures the amount of financing outside of equity
       including short and long-term debt. Financial leverage declined over the
       period, adversely affecting ROCE. Since asset turnover rose substantially
       more than financial leverage declined, the net effect was an increase in
       ROCE.

<u>Problem 11-6</u>

a.   Income tax rate = 1650/2550 = <u>.647</u>

       Interest burden = 2550/(2550+10) = <u>.996</u>

       Profit margin = (2550 + 10)/7120 = <u>.360</u>

       Asset turnover = 7120/7250 = <u>.982</u>

       Leverage = 7250/3860 = <u>1.878</u>

b.   ROCE = .647 x .996 x .360 x .982 x 1.878 = <u>42.8%</u>

c.   Yr. 5   Yr. 9   Impact on change in ROCE

       Tax Burden 628   .647   Favorable
       Interest Burden 989   .996   Favorable
       Operating Margin 245   .360   Major Positive
       Asset Turnover 724   .982   Major Positive
       Financial Leverage   . . . .   1.877   1.878   Unchanged

       ROCE 20.7%   42.8%

The ROCE for Merck more than doubled from 20.7% to 42.8% in Year 9. The two
primary factors behind this improvement were an increase in the operating
margin and an increase in the asset turnover. Merck was able to increase
selling prices or reduce operating costs, or some combination of both. The
higher asset turnover is indicative of greater efficiency because Merck was
able to produce more sales revenue per dollar of assets.

An increase in the tax burden means a lower tax rate, and an increase in the
interest burden means interest is a smaller percentage of pretax income. Both
of these items had a small, but favorable, impact on ROE.

◄ Answers to Cases ►

Case 11-1

a.   1994: [58,950+1,306 (1-.35)] ÷ [(282,896+358,475)/2] = <u>18.65%</u>
      1995: [93,402+1,179 (1-.35)] ÷ [(358,475+435,708)/2] = <u>23.72%</u>
      1996: [103,375+840 (1-.35)] ÷ [(435,708+646,486)/2] = <u>19.21%</u>

b.   1994: 58,950 ÷ [(225,155+297,616)/2] = <u>22.55%</u>
      1995: 93,402 ÷ [(297,616+371,644)/2] = <u>27.91%</u>
      1996: 103,375 ÷ [(371,644+511,945)/2] = <u>23.40%</u>

c.

	Adj. profit margin	Asset turnover	Leverage
1994	58,950/372,245 <u>15.84%</u>	372,245/320,686 <u>1.16</u>	320,686/261,386 <u>1.23</u>
1995	93,402/466,194 <u>20.04%</u>	466,194/397,092 <u>1.17</u>	397,092/334,630 <u>1.19</u>
1996	103,375/659,347 <u>15.68%</u>	659,347/541,097 <u>1.22</u>	541,097/441,795 <u>1.22</u>

d.   Adaptec's ROCE slightly exceeds its ROE in all three years. ROCE would be increased by additional debt in the capital structure. Profit margin appears to drive ROCE over the period. Again, additional leverage would increase ROCE.

e.   As seen above, Adaptec's profit margin plays an important role in its ability to earn high returns. As competition increases, downward pressure will be placed on margins. Thus, the challenge for Adaptec is to maintain its competitive edge.

Case 11-2

		11 %	10 %
a.	1. Return on total assets (A)	8.61	7.70
	2. Disaggregated ROA:		
	Profit margin (A)	4.97	4.94
	Asset turnover (A)	1.73	1.56
	3. Return on LT liabilities & equity (B)	10.96	8.66
	4. Return on common equity ©	21.01	15.27
	5. Equity growth rate (D)	8.63	5.35
	6. Disaggregated ROCE (E):		
	Adjusted profit margin	3.67	3.27
	Asset turnover	1.73	1.56
	Leverage	3.31	2.99

(A)   <u>NI [11] + Int Exp [156] (1 - TR) [158]</u>
       Avg Total Assets [69]

       11: [205.8+101.9 (1-.34)] ÷ [(3016.1+3326.1)/2] = <u>8.61%</u>

10: $[169.0+120.2 \ (1-.34)] \div [(3326.1+3125.9)/2] = $ <u>7.7%</u>

Disaggregated:

    11 profit margin: 273.1/5491.2 = <u>4.97%</u>
    11 asset turnover: 5491.2/3171.1 = <u>1.73</u>

    10 profit margin: 248.3/5030.6 = <u>4.94%</u>
    10 asset turnover: 5030.6/3226.0 = <u>1.56</u>

(B)   <u>NI [11] + Int Exp on Long-Term Debt (1 - TR) [156]</u>
       Avg Long-Term Liabilities + Equity [92 - 78]

     11: $[205.8+43.3 \ (1-.34)] \div [(3016.1-926.9+3326.1-1138.5)/2] = $ <u>10.96%</u>

     10: $[169.0+38.3 \ (1-.34)] \div [(3326.1-1138.5+3125.9-824.1)/2] = $ <u>8.66%</u>

(C)   <u>Net Income [11] - Preferred Dividends [12]</u>
       Average Common Equity [91]

     11: $[205.8-4.3] \div [(901.0+1017.5)/2] = $ <u>21.01%</u>

     10: $[169.0-4.5] \div [(1017.5+1137.1)/2] = $ <u>15.27%</u>

(D)   <u>NI [11] - Total Dividends Paid [12, 121]</u>
       Average Common Equity (C above)

     11: $[205.8-118.7-4.3] \div 959.3 = $ <u>8.63%</u>

     10: $[169.0-106.9-3.6] \div 1077.3 = $ <u>5.43%</u>

(E)   <u>NI [11] - Pref Div [12]</u>   <u>Sales [1]</u>
       Sales [1]   x   Avg Total Assets (A above)

          <u>Avg Total Assets (A above)</u>
    x   Avg Common Equity (C above)

     11:   <u>205.8 - 4.3</u>   <u>5491.2</u>   <u>3171.1</u>
           5491.2   x   3171.1   x   959.3

        = 3.67 x 1.73 x 3.31 = <u>21.01%</u>

     10:   <u>169.0 - 4.5</u>   <u>5030.6</u>   <u>3226.0</u>
           5030.6   x   3226.0   x   1077.3

        = 3.27 x 1.56 x 2.995 = <u>15.27%</u>

b. | Asset Utilization Ratios | 11 | 10 |
|---|---|---|
| Revenues to cash | 181.83 | 284.21 |
| Revenues to receivables | 7.95 | 7.99 |
| Revenues to inventories | 13.00 | 10.62 |
| Revenues to PP&E, net | 4.45 | 4.36 |
| Revenues to Other Assets | 47.96 | 47.01 |
| Revenues to Total Assets | 1.82 | 1.51 |

c. Quaker Oats is improving the return on assets and equity capital. The year to year trend shows increases in all of the ratios. Furthermore, many of the improvements were significant. ROCE increased 38% primarily due to the increase in net income and small reduction in equity. This is borne out by the disaggregated ROCE where the profitability ratio improved significantly. Asset turnover and leverage ratios also contributed to the year to year improvement.

The equity growth rate measures a company's ability to expand through the use of internally generated and retained funds. For Quaker Oats the equity growth rate has increased 59%. This is due to Quaker Oats' increased profitability.

d.

(in millions) Funds Suppliers	Average Funds Supplied	Earnings on Funds Supplied @ 8.61%	Paymts to Supplier of Funds	Accruing to/ (Detracting from)
Current Liabilities	1032.7	88.9	39.9[A]	49.0
L-T Debt	720.75	62.1	27.4[B]	34.7
Other Liabilities	107.9	9.3	—	9.3
Deferred Taxes	347.2	29.9	—	29.9
Preferred Stock	3.3	0.3	4.3[B]	(4.0)
Stockholders' Equity	959.25	82.6	—	82.6
	3171.1	273.1	71.6	

Total income (return) on common equity   201.5

[A] Interest on S-T debt and Other [156], 60.5 (1 - .34) = 39.9

[B] Balance = 27.4

Current liabilities (many interest free) and deferred taxes (interest free) contributed significantly to stockholder's return. Preferred stock reduced the return.

e. 1. Average Gross Productive Assets = Total Assets [69] - Intangible Assets [67] - Net Assets of Discontinued Operations [61 + 68] + Accumulated Depreciation [65] - 20% of Total Other Current Assets [60]

$$\frac{(3016.1+3326.1)-(446.2+466.7)-(160.5+252.2)+(681.9+591.5)-(.2)(114.5+107.0)}{2}$$

= 3122.85

NI [11] + Interest [156] (1 - TR)
Avg. Gross Productive Assets

$$= [205.8 + 101.9 (1 - .34)] \div 3122.85 = \underline{8.74\%}$$

2. NI [11] - Preferred Dividend [12]
Common Shares Outstanding [85 - 90] × Market Price/Sh [137]

Market price per share = (64.875 + 41.75)/2 = 53.3125

$$[205,800,000 - 4,300,000] \div [76,328,721 \times 53.3125] = \underline{4.95\%}$$

Case 11-3

a. The ROCE formula is as follows:

$$\frac{EBIT}{Revenues} \times \frac{Revenues}{Total\ Assets} - \frac{Interest}{Total\ Assets} \times \frac{Assets}{Common\ Equity}$$

$$\times (1 - Income\ tax\ rate)$$

Calculations:

Thompson: [(.322 × .61) - .019] × 1.53 × (1 - .28) = $\underline{19.5\%}$

Southam: [(.073 × 1.29) - .027] × 2.39 × (1 - .43) = $\underline{9.2\%}$

b.

	Thomson	*Southam*
EBIT/Revenues	Lower than early years but trending up recently. Rising margin supports higer ROCE.	Much lower than early years. Flat trend recently. Lower margin leads to lower ROCE.
Interest Turnover	Rose in early years but declined dramatically until Year 11. Lower burden leads to higher ROCE.	Steady increase over period, peaking in Year 4 with decline recently. Higher Interest burden reduces ROCE.
Tax Rate	Steady decline. Lower tax rate leads to higher ROE.	Increased steadily through Year 6. Fallen since, except in last two years. Rising tax rate reduces ROCE.
Asset Turnover	Improved until Year 5. Fluctuating recently. Rising turnover leads to higher ROCE.	Steadily declining ratio. Declining ratio leads to a lower ROCE.

| Leverage | Aggressive expansion led to rising financial leverage. However, ratio has declined to earlier levels. Increased leverage leads to higher ROCE. | Ratio increased dramatically until Year 7, having declined recently. Increased Leverage has been a source of rising ROCE for Southam. |

◄ CHAPTER 12 ►

Profitability Analysis

◄ CHAPTER OUTLINE ►

Profitability analysis is important in analyzing financial statements and complements returns analysis discussed in the prior chapter. Profitability analysis goes behind the accounting measures--sales, cost of sales, operating and non-operating expenses--to assess their sources, persistence, measurement, and key economic relations. Results from this assessment enable us to better estimate both the return and risk characteristics of a company. Profitability analysis also allows us to distinguish between performance primarily attributed to management (operating decisions) from those less related to management decisions (taxes and selling prices).

This chapter describes tools of analysis enabling us to make these distinctions. We also describe break-even analysis and its relevance for assessing profitability. Both analytical and graphic analysis of break-even points are explained. We also describe operating leverage and its importance for profitability analysis. Throughout this chapter we emphasize the application of these analysis tools with several illustrative cases.

◄ CHAPTER OUTLINE ►

▸ **Analyzing Company Profitability**

    Factors in Measuring Company Income

    Two-Phase Analysis of Income

▸ **Analyzing Company Revenues**

    Major Sources of Revenues

    Persistence of Revenues

    Relations between Revenues, Receivables and Inventories

    Revenue Recognition and Measurement

▸ **Analyzing Company Cost of Sales**

    Measuring Gross Profit (Margin)

    Analyzing Changes in Gross Profit

    Interpreting Changes in Gross Profit

▸ **Analyzing Company Expenses**

    Selling Expenses

    Depreciation Expense

    Maintenance and Repairs Expenses

    Amortization of Special Costs

    General and Administrative Expenses

    Financing and Other Expenses

    Income Tax Expenses

    Variation Analysis of Income and Its Components

▸ **Break-Even Analysis**

    Break-Even Analysis Case

    Limitations in Break-Even Analysis

    Uses and Implications of Break-Even Analysis

◄ Learning Objectives ►

- **Describe the importance of profitability analysis and the necessity of analyzing and adjusting income.**

- **Analyze the sources, persistence, measurement and recognition of revenues for assessing profitability.**

- **Explain gross profit and its evaluation using volume, price and costs of sales.**

- **Analyze operating and non-operating expenses using common-size, index number and ratio analyses.**

- **Describe the effective tax rate and the analysis of income tax disclosures.**

◀ Learning Objectives ▶

- **Explain break-even analysis and its relevance in assessing profitability.**

- **Interpret operating leverage and its implications for profitability.**

◄ Answers to Questions ►

1. In the evaluation of the income of an enterprise the analyst is particularly interested in the following questions:

    a. What is the relevant net income and what is its quality?
    b. What elements in the income statements can be used and relied upon for purposes of earning forecasting?
    c. How stable are the major elements on income and expense and what is their trend?
    d. What is the earning power of the enterprise?

2. Net income is not a specific flow awaiting the perfection of a flawless method with which it can be precisely measured. There are a number of reasons for this:

    a. The determination of income is dependent on estimates regarding the outcome of future events. This peering into the future is basically a matter of judgment involving the assessment of probabilities based on facts and estimates.

    b. The accounting standards governing the determination and measurement of income at any given time are the result of the cumulative experience of the accounting profession, regulatory agencies, businessmen, and others. They reflect a momentary equilibrium which is based partly on knowledge and experience and partly on the compromise of widely differing interests and views on methods of measurement. While the accounting profession has moved to narrow the range of acceptable alternative measurement principles, the alternatives nevertheless remain and their complete elimination in the near future is unlikely.

    c. Beyond the problem of honest differences in estimation and other judgments, as well as in the variety of alternative acceptable principles, is the problem arising from the diverse ways in which the judgments and principles are applied. Theoretically, the independent professional accountant should be concerned first and foremost with the fair presentation of the financial statements. He/she should make accounting a "neutral" science which gives expression and effect to economic events but does not affect the results presented. To this end the accountant should choose from among alternative principles those most applicable to the circumstances and should disclose all facts, favorable and adverse, which may affect the user's decision.

       In fact, the accounting profession as a whole has not yet reached such a level of independence and detachment of judgment. It is subject to the powerful pressures on the part of managements who have, or at least feel that they have, a vital interest in the way in which results of operations are presented.

    d. In addition to the above reasons, which are inherent in the accounting process, there exists another reason why there cannot be such a thing as an absolute measure of "real earnings." It is that financial statements are general-purpose presentations designed to serve the diverse needs of many users. Consequently, a single figure of "net income" cannot be relevant to all users and that means that the analyst must use this figure and the additional information disclosed in the financial statements as a starting point and adjust it so as to arrive at a "net income" figure which meets his/her particular interests and objectives.

3. The analysis of the income statements of an enterprise can be conceived as being undertaken at two levels:

    Accounting Principles Used and Their Implication

    The analyst must have a thorough understanding of the principles of income, cost, and expense accounting and measurement employed by the enterprise. Moreover, since most assets, with the exception of cash and receivables actually collectible, represent costs deferred to the future, the analyst must have a good understanding of the principles of asset measurement employed by the enterprise so that he/she can relate them to the income accounting of the enterprise as a means of checking the validity of the accounting. Finally, he/she must understand and assess the implications which the use of one accounting principle, as opposed to another, has on the measurement of the income of an enterprise and its comparison to that of other enterprises.

Tools of Income Statement Analysis

The second level of analysis consists of applying the appropriate tools of analysis to the components of the income statement and the interpretation of the results shown by these analytical measures. The application of these facts are aimed at achieving the objectives of the analysis of results of operations, such as the projection of income, assessment of its stability and quality, and the estimation of earning power.

4. Knowledge of mayor sources of revenues (sales) is important in the analysis of the income statement particularly if the analysis is that of a multimarket enterprise. Each major market or product line may have its own growth pattern, profitability, and future potential.

5. The analysis, evaluation, projection, and valuation of earnings require that these be broken down into categories which share similar characteristics of variability, growth potential, and risk. Similarly, the asset structure and the financing requirements of various segments of an enterprise can vary significantly and thus require separate analysis and evaluation. For example, the credit grantor may be interested in knowing which segments of an enterprise provide funds and which are net users of funds.

    The composition of an enterprise, the relative size and profitability of its various segments, the ability of management to make profitable acquisitions, and the overall performance of management represent additional important information which the analyst seeks from its segmented data.

6. The degree of informative disclosure about the results of operations and the asset base of segments of a business can vary widely. Full disclosure would call for detailed income statements, balance sheets, and statements of cash flows for each significant segment. This is rarely found in practice because of the difficulty of obtaining such breakdowns internally, and also because of management's reluctance to divulge information which could harm the enterprise's competitive position. Short of the disclosure of complete financial statements by the business segment, a great variety of partial detail has been suggested:

    a. Income Statement Data or Revenues Only: In most enterprises this should not present great difficulties.

    b. Gross Profit: This involves complex problems of interdivisional transfer pricing as well as allocation of indirect overhead costs.

    c. Contribution Margin: Contribution margin reporting is based on assigning to each segment the revenues, costs, and expenses for which that segment is solely responsible. It is a very useful concept in management accounting, but for purposes of public reporting it presents problems because there are no generally accepted methods of cost allocation and, consequently, they can vary significantly from company to company and even within one enterprise. Disclosure of allocation methods, while helpful, will not remove all the problems facing the user of such data.

    d. Net Income (after full cost allocation): The further down the income statement we report by segment the more pervasive and the more complex the allocation procedures become. Reporting segment net income would require allocating all joint expenses to each specific business activity on some rational basis even though they may not be directly related to any particular one.

7. The major provisions of SFAS No. 14 are:

    a. It requires that companies report in their annual financial statements the revenues, operating profits, identifiable assets, capital expenditures, and depreciation/depletion/amortization expense of each significant (representing 10 percent or more) industry segments of their operations.

    b. It suggests 10 as a practical limit to the number of industry segments for which a company reports information.

c. If a company derives 10 percent or more of its revenues from sales to a single customer, that fact and the amount of that revenue must be disclosed.

d. Information similar to that required for industry segments also is required for a company's operations in different geographic areas of the world.

8. The financial analyst must be alert to the limitations of public-disclosed segment data. He/she must recognize that the more specific and detailed the information provided, the more likely it is to be based on extensive allocations of costs and expenses. These allocations are often based on such concepts as "equity," "reasonableness," and "acceptability" to managers and these concepts have little relevance to the objectives of financial analysis. Bases of allocating joint expenses are largely arbitrary and subject to differences of opinion as to their validity and precision.

9. Important considerations bearing on the quality and persistence of the sales and revenues trend include:

a. The sensitivity of demand for products to general business conditions.

b. The ability of the enterprise to anticipate trends in demand by the introduction of new/revised products and services.

c. Degree of customer concentration, dependence on major customers, as well as demand stability of major customer groups.

d. Degree of product concentration and dependence on a single segment.

e. Degree of dependence on relatively few "star" salesmen.

f. Degree of geographical diversification of markets.

10. The MD&A requirements focus on results of operations, liquidity, capital resources and the impact of inflation. The SEC desires that MD&As emphasis be redirected to financial results, that forward-looking information should, if possible, be included, and the discussion should focus on trends and implications which are not evident from an examination of the financial statements.

11. In the area of results of operations, MD&A must cover revenue and expense components which are needed for an understanding of results by the reader; major unusual or infrequent events that materially affect reported income from continuing operations; trends or uncertainties that have affected or are likely to affect results and impending changes in cost/revenue relationships such as increases in materials or labor costs. MD&A must also include a discussion of the extent to which material increases in revenues are attributable to increases in prices or to increases in volume or amount of goods or services being sold or to the introduction of new products or services as well as a discussion of the impact of inflation and changing prices on the registrant's revenues and on income from continuing operations.

12. In its instructions to the MD&A requirements, the SEC states that the purpose of the discussion and analysis is to provide investors and others with information relevant to an assessment of the financial condition and results of operations of the registrant as determined by evaluating the amounts and the uncertainty of cash flows from operations and from outside sources.

The instructions for preparation of MD&As make it clear that managements have a great deal of discretion on how to communicate to the reader and what to stress in communications. The aim is meaningful disclosure in narrative form by those in charge of operations who are really in a position to know and who can supply significant additional details not usually found in the financial statements. The results will depend on management's attitudes and objectives.

13. In the analysis of gross profit, the analyst will pay particular attention to: (1) factors which account for the variation in sales and costs of sales, and (2) the relationship between sales and costs of sales and management's ability to control this relationship.

14. Because depreciation is computed in most cases on the basis of time elapsed, the ratio of depreciation expense to income is not a particularly meaningful or instructive relationship. In the evaluation of depreciation expense the ratio of depreciation to gross plant and equipment is more meaningful. The ratio is computed as:

Depreciation Expense ÷ Assets Subject to Depreciation

This ratio can be computed by major categories of assets. The basic purpose is to enable the analyst to detect changes in the composite rate of depreciation used by an enterprise as a means of evaluating its adequacy and of detecting attempts at income smoothing.

15. Maintenance and repair costs vary in significance with the amount invested in plant and equipment as well as with the level of productive activity. They have an effect on the cost of goods sold as well as on the other elements of cost. Since maintenance and repairs contain elements of both fixed and variable costs they cannot vary directly with sales. Thus, the ratio of repairs and maintenance costs to sales, while instructive to compare from year to year or among enterprises, must be interpreted with care. To the extent that the analyst can determine the fixed and the variable portions of maintenance and repairs costs his/her interpretation of their relationship to periodic sales will be more valid.

Repairs and maintenance are, to a significant extent, discretionary costs. That is, the level of expense can, within limits, be regulated by management for a variety of reasons including those aimed at the improvement of reported income or to the preservation of liquid resources. Certain types of repairs cannot, of course, be postponed without resulting breakdowns in productive equipment. But many types of preventive repairs and particularly maintenance can be postponed or skimped on with results whose effects lie mainly in the future. Thus, the level of repair and maintenance costs both in relation to sales and to plant and equipment is of interest to the analyst.

The level of repair and maintenance costs is also important in the evaluation of depreciation expense. Useful lives of assets are estimated by the use of many assumptions including those relating to the upkeep and maintenance of the assets. If, for instance, there is a deterioration in the usual or assumed level of repairs and maintenance, the useful life of the asset will, in all probability, be shortened. That may, in turn, require an upward revision in the depreciation expense or else income will be overstated.

16. The analysis of selling costs has two main objectives:

   (i)   The evaluation over time of the relationship between sales and the costs needed to bring them about.

   (ii)   An evaluation of the trend and the productivity of future-directed selling costs.

The importance of selling costs in relation to sales varies from industry, and from enterprise to enterprise. In some enterprises selling costs take the form of commissions and are, consequently, highly variable in nature, while in others they contain important elements of fixed costs. After allowing for the fixed and variable components of the selling expenses the best way to analyze them is to relate them to sales. The more detailed the breakdown of the selling expense components are, the more meaningful and incisive such analysis will be.

17. Bad debts expense is often regarded as a cost of marketing. Since the expense is importantly tied to the allowance for doubtful accounts it is best evaluated in terms of the relationship between the allowance and gross accounts receivable. The reasons for fluctuations in that relationship can be varied including improvement in the collectibility of receivables or inadequate provisions which result in understated bad debt expense.

18. a. The relationship between the tax accrual and the pretax income, otherwise known as the effective tax rate, is computed as follows:

Income Tax Expense for Period ÷ Income before Income Taxes

b. The analysis of income tax disclosures may be undertaken with specific or specialized objectives in mind. However, the more general objectives of such an analysis are:

- To understand the tax accounting of the enterprise and its impact on income, on related assets and liabilities as well as on the sources and uses of funds or cash.
- To judge the adequacy of the enterprise's tax disclosure.
- To provide a basis for assessing the effect of taxes on future income and funds flows.
- To provide a basis for informed queries to be put to management in order to clear up questions arising during the analysis.
- To identify unusual gains or losses not otherwise disclosed but whose tax effect is highlighted.

19. The basic principle underlying break-even analysis is the behavior of costs. Variable costs vary directly with sales while fixed costs remain essentially constant over a considerable range of sales. Certain costs may contain both fixed and variable elements in them. Examples of such "semivariable" costs are repairs, some materials, indirect labor, fuel, utilities, payroll taxes, and rents which contain a minimum payment provision and are also related to the level of sales. Break-even analysis requires that the variable component of such expenses be separated from the fixed component.

20. The estimation of a variety of possible results by means of break-even analysis requires the use of simplifying assumptions. In most cases these assumptions do not destroy the validity of the conclusions reached. Nevertheless, in reaching such conclusions, the analyst must be fully aware of these assumptions and their possible effect.

The following are some of the more important assumptions implicit in break-even computations:

(1)   The factors comprising the model actually behave as assumed, i.e.:
  a.   That the costs have been reasonably subdivided into their fixed and variable components.
  b.   That variable costs fluctuate proportionally with volume.
  c.   That fixed costs remain fixed over the range relevant to the situation examined.
  d.   That unit selling prices will remain unchanged over the range encompassed by the analysis.

(2)   In addition, there are certain operating and environmental assumptions which emphasize the static nature of any one break-even computation. It is assumed:
  a.   That the mix of sales will remain unchanged.
  b.   That efficiency of operations will remain constant.
  c.   That prices of costs factors will not change.
  d.   That the only factor affecting costs is volume.
  e.   That beginning and end-of-period inventory levels will remain substantially unchanged.
  f.   That there is no substantial change in the general price level during the period.
  g.   Consumer trends will not change in the short run.

The formidable array of assumptions enumerated above points out the susceptibility of break-even computations to significant error. Not all the assumptions are, however, equally important, or, if not holding, will have an equal impact on the validity of conclusions.

21. The variable expense percent measures the relationship between variable costs and sales. It means that, on average, out of every dollar of sales X cents go to meet variable costs, i.e., costs which would not be incurred if the sale did not occur.

The contribution margin ratio is basically the complement of the variable expense percent. It indicates that each dollar of sales generates a contribution of 1-X cents toward meeting fixed expenses and the earning of a profit beyond the break-even point.

22. If an enterprise is reluctant to expand its capacity (and thereby increase its fixed costs and break-even point, assuming that variable costs do not decrease) it may have to consider other alternatives such as:

   a. Foregoing an increase in sales,
   b. Increasing the number of shifts, which could increase variable costs significantly, or
   c. Subcontracting some of its work to outsiders, thus foregoing some of the profit of increased activity.

23. Leverage and fixed costs go together. Financial leverage is the result of relying on fixed costs of funds for a portion of the resources used by the enterprise. Earnings above that fixed cost magnify the return on the residual funds and vice versa. The fixed costs of a business enterprise form the basis of the concept of operating leverage. Until an enterprise develops a volume of sales which is sufficient to cover its fixed costs, it will incur a loss. Once it has covered the fixed costs, further increments in volume will result in more than proportionate increases in profitability.

   An enterprise operating near its break-even point will have relatively larger percentage change of profits or losses for a given change in volume. On the upside the volatility will, of course, be desirable. On the downside, however, it can result in adverse results which are significantly worse than those indicated by changes in sales volume alone.

24. An increase in the break-even point of an enterprise generally increases operating risk. It means that the enterprise is dependent on a higher volume of sales in order to break even. Looked at another way, it means that the enterprise is more vulnerable to economic downturns as compared to its situation with a lower break-even point. There are other repercussions to high levels of fixed costs. For example, a higher break-even point may mean that the enterprise has less freedom of action in fields such as labor relations. A high level of fixed costs makes strikes more expensive and subjects the enterprise to added pressure to submit to higher wage demands.

   The volatility of profits is, among other factors, dependent on the variable expense percent. The low variable-cost enterprise will achieve higher profits for a given increment in volume once break-even operations are reached, than will the high variable-cost enterprise.

◄ Answers to Exercises ►

Exercise 12-1

a. A "diversified" (or conglomerate) company conducts operating activities in unrelated industries. The conglomerate is contrasted to the horizontally or vertically integrated company. Horizontal integration is typified by varied product lines derived from a common material source, such as rubber products for the consumer market, automotive parts, paint products, etc. Vertical integration is characterized by numerous activities involving a single product line such as baking, canning, meat packing, distribution, retailing and real property ownership and management.

b. The difficulty encountered in measuring net profit by industry segment arises in the treatment of joint costs. While revenue and material, labor, and manufacturing costs can usually be identified readily with a given industry segment, some costs serve more than one industry and can be allocated only on an arbitrary basis. When this is done the resulting net profit breakdown is of questionable value since it does not reveal the contribution that each segment is making to the company-wide joint costs.

c. Standard Industries' consolidated income statement reveals at least three possible areas of joint costs.

1. Selling and administrative expense might include costs of central administration and national advertising on a firm-wide basis.

2. Interest expense might pertain to funds borrowed on a firm-wide basis, negotiated and dispensed by top level management.

3. Provision for income taxes is based on the taxable income of the firm as a whole. As a tax it is levied not on each industry segment of a firm but on each separate corporate entity or on a consolidation of the component corporations.

A problem arises because there is difficulty tracing joint costs and furthermore the responsibility for joint costs does not necessarily lie with the industry segments individually. Consequently, when these costs are allocated arbitrarily to the various segments the resulting net profit breakdown is distorted and does not truly reflect the contribution of individual segments.

d. While all gains or losses recognized during a period should generally be included in the determination of net income, any material adjustment which satisfies the following criteria should be excluded: (1) it is directly applicable to the operations of a particular prior period, (2) it is not the result of an economic event that occured after the prior period, (3) it depends on determinations by persons other than management, and (4) it could not previously have been reasonably estimated.

e. In general, an item is treated as extraordinary if it represents an event or transaction that is both unusual in nature and infrequent in occurrence. Items not deemed extraordinary include: asset writedowns/writeoffs, strikes, and gains (losses) from foreign currency transactions and sale of assets used in the business. Under current rules extraordinary items are rare, the most common being gains (losses) from early retirement of debt.

f. The gain on sale of the furniture division should be reported as a discontinued operation, while the assessment of additional taxes (if not accrued for in prior periods) would be expensed in the current period.

Exercise 12-2
10% Revenue Test:

Segment	Sales to affiliated and unaffiliated customers		Test Value	Reportable Segment?
Aerospace	$12,400	≥	$1,420*	Yes
Building	11,300	<	$1,420	No
Ccomputing	500	<	$1,420	No
Total Revenue	$14,200			

   * 10% of total revenue of $14,200

10% Asset Test:

Segment	Identifiable Assets		Test Value	Reportable Segment?
Aerospace	$11,500	≥	$1,328*	Yes
Building	11,360	≥	$1,328	Yes
Computing	420	<	$1,328	No
Total Assets	$13,280			

* 10% of total identifiable assets of $13,280

10% Operating Profit Test:

Segment	Operating Profit	Operating Loss		Test Value	Reportable Segment?
A	$700		≥	$73*	Yes
B		$50	<	$73	No
C	30		<	$73	No
Total	$730				

* 10% of total operating profit of $730

According to the above computations, A and B are reportable segments, and C is not.

Exercise 12-3

a. Reconstruction entries related to taxes for Year 10:

Income Tax Expense [158]	
(1) 153.5	

Deferred Income Taxes (noncurrent) [81]	
	308.4 Beg.
	18.6 (1)
	0.7 (4)
	327.7 End

Tax Effect of Disc. Ops. [144]	
	36.3 (2)

Income Taxes Payable [75]		
(2)	36.3	8.0 Beg
(4)	0.7	134.9 (1)
***	71.9	2.3 (3)
		36.3 End

Tax Effect of Preferred Divs.	
(3) 2.3*	

(1) Tax Expense   153.5
        Deferred Taxes   18.6
        Taxes Payable   134.9

(2) Taxes Payable   36.3
        Tax Effect of Disc. Ops.   36.3

(3) Tax Effect of Preferred Dividends*   2.3
        Taxes Payable   2.3

(4) Income Tax Payable**   0.7
        Deferred Income Tax   0.7

    * Let X = Preferred dividends before income tax
      X (1 - .34) = 4.5 [12]
      X = 6.8

      Then: 6.8 - Tax effect = 4.5
      Tax effect = 2.3

    ** To transfer unexplained balance in Deferred Income Taxes to Income Taxes
Payable.

    *** Assumed income tax paid is $71.9 million (plug).

b.   Item [159] provides information on income tax paid of $90.7 million, which is
     $18.8 million more than the $71.9 million suggested by the analysis above.
     Complete confidence in our understanding of the company's tax accounting would
     require information to explain the main reasons for the discrepancy.

Quaker Oats
Statement Accounting for Variations in Net Income
Year 11 Compared to Year 10

		Increase (Decrease)
Items Tending to Increase NI:	*(in millions)*	*(%)*
Increase in Gross Margin on Sales:		
Increase in Net Sales:		
Net Sales, Year 11	5491.2	
Net Sales, Year 10	5030.6	460.6	9.2%
Deduct Increase in COGS:		
COGS, 11	2839.7	
COGS, 10	2685.9	153.8	5.7%
Net Increase in Gross Margin:		
Gross Margin, 11	2651.5	
Gross Margin, 10	2344.7	306.8	13.1%
Net Decrease in Net Interest Expense:		
Interest Expense, 11	86.2	
Interest Expense, 10	101.8	15.6	(15.3%)
Net Decrease in Loss from Disc. Ops.		
Loss, 11	30.0	
Loss, 10	59.9	29.9	(49.9%)
Total Tending to Increase NI		352.3	
Items Tending to Decrease NI:		
Increase in SGA Expenses:		
SGA, 11	2121.2	
SGA, 10	1844.1	277.1	15.0%
Net Increase in Other Expenses:		
Other Expense, 11	32.6	
Other Expense, 10	16.4	16.2	98.8%
Increase in Income Taxes:		
Income Taxes, 11	175.7	
Income Taxes, 10	153.5	22.2	14.5%
Total Tending to Decrease NI		315.5	
Net Increase in Net Income:		
Net Income, 11	205.8	
Net Income, 10	169.0	36.8	21.8%

Comments:

(1)   Increase in sales due largely to volume increases (per MD&A).

(2) Increase in sales exceeded increase in COGS--leading to increase in gross margin. MD&A cites "lower commodity and packaging costs."

(3) Decrease in net interest expense. MD&A cites "lower financing costs in Brazil."

(4) Most of increase in net income due to smaller loss from discontinued operations--income from continuing operations increased by only 3%.

(5) Large increase in SGA may or may not be positive. Per MD&A increase was due to "higher planned advertising and merchandising," which may or may not increase future profitability.

(6) Large increase in other expenses due in part to $10 million restructuring charge and $17.5 million credit in previous year. This may be an income smoothing device. Foreign exchange gains and losses also lumped into this category.

An important analytical task is to determine how sales and costs will behave in future. Are items of a one-time nature or part of a trend?

Exercise 12-5

a. To determine the amount of income taxes paid in Year 11:

Taxes on Earnings [27]	
(a) 265.9	

Accrued Income Taxes (current liability) [44]			
		46.4	Beg.
(b)	1.1	230.4	(a)
***	220.1	12.1	(c)
		67.7	End

Deferred Taxes (current asset) [155]			
Beg. 37.7			
	1.1		(b)
End 36.6			

Deferred Income Taxes (LT liability) [176]			
		235.1	Beg
(c)	12.1	35.5	(a)
		36.3	End

(a)	Tax expense	265.9	
	Deferred income tax (non-current)		35.5
	Accrued income tax [124A]		230.4
(b)	Accrued income tax (plug)	1.1	
	Deferred income tax (current)		1.1
(c)	Deferred income tax (non-current)	12.1	
	Accrued income tax		12.1

*** Compared to $199.3 [182]

b. Campbell's disclosure of income tax paid ($199.3 million) is $20.8 million less than the $220.1 million suggested by the analysis above. Complete confidence in our understanding of the company's tax accounting would require information to explain the main reasons for the discrepancy.

c.

CAMPBELL SOUP
SCHEDULE TO RECONCILE THE DIFFERENCE BETWEEN STATUTORY
INCOME TAX AND CURRENT FEDERAL INCOME TAX
FOR YEAR 11 (IN MILLIONS)

Statutory Federal income tax (= 667.4 [26] × 34%)		$226.92
Less: Federal benefit on state tax		
State tax currently payable [123]	$23.40	
State income tax (net of federal tax benefit)		
= 667.4 × 3% [135]	20.02	(3.38)
Foreign tax [124]		(21.20)
		$202.34
Add (deduct) permanent differences:		
Other (= 667.4 × 2.5% [139])		16.69
Foreign earnings not taxed or taxed at other		
than Federal rate (= 677.4 × 0.3% [138])		(2.00)
Nondeductible amortization of intangible		
(= 667.4 × 0.6% [137])		4.00
		$221.03
Less Deferred income tax:		
Federal [125]	$(21.90)	
State [126]	(7.50)	
Foreign [127]	(6.10)	(35.50)
Current federal income tax [122]		$185.53

Exercise 12-6

Gross plant assets [161A]	$2,734.9
- land [158]	63.8
- projects in progress [161]	267.0
Subject to depreciation	$2,404.1

a. Accumulated depreciation [162]
   Plant assets subj. to depr.   = 1,017.2 ÷ 2,404.1 = 42.3%

This is a measure of the age of plant assets. The higher the value, the older the assets.

b. Depreciation expense [162A]
   Plant assets subj. to depr.   = 184.1 ÷ 2,404.1 = 7.66%

This is a measure of Campbell's composite rate of depreciation. It should be compared to the value in other years to help detect changes.

c. Depreciation expense [162A]
   Sales [13]   = 184.1 ÷ 6,205.8 = 2.97%

This relation is not particularly meaningful given that depreciation is a fixed cost.

Campbell Soup Company
Statement Accounting for Variation in Net Income
Year 11 Compared to Year 10 (in millions)

			Percentage Change
Items tending to increase net income:			
Decrease in net sales:			
Net sales (Year 11)	$6,204.10		
Net sales (Year 10)	6,205.80	$ (1.70)	0.03%
Deduct: Decrease in cost of product sold:			
Cost of products sold (11)	$4,095.50		
Cost of products sold (10)	4,258.20	162.70	3.82%
Net increase in gross margin		$161.00	
Increase in interest income:			
Interest income (11)	$ 26.00		
Interest income (10)	17.60	8.40	47.73%
Decrease in marketing and selling expense:			
M&S expense (11)	$ 956.20		
M&S expense (10)	980.50	24.30	2.48%
Decrease in net foreign exchange losses:			
Net FX losses (11)	$ 0.80		
Net FX losses (10)	3.30	2.50	75.76%
Decrease in divestiture, restructuring and unusual charges:			
Divestiture, restructuring and unusual charges (11)	$ 0.00		
Divestiture, restructuring and unusual charges (10)	339.10	339.10	100.00%
Total items tending to increase net income		$535.30	
Items tending to decrease net income:			
Decrease in earning of affiliates:			
Earning of affiliates (11)	$ 2.40		
Earning of affiliates (10)	13.50	$ 11.10	82.22%
Increase in administrative expense:			
Administrative expense (11)	$ 306.70		
Administrative expense (10)	290.70	16.00	5.50%
Increase in research and development expense:			
R&D expense (11)	$ 56.30		
R&D expense (10)	53.70	2.60	4.84%
Increase in interest expense:			
Interest expense (11)	$ 116.20		
Interest expense (10)	111.60	4.60	4.12%
Increase in other expense:			
Other expense (11)	$ 26.20		
Other expense (10)	14.70	11.50	78.23%
Increase in minority interest in income:			
Minority interest (11)	$ 7.20		
Minority interest (10)	5.70	1.50	26.32%
Increase in income tax expense:			
Income tax expense (11)	$ 265.90		

Income tax expense (10)	175.00	90.90	51.94%
Total items tending to decrease net income		$138.20	

Net increase in net income:

Net income (11)	$ 401.50		
Net income (10)	4.40	$397.10	9025.0%

Comments:

(1) Sales growth was minimal. The MD&A indicates that sales volume decreased due to "reduced year-end trade promotional activities and the adverse effect of the recession on certain premium products."

(2) Despite sluggish sales growth, gross margin increased significantly due to lower COGS. MD&A cites "benefits from restructuring ... divestitures ... product pruning activities ... productivity improvements ... declining commodity prices." The analyst must try to assess whether the Year 10 restructuring included any expenses properly matched to Year 11.

(3) Interest income increased due to temporary investment of proceeds from borrowings. Interest income will decline to lower levels once these funds are invested in operations.

(4) While marketing and selling expenses decreased by over $14 million, MD&A warns that advertising will increase in Year 12.

(5) Both administrative and other expenses increased due to the effects of incentive compensation plans.

(6) The 9025% increase in net income becomes a 31.2% increase when the effects of the Year 10 restructuring are considered. Note 6 states the after-tax effect of this charge was $301.6 million.

Exercise 12-8

Selling price per unit	$3.50
Variable cost per unit	1.50
Contribution margin	$2.00

a. Break-even point = $100,000/$2 = 50,000 units

b.
Sales ($3.50 × 120,000)	$420,000
Variable costs ($1.50 × 120,000)	180,000
Fixed costs	100,000
Profit at 120,000 units	$140,000

1.
Sales ($3.50 × 138,000)	$483,000
Variable costs ($1.50 × 138,000)	207,000
Fixed costs	100,000
Profit at 138,000 units	$176,000

Increase in profit of $36,000 (25.7%).

```
2.    Sales ($3.50 x 102,000)              $357,000
      Variable costs ($1.50 x 102,000)      153,000
      Fixed costs                           100,000
      Profit at 102,000 units             $104,000
```

Decrease in profit of $36,000 (25.7%).

```
c.  Sales    ($3.50 x 150,000)            $525,000
    Variable costs ($1.50 x 150,000)       225,000
    Fixed costs                            100,000
    Profit at 150,000 units              $200,000

    1.    Sales ($3.15 x 150,000)          $472,500
          Variable costs ($1.50 x 150,000)  225,000
          Fixed costs                       100,000
          Profit at 150,000 units         $147,500
```

Decrease in profit of $52,500 (26.3%).

```
    2.    Sales ($3.50 x 150,000)          $525,000
          Variable costs ($1.20 x 150,000)  180,000
          Fixed costs                       100,000
          Profit at 150,000 units         $245,000
```

Increase in profit of $45,000 (22.5%).

```
    3.    Sales ($3.50 x 180,000)          $630,000
          Variable costs ($1.50 x 180,000)  270,000
          Fixed costs                       100,000
          Profit at 180,000 units         $260,000
```

Increase in profit of $60,000 (30%).

```
    4.    Sales ($3.15 x 180,000)          $567,000
          Variable costs ($1.20 x 180,000)  216,000
          Fixed costs                       100,000
          Profit at 180,000 units         $251,000
```

Increase in profit of $51,000 (25.5%).

Exercise 12-9

a. breakeven point = 40,000 ÷ (10.00 - 6.00) = <u>10,000 copies</u>

At sales volume of 10,000 copies, revenue will be equal to the sum of variable and fixed expenses. For each copy sold after breakeven, income will increase by the contribution margin of $4 per unit.

b.

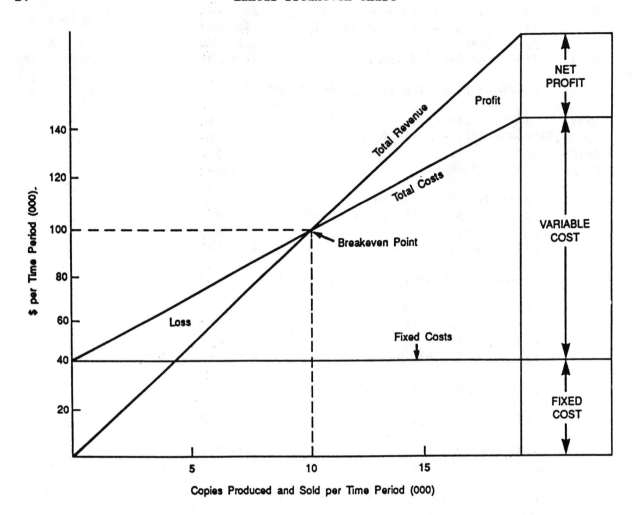

If the graph is drawn to scale, the breakeven point should be 10,000 as in part a.

Exercise 12-10

Let L = lanterns, C = coolers, and T = tents.
Let X = number of units of mix containing 1L, 2C, and 3T.

Break-even point is reached when:

    Sales = Fixed Costs + Variable Costs
    (20X) + 2 (30X) + 3 (50X) = 130,000 + (15X) + 2 (20X) + 3 (25X)
    230 X   = 130,000 + 130 X
    100 X   = 130,000

    X = 1300

Thus, the numbers of units needed to breakeven are 1,300 lanterns, 2,600 coolers, and 3,900 tents.

Proof:	A	B	C	Total
Units	1300	2600	3900	
Sales	$26,000	$78,000	$195,000	$299,000
Variable Costs	19,500	52,000	97,500	169,000
Contribution margin	6,500	26,000	97,500	130,000
Fixed costs				130,000
Income				-0-

Exercise 12-11

Low volume operations mean that fixed costs, which in the case of auto makers are very substantial, must be absorbed by a low number of units produced. Since under the lower of cost or market rule inventory cannot be priced higher than expected sales price less costs of disposal and a normal profit margin, much of that excess overhead must be charged to the period incurred--here the fourth quarter. This is the most likely reason for the losses.

◄ Answers to Problems ►

Problem 12-1

a.
	Variability Ratio	
Time recording devices	441/34	= 13.0
Data communications	1,510/570	= 2.6
Home sewing products	342/276	= 1.2
Hardware for electronics	919/771	= 1.2
Corporate total	3,190/1,310	= 2.4

Note: There are other ways to measure variability. Other possibilities include standard deviation and average percent change.

b. 1.   *Inventory-to-Sales*
   Time recording devices   2,728/4,100   = 67¢
   Home sewing products   526/1,265   = 42¢
   Data communications   1,897/6,886   = 28¢
   Hardware for electronics 287/1,850   = 16¢

   Corporate total   5,438/14,109   = 39¢

   2.   *Inventory-to-Contribution*
   Time recording devices   2,728/412   = $6.62
   Home sewing products   526/342   = $1.54
   Data communications   1,897/1,510   = $1.26
   Hardware for electronics 287/919   = $0.31

   Corporate total   5,438/3,183   = $1.71

c. *Change in income contribution:*

	Yr 2	Yr 3	Yr 4
Data communications	306	120	514
Hardware for electronics	---	771	148
Home sewing products	(2)	(13)	66
Time recording devices	(130)	(277)	378
Corporate	174	601	1,106

d.

	Yr 1	Yr 2	Yr 3	Yr 4
Data communications	44%	59%	48%	47%
Time recording devices	34%	21%	2%	13%
Hardware for electronics	--	--	37%	29%
Home sewing products	22%	20%	13%	11%
Total	100%	100%	100%	100%

e. *Data communications equipment* seems to be the best candidate for investment. Its growth has been steady while the amount of inventory investment required for sales (28¢) and income contribution ($1.26) is relatively low.

The trend of income contribution of *hardware for electronics* is stable and both the amount of investment required for sales (16¢) and income contribution (31¢) compares very well with others.

Home sewing products also shows a stable income contribution trend; however, it should be noted that the amount of sales is decreasing every year and the amount of investment required for sales (42¢) and income contribution ($1.54) do not compare favorably with others.

The least desirable candidate for investment is *time recording devices* whose data compare very poorly with others in all the respects mentioned above.

Problem 12-2

a.

SPYRES MANUFACTURING COMPANY
Comparative Common-Size Income Statements

| | Year Ended December 31 | | % Increase |
	Yr 9	Yr 8	(Decrease)
Net sales	100.0%	100.0%	20.0%
Cost of goods sold	81.7%	86.0%	14.0%
Gross margin on sales	18.3%	14.0%	57.1%
Operating expenses	16.6%	10.2%	98.0%
Income before taxes	1.5%	3.8%	(52.6%)
Income taxes	0.4%	1.0%	(52.0%)
Income after taxes	1.1%	2.8%	(52.9%)

b. Performance in Year 9 was poor when compared with Year 8, and the trend unfavorable. One bright spot was the percentage of Cost of Goods Sold, which decreased in Year 9. However, Operating Expenses climbed sharply, which is somewhat surprising, for there is usually a larger fixed element of these costs than for Cost of Goods Sold. Management should check into the operating expenses, for if they had remained at the 10.2% level in Year 9, income would have been up favorably during Year 9. Operating expenses may have included a future-directed component such as advertising or training costs. The sharp improvement in gross margin may have been due to factors such as the liquidation LIFO inventory layers.

Problem 12-3

a.

	11	10
1. Depr. exp. to assets subject to depr. (A)	6.65%	6.04%
2. Effective interest rate on liabilities (B)	12.7%	11.0%
3. Effective tax rate (C)	42.7%	40.1%
4. COGS and other operating exp. to sales (D)	90.0%	90.0%
5. Net income to total revenues (E)	3.75%	3.36%

Computations:

1. Depreciation Expense [125]
    Gross PP&E [64] - Land*

    *   Land is included in PP&E on the balance sheet. Note 4 [146] discloses that the balance for land for both Years 10 and 11 is $31.0 million.

    Year 11: 125.2 ÷ (1914.6 - 31.0) = 6.65%

    Year 10: 103.5 ÷ (1745.6 - 31.0) = 6.04%

2.   Interest incurred[a]
        Liabilities subject to interest[b]

[a]   Interest expense on: 11   10
            LT debt   43.3   38.3
            ST debt and other   60.5   84.7
            Interest incurred [156]   103.8   123.0

[b]   ST debt [70]   80.6   343.2
        Current portion of LT debt [71]   32.9   32.3
        LT debt [79]   701.2   740.3
                                               814.7   1115.8

        Note: Other liabilities [80] are not considered.

    Year 11: 103.8 ÷ 814.7 = 12.7%

    Year 10: 123.0 ÷ 1115.8 = 11.0%

3.   Tax Expense [8]
        Income before Taxes [7]

    Year 11: 175.7 ÷ 411.5 = 42.7%

    Year 10: 153.5 ÷ 382.4 = 40.1%

4.   Operating Expenses [2 + 4]
        Sales [1]

    Year 11: (2839.7 + 2121.2) ÷ 5491.2 = 90%

    Year 10: (2685.9 + 1844.1) ÷ 5030.6 = 90%

5.   Net Income [11]
        Total Revenues [1]

    Year 11: 205.8 ÷ 5491.2 = 3.75%

    Year 10: 169.0 ÷ 5030.6 = 3.36%

b. There was an increase in depreciation as a percentage of assets subject to depreciation. Before drawing conclusions, the analyst should consider: (1) any change in the mix of depreciable assets, (2) additional years of data for Quaker, and (3) data for other firms in the industry.

The average interest rate paid on liabilities increased by 1.7%. This was primarily due to: (1) repayment of short-term debt near the end of Year 11, and (2) use of the year-end balance in calculating the ratio. If the average amount of short-term debt is used [147], the ratio is 10.4%. In addition, repayments of long-term debt were higher than additions to long-term debt during Year 11. Possibly the debt retired was at a lower interest rate than the new debt taken on.

Per note 16 [158C], the effective tax rate increased slightly primarily due to an increase in state and local taxes and certain miscellaneous items.

The ratio of COGS and operating expenses to sales remains unchanged. However, the disaggregated ratios show there is a decrease in COGS to sales from 53.4% to 51.7% and an increase in SGA to sales from 36.7% to 38.6%. MD&A is informative on these issues. Management cites "lower commodity and packaging costs" for the increase in gross margin. The increase in SGA is due to "higher planned advertising and merchandising."

Quaker Oats' net income to total revenues increased slightly in Year 11. This is due largely to a decrease in losses from discontinued operations and the reduction of interest expense.

Problem 12-4

	Product A		Product B	
	Yr 7	Yr 6	Yr 7	Yr 6
Number of units sold	10,000	7,000	600	900
Selling price per unit	$6.00	$5.00	$50.00	$50.00
Unit cost	$5.00	$4.00	$32.50	$30.00

Causes of change in gross margin:	Change
Product A sales:	
Increased quantity @ Yr 6 prices (3,000 @ $5)	$15,000
Price increase @ Yr 6 quantity (7,000 @ $1)	7,000
Quantity increase x price increase (3,000 @ $1)	3,000
Product A cost of goods sold:	
Increased quantity @ Yr 6 cost (3,000 @ $4)	(12,000)
Increased cost @ Yr 6 quantity (7,000 @ $1)	(7,000)
Cost increase x quantity increase (3,000 @ $1)	(3,000)
Net Increase in Gross Margin from Product A	$ 3,000
Product B sales:	
Decreased quantity @ Yr 6 prices (300 @ $50)	$(15,000)
Product B cost of goods sold:	
Decreased quantity @ Yr 6 cost (300 @ $30)	9,000
Increased cost @ Yr 6 quantity (900 @ $2.50)	(2,250)
Cost increase x quantity decrease (300 @ $2.50)	750
Net Decrease in Gross Margin from Product B	$ (7,500)

Summary:

Net increase from product A	$ 3,000
Less: Net decrease from product B	7,500
Net Decrease in Gross Margin	$ 4,500

Problem 12-5

a. Atlas: $12,000/(1-.4) = $12,000/.6 = $20,000

    Globe: $10,000/(1-.6) = $10,000/.4 = $25,000

b.

	Atlas	Globe
Sales	$18,000	$18,000
Variable costs	7,200	10,800
Fixed costs	12,000	10,000
Net loss	$(1,200)	$(2,800)

c.

	Atlas	Globe
Sales	$27,000	$27,000
Variable costs	10,800	16,200
Fixed costs	12,000	10,000
Net income	$ 4,200	$ 800

d.

	Atlas	Globe
Variable costs	$12,000	$18,000
Fixed costs	12,000	10,000
Total costs	$24,000	$28,000

Required percentage of accounts receivable to be collected to break even:

Atlas: $24,000/$30,000 = <u>80%</u>

Globe: $28,000/$30,000 = <u>93%</u>

e. At break-even point all costs--fixed and variable--are covered. Additional sales beyond the break-even point result in additional variable costs only.

	Atlas	Globe
Expected sales	$30,000	$30,000
Break-even sales	20,000	25,000
Additional sales	$10,000	$ 5,000
Additional variable costs:		
40% of $10,000	4,000	
60% 0f $5,000		3,000

f. <u>Additional net income</u>
Additional cost

Atlas: (10,000 - 4,000) ÷ 4,000 = <u>1.5</u>

Globe: (5,000 - 3,000) ÷ 3,000 = <u>.67</u>

g. Let S = break-even sales in dollars.

Atlas: $S - .4S - .1S - 12,000 = 10,000$
        $S = \underline{\$44,000}$

Globe: $S - .6S - .1S - 10,000 = 10,000$
        $S = \underline{\$66,667}$

h. Present	Atlas	Globe

	Atlas	Globe
Present		
Sales	$30,000	$30,000
Variable costs	12,000	18,000
Fixed costs	12,000	10,000
Income before bad debts	$ 6,000	$ 2,000
Bad debts	3,000	3,000
Net Income	$ 3,000	$(1,000)

	Atlas	Globe
Additional Investment		
Sales	$40,000	$40,000
Variable costs	16,000	24,000
Fixed costs	16,000	14,000
Income before bad debts	$ 8,000	$ 2,000
Bad debts	4,000	4,000
Net Income	$ 4,000	$(2,000)

i. A company with lower fixed costs will have a lower break-even point. This company is at an advantage in a highly competitive market. However, once the break-even point is reached, a company with lower variable costs will be in a much better position because every dollar increase in sales will contribute proportionally more margin due to increased operating leverage.

j. Atlas is in a better position because to realize a contribution margin of 50¢, it incurs only 40¢ in variable costs while Globe has to incur 60¢ in variable costs to realize only 30¢. (Bad debt expenses reduce the contribution margin.)

Problem 12-6

a.

Sales	$10,000,000
Variable costs:	
Cost of sales	6,000,000
Commissions	2,000,000
Contribution margin	$ 2,000,000

Contribution margin ratio = $2,000,000 ÷ $10,000,000 = 20%

Estimated break-even point = 100,000 ÷ .20 = $ 500,000

b. Variable expense percents:

Cost of sales	60%
Commissions	5%
Total	65%

Contribution margin ratio = 100% - 65% = 35%

Fixed costs:	
Sales manager	$ 160,000
3 salespersons @ $30,000 each	90,000
Administrative	100,000
Total	$ 350,000

Estimated break-even point = 350,000 ÷ .35 = $1,000,000

c.

Target income before income tax		$1,900,000
Fixed costs		100,000
Total		$2,000,000

Variable expense percents:

Cost of sales	60%
Commissions	25%
Total	85%

Contribution margin ratio = 100% - 85% = 15%

Estimated sales volume = $2,000,000 ÷ .15 = $13,333,333

d. Let S = sales volume

$$\frac{\$8,500,000}{\$10,000,000} S + \$100,000 = \frac{\$6,500,000}{\$10,000,000} S + \$350,000$$

$$.85 S + \$100,000 = .65 S + \$350,000$$
$$.20 S = \$250,000$$
$$S = \$1,250,000$$

Problem 12-7

a.

Income Tax Expense	
(1) 58.6	
(2) 16.7	
75.3	

Deferred Income Taxes (noncurrent)		
	167.7	Beg
(5) 5.2	16.7	(2)
(6) 11.7		
	167.5	End

Income Taxes Payable		
	20.3	Beg
(3) 0.7	58.6	(1)
(4) 3.8	11.7	(6)
plug 67.5		
	18.6	End

Tax Effect - Disc. Op.	
	0.7 (3)

Tax Effect - Disposal of Disc. Op.	
	3.8 (4)

Tax Effect - Currency Transl.	
	5.2 (5)

(1)	Income tax expense	58.6
	Income taxes payable	58.6

(2)	Income tax expense	16.7	
	Deferred income taxes		16.7

(3)	Income taxes payable	0.7	
	Tax effect - disc. op.		0.7

(4)	Income taxes payable	3.8	
	Tax effect - disposal of disc. op.		3.8

(5)	Deferred income taxes	5.2	
	Tax effect — currency transl.		5.2

(6)	Deferred income taxes	11.7	
	Income taxes payable		11.7
	To close account.		

b.   The plug figure needed to balance the Income Taxes Payable account is $67.5

c.   Year 2 income taxes paid (per SCF)   67.7
     Derived amount of taxes paid   <u>67.5</u>
     Difference   0.2

<u>Problem 12-8</u>

ZETA CORPORATION
Statement Accounting for Variation in Net Income
Year 6 Compared to Year 5

Items tending to increase net income:			*% change*
Increase in gross margin on sales:			
Increase in net sales:			
Net sales, Year 6	186,000		
Net sales, Year 5	<u>155,000</u>	31,000	20.0
Deduct increase in cost of goods sold:			
Cost of goods sold, 6	120,000		
Cost of goods sold, 5	<u>99,000</u>	21,000	21.2
Net increase in gross margin on sales:			
Gross margin, 6	66,000		
Gross margin, 5	<u>56,000</u>	10,000	17.9
Increase in equity in income (loss) of associated company:			
Equity in income, 6	2,000		
Equity in loss, 5	<u>(1,000)</u>	3,000	300.0
Decrease in loss of discontinued operations (net of taxes):			
Loss on disc. ops., 6	1,100		
Loss on disc. ops., 5	<u>1,200</u>	100	8.3
Increase in cumulative effect of change in accounting:			
Cumulative effect, 6	1,000		
Cumulative effect, 5	<u>-0-</u>	<u>1,000</u>	
Total of items tending to increase net income		14,100	

Items tending to decrease net income:
        Increase in S&A expense:
            S&A, 6   37,000
            S&A, 5   33,000   4,000   12.1
        Increase in interest expense:
            Interest expense, 6   10,000
            Interest expense, 5   6,000   4,000   66.7
        Increase in income taxes:
            Income taxes, 6   10,000
            Income taxes, 5   7,800   2,200   28.2
        Increase in minority interest:
            Minority interest, 6   200
            Minority interest, 5   -0-   200
        Increase in loss on disposal of discontinued
        operations:
            Loss on disposal, 6   700
            Loss on disposal, 5   -0-   700
Total of items tending to decrease net income   11,100

Net increase in net income:
        Net income, 6   10,000
        Net income, 5   7,000   3,000   42.9

Interpretation:

   (1)   ZETA has two "below the line" items--discontinued operations and a
          change in accounting principle. While net income increased by 42.9%,
          income from continuing operations increased by 31.7%. (Per note 1, the
          increase in Year 6 income from operations due to the change in
          inventory accounting was only $400.)
   (2)   Per note 3, ZETA acquired most of TRO Company effective December 31,
          Year 6. As the acquisition was accounted for as a purchase, the Year
          5 and 6 income statements do not reflect the results of TRO. Certain
          pro forma information is included in note 3.
   (3)   The 21.2% increase in COGS slightly exceeded the 20% increase in sales,
          leading to a lower gross profit margin despite the accounting change.
   (4)   The increase in equity in income of associated companies helped
          increase net income. The analyst shouls assess whether a dollar of
          income for associated companies is equivalent to a dollar of income for
          ZETA.
   (5)   S&A expenses rose less than sales, contributing to increased income.
   (6)   The increase in interest expense is matched by a similar increase in
          long-term debt.

Problem 12-9
a.

Income Taxes Payable			
(d)	2,700+X	2,000	Beg
		7,700	(b)
		X	(c)
		7,000	End

Deferred Income Taxes			
		2,000	Beg
		1,600	(a)
		3,600	End

Tax Expense		
(a)	1,600	
(b)	8,400	

Tax Effect - Disc. Op.		
	1,000	(b)

Tax Effect - Disposal of Disc. Op.		
	700	(6)

Tax Effect - Accounting Change		
(b)	1,000	

(a) Deferred tax provision (per note 5).

(b) Current tax provision including all parts from income statement. (Note: would be acceptable to make separate entries for each amount).

(c) Taxes payable acquired in purchase of TRO Company (not disclosed).

(d) Estimate of amount paid (plug). SCF states amount paid at $2,600.

b. The Year 6 deferred tax provision of $1,600 represents 50% (after tax) of the timing difference (which is due solely to depreciation per note 5). Therefore:

Depreciation for financial reporting	$6,000
Additional depreciation ($1,600 ÷ 50%)	3,200
Estimated depr. per tax return	$9,200

◄ Answers to Cases ►

<u>Case 12-1</u>

a.

ADAPTEC, INC.
Statement Accounting for Variation in Net Income
1996 Compared to 1995

Items tending to increase net income:			*% change*
Increase in gross profit:			
Increase in net revenues:			
Net revenues, 1996	659,347		
Net revenues, 1995	<u>466,194</u>	193,153	41.4
Deduct increase in cost of revenues:			
Cost of revenues, 1996	275,939		
Cost of revenues, 1995	<u>205,596</u>	70,343	34.2
Net increase in gross profit:			
Gross profit, 1996	383,408		
Gross profit, 1995	<u>260,598</u>	122,810	47.1
Increase in interest income:			
Interest income, 1996	12,694		
Interest income, 1995	<u>7,932</u>	4,762	60.0
Decrease in interest expense:			
Interest expense, 1996	840		
Interest expense, 1995	<u>1,179</u>	<u>339</u>	28.8
Total of items tending to increase net income		127,911	
Items tending to decrease net income:			
Increase in R&D expense:			
R&D expense, 1996	87,628		
R&D expense, 1995	<u>60,848</u>	26,780	44.0
Increase in sales & marketing expense:			
S&M expense, 1996	81,548		
S&M expense, 1995	<u>58,737</u>	22,811	38.8
Increase in general & admin. expense:			
G&A expense, 1996	35,784		
G&A expense, 1995	<u>23,229</u>	12,555	54.0
Increase in write-off of in-process technology:			
Write-off, 1996	52,313		
Write-off, 1995	<u>-0-</u>	52,313	---
Increase in provision for income taxes:			
Provision for I/T, 1996	34,614		
Provision for I/T, 1995	<u>31,135</u>	<u>3,479</u>	11.2
Total of items tending to decrease net income		117,938	
Net increase in net income:			
Net income, 1996	103,375		
Net income, 1995	<u>93,402</u>	9,973	10.7

Interpretation:

(1)   Increase in revenues exceeded increase in cost of revenues, resulting in large increase in gross profit. MD&A cites "increased revenues from

the Company's higher margin products" and "efficiencies in the manufacturing process."

(2) Interest income increased along with the increase in marketable securities. Interest expense decreased as the company continues to pat down its long-term debt.

(3) R&D expense increased more than revenues. This is a good sign as Adaptec must constantly upgrade its product line.

(4) The increases in sales & marketing and general & administrative expenses were not alarmingly high. As indicated in the common-size income statement on page 30 of the 1996 annual report, these items remained at the same percent of net revenues.

(5) The write-off of acquired in-process technology adversely impacted 1996 earnings. As Adaptec continues to acquire other companies in purchase transactions, similar charges will appear in future income statements.

b.

Provision for Income Taxes	
34,614	

Deferred Tax Assets (note 8)		
Beg	11,949	
note 8	6,137	
End	18,086	

Tax-related Current Liabilities (note 2)			
		5,746	Beg
plug	30,279	40,751	note 8
		16,218	End

Per note 2, Adaptec paid $32,869 in taxes in 1996. The figure derived in the T-account analysis ($30,279) is $2,590 lower.

c. 1. Geographic.

2. Income from operations is defined as "net revenues less cost of revenues and operating expenses incurred in supporting the revenues of each geographic area."

3. Write-offs of acquired in-process technology are included as a corporate-level item.

4. The "Singapore, Far East, Other" segment reports the largest intercompany sales because it includes the company's manufacturing facility.

5. Per note 9, intercompany sales "are made at arms-length prices." In such a case, segment profitability is not influenced by artificial forces such as management-determined transfer prices.

6.   The "United States" and "Singapore, Far East, Other" segments are clearly the largest.

United States:	1996	1995	1994
Growth in total revenues	29.7%	24.3%	---
Growth in identifiable assets	64.7%	(20.4)%	---
Operating income/Net revenues	16.4%	14.4%	14.1%
Operating income/Identifiable assets	50.1%	56.2%	35.2%

Given the growth in revenues and operating income, the 1995 decline in identifiable assets is unusual. Growth in the segment's revenues is less that the overall 41.4% growth from part a. Does the company need to expand other segments to maintain high growth? Operating income margin is increasing over time.

Singapore, Far East, Other:	1996	1995	1994
Growth in total revenues	132.4%	61.1%	---
Growth in identifiable assets	110.6%	65.1%	---
Operating income/Net revenues	17.2%	25.3%	19.3%
Operating income/Identifiable assets	29.7%	39.7%	31.0%

As most revenues are from intercompany sales, profitability data is not particularly important. A key figure is the growth in sales to customers, which increased from $382 in 1994 to $49,211 in 1996.

PETERSEN CORP.

	(1) $ of Total Consolidated Revenue				(2) % of Divisional Income to Total Income				(3) Divisional Income as a % of Revenue			
	1	2	3	4	1	2	3	4	1	2	3	4
Manufactured Engineered Products:												
Engineering equipment	28.1	18.3	16.8	17.0								
Other equipment	5.5	3.7	3.5	2.9								
Parts, supplies & services	27.5	18.4	17.3	17.2								
Total	61.1	40.4	37.6	37.1	52.5	30.7	43.5	40.7	5.7	6.0	12.6	11.3
Engineering and Erection Services:	--	--	6.3	14.3	--	--	5.8	12.0	--	--	10.0	8.7
International operations*	--	--	--	--	31.4	17.6	9.6	8.8	--	--	--	--
Total Environmental Systems Group	61.1	40.4	43.9	51.4	83.9	48.3	58.9	61.5	9.2	9.5	14.6	12.3
Graphics Group:												
Frye Copy Systems	23.6	17.3	16.1	15.3	20.2	15.6	13.2	13.6	5.7	7.2	9.0	9.2
Sinclair and Valentine	--	33.0	29.5	23.7	--	28.9	21.8	19.4	--	6.9	8.1	8.4
A. C. Garber	15.3	9.3	10.5	9.6	(4.1)	7.2	6.1	5.5	(1.8)	6.1	6.4	5.9
Total Graphics Group	38.9	59.6	56.1	48.6	16.1	51.7	41.1	38.5	2.8	6.9	8.0	8.2
Total revenues or divisional income	100.0	100.0	100.0	100.0	100.0	100.0	100.0	100.0	6.7	7.9	10.9	10.3

b. The Environmental Systems Group has generally declined in its contribution to total consolidated revenue except in Year 3 when the decline was reversed due to a strong increase in the revenue of the engineering and erection services division. The Graphics Group increased dollar revenue share strongly in Year 1 and has leveled off since. This increase is largely due to the acquisition of Sinclair and Valentine in Year 1.

Note that only income-related data is presented for international operations. In such a case, the analyst must carefully examine the related textual disclosures. In the case of Peterson Corp., these figures consist of royalty income and the Company's equity participation in the income before taxes of the international subsidiaries and affiliates of the group, neither of which are included in revenue.

While the Environmental Systems Group has declined overall in contribution to sales it has grown in contribution to enterprise income. Its income share is much larger than its share in revenues--this is due to greater profitability by the Environmental Systems Group and particularly the Manufactured Engineering Products where profitability (as measured by divisional income as a percentage of revenues) has been growing. While this profitability has declined somewhat from Year 2 to Year 3 it remains at a level considerably higher than the company as a whole.

Case 12-3

a. This case illustrates how poor presentation of tax information in financial statements can make the analyst's task more difficult.

Current and deferred taxes shown in the tabulation include *all* taxes from which taxes relating to discontinued operations and cumulative effect of change in accounting are deducted leaving only those taxes relating to continuing operations.

It is odd that even though there was a charge to income for deferred taxes in x6 the statement of cash flow shows a deduction for deferred taxes not providing cash.

Income Tax Expense ***			
(b)	42	8	(a)

Deferred Income Taxes			
		0	Beg
		42	(b)
		7	(e)
		49	End

Recoverable Income Taxes			
Beg	33		
(f)	23		
End	56		

Income Taxes Payable			
		114	Beg
(a)	8	12	(c)
(e)	7	59	(d)
(g)	71	23	(f)
		122	End

Taxes on Disc. Ops.	
(c) 12	

Tax Effect of Acctg. Change	
(d) 59	

*** alternative approach			
Curr. pay.	63	12	Disc Op
Deferred	42	59	Acctg Change
	34		

Year 6 Tax Entries:

(a)   Income taxes payable   8
            Income tax expense   8

Current taxes related to continuing operations are taxes currently payable of $63 (13+43+7) less $71 (12 related to discontinued operations plus 59 related to cumulative effect of change in accounting) or credit of $8.

(b)   Income tax expense   42
            Deferred income taxes—noncurrent   42

As indicated in tax note (37 + 1 + 4)

(c)   Tax on income from Discontinued Operations   12
            Income taxes payable   12

(d)   Tax effect of accounting change   59
            Income taxes payable   59

(e)   Income taxes payable   7
            Deferred income taxes—noncurrent   7

      To close out the account

(f)   Recoverable income taxes   23
            Income taxes payable   23

      To close out the account

(g)   PLUG—assumed paid

b.   From part a, a debit of $71 is needed to balance the Income Taxes Payable account.

Case 12-4

Income Tax Expense			
(a)	67.4	13.1	(b)
	54.3		

Deferred Income Taxes			
		294.5	Beg
(b)	13.1		
(e)	32.6		
		248.8	End

Income Tax Payable			
		50.0	Beg
(c)	6.0	67.4	(a)
(d)	34.8	32.6	(e)
SCF	41.9		
		67.3	End

Tax Effect - Disc. Ops.			
		6.0	(c)

Tax Effect - Acctg. Change			
		34.8	(d)

(a)   Income tax expense   67.4
          Income tax payable   67.4

(b)   Deferred income tax payable   13.1
          Income tax expense   13.1

(c)   Income tax payable   6.0
          Tax effect—disc operation   6.0

(d)   Income tax payable   34.8
          Tax effect—cum effect   34.8

(e)   Deferred inc tax payable   32.6
          Income tax payable   32.6

      To close out account

Case 12-5

a.

Income Tax Expense			
(a)	507,694	52,149	(b)
	455,545		

Deferred Income Taxes			
		409,090	Beg
(b)	52,149		
(f)	43		
(h)	9,653		
		347,245	End

Income Taxes Payable			
		234,338	Beg
(d)	78,151	507,694	(a)
(g)	19,000	74,068	(c)
plug	662,928	128,581	(e)
		9,653	(h)
		194,255	End

Tax Effect - Extraord. Item		
(c)	74,068	

Prepaid Income Taxes		
Beg	296,861	
(e)	128,581	
End	425,442	

Tax Effect - Acctg. Change		
	78,151	(d)

Additional PIC		
	19,000	(g)

Translation Adjustment		
	43	(f)

(a)	Income tax expense		507,694	
	Income tax payable			507,694
(b)	Deferred income tax		52,149	
	Income tax expense			52,149
(c)	Tax effect—Extraord. Item		74,068	
	Income tax payable			74,068
(d)	Income tax payable		78,151	
	Tax effect—disposal of disc op			78,151
(e)	Prepaid income tax		128,581	
	Income tax payable			128,581

To close out the account

(f)	Deferred income tax payable	43	
	Translation adjustment		43
(g)	Income tax payable	19,000	
	APIC-Tax effect (options)		19,000
(h)	Deferred income tax payable	9,653	
	Income tax payable		9,653

To close out the account.

b.
Year 2 income taxes paid (per SCF)	651,442
Taxes paid (part a)	662,928
Difference	11,486

The difference reflects a discrepancy in our understanding of the company's tax picture based on the disclosures provided in the financial statements. However, the difference is minor compared to the total reported amount of taxes paid.

◄ CHAPTER 13 ►

Earnings-Based Analysis and Valuation

◄ CHAPTER REVIEW ►

Earnings-based financial statement analysis is the focus of this chapter. The two previous chapters examine return and profitability analyses of financial statements. This chapter extends these analyses to consider earnings quality, persistence, valuation, and forecasting. Earnings quality refers to the relevance of earnings in measuring company performance. Its determinants include a company's business environment and its selection and application of accounting principles. Earnings persistence is broadly defined and includes the stability, predictability, variability, and trend in earnings. We also consider earnings management as a determinant of persistence. Our valuation analysis emphasizes earnings and other accounting measures for computing company value. Earnings forecasting considers earning power, estimation techniques, and monitoring mechanisms for analysis.

This chapter describes several useful tools for earnings-based financial analysis. We describe recasting and adjustment of financial statements. We also distinguish between recurring and nonrecurring, operating and nonoperating, and extraordinary and nonextraordinary earnings components. Throughout the chapter we emphasize the application of earnings-based analysis with several illustrations.

◄ CHAPTER OUTLINE ►

▸ **Earnings Quality**

    Measuring Earnings Quality

    Balance Sheet Analysis of Earnings Quality

    External Factors and Earnings Quality

▸ **Earnings Persistence**

    Recasting and Adjusting Earnings for Analysis

    Determinants of Earnings Persistence

    Persistence of Extraordinary Items in Earnings

▸ **Earnings-Based Valuation**

    Relation between Stock Prices and Accounting Data

    Fundamental Valuation Multiples

    Illustration of Earnings-Based Valuation

▸ **Earning Power and Forecasting for Valuation**

    Earning Power

    Earnings Forecasting

    Interim Reports for Monitoring and Revising Earnings Estimates

◄ Learning Objectives ►

- **Describe earnings quality, its measurement and its importance to the analysis of company performance.**

- **Analyze earnings persistence, its determinants and its relevance for earnings forecasting.**

- **Explain recasting and adjusting of earnings and earnings components for analysis.**

- **Describe earnings-based valuation and its relevance for financial analysis.**

- **Analyze earning power and its usefulness for forecasting and valuation.**

◄ Learning Objectives ►

■ **Explain earnings forecasting, its mechanics and its effectiveness in assessing company performance.**

■ **Analyze interim reports and consider their value in monitoring and revising earnings estimates.**

◄ Answers to Questions ►

1. The accounting process of income determination involves a high degree of estimation, and the amount of income reported can vary depending on the assumptions used and the various accounting principles applied. Furthermore, while a single cash outlay is made in a period, the benefits derived from it may cover a number of periods. Cash flows measure the actual inflows and outflows of cash which may not have been caused by transactions that occurred in the same period. Although the concept of income is the result of a series of complex assumptions and conventions and exists only as an approximation of such a measurement system, income is a much more valid measurement of earnings than cash flow.

2. The "quality" of earnings of an enterprise is a measure of the degree of care and unbiased judgment with which they are determined, the extent to which all important and necessary costs have been provided for and the variability which industry conditions subject these earnings to. Analysts must assess the quality of earnings in order to render them comparable to those of other enterprises.

   The quality of earnings depends, among other factors, on:

   (1)   The degree of conservatism with which the estimates of present and future conditions are arrived at. That is, the degree of risk that real estimates or assumptions may prove over-optimistic or downright unwarranted and misleading.

   (2)   Management's discretion in applying GAAP. This requires the analysis of discretionary and future directed costs.

   (3)   The relation between earnings and business risk. The stability, and the growth trend of earnings as well as the predictability of factors which may influence their future levels.

3. Discretionary costs are outlays which management can vary to some extent from period to period in order to conserve resources and/or to influence reported income. Two important categories of discretionary costs are repairs and maintenance and advertising.

   Discretionary costs are readily subject to manipulation by managements who may desire to present a good earnings picture when operational performance is poor in fact. The analyst should realize that an excessive "savings" in the discretionary costs in the current year will inevitably affect future earnings adversely.

4. The significance and the potential value of research and development costs is among the most difficult elements of the financial statements to analyze and interpret. Yet they are important not only because of their relative size but even more so because of their significance for the projection of future results. The analyst must pay careful attention to research and development costs and to the absence of such costs. In many enterprises they represent substantial costs, much of them of a fixed nature, and they can represent the key to future success or failure. We must make a careful distinction between what can be quantified in this area, and consequently analyzed, and what cannot be quantified and must consequently be evaluated in qualitative terms.

   Research and development costs represent a substantial amount in many enterprises. While a quantitative measure of the sizes of expenses is not difficult, it is often difficult to evaluate the quality of research and development costs and their effect on future earnings. There seems to be no clear-cut definition of "research"; therefore, it may not be meaningful to compare the quality of the research and development costs of two companies. The analyst should, in addition to the quantitative evaluation, evaluate such qualitative factors as the caliber of the research staff and organization, the eminence of its leadership, as well as the commercial results of their efforts. Also to be considered is whether the research and development is government-sponsored or company-sponsored.

5. The carrying amounts of most assets appearing in the balance sheet ultimately enter the cost streams of the income statement. Therefore, whenever assets are overstated, the income, both present and cumulative, is overstated because it has been relieved of charges needed to bring such assets down to realizable value. The converse should also hold true, that is, to the extent to which assets are understated, the income, current and cumulative, is also understated.

For similar reasons as above, an overstatement of income can occur because the latter is relieved of charges required to bring the provision or the liabilities up to their proper amounts. Conversely, an overprovision of present and future liabilities or losses results in the understatement of income or in the overstatement of losses.

6. The assets and liabilities of an enterprise hold important clues to an assessment of both the validity and the quality of its earnings. Thus, the analysis of the balance sheet is an important complement to the other approaches of income analysis discussed in the book.

The importance we attach to the amounts at which assets are carried on the balance sheet is due to the fact that, with few exceptions such as cash and land, the cost of most assets enters ultimately the cost stream of the income statement. Thus, we can state the following as a general proposition: Whenever assets are overstated the income, both present and cumulative, is overstated because it has been relieved of charges needed to bring such assets down to realizable values. Similarly, an understatement of provisions and liabilities will result in an overstatement of income because the latter is relieved of charges required to bring the provision or the liabilities up to their amounts. For example, an understatement of the provision for income taxes, product warranties, or pension costs means that income, current and cumulative, is overstated.

Conversely, an overprovision for present and future liabilities or losses results in the understatement of income or in the overstatement of losses. Provisions for future costs and losses which are excessive in amount represent attempts to shift the burden of costs and expenses from future income statements to that of the present.

Bearing in mind the general proposition regarding the effect on income of the amounts at which assets and liabilities are carried in the balance sheet, the critical analysis and evaluation of such amounts represents an important check on the validity of reported income.

7. It is well known that various degrees of risk attach to the probability of the future realization of different types of assets. For example, the future realization of accounts receivable has generally a higher degree of probability than has the realization of deferred research and development costs. Moreover, the future realization of inventory costs can, generally, be predicted with greater certainty than can the future realization of goodwill or deferred start-up costs. As a result, the analysis of the assets carried in the balance sheet by risk-class or risk-category is an important measure of the quality of reported income. Stated another way, if the income determination process results in the deferral of outlays and costs which carry a high degree of risk that they may not prove realizable in the future, then that income is of a lower quality than income which does not involve the creation of such high-risk assets.

8. a. The validity of the sales figure depends on the proper valuation of the accounts receivable which result from it. This valuation must recognize the risk of default in payment. Risk of default should be evaluated and a proper amount of bad debt provision should be charged to income. The relative level of accounts receivable and its relationship to sales can hold clues to improve quality. If an increase in accounts receivable represents merely a shifting of inventory from the company to its customers because of aggressive sales promotion or costly inventories, then these sales accomplish nothing more than "borrowing from the total and thus reduce earnings quality."

b. Overstated inventories lead to overstated profits. In addition to various recording errors, the errors in valuing inventory have a significant effect on reported income. The basic problem arises when costs which should have been written off to expense are retained in the inventory accounts resulting in an overstatement of inventory. Such an overstatement of inventory will result in an overstatement of current income and understatement of future income.

c. The quality of income depends very importantly on the nature of deferred charges. Deferred charges involve estimates of future probabilities and developments, more than any other assets. Inaccurate estimates frequently result in substantial charges in later years, while the incomes in years prior to the one in which the charge occurs are overstated. The risk of failure to attain expectations is relatively higher in the case of deferred charges than in the case of other assets.

9. The concept of earnings quality is so broad that it encompasses many additional factors which can make earnings more reliable or more desirable. These external factors include:

* The effect of changing price levels on the measurement of earnings. In times of rising price levels the inclusion of "inventory profits" or the understatement of expenses such as depreciation lowers in effect the reliability of earnings and hence their quality.

* The quality of foreign earnings is affected by factors such as difficulties and uncertainties regarding the repatriation of funds, currency fluctuations, the political and social climate as well as local customs and regulation. With regard to the latter, the inability to dismiss personnel in some countries in effect converts labor costs into fixed costs.

* Regulation provides another example of external factors which can affect earnings quality. For example, the regulatory environment of a public utility can affect the quality of its earnings if an unsympathetic or even hostile regulatory environment causes serious lags in obtaining rate relief.

* The stability and reliability of earnings sources also affect earnings quality. Defense-related revenues can be regarded as nonrecurring in time of war and affected by political uncertainties in peacetime.

* Finally, some analysts regard complexity of operations and difficulties in their analysis (e.g., highly diversified companies) as factors that negatively affect the quality of earnings.

10. The objective of recasting the income statement is the determination of level of earnings of a given period so that the stable, normal, and continuing elements in the income statement can be separated and distinguished from random, erratic, unusual, or nonrecurring elements which require separate analytical treatment or consideration. Moreover, such recasting also aims at identifying those elements included in the income statement of a given period which should more properly be included in the operating results of one or more prior periods.

11. The analyst will find data needed for the analysis of the results of operations and for their recasting and adjustment in:

* The income statement which is generally subdivided into the following:
    Income from continuing operations
    Income from discontinued operations
    Extraordinary gains and losses
    Cumulative effect of changes in accounting principles.

* The other financial statements and the footnotes thereto.

* Textual disclosures found throughout the published report, including MD&A.

The analyst may also find unusual items segregated within the income statement (generally on a pretax basis) but their disclosure is optional. Such disclosure may not include items which the analyst may regard as significant, noteworthy or unusual and consequently the analyst will consult all the above-mentioned sources as well as, if possible, management in order to obtain the needed facts. These will include facts which affect the comparability and the interpretation of income statements, such as product-mix changes, production innovations, strikes, and raw material shortages which may or may not be included in management's mandatory discussion and analysis of the results of operations.

12. Once the analyst has secured as much information as is possible to obtain, the income statements of a number of years (generally at least five) are recast and adjusted in such a way as to facilitate their future analysis, to evaluate the trend of earnings, as well as to aid in determining the average earning power of the enterprise for the period. While this procedure can be accomplished in one statement it is simpler and clearer to subdivide it into two distinct steps: (1) recasting and (2) adjusting.

The recasting process aims at rearranging the items within the income statement in such a way as to provide the most meaningful detail and the most relevant format needed by the analyst. At this stage the individual items in the income statement may be rearranged, subdivided or tax effected but the total must reconcile to the net income of each period as reported.

The analytical reclassification of items within a period will help in the evaluation of the earnings level. For example, discretionary and other noteworthy expenses should be segregated. The same applies to items such as equity in income or loss of unconsolidated subsidiaries or associated companies which are usually shown net of tax. Items shown in the pretax category must be removed together with their tax effect if they are to be shown below normal "income from continuing operations."

Expanded tax disclosure enables the analyst to segregate factors which reduce taxes as well as those which increase them, enabling an analysis of the degree to which these factors are of a recurring nature. All material permanent differences and credits, such as the investment tax credit, should be included. The analytical procedure involves computing taxes at the statutory rate (currently 35 percent) and deducting tax benefits such as investment tax credits, capital gains rates or tax-free income, and adding factors such as additional foreign taxes, nontax-deductible expenses and state and local taxes (net of federal tax benefit). Immaterial items can be considered in one lump sum labeled as "other."

Analytically recast income statements will contain as much detail as is needed for analysis and are supplemented by explanatory footnotes.

13. Based on data developed in the recast income statements as well as on other available information, certain items of income or loss are assigned to the period to which they most properly belong. This is the adjustment process.

The reassignment of extraordinary items or unusual items (net of tax) to other years must be done with care. For example, the income tax benefit of the carryforward of operating losses should generally be moved to the year in which the loss occurred. The costs or benefits from the settlement of a law suit may relate to one or more preceding years. The gain or loss on disposal of discontinued operations will usually relate to the results of operations over a number of years.

If possible, all years under analysis should be placed on a comparable basis when a change in accounting principle or accounting estimate occurs. If, as is usually the case, the new accounting principle is the desirable one, prior years should, if possible, be restated to the new method, or a notation made regarding a lack of comparability in certain respects. This procedure will result in a redistribution of the "cumulative effect of change in accounting principle" to affected prior years. Changes in estimates can be accounted for only prospectively and generally accepted accounting principles prohibit prior year restatements except in certain specified cases. The analyst's ability to place all years on a comparable basis will depend on availability of information.

Before the trend in earnings can be evaluated it is necessary to obtain the best approximation possible of the earnings level of each year. All items in the income statement must be considered and none can be excluded or "dropped by the wayside." For example, if it is decided that an item in the income statement does not properly belong in the year in which it appears it may be either:

(1)   Shifted (net of tax) to the result of one or a number of other years, or

(2)   If it cannot be identified with another specific year or years, it must be included in the average earnings of the period under analysis.

14.   Analysts must be alert to accounting distortions designed to affect trends. Some of the most common and most pervasive manipulative practices in accounting are designed to affect the presentation of earnings trends. These manipulations are based on the assumptions, generally true, that the trend of income is more important than its absolute size, that retroactive revisions of income already reported in prior periods have little, if any, market effect on security prices and that once a company has incurred a loss, the size of the loss is not as significant as the fact that the loss has been incurred. These assumptions and the propensities of some managements to use accounting as a means of improving the appearance of the earnings trend has led to techniques which can be broadly described as "earnings management."

A number of requirements must be met by the earnings management process so as to distinguish it from outright fraudulent reporting. This process is a rather sophisticated device. It does not rely on outright or patent falsehoods and distortions, but rather uses the wide leeway existing in accounting principles and their interpretation in order to achieve its ends. It is usually a matter of form rather than one of substance. Consequently, it does not involve a real transaction (e.g., postponing an actual sale to another accounting period in order to shift revenue) but only a redistribution of credits or charges among periods. The general objective is to moderate income variability over the years by shifting income from good years to bad years, by shifting future income to the present (in most cases presently reported earnings are more valuable than those reported at some future date) or vice versa.

15.   Earnings management may take many forms. Hereunder are listed some forms to which the analyst should be particularly alert:

*   Changing accounting methods or assumptions with the objective of improving or modifying reported results. For example, to offset the effect on earnings of slumping sales and of other difficulties, Chrysler Corp. revised upwards the assumed rate of return on its pension portfolio, thus increasing income significantly. Similarly, Union Carbide improved results by switching to a number of more liberal accounting alternatives.

*   Misstatements, by various methods, of inventories as a means of redistributing income among the years.

*   The offsetting of extraordinary credits by identical or nearly identical extraordinary charges as a means of removing an unusual or sudden injection of income which may interfere with the display of a growing earnings trend.

16.   There are powerful incentives at work which motivate companies and their employees to engage in income smoothing. Companies in financial difficulties may be motivated to engage in such practices for what they see and justify as their battle for survival. Successful companies will go to great lengths to uphold a hard-earned and well-rewarded image of earnings growths by smoothing those earnings artificially. Moreover, compensation plans or other incentives based on earnings will motivate managements to accelerate the recognition of income by anticipating revenues or deferring expenses.

Analysts must appreciate the great variety of incentives and objectives which lead managements and, at times, second-tier management without the knowledge of top management, to engage in practices ranging from smoothing to the outright falsification of income.

It has been suggested that smoothing is justified if it can help a company report earnings closer to its true "earning power" level. Such is not the function of financial reporting. As we have repeatedly seen in this work, the analyst will be best served by a full disclosure of periodic results and the components which make these up. It is up to the analyst to average, smooth, or otherwise adjust reported earnings in accordance with specific analytical purposes.

The accounting profession has earnestly tried to promulgate rules that discourage practices such as the smoothing of earnings. However, given the powerful propensities of companies and of their owners and employees to engage in such practices, analysts must realize that, where there is a will to smooth or even distort earnings, ways to do so are available and will be found. Consequently, particularly in the case of companies where incentives to smooth are likely to be present, analysts should analyze and scrutinize accounting practices in order to satisfy themselves to the extent possible, regarding the integrity of the income-reporting process.

17. Managements are almost always concerned with the amount of net results of the enterprise as well as with the manner in which these periodic results are reported. This concern is reinforced by a widespread belief that most investors accept the reported net income figures, as well as the modifying explanations which accompany them, as true indices of performance. Extraordinary gains and losses often become the means by which managements attempt to modify the reported operating results and the means by which they try to explain these results. Quite often these explanations are subjective and are slanted in a way designed to achieve the impact and impression desired by management.

18. The basic objectives in the identification and evaluation of extraordinary items by the analyst are:

* To determine whether a particular item is to be considered "extraordinary" for purposes of analysis; that is, whether it is so unusual and nonrecurring in nature that it requires special adjustment in the evaluation of current earnings levels and of future earnings possibilities.

* To decide what form the adjustment for items which are considered as "extraordinary" in nature, should take.

19. *Nonrecurring Operating Gains or Losses.* By "operating" we usually identify items connected with the normal and usual operations of the business. The concept of normal operations is more widely used than understood and is far from clear and well defined. Nonrecurring operating gains or losses are, then, gains or losses connected with or related to operations that recur infrequently and/or unpredictably. Examples include: (1) foreign operations giving rise to exchange adjustments because of currency fluctuations or devaluations, and (2) an unusually severe decline in market prices requires a large writedown of inventory from cost to market.

The analyst in considering how to treat nonrecurring operating gains and losses would do best to recognize the fact of inherent abnormality in business and treat them as belonging to the results of the period in which they are reported.

Recurring Nonoperating Gains or Losses. This category includes items of a nonoperating nature that recur with some frequency. Examples include recurring exchange adjustments, gains and losses on sales of fixed assets, interest income, and the rental received from employees who rent company-owned houses.

While items in this category are often classified as "unusual" in published financial statements, the narrow definition of "nonoperating" which they involve as well as their recurrent nature are good reasons why they should not be excluded from current results by the analyst.

Nonrecurring, Nonoperating Gains or Losses. Of the three categories, this one possesses the greatest degree of "abnormality." Not only are the events here nonrepetitive and unpredictable, but they do not fall within the sphere of normal operations. In many cases these events are not unintended or unplanned. However, they can rarely be said to be totally unexpected. Business is ever subject to the risk of sudden adverse events and to random shocks, be they natural or man-made. In the same manner, business transactions are also subject to unexpected windfalls. Examples in this category include substantial uninsured casualty losses unrelated to normal or expectable operating risks. It can be seen readily that while the above occurrences are, in most cases, of a nonrecurring nature, their relation to the operations of a business varies. All are occurrences in the regular course of business. Even the assets destroyed by acts of nature were acquired for operating purposes and thus were subject to all possible risks.

Of the three categories this one comes closest to meeting the criterion of being "extraordinary." Nevertheless, truly unique events are very rare. What looks at the time as unique may, in the light of experience, turn out to be the symptom of a new set of circumstances. The analyst must bear in mind such possibilities but, barring evidence to the contrary, he/she can regard items in this category as extraordinary in nature and thus omit them from the results of operations of a single year. They are, nevertheless, part of the longer term record of results of the enterprise. Thus, they enter the computation of average earnings, and the propensity of the enterprise to incur such gains or losses must be considered in the projection of future average earnings.

20. a. Whenever there is a gain (whether it is recorded as extraordinary or not), there is an increase in resources. Similarly, a loss results in a reduction of resources. In this sense, an extraordinary gain or loss is not different from a normal or ordinary gain or loss.

    Once an asset is written off as a result of extraordinary loss, that asset will not be available in the future to generate revenues. Conversely, an extraordinary gain will result in an addition of resources on which a future return can be expected. Therefore, the financial analyst should measure the potential effect of the extraordinary events on future earnings and evaluate the likelihood of the occurrence of events causing extraordinary items.

    b. One implication frequently associated with the reporting of extraordinary gains and losses is that they have not resulted from a "normal" or "planned" activity of management and that, consequently, they should not be used in the evaluation of management performance. The analyst should seriously question such a conclusion.

    What is "normal" activity in relation to management's deliberate actions? Whether we talk about the purchase or sale of securities, assets not used in operations, or divisions and subsidiaries that definitely relate to operations, we talk about actions deliberately taken by management with specific purposes in mind. Such actions require, if anything, more consideration or deliberation than ordinary everyday operating decisions because they are usually special in nature and involve substantial amounts of money. The results of such activities always qualify or enhance the results of "normal" operations, thus yielding the final net results.

21. No. Management is entrusted with the control of all assets of an entity in every possible way, including extraordinary events. Their responsibility is not confined to "normal" operations only and we can generally assume that every action taken by the management has some specific purpose in mind, be it "normal operations" or "abnormal operations," to enhance the results of the enterprise. It is extremely rare to see a business event which can be termed completely unexpected or unforeseeable. When it comes to the assessment of results that really count and results that build or destroy value, the distinction of what is normal and what is not fades into insignificance.

22. From a strictly mathematical point of view, the accounting-based equity valuation model is impervious to accounting manipulations under the clean surplus relation. Firms that overstate net income will have higher book values, which will reduce future abnormal earnings. Firms with conservatively measured net income will report lower book values, which will increase future abnormal earnings.

    On the other hand, projections of future profitability are based on current and past financial results. To the extent that accounting manipulations can affect net income forecasts, these manipulations will affect firm valuation.

23. a. The major determinants of the PB ratio are (1) future ROCE, (2) growth in book value, and (3) risk. The major determinants of the PE ratio are: (1) the level of current earnings, (2) trend in future abnormal earnings, and (3) risk.

    b. As illustrated in the chart on page 644 of the text, the joint values of the PB and PE ratios give important insights into the market's expectations regarding earnings growth and future ROCE. To the extent that the analyst can "outguess" the market, he/she will be able to identify mispriced securities.

24. Forecasting must be differentiated from extrapolation. The latter is based on an assumption of the continuation of an existing trend and involves, more or less, a mechanical extension of the trend into the uncharted territory of the future. Forecasting, on the other hand, is based on a careful analysis of as many individual components of income and expense as is possible and a considered estimate of future size taking into consideration interrelationships among the components as well as probable future conditions. Thus, forecasting requires as much detail as is possible to obtain.

25. MD&A often contains a wealth of information on management's views and attitudes as well as on factors which can influence enterprise operating performance. Consequently, the analyst may find much information in these analyses to aid in the forecasting process. Moreover, while not requiring it, the SEC encourages the inclusion in these discussions of forward-looking information.

26. The best possible estimate of the average earnings of an enterprise, which can be expected to be sustained and to repeat with some degree of regularity over a span of future years, is referred to as its earning power. Except in specialized cases, earning power is universally recognized as the single most important factor in the valuation of an enterprise. Most valuation approaches entail in one form or another the capitalization of earning power by a factor or multiplier which takes into account the cost of capital as well as future expected risks and rewards.

The importance of "earning power" is such that most analyses of the income and related financial statements have as one of their ultimate objectives the determination of its amount. Earning power is a concept of financial analysis, not of accounting. It focuses on stable and recurring elements and aims to arrive at the best possible estimate of repeatable average earnings over a span of future years. Accounting, as we have seen, can supply much of the essential information for the computation of earning power. However, the process is one involving knowledge, judgment, experience as well as a specialized investing or lending point of view.

Investors and lenders look ultimately to future cash flows as sources of rewards and safety. Accrual accounting, which underlies income determination, aims to relate sacrifices and benefits to the periods in which they occur. In spite of its known shortcomings, this framework represents the most reliable and relevant indicator of longer term future probabilities of average cash inflows and outflows presently known.

27. Interim financial statements, most frequently issued on a quarterly basis, are designed to fill the reporting gap between the year-end statements. They are used by decision makers as means of updating current results as well as in the prediction of future results.

If a year is a relatively short period of time in which to account for results of operations for many analytical purposes, then trying to confine the measurement of results to a three-month period involves all the more problems and imperfections. Generally, the estimating and adjustment procedures at interim financial statement dates are performed much more crudely than for year-end financial statements. The net result is that the interim reports are less accurate than year-end reports which are audited. Another serious limitation to which the interim reports are subject is the seasonality of activities to which most businesses are subject. Sales may be unevenly distributed over the year and this tends to distort comparisons among the quarterly results of a single year. It also presents problems in the allocation of many costs. Similar allocation problems are encountered with the extraordinary and other nonrecurring elements.

Despite the limitations mentioned above, interim reports can provide useful information if the analysts are fully aware of the possible pitfalls and use them with extreme care. The analyst can overcome some of the seasonality problem by considering in the analysis not merely the results of a single quarter but rather the year-to-date cumulative results.

28. If, as we have seen, a year is a relatively short period of time in which to account for results of operations, then trying to confine the measurement of results to a three month period involves all the more problems and imperfections. For this and other reasons the reporting of interim earnings is subject to limitations and distortions. The intelligent use

of reported interim results requires that we have a full understanding of these possible problem areas and limitations. The following is a review of some of the basic reasons for these problems and limitations as well as their effect on the determination of reported interim results:

Year-End Adjustments. The determination of the results of operations for a year requires a great many estimates, as well as procedures such as accruals and the determination of inventory quantities and carrying values. These procedures can be complex, time consuming, and costly. Examples of procedures requiring a great deal of data collection and estimation includes estimation of the percentage of completion of contracts, determination of cost of work in process, the allocation of under- or over-absorbed overhead for the period and the determination of inventory under the LIFO method. The complex, time-consuming, and expensive nature of these procedures can mean that they are performed much more crudely during interim periods and are often based on records which are less complete than their year-end counterparts. The result inevitably is a less accurate process of income determination which, in turn, may require year-end adjustments which can modify substantially the interim results already reported.

Seasonality. Many enterprises experience at least some degree of seasonality in their activities. Sales may be unevenly distributed over the year and so it may be with production and other activities. This tends to distort comparisons among the quarterly results of a single year. It also presents problems in the allocation of many budgeted costs, such as advertising, research and development, and repairs and maintenance.

29. The mayor disclosure requirements by the SEC with regard to interim reports are:

    (1)   Comparative quarterly and year-to-date abbreviated income statement data--this information may be labeled "unaudited" and must also be included in annual reports to shareholders.
    (2)   Year-to-date statements of cash flows;
    (3)   Comparative balance sheets;
    (4)   Increased pro forma information on business combinations accounted for as purchases;
    (5)   Conformity with the principles of accounting measurement as set forth in the professional pronouncements on interim financial reports;
    (6)   Increased disclosure of accounting changes with a letter from the registrant's independent public accountanting firm stating whether or not it judges the changes to be preferable;
    (7)   Management's narrative analysis of the results of operations, explaining the reasons for material changes in the amount of revenue and expense items from one quarter to the next.
    (8)   Indications as to whether a Form 8-K was flied during the quarter reporting either unusual charges or credits to income or a change of auditors;
    (9)   Signature of the registrant's chief financial of fleer or chief accounting officer.

    The objectives behind these disclosures are:

    (1)   They will assist investors in understanding the pattern of corporate activities throughout a fiscal period.
    (2)   Presentation of such quarterly data will supply information about the trend of business operations over segments of time which are sufficiently short to reflect business turning points.

30. While there have been some notable recent improvements in the reporting of interim results, the analyst must remain aware that accuracy of estimation and the objectivity of determinations are and remain problem areas which are inherent in the measurement of results of very short periods. Also, the limited association of auditors with interim data, while lending as yet some unspecified degree of assurance, cannot be equated to the degree of assurance which is associated with fully audited financial statements. SEC insistence that the professional pronouncements on interim statements be adhered to should offer analysts some additional comfort. However, not all principles promulgated on the subject of interim financial statements result in presentations useful to the analyst. For example, the inclusion of extraordinary items in the results of the quarter in which they occur will require careful adjustment to render them meaningful for purposes of analysis.

While the normalization of expenses is a reasonable intraperiod accounting procedure, the analyst must be aware of the fact that there are no rigorous standards or rules governing its implementation and that it is, consequently, subject to possible abuse. The shifting of costs between periods is generally easier than the shifting of sales; and, therefore, a close analysis of sales may yield a more realistic clue to a company's true state of affairs for an interim period.

Some problems of seasonality in interim results of operations can be overcome by considering in the analysis, not merely the results of a single quarter, but also the year-to-date cumulative results which incorporate the results of the latest available quarter. This is the most effective way of monitoring the results of an enterprise and bringing to bear on its analysis the latest data on operations that are available.

◄ Answers to Exercises ►

Exercise 13-1

a.

	Yr 9	Yr 10	Total 2 years	Average 2 years	Yr 11
Revenues [1]	4879.4	5030.6	9910.0	4955	5491.2
PP&E (net) [66]	959.6	1154.1	2113.7	1056.9	1232.7
Maintenance & Repairs [155]	93.8	96.6	190.4	95.2	96.1
% of Maintenance & Repairs to Revenue	1.92%	1.92%	1.92%	1.92%	1.75%
% of Maintenance & Repairs to PP&E, net	9.77%	8.37%	9.01%	9.01%	7.80%

b.   The percentage of maintenance and repairs to revenues in Year 11 was lower than the percentage for the average. Assuming that the 2-year average is representative of a longer period average, it would appear that management may have been saving on discretionary costs. The percentage of maintenance and repairs to net PP&E may also signal an effort by management to lower costs.

For example, assume total savings equals the difference between the actual expenditure on maintenance and repairs in Year 11 and the amount of spending required to equate the rate of spending implicit in the average percentage to revenues for the preceding years.

```
Implicit spending = 5491.2 x 1.92% =    105.4
Actual spending in Year 11 =              96.1
"Savings"                                  9.3   (8.8% of implicit spending)

PPE (net) x Ave % = 1232.7 x 9.01% =     111.1
Actual                                    96.1
"Savings"                                 15.0   (13.5% of implicit spending)
```

Exercise 13-2

a. The president is correct in designating most of the items described as normal operating expenses which good managements should expect and anticipate. Many views still prevail on how extraordinary items should be presented. They differ with differing conceptions regarding the purposes of the income statement and those of financial statement analysis. Basically, preparers of the income statement should recognize that they have a wide and varied audience and that it is best to give the reader all the information which he or she may need to arrive at an income figure adjusted for his or her own purposes and to abstain from built-in interpretations in such an income statement. The designation of an item of gain or loss as extraordinary carries with it an interpretative message. Consequently, only in those relatively rare cases when an item is both nonoperating and nonrecurring may its designation as extraordinary (based on the preparer's firsthand knowledge of attending circumstances) be useful to the user of financial statements.

b. To qualify for the "extraordinary" presentation category in the income statement the item must be *both* unusual *and* non-recurring in nature. However, the classification of an item as extraordinary for accounting purposes is often dictated by considerations which are not relevant to the objectives of the analyst. Therefore, each analyst should establish his/her own criteria for the classification to suit his/her particular analytical purpose and, if so, how to adjust for it. Some of the frequently used guidelines are:

(1) Nonrecurring operating gains and losses,
(2) Recurring nonoperating gains and losses,
(3) Nonrecurring, nonoperating gains and losses.

c. 1. No. This is an expected business event, although it may not be predictable. It is not different from other events such as increase of import duties and taxes.
    2. No. It may be "nonrecurring," however, it is expected in business.
    3. No. It indicates superior performance by competitors--a frequent occurrence.
    4. No. Tax is legitimate, unavoidable business cost and any change in taxation should affect other companies in the industry as well.
    5. No. Strikes may not be an annual event; however, they are a recurring operational possibility.
    6. No. It is a "nonrecurring" cost of an operating nature.
    7. No. It can occur in any business and it reflects management's planning and judgment.
    8. No. This danger is always inherent in research and development.
    9. No. Same as above.
    10. No. It reveals a failure of credit policy.
    11. No. Capital gains and losses resulting from rental cars should be regarded as operating items of a car rental company.
    12. No. The analyst, however, should carefully analyze the circumstances in order to determine if it qualifies under "nonrecurring" and "nonoperating" event.
    13. No. Amounts involved are generally minor and the operation of the houses should be viewed as a part of the whole operation.

14. Yes. However, it may inform the analyst of the unpreparedness of the management for such event.
15. Yes. It may qualify as a "nonrecurring, nonoperational" event.
16. Yes. Same as above.

Exercise 13-3

a. Many views still prevail on how extraordinary items should be presented. They differ with differing conceptions regarding the purposes of the income statement and those of financial statement analysis. Basically, preparers of the income statement should recognize that they have a wide and varied audience and that it is best to give the reader all the information which he may need to arrive at an income figure adjusted for his/her own purposes and to abstain from built-in interpretations in such an income statement. The designation of an item of gain or loss as extraordinary carries with it an interpretative message. Consequently, only in those relatively rare cases when an item is both non-operating and nonrecurring may its designation as extraordinary (based on the preparer's firsthand knowledge of attending circumstances) be useful to the user of financial statements.

c. The analyst must assess the importance of items presented as extraordinary, the probability of their recurrence, and the likelihood that they represent a symptom of operating conditions which are likely to prevail more in the future than they have in the past. On the basis of such an evaluation he or she will decide how to consider them in the computation of average earnings, average coverage ratios, and average returns on investment, in the evaluation of managements and in the projection of earnings. No further generalization can be very useful in this area.

Exercise 13-4

a. Sales and other revenues should be recognized for interim financial statement purposes in the same manner as revenues are recognized for annual reporting purposes. This means normally at the point of sale or, in the case of services, at completion of the earnings process.

In the case of industries whose sales vary greatly due to the seasonal nature of business, revenues should still be recognized as earned, but a disclosure should be made of the seasonal nature of the business in the notes.

In the case of long-term contracts recognizing earnings on the percentage-of-completion basis, the current state of completion of the contract should be estimated and revenue recognized at interim dates in the same manner as at the normal year end.

b. For interim reporting purposes, product costs (costs directly attributable to the production of goods or services) should be matched with the product and associated revenues in the same manner as for annual reporting purposes.

Period costs (costs not directly associated with the production of particular goods or service) should be charged to earnings as incurred or allocated among interim periods based on an estimate of time expired, benefit received, or other activity associated with the particular interim period(s). Also, if a gain or loss occurs during an interim period and is a type that would not be deferred at year end, the gain or loss should be recognized in full in the interim period in which it occurs. Finally, in allocating period costs among interim periods, the basis for allocation must be supportable and may not be based on merely an arbitrary assignment of costs between interim periods.

The APB allowed for some variances from the normal method of determining cost of goods sold and valuation of inventories at interim dates in *Opinion Number 28*, but these methods are allowable only at interim dates and must be fully disclosed in a footnote to the financial statements. Some companies use the gross profit method of estimating cost of goods sold and ending inventory at interim dates instead of taking a complete physical inventory. This is an allowable procedure at interim dates, but the company must disclose the method used and any significant variances that subsequently result from reconciliation of the results obtained using the gross profit method and the results obtained after taking the annual physical inventory.

At interim dates, companies using the LIFO cost-flow assumption may temporarily have a reduction in inventory level that results in a liquidation of base period tiers of inventory. If this liquidation is considered temporary and is expected to be replaced prior to year end, the company should charge cost of goods sold at current prices. The difference between the carrying value of the inventory and the current replacement cost of the inventory is a current liability for replacement of LIFO base inventory temporarily depleted. When the temporary liquidation is replaced, inventory is debited for the original LIFO value and the liability is removed.

Inventory losses from a decline in market value at interim dates should not be deferred but should be recognized in the period in which they occur. However, if in a subsequent interim period the market price of the written-down inventory increases, a gain should be recognized for the recovery up to the amount of the loss previously recognized. If a temporary decline in market value below cost can reasonably be expected to be recovered prior to year end, no loss should be recognized.

Finally, if a company uses a standard costing system to compute cost of goods sold and to value inventories, variances from standard should be treated at interim dates in the same manner as at year end. However, if variances occur at an interim date that are expected to be absorbed prior to year end, the variances should be deferred instead of being immediately recognized.

c. The APB stated that the provision for income taxes shown in interim financial statements must be based upon the effective tax rate expected for the entire annual period for ordinary earnings. The effective tax rate is, in accordance with previous APB opinions, based on earnings for financial statement purposes as opposed to taxable income which may consider timing differences. This effective tax rate is the combined federal and state(s) income tax rate applied to expected annual earnings, taking into consideration all anticipated investment tax credits, foreign tax rates, percentage depletion capital gains rates, and other available tax planning alternatives. Ordinary earnings do not include unusual or extraordinary items, discontinued operations, or cumulative effects of changes in accounting principles, all of which will be separately reported or reported net of their related tax effect in reports for the interim period or for the fiscal year. The amount shown as the provision for income taxes at interim dates should be computed on a year-to-date basis. For example, the provision for income taxes for the second quarter of a company's fiscal year is the result of applying the expected rate to year-to-date earnings and subtracting the provision recorded for the first quarter. There are several variables in this computation (expected earnings may change, tax rates may change), and the year-to-date method of computation provides the only continuous method of approximating the provision for income taxes at interim dates. However, if the effective rate or expected annual earnings change between interim periods, the change is not reflected retroactively but the effect of the change is absorbed in the current interim period.

Exercise 13-5

The following are general comments. It must be emphasized that the impact will, of course, be quite different on a growth, cyclical, and defensive companies. Nevertheless, the below factors will have some effect on almost all companies.

a.   Within the company, factors that affect:
      (1)   *Earnings per Share*
            (a)   Accounting policy, particularly inventory and depreciation.
            (b)   Sales volume, cost of goods sold, and operating expenses.
            (c)   Quality of management, research.
            (d)   Success of new product introduction.
            (e)   Start-up expense, special items, nonrecurring gains or losses.
            (f)   Expansion programs--internal or through acquisition.
            (g)   Leverage.
            (h)   Overall financial policies.

      (2)   *Dividends per share*
            (a)   Capital expenditure programs.
            (b)   Volatility or stability of net income.
            (c)   Overall financial condition.
            (d)   Alternative uses of cash.
            (e)   Replacement of fixed assets.
            (f)   Stage of life cycle of company--youth, middle, mature.
            (g)   Sinking fund requirements.

      (3)   *Market price per share*
            (a)   Quality of management.
            (b)   Growth rate of net income and earnings per share.
            (c)   Quality of earnings, profit margins, research, competitive environment.
            (d)   Price-earnings ratio accorded—steel, IBM, airlines.
            (e)   Financial management.
            (f)   Trading on equity, leverage.
            (g)   New product development, general outlook.
            (h)   Information disseminated by management so as to allow an intelligent analysis of projects.

b. Economic environmental factors that affect:
    (1) *Earnings per share*
        (a) If the economy turns up or down, and a company makes products whose demand turns with the general economy, earnings will be variable compared to a company whose products are subject to stable or constantly growing demand.
        (b) Government intervention can influence EPS by preventing price rises or forcing uneconomic labor settlements.
        (c) Labor disturbances halting operations, lowering revenues and hence EPS. Companies with poor labor relation policies are subject to such variabilities in earnings.
        (d) Changes in consumer fads or styles of living can cause variance until the affected company catches up again.
        (e) Population shifts out of areas served.
        (f) Changes in tax laws.

    (2) *Dividends per share*
        (a) Tax laws.
        (b) Growth rate of economy encouraging reinvestment.
        (c) Of course, anything affecting EPS affects dividends also—not necessarily immediately, but at least in terms of dividend policy.

    (3) *Market price per share*
        (a) Investor confidence in the ability of the government to cope with problems.
        (b) Cyclical change in economy affecting investor confidence which is reflected in the stock market in general. Research indicates that over 50 percent of price movement of a particular stock is due to price move of the general market.

◀ Answers to Problems ▶

Problem 13-1
a.   Quaker Oats
                       Analytically Recast Income Statements
                          for Years 11, 10, and 9 (in millions)

	Item	11	10	9
Net Sales	1	5,491.2	5,030.6	4,879.4
Interest Income	156	9.0	11.0	12.4
Total Revenue		5,500.2	5,041.6	4,891.8
Costs & Expenses:				
Cost of Sales (A)	2	2,647.0	2,528.1	2,514.0
Selling, General and Admin Exp (B)	4	669.5	605.5	597.0
Repair and Maintenance Expenses (A)	155	96.1	96.6	93.8
Depreciation Expenses (A)	155	125.2	103.5	94.5
Advertising and Merchandising Expenses (B)	155	1,407.4	1,195.3	1,142.7
Research and Development (B)	155	44.3	43.3	39.3
Interest Expenses (C)	5	95.2	112.8	68.8
Foreign Exchange (Gains) Losses	157	(5.1)	25.7	14.8
Amortization of Intangibles	157	22.4	22.2	18.2
Losses (Gains) from plant closing and ops sold	157	8.8	(23.1)	119.4
Miscellaneous Expenses (Income)	157	6.5	(8.4)	(2.9)
Total Costs & Expenses		5,117.3	4,701.5	4,699.7
Income before Taxes		382.9	340.1	192.1
Taxes at 34%	158	130.2	115.6	65.3
Income from Continuing Operations		252.7	224.5	126.8
State & local inc taxes, net of fed benefit (D)	158	(16.7)	(11.9)	(7.7)
ANC benefit (D)	158	0.0	0.0	1.7
Repatriation of foreign earnings (D)	158	(4.3)	(4.8)	2.1
Non-U.S. tax rate differential (D)	158	(8.2)	(9.8)	(8.9)
U.S. tax credit (D)	158	0.2	0.1	0.7
Miscellaneous items—net (D)	158	(6.8)	2.9	3.1
Income (Loss) from discontinued operations (E)	10	(30.0)	(59.9)	54.1
Add LIFO liquidation gain	143	18.9	27.9	31.0
Net Income as reported		205.8	169.0	203.0

		11	10	9
(A) Cost of goods sold	2	2,839.7	2,685.9	2,655.3
Less: Repair and maintenance expenses	155	(96.1)	(96.6)	(93.8)
Less: Depreciation expense	155	(125.2)	(103.5)	(94.5)
Add: LIFO liquidation gain before tax*	143	28.6	42.3	47.0
		2,647.0	2,528.1	2,514.0

* LIFO liquidation gain before tax: Year 11 = 18.9/(1 - .34) = 28.6
                                         Year 10 = 27.9/(1 - .34) = 42.3
                                         Year 9 = 31.0/(1 - .34) = 47.0

		11	10	9
(B) Selling, General and Administrative expenses	4	2,121.2	1,844.1	1,779.0
Less: Advertising and merchandising expenses	155	(1,407.4)	(1,195.3)	(1,142.7)
Less: Research and development	155	(44.3)	(43.3)	(39.0)
		669.5	605.5	597.0
(C) Interest expense	156	101.9	120.2	75.9
Less: Interest allocated to disc ops	156	(6.7)	(7.4)	(7.1)
		95.2	112.8	68.8

(D)   All items marked (D) modify the federal tax at the statutory rate of 34 percent on pretax income from continuing operations and are shown separately for analytical purposes. (For disclosure, see note 16).

(E)   Item [10] provided net of tax results of discontinued operations.

b.   *Comments:*

Unlike reported net income, income from continuing operations has grown significantly over the three years. Income (loss) from discontinuing operations had a marked effect on net results. The LIFO liquidation gains declined over the three year period. Advertising and merchandising expenses increased markedly while repair and maintenance, as well as R & D expenses, remained stable.

Problem 13-2

a.
Campbell Soup Company
Analytically Recast Income Statement
For Years 9 through 11 (in millions)

Refer-ence Item		11	10	9
13	Net sales	$6,204.10	$6,205.80	$5,672.10
24	Equity in earnings of affiliates	2.40	13.50	10.40
19	Interest income	26.00	17.60	38.30
	Total income	$6,232.50	$6,236.90	$5,720.80
	Costs and expenses:			
	Cost of products sold [A]	$3,727.10	$3,893.50	$3,651.80
	Marketing and selling exp [B] . . .	760.80	760.10	605.90
145	Advertising expenses	195.40	220.40	212.90
144	Repair and maintenance	173.90	180.60	173.90
16	Administrative expenses	306.70	290.70	252.10
17	R & D expenses	56.30	53.70	47.70
20	Foreign exchange losses, net	0.80	3.30	19.30
102	Expense due to stock price related incentive programs	15.40	($.10)	17.40
103	Amort of intangible and other assets .	14.10	16.80	16.40
104	Other, net	(3.30)	(2.00)	(1.40)
25	Minority interests	7.20	5.70	5.30
187	Depreciation	194.50	184.10	175.90
18	Interest expense	116.20	111.60	94.10
	Total costs and expenses	$5,565.10	$5,718.40	$5,271.30
	Income before taxes	667.40	518.50	449.50
	Income taxed at 34%	226.92	176.29	152.83
	Income from continuing operations . . .	440.48	342.21	296.67
135	State inc taxes (net of fed tax benefit)*	(20.02)	(6.64)	(3.83)
136	Nondeductible divestitures, restructuring and unusual charges	—	(101.36)	(51.87)
137	Nondeductible amort of intangibles . . .	(4.00)	(1.61)	(1.17)
138	Foreign earnings not taxed or taxed at other than statutory fed rate	2.00	(2.15)	(0.21)
139	Other [C]	(16.96)	(2.23)	(0.11)
22	Divestitures, restructuring and unusual charges	—	(223.81)	(226.38)
28	Net earnings as reported	$ 401.50	$ 4.40	$ 13.10

[A]   Cost of products sold = [14] - depreciation expense - Repair and maintenance

[B]   Marketing and selling expenses = [15] - advertising

[C]   This item also includes the rounding errors

  *   For Year 11, 667.4 × .03 = 20.02

b. *Comments:*

Income from continuing operations increased significantly year after year. Divestitures, restructuring and unusual charges, as well as their tax effects, had significant impacts on net income in 1989 and 1990. R & D expenses rose moderately over the years. Advertising expenses declined in 1991.

Problem 13-3

a. Liabilities assumed:

Accounts payable	$170,000	(unchanged)
Notes payable	50,000	(unchanged)
Bonds payable	200,000	(unchanged)
Total liabilities	$420,000	

Purchase price of Finex	$700,000
Book value of total owner's equity	570,000
Payment in excess of stated book values	$130,000
Add: Decrease in accounts receivable (5%)	7,500
Amount to be allocated to Land, Bldg and Equip	$137,500

Land: [40,000 ÷ (40,000 + 360,000 + 130,000)] × 137,500 = 10,377
Building: [360,000 ÷ (40,000 + 360,000 + 130,000)] × 137,500 = 93,396
Equipment: [130,000 ÷ (40,000 + 360,000 + 130,000)] × 137,500 = 33,727
    Total   137,500

Therefore, the purchase prices are:

Land: $40,000 + $10,377 = $50,377
Building: $360,000 + $93,396 = $453,396
Equipment: $130,000 + $33,727 = $163,727

b.
Finex, Inc. Balance Sheet
As of January 1, Year 2

Cash	$ 55,000	(unchanged)
U.S. government bonds	25,000	(unchanged)
Accounts receivable (net)	142,500	(less 5%)
Merchandise inventory	230,000	(unchanged)
Land	50,377	(restated)
Building	453,396	(restated)
Equipment	163,727	(restated)
Total assets	$1,120,000	
Accounts payable	$ 170,000	(unchanged)
Notes payable	50,000	(unchanged)
Bonds payable	200,000	(unchanged)
Preferred stock	100,000	(unchanged)
Common stock	400,000	(unchanged)
PIC and retained earnings *	200,000	(increase of $130,000)
Total liabilities and capital	$1,120,000	

* Will vary with method of acquisition.

c. Depreciation rates before purchase:

    Building: 7,900 ÷ (360,000 + 35,000) = 2%
    Equipment: 9,000 ÷ (130,000 + 20,000) = 6%

Depreciation expense in Year 2:

    Building: $453,396 x 2%   = $ 9,068
    Equipment: $163,727 x 6%   =   9,824
    Total   = $18,892

Amount to be charged to COGS in Year 2 ($18,892 x 1/3) $6,297
Amount charged to COGS in Year 1 [(7,900÷9,000) x 1/3]   5,633
    Increase in depreciation expense $ 664

			%
Net sales		$860,000	100.0
Cost of goods sold	$546,000		
Add: Increase in depreciation	664	546,664	63.6
Gross profit		$313,336	36.4
Selling & administrative expenses	$240,000		
Add: Increase in depreciation:			
Yr 2: $18,892 - $6,297 = $12,595			
Yr 1: $16,900 - $5,633 = 11,267	1,328		
Bad debt expense	7,500	248,828	28.9
Net operative income		$ 64,508	7.5

d. No, revised net operating income is 7.5% of net sales.

Problem 13-4
Chance of getting the loan from Bank America:

Sales			$500,000
Less:			
10% sales returns		$50,000	
2% sales discount		10,000	60,000
Net Sales			$440,000
Cost of goods sold			
Beg. Inventory ($138,000/1.38)		$100,000	
Purchases	$400,000		
Less:			
2% purchases returned	(8,000)		
1% purchases discount	(4,000)	388,000	
		$488,000	
Less: Ending inventory		138,000	350,000
Gross Margin			$ 90,000

Percent of gross margin to sales = $90,000 ÷ $440,000 = 20.45%

Based on its criteria Bank America would not give a loan to Aspero.

Chance of getting the loan from Bank Boston:

Current liabilities = Purchases ÷ Accounts payable turnover

Accounts payable turnover = 360 ÷ 90 = 4

Accounts payable = 388,000 ÷ 4 = $97,000

Current Assets:
Cash	$ 5,500
Accounts receivable (A)	55,000
Inventory	138,000
Total Current Assets	$198,500

(A)   A/R = Sales ÷ A/R turnover = 440,000 ÷ (360/45) = 55,000

Current ratio = 198,500 ÷ 97,00 = 2.05

Bank Boston *might* give the loan to Aspero.

Problem 13-5

a.   1.   *Company A:*

	Yr 1	Yr 2	Yr 3
Income before effect of expenditure	20	20	20
Depreciation of $10 expenditure	0	5	5
Net income	20	15	15

Company B:

	Yr 1	Yr 2	Yr 3
Income before effect of expenditure	20	20	20
Expensing of $10 expenditure	10	0	0
Net income	10	20	20

2.   *Company A:*
BV, 12/31/Year 1: 50 + 10 = 60
BV, 12/31/Year 2: 60 + 15 = 75
BV, 12/31/Year 3: 75 + 15 = 90

Company B:
BV, 12/31/Year 1: 50 + 0 = 50
BV, 12/31/Year 2: 50 + 20 = 70
BV, 12/31/Year 3: 70 + 20 = 90

3.   *Company A:*
ROCE, Year 2: 15/60 = 25%
ROCE, Year 3: 15/75 = 20%

Company B:
ROCE, Year 2: 20/50 = 40%
ROCE, Year 3: 20/70 = 28.57%

b.   In general, conservative accounting results in lower income and book values in early years. Company B--which immediately expensed the $10 expenditure-- is clearly using more conservative accounting.

c.   *Company A:*
        Value = 60 + [(.25-.15)x60]/1.15 + [(.20-.15)x60]/1.15² = $71.75

        Company B:
        Value = 50 + [(.40-.15)x50]/1.15 + [(.2857-.15)x50]/1.15² = $71.75

        Despite the use of different accounting treatments for the $10 expenditure, the estimated values are equal.

d.   Mathematically, the accounting-based equity valuation model will yield the same value estimates for any accounting system which follows the clean surplus relation. However, to the extent that accounting manipulations can mislead investors and effect the prediction of future earnings, accounting choices can effect firm value.

Problem 13-6
a.   Year 1: 12,500 - (.15)(50,000)   = 5,000   (5,000)
        Year 2: 11,700 - (.15)(56,500)   = 3,226   (3,225)
        Year 3: 11,420 - (.15)(63,845)   = 1,845   (1,843)
        Year 4: 11,860 - (.15)(72,145)   = 1,039   (1,038)
        Year 5: 10,820 - (.15)(72,145)   =   0   (-2)

        Note: Consistent with the example in the text, the figures are based on rounding ROCE to two digits. The figures without rounding are presented in parentheses.

b.   1/1/Year 2: 56,500 + 3,226/1.15 + 1,845/1.15² + 1,039/1.15³ = $60,747
        1/1/Year 3: 63,845 + 1,845/1.15 + 1,039/1.15² = $65,652
        1/1/Year 4: 72,145 + 1,039/1.15 = $72,739
        1/1/Year 5: $72,145

c.   1/1/Year 2: 56,500 + (60,747 - 56,500) x (1+.15/2) = $61,066
        1/1/Year 3: 63,845 + (65,652 - 63,845) x (1+.15/2) = $65,788
        1/1/Year 4: 72,145 + (72,739 - 72,145) x (1+.15/2) = $72,784
        1/1/Year 5: $72,145 (no amounts discounted)

d.   Conservative accounting principles tend to understate net income and book value. As long as the analyst's estimates of future profitability incorporate the eventual reversal of this conservatism under the clean surplus relation, value estimates will not be affected by the accounting.

e.   1/1/Year 2: 1 + (.2071-.15)/1.15 + [(.1789-.15)/1.15²] x [63,845/56,500] +
                    [(.1644-.15)/1.15³] x [72,145/56,500] = 1.09

        1/1/Year 3: 1 + (.1789-.15)/1.15 + [(.1644-.15)/1.15²] x [72,145/56,500]
                    = 1.04

        1/1/Year 4: 1 + (.1644-.15)/1.15] = 1.01

        1/1/Year 5: 1.00

f.　　　"normal" PE = 1.15/.15 = 7.67

1/1/Year 3: 7.67 + [7.67/11,700] x [(1,845-3,226)÷1.15 + (1,039-1,845)÷1.15^2 + (0-1,039)÷1.15^3] - 4,355/11,700 = <u>5.66</u>

1/1/Year 4: 7.67 + [7.67/11,420] x [(1,039-1,845)÷1.15 + (0-1,039)÷1.15^2] - 3,120/11,420 = <u>6.40</u>

1/1/Year 5: 7.67 + [7.67/11,860] x [(0-1,039)÷1.15] - 11,860/11,860 = <u>6.08</u>

◄ Answers to Cases ►

<u>Case 13-1</u>

a.

ADAPTEC, INC.
Analytically Recast Income Statements
1994 through 1996 ($000s)

	1996	1995	1994
Net revenues	$659,347	$466,194	$372,245
Cost of revenues (A)	258,346	189,934	178,037
Research & development exp	87,628	60,848	39,993
Sales & marketing exp	81,548	58,737	46,192
General & administrative exp	35,784	23,229	19,399
Depreciation and amort.	17,593	15,662	11,489
Write-off of in-process technology (B) . .	52,313	0	0
	533,212	348,410	295,110
Income from operations	126,135	117,784	77,135
Interest income	12,694	7,932	5,183
Shareholder settlement	0	0	2,409
Interest Expense	840	1,179	1,306
Income before taxes	137,989	124,537	78,603
Income taxes @ 35% (C)	48,296	43,588	27,511
Income	89,693	80,949	51,092
Add (deduct) tax-related items:			
State taxes (1996: 137,989 x 2.7%) (C)	(3,726)	(2,740)	(2,279)
Lower tax rate on earnings of foreign			
sub (96: 137,989 x 11.8%) (C)	16,283	12,329	8,253
Tax-exempt interest income			
(96: 137,989 x 2.1%) (C)	2,898	2,117	1,258
Other (96: 137,989 x 1.3%) (C)	(1,794)	747	629
Difference (rounding?)	21	0	(3)
Net income as reported	$103,375	$ 93,402	$ 58,950

(A) net of depreciation & amortization

(B) treated as "operating" due to likelihood of recurrence

(C) per note 8

b. Unfortunately, the lack of detailed breakdowns of expenses prevents the analysis from yielding insights beyond those found in earlier cases. Adaptec's footnotes are of little help. Perhaps the most interesting result is the quantification of the tax advantage associated with the Singapore subsidiary. Over the period 1994-96, Adaptec's net income benefitted by $36,865 (or 11.2% of 3/31/96 retained earnings).

c. *R&D Expense to Sales:*
    1994: 39,993/372,245 = 10.7%
    1995: 60,848/466,194 = 13.1%
    1996: 87,628/659,347 = 13.3%

Index Trends:	1994	1995	1996
Net revenues	100	125.2	177.1
R&D expense	100	152.1	219.1

d. Adaptec has increased R&D expenditures (relative to sales) over the last three years. MD&A indicates that the company has "increased staffing levels" and has expanded its focus from primarily SCSI-related products "to include ATM, RAID, serial I/O and infrared technology." On balance, Adaptec's R&D efforts enhance the quality of its earnings.

e. Per note 5, Adaptec has become heavily involved in making strategic business acquisitions. As long as the company uses the purchase method to account for certain transactions, there is a possibility of additional write-offs of in-process technology. Thus, this item should be considered as a recurring operating item.

Case 13-2

a.

Ferro Corp.
Analytically Recast Income Statements
For Years 5 and 6 ($000s)

	Year 6	Year 5
Net Sales	$376,485	$328,005
Cost of Sales (A)	251,846	210,333
Selling & Administration Expenses (B)	48,216	42,140
Repairs & Maintenance (A)	15,000	20,000
Advertising (B)	6,000	7,000
Employee Training Program (B)	4,000	5,000
Research & Development	9,972	8,205
	335,034	292,678
Operating Income	41,451	35,327
Other Income: (C)		
Royalties	710	854
Interest earned	1,346	1,086
Miscellaneous	1,490	1,761
	3,546	3,701
Other Charges: (D)		
Interest Expense	4,055	4,474
Miscellaneous	1,480	1,448
	5,535	5,922
Income before taxes	39,462	33,106
Income taxes @ 48% (before items below) (E)	18,942	15,891
Income from continuing operations	20,520	17,215
Add (deduct) permanent tax differentials:		
Lower tax rate on earnings of consolidated subsidiaries (Year 6: 36,819 × 5.3%) (E)	1,951	1,312
Lower tax rate on equity in income of affiliated companies (6: 36,819 × 1.4%) (E)	516	198
Unrealized foreign exchange loss—not tax deductible (6: 36,819 × 5.3%) (E)	(1,951)	(891)
Add'l US taxes on dividends from subsidiaries, etc. (6: 36,819 × .8%) (E)	(295)	(248)
Investment tax credit (6: 36,819 × 1.5%) (E)	552	223
Miscellaneous tax benefits (6: 36,819 × .4%) —rounded (E)	135	158
Equity in earnings of affiliates (net of tax) (6: 1,394 × .52) (C)	725	262
Unrealized loss on foreign currency translation (net of tax) (6: 4,037 × .52) (D)	(2,099)	(963)
Loss from disposal of chemicals division (net of tax) (5: 7,000 × .52) (A)		(3,640)
Net income as reported	$ 20,054	$ 13,626

(A), (B), etc. indicate related items. For example, repairs and maintenance was separated from cost of goods sold.

b. The factors causing the effective tax rate to be *greater than* the statutory rate include: (1) unrealized foreign exchange translation loss, and (2) additional taxes on dividends from subsidiaries and affiliates. Of these factors, changes in foreign exchange rates may be considered random. Dividend policy is under the control of management.

The factors causing the effective tax rate to be *less than* the statutory rate include: (1) earnings of consolidated subsidiaries taxed at rates less than the US rate, (2) equity in after-tax earnings of affiliates, (3) ITC, and (4) miscellaneous. Of these factors, the ITC is unstable as it depends on government policy.

c. While Ferro's sales grew by only 14.8%, net income from continuing operations increased by 19.2%. However, the increase in the net income to sales ratio may have resulted from "savings" in repairs and maintenance (R&M), advertising, and employee training program expenses. The following analysis explains these "savings":

	Yr 5	Yr 6	Actual Amount	Benchmark*	Difference (savings)
% R&M to Sales	6.1	4.0	$15,000	$22,970	$7,970
% Advertising to Sales	2.1	1.6	6,000	7,910	1,910
% Employee Training to Sales	1.5	1.1	4,000	5,650	1,650
			$25,000	$36,530	$11,530

Year 6 % NI to Sales (on Year 5 basis) would be:

Net income from continuing operations	$20,520
Less "savings" on discretionary items (11,530 × .52) . . .	5,995
Net income on adjusted basis **	$14,525
% of net income to sales (14,525 ÷ 376,485) ***	3.8%

*   Amount of spending required in Year 6 to equal the rate of spending implicit in the Year 5 ratios

** Adjusted to reflect discretionary costs at the same level as prevailed in x5.

*** % of NI to Sales as reported is 5.3%

Note: The disposal of the chemical division may have affected cost patterns.

Case 13-3

(1) The tonnage-of-production method provides an especially good matching of depreciation expense against revenues for Canada Steel's highly cyclical business. A unit-of-production method effectively makes depreciation a variable rather than a fixed cost and, therefore, tends to stabilize earnings. Casting metals is not a high technology business, and actual wear and tear on the equipment is more relevant to replacement need than technological obsolescence.

A switch to straight-line would not eliminate the deferred tax liability as this difference is caused by accelerated methods and shorter lives rather than the difference between the tonnage-of-production and straight-line methods. Moreover, Canada Steel should not attempt to extinguish this liability since it is an interest-free loan from the government which may never have to be repaid as long as new assets are acquired.

A switch to straight-line would leverage profits on any production increase (or decrease) because depreciation expense would be a direct function of *time* rather than *units produced*. However, the quality of earnings could be reduced by a switch to straight-line inasmuch as this method would accentuate the highly cyclical nature of our business and result in an increased net income volatility.

(2)   The reasons for adopting the LIFO method--reducing taxes and increasing cash flow--are still valid. Inflation usually declines during recessions, but this does not mean its recurrence is improbable. Maximizing cash flow remains important to the corporation and shareholders. A return to FIFO would relinquish the tax savings of prior years, although it is true that the balance sheet and income statement would be strengthened by the change.

The quality of earnings is likely to be affected adversely by the lack of consistency in inventory method (two changes in a period of several years) and a perception that the motive in making the change was to increase book value per share, avoid two consecutive unprofitable years, and escape violation of a loan covenant. The $4 million upward adjustment in working capital is a result of increasing the inventory account by this amount, which has the effect of increasing the current ratio as shown below:

	LIFO	FIFO
Current Assets	$10.5	$14.5
Current Liabilities	$ 4.5	$ 4.5
Current Ratio	2.3	3.2

The $0.5 million increment to net income will offset an operating loss of $0.4 million which would not be unexpected on a sales decline of 31%.

In addition, the $2.0 million addition to shareholders' equity from prior years' profits is likely to be far less significant than current profit trends, as Canada Steel has had to disclose regularly in the footnotes to its financial statements the difference in inventory values resulting from the use of LIFO versus FIFO.

(3)   The inventory change will enable Canada Steel to meet the minimum current ratio requirements. However, the stock repurchase program should not be recommended for the following reasons:

a.   The proposed repurchase price of $100 per share is well above book value and recent market prices, suggesting dilution for remaining shareholders.

b.   The potential dividend savings are outweighed by interest costs of $101,000 ($2.0 million × 11% × 0.46 marginal tax rate) to finance the purchase--in other words, leverage is negative.

c. The debt-to-equity ratio is increased significantly from 10% ($2.0 million long-term debt/$17.7 million equity + $2.0 million long-term debt) to 35% ($6.1 million long-term debt/$11.4 million equity + $6.1 million long-term debt). An additional $2.0 million of stock repurchased would raise this ratio to 41% ($8.1 million long-term debt/$11.5 million equity + $8.1 million long-term debt). The increased financial risk is particularly inappropriate for an industry with significant sensitivity to the business cycle. Shrinking shareholders' equity under present circumstances is prudent only by sale of fixed assets, not the incurrence of additional debt.

In summary, each of the foregoing would have a negative impact on the quality of Canada Steel's earnings.

Case 13-4

a.

	1	2	3	4	5	6	7
Net income	1034	1130	1218	1256	1278	1404	1546
BV, beginning	5308	5292	5834	6338	6728	7266	7856
Abnormal earnings (A)	344	442	460	432	403	459	525
PV factor (13%)	.885	.783	.693	.613	.543	.480	.425
PV abnormal earnings	304	346	319	265	219	221	223

(A) abnormal earnings = NI - (.13 x BV, beg)

Value at 1/1/Year 1 = 5308 + 304 + 346 + 319 + 265 + 219 + 221 + 223 = $\underline{\$7,205}$

b. PB ratio = 7205 ÷ 5308 = $\underline{1.36}$

Assuming accurate estimates, a market-based PB of 1.95 implies that Colin is overvalued.

c. PE ratio = 7205 ÷ 1034 = $\underline{6.97}$

Assuming accurate estimates, a market-based PE of 10 implies that Colin is overvalued.

d.

	1	2	3	4	5	6	7	8+
Net income	1034	1130	1218	1256	1278	1404	1546	1546
BV, beginning	5308	5292	5834	6338	6728	7266	7856	8506
Abnormal earnings (A)	344	442	460	432	403	459	525	440
PV factor (13%)	.885	.783	.693	.613	.543	.480	.425	3.270 (B)
PV abnormal earnings	304	346	319	265	219	221	223	1439

(A) abnormal earnings = NI - (.13 x BV, beg)

(B) To discount perpetuity to beginning of Year 1, (1) divide 1439 by 0.13 to arrive at value as of 1/1/Year 8, and multiply by 7-year present value factor of 0.425 [0.425 + 0.13 = 3.270].

Value at 1/1/Year 1 = 5308 + 304 + 346 + 319 + 265 + 219 + 221 + 223 + 1439 = $\underline{\$8,644}$

◄ COMPREHENSIVE CASE ►

Applying Financial Statement Analysis

◄ CHAPTER REVIEW ►

Comprehensive case analysis of the financial statements and notes of Campbell Soup Company is our focus. The three major parts of the book have prepared us to tackle all facets of financial statement analysis. This comprehensive case analysis provides us the opportunity to illustrate and apply these analysis tools and techniques. This case also gives us the opportunity to show how we draw conclusions and inferences from detailed analysis. We review the basic steps of analysis, the building blocks, and attributes of an expert analysis report. Throughout the case we emphasize applications and inferences associated with financial statement analysis.

◄ CHAPTER OUTLINE ►

▸ **Steps in Analyzing Financial Statements**

▸ **Building Blocks of Financial Statement Analysis**

▸ **Reporting on Financial Statement Analysis**

▸ **Specialization in Financial Statement Analysis**

▸ **Comprehensive Case: Campbell Soup Company**

      Preliminary Financial Analysis

      Short-Term Liquidity

      Cash Flow Analysis and Forecasting

      Capital Structure and Solvency

      Return on Invested Capital

      Analysis of Asset Utilization

      Analysis of Operating Performance and Profitability

      Summary Evaluation and Inferences

◂ Learning Objectives ▸

■ **Describe the steps in analying financial statements.**

■ **Review the building blocks of financial statement analysis.**

■ **Explain important attributes of reporting on financial statement analysis.**

■ **Describe implications to financial statement analysis from evaluating companies in specialized industries or with unique characteristics.**

■ **Analyze in a comprehensive manner the financial statements and notes of Campbell Soup Company.**

◄ Answers to Questions ►

1. Financial statement analysis is oriented toward the achievement of definite objectives. In order that the analysis best serve these objectives, the first step is to define them carefully. The thinking and clarification leading up to the definition of objectives is an important part of the analytical process as it insures a clear understanding of objectives, of what is pertinent and relevant, and thus leads to avoidance of unnecessary work. This is indispensable to an effective as well as an efficient analysis: effective in that, given the specifications, it focuses on the most important elements of the financial statements; efficient in that it leads to an analysis with maximum economy of time and effort.

2. The intelligent analyst of financial statement data must always bear in mind that a financial statement is at best an abstraction of an underlying reality. Further mathematical manipulation of financial data can result in second, third, and even further levels of abstractions and the analyst must always keep in mind the business reality behind the figures. No map of the Rocky Mountains can fully convey the grandeur of the terrain. One has to see them in order to appreciate them because maps, like financial statements, are at best, abstractions. That is why analysts must, at some point, leave the financial statements and visit the companies which they analyze in order to get a full understanding of the phenomena revealed by their analysis. This is particularly true because the static reality portrayed by the abstractions found in the financial statements cannot remain static for very long. Reality is constantly changing.

3. The six major "building blocks" of financial analysis which we have studied are:

   1. Short-term liquidity--the ability to meet short-term obligations,

   2. Cash analysis and forecasting--future availability and disposition of cash,

   3. Capital structure and solvency--ability to generate future revenues and meet long-term obligations,

   4. Return on invested capital--ability to provide financial rewards sufficient to attract and retain financing,

   5. Asset utilization (turnover)--Asset intensity in generating revenues to reach a sufficient profitability level, and

   6. Operating performance and profitability--Success at maximizing revenues and minimizing expenses from operating activities over the long run.

   The building block approach to financial statement analysis involves:

   1. The determination of the major objectives which a particular analysis is to achieve.
   2. Arriving at a judgment about which of the six major areas of analysis must be evaluated with what degree of emphasis and in what order of priority.

4. A good analysis separates clearly for the reader the interpretations and conclusions of the analysis from the facts and data upon which they are based. This not only separates fact from opinions and estimates, but also enables the reader to follow the rationale of the analyst's conclusions and allows him/her to modify them as judgment dictates. To this end the analysis should contain distinct sections devoted to:

   1. A brief "Summary and Conclusion" (executive summary) section as well as a table of contents to help the reader decide how much of the report he/she wants to read and which parts of it to emphasize.

   2. General background material on the enterprise analyzed, the industry of which it is a part, and the economic environment in which it operates.

3. Financial and other evidential data used in the analysis as well as ratios, trends, and other analytical measures which have been developed from them.

4. Assumptions as to the general economic environment and other conditions on which estimates and projections are based.

5. A listing of positive and negative factors, quantitative and qualitative, by area of analysis.

6. Projections, estimates, interpretations, and conclusions based on the aforementioned data.

5.   The financial analyst must recognize that there are industries with distinct accounting treatments which arise either from their specialized nature or from the special conditions, such as governmental regulation, to which they are subject. The analysis of the financial statements of such an enterprise requires a thorough understanding of the accounting peculiarities to which they are subject and the analyst must, accordingly, be prepared for this task by studying and understanding of the specialized areas of accounting which affect the analysis.

Examples of specialized industries include oil and gas, life insurance, and public utilities. As in any field of endeavor, specialized areas of inquiry require that specialized knowledge be brought to bear upon them. Financial analysis is, of course, no exception.

◄ Answers to Exercises ►

Exercise CC-1

a.   (6)
b.   (2)
c.   (8)
d.   (1)
e.   (9)
f.   (3)
g.   (5)
h.   (7)
i.   (4)

Solution:

A.   Three firms have zero inventory, (4), (8), and (9). These probably correspond to the firms which have operating expenses instead of cost of goods sold--that is, the investment adviser, the health care company, and the public survey firm.

Company (8) has a very high property, plant and equipment account—it is most likely the *health care company*.

Company (9) has large "Other assets" (which probably represent investments), and high current liabilities--it is the *investment adviser*.

By process of elimination, company (4) is *public survey firm*.

B.   Company (1) has a large plant and equipment account, as well as high long-term debt and interest expense. It is the *utility company*.

C.   Companies (2) and (7) have high R&D expense. This would correspond to the pharmaceutical company and the computing equipment firm.

Since drugs have a shorter shelf-life than computer equipment, the pharmaceutical company will have lower inventory relative to sales. Company (2) is, therefore, the *pharmaceutical company*, while company (7) manufactures *computer equipment*.

D. Company (5) must be the *grocery store*, since it shows very low receivables (few sales on account), and very low net income relative to sales (typical for the industry).

E. Of the two firms left (tobacco manufacturer and brewery), tobacco products require aging. The tobacco manufacturer would keep higher inventories, while a brewery would represent a higher investment in plant and equipment. Company (6) is the *tobacco manufacturer,* and company (3) is the *brewery*.

Alternate Solution:

Industry	Expected Characteristics	Company #
Pharmaceuticals	High R & D	2
Health care	No inventory High plant and equipment No advertising expense No cost of goods sold	8
Utilities	High plant and equipment Large debt (financed with bonds) Low inventories	1
Investment advising	No inventory Low plant and equipment High "other" assets (investments) High interest expense No cost of goods sold	9
Grocery stores	Low NI as % of sales Low receivables Low plant and equipment (operating leases)	5
Computing equipment	High R&D Higher inventory than pharmaceutical company	7
Public opinion surveys	No inventory No R&D No cost of goods sold	4

To distinguish between the tobacco manufacturer (6) and the brewery (3), use the same logic as in the first solution.

The factors that would determine the relative PE ratios are:

1. *Growth in earnings per share:*   *Axel*   *Bike*
    Year 2 to 6   +150%   +54%
    Year 5 to 6   + 21%   +20%

    Assuming net income is comparable as far as accounting practices go, Axel would be likely to have a higher PE ratio because of greater historic growth in earnings per share.

2. *Leverage in capital structure:*   *Axel*   *Bike*
                                           33% of a   None
                                           total capital
                                           structure is debt

    Axel's earnings are likely to be greater, relative to Bike, because of this leverage, so that the growth in per share earnings is likely to be faster, producing greater market appreciation. This is likely to produce a higher PE for Axel. However, Axel does have greater financial risk, which would tend to reduce its PE differential.

3. *Return on common equity, Year 6:*   *Axel*   *Bike*

    $$\frac{2,125}{20,000} = 10.6\% \qquad \frac{2,250}{30,000} = 7.5\%$$

    Axel's greater ROCE is produced by the leverage in the capital structure and will tend to produce a higher PE for the stock as retained earnings can grow faster as long as dividend policies are the same, allowing faster growth of stockholders' investment and reducing the need to finance expansion by selling more stock and thereby diluting earnings per share. [This calculation makes no adjustment for the intangibles carried in the balance sheet—see item 8 below.]

4. *Net income as % of sales:*   *Axel*   *Bike*

    $$\frac{2,125}{30,000} = 7.1\% \qquad \frac{2,250}{30,000} = 7.5\%$$

    The difference is due to Axel's use of debt in its capital structure. If we calculate net income *before* tax and interest (assuming a 50% tax rate), Axel is seen to be more profitable.

                                                                 Axel   *Bike*

	Axel	Bike
NI before tax & interest	4,750,000	4,500,000
Interest expense	500,000	--
NI before tax	4,250,000	4,500,000
NI before tax & interest as % of sales	15.8%	15.0%

Axel's interest payment can be considered by the analyst as a cost of serving the capital structure. Therefore, the truest measure of operating profitability is the ratio of net income before tax and interest to sales. This shows Axel to be marginally more profitable in Year 6, which will tend to produce a faster growth in earnings per share.

5. *Other ratios:*

		Axel	Bike
a.	Current ratio	2.85	2.97
	No significant difference		
b.	Receivables turnover	6.00	8.00
	Implies Bike has a more efficient and strict collection policy		
c.	Ratio of sales to net plant	2.30	1.88
	Suggests Axel is more efficient in utilizing its plant		

6. *Other considerations not able to be evaluated from financial data:*

   a. Reputation of company
   b. Quality of management
   c. Product range and its potential
   d. Accounting policies—inventory, depreciation, amortization of intangibles
   e. Dividend payout and policies (these policies could markedly affect the relative PE ratios to be applied to these two companies if there were some significant differences)
   f. Capital expenditure programs--Will Axel need new plant soon?
   g. Expansion program—internal and via acquisition

7. *Patent position*

   Axel seems to have stronger patent position, but to determine this one would need to know the policy for accounting for these. Does Bike's $100,000 represent net book value of the patents after amortization and Axel's $4 million unamortized cost? Will amortization of Axel's cost be a drain on future earnings? Or do the book values both represent actual unamortized cost and Axel does have a stronger patent position.

8. *Return on tangible book value:*

   Axel: 2,125,000 ÷ 16,000,000 = 13.3%
   Bike: 2,250,000 ÷ 29,900,000 = 7.5%

   The adjustment of book value of equity to tangible amounts increases Axel's return to an even more favorable comparison with Bike.

On most counts, Axel appears to be more efficient and profitable than Bike, and the prospects for greater increases in Axel's earnings per share and market value are likely to produce a higher PE ratio for Axel as long as consideration of the unavailable factors are not unfavorable to Axel.

◄ Answers to Problems ►

<u>Problem CC-1</u>

a.

	Petrochemicals	Pipeline
Revenues (volume x price):		
4950 x $0.47	2326.50	
6290 x $0.187		1176.23
Operating Costs (volume x cost):		
4950 x $0.37	<u>1831.50</u>	
$1176.23 x (1-.27)		<u>858.65</u>
Operating Profits	495.00	317.58

Total operating income = $495 + 317.58 = <u>$812.58</u>

b. Additional information to prepare a forecast of net income would include:

1. Complete schedule of debt outstanding including coupons or estimate of interest costs.
2. Estimate for administration cost (e.g., trendline)
3. Estimate for rental expenses.
4. Estimate for investment income.
5. Tax rates.
6. Complete schedule of preferred shares outstanding including dividend rates.
7. Average number of shares outstanding.

This information can be obtained from the following primary sources: (1) quarterly reports, (2) annual reports, (3) company information packages, (4) prospectuses, (5) management interviews, (6) 10-K filings, and (7) 10-Q filings.

c. 1. Incremental EPS = $\dfrac{\text{incremental operating income} \times (1\text{-tax rate})}{\text{shares outstanding}}$

$\dfrac{\text{volume} \times (\text{price increase per pound}) \times (1\text{-tax rate})}{\text{shares outstanding}}$

= [4,950 x (0.47)(.08) x (1-0.44)] ÷ 305
= <u>$0.34 per share increase</u>

2. Incremental EPS = $\dfrac{\text{volume increase} \times (\text{price-cost}) \times (1\text{-tax rate})}{\text{shares outstanding}}$

= [(4,950)(0.08) x (.47-.37) x (1-0.44) ÷ 305
= <u>$0.07 per share increase</u>

An 8% increase in price alone has far more impact than an 8% increase in volume because higher volume creates an increase in variable costs. If costs rose as much as prices, then the impact on EPS is reduced.

Higher prices often coincide with higher volume if both occur due to an increase in demand greater than any increase in capacity. This is why it is particularly important for analysts to pay attention to industry conditions of supply, demand, capacity, inventories, prices, and costs.

Problem CC-2

a. The principal limitation of the four ratios shown is that they say little about the company's ability to generate cash. It is a lack of cash that ultimately forces a company into bankruptcy. FGC was able to maintain its quick ratio over the period, but working capital declined from $448.7 million in Year 4 to negative $8.3 million in Year 5 and stayed low at a positive $5.4 million in the middle of Year 6. The company also had to rely increasingly on external financing rather than internal sources. The *operating* margin trend over the 2 1/2 years is particularly deceptive in that the margin for the later fiscal periods are much lower after considering rising interest costs.

b. Two better measures to look at are cash flow from operations and the net liquid balance, which are shown with the "Selected Cash Flow Data." The cash flow statement clearly shows that FGC's ability to generate cash has decreased sharply over the last 2 1/2 years. In particular, earnings from continuing operations have fallen from $173.2 million for Year 4 to only $10.4 million for the first 6 months of Year 6. Moreover, noncash working capital items--which declined in Years 4 and 5 (thereby acting as a source of cash)--increased in the first half of Year 6, absorbing $84.1 million (although conceivably seasonal factors might be at work here).

The net liquid balance reflects that part of net working capital which is actually liquid, as opposed to the balance of net working capital, which is relatively illiquid. In the case of FGC, net liquid balance was already negative even *before* the recapitalization of the company in Year 4, indicating that the company was overdependent on short-term external sources of funds. Net liquid balance appears to provide a good leading indicator of default risk.

Other potentially useful measures are times interest earned, return on assets, and return on common equity. Times interest earned looks at the ability of operations to cover the expense of long-term debt. The ratio shows a dramatic decline from a comfortable 2.5 in Year 4 to only 0.06 in the first half of Year 6. A value less than 1.0 is a significant red flag for solvency.

Return on assets and return on equity also indicate FGC's long term financial prospects. Without sufficient returns, the company's debt holders cannot expect security for their claims on income or assets. Return on assets slipped from 8.8% in Year 4 to 0.6% in the first half of Year 6, while return on equity is negative beginning in Year 5. Neither trend is healthy.

c. Based on the information provided, you should seek to sell the bonds, even if it means accepting a bid in the low 50s. The bonds are subordinated debentures which will not have first claim on assets in bankruptcy, and the default risk for this credit appears to be unacceptably high. Industry conditions have deteriorated due to a combination of lower demand and increased supply. Reduced capacity utilization has put downward pressure on prices. The fact that FGC's major competitor is also highly leveraged may reduce the risk of unbridled price competition, although it could also lead to aggressive pricing policies in the event both companies become desperate to spur sales in order to service their large debt burdens. The industries FGC serves are clearly very cyclical, so being highly leveraged places a double strain on the company and calls into serious question the past decisions of management.

Given the poor ability of FGC to generate cash and its weak net liquid balance, indicating too heavy a reliance on external short-term sources of capital, you would be well advised to recommend sale.

Problem CC-3

a.   1.   *The brewing industry compared with the S&P 400:*

The industry and the S&P 400 are very similar in terms of short-term liquidity as indicated by the current ratio and quick ratio. They are similar in the absolute value of the ratios and the trend (both ratios are about the same as in Year 2).

In contrast, there are substantial differences in the long-term financial risk. While the industry has generally experienced a decline in the proportion of debt, the aggregate market data indicates a high level of debt. This divergence in trend is also evident in the flow ratios. While the brewing industry increased interest coverage and relative cash flow ratios, the aggregate market experienced a decline in coverage and relative cash flow.

The total asset turnover ratios are fairly similar although the industry was better. Both units experienced an increase in the net profit margin, but again the industry looked better in the final year. Finally, the industry increased its return on the total assets over time, while the return for the market declined. Therefore, at the end the industry's returns were almost twice as large (7.90 percent vs. 3.97 percent).

To summarize, the brewing industry showed progress in reducing its financial risk and increasing its profits and return on assets. It had a better trend and final position than the market.

2.   *Anheuser-Busch compared with the brewing industry:*

In terms of short-term liquidity, BUD is about the same in Year 6 as in Year 2, but the ratios are consistently below the industry ratios. While there was no deterioration, the firm is clearly less liquid than its industry. It would be important to determine why the firm is able to maintain such a tight short-term posture compared to the rest of the industry.

The firm's long-term debt posture has improved slightly over time in terms of the balance sheet debt to asset ratios. Notably, the industry also has improved, so on a relative basis it is about the same as it was in Year 2. In contrast BUD's interest coverage ratio has declined in absolute terms and relative to the industry. In Years 2, 3, and 4 BUD had coverage of about 12-13 versus 7-8 for the industry; in Year 6 it is about 10 times for BUD versus 11 for the industry. Alternatively, the cash flow ratios for BUD have improved along with the industry.

Total asset turnover has increased for both the firm and the industry. The profit margin performance for the industry was somewhat better—it went from 5.36 percent to 6.16 percent, while BUD was almost constant (6.30 versus 6.17). Notably, this stability in the profit margin is impressive considering the sales growth and industry market share gained by BUD during this time period.

Finally, the return on total assets for BUD has increased over time and has been consistently above the returns for the industry.

In summary, BUD is less liquid than the industry, but is constant on a relative basis. Its financial risk picture is mixed since the debt ratios declined, the interest coverage declined on an absolute and relative basis although it is still a very healthy 10 times, and the cash flow ratios improved. The firm's profit margin was constant but declined on a relative basis but its return on total assets improved absolutely and was constant on a relative basis.

3.   *Anheuser-Busch compared with the S&P 400:*

Again, BUD has maintained its short-term liquidity position, but has liquidity ratios that are consistently below the market. The long-term financial leverage declined over time while the market leverage increased so by Year 6 BUD was much better. This superior position is also reflected in interest coverage which declined somewhat but is still more than twice as large as the market. Also, the cash flow ratios for BUD were the same or lower than the market in Year 2 but are substantially better absolutely and relative to the market in Year 6.

BUD's total asset turnover increased while the market declined slightly. The net profit margin performance was very similar--the market and BUD experienced small declines over the time period. Finally, BUD had a larger return on assets in Year 2 and increased its spread by Year 6 when it was twice as large (3.9 percent vs. 8.89 percent).

In summary, with the exception of the short-term liquidity ratios, BUD was superior in an absolute sense and generally experienced a better trend. As a result, the firm has much lower financial risk and a much higher return on assets.

b. There should be no problem with extending credit to the firm given its declining debt ratios, its strong interest coverage ratios, and its strong cash flow ratio that is already better than the market and generally trending upward compared to a decline for the market.

With the lone exception of the interest coverage ratio which declined in Year 6, all the financial risk measures have been improving on an absolute basis and relative to the market. Even in the case of the coverage ratio, it is still quite large and about 2.5 times the coverage for the aggregate market. Therefore, one would not expect a change in the bond rating based upon these ratios.

◄ Answers to Cases ►

Case CC-2

a. 7,000 = Net income - Cash dividends = 10,000 - 3,000

(10% stock dividend has no effect on total stockholders' equity)

b. Property, plant & equipment   1,000
        Long-term debt   1,000

To record leases at present value of future rental payments.

Statement of cash flows: separate disclosure as non-cash activity

c.

Long-term Debt (incl. current portion)		
	16,200	Beg. balance
repaid in Year 6 2,500	7,500	issuance per SCF
	4,800	from TRO acquisition
	1,000	capital lease (noncash)
	27,000	Ending balance

ZETA's SCF reports "reduction in long-term debt" at $1,500. The only way an external analyst could arrive at this figure is to assume that the capital lease is included in the $7,500 issuance of long-term debt. Unresolved is the question of why the capitalized lease, a non-cash transaction, is seemingly included in this amount.

d.   1. and 2.

ZETA's change in accounting for inventories had the following effects:

Increase (decrease) BALANCE SHEET:	Effect of change to new method in Year 6	Analytical change to restate Year 5 to new method
Inventories	2,800 *	2,000
Tax payable	1,400 **	1,000
Retained earnings	1,400	1,000

*   Cumulative pre-tax effect of $2,000 plus pre-tax effect on Year 6 income from continuing operations (per note 5, statutory tax rate is 50%).

**   50% of $2,800 restatement of cumulative income.

RETAINED EARNINGS:

Beg. balance	0	700 *
Net income	1,400	300 *
Ending balance	1,400	1,000

*   Pro forma income data shows that Year 5 income from continuing operations is increased by $300 based on retroactive application of the accounting change. Thus, the remaining $700 ($1,000 - 300) after-tax effect must pertain to prior years.

INCOME STATEMENT:

Cost of goods sold	(800)	(600)
Tax expense	400	300
Income from continuing operations	400	300
Cumulative effect of change (net of 1,000 tax)	1,000	
Net income	1,400	

3.   The journal entry to record the $1,000 was:

Inventories	2,000	
Taxes payable		1,000
Retained earnings		1,000

There is no effect on cash. The cumulative effect of $1,000 (net) should be included with expenses. It will then be offset by the change in inventories and in tax payable which will all net to zero.

e.   1.   TRO must be a separate entity because minority interest is outstanding. If 100% of TRO had been acquired, we would be unable to determine whether it was maintained as a separate legal entity or dissolved into ZETA.

2. *ZETA Corporation:*

Investment in subsidiary	8,000	
Cash		8,000

Consolidated (per SCF):

Receivables/Inventories	4,200	
Property, plant & equipment	6,000	
Goodwill	2,000	
Current liabilities		3,200
Long-term debt		4,800
Minority interest		400
Cash (net of 4,200 acquired)		3,800

3.

Pro forma revenues (per note 3)	205,000
Reported revenues (without TRO)	186,000
TRO's revenues	19,000

f. 1.

Investment in associated company			
Beginning balance	11,000		
Equity in income (per I/S)	2,000	600	Dividends received (A)
Add'l investment (per SCF)	1,600		
Ending balance	14,000		

(A) Dividends received:

Equity in NI	2,000	
Less undistributed portion	1,400	(per SCF)
Distributed equity	600	

2. *Sources:*

Included in net income	2,000 cr.
Items not affecting cash	(1,400) dr.
Effect on cash from operations . .	600 cr.

Uses:

Investment in associated cos.	1,600 dr.

g. 1.

Minority interest		
	800	Beginning balance
	400	TRO acquisition (note 3)
	200	Share of NI (per I/S)
	1,400	Ending balance

2. No relationship. Minority interest relates to *consolidated* companies, while the investment relates to *unconsolidated* companies.

h.

	LIFO	Difference	FIFO
Beg. inventory	38,000	4,500	42,500
+ Purchases	P	--	P
- End. inventory	(56,000)	(6,000)	(62,000)
= Cost of goods sold	P-18,000	(1,500)	P-19,500

$1,500 less 50% taxes = <u>$750 increase in NI</u>

i. 1. Loss on disposal   1,400
            Property, plant & equipment   1,000
            Inventories   100
            Accounts payable & accruals   300

        Taxes payable   700
            Loss on disposal   700

    2. There was no effect on cash, which is shown as follows:

            Included in net income   (700) dr.
            Items not affecting cash   700   cr.
            Effect on CFO   -0-

    3. The $1,100 operating loss consists of the following gross amounts
        (revenues per note 4; expenses are a plug):

            Revenues   18,000
            Expenses   <u>19,100</u>
            Net loss   (1,100)

        The $1,100 would be part of the SCF as shown below:

            Included in revenues   18,000
            Included in expenses   19,100

        Discontinued operations cannot be segregated because the changes in
        operating current assets and current liability accounts represent both
        continuing and discontinued operations.

j. Amortization of $50 of goodwill ($2,000 ÷ 40 years) will have the following
    effect on the Year 7 SCF:

            In net income 50   dr.
            Items not affecting cash . . <u>50</u>   cr.
            Effect on CFO . . . . . .   -0-

k.   (all amounts per SCF)

	PP&E (net)		
Beginning balance	33,000		
Additions for cash	6,500	6,000	Depreciation expense
TRO acquisition	6,000	1,000	Write-down of disc. ops.
		500	Disposal of equipment
Ending balance	38,000		

Case CC-3

a.   1.   *Short-term liquidity:*

Four of the ratios are indicators of short-term liquidity. KO has a greater current ratio and acid-test ratio. CCE has a significantly higher inventory turnover ratio. Turnover of accounts receivable is virtually the same for both companies. On balance, KO is slightly more liquid, and is in a stronger position since CCE has virtually no cash.

2.   *Capital structure and solvency:*

Looking at the ratio of long-term debt to equity, CCE has significantly greater financial leverage. CCE's large investment in fixed assets and purchased goodwill have been debt financed. This ratio, which ignores short-term debt, exaggerates the difference between the two companies. Total debt to total capital ratios are much closer. CCE's greater dependence on interest-bearing debt and lower profitability result in significantly lower interest coverage as measured by the times interest earned ratio.

3.   *Asset Utilization:*

Both ratios in this category show KO to be superior. Asset turnover and property, plant and equipment turnover are higher for KO. CCE's capital intensive business is responsible for this disparity.

4.   *Profitability:*

KO is clearly the more profitable enterprise by all four measures. The higher gross profit margin is carried down to net income. KO's return on assets and return on common equity also are superior to those of CCE. KO's better competitive position is reflected in its profitability ratios.

b.   Possible analytical adjustments:

1.   Remove purchased goodwill from balance sheets of both companies, reducing assets and shareholders equity by $57 million for KO and $2,935 million for CCE (wiping out shareholders equity).

        Impact: Not material for KO.
                        CCE debt ratios sharply higher because of lower equity.
                        CCE asset turnover improved because of lower assets.
                        CCE ROE and ROCE more than doubled because of lower base.

2.   Remove non-recurring items from income statement of CCE. (From income statement take $104 million gain on sale of operations, less $27 million provision for restructuring, and add from footnote #2 $8.5 million gain on repurchase of debt to equal a net $85.5 million pretax non-recurring gain.) Reduce pretax earnings by $85.5 million for CCE.

        Impact: CCE profitability reduced further in comparison to that of
                        KO (ROA, profit margins, ROE). No other ratios affected.

3.   Add back LIFO reserve to inventory for both companies. Effect is $30 million for KO (cost of goods sold drops and reported profits rise) and $2 million for CCE. Equity increases by same amounts. (Footnote 1 for both companies.)

        Impact: KO current ratio improves slightly.
                        KO inventory turnover decreases.
                        KO debt ratios decline due to higher equity.
                        Effects on CCE immaterial as LIFO reserve relatively small.

4.   Recognize market value of KO investments in excess of carrying value-- $291 million (footnote 2).

        Impact: Higher equity reduces debt ratios and return on equity.
                        Higher assets reduces turnover and return on assets.

5.   Recognize off-balance sheet obligations for KO. KO has guarantees of $133 million (footnote 3).

        Impact: Higher debt ratios for KO. Guarantees also added to assets
                        affecting asset-based ratios: decreasing ROA and turnover.

6. Recognize off-balance sheet obligations for CCE. CCE has operating leases (footnote 3) for which analyst must estimate present value of "liability." One possible calculation follows:

Year	Future value	PV factor *	Present value
9	11,749	0.909	10,680
10	8,436	0.826	6,969
11	6,881	0.751	5,168
12	4,972	0.683	3,396
13	3,485	0.621	2,164
14	3,727 **	0.564	2,102
15	3,727 **	0.513	1,912
16	3,727 **	0.467	1,741
			34,130

*   Assumed interest rate of 10%.

**   Dividing payments beyond Year 13 ($11,181) by Year 13 payment ($3,485) results in 3.21 years. As an approximation, the payments beyond Year 13 are spread equally over Years 14-16.

Impact: Higher debt ratios for CCE.
Current portion of lease obligation reduces CCE current ratio.
Leases would also be added to asset side of balance sheet, affecting all asset based ratios. Lease would increase fixed assets, reducing turnover ratio and ROA.

7. Add pension plan surplus to equity for both companies. Excess of plan assets over projected benefit obligation is $93 million for KO and $46 million for CCE. (Footnote 4 for both companies).

Impact: About the same for both companies as relative impacts the similar. Debt ratios decline due to higher equity. ROCE decreases due to higher equity base.

◄ SUPPLEMENT B ►

Auditing and Financial Analysis

◄ CHAPTER REVIEW ►

Financial statements of a company are the representations of its management. Management bears the primary responsibility for the fairness of presentation and the information disclosure in financial statements. Because of the importance of financial statements, there is demand for their independent verification. Public accounting meets this demand through attestation, or auditing, services. It is probably not coincidental that the more developed an economy and its financial markets, the more important is public accounting. In the U.S., the title "Certified Public Accountant" is acquired by passing a series of examinations and, in most cases, obtaining sufficient experience. While no profession can ensure quality and character in its members, the successful completion of these examinations ensures a minimum level of competence in accounting and auditing practices. Since public accounting firms make up the largest segment of public accounting practice, our consideration of the auditing function and opinion is confined to that segment. There are several real and perceived limitations of auditors' work in practice. Yet the audit firm's function is of critical importance for our analysis. The audit firm's attestation to the fair presentation of financial statements greatly increases their reliability for our analysis as well as the degree and quality of disclosure. Partial or incomplete knowledge of the auditing process is more harmful than none at all. This truth applies to our understanding and knowledge of the audit firm's work and the relevance of the audit opinion.

This supplement provides us an overview of the relevance of auditing for our analysis. It also discusses the types of audit reports and their analysis implications.

◄ CHAPTER OUTLINE ►

▸ **Relevance of Auditing to Analysis**

    Credibility and Competence of the Audit Firm

    Relevance and Limitations of the Audit Report

▸ **Audit Process**

    Generally Accepted Auditing Standards

    Auditing Procedures

▸ **Audit Report**

    Types of Audit Qualifications

    Conditions Yielding Audit Qualifications

▸ **Special Assurance Reports**

▸ **Analysis Implications from Auditing**

    Analysis Implications of the Audit Process

    Analysis Implications of Auditing Standards

    Analysis Implications of Auditor Behavior

    Analysis Implications of Auditor Opinions

    Analysis Implications of Explanatory Language for Uncertainties

    Analysis Implications of the SEC

◄ Learning Objectives ►

- **Describe the relevance of auditing for financial statements.**

- **Explain the importance of the audit firm for our analysis of financial statements.**

- **Describe the audit report (opinion) and its relevance and limitations for our analysis.**

- **Analyze implications of variations in the audit report for financial statement analysis.**

- **Interpret auditing standards specifying an auditor's responsibilities in attesting to the fair presentation of financial statements.**

◄ Answers to Questions ►

1. In relying on the auditor's opinion covering the financial statements subject to review, the analyst must:

   (a) Learn as much as possible about the auditor being relied on.

   (b) Understand fully what the auditor's opinion means and the message it is designed to convey to the user.

   (c) Appreciate the limitations to which the opinion is subject as well as the implications which such limitations hold for the analysis of financial statements covered by the opinion.

2. Auditing standards are broad generalizations which come in three sets:

   (1) *General standards* define the personal qualities required of the independent CPA.

   (2) *Standards of field work* cover the actual execution of the audit and cover the planning of the work, evaluation of the client's system of internal control, and the quality and sufficiency of the evidence obtained.

   (3) *Reporting standards* govern the preparation and presentation of the auditor's report. They are intended to insure that the auditor's position is clearly and unequivocally stated and that the degree of responsibility taken is made clear to the reader.

3. The basic objective of the financial audit is the detection of errors and irregularities which, if undetected, would materially affect the fairness of presentation of financial summarizations or their conformity with generally accepted accounting principles.

   To be economically feasible and justifiable, auditing can aim only at a reasonable level of assurance about the data under review. This means that, under a testing system, assurance can never be complete and that the final audit conclusions are subject to this inherent probability of error.

4. The auditor's opinion deals with:

   (a) the fairness of presentation of the financial statements,

   (b) their conformity with generally accepted accounting principles, and

   (c) disclosure when a material change in accounting principles has occurred.

5. There are four main categories of conditions which require explanatory language, qualification, disclaimer, or adverse opinion:

   (1) Limitations in the scope of the auditor's examination affected by (a) conditions which preclude the application of auditing procedures considered necessary in the circumstances or (b) restrictions imposed by the client.

   (2) The financial statements do not present fairly the financial position and/or results of operations because (a) they fail to conform with generally accepted accounting principles or (b) they do not contain adequate disclosure.

   (3) There exist uncertainties about the future resolution of material matters, the effect of which cannot be estimated or reasonably provided for.

   (4) Inconsistent application of GAAP.

6.	"Except for" qualifications express an opinion on the financial statements except for repercussions stemming from conditions that must be disclosed. They may arise from limitations in the scope of the audit which, because of circumstances beyond the auditor's control or because of restrictions imposed by the audited company, result in a failure to obtain reasonably objective and verifiable evidence in support of events which have taken place. They may arise from a lack of conformity of the financial statements to GAAP.

When there are uncertainties about future events that cannot be resolved or the effect of which cannot be estimated or reasonably provided for at the time the opinion is rendered, such as one due to operating losses or serious financial weakness that calls into question the fundamental assumption that an entity can continue to operate as a going concern, a separate paragraph should refer the reader to the note to the financial statements that provides data about the uncertainty.

In cases of pervasive uncertainty that cannot be adequately measured, an auditor may, but is not required to, issue a disclaimer of opinion rather than merely call the reader's attention to the uncertainty.

7.	a. A disclaimer of opinion is a statement of inability to express an opinion. It must be rendered when insufficient competent evidential matter is available to the audit firm to enable it to form an opinion on the financial statements.

A disclaimer will also result from the existence of uncertainties or unresolved matters when their significance is so great that a "except for" qualification is not appropriate. Substantive reasons for a disclaimer of opinion must always be given.

b. An adverse opinion is rendered in cases when the financial statements are not prepared in accordance with generally accepted accounting principles and this has a significant effect on the fair presentation of those statements. An adverse opinion results generally from a situation in which the auditor has been unable to convince the client to amend the financial statements so that they adhere to generally accepted accounting principles. The issuance of an adverse opinion must always be accompanied by a statement of the reasons for such an opinion.

The difference between adverse opinions and disclaimers of opinion can be best understood in terms of the difference that exists between exceptions that affect the quality of the financial statements on one hand and those which express uncertainties affecting the auditor's opinion on the other. Thus, a situation that may call for an "except for" opinion may, at some point, result in such a degree of pervasive or material disagreements with management that it will require an adverse opinion. Similarly, pervasive and/or material uncertainties may, at some point, require the conversion of an "except for" opinion into a disclaimer of opinion.

8.	The practical effect of explanatory language because of uncertainty is to state the auditor's inability to assess the impact of the contingency, or the likelihood of its occurrence, and to pass on to the reader the burden of its evaluation.

One variety of explanatory language because of uncertainty relates to the question of whether the going-concern assumption in accounting is justified. This question arises when a company is incurring continued operating losses, deficits in the stockholders' equity, working capital insufficiencies, or defaults under loan agreements. In such cases the auditor expresses doubt about the propriety of applying practices implicit in the going-concern concept such as the valuation of fixed assets at cost.

9.	When there has been a material change between periods in accounting principles or in the method of their application, the auditor should refer to the change in explanatory language which follows the opinion paragraph.

10. Auditing is based on a sampling approach to the data under audit. Statistical sampling, while lending itself to many applications in theory, is more limited in actual practice. Thus, most audit tests are based on "judgmental" samples of the data--samples derived by feel, judgment, and evaluation of many factors. Often the size of the sample is necessarily limited by the economics of the accounting practice.

The reader must realize that the auditor does not aim at, nor can ever achieve, complete certainty. Even a review of every single transaction--a process which would be economically unjustifiable--would not achieve complete certainty.

Auditing is a developing art. Even its very basic theoretical underpinnings are far from fully understood or resolved. There is, for instance, no clear relationship between the auditor's evaluation of the effectiveness of the system of internal controls, which is a major factor on which the auditor relies, and the extent of audit testing and the nature of audit procedures employed. If we add to that the fact that the qualities of judgment among auditors can vary greatly, we should not be surprised to find that the history of auditing contains many examples of spectacular failures.

On the other hand, the percentage of failure to the total number of audits performed is very small. The user of audited financial statements can, in general, be reassured about the overall results of the audit function but must remember that there is risk in reliance on its results. Such risks are due to many factors including: the auditor's inability to detect fraud at the highest level and the application of proper audit tests to such an end, the auditor's conception of the range of responsibilities to probe and disclose, and the quality of the audit.

While the audit function will generally justify the reliance which analysts place on audited financial statements, such a reliance cannot be a blind one. The analyst must be aware that the entire audit process is a probabilistic one subject to many risks. Even its flawless application may not necessarily result in complete assurance and most certainly cannot insure that the auditor has gotten all the facts, especially if there is high-level management collusion to withhold such facts. The heavy dependence of the auditing process on judgment will, of necessity, result in a wide range of quality of performance.

11. The auditor maintains that it expresses an opinion on management's statements. Auditor's are very insistent on this point and attach considerable importance to it. It means that, normally, the auditor did not prepare the financial statements nor did it choose the accounting principles embodied in them. Instead, it reviews the financial statements presented by management and ascertains that they are in agreement with the books and records which are audited. The auditor also determines that acceptable principles of accounting have been employed in the preparation of the financial statements, but that does not mean that they are the best principles that could have been used. It is a well-known fact that management will rely on the auditor, as an expert in accounting, to help them pick the principle which, while still acceptable, will come nearest to meeting their reporting objectives. Finally, the auditor will determine that the minimum standards of disclosure have been met so that all matters essential to a fair presentation of the financial statements are included in them.

One could well ask what difference it makes whether the auditor prepared the statements or not so long as it expresses an unqualified opinion on them. The accounting profession has never clearly explained what the implications of this really mean to the user of the financial statements. However, a number of such possible implications should be borne in mind by the analyst:

(a)   The auditor's knowledge about the financial statements is not as strong as that of the preparer who was in more intimate contact with all the factors which gave rise to the transactions. The auditor knows only what it can see on the basis of a sampling process.

(b)   Since many items in the financial statements are not capable of exact measurement, the auditor merely reviews such measurements for reasonableness. These are not the original determinations and unless the auditor can successfully prove otherwise, as in the case of estimates of useful lives of property, management's determination will prevail. Thus, the auditor's opinion contains no reference to "present exactly" or "present correctly" but rather states that the statements "present fairly."

(c)   While the audit firm may be consulted on the use of accounting principles it, as an auditor rather than as preparer of such statements, does not select the principles to be used. Moreover, it cannot insist on the use of the best available principle any more than it is likely to insist on a degree of disclosure above the minimum considered as acceptable.

(d)   While the preparer must, under the rules of double-entry bookkeeping, account for all items, large or small, the auditor is held to less exacting standards of accuracy. Thus, the error tolerances are wider. The auditor leans on the doctrine of materiality which in its basic concept simply means that the auditor need not concern itself, in either the auditing or the reporting phases of its work, with trivial or unimportant matters. What is important or significant is a matter of judgment and the profession has neither defined the concept nor set limits or established criteria to govern the application of the concept of materiality.

12.   The auditor's reference to "generally accepted accounting principles" in its opinion should be well understood by the user of the financial statements. Such reference means that the auditor is satisfied that such principles have authoritative support and that they have been applied "in all material respects." Aside from understanding the operation of the concept of materiality, the analyst must understand that the definition of what constitutes "generally accepted accounting principles" is often vague and subject to significant latitude in interpretation and application. Moreover, not all important areas of accounting are covered by authoritative pronouncements which define acceptable practice.

13.   When the audit firm cannot assess the proper carrying value of an asset or determine the extent of a possible liability or find other uncertainties or contingencies which cannot be determined or measured, it will use explanatory language describing such uncertainties. The analyst using financial statements which contain such explanatory language is faced with a situation where the auditor has passed on to him/her the uncertainty described and, consequently, the task of evaluating its possible impact. The analyst should recognize the situation for what it is and not assume that he/she is dealing with a mere formality designed for the auditor's self-protection. It must be remembered that as between the reader and the auditor, the latter, due to its firsthand knowledge of the company's affairs, is far better equipped to evaluate the nature of the contingencies as well as the probabilities of their occurrence. Thus, the analyst is entitled to expect, but will unfortunately not always get, a full explanation of all factors surrounding the uncertainty.

It must be borne in mind that there are many contingencies and uncertainties which do not call for a qualification but which may nevertheless have very significant impact on the company's financial condition or results of operations. Examples of such contingencies or possibilities are:

* Obsolescence of a major product line.
* Loss of a significant customer.
* Overextension of a business beyond management's capabilities.
* Difficulties in getting production processes operating efficiently and effectively.

14.   Following are some of the circumstances which can point to areas of high audit risk:

(a)   Growth industry or company with need for continuing earnings growth to justify high market price or to facilitate acquisitions.
(b)   Company in difficult financial condition requiring financing urgently and frequently.
(c)   Company with high market visibility issuing frequent progress reports and earnings estimates.

(d)   Management dominated mostly by one or a few strong-willed individuals.
(e)   Personal financial difficulties of members of management.
(f)   Deteriorating operating performance.
(g)   Excessively complex capital structure.
(h)   Management which has displayed a propensity for earnings manipulation.
(i)   Problem industry displaying weaknesses, in such areas as receivable collection, inventories, contract cost overruns, dependence on few products, etc.
(j)   Dealings with insiders on related parties or stockholder lawsuits.
(k)   Turnover of key of officers, legal counsel or auditors.
(l)   Audit conducted by a firm which has experienced a higher than normal incidence of audit failures.

It should be noted, however, that while none of the above situations can be taken for granted to always indicate situations of higher audit risk, they have been shown by experience to have appeared in a sufficient number of problem cases to warrant the analyst's close attention.

15.   a. Adaptec's financial statements were audited by Price Waterhouse LLP. As one of the "Big 6" audit firms, Price Waterhouse has a strong reputation.

   b. Price Waterhouse notes that Adaptec's financial statements for the year ended March 31, 1994 were audited by a different firm.

◄ SUPPLEMENT C ►

Changing Price Levels and Financial Analysis

◄ CHAPTER REVIEW ►

Comparability over time of accounting measures expressed in dollars (monetary unit) is fully valid only if the general purchasing power of the dollar remains unchanged. This is rarely the case. The value of the dollar in terms of purchasing power almost always changes over any length of time. Experience suggests these price-level changes more typically reflect inflation, or a decline in purchasing power. When inflation occurs, the monetary unit becomes increasingly distorted as a measure of actual or physical dimensions of business activities. While the distortive effect of general price-level changes on accounting measures is recognized, preparers of financial statements often prefer to rely on education and disclosure rather than on a restatement of financial statements as a means of conveying price-level effects to users. In times of severe inflation there is increased demand for more formal and systematic measures to adjust for the distortions arising from changes in price levels. The accounting regulatory agencies experimented with supplementary disclosure requirements for price-level adjustments. But these disclosures are currently voluntary. While an important source of company-generated data on the effects of price-level changes on financial statements is no longer available, our analysis needs to understand the nature of the problem and the basic approaches of a solution. Also, certain companies still provide price-level adjusted information and international financial statements often reflect adjustments made necessary by their more serious price-level changes.

This supplement provides us an overview of the methods available for adjusting financial statements for the effects of changing prices and how to interpret these results.

◄ CHAPTER OUTLINE ►

▸ **Analysis When Price Levels Change**

▸ **Capital Maintenance and Income Determination**

  Financial Capital Maintenance

  Physical Capital Maintenance

  Two Accounting Models

▸ **Four Reporting Frameworks**

  Current Cost Accounting

  Constant Dollar Accounting

▸ **Analysis Implications of Price-Level Changes**

  Analysis of Current Cost Measures

  Analysis of Constant Dollar Measures

  Accounting Effects of Inflation

◄ Learning Objectives ►

- **Describe the effects of changing price-levels on financial statements.**

- **Explain capital maintenance and income determination when price levels change.**

- **Describe current cost and constant dollar accounting.**

- **Analyze financial statements restated for the effects of changing price levels.**

- **Interpret financial statements adjusted for changing price levels.**

◄ Answers to Questions ►

1. By making the reporting of the effects of changing prices voluntary, SFAS 89 has basically sanctioned, at least for now, the demise of such reporting. Not surprisingly, a review of published financial statements reveals that very few companies have chosen to report such data voluntarily.

    The FASB arrived at the decision to issue SFAS 89 by a 4 to 3 vote. Substantial forces were at work to bring this about. Research indicated that published SFAS 33 data were not widely used. A great majority of respondents to the exposure draft preceding SFAS 89 favored elimination of the requirements for supplementary disclosure. Companies did not like the work entailed nor did they like the results they had to report.

    All these forces can be readily discerned, but where does this leave financial statement analysts and their need for information in this critical area? The cumulative effect of inflation is substantial and so is the distortion it causes in conventional historical cost accounts. It leads to illusory reported profits, masks the erosion of capital and invalidates many analytical measures. The elimination of supplementary disclosures about the effects of price changes has diminished the sources of reliable information available to financial analysts.

2. The *financial capital maintenance* concept refers to maintaining the purchasing power of invested capital whereas the *physical capital maintenance* concept refers to maintaining the existing operating capability of an enterprise. Under the former concept, cost of goods sold would be stated in constant dollars whereas under the latter concept, cost of goods sold would be stated at the current cost of replacing the units sold.

    For example, assume that 1,000 units are purchased at $10 each when the CPI stood at 100 and 800 units are sold when CPI stood at 110 and the current cost per unit is $12. Under the financial capital maintenance concept, the cost of goods sold would equal $8,800 (800 x 10 x 110/100); whereas under the physical capital maintenance concept, cost of goods sold would equal $9,600 (800 units @ $12). If the 800 units were sold at $15 each, profits under the former concept would be $3,200 ($12,000 - $8,800) and under the latter concept would be $2,400 ($12,000 -$9,600).

3. The following are the four reporting frameworks:

    ■ *Historical Cost/Nominal Dollars (HC/ND)* - the framework under which the conventional primary financial statements are now prepared.
    ■ *Historical Cost/Constant Dollars (HC/CD)* - financial statements restated for general price level changes and expressed in a constant dollar of a given date.
    ■ *Current Cost/Nominal Dollars (CC/ND)* - financial statements restated for specific price changes.
    ■ *Current Cost/Constant Dollars (CC/CD)* - financial statements restated for both specific and general price level changes.

4. *Monetary items* are those which represent a claim to a fixed number of dollars (such as cash, accounts and notes receivable, and investments in bonds), or those representing an obligation to pay a fixed number of dollars (such as accounts, notes, or bonds payable).

    Conversely, *nonmonetary items* are those which do not represent a claim to a fixed number of dollars, such as inventory, property, plant and equipment, common stock, and other common equity accounts. If an item does not qualify as monetary, it must be nonmonetary.

5. One reason monetary gains and losses are poorly understood is that they produce no parallel cash inflows or outflows. Moreover, there is no identifiable change in accounts as a result of a change in the purchasing power of assets and liabilities. These gains and losses are basically the product arrived at by means of a retrospective calculation.

A further objection is that the advantage of borrowing differs from company to company depending on how profitably the assets acquired with debt were employed. Moreover, the largest monetary gains are likely to be shown by highly leveraged companies which may be near insolvency. Thus, the need for concurrent cash flow analysis is critical.

6. The following are some useful generalizations regarding such effects in times of significant inflation:

    a. The larger the proportion of depreciable assets and the higher their age, the greater likelihood of overstatement in unrestated income. Thus, the income of capital intensive companies tends to be affected more than that of others by price level restatements. Accelerated depreciation reduces this effect.

    b. The rate of inventory turnover has a bearing on price level effects. The slower the inventory turnover, the more operating income tends to be overstated, unless the LIFO method is used.

    c. The mix of assets and liabilities as between monetary and nonmonetary is important. A net investment in monetary assets will, in times of rising price levels, lead to purchasing power losses, and purchasing power gains will result from a net monetary liability position.

    d. The methods of financing also have an important bearing on results. The larger the amount of debt, at fixed and favorable rates relative to the inflation rate, and the longer its maturities, the better is the protection against purchasing power losses or the better is the exposure to purchasing power gains.

◄ Answers to Exercises ►

Exercise C-1

a. The historical cost/constant dollar (HC/CD) method of accounting is based on measures of historical prices in dollars, each of which has the same general purchasing power. Historical cost amounts outdated in terms of current prices are restated on a current basis by the application of a general price index (e.g., the Consumer Price Index for All Urban Consumers) to the historical cost amounts.

Measurements of HC/CD amounts are computed by multiplying the components of the historical cost/nominal dollar measurements by the average level of the general price index for the current fiscal year (or the level of the index at the end of the year if comprehensive financial statements are presented) and dividing the result by the level of the index at the date on which the measurement of the associated items was established (that is, the date of acquisition or the date of any measurement not based on historical cost).

b. The principal advantage of the HC/CD method of accounting over the historical cost method is that it assists in the analysis of the effects of changing general price levels. In a period of rising prices, the historical cost method of accounting matches dollars of different purchasing power on the income statement.

c. The current cost method of accounting is based on measuring and reporting assets and expenses associated with the use or sale of assets at their current cost at the balance sheet date or at the date of use or sale.

d. Depreciation expense using the current cost method of accounting would differ from depreciation expense using the historical cost method of accounting because depreciation expense is based on the current rather than historical cost of the fixed asset involved. In a period of rising prices, depreciation expense is likely to be higher using the current cost method of accounting because the current cost of the fixed asset is likely to be higher.

Exercise C-2

a. Interest rate = (21,200 ÷ 20,000) - 1 = 1.06 - 1 = <u>6%</u>

   Amount of interest earned = $21,200 - $20,000 = <u>$1,200</u>

b. To maintain purchasing power, the balance
   on 12/31 should be $20,000 × (121/110) $22,000

   Principal shown in savings book   <u>20,000</u>
   Loss due to inflation   <u>$ 2,000</u>

c. Loss due to inflation (part b) $2,000
   Interest income (part a)   <u>1,200</u> *
   Net *decrease* in wealth   <u>$ 800</u> **

   *   Ignores income taxes payable on the nominal interest income.

   **   Using interest income to mitigate decrease in wealth. However, under this computation no reward (interest) is recognized for the use of your money.

Exercise C-3

Company characteristics that minimize the difference between net income (as reported) and "current cost" earnings:

1. Company uses LIFO.
2. Company has rapid inventory turnover.
3. Company whose cost of goods sold is a small percent of total costs, with high proportion of SG&A.
4. Company with low percent of fixed assets.
5. Company able to increase selling prices (high profit margin).
6. Company with relatively new plant.
7. Company using accelerated depreciation for financial reporting.
8. Company that leases significant portion of fixed assets.
9. Company with large percent of capitalization represented by intangible assets.

                                                              (CFA Adapted)

Exercise C-4

a. Financial policies advantageous in an extended inflationary period include:

   1.   High rate of expansion of manufacturing or production capacity adding significantly to gross plant and equipment and, consequently, to future depreciation requirements.

2. Expansion of the business and fixed assets involves a major decision as to financing of such additions. In an extended inflationary period this use of debt for that purpose would maximize growth. This in turn could add to the company's debt (LT and/or ST) and increase the debt/equity ratio.

3. Expansion of the business involves an increase in inventories and receivables which again could be financed by short-term bank debt (and/or accounts payable).

4. Items 1 and 3 add to the debt of the company and management may decide not to raise equity capital expecting the following developments:

   * an increase in earnings per share resulting from the growth in debt and the high leverage.
   * an evaluation of the price-earnings multiple and therefore more appreciation of the price of the common stock.
   * need for the company to sell less stock than it would have had to if this was done initially.
   * by selling less stock growth rate remains high and P/E is helped.

The above policies could lead to a liquidity problem in a business slowdown ass decsribed below:

1. As the growth of the economy slows down, these factors will adversely affect the company:
   * increase in sales volume will slow down.
   * if the industry is competitive, price cuts may further erode sales.
   * because of increased fixed charges, the break-even point is higher and operating leverage is increased.

2. By having carried the investment through debt financing, the interest charges are higher than would have been the case had some equity been used. This adds to the fixed charges.

3. In an economic slowdown following an inflationary period there is a need to work off inventories due to low sales expectations. The excess is either worked off via price-cutting affecting sales and earnings or over a period of time by producing less—in which case margins decline (because of level of fixed charges).

   Similarly, payments by customers slow down and the receivables are collected with a delay.

   On these two counts substantial funds may be immobilized—while offsetting borrowing on which interest charges must be paid at the same level as in the expansion period—but with a larger negative effect on earnings.

4. The high debt of the company which may have been acceptable in a period of rising earnings and cash flow combined with a liberal interest

coverage, is no longer profitable. Bankers and lenders ask their clients to add to their equity base when the cash flow projections are not met.

At the same time, when the disappointing earnings are reported the PE ratio on the stock may decline just as fast as the earnings if not faster.

The company still needs equity capital, it may have lost the confidence of the bankers and lenders, the confidence of its shareholders, and more important its own self-confidence. As a result it may find it difficult to raise the money it needs.

The factors affected in the balance sheet are:

* Gross plant and equipment--from expansion it may now have to consider divestiture.

* Inventories and receivables--have to be reduced rapidly, a difficult task in a rough environment.

* Short-term bank loans--they come due, but the banks are not as eager to renew them.

* Long-term debt--may rise if the change is anticipated soon enough to refinance short-term obligations.

* Equity--was increasing at a comfortable clip via retained earnings; must now be built up via stock offerings. The additions to paid-in capital from such offerings are much lower than they would have been in a period of expansion.

b. Two important ways of overstating earnings in a period of inflation are:

1. The vast majority of enterprises worldwide compute their depreciation for shareholders' reports based on the historical cost of their plant and equipment. The historical cost of plant is much lower than its replacement cost after an inflationary period and, as a result, the charge for depreciation is understated.

2. Companies using the FIFO method for valuing their inventories could have higher net income compared to a company using the LIFO method.

c. An overstatement of ROCE can occur in the following ways:

1. By overstating net earnings based on depreciation of historical cost—which could be much lower than replacement value--and if inventories are valued using the FIFO method.

2.   The net worth of the company itself may be understated because:

Net Worth = Total Assets - Liabilities

If total assets are worth more because their replacement is higher than the historical cost valuation, then net worth should also be revalued. An upward valuation of net worth and a downward adjustment to net earnings are appropriate, resulting in a much lower than reported return.

(CFA Adapted)

◄ Answers to Problems ►

Problem C-1

TREK CO.
General Price-Level Gain or Loss, Year 2

		Conventional	Conversion Factor	Restated
Net Monetary Assets, 1/1/2:				
Cash	50,000			
Mortgage Payable	(100,000)	(50,000)	165/150	(55,000)
Net Monetary Assets, 12/31/2				(50,000)
Net General Price-Level Gain				5,000

Income Statement, Year 2

	Conventional	Conversion Factor	Restated
Depreciation Expense	8,000	165/150	8,800
General Price-Level Gain (above)			(5,000)
Net Income (Loss)			(3,800)

Balance Sheet As of 12/31/2

	Conventional	Conversion Factor	Restated
ASSETS			
Cash	50,000	monetary	50,000
Land	50,000	165/150	55,000
Building	200,000	165/150	220,000
Less: Accumulated Depreciation	(8,000)	165/150	(8,800)
Total Assets	292,000		316,200
LIABILITIES AND OWNERS' EQUITY			
Liabilities			
Mortgage Payable	100,000	monetary	100,000
Owners' Equity			
Capital, 1/1/2	200,000	165/150	220,000
Less: Net Income (loss), Year 2	(8,000)		(3,800)
Capital, 12/31/2	192,000		216,200
Total Liabilities and Capital	292,000		316,200

EDDY CO.
Worksheet to Prepare CC/ND Financial Statements

INCOME STATEMENT	HC/ND	Adjustments Dr.	Adjustments Cr.	CC/ND
Sales	400,000			400,000
Cost of goods sold	105,000	(1) 45,000		150,000
Selling & admin. expenses	55,000			55,000
Depreciation expense	25,000	(2) 5,000		30,000
Interest expense	25,000			25,000
Income tax expense	42,000			42,000
	252,000			302,000
Current operating income	148,000			98,000
Realized Holding Gain:				
On inventory sold			(1) 45,000	45,000
On use of buildings and equipment			(2) 5,000	5,000
Total realized holding gain				50,000
Realized income	148,000			148,000
Unrealized Holding Gains (loss):				
On ending inventory		(3A) 6,000	(3) 10,000	4,000
On property, plant, & equipment		(4A) 20,000	(4) 30,000	
		(5) 9,000	(5A) 5,000	6,000
		29,000	35,000	
Unrealized holding gains 12/31/2				10,000
Net income	148,000			158,000

(1) The difference between CC of $150,000 and HC of $105,000.
(2) The difference between CC of $30,000 and HC of $25,000.
(3) The difference between CC of $75,000 and HC of $65,000 for inventories on 12/31/2.
(3A) The difference between CC of $41,000 and HC of $35,000 for inventory on 1/1/2.
(4) The difference between CC of $300,000 and HC of $270,000 for PP&E on 12/31/2.
(4A) The difference between CC of $290,000 and HC of $270,000 for PP&E on 1/1/2.
(5) The difference between CC of $84,000 and HC of $75,000 for accumulated depreciation on 12/31/2.
(5A) The difference between CC of $55,000 and HC of $50,000 for accumulated depreciation on 1/1/2.

BALANCE SHEET

	HC/ND	Adjustments Dr.	Adjustments Cr.	CC/ND
Cash	5,000			5,000
Accounts receivable	30,000			30,000
Inventories	65,000	(3) 10,000		75,000
Total current assets	100,000			110,000
Property, plant, and equipment	270,000	(4) 30,000		300,000
Accumulated depreciation	(75,000)		(5) 9,000	(84,000)
Property, plant, and equipment—net	195,000			216,000
Total Assets	295,000			326,000
Current liabilities	47,000			47,000
Long-term liabilities	60,000			60,000
Deferred income tax	3,000			3,000
Total Liabilities	110,000			110,000
Common stock	165,000			165,000
Retained earnings, 12/31/2	20,000			20,000
Unrealized holding gains 1/1/2			(3A) 6,000 (4A) 20,000	21,000
			26,000	
Unrealized holding gains for Year 2		(5A) 5,000		10,000
Unrealized holding gains 12/31/2		5,000		31,000
Total shareholders' equity	185,000			216,000
Total Liabilities and Shareholders' Equity	295,000			326,000

(1) The difference between CC of $150,000 and HC of $105,000.
(2) The difference between CC of $30,000 and HC of $25,000.
(3) The difference between CC of $75,000 and HC of $65,000 for inventories on 12/31/2.
(3A) The difference between CC of $41,000 and HC of $35,000 for inventory on 1/1/2.
(4) The difference between CC of $300,000 and HC of $270,000 for PP&E on 12/31/2.
(4A) The difference between CC of $290,000 and HC of $270,000 for PP&E on 1/1/2.
(5) The difference between CC of $84,000 and HC of $75,000 for accumulated depreciation on 12/31/2.
(5A) The difference between CC of $55,000 and HC of $50,000 for accumulated depreciation on 1/1/2.